JOHN WILLIS

SCREEN WORLD

1997

VOLUME 48

ASSOCIATE EDITOR
BARRY MONUSH

1955

1958

1960

1965

1965

1967

1973

1975

1988

SIDNEY POITIER

one of the cinema's ground breaking actors, who helped tear down racial barriers while giving performances of intelligence, depth and integrity.

FILMS: From Whence Cometh My Help (Documentary, 1949), No Way Out (1950), Cry, the Beloved Country (1951), Red Ball Express (1952), Go, Man, Go! (1954), Blackboard Jungle (1955), Goodbye, My Lady (1956), Edge of the City (1957), Something of Value (1957), Band of Angels (1957), The Mark of the Hawk (1958), The Defiant Ones (Academy Award nomination, 1958), Virgin Island (1958), Porgy and Bess (1959), All the Young Men (1960), Paris Blues (1961), A Raisin in the Sun (1961), Pressure Point (1962), Lilies of the Field (Academy Award for Best Actor, 1963), The Long Ships (1964), The Greatest Story Ever Told (1965), The Bedford Incident (1965), A Patch of Blue (1965), The Slender Thread (1965), Duel at Diablo (1966), To Sir, With Love (1967), In the Heat of the Night (1967), Guess Who's Coming to Dinner (1967), For Love of Ivy (1968), The Lost Man (1969), They Call Me MISTER Tibbs! (1970), King: A Filmed Record...Montgomery to Memphis (1970), The Organization (1971), Brother John (1971), Buck and the Preacher (1972; and director), A Warm December (1973; and director), Uptown Saturday Night (1974; and director), The Wilby Conspiracy (1975), Let's Do It Again (1975; and director), A Piece of the Action (1977; and director), Stir Crazy (1980; director only), Hanky Panky (1982; director only), Fast Forward (1985; director only), Shoot to Kill (1988), Little Nikita (1988), Ghost Dad (1990; director only), Sneakers (1992), The Jackal (1997)

Ralph Fiennes, Kristin Scott Thomas in *The English Patient*
Academy Award Winner for Best Picture of 1996
© Miramax Films

CONTENTS

EDITOR: JOHN WILLIS

ASSOCIATE EDITOR: BARRY MONUSH

Staff: William Camp, Jimmie Hollifield, II,

Tom Lynch, John Sala

Acknowledgements: Bendix Anderson, Ed Arentz, Arrow Releasing, Artistic License, Castle Rock Entertainment, Cinepix Films Properties, Cline & White, Tommy Crudup, Richard D'Attile, Gerard Dapena, Dennis Davidson Associates, Alex Dawson, Samantha Dean, The Film Forum, Gramercy Pictures, Clairborne Hancock, Kino International, Steve Ledezma, Leisure Time Features, LIVE Entertainment, Mike Maggiore, Mark Mauceri, David Mazor, Miramax Films, Julia Moberg, David Munro, New Line Cinema/Fine Line Features, New Yorker Films, October Films, PMK Publicity, Phaedra Films, Sony Pictures Entertainment, Sheldon Stone, Strand Releasing, Paul Sugarman, Twentieth Century Fox, Universal Pictures, Jen Wallace, Walt Disney Pictures, Glenn Young, Zeitgeist Films.

1. Tom Cruise 2. Mel Gibson 3. John Travolta 4. Arnold Schwarzenegger

5. Sandra Bullock 6. Robin Williams 7. Sean Connery 8. Harrison Ford

9. Kevin Costner 10. Michelle Pfeiffer 11. Jim Carrey 12. Michael Douglas

13. Demi Moore 14. Brad Pitt 15. Glenn Close 16. Denzel Washington

TOP BOX OFFICE STARS OF 1996

17. Goldie Hawn

18. Eddie Murphy

19. Rene Russo

20. Meg Ryan

1996 RELEASES
January 1 Through December 31, 1996

21. Will Smith

22. Helen Hunt

23. Pierce Brosnan

24. Bruce Willis

25. Jack Nicholson

Tommy Lee Jones

Barbra Streisand

Jeff Goldblum

Ed Harris, Sally Field

EYE FOR AN EYE

(PARAMOUNT) Producer, Michael I. Levy; Co-Producer, Michael Polaire; Director, John Schlesinger; Screenplay, Amanda Silver, Rick Jaffa; Based on the novel by Erika Holzer; Photography, Amir M. Mokri; Designer, Stephen Hendrickson; Editor, Peter Honess; Costumes, Bobbie Read; Music, James Newton Howard; Associate Producer, Kathryn Knowlton; Casting, Mali Finn; a Michael I. Levy production; Dolby Stereo; Deluxe color; Rated R; 101 minutes; January release

CAST

Karen McCann	Sally Field
Mack McCann	Ed Harris
Julie McCann	Olivia Burnette
Megan McCann	Alexandra Kyle
Robert Doob	Kiefer Sutherland
Detective Sergeant Denillo	Joe Mantegna
Dolly Green	Beverly D'Angelo
Peter Green	Darrell Larson
Angel Kosinsky	Charlayne Woodard
Sidney Hughes	Philip Baker Hall
Martin	Keith David
Hispanic Housewife	Wanda Acuna
Her Husband	Geoffrey Rivas
Judge Younger	Armin Shimerman
Susan Juke	Natalija Nogulich
Howard Bolinger	Nicholas Cascone
Maria	Stella Garcia
Aunt McCann	Justine Johnson

and Wayne Pere (French Teacher), Joan Crowe (Michelle), Ross Bagley (Sean), Jane Morris (County Clerk), Cynthia Rothrock (Tina), Bobby J. Foxworth (Man following Karen), Manny Rodriguez (Gun Instructor), Michael Podwal (Pilates Instructor), Sierra Pecheur (Teacher), Zack Eginton (Obnoxious Boy), Kim Kim (Shopkeeper), A.C. Weary (Newscaster), Brenda Smith (Waitress), Ron Dean (Detective at McCann House), David Courier, Ellis E. Williams (Crime Scene Policemen), David Barrera (Precinct Officer), Scott Waara (Detective), Tom Lillard (Bailiff); Parents of Murdered Children: Angela Paton (Moderator), Donal Logue (Tony), William Mesnick (Albert Gratz), Rondi Reed (Regina Gratz), Cherie Franklin, Francesca P. Roberts, Marie Chambers, Rolando Molina, Ernie Vincent, Teddy Vincent, Minnie Summers Lindsey; Media Museum: Michael Buchman Silver (Assistant), Eric Morris (Columnist), Iris Fields, Jeremy Eynon (Office Staff); Traffic Jam: Fort Atkinson (Angry Man), Evelyn Parke (911 Caller), Dolores Velazquez, Pablo Velazquez (Hispanic Couple); Downtown: Patricia Belcher, Alesia Jones (Quarreling Women), Maurice Sherbanee (TV Salesman), Bob Clendenin (Hotel Clerk), Larry Polson (Yelling Man); Sharon D. Chase, Janet Dey, Buzz Barbee, Nino Polito (Mourners).

Karen McCann, shattered that the man who murdered her daughter has been set free on a legal technicality, swears to find justice her own way.

©Paramount Pictures

Joe Mantegna, Sally Field

Kiefer Sutherland

Sally Field

DUNSTON CHECKS IN

(20TH CENTURY FOX) Producers, Todd Black, Joe Wizan; Executive Producer, Rodney Liber; Director, Ken Kwapis; Screenplay, John Hopkins, Bruce Graham; Story, John Hopkins; Photography, Peter Collister; Designer, Rusty Smith; Editor, Jon Poll; Co-Producer, Jason Blumenthal; Music, Miles Goodman; Costumes, Alina Panova; Orangutan Trainer, Larry Madrid; Casting, Linda Lowy, John Brace; Second Unit Director/Stunts, Walter Scott; a Joe Wizan/Todd Black production; Dolby Stereo; Deluxe color; Rated PG; 88 minutes; January release

CAST

Robert Grant	Jason Alexander
Mrs. Dubrow	Faye Dunaway
Kyle Grant	Eric Lloyd
Lord Rutledge	Rupert Everett
Brian Grant	Graham Sack
La Farge	Paul Reubens
Lionel Spalding	Glenn Shadix
Victor	Nathan Davis
Mrs. Dellacroce	Jennifer Bassey
Nancy	Judith Scott
Murray	Bruce Beatty
Norm	Danny Comden
Artie	Steven Gilborn
Mrs. Winthrop	Lois de Banzie
Mrs. Feldman	Natalie Core
Dunston	Sam

and Eugenia Hamilton (Frau Biedermeyer), Michelle Bonilla (Consuelo), Alexander Walters (William),Toribio Prado (Bernard), Bree Turner (French Girl), Kevin Kraft (Desk Clerk), Per Siragusa, Ray K. Morris (Maintenance Men), Ernest Perry, Jr. (Doorman), Frank Kopyc (Night Doorman), Lynne Marie Stewart (Cucumber Woman), Marceline Hugot (Mrs. Harrison), Cynthia Martells (Ms. Pink), Michael McCarty (Tex), Katherine Olsen (Mrs. Tex), Cynthia Madvig (Kimberly), Ken Patrick Martin (Waiter), Karen Maruyama (Telephone Operator), Rita Minor, Victoria Kemsley (Maids), Ray Chang, Nicholas Garr, Roderick Bascom, Paula Malcomson (Bellmen), Neriah Davis (Ferrari Girl), Toni Perrotta (Maid), Jim Ishida (Bali Majestic Guest), Sunni (Bali Majestic Clerk), Tracy Zahoryin (Fashion Model), Bob Bergen, Frank Welker (Special Vocal Effects)

Tired of his life of crime, an organgutan flees his criminal owner, a jewel thief who has checked into the posh Majestic Hotel..

© 20th Century Fox

Eric Lloyd, Sam

Paul Reubens, Faye Dunaway, Jason Alexander

George Clooney, Quentin Tarantino

FROM DUSK TILL DAWN

(MIRAMAX) Producers, Gianni Nunnari, Meir Teper; Executive Producers, Lawrence Bender, Robert Rodriguez, Quentin Tarantino; Co-Producers, Elizabeth Avellan, Paul Hellerman, Robert Kurtzman, John Esposito; Director/Editor, Robert Rodriguez; Screenplay, Quentin Tarantino; Story, Robert Kurtzman; Photography, Guillermo Navarro; Designer, Cecilia Montiel; Costumes, Graciela Mazon; Music, Graeme Revell; Special Make-up Effects, Kurtzman, Nicotero & Berger EFX Group, Inc.; Visual Effects Supervisors, Daniel A. Fort, Diana Dru Botsford; Casting, Johanna Ray, Elaine J. Huzzar; a Dimension Films presentation of a Band Apart in association with Los Hooligans productions; Dolby SDDS Stereo; Color; Rated R; 108 minutes; January release

CAST

Jacob Fuller	Harvey Keitel
Seth Gecko	George Clooney
Richard Gecko	Quentin Tarantino
Kate Fuller	Juliette Lewis
Border Guard/Chet Pussy/Carlos	Cheech Marin
Frost	Fred Williamson
Santanico Pandemonium	Salma Hayek
Old Timer	Marc Lawrence
Texas Ranger Earl McGraw	Michael Parks
Newscaster Kelly Houge	Kelly Preston
Sex Machine	Tom Savini
FBI Agent Stanley Chase	John Saxon
Razor Charlie	Danny Trejo
Scott Fuller	Ernest Liu
Pete Bottoms	John Hawkes
Red-Headed Hostage	Heidi McNeal
Blonde Hostage	Aimee Graham
Hostage Gloria	Brenda Hillhouse
Titty Twister Guitarist & Vocalist	Tito Larriva
Titty Twister Saxophonist	Pete Atasanoff
Titty Twister Drummer	Johnny Vatos Hernandez
Mouth Bitch Victim	Gino Crognale
Santanico Victim	Greg Nicotero
Danny	Cristos
Manny	Mike Moroff
Big Emilio	Ernest Garcia

and Danny the Wonder Pony (Himself), Michelle Berube, Neena Bidasha, Veena Bidasha, Ungela Brockman, Madison Clark, Maria Diaz, Rosalia Hayakawa, Janine Jordae, Jacque Lawson, Houston Leigh, Janie Liszewski, Tia Texada (Dancers), Jon Fidele, Jake McKinnon, Michael McKay, Josh Patton, Walter Phelan, Wayne Toth, Henrik Von Ryzin (Monsters)

A pair of criminal brothers, on the run from the police, kidnap a minister and his children and end up at the bizarre Titty Twister bar.

© Dimension Films

BED OF ROSES

(NEW LINE CINEMA) formerly *Amelia and the King of Plants*; Producers, Allan Mindel, Denise Shaw; Executive Producers, Joseph Hartwick, Lynn Harris; Director/Screenplay, Michael Goldenberg; Photography, Adam Kimmel; Designer, Stephen McCabe; Editor, Jane Kurson; Costumes, Cynthia Flynt; Co-Producer, Michael Haley; Music, Michael Convertino; Casting, Meg Simon; a Mindel/Shaw production; Dolby SDDS Stereo; Technicolor; Rated PG; 87 minutes; January release

CAST

Lewis Farrell	Christian Slater
Lisa Walker	Mary Stuart Masterson
Kim	Pamela Segall
Danny	Josh Brolin
Randy	Brian Tarantina
Mom	Debra Monk
Alice	Mary Alice
Simon	Kenneth Cranham
Wendy	Ally Walker
Grandma Jean	Anne Pitoniak
Dad	R.M. Haley
Aunt Meg	Cass Morgan
Francine	Gina Torres
Fayard	Nick Tate
Jimmy	Victor Sierra
Sam	Michael Mantell
Jason	Zachary Chaltiel
Lisa's Secretary	Claire Mari Jacobs

and Paul Cassell (1st Executive), Yvonne Zima (Young Lisa), Desire Casado (Amelia), Aldis Hodge (Prince), Jessica Brooks Grant (Queen), Jonathan Nocera (King), Leah Pepper (Sara), Donna Jean Fogel (Student Teacher), S.A. Griffin (Stanley), Edith Blume (Mumuu Woman), Liz Sinclair (Sad Woman)

Lisa, a workaholic investment banker, begins receiving a steady stream of flowers from a secret admirer in this romantic comedy.

© New Line Cinema

Mary Stuart Masterson, Christian Slater

Pamela Segall

Mary Stuart Masterson

Christian Slater

ONCE UPON A TIME ... WHEN WE WERE COLORED

(BET PICTURES) Producers, Tim Reid, Michael Bennett; Executive Producer, Butch Lewis; Director, Tim Reid; Screenplay, Paul W. Cooper; Based on the book by Clifton L. Taulbert; Co-Producers, Clifton L. Taulbert, Paulette Millichap; Photography, John Simmons; Designer, Michael Clausen; Editor, David Pincus; Music, Steve Tyrell; Costumes, Winnie D. Brown; Casting, Jaki Brown-Karman; a United Image Entertainment production; Deluxe Color; Rated PG; 111 minutes; January release

Paula Kelly, Karen Malina White, Al Freeman, Jr., Deinoyos Llerena

CAST

Poppa	Al Freeman, Jr.
Ma Ponk	Phylicia Rashad
Melvin	Leon
Cleve	Richard Roundtree
Miss Maybry	Polly Bergen
Mama Pearl	Paula Kelly
Mr. Walter	Bernie Casey
Preacher Hurn	Isaac Hayes
Cliff Taulbert at 16	Damon Hines
Miss Annie	Anna Maria Horsford
Uncle Sammy, age 19/Narrator	Phill Lewis
Mr. Will	Taj Mahal
Nila Fontaine	Iona Morris
Cliff Taulbert (12 yrs.)	Willie Norwood, Jr.
Miss Alice	Salli Richardson
Mary Taulbert	Karen Malina White
Sammy (7 yrs.)	Braxton Brown, III
Straw Boss	Frank Taylor
Cliff (newborn)	Montrel Johnson
Cliff (2 months)	Deionyos Llerena
Moss Jones	Ben Epps
Willie Jones	Tyrone Hicks
Cliff (5 yrs.)	Charles Earl "Spud" Taylor, Jr.
Moses Taulbert	Winston Hemingway
Mr. Bob	Sean Bridgers
Colored Man, KKK Crowd	Edward Allen
Klansmen	Don Tilly, George Hasenstaab
Clarence, School Bully	Deji Olasimbo
Henry, School Bully	Angelo Pope
Sammy (12 yrs.)	Brandon Crawford
Miss Maxey	Daphne Maxwell Reid
Fight Commentator	Neil Ross
Cooter Man	Ralph Wilcox
Lurlean	Beatrice Bush
Cousin Bobby (12 yrs.)	Carter Gaston
Road Manager	Stan Kelly
Louise	Ashanti Blaize
Barker	Mark Britt
Dr. Duke	Rick Warner
Stanley, Field Worker	Darren Law
Mr. Barnes	David Lenthall
A&D Business Man	Kenneth Sprunt, Jr.
Hatti Mae	Sherita Starks
Miss Doll	Crystal Fox
Mr. Stein	Joe Inscoe
Bill Crocket	Nate Bynum
Brother Stanley	Wayne Dehart
Lillie Short	Schree "Tina" Lewis
Field Worker #2	Bobby Graham

and Dave McIntyre, Thym Kennedy, Darren Beatty (Juke Joint Patrons), David Lomax (Juke Joint Fighter)

Author Clifton Taulbert recalls his boyhood growing up in segregated Mississippi in the 1940s.

© BET Pictures

Phylicia Rashad   Leon

Charles Earl "Spud" Taylor Jr.

Richard Roundtree   Isaac Hayes

DON'T BE A MENACE TO SOUTH CENTRAL WHILE DRINKING YOUR JUICE IN THE HOOD

(MIRAMAX) Producers, Keenen Ivory Wayans, Eric L. Gold; Executive Producers, Mark Burg, Dan Genetti; Director, Paris Barclay; Screenplay, Shawn Wayans, Marlon Wayans, Phil Beauman; Photography, Russ Brandt; Editors, William Young, Marshall Harvey; Music, John Barnes; Co-Executive Producers, Shawn Wayans, Marlon Wayans; Designer, Aaron Osborne; Costumes, Valari Adams; Casting, Robi Reed-Humes, Tony Lee; an Island Pictures presentation of an Ivory Way production; Dolby Digital Stereo; Deluxe color; Rated R; 88 minutes; January release

CAST

Ashtray	Shawn Wayans
Loc Dog	Marlon Wayans
Dashiki	Tracey Cherelle Jones
Preach	Chris Spencer
Crazy Legs	Suli McCullough
Toothpick	Darrell Heath
Loc Dog's Grandma	Helen Martin
Doo Rag	Isaiah Barnes
Ashtray's Father	Lahmard Tate
Mailman	Keenen Ivory Wayans
Dave the Crackhead	Keith Morris

and Craig Wayans (Thug #1), Casey Lee (Birthday Boy Thug), Joe "Nub" Scott (Birthday Cake Boy), Kim Wayans (Mrs. Johnson), Vivica Fox (Ashtray's Mother), Lee Scott (Flashback Girl), Marian Reynolds (Flashback Mother), Tommy Morgan, Jr. (Car Jacker), Virginia Watson (Loc Dog's Mom), Gabriel Alexander (Jheri Curl Kid), Scott Randle (Doughboy), Wesley Eugene (Tre), Tedero Jones, Jr. (Ricky), Queline Young (A.K.), Alex Thomas (Al Dog), Reginald Green (Gang Member), Samuel Monroe, Jr. (Sam), Kwame Ganon (Driver with Curlers), Warren "Zubari" Washington, Don "Mazi" Mitchell (Cellular Phones), Benjamin Everitt (The Man), Toshi Toda (Korean Store Owner), Tamayo Otsuki (Korean Woman), Ahmad Reese (Low Rider Gangsta), Lester Barrie (Preacher), Vivian "Rappin' Granny" Smallwood (Sister Williams), Omar Epps (Malik), Jeffrey Anderson-Gunter (Homeless Man), Cynthia Madvig (Secretary), James Van Patten (Harvard Man), Alan Abelew (Recruiter), Michael Adler (Man in White Coat), Don Reed (Driving Instructor), Faizon Love (Rufus), Bernie Mac (Officer Self Hatred), Mik Scriba (Officer with Bullhorn), Kirk Kinder (Prison Guard), A.J. Jamal (The Cellmate), Antonio Fargas (Old School), La Wanda Page (Old School's Mom), Yvette Wilson (Nurse), Guy Torry (Doo Rag's Father), Travon Jamar (Drug Thug #1), Damien Wayans (Cousin with Bag), Charles Edward Bennett (Jiffy Pop), Paula Jai Parker (Drunk Party Girl), Lisa Morgan (Sabomboo), Tiara English (La Quanda), Terri J. Vaughn (Keisha), Xavier Cook (Child Support Man), Mitchell Marchand (Mitchell), J.W. Smith (Det. Cliche), Kelly Vaughn (Snowflake)

Spoof of current films about troubled black youths, in which young Ashtray is sent back to the 'hood to live with his father.

© Paramount

David Spade, Chris Farley

Marlon Wayans, Tracey Cherelle Jones, Shawn Wayans

BLACK SHEEP

(PARAMOUNT) Producer, Lorne Michaels; Executive Producers, Robert K. Weiss, C.O. Erickson; Director, Penelope Spheeris; Screenplay, Fred Wolf; Photography, Daryn Okada; Editor, Ross Albert; Costumes, Jill Ohanneson; Co-Producer, Dinah Minot; Music, William Ross; Casting, Deborah Aquila, Jane Shannon; a Lorne Michaels production; Dolby Stereo; Deluxe color; Rated PG-13; 87 minutes; February release

CAST

Mike Donnelly	Chris Farley
Steve Dodds	David Spade
Al Donnelly	Tim Matheson
Governor Tracy	Christine Ebersole
Drake Sabitch	Gary Busey
Robbie Mieghem	Grant Heslov
Roger Kovary	Timothy Carhart
Neuschwander	Bruce McGill
Scott Colleary	Michael Patrick Carter
Clyde Spinoza	Boyd Banks
Motorcycle Cop	David St. James
State Trooper	Skip O'Brien

and Branden R. Morgan (Fan), "Gypsy" Spheeris (Pocket Pool Lady), John Ashker (Jim Blaine), William Howell (Rastafarian), Austin Kottke, Toby Scott Ganger (Tough Kids), Dylan Lucas (Ricky), James Noah (Mayor), Chris Owen (Hal), Jonathan Everett Lewis (Carl), Larita Shelby (Reporter), Karen Kahn (Anchor Woman), Laura Weekes (TV Reporter), Tucker Smallwood (Election Analyst), Mark Thomas McLaughlin, Steve Neil Turner, Matt David Lukin, Daniel Joe Peters (Mudhoney), Kevin P. Farley, John Farley (Bouncers), Patrick Pankhurst (Donald Tracy), Luke Dickinson (Andrew Tracy), Fred Wolf (Ronald Forte), Patricia Place (Woman at Party), Annie O'Donnell (Election Worker), Kathleen O'Malley (Mrs. Oneacre), Jean Speegle Howard (Elderly Woman), Drew Wilson (Elderly Man), Michele Burkette (Police Woman), Andrew Breymann (Hillbilly Kid)

Gubernatorial candidate Al Donnelly, embarrassed by his underachieving brother Mike, hires campaign worker Steve Dodds to keep him out of trouble.

© Miramax

WHITE SQUALL

(HOLLYWOOD PICTURES) Producers, Mimi Polk Gitlin, Rocky Lang; Executive Producer/Director, Ridley Scott; Screenplay, Todd Robinson; Co-Producers, Nigel Wooll, Todd Robinson; Photography, Hugh Johnson; Designers, Peter J. Hampton, Leslie Tomkins; Editor, Gerry Hambling; Costumes, Judianna Makovsky; Music, Jeff Rona; Special Effects, Joss Williams; Casting, Louis Di Giaimo; Stunts, Eddie Stacey; Distributed by Buena Vista Pictures; a Scott Free production, presented in association with Largo Entertainment Inc.; Dolby Digital Stereo; Panavision; Technicolor; Rated PG-13; 127 minutes; February release

Jason Marsden, Jeff Bridges, Scott Wolf, Balthazar Getty

CAST

Christopher Sheldon "Skipper"	Jeff Bridges
Dr. Alice Sheldon	Caroline Goodall
McCrea	John Savage
Chuck Gieg	Scott Wolf
Frank Beaumont	Jeremy Sisto
Gil Martin	Ryan Phillippe
Robert March	David Lascher
Dean Preston	Eric Michael Cole
Shay Jennings	Jason Marsden
Francis Beaumont	David Selby
Girard Pascal	Julio Mechoso
Sanders	Zeljko Ivanek
Tod Johnstone	Balthazar Getty
Tracy Lapchick	Ethan Embry
Charles Gieg	Jordan Clarke
Middy Gieg	Lizbeth Mackay
Peggy Beaumont	Jill Larson
Cuban Commander	James Medina
Tyler	James Rebhorn
Girl in Brothel	Nicole Ann Samuel
Ms. Boyde	Becky Ann Baker
Bregitta	Camilla Overbye Roos

and Nathaniel Ives (Relief Bo'sun), Chris Condon, Andrew Hartley, Peyton Thomas (Crew Members), Jordan Scott, Nynne Christiansen, Charlotte Anderson, Lene Kristensen, Anja Clausen, Anita Weider, Emily Chittell, Mette Hocke (Danish School Girls)

Thirteen young men, members of the Ocean Academy, sign up as crew members aboard the Albatross, an experience that ends in tragedy when a storm arises and capsizes the ship.

John Savage   Ethan Embry

Eric Michael Cole, Scott Wolf, Jason Marsden, Jeff Bridges, David Lascher, Caroline Goodall, Jeremy Sisto, Peyton Thomas, Julio Mechoso

THE JUROR

(COLUMBIA) Producers, Irwin Winkler, Rob Cowan; Executive Producer, Patrick McCormick; Director, Brian Gibson; Screenplay, Ted Tally; Based on the novel by George Dawes Green; Photography, Jamie Anderson; Designer, Jan Roelfs; Music, James Newton Howard; Costumes, Colleen Atwood; Editor, Robert Reitano; Casting, Louis DiGiaimo; an Irwin Winkler production; Dolby SDDS Stereo; Panavision; Technicolor; Rated R; 116 minutes; February release

CAST

Annie Laird	Demi Moore
The Teacher	Alec Baldwin
Oliver	Joseph Gordon-Levitt
Juliet	Anne Heche
Eddie	James Gandolfini
Tallow	Lindsay Crouse
Louie Boffano	Tony Lo Bianco
Judge Weitzel	Michael Constantine
Boone	Matt Craven
Bozeman	Todd Susman
Joseph Boffano	Michael Rispoli
Inez	Julie Halston
DeCicco	Frank Adonis
Rodney	Matthew Cowles
Forewoman	Polly Adams
Accountant	Jack Gilpin
Stockbroker	Chuck Cooper
Musician	Charlie Landry
Locksmith	Tom Signorelli
Housewife	Frances Foster
Matron	Robin Moseley
Mrs. Riggio	Rosemary De Angelis
Thomas Riggio	Joseph Perrino
Carew	James Michael McCauley
Walters	William Hill
Court Clerk	Randy Jurgensen
Frankie	Chuck Zito
Dom	Steve Santususso
Archangelo	Peter Rini

and Gayle Scott (Party Singer), Gary R. Wordham (Flirting Intern), Anne Bobby, Fiona Gallagher (Ticket Agents), Luisa Huertas (Car Rental Agent), Daniel Martinez (Jeep Guy), Melissa Murray (Lainie), Brett Barsky (Jesse), Denise Burse (Secretary), Jose Senteno (Gold Tooth), Kalani Queypo, Alejandro Garcia (Deer Dancers), Rauol Morales, Marco Quezaza (Shooters), Jose Jara (Gunman)

In order to insure an acquital for mobster Louie Boffano, a member of the juror has her life threatened by a hired gunman.

Joseph Gordon-Levitt, Demi Moore

James Gandolfini, Demi Moore

Michael Rispoli, Alec Baldwin, Tony Lo Bianco, Peter Rini

Anne Heche, Joseph Gordon-Levitt

Christian Slater

John Travolta, Christian Slater

Samantha Mathis

BROKEN ARROW

(20TH CENTURY FOX) Producers, Mark Gordon, Bill Badalato. Terence Chang; Executive Producers, Christopher Godsick, Dwight Little; Director, John Woo; Screenplay, Graham Yost; Photography, Peter Levy; Designer, Holger Gross; Editors, John Wright, Steve Mirkovich, Joe Hutshing; Co-Producer, Allison Lyon Segan; Music, Hans Zimmer; Costumes, Mary Malin; Casting, Donna Isaacson; a Mark Gordon production in association with WCG Entertainment; Dolby Stereo; Super 35 Widescreen; Deluxe color; Rated R; 108 minutes; February release

CAST

Vic Deakins	John Travolta
Riley Hale	Christian Slater
Terry Carmichael	Samantha Mathis
Colonel Max Wilkins	Delroy Lindo
Pritchett	Bob Gunton
Giles Prentice	Frank Whaley
Kelly	Howie Long
Lt. Colonel Sam Rhodes	Vondie Curtis-Hall
Chairman, Joint Chief of Staff	Jack Thompson
Johnson	Vyto Ruginis
Lt. Thomas	Ousaun Elam
Max	Shaun Toub
Novacek	Casey Biggs
Shepherd	Jeffrey J. Stephen
Frakes	Joey Box
Daly	Jon W. Kishi
Brandt	Myke Schwartz
Lt. Reed	Jim Palmer
Jim	Vince Deadrick, Sr.
McKeller	Charlie Brewer
Miller	Gary Epper
Carl	Mario Roberts
Moss	J.N. Roberts
Secretary of Defense Baird	Kurtwood Smith
Air Force General Creely	Daniel von Bargen
Chairman Aid	Bruce E. Holman
General Boone	Carmen Argenziano
Park Ranger Baker	James G. MacDonald
I.R. Crewman	French Stewart
Pentagon Assistant	Jim Moyle
Major Hunt	Chris Mulkey
Captain Johnson	Henry Murph
Captain Wright	Tom Waddell
Wanda	Rosemary Schoppman

Military pilot Riley Hale tries to stop his partner Vic Deakins, who has stolen a pair of nuclear warheads.

© *20th Century Fox*

Howie Long

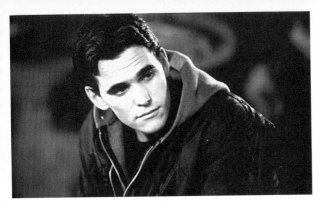

Matt Dillon

Timothy Hutton

Mira Sorvino

Matt Dillon, Lauren Holly

Timothy Hutton, Annabeth Gish

Michael Rapaport

BEAUTIFUL GIRLS

(MIRAMAX) Producer, Cary Woods; Executive Producers, Cathy Konrad, Bob Weinstein, Harvey Weinstein; Co-Producer, Alan C. Blomquist; Director, Ted Demme; Screenplay, Scott Rosenberg; Photography, Adam Kimmel; Designer, Dan Davis; Editor, Jeffrey Wolf; Costumes, Lucy W. Corrigan; Music, David A. Stewart; Associate Producers, Scott Rosenberg, Joel Stillerman; Casting, Margery Simkin; a Woods Entertainment production; Dolby Stereo; Deluxe color; Rated R; 107 minutes; February release

CAST

Tommy "Birdman" Rowland	Matt Dillon
Michael "Mo" Morris	Noah Emmerich
Tracy Stover	Annabeth Gish
Darian Smalls	Lauren Holly
Willie Conway	Timothy Hutton
Gina Barrisano	Rosie O'Donnell
Kev	Max Perlich
Jan	Martha Plimpton
Marty	Natalie Portman
Paul Kirkwood	Michael Rapaport
Sharon Cassidy	Mira Sorvino
Andera	Uma Thurman
Stanley "Stinky" Womack	Pruitt Taylor Vince
Sarah Morris	Anne Bobby
Dick Conway	Richard Bright
Steve Rossmore	Sam Robards
Bobby Conway	David Arquette
Victor	Adam Le Fevre
Frank Womack	John Carroll Lynch
Kristen Rossmore	Sarah Katz
Sharon's Mother	Camille D'Ambrose
Chip	Martin Rubin
Peter the Eater	Tom Gibis

and Allison Levine (Waitress at Moonlight Mile), Earl R. Burt (Bartender), Gregory Dulli (Lead Singer, Afghan Whigs), Trent Nicholas Thompson "TNT" (Michael Morris, Jr.), Nicole Ranallo (Cheryl Morris), Joyce Lacey, Matthew Nathan Castens (Reunion Classmates), Anne W. Erickson (Coffee Shop Waitress), Ollie Osterberg, Sterilng Robson, Edward Kaspszak (Drinkers), John Scurti (Ticket Agent), Herbie Ade (Bar Owner), Ben Gooding (Customer), Frank Anello (Irv), Lucky the Saint Bernard ("Elle Macpherson")

Willie Conway returns to his working class town for a class reunion and hooks up with his old friends, who don't seem to have outgrown their problems with women.

©Miramax Films

Natalie Portman

Max Perlich, Noah Emmerich

Timothy Hutton, Rosie O'Donnell, Matt Dillon

Uma Thurman

17

HAPPY GILMORE

(UNIVERSAL) Producer, Robert Simonds; Executive Producers, Brad Grey, Bernie Brillstein, Sandy Wernick; Director, Dennis Dugan; Screenplay, Tim Herlihy, Adam Sandler; Photography, Arthur Albert; Designers, Perry Andelin Blake, William Heslup; Editor, Jef Gourson; Co-Producers, Warren Carr, Jack Giarraputo; Costumes, Tish Monoghan; Music, Mark Mothersbaugh; Casting, Joanna Colbert; a Bernie Brillstein-Brad Grey/Robert Simonds production; Dolby DTS Stereo; Deluxe color; Rated PG-13; 92 minutes; February release

CAST

Happy Gilmore	Adam Sandler
Shooter McGavin	Christopher McDonald
Virginia Venit	Julie Bowen
Grandma	Frances Bay
Chubbs Peterson	Carl Weathers
Otto	Alan Covert
IRS Agent	Robert Smigel
Himself	Bob Barker
Mr. Larson	Richard Kiel
Doug Thompson	Dennis Dugan
Jeering Fan	Joe Flaherty
Himself	Lee Trevino
Potter	Kevin Nealon
Announcer	Verne Lundquist
Happy's Waterbury Caddy	Jared Van Snellenberg
Coach	Ken Camroux
Assistant Coach	Rich Elwood
Terry	Nancy McClure

and Helena Yea (Chinese Lady), William Sasso, Dee Jay Jackson (Movers), Ellie Harvie (Registrar), Ian Boothby (Guy on Green), Andrew Johnston (Crowd Guy—Waterbury), Kimberly Restell (Crowd Girl—Waterbury), Fred Perron (Waterbury Heckler), Helen Honeywell (Crazy Old Lady), Paul Raskin (Starter—Waterbury), William Samples (Starter—AT&T), John Shaw (Daniel Lafferty), Ted Deeken (Auctioneer), John Destry (Zamboni Driver), Jim Crescenzo (Shooter's AT&T Caddy), Brett Armstrong (Shooter's Tournament Caddy), Stephen Tibbetts, Edward Lieberman (Pro Golfers), Donald MacMillan (Young Happy), Louis O'Donoghue (Happy's Dad), Lisanne Collett (Happy's Mom), Stephen Dimopolous (Italian Guy), Douglas Newell (Starter—Pro-Am), Frank L. Frazier (Blue Collar Fan), David Kaye (Reporter), Zachary Webb (Batting Kid), Simon Webb (Doctor), Mark Lye (Himself), Betty Linde (Elderly Woman), Dave Cameron, Lou Kliman (Reporters), Brent Chapman (Official), Jessica Gunn (Signed Chest Woman), Phillip Beer (Cowboy Joe), Fat Jack (Jack Beard), Michelle Holdsworth (Babe on Green), Charles L. Brame (Abraham Lincoln), Ben Stiller

Hot tempered hockey player Happy Gilmore changes sports and becomes a pro golfer.

©Universal Pictures

Bob Barker, Adam Sandler

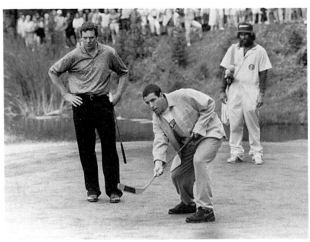

Christopher McDonald, Adam Sandler

Julie Bowen, Frances Bay, Adam Sandler

Carl Weathers, Adam Sandler

Ellen DeGeneres, Bill Pullman

MR. WRONG

(TOUCHSTONE) Producer, Marty Katz; Executive Producer, David Hoberman; Director, Nick Castle; Screenplay, Chris Matheson, Kerry Ehrin, Craig Munson; Photography, John Schwartzman; Designer, Doug Kraner; Editor, Patrick Kennedy; Co-Producer, Ira Shuman; Music, Craig Safan; Costumes, Ingrid Ferrin; Casting, Jane Jenkins, Janet Hirshenson; a Mandeville Films/Marty Katz production; Distributed by Buena Vista Pictures; Dolby Stereo; Technicolor; Rated PG-13; 92 minutes; February release

CAST

Martha Alston	Ellen DeGeneres
Whitman Crawford	Bill Pullman
Inga	Joan Cusack
Jack Tramonte	Dean Stockwell
Mrs. Crawford	Joan Plowright
Walter	John Livingston
Dick Braxton	Robert Goulet
Jane	Ellen Cleghorne
Annie	Hope Davis
Bob	Brad Henke
Nancy Culpepper	Christine Cattell
Mr. Alston	Peter White
Mrs. Alston	Polly Holliday
Stuart	Briant Wells
Consuela	Camille Saviola
Missy	Maddie Corman
Cody	Jonathan Hernandez
Nicole	Victoria Flores
Themselves	Louie Anderson, Casey Kasem, Jean Kasem

and Hector Elias (Mexican Detective), Frank Roman (Mexican Lieutenant), Shea Farrell (James), Frank Lugo (Priest), Johnny Miller (Old Man), John Cothran, Jr. (Owner), Wayne Alexander (Man at Opera), Jamie McGurk (Waitress), Christopher Kriesa, Frederick Dawson (Cops), Gil Combs (Flower Truck Delivery Man), Charlene Castle (Woman at Wedding), Bob Harvey (Bartender), Mickey Harrison (Elder Neighbor), Jenny Turnham (Aunt Belinda)

Martha Alston thinks she has found the perfect lover in Whitman Crawford until his increasingly strange behavior causes her to want out of the relationship.

© Touchstone Pictures

John Livingston, Ellen DeGeneres

Joan Plowright, Bill Pullman, Ellen DeGeneres

Ellen Cleghorne, Ellen DeGeneres

CITY HALL

(COLUMBIA) Producers, Edward R. Pressman, Ken Lipper, Charles Mulvehill, Harold Becker; Director, Harold Becker; Screenplay, Ken Lipper, Paul Schrader, Nicholas Pileggi, Bo Goldman; Photography, Michael Seresin; Designer, Jane Musky; Editors, Robert C. Jones, David Bretherton; Costumes, Richard Hornung; Music, Jerry Goldsmith; Casting, John Lyons; a Castle Rock Entertainment presentation of an Edward R. Pressman/Ken Lipper production; Dolby SDDS Stereo; Technicolor; Rated R; 111 minutes; February release

CAST

Mayor John Pappas	Al Pacino
Kevin Calhoun	John Cusack
Marybeth Cogan	Bridget Fonda
Frank Anselmo	Danny Aiello
Judge Walter Stern	Martin Landau
Abe Goodman	David Paymer
Paul Zapatti	Tony Franciosa
Larry Schwartz	Richard Schiff
Sydney Pappas	Lindsay Duncan
Detective Eddie Santos	Nestor Serrano
Detective Holly	Mel Winkler
Elaine Santos	Lauren Velez
Maria Santos	Chloe Morris
Randy Santos	Ian Quinlan
Nettie Anselmo	Roberta Peters
Vinnie Zapatti	Angel David
Tino Zapatti	Larry Romano
Wakeley	Rob LaBelle
James Bone	Ray Aranha
James Bone, Jr.	Jaliyl Lynn
Peter Ragan	John C. Vennema
Murray Safire	Steve Aronson

and Jerome X. Donovan (Seymour Harris), Mark Lonow (Lenny Lasker), Murphy Guyer (Captain Florian), John Finn (Commissioner Coonan), Richard Gant (Deputy Commissioner Samuels), Tamara Tunie (Leslie Christos), Fran Brill (Angie), Brian Murray (Corporation Council), John Slattery (Intel Detective—George), Benny Nieves (Intel Detective—Jaime), Miguel Sierra (Israel Torres), Sylvia Kauders (Gussie), Brenda Thomas (Clara), Gerry Vichi (Milton), Ernest F. Hollings (Senator Marquand), Jordan Baker (Mrs. Marquand), Rev. Leonard Chapman (Rev. Chapman), Tony Capone (Billy—Carousel), Jennifer Prescott (Julie—Carousel), Rev. Joseph Kelly, S.J. (Hospital Priest), Harry Bugin (Morty the Waiter), Ron L. Cox (Prosecutor), Kaity Tong, Amy Atkins, Brenda Pressley, Michael O'Looney, Carl White, Mary Murphy, Justin Ashforth, Charles Gemmill, Gina Rice (Field Reporters), Roma Torre, Jack Cafferty, Lewis Dodley, Edward I. Koch (Newscasters), Stanley Anderson (Train Conductor), Sally Mayes (Floyd Diner Waitress), Lucia Mendoza (Elaine Santos' Sister), Geoffrey Wade (Gracia Mansion Butler), Gloria K. Smith, James F. Gainer (Vocalists)

The death of an innocent boy during a shooting in Brooklyn unlocks a scandal in the New York mayor's office.

© Castle Rock Entertainment

John Cusack, Al Pacino

David Paymer   Martin Landau

Bridget Fonda, John Cusack

Danny Aiello

Kermit, Gonzo, Kevin Bishop, Rizzo

MUPPET TREASURE ISLAND

(WALT DISNEY PICTURES) Producers, Martin G. Baker, Brian Henson; Executive Producer, Frank Oz; Director, Brian Henson; Screenplay, Jerry Juhl, Kirk R. Thatcher, James V. Hart; Suggested by the Robert Louis Stevenson novel; Photography, John Fenner; Designer, Val Strazovec; Music, Hans Zimmer; Line Producer, Selwyn Roberts; Songs, Barry Mann, Cynthia Weil; Editor, Michael Jablow; Costumes, Polly Smith; Special Effects Producer, Thomas G. Smith; Casting, Mike Fenton, Alison Cowitt, Suzanne Crowley, Gilly Poole; from Jim Henson Productions; Distributed by Buena Vista Pictures; Dolby Digital Stereo; Technicolor; Rated G; 99 minutes; February release

CAST

Long John Silver	Tim Curry
Jim Hawkins	Kevin Bishop
Billy Bones	Billy Connolly
Mrs. Bluveridge	Jennifer Saunders
The Great Gonzo/Dr. Bunsen Honeydew/Waldorf	Dave Goelz
Kermit the Frog (Captain Smollett)/Rizzo the Rat/Beaker	Steve Whitmire
Statler/Blind Pew/Mad Monty/Butler	Jerry Nelson
Bad Polly/Black Dog/Spa'am	Kevin Clash
Clueless Morgan	Bill Barretta
Sweetums	John Henson
Miss Piggy (Benjamina Gunn)/Fozzie Bear/Sam Eagle	Frank Oz
Short Stack Stevens	Danny Blackner
Black Eyed Pea	Peter Geeves
Easy Pete	Harry Jones
Captain Flint	David Nicholls
Calico Jerry	Frederick Warder

After young Jim Hawkins gets hold of a valuable treasure map he joins up with Captain Smollett and his crew to set sail to find the loot. Previous versions of the classic novel were produced by MGM in 1934 with Wallace Beery as Long John Silver and Jackie Coogan as Jim Hawkins; Walt Disney in 1950 with Robert Newton as Silver and Bobby Driscoll as Jim; and National General in 1972 with Orson Welles. Newton played the role again in the Australian film Long John Silver *which was released in the US by DCA in 1955.*

Kermit, Miss Piggy

Sam Eagle, Kermit, Tim Curry, Kevin Bishop, Gonzo

BEFORE AND AFTER

(HOLLYWOOD PICTURES) Producers, Barbet Schroeder, Susan Hoffman; Executive Producers, Roger Birnbaum, Joe Roth; Director, Barbet Schroeder; Screenplay, Ted Tally; Based on the book by Rosellen Brown; Photography, Luciano Tovoli; Designer, Stuart Wurtzel; Editor, Lee Percy; Costumes, Ann Roth; Co-Producer, Chris Brigham; Music, Howard Shore; Associate Producer, Jonathan Glickman; Casting, Howard Feuer; a Schroeder/Hoffman production, presented in association with Caravan Pictures; Distributed by Buena Vista Pictures; Dolby Digital Stereo; Technicolor; Rated PG-13; 108 minutes; February release

CAST

Carolyn Ryan	Meryl Streep
Ben Ryan	Liam Neeson
Jacob Ryan	Edward Furlong
Judith Ryan	Julia Weldon
Panos Demeris	Alfred Molina
Fran Conklin	Daniel von Bargen
Wendell Bye	John Heard
Terry Taverner	Ann Magnuson
Marian Raynor, Prosecutor	Kaiulani Lee
Dr. Tom McAnally	Larry Pine
Panos' Assistant	Ellen Lancaster
Judge Grady	Wesley Addy
T.J.	Oliver Graney
T.J.'s Mom	Bernadette Quigley
Dr. Ryan's Assistant	Pamela Blair
Dr. Trygve Hanson	John Wylie
Doctor #1	John Deyle
Young Policeman	Tim Cavanaugh
Hardware Clerk	John Webber
TV Reporter	Jay Potter
Bailiff	Sharon Ullrick
Journalists	Robert Westenberg, Susan Pratt

Carolyn and Ben Ryan are distraught when their teenage son Jacob disappears after his girlfriend has been found murdered.

Meryl Streep, Liam Neeson, Edward Furlong

Alfred Molina, Liam Neeson, Meryl Streep, Edward Furlong

Julia Weldon, Liam Neeson, Meryl Streep, Edward Furlong

Julia Roberts, John Malkovich

Julia Roberts, John Malkovich

George Cole, Kathy Staff, Bronagh Gallagher, Michael Sheen, Julia Roberts

Julia Roberts

MARY REILLY

(TRISTAR) Producers, Ned Tanen, Nancy Graham Tanen, Norma Heyman; Executive Producer, Lynn Pleshette; Director, Stephen Frears; Screenplay, Christopher Hampton; Based on the novel by Valerie Martin; Co-Producer, Iain Smith; Photography, Philippe Rousselot; Designer, Stuart Craig; Editor, Lesley Walker; Costumes, Consolata Boyle; Music, George Fenton; Casting, Leo Davis, Juliet Taylor; Dolby SDDS Stereo; Technicolor; Rated R; 108 minutes; February release

CAST

Mary Reilly . . . . Julia Roberts
Dr. Henry Jekyll/Mr. Hyde . . . . John Malkovich
Mr. Poole. . . . . George Cole
Mary's Father. . . . . Michael Gambon
Mrs. Kent . . . . Kathy Staff
Mrs. Farraday . . . . Glenn Close
Bradshaw . . . . Michael Sheen
Annie. . . . . Bronagh Gallagher
Mary's Mother. . . . . Linda Bassett
Haffinger . . . . Henry Goodman
Sir Danvers Carew . . . . Ciaran Hinds
Young Mary . . . . Sasha Hanau
Young Woman . . . . Moya Brady
Young Whore . . . . Emma Griffiths Malin
Doctor. . . . . David Ross
Vicar . . . . Tim Barlow
Screaming Girl. . . . . Isabella Marsh
Screaming Girl's Mother . . . . Wendy Nottingham
Screaming Girl's Father . . . . Richard Leaf
Inspector . . . . Stephen Boxer
Policeman . . . . Bob Mason
and Ellie Crockett, Robbi Stevens, Kadamba, Evelyn Doggart, Piu Fan Lee, Mimi Potworowska, Samantha Hones, Julia Hagen (Farraday Girls)

Mary Reilly, a servant in the house of Dr. Henry Jekyll, finds herself drawn to the Doctor's mysterious assistant, Mr. Hyde.

©TriStar Pictures

UNFORGETTABLE

(MGM) Producers, Dino De Laurentiis, Martha De Laurentiis; Executive Producers, Andrew Lazar, Rick Dahl, William Teitler; Director, John Dahl; Screenplay, Bill Geddie; Photography, Jeffrey Jur; Designer, Rob Pearson; Editors, Eric L. Beason, Scott Chestnut; Costumes, Terry Dresbach, Glenne Campbell; Music, Christopher Young; Line Producer, Lucio Trentini; Casting, Carol Lewis; a Dino De Laurentiis presentation; Dolby Digital DTS Stereo; Deluxe color; Rated R; 111 minutes; February release

CAST

David Krane	Ray Liotta
Martha Briggs	Linda Fiorentino
Don Bresler	Peter Coyote
Stewart Gleick	Christopher McDonald
Curtis Avery	David Paymer
Michael Stratton	Duncan Fraser
Cara Krane	Caroline Elliott
Lindy Krane	Colleen Rennison
Kelly	Kim Cattrall
Mary Krane	Stellina Rusich
Eddie Dutton	Kim Coates
Sheila Wills	Suzy Joachim
Joseph Bodner	Garwin Sanford
Donna Berman	Jenafor Ryane
Boyfriend	Jimmy Broyden
Assistant Pharmacist	Dean Choe
Pharmacist	Mike Crestjo
Media	Joanna Piros
Media #2	Kevin Hayes
Colleague	Cheryl Wilson
George Guard #1	Nathaniel Deveaux
Andy Guard #1	Dwight McFee
Building Manager	Claudio de Victor
Priest	Arlen Jones
Mother	Sidonie Boll
Small Son	Eric Pospisil

and Rondel Reynoldson (Nurse Karen), Brock Chapman (Young Eddie Dutton), Bob Wilde (Eddie's Dad), Cory Dagg (Lawyer), Robert Metcalfe (District Attorney), Henry Watson (Judge), William B. Davis (Dr. Smoot), Tong Lung (Police Sketch Artist), Robin Douglas (Receptionist), Callum Keith Rennie (Drug Dealer), Roland Corkum (Priest at Wedding), Leslie Graham (Nurse), David Sobolov (Paramedic), Kate Lancaster, Tom Davies (Nude Corpses), Dave St. Pierre (Sexy Guy), Isabel Price, Dale Villeneuve (Sexy Girls), Azalea Davila (Eddie's Girlfriend)

Hoping to identify his wife's murderer Dr. David Krane attempts to inject himself with the dead woman's memories by way of an experimental memory transfer formula.

©Metro Goldwyn Mayer

Robert Musgrave, Luke Wilson, Owen C. Wilson

Linda Fiorentino, Ray Liotta, David Paymer

BOTTLE ROCKET

(COLUMBIA) Producers, Polly Platt, Cynthia Hargrave; Executive Producers, James L. Brooks, Richard Sakai, Barbara Boyle, Michael Taylor; Director, Wes Anderson; Screenplay, Owen C. Wilson, Wes Anderson; Photography, Robert Yeoman; Designer, David Wasco; Editor, David Moritz; Costumes, Karen Patch; Music, Mark Mothersbaugh; Co-Producers, Ray Zimmerman, L.M. Kit Carson; Casting, Liz Keigley; a Boyle-Taylor production, a Gracie Films production; Dolby SDDS; Technicolor; Rated R; 95 minutes; February release

CAST

Didgnan	Owen C. Wilson
Bob Mapplethorpe	Robert Musgrave
Anthony Adams	Luke Wilson
Inez	Lumi Cavazos
Mr. Henry	James Caan
Dr. Nichols	Ned Dowd
Grace	Shea Fowler
Bernice	Haley Miller
Future Man	Andrew Wilson
H. Clay Murchison	Brian Tenenbaum
Stacy Sinclair	Jenni Tooley
Temple	Temple Nash
Bookstore Employee	Dipak Pallana
Bookstore Manager	Darryl Cox
Rob	Stephen Dignan
Wife in Motelroom	Julie Mayfield
Husband in Motelroom	Don Phillips, Jr.
Carmen	Anna Cifuentes
Rocky	Donny Caicedo
Anita	Melinda Renna
Man in Bar	Richard Reyes
Man outside Bar	Julio Cedillo
Hector Mapplethorpe	Teddy Wilson
Applejack	Jim Ponds

and Takayuki Kubota (Rowboat), Kumar Pallana (Kumar), Haskel Craver (Jackson), Jill Parker-Jones (Motel Manager), Nena Smarz (Maid), Hector Garcia, Daniel R. Padgett (Freezer Guys), Russell Towery, Ben Loggins (Cops), Linn Mullin (Detective)

©Columbia Pictures

UP CLOSE & PERSONAL

(TOUCHSTONE) Producers, Jon Avnet, David Nicksay, Jordan Kerner; Executive Producers, Ed Hookstratten, John Foreman; Director, Jon Avnet; Screenplay, Joan Didion, John Gregory Dunne; Suggested by the book *Golden Girl* by Alanna Nash; Co-Producers, Lisa Lindstrom, Martin Huberty; Photography, Karl Walter Lindenlaub; Designer, Jeremy Conway; Editor, Debra Neil-Fisher; Costumes, Albert Wolsky; Music, Thomas Newman; Song: "Because You Loved Me" by Diane Warren/performed by Celine Dion; Casting, David Rubin; an Avnet/Kerner production, presented in association with Cinergi Pictures Entertainment; Distributed by Buena Vista Pictures; Dolby Digital Stereo; Technicolor; Rated PG-13; 124 minutes; March release

Michelle Pfeiffer, Robert Redford

CAST

Warren Justice	Robert Redford
Tally Atwater	Michelle Pfeiffer
Marcia McGrath	Stockard Channing
Bucky Terranova	Joe Mantegna
Joanna Kennelly	Kate Nelligan
Ned Jackson	Glenn Plummer
John Merino	James Rebhorn
Rob Sullivan	Scott Bryce
Fernando Buttanda	Raymond Cruz
Luanne Atwater	Dedee Pfeiffer
Dan Duarte	Miguel Sandoval
Buford Sells	Noble Willingham
Tom Orr	James Karen
Vic Nash	Brian Markinson

and Michael Laskin (IBS Director), Robert Keith Watson (IBS Makeup Man), Lily Nicksay (Star Atwater), Joanna Sanchez (Ileana), Daniel Zacapa (Harvey Harris), Heidi Swedberg (Sheila), Fern Buchner (WMIA Makeup Woman), Miguel Perez (WMIA Floor Manager), Nicholas Cascone (WMIA Director), Kenneth Fuchs (WMIA Assistant Director), Julie Foreman (WMIA Producer), Edwina Moore (WMIA Co-Anchor), Patti Davis Suarez (WMIA Reporter), Marc Macaulay (Police Spokesman), Ed Amatrudo, Ana Azcuy, Peter D'Oench, Dave Game, Michelle Gillen, Eliott Rodriguez, Jennifer Valoppi (Miami Reporters), Yareli Arizmendi (Inez Cifuentes), Salvador Levy (Congressman Diaz), Manny Suarez (Diaz Aide), Neil Giuntoli (Trailer Park Manager), Jason Sanford (Photographer), Michael Villani (Doug Dunning), Elizabeth Ruscio (Lulu Delano), Michael Shamus Wiles (WFIL Cameraman), Nigel Gibbs (WFIL Floor Manager), Mary Elizabeth Sheridan, Marian Lamb Bechtelheimer (98 Year Old Twins), Natalie Barish, Wanda Lee Evans, Charles Noland, Charles Martiniz, Charles C. Stevenson Jr., Cynthia Szigeti (Focus Group), Guillermo Gentile (Chess Player), Fabian (Himself), Richard Alliger (Right to Life Protester), Ginny Graham (Homeless Woman), Frederick Strother (City Councilman), Larry John Meyers (Murray Gordon), Andy Prosky (Cord Otavio), Bruce Gray (Gabe Lawrence), Norman Parker (Mark Lindner), Lori New (Merino's Secretary), Charlie Holliday (Priest), Leontine Guilliard (Guard Shay), Johnnie Hobbs, Jr. (Warden), Tom McCarthy (Negotiator), Roger Rathburn (Gary Logan), Dennis Dun (Satellite Technician), Rhonda Overby (WFIL Reporter), Lexie Bigham (Convict), Jack Shearer (Prison Expert), Andrew Glassman(Shouting Questioner), Rick Warner (Spokesman), Joe B. Shapiro (Waiter), Rosie Malek-Yonan (Boarding Agent), Chris Stone (Backstage Floor Manager).

Robert Redford, Joe Mantegna

Newsman Warren Justice takes Tally Atwater under his wing and helps her to become a top tv newscaster. The film received an Oscar nomination for song ("Because You Loved Me").

©*Touchstone Pictures*

Stockard Channing, Michael Villani, Michelle Pfeiffer

Kate Nelligan, Robert Redford

DOWN PERISCOPE

(20TH CENTURY FOX) Producer, Robert Lawrence; Executive Producer, Jack Cummins; Director, David S. Ward; Screenplay, Hugh Wilson, Andrew Kurtzman, Eliot Wald; Story, Hugh Wilson; Photography, Victor Hammer; Designer, Michael Corenblith; Editors, William Anderson, Armen Minasian; Co-Producer, Stanley Wilson; Music, Randy Edelman; Costumes, Luke Reichle; Casting, Ferne Cassel; a Robert Lawrence production; Dolby Stereo; Deluxe color; Rated PG-13; 92 minutes; March release

CAST

Lt. Commander Tom Dodge	Kelsey Grammer
Lt. Emily Lake	Lauren Holly
Executive Officer Marty Pascal	Rob Schneider
Howard	Harry Dean Stanton
Rear Admiral Yancy Graham	Bruce Dern
Captain Carl Knox	William H. Macy
Seaman Buckman	Ken Hudson Campbell
Seaman Nitro	Toby Huss
Planesman First Class Jefferson Jackson	Duane Martin
Seaman Stanley "Spots" Sylversterson	Jonathan Penner
Engineman First Class Brad Stepanak	Bradford Tatum
Sonarman Second Class E.T. "Sonar" Lovacelli	Harland Williams
Admiral Dean Winslow	Rip Torn
Orlando Radioman	James Martin, Jr.
Orlando Ensign	Jordan Marder
Orlando XO	Matt Landers
Orlando Sonarman	Joseph Latimore
Stingray Radioman	Patton Oswalt
Helmsman	Joe Soto
Young Sailor	John Shepherd
Trawler Captain	Pierrino Mascarino
Fishermen	Dennis Fimple, Ancel Cook
Supportive Admiral	James Harper
Admirals	Rudy Hornish, Tommy Terrell
Secretary	Elliot Easton
Orlando Young Sailor	Michael William Connors

and Paul Tranghese (Sailor #2), Mitch Danton (Conn Tower Officer), Jackson Sleet (Torpedo Man), Annie Talbot (Singing Waitress), Eugene Daniel, Bob Dini, Andrew English, Steve Giralo, Robert Grochau, Jamie James, Joseph Keawkalaya, Todd Odom (Singing Sailors)

Lt. Commander Thomas Dodge is dismayed to learn that he has been assigned to a junked World War II submarine manned by a motley crew of misfit sailors.

Bradford Tatum, Rob Schneider, Kelsey Grammer

Ken Hudson Campbell, Lauren Holly

Kelsey Grammer (c)

Frances McDormand, John Carroll Lynch

Steve Buscemi, Peter Stormare

Harve Presnell, William H. Macy

FARGO

(GRAMERCY) Producer, Ethan Coen; Executive Producers, Tim Bevan, Eric Fellner; Director, Joel Coen; Screenplay, Ethan Coen, Joel Coen; Line Producer, John Cameron; Photography, Roger Deakins; Designer, Rick Heinrichs; Costumes, Mary Zophres; Music, Carter Burwell; Editor, Roderick Jaynes; Casting, John Lyons; a PolyGram Filmed Entertainment presentation in association with Working Title Films; Dolby Stereo; DuArt color; Rated R; 97 minutes; March release

CAST

Marge Gunderson	Frances McDormand
Carl Showalter	Steve Buscemi
Jerry Lundegaard	William H. Macy
Gaer Grimsrud	Peter Stormare
Wade Gustafson	Harve Presnell
Norm Gunderson	John Carroll Lynch
Jean Lundegaard	Kristin Rudrüd
Scotty Lundegaard	Tony Denman
Irate Customer	Gary Houston
Irate Customer's Wife	Sally Wingert
Salesman	Kurt Schweickhardt
Hookers	Larissa Kokernot, Melissa Peterman
Shep Proudfoot	Steven Reevis
Reilly Diefenbach	Warren Keith
Morning Show Host	Steve Edelman
Morning Show Hostess	Sharon Anderson
Stan Grossman	Larry Brandenburg
State Trooper	James Gaulke
Victim in Field	*°?
Victim in Car	Michelle Suzanne Le Doux
Lou	Bruce Bohne
Cashier	Petra Boden
Mike Yanagita	Steve Park
Customer	Wayne Evenson
Officer Olson	Cliff Rakerd
Hotel Clerk	Jessica Shepherd
Airport Lot Attendant	Peter Schmitz
Mechanic	Steve Shaefer
Escort	Michelle Hutchinson
Man in Hallway	David Lomax
Himself	José Feliciano
Night Parking Attendant	Don William Skahill
Mr. Mohra	Bain Boehlke
Valerie	Rose Stockton
Bismarck Cops	Robert Ozasky, John Bandemer
Bark Beetle Narrator	Don Wescott

Car salesman Jerry Lundegaard, hoping to erase a debt, hires a team of hoods to kidnap his wife, intending to collect a portion of the ransom money from his wife's wealthy father. 1996 Academy Awards Winner for Best Actress (Frances McDormand) and Original Screenplay. The film received additional nominations for picture, director, supporting actor (William H. Macy), cinematography and film editing.

©Gramercy Pictures

Steve Buscemi, Michelle Hutchinson

Shirley MacLaine and Audrey Hepburn in *The Children's Hour*

Two men dance together in an 1895 experimental film from the Thomas Edison Studio

Producer/director Jeffrey Friedman, co-executive producer/narrator Lily Tomlin, producer/director Rob Epstein

Marlene Dietrich in *Morocco*

THE CELLULOID CLOSET

(SONY CLASSICS) Producers/Directors, Rob Epstein, Jeffrey Friedman; Executive Producer, Howard Rosenman; Co-Producer, Michael Lumpkin; Co-Executive Producer/Narrator, Lily Tomlin; Narration Written by Armistead Maupin; Story, Rob Epstein, Jeffrey Friedman, Sharon Wood; Based on the book by Vito Russo; Photography, Nancy Schreiber; Editors, Jeffrey Friedman, Arnold Glassman; Art Director, Scott Chamblis; Music, Carter Burwell; Vocal Performance, k.d. lang; Associate Producers, Wendy Braitman, Michael Ehrenzweig, Caryn Mendez; a Home Box Office presentation in association with Channel 4, ZDF/arte, Brillstein-Grey Entertainment, Hugh M. Hefner, James C. Hormel & Steve Tisch of a Telling Pictures production; Color; Rated R; 102 minutes; March release. Documentary chronicling 100 years of the depiction of gay characters in motion pictures.

WITH

Tony Curtis, Armistead Maupin, Susie Bright, Whoopi Goldberg, Jan Oxenberg, Harvey Fierstein, Quentin Crisp, Richard Dyer, Jay Presson Allen, Arthur Laurents, Gore Vidal, Farley Granger, Stewart Stern, Paul Rudnick, Shirley MacLaine, Barry Sandler, Mart Crowley, Antonio Fargas, Tom Hanks, Ron Nyswaner, Daniel Melnick, Harry Hamlin, John Schlesinger, Susan Sarandon

This film originally premiered on HBO in January of 1996.

© HBO

Eric Roberts, Marlee Matlin, Lee Grant

IT'S MY PARTY

(back row) George Segal, Bronson Pinchot, Dimitra Arlys; (middle row) Gregory Harrison, Eric Roberts, Lee Grant, Paul Regina; (front row) Olivia Newton-John, Marlee Matlin, Margaret Cho

(UNITED ARTISTS) Producers, Joel Thurm, Randal Kleiser; Executive Producers, Robert Fitzpatrick, Gregory Hinton; Director/Screenplay, Randal Kleiser; Photography, Bernd Heinl; Designer, Clark Hunter; Editor, Ila von Hasperg; Music, Basil Poledouris; Costumes, Daniele King; Line Producer, Harry Knapp; Casting, Joel Thurm, Steven Fertig; an Opala production; Distributed by MGM/UA; DTS Digital Stereo; Deluxe color; Rated R; 110 minutes; March release

CAST

Charlene Lee	Margaret Cho
Rodney Bingham	Bruce Davison
Amalia Stark	Lee Grant
Andrew Bingham	Devon Gummersall
Brandon Theis	Gregory Harrison
Daphne Stark	Marlee Matlin
Damian Knowles	Roddy McDowall
Lina Bingham	Olivia Newton-John
Monty Tipton	Bronson Pinchot
Tony Zamara	Paul Regina
Paul Stark	George Segal
Nick Stark	Eric Roberts
Zack Phillips	Steven Antin
Fanny Kondos	Dimitra Arlys
Jack Allen	Christopher Atkins
Douglas Reedy	Dennis Christopher
Dr. David Wahl	Ron Glass
Joel Ferris	Lou Liberatore
Matt Paulson	Victor Love
Greg King	Peter Murnik
Soli Real	Felix A. Pire
Tim Bergen	Joel Polis
Joe Lovett	Jon David Weigand
Sara Hart	Sally Kellerman
Bill Hart	Robert Fitzpatrick
Pat Bergen	Talia Paul
Jim Bixby	Eugene Robert Glazer
Brandon's Mother	Nina Foch
Carl Fertig	David Knapp

and Jim Kline (Cowboy), Raul Seymour (Gym Rat), Mike Pointer (Alex), David Medina (Juan), Rhapsody (Miss Texas-at-Large), Brian To (Boy in Pool), David Holladay (Gene), Michael Kearns (Party Guest), Matthew Rickard (Young Andrew), Steve Kmetko (Newscaster), Greg Louganis (Dan Zuma).

Eric Roberts, Gregory Harrison

Eric Roberts, Bruce Davison

Nick Stark, suffering from AIDS and realizing that his end is near, gathers everyone he loves for one final, two-day farewell party.

©United Artists

Nathan Lane

Gene Hackman, Dianne Wiest

Robin Williams, Christine Baranski

Nathan Lane, Hank Azaria, Robin Williams

THE BIRDCAGE

(UNITED ARTISTS) Producer/Director, Mike Nichols; Executive Producers, Neil Machlis, Marcello Danon; Screenplay, Elaine May; Based on the stage play *La Cage aux Folles* by Jean Poiret and the script written by Francis Veber, Edouard Molinaro, Marcello Danon and Jean Poiret; Photography, Emmanuel Lubezki; Designer, Bo Welch; Editor, Arthur Schmidt; Costumes, Ann Roth; Choreographer, Vincent Paterson; Associate Producer, Michele Imperato; Hair and Make-up Designers, J. Roy Helland, Peter Owen; Casting, Juliet Taylor, Ellen Lewis; Distributed by MGM/UA; Dolby DTS Stereo; Technicolor; Rated R; 119 minutes; March release

Robin Williams, Nathan Lane

CAST

Armand Goldman	Robin Williams
Senator Keeley	Gene Hackman
Albert	Nathan Lane
Louise Keeley	Dianne Wiest
Val Goldman	Dan Futterman
Barbara Keeley	Calista Flockhart
Agador	Hank Azaria
Katharine	Christine Baranski
Harry Radman	Tom McGowan
Photographer	Grant Heslov
Cyril	James Lally
Celsius	Luca Tommassini

The Goldman Girls . . . . Luis Camacho, André Fuentes, Anthony Richard Gonzalez, Dante Lamar Henderson, Scott Kaske, Kevin Alexander Stea

Waiter in Club	Tim Kelleher
TV Woman in Van	Ann Cusack
TV Man in Van	Stanley DeSantis
Club Hostess	J. Roy Helland
Fishmonger	Anthony Giaimo
Bakery Man	Lee Delano
Senator Eli Jackson	David Sage
TV Hosts	Mike Kinsley, Tony Snow
Kelley's Maid	Dorothy Constantine
Black Girl on TV	Trina McGee-Davis

and Barry Nolan, Amy Powell, Ron Pitts, James Hill, Mary Major (TV Reporters), Steven Porfido (State Trooper), John D. Pontrelli (Waiter in Cafe), Herschel Sparber (Big Guy in Park), Francesca Cruz (Katharine's Secretary), Brian Reddy, Jim Jansen (TV Editors), Al Rodrigo (Latino Man in Club), Marjorie Lovett, Sylvia Short (Matrons), James H. Morrison (Pastor), Rabbi Robert K. Baruch (Rabbi).

Night club owner Armand Goldman and his lover Albert, a female imper-sonator, are faced with having to meet with the conservative parents of the fiancee of Armand's son. Remake of the French film La Cage aux Folles *which starred Ugo Tognazzi (Armand) and Michel Serrault (Albin/Albert) and was released in the U.S. in 1979 by United Artists. This film received an Oscar nomination for art direction.*

©United Artists

Luca Thomassini, Nathan Lane

Hank Azaria, Dan Futterman, Robin Williams

Robin Williams, Hank Azaria

FLIRTING WITH DISASTER

(MIRAMAX) Producer, Dean Silvers; Executive Producers, Bob Weinstein, Harvey Weinstein; Co-Executive Producer, Trea Hoving; Co-Producer, Kerry Orent; Director/Screenplay, David O. Russell; Photography, Eric Edwards; Designer, Kevin Thompson; Editor, Christopher Tellefsen; Costumes, Ellen Lutter; Music, Stephen Endelman; Casting, Ellen Parks, Risa Bramon Garcia; a Dean Silvers production; Dolby Digital Stereo; Technicolor; Rated R; 92 minutes; March release

CAST

Mel Coplin	Ben Stiller
Nancy Coplin	Patricia Arquette
Tina Kalb	Téa Leoni
Mrs. Coplin	Mary Tyler Moore
Mr. Coplin	George Segal
Richard Schlicting	Alan Alda
Mary Schlicting	Lily Tomlin
Paul	Richard Jenkins
Tony	Josh Brolin
Valerie Swaney	Celia Weston
Lonnie Schlicting	Glenn Fitzgerald
Jane	Beth Ostrosky
Sandra	Cynthia Lamontagne
Fritz Boudreau	David Patrick Kelly
Mitch	John Ford Noonan
B&B Lady	Charlet Oberly

Mel Coplin, feeling that his life is incomplete, teams up with pyschologist Tina Kalb to track down his biological parents.

©Miramax

Lily Tomlin, Alan Alda, Glenn Fitzgerald

Mary Tyler Moore, George Segal

David Patrick Kelly, Ben Stiller

Téa Leoni, Ben Stiller

Josh Brolin, Téa Leoni, Ben Stiller, Richard Jenkins, Patricia Arquette

Madonna, Spike Lee, Theresa Randle

GIRL 6

(FOX SEARCHLIGHT) Producer/Director, Spike Lee; Executive Producer, Jon Kilik; Screenplay, Suzan-Lori Parks; Photography, Malik Hassan Sayeed; Designer, Ina Mayhew; Editor, Sam Pollard; Songs, Prince; Associate Producer, Cirri Nottage; Costumes, Sandra Hernandez; Casting, Aisha Coley; a 40 Acres and a Mule Filmworks Production; Dolby DTS Stereo; Technicolor; Rated R; 105 minutes; April release

CAST

Girl 6	Theresa Randle
Shoplifter	Isaiah Washington
Jimmy	Spike Lee
Boss # — Lil	Jenifer Lewis
Girl # 39	Debi Mazar
Caller # 1 — Bob	Peter Berg
Scary Caller # 30	Michael Imperioli
Girl # 19	Dina Pearlman
Girl # 42	Maggie Rush
Girl # 4	Desi Moreno
Salesgirls	Kristen Wilson, K Funk, Debra Wilson
Girl # 75	Naomi Campbell
Girl # 12	Gretchen Moll
Girl # 29 — Punkster	Shari Freels
Caller # 4 — Beach	Richard Belzer
Caller # 33 — Wall Street	Larry Pine
Caller # 8 — Martin	Coati Mundi
Caller # 8 — Christine	Delilah Cotto
Caller # 6	Anthony Nocerino
Caller # 18	Tom Byrd III
Caller # 14	Bray Poor
Caller # 3 and # 16	Joseph Lyle Taylor
Boss # 3	Madonna
Boss #2 — Male in Office	Arthur Nascarella
Murray, the Agent	John Turturro
Director # 1 — NY	Quentin Tarantino
Director #2 — LA	Ron Silver
Rob	John Cameron Mitchell
Herself	Halle Berry

and Mica Hughes (Director's Assistant), Leonard Thomas (Co-Agent), Joie Susannah Lee (Switchboard Operator), Rolonda Watts (Reporter Nita), Carol Jenkins (Newscaster Carol), Jim Jensen (Newscaster Jim), Jacqueline McAllister (Angela), Novella Nelson (Angela's Aunt), Billie Neal (Angela's Mother), Susan Batson (Acting Coach), Ranjit Chowdhry (Indian Shopkeeper), Rita Wolf (Wife of Indian Shopkeeper), Andrea Navedo, Lesley-Camille Troy, Michele Kelly (Phone Girls), Yohan Lim (Korean Deli Owner), Keith Smith (2nd A.D.), Nelson Vasquez (Ronnie, the Guard), Al Palagonia (Man Mistaken for Bob Regular), Jeff Ward, Chuck Jeffreys, Andy Duppin, Jalil Lynch, David Lomax (Bad Guys), Carlo Vogel, Brian Konowal (Male Assistants), Jennifer Ramos, Jennifer Lee, Tomoko Hagane, Genevieve Yraola, Jennifer Ceballos (Topless Dancers).

Unable to secure work as an actress, a young woman gets a job as a phone sex operator and finds herself being lured into the fantasy of the business.

©Fox Searchlight Pictures

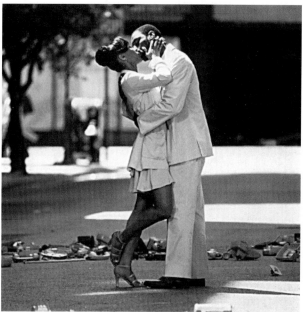

Theresa Randle, Isaiah Washington

Leonard Thomas, Theresa Randle

Spike Lee, Jenifer Lewis, Theresa Randle

A FAMILY THING

(UNITED ARTISTS) Producers, Robert Duvall, Todd Black, Randa Haines; Executive Producer, Michael Hausman; Director, Richard Pearce; Screenplay, Billy Bob Thornton, Tom Epperson; Photography, Fred Murphy; Designer, Linda DeScenna; Editor, Mark Warner; Music, Charles Gross; Costumes, Joe I. Tompkins; Co-Producer, Brad Wilson; Casting, Victoria Thomas; a Todd Black & Randa Haines/Butchers Run Films production; Distributed by MGM/UA; DTS Stereo; Super 35 Widescreen; Color; Rated PG-13; 109 minutes; March release

CAST

Earl Pilcher, Jr.	Robert Duvall
Ray Murdock	James Earl Jones
Virgil Murdock	Michael Beach
Aunt T.	Irma P. Hall
Ruby	Grace Zabriskie
Ann Murdock	Regina Taylor
Carrie	Mary Jackson
Karen	Paula Marshall
Earl, Sr.	James Harrell
Kindra	Lauren Leigh Phillips
Danielle	Ashleigh Jordan
Sonny	David Keith
Young Aunt T.	Saundra Quarterman
Willa Mae	Patrice Pitman Quinn
Junior Turner	Don James
Dr. Parks	Jim Sanderson
Young Carrie Pilcher	Karla Harscheid
Maotis	Crystal Laws Green
Little Raymond	Marquis Ramone Colquitt
Brother Conners	Nathan Lee Lewis
Woman in Apartment	Katharine Mitchell
Sunburned Man	Xander Berkeley
Waitress	Willo Hausman
Tommy	Rufus Thomas

and Richard Lexsee, Ramsey Harris, J. Antonio Moon (Truckjackers), Meg Thalken (Doctor), Jeri Boyle (Old Lady), Tommy Bush (Old Man), Jacqueline Williams (Woman at Hospital), Wandachristine (Woman at City Hall), Roy Hytower (Man at Gas Station), John Mikels (Policeman), Asa Harris (Woman Brithday Friend), Bernard Mixon (Birthday Husband), Paulette McDaniels (Birthday Girl), Phillip Edward Van Lear (Club Manager), Antoine Roshell (Young Man in Car), Greg Hollimon (Man #2), Reginald C. Hayes (Virgil's Friend)

When Earl Pilcher, Jr. receives a letter explaining that his real mother was black, he travels to Chicago to meet the half-brother he has never known.

©*United Artists*

James Earl Jones, Robert Duvall

Robert Duvall, Irma P. Hall, James Earl Jones, Michael Beach

Irma P. Hall, Robert Duvall

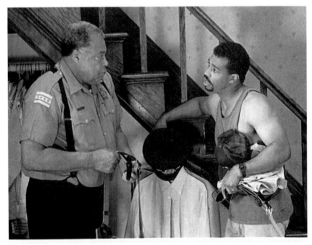

James Earl Jones, Michael Beach

SGT. BILKO

Steve Martin, Dan Aykroyd, Phil Hartman

(UNIVERSAL) Producer, Brian Grazer; Director, Jonathan Lynn; Screenplay, Andy Breckman; Based on the tv series "You'll Never Get Rich/The Phil Silvers Show" created by Nat Hiken; Photography, Peter Sova; Designer, Lawrence G. Paull; Editor, Tony Lombardo; Co-Producer, Mary McLaglen; Music, Alan Silvestri; Costumes, Susan Becker; Casting, Jane Jenkins, Janet Hirshenson; an Imagine Entertainment presentation; DTS Stereo; Super 35 Widescreen; Deluxe color; Rated PG; 94 minutes; March release

CAST

Master Sgt. Ernest G. Bilko	Steve Martin
Colonel Hall	Dan Aykroyd
Major Thorn	Phil Hartman
Rita Robbins	Glenne Headly
Wally Holbrook	Daryl Mitchell
Dino Paparelli	Max Casella
Duane Doberman	Eric Edwards
Tony Morales	Dan Ferro
Sgt. Henshaw	John Marshall Jones
Sam Fender	Brian Leckner
Luis Clemente	John Ortiz
Sgt. Raquel Barbella	Pamela Segall
Mickey Zimmerman	Mitchell Whitfield
Major Ebersole	Austin Pendleton
Lt. Oster	Chris Rock
Lt. Monday	Catherine Silvers
Captain Moon	Steve Park
Mrs. Hall	Debra Jo Rupp
General Tennyson	Richard Herd
Master Sergeant Sowicki	Steve Kehela
First Engineer	Dale Dye
Minister	Charles Stevenson
Mr. Robbins	Rance Howard
Nelson	Christopher Paul Hart
Bartender	Steph Benseman
Blackjack Dealer	Sammy Micco
Assistant Casino Manager	Ursula Burton
G.H.Q. Corporal	Carol Rosenthal
First Technician	Henry Hayashi
Schoolboy Actor	Anthony Monroy-Marquez
Schoolgirl Actress	Lauren Kate Weinger
Janet	Tami-Adrian George
Himself	Travis Tritt
Radio Disc Jockey	Reno Wilson
Second Technician	Sally Ann Brooks
Soldier	Derek Basco
Telephone Operator	Carmela Rappazo
Soldiers	Dwayne Chattman, Clifton Gonzalez
Vegas Women	Andrea Robinson, Lynn Tulaine
Corporal #2	Cheryl Francis Harrington
Boxing Trainer	Michael D. Starks
Craps Dealer	David E. Cousin
D.O.D. Dignitary	Allan Bragg
Pit Boss	Frank Romano
Valet Parker	Russell Bobbitt

Steve Martin

Sgt. Bilko's lackadaisical way of running the Ft. Baxter motor pool is threatened by the arrival of his uptight nemesis Major Thorn. Based on the CBS tv series "You'll Never Get Rich" (later retitled "The Phil Silvers Show") which ran from 1955-59 and starred Phil Silvers (Bilko), and Paul Ford (Col. Hall).

Steve Martin, Glenne Headly

DENISE CALLS UP

(SONY PICTURES CLASSICS) Producer, J. Todd Harris; Executive Producers, John Davis, Stephen Nemeth; Director/Screenplay, Hal Salwen; Co-Producer, Michael Cozell; Photography, Michael Mayers; Editor, Gary Sharfin; Designer, Susan Bolles; Costumes, Edi Giguere; Casting, Sheila Jaffe, Georgianne Walken; a Davis Entertainment and Skyline Entertainment Partners in association with Dark Matter Productions presentation; Dolby Stereo; Color; Rated PG-13; 80 minutes; March release

CAST

Denise	Alanna Ubach
Frank	Tim Daly
Barbara	Caroleen Feeney
Martin	Dan Gunther
Gale	Dana Wheeler-Nicholson
Jerry	Liev Schreiber
Linda	Aida Turturro
Gale's Aunt Sharon	Sylvia Miles
The Cab Driver	Jean Claude Lamarre
Dr. Brennen	Mark Blum
Jerry as a Little Boy	Hal Salwen

Comedy about seven young professionals who have formed a stronger bond with their computers and telephones than with one another.

© Sony Pictures Classics

Liev Schreiber

Alanna Ubach

Tim Daly

Dan Gunther

Caroleen Feeney

Dana Wheeler Nicholson

RACE THE SUN

(TRISTAR) Producers, Richard Heus, Barry Morrow; Executive Producer, David Nichols; Director, Charles T. Kanganis; Screenplay, Barry Morrow; Photography, David Burr; Designer, Owen Paterson; Editor, Wendy Greene Bricmont; Music, Graeme Revell; Casting, Sharon Bialy; a Morrow/Heus production; Dolby SDDS Stereo; Technicolor; Rated PG; 105 minutes; March release

CAST

Sandra Beecher	Halle Berry
Frank Machi	James Belushi
Commissioner Hawkes	Bill Hunter
Daniel Webster	Casey Affleck
Cindy Johnson	Eliza Dushku
Jack Fryman	Kevin Tighe
Eduardo Braz	Anthony Ruivivar
Gilbert Tutu	J. Moki Cho
Marco Quito	Dion Basco
Uni Kakamura	Sara Tanaka
Oni Nagano	Nadja Pionilla
Luana Kanahele	Adriane Napualani Uganiza
Hans Kooiman	Steve Zahn
Judd Potter	Robert Hughes
Ed Webster	Jeff Truman
Steve Fryman	Joel Edgerton
Bob Radford	Tyler Coppin
Mr. Cronin	Marshall Napier
Barb Webster	Gabrielle Hammond
Mrs. Chang	Robyn Moore
Guy	Michael Burgess

and John Alan Su (Another Teacher), John Negro Ponte (Detention Teacher), Marc Gray (Academy Student), Jo-Anne Cahill (Weigh-in Judge), Rick Adams (Stanford University Guy), Rostislav Orel (Pavel), Archer Lyttle (Tom Foote), Piero von Arnim (Gautier), Amanda Wenban (Alice Springs Reporter), Jimmy Sadeli (Hawaiian Reporter), Clarence Dahy, Harry Pavlidis, Franko Milostnik (Reporters), Tim Aris (Scrutineer), Monroe Reimers (Football Coach), Jeamin Lee, Kuni Hashimoto (Oni's Parents), Vera Hong (Detention Student), Prasitt Clifton (Basket Maker)

Science teacher Sandra Beecher encourages some of her misfit students to build and race an experimental car powered by the sun.

©TriStar Pictures

Casey Affleck, Halle Berry, Dion Basco, Adriane Napualani Uganiza, Nadja Pionilla, J. Moki Cho, Sara Tanaka, Anthony Ruivivar, Eliza Dushku, James Belushi

Halle Berry

CARRIED AWAY

(FINE LINE FEATURES) Producers, Lisa M. Hansen, Paul Hertzberg; Executive Producers, Bruno Barreto, Amy Irving, Robert Dattila; Co-Producer, Catalaine Knell; Director, Bruno Barreto; Screenplay, Ed Jones, Dale Herd; Based on the novel *Farmer* by Jim Harrison; Photography, Declan Quinn; Designer, Peter Paul Raubertas; Editor, Bruce Cannon; Costumes, Grania Preston; Music, Bruce Broughton; Line Producer, Russell D. Markowitz; a CineTel Films presentation; Dolby Stereo; Color; Rated R; 107 minutes; March release

CAST

Joseph Svenden	Dennis Hopper
Rosealee Henson	Amy Irving
Catherine Wheeler	Amy Locane
Joseph's Mother	Julie Harris
Major Wheeler	Gary Busey
Dr. Evans	Hal Holbrook
Robert Henson	Christopher Pettiet
Lily Henson	Priscilla Pointer
Catherine's Mother	Gail Cronaeur

Joseph, a small town teacher, begins an affair with Catherine, a 17-year-old student, despite his relationship with fellow teacher Rosealee.

©FineLine Features

Amy Irving, Dennis Hopper

Laura Linney, Richard Gere

Frances McDormand, Richard Gere, Edward Norton

Richard Gere

Richard Gere, Edward Norton

Alfre Woodard, Laura Linney

Laura Linney

PRIMAL FEAR

(PARAMOUNT) Producer, Gary Lucchesi; Executive Producer, Howard W. Koch, Jr.; Director, Gregory Hoblit; Screenplay, Steve Shagan, Ann Biderman; Based on the novel by William Diehl; Photography, Michael Chapman; Designer, Jeannine Oppewall; Costumes, Betsy Cox; Editor, David Rosenbloom; Music, James Newton Howard; Casting, Deborah Aquila, Jane Shannon; presented in association with Rysher Entertainment; a Gary Lucchesi production; Dolby Stereo; Deluxe color; Rated R; 130 minutes; April release

CAST

Martin Vail	Richard Gere
Janet Venable	Laura Linney
John Shaughnessy	John Mahoney
Judge Miriam Shoat	Alfre Woodard
Dr. Molly Arrington	Frances McDormand
Aaron Stampler/Roy	Edward Norton
Yancy	Terry O'Quinn
Tommy Goodman	Andre Braugher
Joey Pinero	Steven Bauer
Abel Stenner	Joe Spano
Martinez	Tony Plana
Archbishop Rushman	Stanley Anderson
Naomi Chance	Maura Tierney
Alex	Jon Seda
Connerman	Reg Rogers
Weil	Kenneth Tigar
Woodside	Brian Reddy
M.C.	Christopher Carroll
Lou	Wendy Cutler
Turner	Ron O.J. Parson
Vail's Secretary	Sigrid K. Zahner
WLS Anchors	Diann Burns, Linda Yu
WLS Location Reporter	Andy Shaw
WBBM Anchors	Mary Ann Childers, Lester D. Holt
WBBM Location Reporters	Sylvia Gomez, Jon Duncanson
WGN Anchors	David Eckert, Robert Jordan
WGN Location Reporters	Joanie Lum, Randy Salerno
Postman	Kyle Colerider-Krugh
Joe	Joseph Luis Caballero
Young Boy	Randall Slavin
Sergeant	Mike Bacarella
Precinct Jailer	Turk Muller
Cop	Joe Kosala
Bartender	Lenny Wilson
Bailiff	Peter Schreiner
Old Man	Joseph R. Ryan
Linda	Azalea Davila

and Wayne Wright (Court Clerk), Tony Fitzpatrick (Duty Officer), Clarence Williams Jr. (Arresting Cop), Rosalie V. Lewis (Stenographer), Dwight Brad Dyer (Prison Guard)

Criminal defense attorney Martin Vail takes on the case of an altar boy accused of killing of a beloved Chicago archbishop. This film received an Oscar nomination for supporting actor (Edward Norton).

©Paramount Pictures Corporation

Andre Braugher, Edward Norton, Richard Gere

Richard Gere

Richard Gere, Laura Linney

John Mahoney, Alfre Woodard, Richard Gere

FAITHFUL

(NEW LINE CINEMA/SAVOY) Producers, Jane Rosenthal, Robert De Niro; Executive Producers, Peter Gatien, Dan Lauria; Director, Paul Mazursky; Screenplay, Chazz Palminteri, based on his play; Co-Producer, Geoffrey Taylor; Photography, Fred Murphy; Designer, Jeffrey Townsend; Editor, Nicholas C. Smith; Costumes, Hope Hanafin; Music, Phillip Johnston; Line Producer, Nan Berstein Freed; Associate Producer, Henry Bronchtein; Casting, Ellen Chenoweth; a Price Entertainment presentation in association with Miramax Films of a Tribeca production; Stereo; Color; Rated R; 88 minutes; April release

CAST

Margaret O'Donnell	Cher
Tony	Chazz Palminteri
Jack O'Donnell	Ryan O'Neal
Dr. Susskind	Paul Mazursky
Debbie	Amber Smith
Maria	Elisa Leonetti
Maria's Boyfriend	Mark Nassar
Young Men at Rolls	Stephen Spinella, Jeffrey Wright
Little Tony	David Merino
Tony's Father	Steven Randazzo
Tony's Mother	Olinda Turturro
Jewelry Store Salesman	Max Norat
Saleslady	Allison Janney
Priest	Chris O'Neill
Foreman	Michael Mulheren
Trucking Dispatcher	Jerry Walsh
Teacher	Gianna Ranaudo
Kids	Omar Sharif Scroggins, Zakee Howze
Young Guys in Car	Paul Ronan, Steve Carreri

Black comedy about a woman who, on her twentieth wedding anniversary, discovers that her husband has hired a hit man to kill her.

©*New Line Productions/Savoy*

Chazz Palminteri, Cher

Chazz Palminteri, Ryan O'Neal

Cher, Chazz Palminteri

Cher

Regina King, Martin Lawrence

Lynn Whitfield, Martin Lawrence

Lynn Whitfield

A THIN LINE BETWEEN LOVE AND HATE

(NEW LINE CINEMA) Producers, Douglas McHenry, George Jackson; Executive Producer/Director/Story, Martin Lawrence; Screenplay, Martin Lawrence, Bentley Kyle Evans, Kenny Buford, Kim Bass; Co-Producers, David Raynr, Suzanne Broderick, William C. Carraro; Photography, Francis Kenny; Designer, Simon Dobbin; Editor, John Carter; Costumes, Eduardo Castro; Music, Roger Troutman; Associate Producer, Peaches Davis; Casting, Mary Gail Artz, Barbara Cohen; a Savoy Pictures co-presentation of a Jackson-McHenry production in association with You Go Boy! productions; Stereo; Super 35 Widescreen; Color; Rated R; 108 minutes; April release

CAST

Darnell Wright	Martin Lawrence
Brandi Web	Lynn Whitfield
Mia	Regina King
Tee	Bobby Brown
Ma Wright	Della Reese
Erica	Malinda Williams
Earl	Daryl Mitchell
Smitty	Roger E. Mosley
Adrienne	Simbi Khali
Nikki	Tangie Ambrose
Gwen	Wendy Robinson
Peaches	Stacii Jae Johnson
Reggie	Miguel A. Nunez, Jr.
Manny	Faizon Love
Marvis	Michael Bell
Rodney	Dartanyan Edmunds
Parking Attendant	Greer Bohanon
Club Security #1	Michael Taliferro
Tyrone	Tiny Lister
Bartender	Tracy Morgan
Officers	Tom Stillman, Arkay Stevens
Officer Evans	Charles Walker

Selfish womanizer Darnell Wright finds his life in danger after he woos and then dumps emotionally unstable Brandi Web.

© *New Line Productions*

Martin Lawrence, Bobby Brown

41

JAMES AND THE GIANT PEACH

(WALT DISNEY PICTURES) Producers, Denise Di Novi, Tim Burton; Executive Producer, Jake Eberts; Director, Henry Selick; Screenplay, Karey Kirkpatrick, Jonathan Roberts, Steve Bloom; Based upon the book by Roald Dahl; Photography, Pete Kozachik, Hiro Narita; Co-Producers, Brian Rosen, Henry Selick; Music/Original Songs, Randy Newman; Editor, Stan Webb; Designer, Harley Jessup; Casting, Robin Gurland, Brian Chavanne, Ros and John Hubbard; Animators, Anthony Scott, Michael Belzer, Timothy Hittle, Trey Thomas, Justin Kohn, Christopher Gilligan, Richard C. Zimmerman, Steven A. Buckley, Guionne LeRoy, Michael W. Johnson, Josephine T. Huang, Daniel K. Mason, Paul Berry, Kent Burton, Tom St. Amand, Webster Colcord, Chuck Duke; Visual Effects Supervisor, Pete Kozachik; Distributed by Buena Vista Pictures; a Denise Di Novi production, presented in association with Allied Filmmakers; Dolby Digital Stereo; Technicolor; Rated PG; 80 minutes; April release

CAST

James Henry Trotter . . . . Paul Terry
Aunt Spiker . . . . Joanna Lumley
Aunt Sponge . . . . Miriam Margolyes
The Old Man . . . . Pete Postlethwaite
James' Father . . . . Steven Culp
James' Mother . . . . Susan Turner-Cray
Girl With Telescope . . . . Cirocco Dunlap
Newsboy . . . . Chae Kirby
Hard Hat Man . . . . Jeff Mosley
Cabby . . . . Al Nalbandian
Innocent Girl . . . . Emily Rosen
Beat Cop . . . . Mike Starr
Street Kid . . . . Mario Yedidia
Reporters . . . . J. Stephen Coyle, Michael Girardin, Tony Haney

VOICE CAST

Grasshopper . . . . Simon Callow
Centipede . . . . Richard Dreyfuss
Ladybug . . . . Jane Leeves
Glowworm . . . . Miriam Margolyes
Spider . . . . Susan Sarandon
Earthworm . . . . David Thewlis

Fantasy mixing live action and stop-action animation about a lonely boy who climbs inside a giant peach and takes off for New York City. This film received an Oscar nomination for original musical score.

©The Walt Disney Company

KIDS IN THE HALL
BRAIN CANDY

(PARAMOUNT) Producer, Lorne Michaels; Executive Producers, Tom Rosenberg, Sigurjon Sighvatsson, David Steinberg; Co-Producers, Barnaby Thompson, Richard S. Wright; Director, Kelly Makin; Screenplay, Norm Hiscock, Bruce McCulloch, Kevin McDonald, Mark McKinney, Scott Thompson; Photography, David A. Makin; Designer, Gregory P. Keen; Editor, Christopher Cooper; Music, Craig Northey; Costumes, Delphine White; Line Producer, Martin Walters; Casting, Ross Clydesdale; a Lakeshore Entertainment presentation of a Lorne Michaels production; Dolby Stereo; Deluxe color; Rated R; 88 minutes; April release

CAST

Marv/Psychiatrist/New Guy/Raymond . . . . Dave Foley	
Alice/Cisco/Grivo/Worm Pill Scientist/	
Cop #2/Cancer Boy/White Trash Man . . . . Bruce McCulloch	
Chris Cooper/Chris' Dad/Doreen/Lacey . . . . Kevin McDonald	
Simon/Don Roritor/Cabbie/Gunter/Cop #1/	
Nina Bedford/Melanie/Drill	
Sergeant/White Trash Woman . . . . Mark McKinney	
Baxter/Mrs. Hurdicure/Wally/Malek/	
The Queen/Scientist Phil/Raj/Clemptor . . . . Scott Thompson	
Ginny . . . . Kathryn Greenwood	
Raymond's Kids. . . . . Amy Smith, Lachlan Murdoch	
Groupies . . . . Nicole deBoer, Krista Bridges	
Wally's Son. . . . . Christopher Redman	
Wally's Daughter. . . . . Erica Lancaster	
Natalie . . . . Jackie Harris	
Panicky Assistant. . . . . Jonathan Wilson	
Mai Tai Waiter . . . . Tony Ning	
Young Chris . . . . Jason Barr	
Old Man in Audience . . . . Jack Jessop	
Woman in Audience. . . . . Sharon Dyer	
Tom Jones Girl . . . . Diane Flacks	

and Barbara Lynn Redpath, Jason D'Addario, Carrie Betker, Elijah R. Brown, Trenton Howe, Pat Patterson, Kay Hawtrey (Wally's Neighbors), Luciano Casimiri (Doorman), Janeane Garofalo (Woman at Party), Adam Reid (Scarred Teenager), Larry Mannell, Donald Tripe, Kirsten Johnson, Lindsay Leese (Scientists), Andy Jones (Monkey Scientist), Thom Bell (Old Man in Pie), Eric Tunney (Wally's Lover), Ann Holloway (Disco Woman), Amanda Payton Stewart (Young Disco Woman), Sherry Hilliard (Coma Queen), Jenni Soosar, Ingrid Hart (Runners-Up), Jared Wall (Miguel), Paul Bellini (Himself), Brendan Fraser (Uncooperative Patient)

A scientist creates a mood-altering drug that latches on to a person's happiest memories and puts them in an eternal state of euphoria.

© Paramount Pictures/Lakeshore Entertainment

Scott Thompson

Bruce McCulloch, Mark McKinney

Mark McKinney, David Foley

Bruce McCulloch, Kevin McDonald, Mark McKinney, Scott Thompson and David Foley

GETTING AWAY WITH MURDER

(SAVOY) Producers, Frank Price, Penny Marshall; Executive Producers, Elliott Abbott, Frederic W. Brost; Director/Screenplay, Harvey Miller; Photography, Frank Tidy; Designer, John Jay Moore; Editor, Richard Nord; Music, John Debney; Costumes, Judy Gellman; Associate Producer, Gail Sicilia; Casting, Sheila Jaffe, Georgiane Walken; a Rank Distributors release of a Price Entertainment/Parkway productino; Dolby Stereo; Technicolor; Rated R; 92 minutes; April release

CAST

Jack Lambert	Dan Aykroyd
Inga Mueller	Lily Tomlin
Max Mueller/Karl Luger	Jack Lemmon
Gail Holland	Bonnie Hunt
Marty Lambert	Brian Kerwin
Judge	Jerry Adler
Psychiatrist	Andy Romano
Sgt. Roarke	Robert Fields
Detective Stanley	J.C. Quinn
Waitress Patti	Susan Forristal
Liz Lambert	Marissa Chibas
Chemistry Lab Professor	Jon Korkes
Old Man	Jack Jessup
Old Woman	Judy Sinclair
Lawyer Brownell	Dave Nichols
Electronic Salesman	Damon D'Oliveira
Bartender	Wayne Robson

and Kathleen Marshall, Jacqueline Klein, Alex Appel, Jillian Hirasawa, Rino Romano (Students), Richard Blackburn, Thomas Mitchell (Nazi Sympathizers), Richard Liss, Kevin Frank, Ann Marie MacDonald, Caroline Yeager (Marty's Party Guests), Bernard Shaw, Bobbie Battista, John McLaughlin, Morton Kondracke, Fred Barnes, Eleanor Clift, Roy Hobbs, Heather Kahn (Themselves), Brett Moon, Ryan Moon (Inga's Twins), Victor Chan (Waiter), Dick Callahan, Diane Douglass, Mary Ann Coles (Mueller's Neighbors), Howard Glassman (Radio Talk Show Host), Jamie Harrold (Jack's Step Son), Camille James Adams (Postal Clerk), Gabriel Regev (Israeli Defense Minister), Colleen Reynolds, Janet Land (Ferry Women), Johnnie Chase (Detective), Luke Costello, Kerry MacDonald (Halloween Kids), Ron Hartman (Cemetery Minister), Brian Kennington (Court Clerk), Herb Lovelle (Blind Man), Robert Morgenroth (Newscaster), Doug O'Keeffe (Gail's Date), Jerry Savoy (Cab Driver), Helen Taylor (Veterinarian), Nicholas Pasco (Cop in Jail).

Black comedy in which ethics professor Jack Lambert is faced with a moral dilemma when the media accuses his kindly next door neighbor of being a notorious Nazi war criminal. © Savoy Pictures

Dan Aykroyd, Lily Tomlin

Dan Aykroyd, Jack Lemmon

FEAR

(UNIVERSAL) Producers, Brian Grazer, Ric Kidney; Executive Producer, Karen Kehela; Director, James Foley; Screenplay, Christopher Crowe; Photography, Thomas Kloss; Designer, Alex McDowell; Editor, David Brenner; Music, Carter Burwell; Costumes, Kirsten Everberg; Casting, Debra Zane; an Imagine Entertainment presentation of a Brian Grazer production; DTS Stereo; Panavision; Deluxe color; Rated R; 95 minutes; April release

CAST

David McCall	Mark Wahlberg
Nicole Walker	Reese Witherspoon
Steve Walker	William Petersen
Laura Walker	Amy Brenneman
Margo Masse	Alyssa Milano
Toby	Christopher Gray
Logan	Tracy Fraim
Hacker	Gary John Riley
Terry	Jason Kristofer
Knobby	Jed Rees
Gary Rohmer	Todd Caldecott
Eddie Clark	John Oliver
Larry O'Brien	David Fredericks
Counterman	Ravinder Toor
Alex McDowell	Andrew Airlie
Julie Masse	Jo Bates
Kid at Door	Will Sengotta
Peterman	L. Harvey Gold
Kaiser	Banner

Nicole's romance with David McCall turns from romantic to deadly when the young man begins to show his volatile and dangerous side.

© Universal City Studios, Inc.

Mark Wahlberg, Reese Witherspoon

MRS. WINTERBOURNE

(TRISTAR) Producers, Dale Pollock, Ross Canter, Oren Koules; Executive Producer, Patrick Palmer; Director, Richard Benjamin; Screenplay, Phoef Sutton, Lisa-Maria Radano; Based upon the novel *I Married a Dead Man* by Cornell Woolrich; Photography, Alex Nepomniaschy; Designer, Evelyn Sakash; Editors, Jacqueline Cambas, William Fletcher; Costumes, Theoni V. Aldredge; Music, Patrick Doyle; Casting, Nancy Foy; an A&M Films production; SDDS Dolby Stereo; Technicolor; Rated PG-13; 104 minutes; April release

CAST

Grace Winterbourne . . . . Shirley MacLaine
Connie Doyle . . . . Ricki Lake
Bill Winterbourne/Hugh Winterbourne . . . . Brendan Fraser
Paco . . . . Miguel Sandoval
Steve DeCunzo . . . . Loren Dean
Father Brian . . . . Peter Gerety
Christine . . . . Jane Krakowski
Lieutenant Ambrose . . . . Debra Monk
Renee . . . . Cathryn De Prume
Sophie . . . . Kate Hennig
Patricia Winterbourne . . . . Susan Haskell
Baby Hughie . . . . Justin Van Lieshout, Alec Thomlison
Susan . . . . Jennifer Irwin
Dr. Hopley . . . . Victor Young
Steve's Pal . . . . Tony Munch
Homeless Man . . . . Nesbitt Blaisdell
Conductors . . . . David Lipman, Jim Feather
Woman on Train . . . . Irene Pauzer
Vera . . . . Bertha Leverone
Detective at Steve's . . . . Johnie Chase
Ambrose's Assistant . . . . Craig Eldridge
Nurse . . . . Paula Prentiss
and Jack Mosshammer, Santino Buda, Marco Kyris (Scuzzy Friends), Thomas Joyce (Jeweler), Tom Harvey (Ty Winthrop), Caroline Yli-Loumi (Florist), Peter Fleming (Wedding Planner), Joa Gamelin (Wedding Gown Designer), Colin Fox, Joan Luchak, Melanie Zuber (Wedding Guests), Bob McAlpine, Rob Gusevs, Shawn Eisenberg, Glyn Stephens (Music Combo)

Following a train wreck, Connie Doyle, who has just given birth, is mistaken for the bride of the late Bill Winterbourne by the groom's wealthy family. © TriStar Pictures Inc.

Ricki Lake, Brendan Fraser

Paula Prentiss

Ricki Lake, Shirley MacLaine

Loren Dean, Ricki Lake, Brendan Fraser

THE LAST SUPPER

(SONY PICTURES) Producers, Matt Cooper, Larry Weinberg; Executive Producer, David Cooper; Co-Executive Producers, Jonathan Penner, Stacy Title; Director, Stacy Title; Screenplay, Dan Rosen; Co-Producers, Lori Miller, Dan Rosen; Photography, Paul Cameron; Designer, Linda Burton; Editor, Luis Colina; Music, Mark Mothersbaugh; Casting, Debra and Bonnie Zane; a Vault Inc. production; Dolby Stereo; Color; Rated R; 94 minutes; April release

Ron Eldard, Cameron Diaz, Courtney B. Vance, Annabeth Gish and Jonathan Penner

CAST

Paulie	Annabeth Gish
Norman Arbuthnot	Ron Perlman
Jude	Cameron Diaz
Marc	Jonthan Penner
Luke	Courtney B. Vance
Pete	Ron Eldard
Zack	Bill Paxton
Sheriff Stanley	Nora Dunn
Deputy Hartford	Dan Rosen
Girl in Coffee Shop	Amber Taylor
Jerk in Coffee Shop	Matt Cooper
Reverend Hutchens	Charles Durning
Dominant Male	Mark Harmon
Iowa Resident at Door	Gil Segel
Abortion Activist	Rachel Chagall
Nation Man	Warren Hutcherson
Homeless Basher	Nick Sadler
Tow Truck Guy	Steve Welch
Illegal Alien Hater	Amy Hill
Young Jude	Carly Weber
Anti-Environmentalist	Jason Alexander
Skin Head	Frederick Lawrence
Illiterate Librarian	Pamela Gien
Heather	Bryn Erin
Businessman with White Socks	Larry Weinberg
Jenny	Elisabeth Moss

Five liberal graduate students invite various conservatives to dinner with the intention of eliminating them. © The Vault Inc.

SUNSET PARK

(TRISTAR) Producers, Danny DeVito, Michael Shamberg, Dan Paulson; Executive Producer, Elizabeth Cantillon; Co-Producers, Mary Kane, Cara Buonincontri; Director, Steve Gomer; Screenplay, Seth Zvi Rosenfeld, Kathleen McGhee-Anderson; Photography, Robbie Greenberg; Designer, Victoria Paul; Editor, Arthur Coburn; Costumes, Carl Ramsey; Music, Miles Goodman, Kay Gee; Casting, Robi Reed-Humes, Tony Lee, Andrea Reed; a Jersey Films production in association with Daniel L. Paulson productions; Dolby SDDS Stereo; Technicolor; Rated R; 100 minutes; April release

CAST

Phyllis Saroka	Rhea Perlman
Shorty	Fredro Starr
Mona	Carol Kane
Spaceman	Terrence DaShon Howard
Barbara	Camille Saviola
Busy-Bee	De'Aundre Bonds
Butter	James Harris
Andre	Anthony Hall
Drano	Antwon Tanner
Kurt	Shawn Michael Howard
Boo Men	Guy Torry
Morris Bernstein	Scott Burkholder
Dominic	John Aprea
Mr. Santiago	John Vargas
Carla	Rhonda Stubbins White
Washington Heights Coach	Steffen Foster
Judge Meyer	Hattie Winston
Referees	Tim Hutchinson, Charles E. Thompson, Curtis McGee
East Flatbush Player	Paul Johnson
Shirley	Tracy Vilar
Sal the Janitor	Michael Mack
Kid Gloc	Lucien Lewis
Coney Island Player	Eric George
Dreadlock Guy	Gary Dourdan

and Silk Willie Dunn (School Bus Driver), Melissa Berger (Cop at Apartment), Trula Marcus (Marisa), Vincent Pastore (Charlie the Super), A. Doran Reed (Carlton Palmer), Bee-Be Smith (Regina), Malinda Williams (Cherl), Jay Della, Christopher McHale (Bar Customers)

Despite protests Phyllis Saroka accepts the challenge of coaching the boys basketball team at Sunset Park High. © TriStar Pictures

Fredro Star, Antwon Tanner, Anthony Hall, James Harris, Rhea Perlman

MULHOLLAND FALLS

(MGM) Producers, Richard D. Zanuck, Lili Fini Zanuck; Director, Lee Tamahori; Screenplay, Pete Dexter; Story, Pete Dexter, Floyd Mutrux; Photography, Haskell Wexler; Designer, Richard Sylbert; Editor, Sally Menke; Costumes, Ellen Mirojnick; Music, Dave Grusin; Executive Producer, Mario Iscovich; Casting, Shari Rhodes, Joseph Middleton; Presented in association with Largo Entertainment; from MGM/UA Distribution; DTS Stereo; Deluxe color; Rated R; 107 minutes; April release

Melanie Griffith, Nick Nolte

CAST

Max Hoover	Nick Nolte
Katherine Hoover	Melanie Griffith
Ellery Coolidge	Chazz Palminteri
Eddie Hall	Michael Madsen
Arthur Relyea	Chris Penn
Col. Nathan Fitzgerald	Treat Williams
Allison Pond	Jennifer Connelly
F.B.I. Special Agent McCafferty	Daniel Baldwin
Jimmy Fields	Andrew McCarthy
General Thomas Timms	John Malkovich
The Chief	Bruce Dern
Captain	Kyle Chandler
Earl	Ed Lauter
Flynn	William Petersen
Flynn's Guest at Dinner	Rob Lowe
Esther	Louise Fletcher
Perino's Matire 'd	Larry Garrison
Lolita	Chelsea Harrington
Bar Woman	Johna Johnson
Staff Car Sergeant	Rick Johnson
Staff Car Driver	Britt Burr
Cigarette Girl	Melinda Clarke
Foreman	Ernie Lively
Coroner	Richard Sylbert
Assistant Coroner	Michael Krawic
Kenny Kamins	Titus Welliver

and Robert Peters (Cop #1), Father William M. Thigpen (Priest), Drew Pillsbury (Chief Assistant), Brad Hunt (Guard), Aaron Neville (Nite Spot Singer), Buddy Joe Hooker (DC-3 Pilot), Eddie Caicedo (Gasping Patient), Price Carson (Honor Guard), Azalea Davila, Sky Solari (Perino's Girls), Alisa Christiensen (Spaghetti Girl)

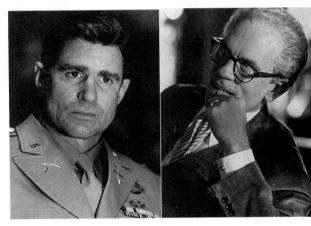

Treat Williams   John Malkovich

Four L.A. cops, nicknamed the "Hat Squad," investigate the murder of a young woman whose broken body has been discovered at a construction sight.
© Metro-Goldwyn-Mayer

Chris Penn, Nick Nolte, Michael Madsen, Chazz Palminteri

THE QUEST

(UNIVERSAL) Producer, Moshe Diamant; Executive Producer, Peter MacDonald; Director, Jean-Claude Van Damme; Screenplay, Steven Klein, Paul Mones; Story, Frank Dux, Jean-Claude Van Damme; Line Producer, Jason Clark; Photography, David Gribble; Designer, Steve Spence; Editors, John F. Link William J. Meshover; Associate Producers, Jack Frost Sanders, Eugene Van Varenberg; Costumes, Joseph Porro; Music, Randy Edelman; Fight Choreographer, Steven Lambert; Casting, James F. Tarzia; an MDP Worldwide presentation of a Moshe Diamant production; DTS Digital Stereo; Super 35 Widescreen; Deluxe color; Rated PG-13; 95 minutes; April release

CAST

Chris Dubois	Jean-Claude Van Damme
Lord Edgar Dobbs	Roger Moore
Maxie Devine	James Remar
Carrie Newton	Janet Gunn
Harry Smith	Jack McGee
Khao	Aki Aleong
Khan	Abdel Qissi
Riggi	Louis Mandylor
Master Tchi	Chang Ching Peng Chaplin
Officer O'Keefe	Ryan Cutrona
Red	Shane Meier
Billy	Matt Lyon
Phang	Jen Sung Outerbridge
Chinese Fighter	Peter Wong
Sumo Fighter	Kitao
German Fighter	Habby Heske
Brazilian Fighter	Cesar Carneiro
French Fighter	Takis Triggelis
Turkish Fighter	Azdine Nouri
Greek Tighter	Stefanos Miltsakakis
Spanish Fighter	Peter Malota
African Fighter	Ellis Winston
Okinawan Fighter	Ong Soo Han
Russian Fighter	Brick Bronsky
Korean Fighter	Ip Choi Nam
Scottish Fighter	Michael Ian Lambert

and Gordon Masten (Bartender), Zev Revach (Turk Captain), Manon Marcoux (Nanny), Kristopher Van Varenberg (Young Chris), Cherdpong Laoyant (Dining Salon Bangkok Waiter), Vichai Indtrasathit (Tibetan Monk in New York), Chai Chapanond (Lama Announcer), H. Rudy Gontha (Innkeeper), Jodie Charattanawet (Annan), Tara Nichelle Biberstein (Little Girl), Jason Cavalier, Rik Kiviaho, Anderson C. Bradshaw (Youths), Michael Caloz, Camelia Lightbourne (Childern), Emilio Migliozzi (Riggi's Mug), Brauno Belfiore, Michael Davila, Magnus Ljungberg, Joseph Dykes, Martin Gerber, Lindsay Sargeant, Scott Wilson, Paul Moses (Fighters' Entourage)

A New York pickpocket, on the run from the police, ends up in the Far East where he enters a prestigious martial arts contest.

Roger Moore, Jean-Claude Van Damme

Jean-Claude Van Damme (r)

THE SUBSTITUTE

(ORION) Producers, Morrie Eisenman, Jim Steele; Director, Robert Mandel; Screenplay, Roy Frumkes, Rocco Simonelli, Alan Ormsby; Executive Producers, Devora Cutler, Steven Bakalar; Photography, Bruce Surtees; Designer, Ron Foreman; Editor, Alex Mackie; Music, Gary Chang; Co-Producer, Juanita Diana; a Live Entertainment presentation of a Dinamo/H2 production; Dolby Stereo; Color; Rated R; 114 minutes; April release

CAST

Shale	Tom Berenger
Jane Hetzko	Diane Venora
Rolle	Ernie Hudson
Juan Lacas	Marc Anthony
Mr. Sherman	Glenn Plummer
Lisa	Maria Celedonio
Jerome	Sharron Corley
Joey Six	Raymond Cruz
Rem	Luis Guzman
Wellman	Richard Brooks
Hollan	William Forsythe
John Janus	Willis Sparks
Johnny Glades	Rodney A. Grant
Tay	Maurice Compte
Rodriguez	Vincent Laresca
Kod Punk	Ian Marioles
Michael	David Spates
Frank	David Hayes
Anna Dillon	Peggy Pope
Wolfson	Cliff DeYoung

and Steve Zurk (P.E. Coach), Mike Benitez (Chemistry Teacher), Jody Wilson (Mrs. Andrewson), Steve Dumochel (Buyer), Noelle Beck (Deidre), Mercedes Eriquel (High School Nurse)

After his girlfriend is assaulted by a gang of students, mercenary Shale poses as a substitute to seek out and punish the guilty parties.

Glenn Plummer, Tom Berenger

Janeane Garofalo

Janeane Garofalo, Uma Thurman

Ben Chaplin, Hank

Uma Thurman, Janeane Garofalo

THE TRUTH ABOUT CATS AND DOGS

(20TH CENTURY FOX) Producer, Cari-Esta Albert; Executive Producers, Richard Hashimoto, Audrey Wells; Director, Michael Lehmann; Screenplay, Audrey Wells; Photography, Robert Brinkmann; Designer, Sharon Seymour; Editor, Stephen Semel; Music, Howard Shore; Costumes, Bridget Kelly; Casting, Debra Zane; a Noon Attack production; Dolby Stereo; Deluxe color; Rated PG-13; 97 minutes; April release

CAST

Noelle Slusarsky	Uma Thurman
Abby Barnes	Janeane Garofalo
Brian	Ben Chaplin
Ed	Jamie Foxx
Roy	James McCaffrey
Eric	Richard Coca
Mario	Stanley DeSantis
Susan	Antoinette Valente
Bee Man	Mitch Rouse
Emily	La Tanya M. Fisher
Child Model	Faryn Einhorn
Radio Caller/Bookstore Man	David Cross
Radio Caller	Mary Lynn Rajskub
Bookstore Man	Bob Odenkirk
Bookstore Cashier	Dechen Thurman
Mother	Victoria Edwards
Saleswoman	Lisa Marie Russell
Irate Director	Robert Brinkmann

and Josiah Polhemus, Nigel Gibbs, David Phelps, Linda Porter, Michael Burke, Vanessa J. Wells (Newscast Auditioners), Hank the Dog (Hank)

After radio talk show host Abby Barnes lies about herself to caller Brian, she asks her friend Noelle to pass herself off as Abby when Brian insists on a face-to-face meeting.

© Twentieth Century Fox

I SHOT ANDY WARHOL

(ORION) Producers, Tom Kalin, Christine Vachon; Executive Producers, Lindsay Law, Anthony Wall; Director, Mary Harron; Screenplay, Mary Harron, Daniel Minahan; Photography, Ellen Kuras; Editor, Keith Reamer; Music, John Cale; Designer, Thérèse Deprez; Costumes, David Robinson; Casting, Barden, Hopkins and Smith; a Playhouse International Pictures presentation in association with the Samuel Goldwyn Company and BBC Arena; Dolby Digital Stereo; Technicolor; Not rated; 106 minutes; May release

Lili Taylor

CAST

Valerie Solanas	Lili Taylor
Andy Warhol	Jared Harris
Candy Darling	Stephen Dorff
Stevie	Martha Plimpton
Jeremiah	Danny Morgenstern
Maurice Girodias	Lothaire Bluteau
Ondine	Michael Imperioli
Paul Morrissey	Reg Rogers
Brigid Berlin	Coco McPherson
Gerard Malanga	Donovan Leitch
Viva	Tahnee Welch
Fred Hughes	Craig Chester
Billy Name	James Lyons
Iris	Anna Thomson
Jackie Curtis	Jamie Harrold
Ultra Violet	Myriam Cyr
Tom Baker	Bill Sage
Susan	Lorraine Farris
Danny	Victor Browne
Rotten Rita	Billy Erb
Laura	Jill Hennessy
Amphetamine Head	Kevin Rendon
Isabelle De Courcy	Caroline Benezet-Brown
Comtesse De Courcy	Anh Duong
Mario Amaya	Massimo Audiello
Warhol Superstars	Christina McKay, Eugenie McKay
Louis Solanas	Mark Margolis

and Dawn Didawick (Waitress), Georgia Hubley, Ira Kaplan, James McNew, Tara Key (The Party Band), Faith Greer (Mrs. Warhola), Jeff Webster (Assistant D.A. Lanklar), Lola Pashalinski (Psychiatrist), Henry Cabot Beck, Christopher Cook (Reporters), Edoardo Ballerini (Editor of School Paper), Gabriel Mick (Clean Cut Boy), Mariah Quinn (Jean), Fenton Lawless (John Who Likes Golf Shoes), Laura Ekstrand (Marilyn), Michelle Hurst (Nedick's Manager), Michael Stumm (Chelsea Manager), Justin Theroux (Mark the Revolutionary), Eric Mabius (Revolutionary No. 2), Peter Friedman (Alan Burke), Isabel Gillies (Alison), Davis Hall (Alan Burke Show Director), Paco Juanas (Flamenco Guitarist), Steve Itkin (Police Chief on TV), Bill Lin, Debbon Ayer, Anna Grace (Passerbys), Daniel Haughey (The Pornographer), Lynn Cohen (Hotel Concierge)

Martha Plimpton

Donovan Leitch

The true story of feminist Valerie Solanas, her involvement with Andy Warhol's New York party crowd of the 1960s and her attempt on the noted artist's life.   © Orion Pictures Corp.

Lothaire Bluteau   Stephen Dorff

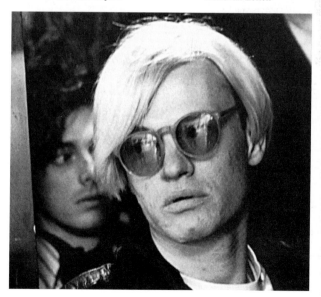
Jared Harris

THE GREAT WHITE HYPE

(20TH CENTURY FOX) Producers, Fred Berner, Joshua Donen; Director, Reginald Hudlin; Screenplay, Tony Hendra, Ron Shelton; Photography, Ron Garcia; Designer, Charles Rosen; Editor, Earl Watson; Co-Producers, Barry Berg, Neil Leifer; Music, Marcus Miller; Costumes, Ruth Carter; Casting, Eileen Mack Knight; an Atman Entertainment/Fred Berner Films production; Dolby Stereo; Deluxe color; Rated R; 90 minutes; May release

CAST

Revered Fred Sultan	Samuel L. Jackson
Mitchell Kane	Jeff Goldblum
Terry Conklin	Peter Berg
Sol	Jon Lovitz
Peter Prince	Corbin Bernsen
Julio Escobar	Cheech Marin
Johnny Windsor	John Rhys-Davies
Bambi	Salli Richardson
Hassan El Ruk'n	Jamie Foxx
Artemus St. John Saint	Rocky Caroll
Roper's Manager	Albert Hall
Vivian	Susan Gibney
Marvin Shabazz	Michael Jayce
Palace Guards	Duane Davis, Lamont Johnson, Lydell M. Cheshier Randy "Roughhouse" Harris
James "The Grim Reaper" Roper	Damon Wayans
Artie	Sam Whipple
Fight Announcers	Stu Nahan, Ferdie Pacheco, M.D.
Press Member #1	Al Rodrigo
Lee the Drummer	Phil Buckman
Angel	Renee Ammann
Michael Katz	Walter Addison
Chairman Jerry Schwartz	Michael Fairman

and Bert Randolph Sugar, Tim Kawakami, Brian Setzer, Method Man (Themselves), Jonathan P. Hicks, Craig Modderno (Sports Writers), Brad Blaisdell, James Hardie (Press Corps), Nedra Volz (Old Lady), Rick Scarry (White Middle American), Elizabeth LaRou, Alyson Croft, Christal L. House (Pretty Young Women), Richard Steele (Referee), Anthony "A.J." Johnson (Sultan's Valet), Irv L. Dotten, Deezer D., Reno Wilson (Roper's Cronies), Art Evans (Minister), G. John Slagle (Kane's Cameraman), Leon Frederick, James H. Hays (Roper's Cornermen)

Hoping to build up dwindling audience interest, fight promoter Fred Sultan talks white rock star Terry Conklin into fighting black heavyweight champ James Roper, whom he had defeated in the distant past.

Samuel L. Jackson, Rocky Caroll, Salli Richardson, Jon Lovitz

Peter Berg

Jeff Goldblum

Cheech Marin, Samuel L. Jackson

THE CRAFT

(COLUMBIA) Producer, Douglas Wick; Executive Producer, Ginny Nugent; Director, Andrew Fleming; Screenplay, Peter Filardi, Andrew Fleming; Story, Peter Filardi; Photography, Alexander Gruszynski; Designer, Mark Dobrowolski; Editor, Jeff Freeman; Music, Graeme Revell; Costumes, Deborah Everton; Co-Producer, Lisa Tornell; Visual Effects, Sony Imageworks; a Douglas Wick production; Dolby SDDS Stereo; Technicolor; Rated R; 100 minutes; May release

CAST

Sarah	Robin Tunney
Nancy	Fairuza Balk
Bonnie	Neve Campbell
Rochelle	Rachel True
Chris	Skeet Ulrich
Laura Lizzie	Christine Taylor
Mitt	Breckin Meyer
Trey	Nathaniel Marston
Mr. Bailey	Cliff De Young
Lirio	Assumpta Serna
Grace	Helen Shaver
Jenny	Jeanine Jackson
Doctor	Brenda Strong
Laura's Friends	Elizabeth Guber, Jennifer Greenhut
Vagrant	Arthur Senzy
Monsieur Thepot	Endre Hules
Swimming Coach	Mark Conlon

and Christine Louise Berry (Stewardess), William Newman (Street Preacher), Erin Tavin (Homeless Mother), Rod Britt (Priest), Brogan Roche (Insurance Man), Rebecca McLaughlin (Biology Teacher), Tony Genaro (Bus Driver), Janet Rotblatt (Homeroom Teacher), Jason Filardi (Paramedic), Karyn J. Dean, Danielle Koenig (Whispering Girls), Janet Eilber (Sarah's Mother), Esther Scott (Nurse)

Outsider Sarah, newly arrived at a Los Angeles high school, finds herself joining a mysterious trio of girls who happen to practice witchcraft.

© Columbia Pictures Industries, Inc.

Neve Campbell, Fairuza Balk, Robin Tunney, Rachel True

Lukas Haas, Winona Ryder

BOYS

(TOUCHSTONE) Producers, Peter Frankfurt, Paul Feldsher, Erica Huggins; Executive Producers, Ted Field, Scott Kroopf, Robert W. Cort; Director/Screenplay, Stacy Cochran; Based on the short story "Twenty Minutes" from the book *Dusk* by James Salter; Co-Producer, Rudd Simmons; Photography, Robert Elswit; Designer, Dan Bishop; Editor, Camilla Toniolo; Costumes, Lucy W. Corrigan; Music, Stewart Copeland; Casting, Todd Thaler; an InterScope Communications/PolyGram Filmed Entertainment production; Distributed by Buena Vista Pictures; Dolby Digital Stereo; Technicolor; Rated PG-13; 88 minutes; May release

CAST

Patty Vare	Winona Ryder
John Baker, Jr.	Lukas Haas
Officer Kellogg Curry	John C. Reilly
Fenton Ray	James LeGros
Bud Valentine	Skeet Ulrich
John Cooke	Charlie Hofheimer
John Murphy	Spencer Vrooman
John Phillips	Wiley Wiggins
John Van Slieder	Russell Young
Jon Heinz	Christopher Pettiet
Jilly	Catherine Keener
Officer Bill Martone	Bill Sage
Liz Curry	Maddie Corman
Baker's Mom	Jessica Harper
Baker's Dad	Chris Cooper

and Matt Malloy (Bartender), Marty McDonough (Teacher), Vivienne Shub (Frances), Andy Davis (Jonathan Marco), David Newsom (Curt), James Gardiner (Kellogg Curry, Jr.), Cheryl Goode (Beer Girl), John J. Fitzpatrick (Steve Hunt), Gregorio Rosenblum (Dr. Paz), Miranda Syp (Ellen Vare), Robert Carlton (Tom Vare), John Reeves (Phil Rains, Esq.), Carter McNeese (Floor Waxer), Angela Hall (Officer Julie Leroux), Bob Moore (Officer Darryl Cane), David Paulson (Lt. Love)

High School senior John Baker, Jr. discovers a mysterious woman who has fallen from her horse near the grounds of his boarding school and decides to take her back to his dorm room.

© Buena Vista Pictures Distribution, Inc.

Lukas Haas, Russell Young, Christopher Pettiet, Wiley Wiggins

Sharon Stone, Rob Morrow

Peter Gallager, Rob Morrow

LAST DANCE

(TOUCHSTONE) Producer, Steven Haft; Executive Producer, Richard Luke Rothschild; Co-Producer, Chuck Binder; Director, Bruce Beresford; Screenplay, Ron Koslow; Story, Steven Haft, Ron Koslow; Photography, Peter James; Designer, John Stoddart; Editor, John Bloom; Music, Mark Isham; Costumes, Colleen Kelsall; Casting, Shari Rhodes, Joseph Middleton; a Steven Haft production; Distributed by Buena Vista Pictures; Dolby Digital Stereo; Technicolor; Rated R; 103 minutes; May release

CAST

Cindy Liggett	Sharon Stone
Rick Hayes	Rob Morrow
Sam Burns	Randy Quaid
John Hayes	Peter Gallagher
The Governor	Jack Thompson
Jill	Jayne Brook
Legal Aid Attorney	Pamala Tyson
Billy	Skeet Ulrich
Doug	Don Harvey
Reggie	Diane Sellers
Frances	Patricia French
Rusk	Jeffery Ford
Detective Vollo	Dave Hager
Louise	Christine Cattell
Helen	Peg Allen
Governor's Wife	Peggy Walton Walker
Carolyn	Deena Dill
Etta	Diana Taylor
Stripper in Bar	Mimi Craven
McGuire	John Cunningham
Betty	Randy Hresko
Grace	Charlotte Hackman
Warden Rice	Ralph Wilcox
Warden Laverty	Ken Jenkins
Reverend Cummins	Joe Inscoe
Officer Mulkey	Elizabeth Omilami
Governor's Receptionist	Sandra Thigpen
Governor's Aide	Michael Montgomery
Debbie	Rachel Glass
Matt	Kyle Hester
Sue Hunt	Ginny Parker
Tiffany Hunt	Kaitlyn Kenney
Paul Faring	Kenneth Schulz

and Dennis Ferrier, Demetria Kalodimos, Jeff McAtee, Cynthia Williams, Ava P. Philson, Carlene Moore (Reporters), Ted Manson (Judge Gorman), William Thorp (Motorboat Pilot), Richard Cowl (Judge Butler), Dionne Gardner (Dress Shop Sales Girl), Asha J. King (Linda's Daughter), B.J. Brown (Drill Instructor), Thomas "Kirk" Hawkins (Sea Plane Pilot), Susan Jeffery (Party Clown), Trilby Beresford (Title Sequence Girl), Dottie Snow (Cindy's Aunt), Kuldeep Narain (Tour Guide), and Charles S. Dutton.

Attorney Rick Hayes becomes convinced that Cindy Liggett, waiting on death row for 12 years, has been given an unjust sentence.

© Touchstone Pictures

Randy Quaid, Skeet Ulrich, Rob Morrow

Sharon Stone

THE PALLBEARER

(MIRAMAX) Producers, Jeffrey Abrams, Paul Webster; Executive Producers, Bob Weinstein, Harvey Weinstein, Meryl Poster; Director, Matt Reeves; Screenplay, Jason Katims, Matt Reeves; Line Producer, Nellie Nugiel; Co-Producer, Jason Katims; Photography, Robert Elswit; Designer, Robin Standefer; Editor, Stan Salfas; Music, Stewart Copeland; Costumes, Donna Zakowska; Casting, Billy Hopkins, Suzanne Smith, Kerry Barden; an Abrams/Katims/Webster production; Dolby Stereo; Color; Rated PG-13; 97 minutes; May release

CAST

Tom Thompson	David Schwimmer
Julie DeMarco	Gwyneth Paltrow
Brad	Michael Rapaport
Cynthia	Toni Collette
Tom's Mom	Carol Kane
Lauren	Bitty Schram
Ruth Abernathy	Barbara Hershey
Scott	Michael Vartan
Jared	Matthew Faber
Sylvie	Robin Morse
The Job Interviewer	Edoardo Ballerini
The Undertaker	Tony Machine
Minister	Robert Katims
The Abernathy Cousins	Greg Grunberg, David Vadim, Zak Orth
The Pallbearers	Kevin Corrigan, Joseph D'Onofrio, John Mudd, Eric Morace
Aunt Lucille	Elizabeth Franz
Roller Coaster Rider	Marnie Pomerantz
Philip DeMarco	Mark Margolis
Suzanne DeMarco	Jean DeBaer
Maitre D'	George Masters
The Other Tom	Todd Schrenk
Rabbi	Rabbi Joel Zion
Wedding Guests	Sal Maneri, Gwen Goldsmith

Tom Thompson receives a phone call from a myterious woman asking him to be the pallbearer at the funeral of an old classmate he can't seem to remember. © Miramax Films

Gwyneth Paltrow, David Schwimmer

David Schwimmer, Barbara Hershey

Bitty Schram, Toni Collette, Gwyneth Paltrow, Michael Rapaport, David Schwimmer, Barbara Hershey, Michael Vartan

DEAD MAN

(MIRAMAX) Producer, Demetra J. MacBride; Director/Screenplay, Jim Jarmusch; Photography, Robby Muller; Editor, Jay Rabinowitz; Music, Neil Young; Designer, Robert Ziembicki; Co-Producer, Karen Koch; Costumes, Marit Allen; Casting, Ellen Lewis, Laura Rosenthal; a Pandora Film, JVC and Newmarket Capital Group, L.P. presentation of a 12-Gauge Production; U.S. - German - Japanese; Dolby Stereo; Black and white; Rated R; 120 minutes; May release

CAST

William Blake	Johnny Depp
Nobody	Gary Farmer
Cole Wilson	Lance Henriksen
Conway Twill	Michael Wincott
Thell Russell	Mili Avital
Salvatore "Sally" Jenko	Iggy Popp
Benmont Tench	Jared Harris
Big George Drakoulious	Billy Bob Thornton
Train Fireman	Crispin Glover
Johnny "The Kid" Pickett	Eugene Byrd
Nobody's Girlfriend	Michelle Thrush
Charlie Dickinson	Gabriel Byrne
John Scholfield	John Hurt
Trading Post Missionary	Alfred Molina
John Dickinson	Robert Mitchum
Marvin (Older Marshall)	Jimmie Ray Weeks
Lee (Younger Marshall)	Mark Bringelson
Man with Gun in Alley	Gibby Haines
Man at End of Street	George Duckworth
Man with Wrench	Richard Boes
Old Man with Wanted Posters	Mike Dawson
Men at Trading Post	John Pattison, Todd Pefiffer

and Leonard Bowechop, Cecil Cheeka, Michael McCarty (Makah Village), Thomas Bettles (First Young Nobody), Daniel Chas Stacy (Second Young Nobody), Peter Schrum (Drunk), John North (Mr. Olafsen), and Steve Buscemi.

Accountant William Blake arrives in the desolate and decrepit Western town of Machine to take a job at the Dickinson Metalworks.

'© Miramax Film

Alfred Molina, Johnny Depp, Gary Farmer

Robert Mitchum

Maggie Han, Robert Wuhl

OPEN SEASON

(LEGACY) Producer, Daniel Raskov; Executive Producer, Ron Shelton; Director/Screenplay, Robert Wuhl; Co-Producer, Karen Koch; Photography, Stephen Lighthill; Editor, Seth Flaum; Designer, Linda Burton; Music, Marvin Hamlisch; Casting, Ed Johnston; a Republic Pictures presentation of a Frozen Rope production, 1993; Ultra-Stereo; Color; Rated R; 97 minutes; May release

CAST

Stuart Sain	Robert Wuhl
Billy Patrick	Rod Taylor
George Plunkett	Gailard Sartain
Rachel Rowen	Helen Shaver
Cary Sain	Maggie Han
Leon	Steve White
Herbert Goodfellow	Timothy Arrington
Doris Hays-Britton	Dina Merrill
Eric Schlockmeister	Saul Rubinek
Scarface	Lloyd Adams
Nun/Spoon Nettles	Marcy King
Hunk Cop	Rick Forsayeth
Kerwin Kessler	Barry Flatman
Peter Carter	Howard Hoover
Sam	Dwight Bacquie
Mark	Burke Lawrence
Leon	Steven C. White
Girl with Hat	Catherine Kellner
Zachariah Boone	Roger Dunn
Sarah Boone	Maggie Butterfield
Isadiah Boone	Drew Jurecka
Hannah Boone	Jaya Karsemeyer
Rock Maninoff	Tom Selleck
Xanex	Alan Thicke
Homer	Jimmie Walker
Hamlet	Joe Piscopo
Themselves	Bob Costas, Larry King, Tony Guida, Regis Philbin

and Elizabeth Goodyear, Craig Eldridge, Frank Moore (Reporters), Dolores Toth, Marilyn Boyle, Faye Deabreu (Ladies), O.J. Kane, Sarah Beth Clark (Students), Conrad Coates, Jude Gerard Prest, Cliff Turner, Lindsay Leese (Fielding Reps), Hadely Sandiford (Dr. Jeffries), Darlene Cooke (Mrs. Jeffries), Vladimir Pritsker (Yuri Nolibow), Mila Kaney (Mila Nolibow), George Buza (Orly Travis), Alexe Duncan (Molly Travis), Colin Fox (Jackson Carp), Andrew Moody (Floor Manager), Griz the Dog (Tofu the Dog), Jackie Harris (Amanda), Bruce Beaton (Carson), Joanna Hartley (Linda Carlisle), Kate Asner (Harriet), Danny Smith (Buck Greene, Rookie Messenger), Jonathan Hartman (Angel), Suzanne Krull (Mona), Suzanne Barker (Susan Steenland), Alex Laurier (Peter Miles), Jovanni Sy (Gossage), Marvin Ishmael (Rawly), Aimee Brooks (Clinique), Johnny Moran (Deltoid), Eric Greenberg (Organic Waiter), Barbara Koldys Capelli, Tracy Hudak, Steve Epstein, Raymond DeMarco (People-on-Street), Peter Ferri (Dr. H. Roth Castell)

Comedy about an employee of the Fielding Ratings Company who rises to power after an error in the ratings system causes public television to become the country's top-rated network.

© Frozen Rope Productions, Inc

ORIGINAL GANGSTAS

Dawn Stern, Christopher B. Duncan, Timothy Lewis

Isabel Sanford, Oscar Brown, Jr.

(ORION) Producer, Fred Williamson; Director, Larry Cohen; Screenplay, Aubrey Rattan; Photography, Carlos Gonzalez; Editors, David Kern, Peter B. Ellis; Music, Vladimir Horunzhy; Designer, Elayne Barbara Ceder; Costumes, Lisa Moffie; Casting, Craig Campobasso; from Po'Boy productions; Dolby DTS Stereo; Astro Film color; Rated R; 99 minutes; May release

CAST

John Bookman	Fred Williamson
Jake Trevor	Jim Brown
Laurie Thompson	Pam Grier
Reverend Dorsey	Paul Winfield
Gracie Bookman	Isabel Sanford
Marvin Bookman	Oscar Brown, Jr.
Slick	Richard Roundtree
Bubba	Ron O'Neal
Spyro	Christopher B. Duncan
Damien	Eddie Bo Smith, Jr.
Kayo	Dru Down
Dink	Shyheim Franklin
Detective Slatten	Robert Forster
Mayor	Charles Napier
Michael Casey	Wings Hauser
Detective Waits	Frank Pesce
Marcus	Godfrey C. Danchimah
Blood	Tim Rhoze
Thelma/Mrs. Jones	Seraiah Carol
Princess	Dawn Stern
Kenny Thompson	Timothy Lewis
Lisa Bookman	Linda Marie Bright
Bobby	Kevin Watson
Doctor	Anthony Snowden
TV Announcer	Nick Edenetti
TV News Reporter	Jacqueline Swike
Ladies in Gym	Kimberly Shufford, Idella Haywood

and 1st Baptist Church Choir (Christian Chapel Choir), Raymond Taylor (Boy Left in Street), Scarface (Rebel Guard at Party), Bushwick Bill (Party Cigar Smoker), Dani Girl (Dancer at Party), Luniz (Customers at Thelma's Cafe), The Chi-Lites (Themselves)

John Bookman returns to his hometown of Gary, Indiana where the gang he helped create 30 years earlier, The Rebels, have now made the streets too dangerous for the residents. © Orion Pictures Corp.

Jim Brown, Ron O'Neal, Richard Roundtree, Pam Grier, Fred Williamson

Elijah Wood, Paul Hogan

Flipper, Elijah Wood

FLIPPER

(UNIVERSAL) Producers, James J. McNamara, Perry Katz; Executive Producer, Lance Hool; Director/Screenplay, Alan Shapiro; Based on the Motion Picture Screenplay by Arthur Weiss and Story by Ricou Browning and Jack Cowden; Photography, Bill Butler; Designer, Thomas A. Walsh; Editor, Peck Prior; Co-Producers, Conrad Hool, Darlene Spezzi; Associate Producer, Doug Merrifield; Costumes, Matthew Jacobsen; Music, Joel McNeely; Vocal Performance by Crosby, Stills and Nash; Underwater Director of Photography, Pete Romano; Casting, Julie Ashton-Barson; a co-presentation of The Bubble Factory of an American Film/Perry Katz production; DTS Stereo; Super 35 Widescreen; Deluxe color; Rated PG; 96 minutes; May release

Chelsea Field   Isaac Hayes

CAST

Sandy Ricks	Elijah Wood
Porter Ricks	Paul Hogan
Dirk Moran	Jonathan Banks
Bounty Fishermen	Robert Deacon, Mark Casella, Luke Halpin
Fisherman's Wife	Ann Carey
Tommy	Bill Kelley
Cathy	Chelsea Field
Marvin	Jason Fuchs
Little Girl	Lindsay Treco
Kim	Jessica Wesson
Russ	Mal Jones
Mr. Dunnahy	Louis Seeger Crume
Bartender	Bill Nolan
Buck	Isaac Hayes
Sandy's Mom	Mary Jo Faraci
Sandy's Sister	Allison Bertolino

Rebellious teen Sandy Ricks comes to a remote island to live with his uncle and finds himself befriending an orphaned dolphin. Based on the 1963 MGM film, its 1964 sequel Flipper's New Adventure, and the subsequent NBC tv series (1964-68) all of which featured Luke Halpin as Sandy Ricks; Halpin appears in this film as a fisherman.

Flipper

HEAVEN'S PRISONERS

(SAVOY) Producers, Albert S. Ruddy, Andre E. Morgan, Leslie Greif; Executive Producers, Hildy Gottlieb, Alec Baldwin; Co-Producer, Gray Frederickson; Director, Phil Joanou; Screenplay, Charley Peyton, Scott Frank; Based upon the novel by James Lee Burke; Photography, Harris Savides; Designer, John Stoddart; Editor, William Steinkamp; Costumes, Aude Bronson-Howard; Music, George Fenton; Associate Producer, Michael Alan Kahn; Casting, Linda Phillips-Palo; a New Line Cinema and Savoy Pictures presentation, in association with Rank Film Distributors and PVM Entertainment of a Ruddy Morgan production; Dolby SDDS Digital Stereo; Technicolor; Rated R; 126 minutes; May release

CAST

Dave Robicheaux	Alec Baldwin
Annie Robicheaux	Kelly Lynch
Robin Gaddis	Mary Stuart Masterson
Bubba Rocque	Eric Roberts
Claudette Rocque	Teri Hatcher
Minos P. Dautrieve	Vondie Curtis Hall
Batist	Badja Djola
Alafair	Samantha Lagpacan
Didi Giancano	Joe Viterelli
Jerry Falgout	Tuck Milligan
Victor Romero	Hawthorne James
Eddie Keats	Don Stark
Toot	Carl A. McGee
Detective Magelli	Paul Guilfoyle
Priest	Chris Krisea
Dom	Saul Stein
Tony	Chuck Zito
Spanish Nun	Socorro Santiago
Nun	Patricia Huston
Jungle Room Bartender	Don Yesso
Jungle Room Patron	Anne Schedeen
Johnny Dartez	Joe Hess
Sheriff Len Whitley	Gray Frederickson

and Lenore Banks (Driver), Don Brady (Apartment Man), Marion Zinser (Apartment Woman), Glenn Gomez (Piano Mover), James "Hooks" Reynolds (Truck Driver), Tom Burgess (Prison Guard), Herman Myles, Sr. (Clarence), Jerry Procanik (Patron), Connie Whittemore (Stripper)

Ex-cop Dave Robicheaux is drawn back into a world of violence after he begins investigating a mysterious crash from which he had pulled its sole survivor, a Salvadoran girl, from the wreckage.

© New Line Productions, Inc. and Savoy Pictures

Kelly Preston, Alec Baldwin

Mary Stuart Masterson, Alec Baldwin

Brendan Sexton, Jr., Heather Matarazzo

WELCOME TO THE DOLLHOUSE

(SONY CLASSICS) Producer/Director/Screenplay, Todd Solondz; Executive Producer, Donna Bascom; Photography, Randy Drummond; Designer, Susan Block; Editor, Alan Oxman; Music, Jill Wisoff; Casting, Ann Goulder; a Suburban Pictures presentation; Color; Rated R; 87 minutes; May release

CAST

Dawn Wiener	Heather Matarazzo
Lolita	Victoria Davis
Cookie	Christina Brucato
Cynthia	Christina Vidal
Chrissy	Siri Howard
Brandon McCarthy	Brendan Sexton, Jr.
Jed	Telly Pontidis
Lance	Herbie Duarte
Troy	Scott Coogan
Missy Wiener	Daria Kalinina
Mark Wiener	Matthew Faber

and Josiah Trager (Kenny), Ken Leung (Barry), Dimitri Iervolino (Ralphy), Rica Martens (Mrs. Grissom), Angela Pietropinto (Mrs. Wiener), Bill Buell (Mr. Wiener), Eric Mabius (Steve Rodgers), Stacey Moseley (Mary Ellen Moriarty), Will Lyman (Mr. Edwards), Elizabeth Martin (Mrs. Iannone), Zsanne Pitta (Ginger Friedman), Richard Gould (Mr. Kasdan), Beverly Hecht (Steve's Girlfriend), Teddy Coluca (Police Sergeant), Tommy Fager (Tommy McCarthy), James O'Donoghue (Mr. McCarthy)

Passive teenager Dawn Wiener accepts the verbal abuse of her peers while enduring high school. © Sony Pictures Entertainment Inc.

SPY HARD

(HOLLYWOOD) Producers, Rick Friedberg, Doug Draizin, Jeffrey Konvitz; Executive Producers, Robert L. Rosen, Leslie Nielsen; Director, Rick Friedberg; Screenplay, Rick Friedberg, Dick Chudnow, Jason Friedberg, Aaron Seltzer; Story, Jason Friedberg, Aaron Seltzer; Photography, John R. Leonetti; Designer, William Creber; Editor, Eric Sears; Costumes, Tom Bronson; Opening Title Sequence, "Weird Al" Yankovic; Music, Bill Conti; Casting, Fern Champion, Mark Paladini; a Friedberg/Draizin/Konvitz production; Distributed by Buena Vista Pictures; Dolby Digital Stereo; Technicolor; Rated PG-13; 81 minutes; May release

Leslie Nielsen, Nicollette Sheridan

CAST

Dick Steele (Agent WD-40)	Leslie Nielsen
Veronique Ukrinsky (Agent 3.14)	Nicollette Sheridan
The Director	Charles Durning
Miss Cheevus	Marcia Gay Harden
Norman Coleman	Barry Bostwick
Kabul	John Ales
General Rancor	Andy Griffith
Professor Ukrinsky	Elya Baskin
McCluckey	Mason Gamble
Slice	Carlos Lauchu
Victoria/Barbara Dahl	Stephanie Romanov

and Curtis Armstrong (Pastry Chef), Tina Arning, Gayle Obodzinski (Dancers), William Barillaro (Blind Driver), Michael Berryman (Bus Patron with Oxygen Mask), Julie Brown (Cigarette Girl), Stephen Burrows (Agent Burrows), Keith Campbell, Carl Ciarfalio (Thugs), Johnny Cocktails (Postal Worker), Wayne Cotter (Male Dancer), Rick Cramer (Rancor Terrorist Helmlich), Eddie Deezen (Rancor Guy Who Gets Spit On), Joey Dente (Dead Wise Guy Goombah), Paul Eliopoulos, Hollis Hill (Agents), Andrew Christian English (Paratrooper), Brad Garrett (Voice for Short Rancor Guard), Michael Lee Gogin (Short Rancor Guard), Bruce Gray (The President), Brian Howe (Clubhouse Bartender), Nia James (Rancor Terrorist), Valentino Johnson (Michael Jackson Look-alike), Elizabeth Kaitan (Helicopter Ticket Agent), John Kassir (Rancor Guard at Intercom), Diane Klimaszewski, Elaine Klimaszewski (Twins), Austin Kottke (Boy with Balloons), Clyde Kusatsu (Noggin), Kelly Lange, Desiree More (Themselves), Michael Leahs (Jogger), Tara León (Manicurist), Bruno Marcotulli (Sad Mime), Esau McKnight (Warrior on Cell Phone Skippy), Katherine Moffat (Agent Moffat), Fran Montano (Carny at Weapons Lab), Ron Morgan (Weapons Lab Worker), Joanne Nerlino (Machine Gun Packing Nun Leader), Mil Nicholson (English Countdown Lady), Gary Owens (M.C. for Rancor Extortion Video), Tyler Patton (Punk Leader), Julie Payne (Mother Superior), Pee Wee Piamonti (Fighting Rancor Guard), Jeff Sanders (Bird-Calling Rancor Guard), Thom Sharp (Agent Sharp), Shari Shattuck (Stewardess), Pat Tanzillo (Agent Tanzillo), Thuy Trang (Masseuse), Angela Visser (Gorgeous Blonde), Reid Worthington (Balloon Popping Boy), Maxi Anderson, Billie Barnum, Maria Del Rey, Linda Harmon, Darlene Koldenhoven, Carol Lombard, Jeanie Long, Joanne Nerlino, Sally Stevens, Tata Vega, Jeannine Wagner, Julia Waters, Maxine Waters (Singing Nuns); Friends Who Stopped By: Dr. Joyce Brothers (Steele's Tag Team Member), Ray Charles (Bus Driver), Roger Clinton (Agent Clinton), Robert Culp (Businessman), Fabio (Himself), Robert Guillaume (Agent Steve Bishop), Hulk Hogan (Steele's Tag Team Member), Pat Morita (Brian the Waiter), Alexandra Paul (Woman in Murphy Bed), Mr. T (Agency Helicopter Pilot), Alex Trebek (Agency Tape Recorder Voice Over)

Agent Dick Steele is called back into active service to stop his nemesis General Rancor from controlling the world.

© Hollywood Pictures Company

Leslie Nielsen

Nicollette Sheridan, Leslie Nielsen

Leslie Nielsen, Andy Griffith

Draco, Dennis Quaid

Dennis Quaid, David Thewlis

Pete Postlethwaite, Dina Meyer, Dennis Quaid

Julie Christie, Dennis Quaid

DRAGONHEART

(UNIVERSAL) Producer, Raffaella De Laurentiis; Executive Producers, David Rotman, Patrick Read Johnson; Director, Rob Cohen; Screenplay, Charles Edward Pogue; Story, Patrick Read Johnson, Charles Edward Pogue; Co-Producer, Hester Hargett; Photography, David Eggby; Designer, Benjamin Fernandez; Editor, Peter Amundson; Music, Randy Edelman; Costumes, Thomas Casterline, Anna Sheppard; Special Effects Supervisor, Kit West; Character Animation Supervisor, James Straus; Dragon Designer, Phil Tippet; Casting, Margery Simkin; a Rafaella De Laurentiis production; Dolby DTS Stereo; Panavision; Deluxe color; Rated PG-13; 103 minutes; May release

CAST

Bowen	Dennis Quaid
Einon	David Thewlis
Gilbert	Pete Postlethwaite
Kara	Dina Meyer
Felton	Jason Isaacs
Brok	Brian Thompson
Young Einon	Lee Oakes
Hewe	Wolf Christian
Redbeard	Terry O'Neill
King Freyne	Peter Hric
Felton's Minx	Eva Vejmelkova
Swamp Village Chief	Milan Bahul
Young Kara	Sandra Kovacicova
Boy in Field	Kyle Cohen
Aislinn's Chess Partner	Thom Baker
Aislinn	Julie Christie
Voice of Draco	Sean Connery

and the voice of John Gielgud

The last of the firebreathing dragons, Draco, joins forces with Bowen to put an end to the evil rule of tryanical Einon. This film received an Oscar nomination for visual effects. © Universal City Studios, Inc.

Jean Reno

Tom Cruise, Ving Rhames

Tom Cruise, Henry Czerny

Kristin Scott Thomas

Tom Cruise

MISSION: IMPOSSIBLE

(PARAMOUNT) Producers, Tom Cruise, Paula Wagner; Executive Producer, Paul Hitchcock; Director, Brian De Palma; Screenplay, David Koepp, Robert Towne; Story, David Koepp, Steven Zaillian; Based on the television series created by Bruce Geller; Photography, Stephen H. Burum; Designer, Norman Reynolds; Editor, Paul Hirsch; Special Make-Up Effects, Rob Bottin; Visual Effects Supervisor, John Knoll; Costumes, Penny Rose; Music, Danny Elfman; *Mission: Impossible* Theme by Lalo Schifrin; Casting, Mali Finn, Patsy Pollock; a Cruise/Wagner production; Dolby Stereo; Panavision; Deluxe color; Rated PG-13; 110 minutes; May release

CAST

Ethan Hunt	Tom Cruise
Jim Phelps	Jon Voight
Claire	Emmanuelle Beart
Kittridge	Henry Czerny
Krieger	Jean Reno
Luther	Ving Rhames
Sarah Davies	Kristin Scott-Thomas
Max	Vanessa Redgrave
Jack Harmon	Emilio Estevez
Frank Barnes	Dale Dye
Golitsyn	Marcel Iures
Zozimov	Ion Caramitru
Hannah	Ingeborga Dapkunaite
Druken IMF Agents	Valentina Yakunina, Marek Vasut
Kittridge Technician	Nathan Osgood
TV Interviewer	John McLaughlin
CIA Analyst William Donloe	Rolf Saxon
Matthias	Karel Dobry
Max's Companion	Andreas Wisniewski
Diplomat Rand Housman	David Shaeffer
Mayor Brandl	Rudolf Pechan
Jaroslav Reid	Gaston Subert
Denied Area Security Guards	Ricco Ross, Mark Houghton
Sky News Man	Bob Friend
Flight Attendant	Annabel Mullion
CNN Reporter	Garrick Hagon
Cleaning Woman	Jirina Trebicka
Kiev Room Agents	Andrzei Borkowski, Maya Dokic, Sam Douglas, Oleg Fedorov, Carmela Marner, Mimi Potworowska
Train Engineer	David Schneider
Executive on Train	Helen Lindsay
CIA Agent	Pat Starr
CIA Lobby Guard	Richard D. Sharp
CIA Escort Guard	Randall Paul
CIA Agent	Suzanne Doucette
Public Official	Graydon Gould
MI5 Agent	Tony Vogel
Large Man	Michael Rogers
Margaret Hunt	Laura Brook
Donald Hunt	Morgan Deare
Steward on Train	David Phelan
Air Stewardess	Melissa Knatchbull

American agent Ethan Hunt must prevent a computerized list of secret agents from falling into enemy hands. Based on the CBS tv series that ran from 1966 to 1973 and starred Peter Graves as Jim Phelps.

© Paramount Pictures Corp.

Tom Cruise

Tom Cruise, Emmanuelle Beart

Tom Cruise, Jon Voight

EDDIE

(TOUCHSTONE) Producers, David Permut, Mark Burg; Executive Producers, Ron Bozman, Steve Zacharias, Jeff Buhai; Director, Steve Rash; Screenplay, Jon Connolly, David Loucka, Eric Champnella, Keith Mitchell, Steve Zacharias, Jeff Buhai; Story, Steve Zacharias, Jeff Buhai, Jon Connolly, David Loucka; Co-Producer, Andrew Gunn; Photography, Victor Kemper; Designer, Dan Davis; Editor, Richard Halsey; Costumes, Molly Maginnis; Music, Stanley Clarke; Casting, Reuben Cannon & Associates; a David Permut production, presented in association with PolyGram Filmed Entertainment/Island Pictures; Distributed by Buena Vista Pictures; Dolby Digital Stereo; Technicolor; Rated PG-13; 100 minutes; May release

Lisa Ann Walter, Whoopi Goldberg

CAST

Edwina "Eddie" Franklin	Whoopi Goldbreg
Wild Bill Burgess	Frank Langella
Coach Bailey	Dennis Farina
Assistant Coach Zimmer	Richard Jenkins
Claudine	Lisa Ann Walter
Joe Nader	John Benjamin Hickey
Beth Hastings	Troy Beyer
Nate Wilson	John Salley
Terry Hastings	Rick Fox

and Malik Sealy (Stacy Patton), Mark Jackson (Darren Taylor), Dwayne Schintzius (Ivan Radovadovitch), Greg Ostertag (Joe Sparks), Vernel Singleton (Jamal Duncan), Marv Albert, Chris Berman, Walt Frazier, Donald Trump, Mujibur Rahman, Sirajul Islam, Rudolph W. Giuliani, Edward Koch, Fabio (Themselves), Aasif Mandvi (Mohammed), Johnny Williams (Big Al), Albert Pisarenkov (Mischa), Isiah Whitlock, Jr. (Rick), James K. Flynn (MSG Announcer), Gary Payton (Rumeal Smith), George O. Gore II (Malik Jones), Zachary Simmons Glover (Jerome), Jermaine Maurice Butler (Suli), Davenia McFadden (Rae Jones), Lou Criscuolo (Fred), Sylvia Harman (Helen), Jonathan Marten (Bag #1 Eric), Ethan Edward Marten (Bag #2 Keith), Melrose Larry Green (Colorful Fan), Norman "Max" Maxwell (Fair Weather Fan), Moses Gibson (Odell), Alexandra Adi (ESPN Radio Producer), Jim Gloster (L.A. bellhop), Kristian Damian (Young Malik), Allan Lindo (Young Jerome), Scott Owen Cumberbatch (Young Suli), Ana Divac (Party Girl), Julie Araskog (Frazier Radio Producer), Spud Webb, Glenn "Doc" Rivers, Jon Koncak (Atlanta Hawks), Vlade Divac, Corie Blount, Cedric Ceballos, "Pig" Miller, Nick Van Exel (Los Angeles Lakers), Kurt Rambis (Lakers Head Coach), John "Hot Rod" Williams, Brad Daugherty, John S. Battle, Bobby Phills, Terrell Brandon (Cleveland Cavaliers), Alex English (Cavaliers Head Coach), Rob Ryder (Cavaliers Assistant Coach), Dennis Rodman, Avery Johnson, Vinny Del Negro, J.R. Reid, Cory Alexander, Jack Haley (San Antonio Spurs) Olden Polynice, Walt Williams, Randy Brown, Tyus Edney, Brian Grant, Mitch Richmond, Duane Causwell (Sacramento Kings), Sam Mitchell, Dale Davis (Indiana Pacers), Danny Manning, Joe Kleine, Danny Schayes, Elliot Perry, Wayman Tisdale (Phoenix Suns), Larry Johnson, Muggsy Bogues, David Wingate, Scott Burrell, Joe Wolf (Charlotte Hornets), Anthony Mason, Herb Williams, John Starks (Pickup Players), David Dwyer, J. Don Ferguson, Mick McGovern, Jerry J. Heater, Zelton Steed (Game Referees), Gary T. McTague, Patt Noday, Dorothy Recasner Brown, Steve Coulter, Ron Clinton Smith (Locker Room Reporters), Al Trautwig (NYC TV Reporter), John DiMaggio (Construction Worker), Armand Dahan (Street Vendor), Daniel D. Bannister, Tyrone Bell, Marcus P. Blucas, Demetrius Calip, Ray Lawson (Bench Knicks), Gene Banks (Knicks Asst. Coach), Bret Wood (Knicks Trainer), Mitchell Gordon (Dancing Knicks Fan), Alan Scott (Rowdy Fan), Joseph Sinacori (Joe the Cop), Rachel Pond (Owner's Box Hostess), Beau Nix (Game Scorer), Charles Martin, George Halgas (St. Louis Businessmen), Anthony Lopez, Sr. (Youth Ref), Kim Delgado (Businessman), Bernie Engel (Elderly Fan), Joseph Anthony Battaglia, Thomas Nial (Angry Fans), Ebony Jo-Ann (Patton's Mama), Eartha D. Robinson (Knicks Choreographer), Gene Anthony Ray, Michelle Bagby, Ben Bagby, Kimberly Marie Bailey, T'Fani Bose, Heather Atwood Brody, Debbie Caddell, Joy Davis, Michelle Fernandez, Felicia Fritz, Cezette Gregory, Sandy Heddings, Candy House, Arnella Jarrett, Heather Jones, Melissa Marlowe, Lia Panos, Nicole Price, Katrina Simmons, Shannon Spivey, Julie C. Wells, Tara Wood (Dancers)

As a publicity ploy limo driver and avid basketball fan Eddie Franklin is hired as head coach for the last place New York Knicks.

© Hollywood Pictures Company

Frank Langella, Whoopi Goldberg

Malik Sealy, Whoopi Goldberg

THE PHANTOM

(PARAMOUNT) Producers, Robert Evans, Alan Ladd, Jr.; Executive Producers, Dick Vane, Joe Dante, Graham Burke, Greg Coote, Peter Sjoquist, Bruce Sherlock; Director, Simon Wincer; Screenplay/Co-Producer, Jeffrey Boam; Based on the Phantom Characters Created by Lee Falk; Photography, David Burr; Designer, Paul Peters; Editors, O. Nicholas Brown, Bryan H. Carroll; Costumes, Marlene Stewart; Casting, Deborah Aquila, Jane Shannon Smith; a Village Roadshow Pictures production, presented in association with Robert Evans and The Ladd Company; Dolby DTS Stereo; Panavision; Deluxe color; Rated PG; 101 minutes; June release

Kristy Swanson, Billy Zane

CAST

Phantom (Kit Walker)	Billy Zane
Diana Palmer	Kristy Swanson
Xander Drax	Treat Williams
Sala	Catherine Zeta Jones
Quill	James Remar
Kabai Sengh	Cary-Hiroyuki Tagawa
Uncle Dave	Bill Smitrovich
Morgan	Casey Siemaszko
Charlie Zephro	David Proval
Ray Zephro	Joseph Ragno
Lilly Palmer	Samantha Eggar
Jimmy Wells	Jon Tenney
Phantom's Dad	Patrick McGoohan
Captain Horton	Robert Coleby
Police Commissioner Farley	Al Ruscio
Mayor Krebs	Leon Russom
Falkmoore	Bernard Kates
Al the Cabby	John Capodice
Mounted Cop	Bob Kane
Cycle Cops	William Jones, John Prosky
Dr. Fleming	Alan Zitner
Corporal Weeks	Dane Carson
Zak	Chatpong "Jim" Petchlor
Breen	Dane Farwell
Styles	Jared Chandler
Guran	Radmar Agana Jao

and William Zappa (Ugly Pirate), Agoes Widjaya Soedjarwo (Pirate #1), Clint Lilley (Gangster #1), Jo Phillips (Pilot), Austin Peters (Boy Phantom), Victor Madrona (Shaman), Valerie Flueger (Receptionist), Rod Dailey (Short Order Cook)

The Phantom, a mysterious crime fighter, battles the evil Xander Drax who hopes to possess the three Skulls of Touganda, which together can give him unlimited power. © Paramount Pictures Corp.

Billy Zane

Treat Williams

Patrick McGoohan, Billy Zane

Nicolas Cage

Nicolas Cage, Sean Connery

David Morse, Ed Harris

THE ROCK

(HOLLYWOOD PICTURES) Producers, Don Simpson, Jerry Bruckheimer; Executive Producers, William Stuart, Sean Connery, Louis A. Stroller; Director, Michael Bay; Screenplay, David Weisberg, Douglas S. Cook, Mark Rosner; Story, David Weisberg, Douglas S. Cook; Photography, John Schwartzman; Designer, Michael White; Editor, Richard Francis-Bruce; Music, Nick Glennie-Smith, Hans Zimmer; Costumes, Bobbie Read; Stunts, Kenny Bates; Casting, Heidi Levitt, Billy Hopkins; a Don Simpson and Jerry Bruckheimer production; Distributed by Buena Vista Pictures; Dolby Digital Stereo; Super 35 Widescreen; Technicolor; Rated R; 136 minutes; June release

CAST

Patrick Mason	Sean Connery
Stanley Goodspeed	Nicolas Cage
General Francis X. Hummel	Ed Harris
Major Tom Baxter	David Morse
Marine Captain Hendrix	John C. McGinley
Sergeant Crisp	Bokeem Woodbine
Private Scarpetti	Jim Maniaci
Private Gamble	Greg Collins
Hummel Marine "A"	Jack Yates
Hummel Marine "B"	Juan A. Riojas
Hummel Marine "C"	Joseph Patrick Kelly
Captain Frye	Gregory Sporleder
Captain Darrow	Tony Todd
Private Cox	Brendan Kelly
Private McCoy	Steve Harris
Eddie Paxton	William Forsythe
Marvin Isherwood	Todd Louiso
Chef	Fred Salvallon
F.B.I. Director Womack	John Spencer
Jade Angelou	Claire Forlani
Lt. Col. Callahan	Tucker Smallwood
Marine That Dies	Ingo Neuhas
Charles Anderson	Michael Biehn
Carla Pestalozzi	Vanessa Marcil
Park Ranger Bob	Raymond O'Connor
Tourists	Janie Sanguinetti, Luenell, John W. Love Jr.
Benny	William Newman
Dr. Ling	David Bowe
Agent Margie Wood	Raquel Krelle
Louis Linstrom	Howard Platt
Seal Boyer	Dennis Chalker
Seal Reigert	Marshall Teague
Seal Dando	Duffy Gaver
Special Agent Shepard	Danny Nucci
Cobra Helicopter Pilots	Chuck P. Aaron, Steve Bligh, Chuck Tamburro, Mike Tamburro
Sikorsky Pilots	O.C. Anderson, Par Knutsen, Calvin Coady
Navy Seals	Steve Decker, Billy Devlin, Joseph Hawes, Mike Mahrer Carlos Sandoval, Rick Toms
Francis Reynolds	Willie Garson
F.B.I. Radar Technicians	John Nathan, Robert M. Anselmo
Military Official	Jack Ford

and T. J. Hageboeck (F.B.I. Agent Cord), Dwight Hicks (F.B.I. Agent Star), Ralph Peduto (F.B.I. Agent Hunt), Anthony Clark (Paul the Hotel Barber), Andy Ryan (Lab Tech), Hans Georg Struhar (Valet), Sean Skelton (Kid on Motorcycle), Sam Whipple (Larry Henderson), Leonard McMahan (Cable Car Conductor), Robert C. Besgrove, Richard Conti, Cully Fredricksen, Marco Kyris, Michael Edward Rose (F.B.I. Agents), Anthony Guidera (Lead F-18 Pilot), James Caviezel (Rear F-18 Pilot), G. Rudy Mettia, John Enos III (Sea Stallion Pilots), Ken Kells (Spotter), Joe Bradley (Angry Tourist), Harry Humphries (Admiral), Victoria Redstall (Secretary), Charles Johnson (Marlin), Celeste Weaver (Stacy Richards), Tom Towles, Ronald Simmons, Robert Ben Rajab (Alcatraz Park Rangers), Buck Kartalian (Reverend), David Marshall Grant

Chemical/biological weapons expert Stanley Goodspeed enlists the aide of federal prisoner John Patrick Mason, the only man known to have escaped from Alcatraz prison, to help him stop a crazed general who has taken over Alcatraz Island with the intention of destroying San Francisco with poison gas. This film received an Oscar nomination for sound.

Sean Connery, Nicolas Cage

David Morse, Ed Harris, John C. McGinley

Vanessa Marcil, Nicolas Cage

Sean Connery, Nicolas Cage

THE CABLE GUY

(COLUMBIA) Producers, Andrew Licht, Jeffrey A. Mueller, Judd Apatow; Executive Producers, Brad Grey, Bernie Brillstein, Marc Gurvitz; Director, Ben Stiller; Screenplay, Lou Holtz, Jr.; Photography, Robert Brinkmann; Designer, Sharon Seymour; Editor, Steven Weisberg; Costumes, Erica Edell Phillips; Music, John Ottman; Co-Producer, William Beasley; Casting, Juel Bestrop; a Bernie Brillstein/Brad Grey production of a Licht/Mueller Film Corp. production; Dolby SDDS Stereo; Super 35 Widescreen; Technicolor; Rated PG-13; 94 minutes; June release

CAST

Cable Guy (Chip Douglas)	Jim Carrey
Steven Kovacs	Matthew Broderick
Robin Harris	Leslie Mann
Rick	Jack Black
Earl Kovacs	George Segal
Mrs. Kovacs	Diane Baker
Sam Sweet	Ben Stiller
Himself	Eric Roberts
Medieval Waitress	Janeane Garofalo
Medieval Host	Andy Dick
Steven's Boss	Harry O'Reilly
Sales Manager	David Cross
Steven's Secretary	Amy Stiller
Robin's Date	Owen Wilson

and Keith Gibbs, Tommy Hinkley, Shawn Michael Howard, Jeff Kahn, Suli McCullough, Jeff Michalski, Joel Murray, Andrew Shaifer (Basketball Players), Cameron Starman (Cable Boy), Kathy Griffin (Cable Boy's Mother), Jeremy Applegate, Adam Consolo, Michael Fossat, Kennedy Kabasares, Robert L. Rasner (Medieval Times Serfs), Misa Koprova (Raul), Aki Aleong, Dona Hardy, Lloyd Kino, Sara Lowell, Cynthia Mason, Michael Rivkin, Harper Roisman, Sandra Thigpin, Sean Whalen, Marty Zagon (Karaoke Party Guests), Staci Flood, Mary Lee, Raydeen Revilla, Darlene Worley (Karaoke Video Dancers), Cynthia Lamontagne (Restaurant Hostess), James O'Conell (Bathroom Attendant), Douglas Robert Jackson (Bathroom Patron), Charles Napier, Christopher Michael (Arresting Officers), Charles Knox Robinson, III (Steven's Lawyer), John O'Donohue (Prison Guard), Lydell M. Chesier, Jason Larimore, Ahmad Reese, Emilio Rivera (Jail Inmates), Bob Odenkirk (Steven's Brother), Julie Hayden (Steven's Sister), Annabelle Gurwitch (Steven's Sister-in-Law), Blake Boyd (Steven's Brother-in-Law), Lisa D'Agostino (Newsroom Researcher), Tabitha Soren, Rikki Klieman, Robert Simels (Themselves), Leonard Turner (Sam Sweet Judge), Carlo Allen (Sam Sweet Court Clerk), Conrad Janis (Father, "Double Trouble"), Thomas Scott (Sam at 8 yrs.), Steven Scott (Stan at 8 yrs.), Christine Devine (Anchor Woman), Mark Thompson (Newsroom Reporter), Wendy Walsh (Reporter Outside Courtroom), Marion Dugan (Robin's Neighbor), Bill Beasley (Nuclear Dad), Christine Beasley (Nuclear Mom), Adam Beasley, Devon Beasley (Nuclear Kids), Barbara Babbin, Frank Davis, Julian Reyes (Bar Patrons), Kyle Gass (Couch Potato), David Bowe (Helicopter Paramedic), Bobby Zajonc (Pilot)

After convincing the cable guy to give him additional channels for free, Steven Kovacs discovers that he can't get the needy fellow out of his life.

Matthew Broderick, Jim Carrey

Jim Carrey

Jim Carrey, Matthew Broderick

Jim Carrey, George Segal, Diane Baker

68

John Lynch, Robin Wright

Stockard Channing

MOLL FLANDERS

(MGM) Producers, John Watson, Richard B. Lewis, Pen Dnsham; Executive Producer, Morgan O'Sullivan; Director/Screenplay/Screen Story, Pen Densham; Based on the character from the novel by Daniel DeFoe; Photography, David Tattersall; Designer, Caroline Hanania; Editors, Neil Travis, James R. Symons; Costumes, Consolata Boyle; Music, Mark Mancina; Casting, Ros and John Hubbard; a Trilogy Entertainment Group production, presented in association with Spelling Films; Dolby DTS Sereo; Panavision; Deluxe color; Rated PG-13; 123 minutes; June release

CAST

Moll Flanders	Robin Wright
Hibble	Morgan Freeman
Mrs. Allworthy	Stockard Channing
Artist	John Lynch
Mrs. Mazzawatti	Brenda Fricker
Edna	Geraldine James
Flora	Aisling Corcoran
Priest	Jim Sheridan
Artist's Father	Jeremy Brett
Artist's Mother	Britta Smith
Polly	Cathy Murphy
Mary	Emma McIvor
Alice	Maria Doyle Kennedy
Orphanage Woman	Ger Ryan
Magistrate	Harry Towb
Mr. Mazzawatti	Alan Stanford
Mazzawatti Daughters	Eileen McCloskey, Nicola Teehan
Mazzawatti Butler	Chris Curran
Kindly Sister	Rynagh O'Grady
Disciplinary Nun	Maria Hayden
Allworthy Maid	Janet Moran
Physician	Kieran Hurley
Mother Superior	Mary McEvoy
Deilvery Man	Brendan Conroy
Moll's Mother	Rita Hamill
Doctor of Sorts	Birdy Sweeney
Mr. 100 Guineas	Brendan Cauldwell

and Mal Whyte (Bald Cleric), Barry Barnes (Older Brother), Paul Hickey (Younger Brother), Tom Jordan (Greying Father), Charlotte Bradley (Artist's Sister), Brian deSalvo (Artist's Butler), Brian Munn (Carriage Driver), Gina Moxley (Girl at Confessional), Jonathan Ryan (Goldsmith), Pat Leavy (Widow), Stanley Townsend (Gambler), Tom Lawlor (Shop Owner), Gerry Walsh (Man with Blunderbuss), Joe Savino (Threatening Man), Gary Whelan (Prison Guard), Helene Montague (Woman with Baby), Eileen Reid (Smallpox Woman), Brendan Dempsey (Lord with Dog), Ardal O'Hanlon (Gentleman from East Chiswick), Conor Lovett (Footman), Teacel Hines (Young Footman), Des Braiden (Gatekeeper), Elizabeth McKnight, E'Dena Hines (Maids), Audrey Tom (Red Dress Prostitute), Magael McLaughlin, Courtney King, Carl Jahme (Allworthy)

Hibble tells of the life of Moll Flanders and how she hoped to escape from her lowly existence as she went from poverty stricken London to a whore house to a love affair with a struggling artist. Previous film version The Amorous Adventures of Moll Flanders *(Paramount, 1965) starred Kim Novak.* © Metro-Goldwyn-Mayer, Inc.

Robin Wright, Eileen McClosky, Brenda Fricker, Harry Towb

Morgan Freeman, Aisling Corcoran

Victor, Quasimodo, Hugo, Laverne

Quasimodo

Esmeralda, Phoebus

Hugo, Victor, Laverne, Esmeralda, Quasimodo

THE HUNCHBACK OF NOTRE DAME

(WALT DISNEY PICTURES) Producer, Don Hahn; Directors, Gary Trousdale, Kirk Wise; Animation Story, Tab Murphy; Based on the novel *Notre Dame de Paris (The Hunchback of Notre Dame)* by Victor Hugo; Animation Screenplay, Tab Murphy, Irene Mecchi, Bob Tzudiker, Noni White, Jonathan Roberts; Music, Alan Menken; Lyrics, Stephen Schwartz; Co-Producer, Roy Conli; Associate Producer, Phil Lofaro; Art Director, David Goetz; Artistic Coordinator, Randy Fullmer; Editor, Ellen Keneshea; Artistic Supervisors: Story, Will Finn; Layout, Ed Ghertner; Background, Lisa Keene; Clean Up, Vera Lanpher-Pacheco; Visual Effects, Christopher Jenkins; Computer Graphics Imagery, Kiran Bhakta Joshi; Production Manager, Patricia Hicks; Distributed by Buena Vista Pictures; Dolby Digital Stereo; Technicolor; Rated G; 85 minutes; June release

CAST

Hugo	Jason Alexander
Quasimodo's Mother	Mary Kay Bergman
Brutish Guard	Corey Burton
Guards/Gypsies	Jim Cummings
Oafish Guard	Bill Fagerbakke
Quasimodo	Tom Hulce
Frollo	Tony Jay
Clopin	Paul Kandel
Victor	Charles Kimbrough
Phoebus	Kevin Kline
Singing Voice of Esmeralda	Heidi Mollenhauer
Esmeralda	Demi Moore
Guards/Gypsies	Patrick Pinney
The Old Heretic	Gary Trousdale
Archdeacon	David Ogden Stiers
Baby Bird	Frank Welker
Laverne	Mary Wickes
Additional Laverne Dialogue	Jane Withers

and Jack Angel, Joan Barber, Scott Barnes, Bob Bergen, Mary Kay Bergman, Susan Blu, Maureen Brennan, Rodger Bumpass, Corey Burton, Victoria Clark, Philip Clarke, Jennifer Darling, Debi Derryberry, Jonathan Dokuchitz, Bill Farmer, Laurie Faso, Merwin Foard, Dana Hill, Judy Kaye, Eddie Korbich, Alix Korey, Michael Lindsay, Sherry Lynn, Mona Marshall, Howard McGillin, Mickie McGowan, Anna McNeely, Bruce Moore, Denise Pickering, Phil Proctor, Jan Rabson, Peter Samuel, Kath Soucie, Gordon Stanley, Mary Stout, Marcelo Tubert (Additional Voices)

The deformed bell-ringer of Notre Dame, Quasimodo, who yearns to be accepted by the outside world, falls in love with the beautiful gypsy girl Esmeralda, whom he helps hide from the authorities in the cathedral. Previous film versions of Victor Hugo's novel starred Lon Chaney (1923), Charles Laughton (1939), and Anthony Quinn (1956). This film received an Oscar nomination for original musical score.

© Disney Enterprises, Inc.

Quasimodo

Frollo, Quasimodo

Esmeralda, Quasimodo

Clopin, Quasimodo

THE LOW LIFE

(CFP) Producers, Donald Zuckerman, Tobin Heminway; Director, George Hickenlooper; Screenplay, John Enbom, George Hickenlooper; Story, John Enbom; Co-Producers, Dan Etheridge, Martin Yu; Executive Producers, Mark Blum, George Hickenlooper, Gary Siegler, Leslie Zuckerman; Photography, Richard Crudo; Designer, Deborah Smith; Costumes, Alexandra Welker; Editors, Yaffa Lerea, Jim Makiej; Music, Bill Boll; Line Producer, Karen S. Shapiro; Casting, Heidi Levitt, Rick Montgomery, Dana Parada; from Cabin Fever Entertainment and Cinepix Film Properties Inc.; Color; Rated R; 98 minutes; June release

CAST

John	Rory Cochrane
Bevan	Kyra Sedgwick
Chad	Ron Livingston
Leonard	Christian Meoli
Suzie	Sara Melson
Mike, Jr.	James Le Gros
Andrew	Sean Astin
Mike, Sr.	J.T. Walsh
"Little Tramp" Woman	Shawnee Smith
Hollywood Mogul	Jefferson Mays
Uncle Darr	Brent J. Williams
Louis	Antoni Cornoe
Latina Girlfriend	Angela Aviles
Matthew Greenberg	Mark Blum
Craig	Channon Roe
Bartender	Michael Massee
Patrick	Patrick Ladislav
Poet	Renee Zellweger

and Otto Coelho (Chuck), Timothy Gallaher (Performer Artist/UFO), Jan Boyer (Waitress), Donald Zuckerman (Married Attorney), Jon Beatty (Office Supervisor), F. Joseph Schulte (Temp Office Manager), Marianne Meullerleile (Temp Dispatcher), Rommel Hyacinth (Haitian Man), Kristina Loggia (Andy's Sister), Bernie Lane (Andy's Father), George Hickenlooper, Sr. (Priest), Mark Moran (Jorge), Harold Jose Martinez (Julio's Friend), Esther Scott (Mrs. Raymond), James Katsuki Taenaka (Wineshop Clerk), Michael Beugg, James Blevins, Tobin Heminway, Mark Anthony Little (Police Officers)

John, a recent Yale graduate who has ended up at a dead end temp job, finds his emotionally deadened outlook on life challenged by his hyper, needy new roommate Andrew.

© CFP Distribution

Sean Astin, Rory Cochrane

Pruitt Taylor Vince, Shelley Winters

HEAVY

(CFP) Producer, Richard Miller; Director/Screenplay, James Mangold; Photography, Michael Barrow; Designer, Michael Shaw; Music, Thurston Moore; Editor, Meg Reticker; Executive Producer, Herbert Beigel; Casting, Todd Thaler; a Richard Miller production; Dolby Stereo; DuArt color; Not rated; 105 minutes; June release

CAST

Victor	Pruitt Taylor Vince
Callie	Liv Tyler
Dolly	Shelley Winters
Delores	Deborah Harry
Leo	Joe Grifasi
Jeff	Evan Dando
Grey Man in Hospital	David Patrick Kelly
Darlene	Marian Quinn
Donna	Meg Hartig
Jean	Zandy Hartig
Tony	Peter Ortel

A shy, overweight pizza chef finds himself falling in love with the beautiful new waitress his mother has hired to work at their tavern.

© CFP Distribution

Liv Tyler

STRIPTEASE

(COLUMBIA) Producer, Mike Lobell; Executive Producer, Joseph Hartwick; Director/Screenplay, Andrew Bergman; Based on the novel by Carl Hiaasen; Photography, Stephen Goldblatt; Designer, Mel Bourne; Editor, Anne V. Coates; Costumes, Albert Wolsky; Music, Howard Shore; Choreographer, Marguerite Pomerhn Derricks; Casting, John Lyons; a Castle Rock Entertainment presentation of a Lobell/Bergman production; SDDS Stereo; Technicolor; Rated R; 115 minutes; June release

CAST

Erin Grant	Demi Moore
David Dilbeck	Burt Reynolds
Al Garcia	Armand Assante
Shad	Ving Rhames
Darrell Grant	Robert Patrick
Malcolm Moldovsky	Paul Guilfoyle
Orly	Jerry Grayson
Angela	Rumer Willis
Erb Crandal	Robert Stanton
Jerry Killian	William Hill
Alan Mordecai	Stuart Pankin
Monique, Jr.	Dina Spybey
Sabrina Hepburn	Pasean Wilson
Urbana Sprawl	Pandora Peaks
Lorelei	Barbara Alyn Woods
Ariel Sharon	Kimberly Flynn
Tiffany Glass	Rena Riffel
Rita	Siobhan Fallon
Alberto	Gary Basaraba
Paul Guber	Matthew Baron
Willie Rojo	Gianni Russo
Chris Rojo	José Zuñiga
Pierre	Anthony Jones
Chico	Eduardo Yañez
Nico	Antoni Corone
Donna Garcia	Frances Fisher
Andy	Teddy Bergman
Judge Fngerhut	Louis Seeger Crume

and Aymee Garcia (Temp), Deborah Magdalena (Secretary), Keone Young (Ling), Johnny Cocktails (DJ), Anthony Giaimo (Medical Examiner), Jerry Pacific (Parking Valet), Anna Lobell (Video Clerk), Diane Adams (Hospital Volunteer), Chad Ayers (Young Christian), April Sharpe (Seaquarium Guide), Maria Gennaro (TV Reporter), Keith Blaney, Marc Chaykin (Bachelors), Edward Goldstein (Bartender), Christi Bauerle (Cocktail Waitress), Yoshi Obata, Tony Toyoda, Scott Oughterson (Businessmen in Club), Ted Niarhos, Jr., Darreck Crane, Marco Assante (Patrons in Club)

Desperate to raise enough money to regain custody of her daughter, Erin Grant takes a job stripping at a Fort Lauderdale nightclub. Rumer Willis is Demi Moore's real-life daughter. © Castle Rock Entertainment

Burt Reynolds

Rumer Willis, Demi Moore

Robert Patrick

Ving Rhames

73

LONE STAR

(SONY PICTURES CLASSICS) Producers, R. Paul Miller, Maggie Renzi; Executive Producer, John Sloss; Director/Screenplay/Editor, John Sayles; Photography, Stuart Dryburgh; Designer, Dan Bishop; Costumes, Shay Cunliffe; Music, Mason Daring; Associate Producer, Jan Foster; Casting, Avy Kaufman; a Castle Rock Entertainment presentation of a Rio Dulce production; Dolby Stereo; Super 35 Widescreen; Color; Rated R; 134 minutes; June release

CAST

Sheriff Sam Deeds	Chris Cooper
Pilar	Elizabeth Peña
Delmore Payne	Joe Morton
Mercedes Cruz	Miriam Colon
Mayor Hollis Pogue	Clifton James
Sheriff Charlie Wade	Kris Kristofferson
Otis Payne	Ron Canada
Sheriff Buddy Deeds	Matthew McConaughey
Bunny	Frances McDormand
Chet Payne	Eddie Robinson
Cliff	Stephen Mendillo
Mikey	Stephen J. Lang
Celie	Oni Faida Lampley
Molly	Eleese Lester
Deputy Travis	Joe Stevens
Amado	Gonzalo Castillo
Enrique	Richard Coca
Fenton	Tony Frank
Young Hollis	Jeff Monahan
Priscilla Worth	LaTanya Richardson
Athens	Chandra Wilson
Shadow	Damon Guy

and Dee Macaluso (Anglo Mother),Luis Cobo (Mexican-American Father), Marco Perella (Anglo Father), Don Phillips (Principal), Mary Jane R. Hernandez (Mexican-American Mother), Jesse Borrego (Danny), Carina Martinez (Paloma), Tony Plana (Ray), Richard A. Jones (Ben Wetzel), Beatrice Winde (Minnie Bledsoe), Gabriel Casseus (Young Otis), Randy Stripling (Roderick), Richard Reyes (Jorge), Olga Luna (Waitress), Juan Vega III (Cook), Lizzie Curry Martinez (Girl), Leo Burmester (Cody), Carmen de Lavallade (Carolyn), Vanessa Martinez (Young Pilar), Tay Strathairn (Young Sam), Sam Vlahos (Pete), Maricela Gonzalez (Anselma), Tony Amendola (Chucho Montoya), Gilbert R. Cuellar, Jr. (Eladio), James Borrego (Young Chucho), Gordon Tootoosis (Wesley Birdsong), Lisa Suarez (Marisol), Jesús Ramirez (Driver), John Griesemer (Voice of Football Announcer), Eduardo Martinez (Jamie), Azalea Mendez (Young Mercedes)

After a skeleton is found in the desert, Sam Deeds, sheriff in a small Texas town, opens up the investigation on a 40-year-old murder which involves his legendary father, Sheriff Buddy Deeds.

Chris Cooper

Eddie Robinson, Ron Canada

Matthew McConaughey

Kris Kristofferson

Elizabeth Pena

Joe Morton

Jada Pinkett, Eddie Murphy

Dave Chappelle

Eddie Murphy, Jada Pinkett

John Ales, Eddie Murphy

THE NUTTY PROFESSOR

(UNIVERSAL) Producers, Brian Grazer, Russell Simmons; Executive Producers, Jerry Lewis, Karen Kehela, Mark Lipsky; Director, Tom Shadyac; Screenplay, David Sheffield, Barry W. Blaustein, Tom Shadyac, Steve Oedekerk; Based on the motion picture written by Jerry Lewis, Bill Richmond; Photography, Julio Macat; Designer, William Elliott; Editor, Don Zimmerman; Co-Producer, James D. Brubaker; Visual Effects Supervisor, Jon Farhat; Special Makeup Effects, Rick Baker; Costumes, Ha Nguyen; Music, David Newman; Casting, Aleta Chappelle; an Imagine Entertainment presentation of a Brian Grazer production; Digital DTS Stereo; Deluxe color; Rated PG-13; 95 minutes; June release

Eddie Murphy

CAST

Prof. Sherman Klump/Buddy Love/ Lance Perkins/Papa Klump/ Mama Klump/Grandma Klump/Ernie Klump	Eddie Murphy
Carla Purty	Jada Pinkett
Harlan Hartley	James Coburn
Dean Richmond	Larry Miller
Reggie Warrington	Dave Chappelle
Jason	John Ales
Dean's Secretary	Patricia Wilson
Ernie Klump, Jr.	Jamal Mixon
Fit Woman	Nichole McAuley
Health Instructor	Hamilton Von Watts
Asian Man	Chao-Li Chi
Host	Tony Carlin
Bartender	Quinn Duffy
Band Leader	Doug Williams
Students	David Ramsey, Chaz Lamar Shepherd, Steve Monroe
Sad Fat Girl	Lisa Halpern
Doctors	Mark McPherson, John Prosky, Michael Rothhaar
Nurse	Sara Ballantine
Cop	Greg Natale
Guy in Crowd	Roy Werner
Woman in Crowd	Retha Jones
Security Guard	Joe Greco

and Nick Kokotakis (Waiter), Stanley D. Petter III (Fireman), Mohammad Mohsen (Bodybuilder), Michael D. Starks (Boxing Trainer), Julianne Christie (Sporting Goods Clerk), Christie Blanchard-Power (Dignitary), Alexia Robinson, Lisa Boyle, Athena Massey (Sexy Girls), Judith Woodbury (Wellman College Alumni)

Shy and overweight college professor Sherman Klump invents a formula that turns him into a slimmer, more outgoing persona, Buddy Love. Remake of the 1963 Paramount film that starred Jerry Lewis and Stella Stevens. 1996 Academy Award winner for Best Makeup.

Eddie Murphy

Eddie Murphy

Eddie Murphy, Larry Miller

INDEPENDENCE DAY

Will Smith, Harry Connick, Jr.

Harvey Fierstein, Jeff Goldblum

(20TH CENTURY FOX) Producer, Dean Devlin; Executive Producers, Roland Emmerich, Ute Emmerich, William Fay; Director, Roland Emmerich; Screenplay, Dean Devlin, Roland Emmerich; Photography, Karl Walter Lindenlaub; Designers, Oliver Scholl, Patrick Tatopoulos; Editor, David Brenner; Music, David Arnold; Costumes, Joseph Porro; Associate Producer, Peter Winther; Visual Effects Supervisors, Volker Engel, Douglas Smith; Digital Effects Supervisor/Producer, Tricia Ashford; Alien Creature Effects, Patrick Tatopoulos; a Centropolis Entertainment production; Dolby Stereo; Super 35 Widescreen; Deluxe Color; Rated PG-13; 145 minutes; July release

CAST

Captain Steven Hiller	Will Smith
President Thomas J. Whitmore	Bill Pullman
David Levinson	Jeff Goldblum
Marilyn Whitmore	Mary McDonnell
Julius Levinson	Judd Hirsch
General William Grey	Robert Loggia
Russell Casse	Randy Quaid
Constance Spano	Margaret Colin
Albert Nimziki	James Rebhorn
Marty Gilbert	Harvey Fierstein
Major Mitchell	Adam Baldwin
Dr. Brakish Okun	Brent Spiner
Miguel	James Duval
Jasmine Dubrow	Vivica A. Fox
Alicia	Lisa Jakub
Dylan	Ross Bagley
Patricia Whitmore	Mae Whitman
Captain Watson	Bill Smitrovich
Tiffany	Kiersten Warren
Captain Jimy Wilder	Harry Connick, Jr.
Troy	Guiseppe Andrews
Dr. Isaacs	John Storey

and Frank Novak (Teddy), Devon Gummersall (Philip), Leland Orser, Vivian Palermo (Techies/Med. Assts.), Mirron E. Willis, Ross Lacy (Aides), David Pressman (Whitmore's Aide), Raphael Sbarge (Commander/Tech.), Bobby Hosea, Dan Lauria (Commanding Officers), Steve Giannell, Eric Paskel (Radar Techs), Carlos LaCamara (Radar Operator), John Bennett Perry, Troy Willis (Secret Servicemen), Tim Kelleher (Technician), Wayne Wilderson (Area 51 Technician), Jay Acovone (Area 51 Guard), James Wong, Thom Barry, Jana Marie Hupp (SETI Techs), Matt Pashkow (2nd Officer), Robert Pine (Chief of Staff), Marisa Morell, Michael Winther, Dexter Warren, Paul LeClair (Co-Workers), Capt. Michael "Chewy" Vacca (Lt. Peterson), David Chanel (Secret Service Agent), John Capodice (Mario), Greg Collins (Military Aide), Derek Webster (Sky Crane Pilots), Mark Fite, Eric Neal Newman (Pilots), Levani, Kristof Konrad (Russian Pilots), Kevin Sifuentes (Tank Commander), Elston Ridgle (Soldier), Randy Oglesby, Jack Moore (Mechanics), Barry Del Serman (Street Preacher), Lyman Ward (Secret Service Guy), Anthony Crivello (Lincoln) Richard Speight, Jr. (Ed), Barbara Beck (Monica Soloway), Joe Fowler, Andrew Warne, Sharon Tay (Reporters), Peter Jozef Lucas (Russian Reporter), Yelena Danova (Russian Newscaster), Derek Kim (Korean Newscaster), Vanessa J. Wells (Newscaster), Jessika Cardinahl (German Video Newscaster), Gary W. Cruz, Ron Pitts, Wendy L. Walsh, Christine Devine, Mark Thompson, Jack Germond, Morton Kondracke (Video Newscasters), Ernie Anastos (Rex Black NY Newscaster), Cinckevin Cooney (Atlantic Air), Rance Howard (Chaplain), Nelson Mashita (Japanese Tech), Jeff Phillips (B-2 Pilot), Sayed Badreya (Arab Pilot), Adam Tomei (Sailor), John Bradley (Lucas), Kimberly Beck (Housewife), Thomas F. Duffy (Lieutenant), Andrew Keegan (Older Boy), Jon Matthews (Thomson), Jim Piddock (Reginald), Fred Barnes, Eleanor Clift, Jerry Dunphy, John McLaughlin, Barry Nolan, George Putnam (Themselves), Eric Michael Zee (Northridge Field Reporter), Pat Skipper (Redneck), Carlos Lara (Butler), Lee Strauss (Elvis Fanatic), Lisa Star (Woman on Roof), Malcolm Danare (Intellectual on Roof), Arthur Brooks (Trucker on Roof), Michael G. Moertl (Thief), James J. Joyce (Master C.P.O.), Joyce Cohen (Kim Peters Reporter), Julie Moran (Entertainment Tonight Reporter), Robin Groth (Flagstaff News Anchor), Richard Pachorek (LAPD Helicopter Pilot), Dakota (Boomer), Gary Hecker (Alien Vocal Effects), Frank Welker (Special Vocal Effects)

Gigantic alien spaceships appear over various cities, ready to obliterate the earth, causing the world citizens to rally together to fight. 1996 Academy Award winner for Best Visual Effects. The film received an additional nomination for sound.

© Twentieth Century Fox

Brent Spiner, Bill Pullman, James Rebhorn

Robert Loggia, Bill Pullman

Mary McDonnell

Ross Bagley, Vivica A. Fox

Margaret Colin, Mae Whitman, Jeff Goldblum, Judd Hirsch

PHENOMENON

(TOUCHSTONE) Producers, Barbara Boyle, Michael Taylor; Executive Producers, Charles Newirth, Jonathan Krane; Director, Jon Turteltaub; Screenplay, Gerald DiPego; Photography, Phedon Papamichael; Designer, Garreth Stover; Editor, Bruce Green; Music, Thomas Newman; Costumes, Betsy Cox; Casting, Renee Rousselot; a Barbara Boyle and Michael Taylor production; Distributed by Buena Vista Pictures; Dolby Digital Stereo; Panavision; Technicolor; Rated PG; 124 minutes; July release

CAST

George Malley	John Travolta
Lace Pennamin	Kyra Sedgwick
Nate Pope	Forest Whitaker
Doc	Robert Duvall
Al	David Gallagher
Glory	Ashley Buccille
Tito	Tony Genaro
Banes	Sean O'Bryan
Jack Hatch	Bruce Young
Jimmy	Michael Milhoan
Ted Rhome	Vyto Ruginis
Ella	Elisabeth Nunziato
Professor Ringold	Jeffrey DeMunn
Dr. Wellin	Richard Kiley
Alberto	Mark Valim
Roger	Troy Evans
Bonnie	Ellen Geer
Pete	James Keane
Marge	Susan Merson
Cal	James Cotton
Niedorf	Brent Spiner
Ella's Father	Tony A. Mattos
Major Benz	Anni Long
Reporter	Mark Soper
Sick Boy's Father	Daniel Zacapa
Intense Man at Library Fair	Justin DiPego
Taunting Man at Library Fair	Cab Covay
May	Jewel Benedict
Man in Orchard	Carl Parker
Agents	Tom Fridley, Eric G. Tignini
Customer at Malley's	Richard Gross
Celia	Beth Kennedy

and Mariann V. Carothers (Furniture Store Owner), Isaac Reiswig (Man in Crowd), Claudia Crespin (Woman in Crowd), Michael Forner, Joseph A. Nicosia, Dan Partain (Men at Bar), Betsy Berryhill (Woman at Bar), Jack Chouchanian (Technician #1), Sage Callaway (Officer)

After being dazzled by a mysterious light from above, small town garage mechanic George Malley finds himself possessing phenomenal intelligence and unexplainable powers.

© Touchstone Pictures

Kyra Sedgwick, John Travolta

Forest Whitaker, John Travolta

John Travolta, Robert Duvall

Kyra Sedgwick, David Gallagher, Ashley Buccille

HARRIET THE SPY

(PARAMOUNT) Producer, Marykay Powell; Executive Producer, Debby Beece; Director, Brownwen Hughes; Screenplay, Douglas Petrie, Theresa Rebeck; Adaptation, Greg Taylor, Julie Talen; Based upon the novel by Louise Fitzhugh; Photography, Francis Kenny; Designer, Lester Cohen; Editor, Debra Chiate; Costumes, Donna Zakowska; Co-Producer, Nava Levin; Music, Jamshied Sharifi; Casting, Jill Greenberg Sands; a Rastar production, presented in association with Nickelodeon Movies; Dolby Stereo; Deluxe color; Rated PG; 101 minutes; July release

CAST

Harriet Welsch . . . . Michelle Trachtenberg
Sport . . . . Gregory Smith
Janie . . . . Vanessa Lee Chester
Ole Golly . . . . Rosie O'Donnell
Mrs. Welsch . . . . J. Smith-Cameron
Mr. Welsch . . . . Robert Joy
Agatha K. Plummer . . . . Eartha Kitt
Marion Hawthorne . . . . Charlotte Sullivan
Rachel Hennessy. . . . . Teisha Kim
Beth Ellen Hansen . . . . Cecilley Carroll
Boy With Purple Socks. . . . . Dov Tiefenbach
Carrie Andrews. . . . . Nina Shock
Pinky Whitehead. Conor Devitt
Laura Peters . . . . Alisha Morrison
Miss Elson. . . . . Nancy Beatty
Harrison Withers . . . . Don Francks
George Waldenstein . . . . Eugene Lipinski
Sport's Dad. . . . . Gerry Quigley
Janie's Mother. . . . . Jackie Richardson
Windchime Lady. . . . . Mercedes Enriquez
Mrs. Hong Fat . . . . Mung-Ling Tsui
Mr. Hong Fat . . . . Ho Chow
Frankie Hong Fat. Byron Wong
Bruno Hong Fat. . . . . Paul Lee
Paige Hong Fat . . . . Kim Lieu
Grandpa Hong Fat. . . . . Kwok-Wing Leung
Maid. . . . . Sally Cahill
Dr. Wagner. . . . . Roger Clown
and Jamie Jones (Pickpocket), Bob Windsor (Dog Delivery Guy), Gladys O'Connor (Woman With Purse), Vic Ho (Acupuncturist), Roland Kirouac, Jr. (Choreographer), Maury Chaykin (Director)

Determined to be a famous writer when she grows up, Harriet Welsch travels her special spy route, observing the world around her and jotting down what she sees in her secret spy notebook.

Vanessa Lee Chester, Gregory Smith, Michelle Trachtenberg, Rosie O'Donnell

Michelle Trachtenberg

MANNY & LO

(SONY CLASSICS) Producers, Dean Silvers, Marlen Hecht; Executive Producer, Klaus Volkenborn; Director/Screenplay, Lisa Krueger; Photography, Tom Krueger; Designer, Sharon Lomofsky; Editor, Colleen Sharp; Music, John Lurie; Costumes, Jennifer Parker; Casting, Ellen Parks; a Pope Entertainment Group and Klaus Volkenborn presentation; Color; Rated R; 97 minutes; July release

CAST

Elaine . . . . Mary Kay Place
Amanda (Manny) . . . . Scarlett Johansson
Laurel (Lo) . . . . Aleksa Palladino
Mr. Humphreys. Paul Guilfoyle
Joey . . . . Glenn Fitzgerald
Chuck . . . . Cameron Boyd
Georgine . . . . Novella Nelson
Connie . . . . Angie Phillips
Chuck's Mom . . . . Monica Smith
and Dean Silvers, Marlen Hecht, Forrest Silvers, Tyler Silvers (Suburban Family), Lisa Campion (Convenience Store Clerk), Susan Decker, Marla Zuk, Bonnie Johnson (Baby Store Customers), Melissa Johnson (Child), Melanie Johansson, Karsten Johansson, Hunter Johansson, Vanessa Johansson (Golf Course Family), David DeStaebler, Mark Palmieri (Golf Course Cops), Tony Arnaud (Sheriff), Nicholas Lent (Lo's Baby)

11-year-old Manny and her 16-year-old sister Lo live a life on the road after running away from separate foster homes.

Scarlett Johansson, Mary Kay Place, Aleksa Palladino

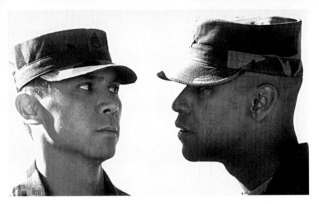

Lou Diamond Phillips, Denzel Washington

Meg Ryan

Lou Diamond Phillips

Regina Taylor, Denzel Washington

Denzel Washington

Denzel Washington, Scott Glenn

COURAGE UNDER FIRE

(20TH CENTURY FOX) Producers, John Davis, Joseph M. Singer, David T. Friendly; Executive Producers, Joseph M. Caracciolo, Debra Martin Chase; Director, Edward Zwick; Screenplay, Patrick Sheane Duncan; Photography, Roger Deakins; Designer, John Graysmark; Costumes, Francine Jamison-Tanchuck; Editor, Steven Rosenblum; Music, James Horner; Casting, Mary Colquhoun; a Fox 2000 Pictures presentation of a Davis Entertainment Company/Joseph M. Singer production; Dolby Stereo; Color; Rated R; 116 minutes; July release

Seth Gilliam, Meg Ryan

CAST

Lt. Colonel Nathaniel Serling	Denzel Washington
Captain Karen Walden	Meg Ryan
Monfriez	Lou Diamond Phillips
General Hershberg	Michael Moriarty
Ilario	Matt Damon
Bruno	Bronson Pinchot
Altameyer	Seth Gilliam
Meredith Serling	Regina Taylor
Banacek	Zeljko Ivanek
Gartner	Scott Glenn
Rady	Tim Guinee
Boylar	Tim Ransom
Patella	Sean Astin
Robins	Armand Darrius
Bobcat 5	Mark Adair-Rios
Chelli	Ned Vaughn
Jenkins	Manny Perez
Egan	David McSwain
Thompson	Sean Patrick Thomas
Joel Walden	Ken Jenkins
Geraldine Walden	Kathleen Widdoes
Anne Marie Walden	Christina Stojanovich
Nathan Serling, Jr.	Lucky Luciano
Joleen Serling	Erica C. Newman
Brian Serling	Jamal A. Mays
Josie Serling	Ashlee Jordan Pryor
Maria	Michole White
Hillerman	Jeffrey Waid
Drill Team Commander	Patrick Young
Soldier	Jimmy Ray Pickens
Coffee Sergeant	Jack Watkins
Cadres	Matt Sigloch, James Paul Morse
McQuillan	Bruce McGill
Teegarden's Crew Chief	Rory J. Aylward
Refueler	Kyle Mickaelian
Orderly	Michael Dolan
The President	John Roarke
Questioner	Tom Schanley
Iraqi Tank Commander	Bob Apisa
Laughing Gunner	Daniel Gonzalez
Speaker	Albert Hall
Don Boylar	Richard Venture
Louise Boylar	Diane Baker
Annie	Amy Hathaway
Delinquent Soldier	Reed Frerichs
Rowtero	Julius Carter

Michael Moriarty, Danzel Washington

Tormented by a mishap during a battle in which he accidentally caused the death of his own men, Nat Serling is asked to investigate the circumstamces behind the proposal that Capt. Karen Walden receive the Medal of Honor.

© Twentieth Century Fox

Meg Ryan, Matt Damon

WALKING AND TALKING

(MIRAMAX) Producers, Ted Hope, James Schamus; Executive Producers, Dorothy Berwin, Scott Meek; Director/Screenplay, Nicole Holofcener; Photography, Michael Spiller; Designer, Anne Stuhler; Editor, Alisa Lepselter; Costumes, Edi Giguere; Music, Billy Bragg; Casting, Avy Kaufman; a Channel Four Films/Team/Pandora/Mikado and Electric presentation of a Good Machine/Zenith production; Ultra Stereo; DuArt color; Rated R; 86 minutes; July release

CAST

Amelia	Catherine Keener
Laura	Anne Heche
Andrew	Liev Schreiber
Frank	Todd Field
Bill	Kevin Corrigan
Peter	Randall Batinkoff
Amelia's Therapist	Joseph Siravo
Laura's Devil-Seeing Patient	Vincent Pastore
Andrew's Mom	Lynn Cohen
Andrew's Dad	Lawrence Holofcener
Young Amelia	Amy Braverman
Young Laura	Miranda Stuart Rhyne
The Vet	Brenda Thomas Denmark
Laura's Sexy Patient	Rafael Alvarez
Ellen the Waitress	Ritamarie Kelly
Actor in Play	Steve Cohen
Peter's Friend	Jordan Levinson
Amelia's Co-Worker	Heather Gottlieb
Cat Sympathizer	Nitza Wilon
Amelia's Neighbor (Gum Puller)	Allison Janney
Amelia's Neighbor (Betsy)	Alice Drummond
Virginia	Louise Yanofsky
Rick	Michael Kroll
Aunt Cynthia	Isa Thomas
Big Jean, the Cat	Spatz

Laura dreads telling her closest friend Amelia that she has decided to end her life as a single woman and marry Frank.

© Miramax Films

Liev Schreiber, Catherine Keener, Anne Heche, Todd Field

Catherine Keener, Anne Heche

FLED

(MGM) Producer, Frank Mancuso, Jr.; Executive Producer/Screenplay, Preston A. Whitmore, II; Director, Kevin Hooks; Photography, Matthew F. Leonetti; Designer, Charles Bennett; Editors, Richard Nord, Joseph Gutowski; Costumes, Jennifer Bryan; Music, Graeme Revell; Associate Producer, Vikki Williams; Casting, Amanda Mackey Johnson, Cathy Sandrich; a Frank Mancuso, Jr. production; Distributed by MGM/UA; DTS Stereo; Deluxe color; Rated R; 98 minutes; July release

CAST

Piper	Laurence Fishburne
Dodge	Stephen Baldwin
Gibson	Will Patton
Pat Schiller	Robert John Burke
Lieutenant Clark	Robert Hooks
Santiago	Victor Rivers
Chris Paine	David Dukes
Warden Nichols	Ken Jenkins
Mantajano	Michael Nader
Faith/Cindy	Brittney Powell
Cora	Salma Hayek
Herb Foster	Steve Carlisle
Officer Thornhill	Brett Rice

and J. Don Ferguson (Chairman), Kathy Payne (Margaret Parks), Bob Apisa (Jose Marti), Gary Yates (Sgt. Bailey), Jon Huffman (Milliner), Anderson Martin (Officer Kevin), Bob Hannah (Mason), Margo Moorer (Waitress), Angela Mills (Jocelyn), Michael Hooks (Vonte), Joe Torry (Bo Grant), Bill Bellamy (Ray), RuPaul (Himself), Robby Preddy (Zestos Waitress), Taurean Blacque (Les), K. Addison Young (Puffy), Libby Whittemore (Sandra), Meredith Gordon (Officer), David Dwyer (Sgt. Leonard), Michael H. Moss (Dispatcher), James Michael Hill (Man in the Bathroom), Tom Turbiville (Security Guard), Charles Gershon, Molli D. Gershon, Brannon Bates, Katie Glendinning, Phonz Bass, Karl D. Gardner (Gondola Passenger).

Piper and Dodge escape from prison through the backwoods of Georgia, hoping to retrieve some stolen money and an incriminating computer disk.

© Metro-Goldwyn-Mayer, Inc.

Stephen Baldwin, Laurence Fishburne

MULTIPLICITY

(COLUMBIA) Producers, Trevor Albert, Harold Ramis; Executive Producer, Lee R. Mayes; Director, Harold Ramis; Screenplay, Chris Miller, Mary Hale, Lowell Ganz, Babaloo Mandel; Based on the short story by Chris Miller; Photography, Laszlo Kovacs; Designer, Jackson DeGovia; Editors, Pem Herring, Craig Herring; Costumes, Shay Cunliffe; Music, George Fenton; Visual Effects Supervisor, Richard Edlund; Co-Producer, Whitney White; Casting, Howard Feuer; a Trevor Albert production; Dolby SDDS Stereo; Panavision; Technicolor; Rated PG-13; 117 minutes; July release

Michael Keaton, Michael Keaton, Michael Keaton, Michael Keaton

CAST

Doug Kinney/Two/Three/Four	Michael Keaton
Laura Kinney	Andie MacDowell
Zack Kinney	Zack Duhame
Jennifer Kinney	Katie Schlossberg
Dr. Leeds	Harris Yulin
Del King	Richard Masur
Vic	Eugene Levy
Noreen	Ann Cusack
Ted	John DeLance
Franny	Judith Kahan
Paul	Obba Babatunde
Walt	Brian Doyle-Murray
Robin	Julie Bowen
Beth	Dawn Maxey
Patti	Kari Coleman
Coach Jack	Steven Kampmann
Irate Football Parents	Michael Milhoan, Skip Stellrecht
Maitre D'	James Piddock
Ballet School Receptionist	Robin Duke
Den Mother	Suzanne Herrington
Laura's Father	Robert Ridgley
Building Inspector	Glenn Shadix
Construction Worker	Dennis R. Lyell
Lab Technician Twins	Richard Plon, Harold Plon
Man in Restaurant	George D. Wallace
Woman in Restaurant	Justine A. Johnston

Finding it increasingly difficult to cope with his busy schedule Doug Kinney has himself scientifically cloned.

© Columbia Pictures Industries, Inc.

Michael Keaton, Michael Keaton, Michael Keaton

Andie MacDowell, Michael Keaton

Zack Duhame, Katie Schlossberg, Michael Keaton, Andie MacDowell

KINGPIN

Woody Harrelson, Vanessa Angel, Randy Quaid

Bill Murray

(MGM) Producers, Brad Krevoy, Steve Stabler, Bradley Thomas; Executive Producer, Keith Samples; Director, Peter Farrelly, Bobby Farrelly; Screenplay, Barry Fanaro, Mort Nathan; Photography, Mark Irwin; Designer, Sidney Jackson Bartholomew, Jr.; Editor, Christopher Greenbury; Co-Producers, Jim Burke, John Bertolli; Associate Producer, James B. Rogers; Music, Freedy Johnston; Costumes, Mary Zophres; Casting, Rick Montgomery, Dan Parada; a Rysher Entertainment presentation of a Motion Picture Corporation of America production of a Farrelly Brothers' Movie; DTS Stereo; Super 35 Widescreen; Deluxe color; Rated PG-13; 113 minutes; July release

CAST

Roy Munson	Woody Harrelson
Ishmael	Randy Quaid
Claudia	Vanessa Angel
Ernie McCracken	Bill Murray
The Gambler	Chris Elliott
Mr. Boorg	William Jordan
Owner of Stiffy's	Richard Tyson
Landlady	Lin Shaye
Thomas	Zen Gesner
Mrs. Boorg	Prudence Wright Holmes
Stanley Osmanski	Rob Moran
Calvert Munson	Danny Green
Young Roy	Will Rothhaar

and Mark Charpentier, Brad Faxon, Billy Andrade, Paul DeWolf (1979 Bowling Buddies), Jilly Lytle (Odor Eater Babe), Willie Beauchene (Bunion Boy), Sayed Badreya (Fatima), Linda Carola (1979 Waitress), Monica Shay (1979 Diner Floozy), Danny Murphy (Beaver Valley Bowling Manager), David Shackelford (Red Neck Stutterer), Mike Cerrone, Mike Cavallo, Rick Barker, Paul Pelletier, Tom Leasca, Tom Lupo (Beaver Bowl Hustlers), Jimmy Shay (Invisible Hustler), Hank Brandt (Bowling Priest), Suzan Hughes (Cocktail Waitress), Michael Corrente, Herbie Flynn (Scranton Winos), Joe "Smokey" Krawlicky (Pennsylvania Hall O' Fame Bowler), Googy Gress (Lancaster Bowl Manager), Hillary Matthews (Mother With Carriage), Ryan & William Heggs (Baby in Carriage), Willie Garson (Purse Snatcher), Nancy Frey-Jarecki (Sarah Boorg), Robby Thibeau (Lucas Boorg), Helen Manfull (Grandma Boorg), Terry Mullany, Brian Stube, Jim Blake, Chris Spain (Amish Saw Guys), Rose Smith-Lotenero (Amish Babe), Michelle Matheson (Rebecca), Nicholas Greenbury, Andrew Greenbury (Amish Kids), Pucky Lippincott (Amish Bellringer), Mark "Chief" Wasler (Make-out King), Gretchen Treser (Make-out Queen), Patrick Healy (Urinal Boy), Sean P. Gildea (McKnight Bowl Bartender), Jackie Flynn (Dog Boy), Jonathan Richman, Tommy Larkins (Tavern Band), Bob Weeks (Waiter), Roger Clemens (Skidmark), Libby Langdon (Skidmark's Squirrel), Liza, Wallace Lester, Mark Pauperas, Sid Greenbud, Kipp Stroden, Sidney J. Bartholomew, Jr. (Tavern Drunks), Rosey Brown, John Jordan, Mark Miosky (Skidmark's Friends), John Woodin, Gordie Merrick, Steven R. Gehrke, Clem "Mandingo" Franek (Bowling Steelworkers), Kathy Farrelly, Stacy Lundin (Bowling Biker Babes), Jonathan "Earl" Stein, Alex Stohn (Bowling Farmers), Lori Bagley (Beautiful Dancers), Jo Marcus, Cecile Krevoy, Mary Stohn (Sexy Senior Bowlers), Steve Tyler (Gas Station Attendant), The Artist Formerly Known as Docky (Uncle Willy), John Stroehman, Louis Charles Consolo (Stiffy's Goons), Joanne Wolfe, Danielle Parsons (Silver Legacy Waitress), Jane Pratt (TV Interviewer), Steve Stabler (TV Cameraman), Elizabeth Jordan, Cynthia Farrelly Gesner (Silver Legacy Maids), Brian Mone (Psycho Guy), Taryn Chilivis (Cute Mother), Lisa Stohard, Melinda Kocsis, Rachel Wagner, Victoria Scott (Unified Fund Moms), Joshua Nelson (Unififed Fund Kid), Kevin O'Brien (Pizza Guy), Nancy Farrelly (Nouchi's Gal), Warren Tashjian (Courtesy Call Guy), Mariann Farrelly, Aggie Byers (Tournament Sign-up Ladies), John Popper (Bowling Tournament Announcer), Don Julio, Kevin Civale, Brian Voss, Mark Roth, Justin Hromek, Ron Palumbi, Jr., Parker Bohn III, Randy Pederson (Pro Bowlers), John Cioffoletti (Philips Head Bowler), Jon Dennis, Chris Schenkel, Chris Berman (Themselves), Clint Allen (Store Clerk), Urge Overkill (National Anthem Band), Jessica Byers, Julie Byers (Big Ern's Valets), Preston Thomas, Jeff Thomas (Tournament Liaisons), Morganna (Herself), Jim Ahern (Sport), John Neary (Mission Priest), Kenny Griswold, George Bedard, Joe Lewis (Barflies), George Christy (Stiffy's Announcer), Andy Taylor (Custodian), Brad Norton (MIA Guy), Blues Traveler (Amish Band), Scott Gasbarro (Amish Dancing Dude)

Washed up, former bowling-pro Roy Munson discovers an Amish bowling wiz named Ishmael and takes him to the winner-take-all tournament in Reno, hoping to get rich.

© Rysher Entertainment

Woody Harrelson, Vanessa Angel, Randy Quaid

CHAIN REACTION

(20TH CENTURY FOX) Producers, Arne L. Schmidt, Andrew Davis; Executive Producers, Richard D. Zanuck, Erwin Stoff; Director, Andrew Davis; Screenplay, J.F. Lawton, Michael Bortman; Story, Arne L. Schmidt, Rick Seaman, Josh Friedman; Photography, Frank Tidy; Designer, Maher Ahmad; Editors, Donald Brochu, Dov Hoenig, Arthur Schmidt; Music, Jerry Goldsmith; Visual Effects Supervisor, Nick Davis; a Zanuck Company/Chicago Pacific Entertainment/Arne L. Schmidt production; Dolby Stereo; Astro Film color; Rated PG-13; 106 minutes; August release

Rachel Weisz, Keanu Reeves

CAST

Eddie Kasalivich	Keanu Reeves
Paul Shannon	Morgan Freeman
Lily Sinclair	Rachel Weisz
FBI Agent Ford	Fred Ward
FBI Agent Doyle	Kevin Dunn
Lyman Earl Collier	Brian Cox
Maggie McDermott	Joanna Cassidy
Ed Rafferty	Chelcie Ross
Dr. Alistair Barkley	Nicholas Rudall
Lu Chen	Tzi Ma

and Research Team: Krzysztof Pieczynski (Lucasz Screbneski), Julie R. Peal (Emily Pearl), Godfrey C. Danchimah, Jr. (Chidi Egbuna), Gene Barge (James Washington), Nathan Davis (Morris Grodsky), Aaron Williams (Lab Techie #3), Daniel H. Friedman (Video Dan); FBI Agents: Johnny Lee Davenport (Caleb Williams), James Sie (Ken Lim), Joan Kohn (Sarah Fine), Juan Ramirez (Raymond Pena), Nydia Rodriguez Terracina (Gabrielle Guerrera), Scott Benjaminson (Stuart Showcroft), Ned Schmidtke (Wisconsin Chief Schmidke), Randall Arney, Noelle Bou-Sliman (DC Technicians); Cops: Joe Kosala (Sgt. Joe Byczkowski), Ron Dean (Sgt. Nick Zingaro), Miguel Nino (Officer Miguel), Turk Muller (Dane County Cop), Neil Flynn (State Trooper Nemitz), Michael Skewes (State Trooper Schwartz); Shannon's Staff: Margaret Travolta (Anita Fermi), Jacqueline Arthur (Jackie Mann), Tom Mula (Chicago Administrator), Denise Price (Receptionist), Rick LeFevour (Matthew Haig), Charley Sherman (Justin Tidy), Gina Raffin (Colleen Dryden); Reporters: Pam Zekman (Rita Bliss), Lisa Tejero (Dolores Enrique), David Pasquesi (Al Vanzetti), John Drummond (Drummond), Catherine Lemkau, Tell Draper (TV Reporters); Danny Goldring (Clancy Butler), Eddie Bo Smith, Jr. (Yusef Reed), Michael Gaylord James (Jim Gaylord), Ken Moreno (Naldo Partida), Allen Hamilton (Senator Phil Schmidt), Dick Cusack (Senate Chairman), Nick Kusenko (Staff Member Stennis), David Michael Gee (Senate Guard), Stanley M. Span (Firechief #1), Ann Whitney (Barkley's Lawyer), Rich Komenich (Bar Patron), Afram Bill Williams, Will Zahrn (Bridge Controllers), John W. Hardy (Train Porter), Mary Seibel (Older Woman on Train), Nina Beesley (Flower Shop Owner), Mike Shannon (DC Flower Delivery Man), Billy Haynes (Doorman), Walter Doggett (Gate Guard), Jack Kandel (Panhandler), Timothy Maxwell (Homeless Husband), Leslie Mikol (Homeless Wife), Rio Zavala (Homeless Man); C-Systems Staff: Mark Morettini (Romano), Soseh Kevorkian (Evelyn), Christopher Holloway (Max Holloway), Jim Ortlieb (Orbit), Cherl Hamada (Hamada), Mike Gray (Swizlard), Joe Guastaferro (Tunnel Foreman).

When a research laboratory is destroyed, two of its top scientists, Eddie Kasalivich and Lily Sinclair, find themselves on the run when the finger of guilt points at them.

©Twentieth Century Fox

Morgan Freeman, Brian Cox

Kevin Dunn, Fred Ward

Keanu Reeves

87

JOHN CARPENTER'S
ESCAPE FROM L.A.

(PARAMOUNT) Producers, Debra Hill, Kurt Russell; Director, John Carpenter; Screenplay, John Carpenter, Debra Hill, Kurt Russell; Based on characters created by John Carpenter, Nick Castle; Photography, Gary B. Kibbe; Designer, Lawrence G. Paull; Editor, Edward A. Warschilka; Costumes, Robin Michel Bush; Music, Shirley Walker, John Carpenter; Visual Effects Supervisor, Kimberly K. Nelson; Presented in association with Rysher Entertainment; Dolby Stereo; Panavision; Deluxe color; Rated R; 100 minutes; August release

CAST

Snake Plissken	Kurt Russell
Utopia	A.J. Langer
Map to the Stars Eddie	Steve Buscemi
Cuervo Jones	George Corraface
Malloy	Stacy Keach
Brazen	Michelle Forbes
Hershe	Pam Grier
Saigon Shadow	Jeff Imada
President	Cliff Robertson
Taslima	Valeria Golino
Pipeline	Peter Fonda
Blonde Hooker	Ina Romeo
Duty Sergeant	Peter Jason
Police Anchor	Jordan Baker
Woman on Freeway	Caroleen Feeney
Congressman	Paul Bartel
Com Officer	Tom McNulty
Surgeon General of Beverly Hills	Bruce Campbell
Surfer	Breckin Meyer
Skinhead	Robert Carradine
Cloaked Figure	Shelly Desai
Test Tube	Leland Orser
Narrator	Kathleen Blanchard
Mescalitos	William Luduena, Gabriel Castillo
Jacket Mescalito	William Peña
U.S. Cleric Justice	David Perrone

In futuristic Los Angeles, where the city has broken off from the mainland and become a deportation center for criminals, Snake Plissken is recruited to locate a valuable doomsday device brought there by the President's rebellious daughter, Utopia. Sequel to the 1981 Embassy Pictures release Escape From New York, *which also starred Kurt Russell and was directed by John Carpenter.* ©Paramount Pictures

Kurt Russell

Kurt Russell, Bruce Campbell

Kurt Russell, Peter Fonda

Kurt Russell, Pam Grier, Steve Buscemi

JACK

(HOLLYWOOD PICTURES) Producers, Ricardo Mestres, Fred Fuchs, Francis Ford Coppola; Executive Producer, Doug Claybourne; Director, Francis Ford Coppola; Screenplay, James DeMonaco, Gary Nadeau; Photography, John Toll; Designer, Dean Tavoularis; Editor, Barry Malkin; Costumes, Aggie Guerard Rodgers; Music, Michael Kamen; Casting, Linda Phillips Palo, Rosalie Joseph; an American Zoetrope/Great Oaks production; Distributed by Buena Vista Pictures; Dolby Digital Stereo; Technicolor; Rated PG-13; 113 minutes; August release

CAST

Jack Powell	Robin Williams
Karen Powell	Diane Lane
Brian Powell	Brian Kerwin
Miss Marquez	Jennifer Lopez
Lawrence Woodruff	Bill Cosby
Dolores Durante	Fran Drescher
Louis Durante	Adam Zolotin
Edward	Todd Bosley
John-John	Seth Smith
George	Mario Yedidia
Johnny Duffer	Jeremy Lelliott
Phoebe	Jurnee Smollett
Jane	Dani Faith
Victor	Hugo Hernandez
Eric	Rickey D'Shon Collins
Paulie	Michael McKean
Angry Man	Edward Lynch
Bartender	Don Novello
Dr. Benfante	Allan Rich
Dr. Lin	Keone Young
Poppy	Irwin Corey
Principal McGee	Al Nalbandian
High School Principal	Dwight Hicks
Lucy	Allison Whitbeck
Boy in Classroom	Sam Ritzenberg
Eric's Brother	Terry Ricardo Jefferson II
Mario	Studio Gutierrez
Big Joe	Joe Akins
Kendra	Kendra Sutherland
Allison	Ashlee Lauren

and Wilma Bonet, Abigail Van Alyn, Rainer Judd, Marcella Pabros, Jennifer Garces (Nurses), Marc Coppola, Terry McGovern, Kim Wonderly (Radio Personalities), Bria Neuenschwander (Drugstore Clerk), Steven Anthony Jones (Officer at Jail), Jeannette Etheredge, Jacqui De La Fontaine (Cats), Josh Kornbluth (Pack of Cigarettes), Helen Shumaker (Martini), Pete Escovedo with The New Morty Show, Pete Escovedo, Morty Okin, John Quam, Andrew Higgins, David Murotake, Whitney Wilson, David Rubin, Carroll Ashby, Juan Escovedo, Ray Loeckle, Mike Moore, Peter Michael Escovedo, Van Hughes (Conga Band), Michael Madland (Louis at 18), Matt Kroot (Edward at 18), Ryan Kennedy (George at 18), Tyler Smith (John-John at 18), Jesse James Chisholm (Johnny Duffer at 18), Jonathan A. Turner (Eric at 18), Kamela Peart (Phoebe at 16), Jennifer Hagan (Jane at 16)

A 10-year-old boy, Jack Powell, born with a condition causing him to age four times faster than normal, finally realizes his dream of attending school with other children, entering the 5th grade.

©Hollywood Pictures Company

Fran Drescher, Adam Zolotin, Robin Williams

Robin Williams, Brian Kerwin

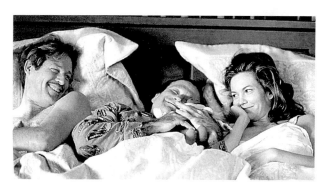

Brian Kerwin, Robin Williams, Diane Lane

Bill Cosby, Robin Williams

EMMA

(MIRAMAX) Producers, Patrick Cassavetti, Steven Haft; Executive Producers, Bob Weinstein, Harvey Weinstein; Director/Screenplay, Douglas McGrath; Based on the novel by Jane Austen; Photography, Ian Wilson; Designer, Michael Howells; Editor, Lesley Walker; Music, Rachel Portman; Costumes, Ruth Myers; Associate Producer, Donna Grey; a Matchmaker Films production/Haft Entertainment production; Dolby Stereo; Color; Rated PG; 111 minutes; August release

CAST

Emma Woodhouse	Gwyneth Paltrow
Harriet Smith	Toni Colette
Mr. Elton	Alan Cumming
Mr. Knightley	Jeremy Northam
Frank Churchill	Ewan McGregor
Mrs. Weston	Greta Scacchi
Mrs. Elton	Juliet Stevenson
Jane Fairfax	Polly Walker
Miss Bates	Sophie Thompson
Mrs. Bates	Phyllida Law
Mr. Weston	James Cosmo
Mr. Woodhouse	Denys Hawthorne
Mrs. Goddard	Kathleen Byron
Mr. Martin	Edward Woodall
Little Boy	Brett Miley
John Knightley	Brian Capron
Isabella	Karen Westwood
Footman	Paul Williamson
Miss Martin	Rebecca Craig
Mrs. Martin	Angela Down
Mr. Cole	John Franklyn Robbins
Bate's Maid	Ruth Jones

Emma Woodhouse, hoping to help others lead the sort of good life she herself believes she lives, takes Harriet Smith under her wing, hoping to find the plain young lady a suitable husband. 1996 Academy Award winner for original musical or comedy score.

© Miramax Films

Gwyneth Paltrow

Greta Scacchi

Gwyneth Paltrow, Jeremy Northam

Ewan McGregor

Alan Cumming, Gwyneth Paltrow

Gwyneth Paltrow, Jeremy Northam

Gwyneth Paltrow, Toni Collette

Juliet Stevenson, Alan Cumming

Alan Cumming, Juliet Stevenson, Polly Walder, Ewan McGregor

BASQUIAT

(MIRAMAX) Producers, Jon Kilik, Randy Ostrow, Joni Sighvatsson; Executive Producers, Peter Brant, Joseph Allen, Michiyo Yoshizaki; Director/Screenplay, Julian Schnabel; Story/Co-Producer, Lech Majewski; Story Developer, Michael Thomas Holman; Photography, Ron Fortunato; Designer, Dan Leigh; Costumes, John Dunn; Music, John Cale; Editor, Michael Berenbaum; a Peter Brant/Joseph Allen production; Dolby Stereo; Color; Rated R; 108 minutes; August release

CAST

Jean Michel Basquiat . . . . Jeffrey Wright
Rene Ricard . . . . Michael Wincott
Benny Dalmau . . . . Benicio Del Toro
Gina Cardinale . . . . Claire Forlani
Andy Warhol . . . . David Bowie
Bruno Bischofberger . . . . Dennis Hopper
Albert Milo . . . . Gary Oldman
The Interviewer . . . . Christopher Walken
The Electrician . . . . Willem Dafoe
Shenge . . . . Jean Claude Le Marre
Mary Boone . . . . Parker Posey
Annina Nosei . . . . Elina Lowensohn
Henry Geldzahler . . . . Paul Bartel
Big Pink . . . . Courtney Love
Cynthia Kruger . . . . Tatum O'Neal
Tom Kruger . . . . Chuck Pfeifer
Rockets . . . . Rockets Redglare
Esther Milo . . . . Esther G. Schnabel
Jack Milo . . . . Jack Schnabel
Jacqueline Milo . . . . Lola Schnabel
Themselves . . . . Peter McGough, David McDermott, Nemo
Mr. Chow . . . . Michael Chow
Christine . . . . Olatz Maria Schnabel
Stella . . . . Stella Schnabel
Maitre'd at Ballato's . . . . Steven Randazzo
Counterman at Deli . . . . Michael Badalucco
Giorgio . . . . Frances Dumaurier
Guard at Hospital . . . . Joseph R. Gannascoli
Matilde . . . . Hope Clarke
Young Jean Michel . . . . Brian Wright
and Tarmo Urb (Lech), Denise Burse (Mary on TV), Robert Alexander (Band Guy), Vincent Larseca (Vincent), Paul Outlaw (Paul), Leonard Jackson (Jean Michel's Father), Dave Shelley (Photographer), Fredrick Weller (Frank), Rene Rivera (Juan), Sam Rockwell, Ron Brice (Thug), William Seymour (Mr. Chow's Matire'd), Linda Larkin (Fan), Julie Araskog (Julie), Richard Butler, Joe Glasco, Steven Parenago, Jose Luis Ferrer, Irene Kiss, Richard the Ox (Medieval Villagers), Isabella Rossellini (Party Guest)

The true story of painter Jean-Michel Basquiat and his brief period of acclaim in the New York art world before his death at the age of 27.

Jeffrey Wright, David Bowie, Gary Oldman, Dennis Hopper

Courtney Love, Jeffrey Wright

Jeffrey Wright

Jeffrey Wright, Benicio Del Toro

MATILDA

(TRISTAR) Producers, Danny DeVito, Michael Shamberg, Stacey Sher, Liccy Dahl; Executive Producers, Michael Peyser, Martin Bregman; Director, Danny DeVito; Screenplay/Co-Producers, Nicholas Kazan, Robin Swicord; Based on the book by Roald Dahl; Photography, Stefan Czapsky; Designer, Bill Brzeski; Editors, Lynzee Klingman, Brent White; Costumes, Jane Ruhm; Music, David Newman; Associate Producer, Joshua Levinson; Casting, David Rubin, Renée Rousselot; a Jersey Films production; Dolby SDDS Stereo; Super 35 Widescreen; Technicolor; Rated PG; 93 minutes; August release

Danny DeVito, Mara Wilson, Rhea Perlman

CAST

Matilda Wormwood	Mara Wilson
Harry Wormwood	Danny DeVito
Zinnia Wormwood	Rhea Perlman
Miss Honey	Embeth Davidtz
Agatha Trunchbull	Pam Ferris
FBI Agents	Paul Reubens, Tracey Walter
Michael	Brian Levinson
Miss Phelps	Jean Speegle Howard
Matilda, 4 years	Sara Magdalin
Roy	R.B. Robb
Luther	Goliath Gregory
Waiter	Fred Parnes
Lavender	Kiami Davael
Julius Rottwinkle	Leor Livneh Hackel
Amanda Thripp	Jacqueline Steiger
Bruce Bogtrotter	Jimmy Karz
Nigel Hicks	Michael Valentine
Charles	Liam Kearns
Magnus	Mark Watson
Hortensia	Kira Spencer Hesser
Nearby Boy	J.C. Alexander
Older Boy	Malone Brinton
Cookie	Marion Dugan

and Joshua Alvarez, Max E. Blum, Erin M. Gray, Misty L. Oppenheim, Christopher Shepard Hughes, Rachel Snow (Children at Assembly), Craig Lamar Traylor, Jennifer Key, Marty Bautista, Anthony Hernandez, Raina Cease, Jonathan Cease, Vinnie Buffolino, Marcella Sassano, Johnny Thomas III, Shannon Hughes, Christel Khalil, Cassie Colaw, Justin Stout, Cindy Tran, Jonathan Feyer (Children in Classroom), Alissa and Amanda Graham, Trevor and James Gallagher (Matilda, Newborn), Kayla and Kelsey Fredericks (Matilda, 9 months), Amanda and Caitlin Fein (Matilda, Toddler), Nicholas Cox (Michael, 6 years), Amanda and Kristin Summers (Miss Honey, 2 years), Phoebe Pearl (Miss Honey, 5 years), Kathy Lynn Barbour, Donna Spangler (Million $ Sticky Showgirls), Marianne Curan, Penny Holland, Richard E. Coe (Million $ Sticky Contestants), Mr. Speaker, Sir Isaac, Wayne (Newts)

Young Matilda, a genius in love with books, is sent by her uncaring parents to Crunchem Hall run by the cruel, sadistic principal Agatha Trunchbull.

Pam Ferris

Sara Magdalin

Mara Wilson, Embeth Davidtz

THE FAN

(TRISTAR) Producer, Wendy Finerman; Executive Producers, Bill Unger, James W. Schotchdopole, Barrie M. Osborne; Director, Tony Scott; Screenplay, Phoef Sutton; Based on the book by Peter Abrahams; Photography, Dariusz Wolski; Designer, Ida Random; Editors, Christian Wagner, Claire Simpson; Co-Producer, Margaret French Isaac; Costumes, Rita Ryack, Daniel Orlandi; Music, Hans Zimmer; Casting, Ellen Lewis; a Mandalay Entertainment presentation of a Wendy Finerman and Scott Free production; Dolby SDDS Stereo; Panavision; Technicolor; Rated R; 117 minutes; August release

CAST

Gil Renard	Robert De Niro
Bobby Rayburn	Wesley Snipes
Jewel Stern	Ellen Barkin
Manny	John Leguizamo
Juan Primo	Benicio Del Toro
Ellen Renard	Patti D'Arbanville-Quinn
Tim	Chris Mulkey
Richie Renard	Andrew J. Ferchland
Sean Rayburn	Brandon Hammond
Coop	Charles Hallahan
Garrity	Dan Butler
Bernie	Kurt Fuller

and Michael Jace (Scalper), Frank Medrano (Bartender Leon), Don S. Davis (Stook), John Kruk (Lanz), Stoney Jackson (Zamora), Brad Henke (Tjader), Drew Snyder (Burrows), Edith Diaz (Elvira), Walter Addison (Det. Lewis), Wayne Duvall (Det. Baker), Joe Pichler (Sick Sean), James G. MacDonald (Sick Sean's Dad), Tuesday Knight (Nurse), Marla Sucharetza (Angie), Nikki Lee (Dawna), Marjorie Lovett (Stanford Woman), Michael Andolini (Man behind Gil), M.C. Gainey (Man behind Man), Michael Bofshever (Little League Coach), Kirk Ward (The Giant Mascot), Eric Bruskotter (Catcher), Kirk D. Terry, Abraham Flores, Dennis Neil Henderson (Umpires), Aaron Neville (Opening Game Singer), Jerry Saslow, Michael P. Byrne, Bret Lewis, Roger Lodge, Ron Pitts (Reporters), Stanley DeSantis (Stoney), Jack Black (Broadcast Technician), Thomas Duffy (Figgy), Don Fischer, Veron Guichard II (Cops), Kim Robillard (Jefferson Sporting Goods Clerk), Keith Leon Williams (Stadium Official), Chanté Moore (Primo Tribute Singer), Paul Herman (Seedy Suit Guy), Robert Louis Kempf (Baggage Attendant), Jesse Ibara (Padres Pitcher), James Betzsold (Padres Catcher), Chris Fick (Giants Left Fielder), Ben Hines (Giants 1st Baseman), Rick Magnante (Giants 3rd Base Coach), Carl Mergenthaler, Clayton Holt, Lennox Brown, Troy Cephers, Freeman White (Bobby's Teammates), Bruce Hines (Umpire End Game), Adam Druxman (Paparazzi), Kathy Stewart, Carolyn Washington, Nikki Hart, Bo Daniels, Randal Salguero, Tracy Leanne Mandac (Fans), Gregg Tome (Det. Schmerg), Sonya Bertelson (Waitress), Brian Freifield (Art), Jennifer Stander (Store Employee), Roy Conrad, Richard Riehle, Earl Billings, John Carroll Lynch, Tim Monsion, Ralph Bertelle, Norm Compton (Shopkeepers)

The San Francisco Giants' star ballplayer, Bobby Rayburn, finds himself increasingly in danger because of an obsessive, unhinged fan.

© TriStar Pictures, Inc.

Wesley Snipes, Robert De Niro, Andrew J. Ferchland

THE WIFE

(ARTISTIC LICENSE FILMS) Producers, Scott Macaulay, Robin O'Hara; Executive Producers, Micheal D. Aglion, Pierre Edelman; Director/Screenplay, Tom Noonan; Based on his play *Wifey*; Photography, Joe DeSalvo; Designer, Dan Ouellette; Costumes, Kathryn Nixon; Editor, Richmond Arrley; Music, Ludovico Sorret; a CIBY 2000 production of a Genre Film; Color; Not rated; 105 minutes; August release

CAST

Rita	Julie Hagerty
Jack	Tom Noonan
Cosmo	Wallace Shawn
Arlie	Karen Young

Two New Age therapists, Jack and Rita, invite one of their patients, Cosmo and his unstable wife, Arlie, to dinner.

© Ciby 2000

Tom Noonan, Wallace Shawn

Wallace Shawn, Julie Hagerty

A VERY BRADY SEQUEL

(PARAMOUNT) Producers, Sherwood Schwartz, Lloyd J. Schwartz, Alan Ladd, Jr.; Director, Arlene Sanford; Screenplay, Harry Elfont, Deborah Kaplan, James Berg, Stan Zimmerman; Story, Harry Elfont, Deborah Kaplan; Based on Characters Created by Sherwood Schwartz; Photography, Mac Ahlberg; Designer, Cynthia Charette; Editor, Anita Brandt-Burgoyne; Co-Producers, Michael Fottrell, Kelliann Ladd; Costumes, Rosanna Norton; Music, Guy Moon; Casting, Deborah Aquila, Jane Shannon Smith; a Ladd Company/Sherwood Schwartz production; Dolby Stereo; Deluxe color; Rated PG-13; 89 minutes; August release

CAST

Carol Brady	Shelley Long
Mike Brady	Gary Cole
Greg Brady	Christopher Daniel Barnes
Marcia Brady	Christine Taylor
Peter Brady	Paul Sutera
Jan Brady	Jennifer Elise Cox
Bobby Brady	Jesse Lee
Cindy Brady	Olivia Hack
Alice	Henriette Mantel
Roy Martin/Trevor Thomas	Tim Matheson
Explorer/Dead Husband	Whip Hubley
Auctioneer	Whitney Rydbeck
Art Patrons	Sue Casey, Gregory White
Ms. Cummings	RuPaul
Ms. Cumming's Daughter	Diana Theodore
Brent the Lifeguard	David Ramsey
Jason the Lifeguard	Phil Buckman
Mr. Phillips	Steven Gilborn
Flower Delivery Guy	Michael Weatherred
Charity Chairperson	Yvonne Farrow
Sergio	David Spade
Themselves	Zsa Zsa Gabor, Rosie O'Donnell
Construction Worker	Skip O'Brien
Kathy Lawrence	Jennifer Aspen
Coffee Shop Guy	Ian M. Galespie
Warren Mulaney	Brian Van Holt
Coffee Customer	Bodhi Pine Elfman
Detective	Richard Belzer
Dr. Whitehead	John Hillerman
Jeannie	Barbara Eden

and Connie Ray (Flight Attendant), Don Nahaku (Car Rental Guy), Anthony J. Silva, Jr. (Hotel Concierge), Laura Weekes (George Glass's Mother), Bill Applebaum (George Glass's Father), Michael Lundberg (George Glass), Sidney Liufau (Security Guard)

Roy Martin pretends to be Carol Brady's supposedly-deceased first husband in order to locate a precious horse statue that the Brady family has in their possession. The second feature film based on the ABC tv series "The Brady Bunch" (1969-74), following The Brady Bunch Movie, *with all of the cast principals repeating their roles.*

© Paramount Pictures Corp.

Christine Taylor, Paul Sutera, Jesse Lee, Tim Matheson, Jennifer Elise Cox, Olivia Hack, Christopher Daniel Barnes

Shelley Long   Gary Cole

GIRLS TOWN

(OCTOBER) Producer, Lauren Zalaznick; Co-Producers, Sarah Vogel, Kelley Forsyth; Director, Jim McKay; Screenplay, Jim McKay, Denise Casano, Anna Grace, Bruklin Harris, Lili Taylor; Photography, Russell Fine; Designer, David Doernberg; Costumes, Carolyn Grifel; Editors, Jim McKay, Alex Hall; Music, Guru; Casting, Adrienne Stern; a C-Hundred Film Corp. and Boomer Pictures presentation; Color; Rated R; 90 minutes; August release

CAST

Patti	Lili Taylor
Angela	Bruklin Harris
Emma	Anna Grace
Nikki	Aunjanue Ellis
Marlys	Asia Minor
Jessie (Boom Box Guy)	Carl Kwaku Ford
Dylan	Guillermo Diaz
Teacher	Shondalon
Nikki's Mom	Ernestine Jackson
Eddie	John Ventimiglia
Cora	Mary Joy
Angela's Mom	Stephanie Berry
Benita	Yassira
Cam	Nathaniel Freeman
Anthony	Michael Imperioli
Richard Helms	Tom Gilroy
Helms' Co-Worker	Andrew Vandusen

Three high school girls react with rage after a tragedy befalls one of their friends.

© October Films

Lili Taylor, Anna Grace, Bruklin Harris

SHE'S THE ONE

(FOX SEARCHLIGHT) Producers, Ted Hope, James Schamus, Edward Burns; Executive Producers, Robert Redford, Michael Nozik; Director/Screenplay, Edward Burns; Co-Executive Producer, John Sloss; Photography, Frank Prinzi; Designer, William Barclay; Editor, Susan Graef; Costumes, Susan Lyall; Music, Tom Petty; a Good Machine/Marlboro Road Gang production in association with South Fork Pictures; Dolby Digital Stereo; Color; Rated R; 96 minutes; August release

CAST

Renee	Jennifer Aniston
Hope	Maxine Bahns
Mickey Fitzpatrick	Edward Burns
Heather	Cameron Diaz
Mr. Fitzpatrick	John Mahoney
Francis Fitzpatrick	Mike McGlone
Molly	Amanda Peet
Ron	Frank Vincent
Carol	Anita Gillette
Connie	Leslie Mann
Tom	Malachy McCourt
Older Woman	Beatrice Winde
Older Man	Eugene Osborne Smith
Mr. Deluca	Robert Weil
Father John	Tom Tammi
Doorman	Raymond De Marco
Scott	Ron Farrell

Mickey tries to find independence and happiness driving a cab until he meets free-spirited Hope; meanwhile Mickey's brother Francis neglects his wife Renee to have an affair with Mickey's ex, Heather.

©Fox Searchlight Pictures

Edward Burns, Maxine Bahns, Cameron Diaz, Jennifer Aniston, Mike McGlone

Mike McGlone, Jennifer Aniston

ALASKA

(COLUMBIA) Producers, Carol Fuchs, Andy Burg; Co-Producer, Gordon Mark; Director, Fraser C. Heston; Screenplay, Andy Burg, Scott Myers; Photography, Tony Westman; Designer, Douglas Higgins; Editor, Rob Kobrin; Music, Reg Powell; Casting, Mary Gail Artz, Barbara Cohen; a Castle Rock Entertainment presentation of a Fuchs/Burg production; SDDS Stereo; Super 35 Widescreen; Technicolor; Rated PG; 110 minutes; August release

CAST

Jessie Barnes	Thora Birch
Sean Barnes	Vincent Kartheiser
Jake Barnes	Dirk Benedict
Perry	Charlton Heston
Koontz	Duncan Fraser
Ben	Gordon Tootoosis
Charlie	Ben Cardinal
Chip	Ryan Kent
Sergeant Grazer	Don S. Davis
Mrs. Ben	Dolly Madsen
Trooper Harvey	Stephen E. Miller
Chip's Father	Byron Chief Moon
Florence	Kristin Lehman
Burly Fisherman	Adrien Dorval
Cubby	Agee

Young Jessie and Sean set out to find their father whose plane has crashed somewhere in the mountains of Alaska.

©Castle Rock Entertainment

Thora Birch, Vincent Kartheiser, Agee

Charlton Heston

THE ISLAND OF DR. MOREAU

(NEW LINE CINEMA) Producer, Edward R. Pressman; Executive Producers, Tim Zinnemann, Claire Rudnick-Polstein; Director, John Frankenheimer; Screenplay, Richard Stanley, Ron Hutchinson; Based on the novel by H.G. Wells; Photography, William A. Fraker; Designer, Graham "Grace" Walker; Editor, Paul Rubell; Special Creature and Make Up Effects, Stan Winston; Music, Gary Chang; Costumes, Norma Moriceau; Casting, Valerie McCaffrey; an Edward R. Pressman production; Dolby SDDS Stereo; Super 35 Widescreen; Color; Rated PG-13; 95 minutes; August release

Marlon Brando

CAST

Dr. Moreau	Marlon Brando
Montgomery	Val Kilmer
Edward Douglas	David Thewlis
Aissa	Fairuza Balk
Hyena-Swine	Daniel Rigney
Azazello	Temuera Morrison
Majai	Nelson De La Rosa
Assassimon	Peter Elliott
Lo-Mai	Mark Dacascos
Sayer of the Law	Ron Perlman
M'Ling	Marco Hofschneider
Waggdi	Miguel Lopez
Boar Man	Neil Young
Bison Man	David Hudson
Fox Lady	Clare Grant
Sow Ladies	Kitty Silver, Fiona Mahl
Kiril	William Hootkins
Captain	Agoes Soedjarvo
Soldiers	Ron Vreeken, Lou Horvath

David Thewlis

Plane crash survivor Edward Douglas finds himself on a mysterious island where Dr. Moreau is experimenting with transforming animals into humans. The H.G. Wells novel was previously filmed in 1933 as Island of Lost Souls, *with Charles Laughton (as Moreau), and in 1977 with Burt Lancaster.*

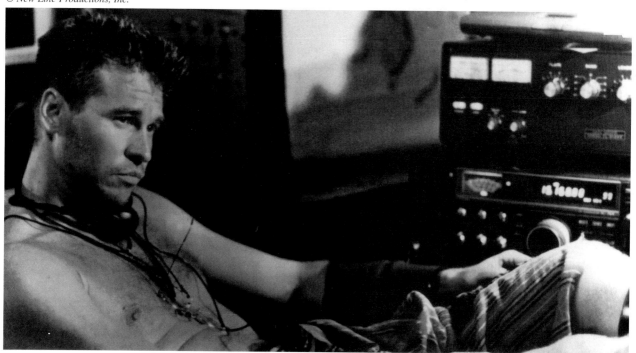

Val Kilmer

Brock Pierce, Sinbad

Brock Pierce, Sinbad

James Naughton, Brock Pierce, Sinbad, Lisa Eichhorn, Blake Boyd

Sinbad, Brock Pierce

FIRST KID

(WALT DISNEY PICTURES) Producers, Roger Birnbaum, Riley Kathryn Ellis; Executive Producers, Sinbad, Dale De La Torre, Tim Kelleher; Co-Producer, Jeffrey Chernov; Director, David Mickey Evans; Screenplay, Tim Kelleher; Photography, Anthony B. Richmond; Designer, Chester Kaczenski; Editor, Harry Keramidas; Costumes, Grania Preston; Music, Richard Gibbs; Casting, Shari Rhodes, Joseph Middleton; Presented in association with Caravan Pictures; Dolby Digital Stereo; Technicolor; Rated PG; 101 minutes; August release

CAST

Sam Simms	Sinbad
Luke Davenport	Brock Pierce
Dash	Blake Boyd
Woods	Timothy Busfield
Morton	Art La Fleur
Wilkes	Robert Guillaume
Linda Davenport	Lisa Eichhorn
President Davenport	James Naughton
Susan Lawrence	Fawn Reed
Katie Warren	Erin Williby
Rob	Zachery Ty Bryan
James	Michael Krawic
Speed	Bill Cobbs
Andre	Jemar Jewann Jefferson
Yo-Yo	Daniel Baron
Peterson	Joe Inscoe
Clark	J. Michael Hunter
Harold	Tomas Arana
Eddie	Doug MacArthur Williams

and Helen Hedman, Jacqueline Chernov (Teachers), Jonthan Cabot Wade, Andrew T. Wood, Lee Sparks (Kids), Sonny Bono (Himself), Henry Strozier (General), Elisabeth Noone (President's Secretary), Peyton Chesson-Fohl (Roller Blade Kid), Heather Kirk, Kristi Cobb (Katie's Friends), Scott Evans (Uniformed Agent), Bob Child (Security Officer), Patsy Grady Abrams (Cleaning Lady), Richard Trask (Walter), Derek Leonidoff (Donut Kid), Sylvia "Small Frie" Cannon (Coffee Kid), Melissa Johnston (Reporter), Raynor Scheine (Maintenance Worker), Melanie Hastings (Local News Anchor), Steve Kmetko (Famous News Anchor), Ricardo Miguel Young (Inside Copy Anchor), Mark Nassar, Brett Zebrowski (Secret Service Agents), Robert Earl Stoudamire (Little Boy), Stephanie Lloyd (Local Weather Person), Emma Stock (Snake Screamer), Stephen Caywood (Body Double), Audra Wilks (Waitress)

The undisciplined son of the President of the United States meets his match when Secret Service Agent Sam Simms is assigned to look after the boy.

©Disney Enterprises

THE SPITFIRE GRILL

(COLUMBIA) Producer, Forrest Murray; Executive Producer, Warren G. Stitt; Co-Producers, Edward E. Vaughn, Marci Liroff; Director/Screenplay, Lee David Zlotoff; Photography, Rob Draper; Editor, Margie Goodspeed; Designer, Howard Cummings; Costumes, Louise Mingenbach; Music, James Horner; Casting, Marci Liroff; a Castle Rock Entertainment presentation of a Gregory Production in association with the Mendocino Corporation; Ultra-Stereo; Deluxe color; Rated PG-13; 116 minutes; August release

CAST

Percy Talbott	Alison Elliott
Hannah Ferguson	Ellen Burstyn
Shelby Goddard	Marcia Gay Harden
Nahum Goddard	Will Patton
Joe Sperling	Kieran Mulroney
Sheriff Gary Walsh	Gailard Sartain
Johnny B./Eli	John M. Jackson
Effy Katshaw	Louise De Cormier
Rebecca Goddard	Ida Griesemer
Molly Goddard	Lincoln & Emerson Grow
Meeshack Boggs	Sam Lloyd, Sr.
Jolene	Lisa Louise Langford
Stuart	Forrest Murray
Customers	Patty Smith, Dennis Mientka, Stuart Jackson
Neighbor	Faith Caitlin
Town Member #2	Janet St. Onge
Deputy	Jim Hogue
Clare	Stacy Becker
Aaron Sperling	Cliff Levering
Woman at Bar	Monica Callan
Man at Bar	Richard Addis

After being released from prison Percy Talbott relocates to the small Maine town of Gilead where she takes a job as a waitress at the Spitfire Grill.

©Castle Rock Entertainment

Alison Elliott, Ellen Burstyn, Marcia Gay Harden

Ellen Burstyn, Alison Elliott

Alison Elliott

Alison Elliott, Ellen Burstyn, Marcia Gay Harden

THE TRIGGER EFFECT

(GRAMERCY) Producer, Michael Grillo; Executive Producers, Walter Parkes, Laurie MacDonald, Gerald R. Molen; Director/Screenplay, David Koepp; Photography, Newton Thomas Sigel; Designer, Howard Cummings; Editor, Jill Savitt; Associate Producers, Fernando Altschul, Michele Weisler; Music, James Newton Howard; Casting, Nancy Nayor; an Amblin Entertainment production; DTS Stereo; Eastman color; Rated R; 98 minutes; August release

CAST

Matthew	Kyle MacLachlan
Annie	Elisabeth Shue
Joe	Demot Mulroney
Raymond	Richard T. Jones
Steph	Bill Smitrovich
Gary	Michael Rooker
Sarah	Tori Kristiansen, Tyra Kristiansen
Johnny	Rick Worthy
Trendy German Guy	Edhem Barker
Tripping Guy	Tyrone Tann
Hand Holding Guy	David O'Donnell
Hand Holding Girl	Monica Torres
Double Date Guy	Greg Grunberg
Double Date Girl	Kerri Vickers
Counter Girls	Christina Alvarado, Victoria Fleming
Babysitter	Molly Morgan
Mr. Schaefer	Philip Bruns
Drugstore Announcer	Kirk Fox
Pharmacist	William Lucking
Arguing Customer	Rosanna Huffman
Ball Bouncer	Andy Walker
Security Guard	Carl Ciarfalio
Admitting Nurse	Wanda-Lee Evans
Gun Shop Clerk	Richard Schiff
Prowler	Jack Noseworthy
Raji	Shishir Kurup

and Gary Bayer (Middle Aged Neighbor), Conor O'Farrell, Eugene Collier (Police Officers), Devoy White (Waiter), Amanda Grillo (Girl at Ice Cream Truck), Parker Swanson (Medic), Jonathan Mumm (Man at Table), Elizabeth Gandy (Cafe Waitress), Dorian Dunbar (Kari)

A power failure puts Matt and Annie on edge when they have trouble obtaining the medicine for their infant daughter.

©Gramercy Pictures

Kyle MacLachlan

Kyle MacLachlan, Elisabeth Shue

Richard T. Jones

Kyle MacLachlan, Elisabeth Shue, Dermot Mulroney

BULLETPROOF

(UNIVERSAL) Producers, Robert Simonds; Executive Producers, Brad Grey, Bernie Brillstein, Sandy Wernick, Eric L. Gold; Director, Ernest Dickerson; Screenplay, Joe Gayton, Lewis Colick; Story, Joe Gayton; Photography, Steven Bernstein; Designers, Perry Andelin Blake, William F. Matthews; Editor, George Folsey, Jr.; Co-Producers, Ira Shuman, Jack Giarraputo; Costumes, Marie France; Music, Elmer Bernstein; Casting, Joanna Colbert; a Bernie Brillstein-Brad Grey/Robert Simonds/Gold-Miller production; DTS Digital Stereo; Super 35 Widescreen; Deluxe color; Rated R; 85 minutes; September release

CAST

Rock Keats	Damon Wayans
Archie Moses	Adam Sandler
Frank Colton	James Caan
Bledsoe	Jeep Swenson
Capt. Jensen	James Farentino
Traci Flynn	Kristen Wilson
Detective Sulliman	Larry McCoy
Detective Jones	Allen Covert
Finch	Bill Nunn
Charles	Mark Roberts
Disneyland Cop	Mark Cassella

and Andrew Shaifer (Cop at Airport), Monica Potter (Biker's Woman), Jonathan Loughran (Rookie Cop), Steve White (Veteran Cop), Gwen McGee (Surgeon), Charmaine Craig (Waitress), Jill Holden (Gruesome Lady), Renee Paidle (Porn Woman), Adam Voughn (Porn Man), Xander Berkeley (Gentry), Sal Landi (Cole), David Labiosa (Rigo), Conrad Goode (Biker), Maury Sterling (Skinny Guy), Scotty Hoxby (Lindsay), Victor Aaron (Hispanic Man), Jacqueline Dickerson (Bartender), Donna M. Duffy (Anesthesiologist), Janice Rivera, Loetta Ernest, Cindy Barrera (Senoritas), Ford Scott (Arizona Highway Patrol), William Proctor, Garret T. Sato (Bad Guys), Paule Stewart (Moses' Mom)

Having been accidentally shot by his best friend, Archie Moses, during a botched drug bust, Rock Keats recovers, only to be assigned to bring his fugitive buddy back to L.A. to supply evidence against a powerful drug lord.

©Universal City Studios, Inc.

Damon Wayans, Adam Sandler

Damon Wayans, Adam Sandler

KILLER: A JOURNAL OF MURDER

(LEGACY) Producers, Janet Yang, Mark Levinson; Executive Producers, Oliver Stone, Melinda Jackson; Director/Sreenplay, Tim Metcalfe; Based on the book by Thomas E. Gaddis and James O. Long; Photography, Ken Kelsch; Designer, Sherman Williams; Editor, Richard Gentner; Costumes, Kathryn Morrison; Associate Producers, George Linardos, Lisa Moiselle; Casting, Amanda Mackey, Cathy Sandrich; a Spelling Films presentation of an Ixtlan Production in association with Breakheart Films; Dolby Stereo; Color; Rated R; 91 minutes; September release

CAST

Carl Panzram	James Woods
Henry Lesser	Robert Sean Leonard
Elizabeth Wyatt	Ellen Greene
Esther Lesser	Cara Buono
R.G. Greiser	Robert John Burke
Warden Charles Casey	Steve Forrest
Sam Lesser	Jeffrey DeMunn
Richard Lesser	Christopher Petrosino
Warden Quince	Richard Riehle
Karl Menninger	John Bedford Lloyd
Old Henry Lesser	Harold Gould
Judge Kingman	Conrad McLaren
Sally	Lili Taylor

and Richard Council (Cop), Rob Locke Jones (Junkie), Michael Jeffrey Woods (Harry Sinclair), Rainor Scheine (Trusty), Eddie Cairis (Young Carl Panzram), Seth Romitelle (Teenage Carl Panzram), John MacKay (Jack Turner), James Murtaugh (Walter Bailey), Richard Spore (Jury Foreman), Christopher Wynkoop (Minister), Stephen Mendillo (Hiram the Guard), Richard Gartner (Hangman), Martha A. Woods (Bartender)

True story about the relationship that develops at Leavenworth prison between ruthless serial murderer Carl Panzram and a sympathetic guard Henry Lesser who encourages the prisoner to write about his experiences.
©Spelling Films

James Woods, Robert Sean Leonard

Cara Buono, Robert Sean Leonard

FLY AWAY HOME

(COLUMBIA) Producers, John Veitch, Carol Baum; Executive Producer, Sandy Gallin; Director, Carroll Ballard; Screenplay, Robert Rodat, Vince McKerwin; Based on the autobiography by Bill Lishman; Photography, Caleb Deschanel; Designer, Séamus Flannery; Editor, Nicholas C. Smith; Costumes, Marie-Sylvie Deveau; Music, Mark Isham; Song: "10,000 Miles" performed by Mary Chapin Carpenter; Casting, Reuben Cannon, Deirdre Bowen; a Sandollar Production; Dolby SDDS Stereo; Technicolor; Rated PG; 108 minutes; September release

CAST

Thomas Alden	Jeff Daniels
Amy Alden	Anna Paquin
Susan Barnes	Dana Delany
David Alden	Terry Kinney
Barry Strickland	Holter Graham
Glenn Seifert	Jeremy Ratchford
Amy's Mother	Deborah Verginella
General	Michael J. Reynolds
Dr. Killian	David Hemblen
Developer	Ken James
Jackie	Nora Ballard
Laura	Sarena Paton

and Carmen Lishman, Christi Hill (Older Girls), Judith Orban (Teacher), Jeff Braunstein (Chairman), John Friesen (Smalltown Businessman), Chris Benson (Farmer), Kevin Jubinville (Military Police), Philip Akin (Air Force Reporter), Gladys O'Connor (Farm Woman), Geoff McBride (Clerk), Dick Callahan (Customs Inspector), Cheryl MacInnis, Mark Wilson, J. Craig Sandy (Reporters), Wendy Walsh, Larry McCormick, Richard Saxton, Linden Chiles (Television Anchor), Timm Zemanek (Husband), Diane Douglass (Wife), Azura Bates (Bratty Sister), Jonathan Bates, Michael Vollans (Bratty Brothers), Michael Copeman (Gun Shop Owner), John E. Nelles (Tower Supervisor), Jeffrey W. Poulis, Christopher Lorenz (Tower Operators), Melissa Tanti (Dune Woman)

After his daughter Amy adopts a family of goslings, Thomas Alden comes up with the outrageous idea of getting the birds to migrate south by following him and Amy in makeshift planes. This film received an Oscar nomination for cinematography.

Anna Paquin, Jeff Daniels

Jeff Daniels

Dana Delany, Anna Paquin

Anna Paquin

Dustin Hoffman, Dennis Franz, Sean Nelson

Dennis Franz, Sean Nelson

Dustin Hoffman

AMERICAN BUFFALO

(SAMUEL GOLDWYN CO.) Producer, Gregory Mosher; Executive Producer, John Sloss; Director, Michael Corrente; Screenplay, David Mamet, based on his play; Photography, Richard Crudo; Designer, Daniel Talpers; Costumes, Deborah Newhall; Music, Thomas Newman; Editor, Kate Sanford; Co-Producer, Sarah Green; Casting, Billy Hopkins, Suzanne Smith, Kerry Barden; Presented in association with Capitol Films, produced in association with Punch Productions; Dolby Stereo; Color; Rated R; 88 minutes; September release

CAST

Walter "Teach" Cole	Dustin Hoffman
Donny Dubrow	Dennis Franz
Bobby	Sean Nelson

Realizing that the buffalo head nickel he sold a customer from his junk shop is worth more than he charged, Donny Dubrow reluctantly enlists the aid of his friend Teach to steal it back. The original 1977 Broadway production starred Robert Duvall (Teach), Kenneth McMillan (Donny), and John Savage (Bobby).

©The Samuel Goldwyn Company

Dennis Franz, Dustin Hoffman

John Turturro, Illeana Douglas, Eric Jerome Kirkland, Irving Eugene Washington III, Kurt Jackson, Michael Saulsberry

Eric Stoltz, Illeana Douglas, John Turturro, Patsy Kensit

GRACE OF MY HEART

(GRAMERCY) Producers, Ruth Charny, Daniel Hassid; Executive Producer, Martin Scorsese; Director/Screenplay, Allison Anders; Photography, Jean Yves Escoffier; Designer, Francois Seguin; Supervising Editor, Thelma Schoonmaker; Editors, James Keiw, Harvey Rosenstock; Line Producer, Elliot Rosenblatt; Music, Larry Klein; Music Supervisor, Karyn Rachtman; Song: "God Give Me Strength" by Burt Bacharach and Elvis Costello; Costumes, Susan Bertram; Casting, Russell Gray; a Cappa production; DTS Stereo; CFI Color; Rated R; 115 minutes; September release

Matt Dillon (c)

CAST

Denise Waverly (Edna Buxton)	Illeana Douglas
Jay Phillips	Matt Dillon
Howard Caszatt	Eric Stoltz
John Murray	Bruce Davison
Cheryl Steed	Patsy Kensit
Joel Millner	John Turturro
Doris Shelly	Jennifer Leigh Warren
Mrs. Buxton	Christina Pickles
Kelly Porter	Bridget Fonda
Dress Saleswoman	Sissy Boyd
Talent Show Contestant	Jill Sobule
M.C. at Talent Show	Tegan West
Audition Record Producer	Richard Schiff
Betty	Natalie Venetia Belcon
Sha Sha	Kathy Barbour
Waitress in Diner	Diane Robin

The Stylettes .... "Portrait": Eric Jerome Kirkland Irving Eugene Washington III, Kurt Jackson, Michael Saulsberry

Receptionists	Drena De Niro, Amanda De Cadenet
Girl in Coffee Shop	Jade Gordon
Annie	Tracy Vilar
Brill Building Songwriter	Martin Valinsky
Radio Station Receptionist	Lita Stevens
Brill Building Hallway Singers	"For Real"
Record Producer	Larry Klein
Matthew Lewis	Chris Isaak

Click Brothers .... The Williams Brothers (David Williams, Andrew Williams)

Marion	Lucinda Jenney
Girl in Howard's Bed	Deidre Lewis
Baby Luma	Buster
Cab Driver	John Nacco
Kindly Nurse	Lynne Adams
Luma	Brittany English Stevens
Annie's Son	Johnny Thomas III
Journalist	Harry Victor

The Riptides .... "Redd Kross": Jeffrey McDonald, Steven McDonald, Brian Reitzell

Riptides Dancing Girls	Christina Ehrlich, Melanie A. Gage
TV Interviewer	Albert Macklin
Riptides Engineer	J Mascis
Theremin Player	Robert Brunner
Security Expert	Chris Shearer
Singers on Beach	China Kantner, Paige Dylan, Alicia Jaffee
Singers in Tree	Alice Cohen, Lita Hernandez, Delia Gonzalez
Dr. Jones "Jonesy"	David Clennon
Crying Woman at Funeral	Precious Chong
Voice of Guru Dave	Peter Fonda
Commune Guitarist	Shawn Colvin

Bruce Davison

After winning a talent contest Denise Waverly earns a record contract but finds that the company is more interested in her abilities as a songwriter than a singer. Over the course of several years and assorted relationships she becomes a success in that field but longs to put out a record of her own.

© *Gramercy Pictures*

Natalie Venetia Belcon, Jennifer Leigh Warren, Kathy Barbour

Goldie Hawn, Diane Keaton, Bette Midler

Sarah Jessica Parker, Bette Midler

THE FIRST WIVES CLUB

(PARAMOUNT) Producer, Scott Rudin; Executive Producers, Ezra Swerdlow, Adam Schroeder; Director, Hugh Wilson; Screenplay, Robert Harling; Based on the novel by Olivia Goldsmith; Photography, Donald Thorin; Designer, Peter Larkin; Editor, John Bloom; Costumes, Theoni V. Aldredge; Co-Producer, Thomas Imperato; Music, Marc Shaiman; Casting, Ilene Swerdlow; a Scott Rudin production; Dolby Stereo; Deluxe color; Rated PG; 102 minutes; September release

CAST

Elise Elliot Atchison	Goldie Hawn
Brenda Morelli Cushman	Bette Midler
Annie MacDuggan Paradise	Diane Keaton
Gunilla Garson Goldberg	Maggie Smith
Shelly	Sarah Jessica Parker
Morty Cushman	Dan Hedaya
Cynthia Swann Griffin	Stockard Channing
Bill Atchison	Victor Garber
Aaron Paradise	Stephen Collins
Phoebe LaVelle	Elizabeth Berkley
Dr. Leslie Rosen	Marcia Gay Harden
Duarto Feliz	Bronson Pinchot
Chris Paradise	Jennifer Dundas
Catherine MacDuggan	Eileen Heckart
Uncle Carmine	Philip Bosco
Dr. Morris Packman	Rob Reiner
Gil Griffin	James Naughton
Jason Cushman	Ari Greenberg
Teresa	Aida Linares
Themselves	Ivana Trump, Gloria Steinem, Edward I. Koch, Kathie Lee Gifford
Auctioneer	Christopher Burge
Mr. Christian	Stephen Pearlman
Ms. Sullivan	J. Smith-Cameron
Man in Bed	Walter Bobbie
Woman in Bed	Kate Burton
Mark Loest	Greg Edelman
Eric Loest	Mark Nelson
Mohammed	Harsh Nayyar
Newscaster	Sue Simmons
Brett Artounian	Timothy Olyphant
Maurice	Edward Hibbert
Hostess	Teresa DePriest
Busboy	Johnny Sanchez
Federal Marshals	J.K. Simmons, Stephen Mendillo
Karen	Robin Morse
Broadway Director	Peter Frechette
The Cantor	Mark Perman
Waiter	George Vlachos
Contractor	Armand Dahan
Elise's Fan	Lea De Laria
Jilted Lover	Debra Monk
Chris' Friend	Jennifer Lam
Young Brenda	Michele Brilliant
Young Elise	Dina Spybey
Young Annie	Adria Tennor
Young Cynthia	Julieherea DeStefano
"A Certain Age" Cast	Paul Hecht, Anne Shropshire, Chelsea Altman, Eric Martin Brown
Dancers	Nancy Ticotin, Roxane Barlow, Amy Heggins

and Heather Locklear

Three middle-aged women, dumped by their respective husbands for younger women, bond together to take revenge. This film received an Oscar nomination for original musical or comedy score.

©*Paramount Pictures Corp.*

Bronson Pinchot, Sarah Jessica Parker, Maggie Smith

Bette Midler, Goldie Hawn, Diane Keaton

Elizabeth Berkley, Goldie Hawn

Marcia Gay Harden, Diane Keaton

Diane Keaton, Bette Midler, Goldie Hawn

Stephen Collins, Dan Hedaya, Victor Garber

Diane Keaton

LAST MAN STANDING

(NEW LINE CINEMA) Producers, Walter Hill, Arthur Sarkissian; Executive Producers, Sara Risher, Michael De Luca; Director/Screenplay, Walter Hill; Based on the story by Ryuzo Kikushima, Akira Kurosawa; Co-Producer, Ralph Singleton; Photography, Lloyd Ahern; Designer, Gary Wissner; Editor, Freeman Davies; Music, Ry Cooder; Costumes, Dan Moore; Casting, Mary Gail Artz, Barbara Cohen; an Arthur Sarkissian production of a Lone Wolf Film; Dolby Stereo; Panavision; Deluxe color; Rated R; 102 minutes; September release

CAST

John Smith	Bruce Willis
Sheriff Ed Galt	Bruce Dern
Joe Monday	William Sanderson
Hickey	Christopher Walken
Doyle	David Patrick Kelly
Felina	Karina Lombard
Fredo Strozzi	Ned Eisenberg
Lucy Kolinski	Alexandra Powers
Giorgio Carmonte	Michael Imperioli
Captain Tom Pickett	Ken Jenkins
Jack McCool	R.D. Call
Deputy Bob	Ted Markland
Wanda	Leslie Mann
Finn	Patrick Kilpatrick
Comandante Ramirez	Luis Contreras
Gas Station Attendant	Raynor Scheine
Jacko the Giant	Tiny Ron
The Undertaker	John Paxton
Berto	Michael Cavalieri
Santo	Hannes Fritsch
Docker	Michael Strasser
Burke	Matt O'Toole
The Madam	Lin Shaye

and Larry Holt (Border Patrolman), Allan Graf (Convoy Driver), Cassandra Gava (Barmaid), Randy Hall (Doyle Thug), Jimmy Ortega, Tom Rosales (Ramirez Bodyguards), Dean Rader-Duval (Donnie), Michael Prozzo (Roca), Chris Doyle, Jim Palmer (Brothel Thugs), Randy Hall, Kerry Lynch, Paul Lyons, Rick Merring, Michael McBride, Scott Pierce, Ed Rote, Scott Strand, Jim Wilkey (Doyle Gang), Andrew Alden, Arnie Alpert, Dana Bambo, Philip Ciano, Robert Coffee, Michael Cordeiro, Sonny D'Angelo, Carmine Grippo, Timothy Gallegos, Michael Lerner, Ken Medlock, Bill Rochon, Joe Kay, Rocky Reyna Galiente (Strozzi Gang)

A mysterious con man arrives in the dingy town of Jericho, Texas, where he becomes involved in a bloody war between two rival gangs. Previous film versions of this story were Yojimbo *(1961) and* A Fistful of Dollars *(1964).*

©New Line Productions, Inc.

Bruce Willis

Bruce Dern

Christopher Walken

Karina Lombard

Alexandra Powers

Stanley Tucci, Tony Shalhoub

Stanley Tucci,, Ian Holm

Campbell Scott, Isabella Rossellini

Minnie Driver

BIG NIGHT

(SAMUEL GOLDWYN CO.) Producer, Jonathan Filley; Executive Producers, Keith Samples, David Kirkpatrick; Directors, Campbell Scott, Stanley Tucci; Screenplay, Joseph Tropiano, Stanley Tucci; Photography, Ken Kelsch; Designer, Andrew Jackness; Editor, Suzy Elmiger; Music, Gary DeMichele; Costumes, Juliet Polcsa; Co-Producers, Elizabeth W. Alexander, Peter Liguori, Oliver Platt; a Rysher Entertainment presentation; Dolby Stereo; Color; Rated R; 107 minutes; September release

CAST

Secondo Pilaggi . . . . Stanley Tucci
Primo Pilaggi . . . . Tony Shalhoub
Gabriella . . . . Isabella Rossellini
Pascal . . . . Ian Holm
Phyllis . . . . Minnie Driver
Cristiano . . . . Marc Anthony
Bob . . . . Campbell Scott
Ann . . . . Allison Janney
Man in Restaurant . . . . Larry Block
Woman in Restaurant . . . . Caroline Aaron
Stash . . . . Andrei Belgrader
Loan Officer . . . . Peter McRobbie
Leo . . . . Liev Schreiber
Alberto . . . . Pasquale Cajano
Singer . . . . Christine Tucci
Charlie . . . . Gene Canfield
Ida . . . . Tina Bruno
Chubby . . . . Peter Appel
Man on Truck . . . . Jack O'Connell
Chubby's Wife . . . . Karen Shallo
Lenore . . . . Alvaleta Guess
Dean . . . . Tamar Kotoske
Father O'Brien . . . . Robert W. Castle
Joan . . . . Susan Floyd
Natalie . . . . Dina Spybey
Jameson . . . . Seth Jones

Hoping to boost business at their Italian restaurant at the Jersey Shore brothers Secondo and Primo Pilaggi plan to host a big dinner at their establishment in honor of singer Louis Prima.

EXTREME MEASURES

(COLUMBIA) Producer, Elizabeth Hurley; Executive Producer, Andrew Scheinman; Co-Producer, Chris Brigham; Director, Michael Apted; Screenplay, Tony Gilroy; Based on the book by Michael Palmer; Photography, John Bailey; Designer, Doug Kraner; Editor, Rick Shaine; Costumes, Susan Lyall; Music, Danny Elfman; Casting, Linda Lowy; a Castle Rock Entertainment presentation of a Simian Films production; Dolby Stereo; Panavision; Technicolor; Rated R; 118 minutes; September release

Gene Hackman, Hugh Grant

CAST

Dr. Guy Luthan	Hugh Grant
Dr. Lawrence Myrick	Gene Hackman
Jodie Trammel	Sarah Jessica Parker
Frank Hare	David Morse
Burke	Bill Nunn
Bobby	John Toles-Bey
Dr. Jeffery Manko	Paul Guilfoyle
Dr. Judith Gruszynski	Debra Monk
Claude Minkins	Shaun Austin-Olsen
Teddy Dolson	Andre De Shields
Dr. Mingus	J.K. Simmons
Detective Stone	Peter Appel
Helen	Diana Zimmer
Ruth Myrick	Nancy Beatty
Dr. Gene Spitelli	Gerry Becker
Izzy	Gene Ruffini
Stone's Partner	Bill MacDonald
Mr. Randall	Peter Maloney
Cop	Johnie Chase
Criminal	Noam Jenkins
Myrick's Daughter	Larissa Lapchinski
Granddaughter	Phallon Carpino
Dr. Garlock	Ross Petty
Shelter Supervisor	Todd Stewart
Medical Examiner	Lawrence Arancio

and D. Garnet Harding, Simon Reynolds, Derwin Jordan, Tara Rosling, Martin Roach, Bernard Browne, Sanjay Talwar (ER Doctors), Christina Collins, Arlene Duncan, Cheryl Swarts (ER Nurses), Vincent Marino (Janitor), Marcia De Bonis (Pam), John Ventimiglia (Det. Manning), John Heffernan (Cartman), Raynor Scheine (Half-Mole), John Trudell (Tony), Nelson Vasquez (Skicap), Vincent Laresca (Patches), Denis Akiyama (Prof. Asakura), Kim Roberts (Home Nurse), Gerry Quigley (Party Guest), Teresa Yenque (Neighbor), Chris Edwards (Uniform Cop), David Eisner (Guy's Lawyer), Dana Stevens (Prosecutor), Michael J. Reynolds (Judge), David Cronenberg (Hospital Lawyer), Desi Moreno (Toll Collector), Marc Gosselin (Jodie's Brother), Jackie Richardson, Marium Carvell (Triphase Nurses), Marilyn McDonald (Mole Lady)

The traumatic death of a homeless man from bizarre symtoms causes Dr. Guy Luthan to investigate the mysterious circumstances that brought the patient to the hospital in the first place.

©Castle Rock Entertainment

David Morse, Bill Nunn

Sarah Jessica Parker

David Cronenburg (c), Paul Guilfoyle

ED'S NEXT MOVE

(ORION CLASSICS) Producer, Sally Roy; Director/Screenplay, John Walsh; Photography, Peter Nelson; Editor, Pamela Martin; Designer, Kristin Vallow; Music, Benny Golson; Costumes, Maura Sircus; Associate Producer, Joshua Astrachan; Casting, Susan Shopmaker; an Ed's Films production; Ultra Stereo; Deluxe color; Rated R; 88 minutes; September release

CAST

Eddie Brodsky	Matt Ross
Lee Nicol	Callie Thorne
Ray Obregon	Kevin Carroll
Anne	Cathy Curtin
Hospital Kid	Timothy Pilato
Greedy Roommate	Ramon Moses
Sloppy Roommate	Eric Weiner
Pot-Smoking Roommate	Joshua Astrachan
Fiche Lock Roommate	David Pittu
Beach Blanket Roommate	Devin Eggleston
Hyper-Wary Tenant	Robert Margolis
Dr. Banarjee	Ramsey Faragallah
Angry Actress	Michael Huston
Brush With Happiness Guy	Voltaire
Weather Video Guy	Will Arnett
Woman at Party	Joy Findlay
Performance Artist	Veronika Korvin
Numbers Woman	Liz Tuccillo
Bond Trader Jordan	Rick Kaplan
Bond Trader Bryce	Joseph Fuqua
Translators	Cynthia Kaplan, Dale Carman
Elenka	Nina Sheveleva

and Peter Jacobson (Yalta Coffee Shop Owner), A.J. Brentano ("Nitty Gritty" Disputer), Reine Hewitt, Kelly Yusko (Girls in Coffee Shop), Ned Ringleh (Nice Guy Salesman), Merrill Holtzman (Nice Guy), Lisa Harris (Woman Nice Guy Hits On), Helene Weintraub, Gloria Goldman (Cloister's Ladies), Steven Arvanites (Bubble Wrap Sculptor), Haras Ginsberg (Art Student), Conrad Wolfson (Liquor Store Clerk), Aunjanue Ellis (Erica), Roxanne Manzano (Teacher), Andy Buelvas (School Kid), R.E. Rodgers (Officer Sanchez), Oliver Wadsworthy (Video Camera Guy), Jimmy Cummings (Lee's Boyfriend)

Dumped by his girlfriend, Midwesterner Eddie Ross moves to New York where he struggles with the dating scene until he meets musician Lee Nicol.

©Orion Pictures Corp.

Matt Ross, Callie Thorne

Kevin Carroll, Matt Ross

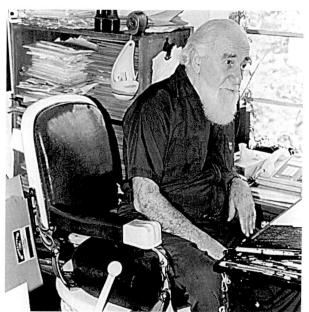

Al Hirschfeld

THE LINE KING: THE AL HIRSCHFELD STORY

(CASTLE HILL) Producer/Director/Screenplay, Susan W. Dryfoos; Associate Producer/Editor, Angelo Corrao; Photography, Richard Blofson, Jeffrey Grunther; Animation Editor, Nick Mavroson, The Image Group, NY; a Times History production; Color; Not rated; 87 minutes; September release. A look at the life and work of caricaturist Al Hirschfeld.

WITH

Al Hirschfeld, Carol Channing, Colleen Dewhurst, Margo Feiden, Jules Feiffer, Arthur Gelb, Brendan Gill, Eric Goldberg, Adam Gopnik, Philip Hamburger, Katharine Hepburn, Kitty Carlisle Hart, Dolly Haas Hirschfeld, Nina Hirschfeld, Stefan Kanfer, Louise Kerz, Paula Laurence, Dr. Calvin F. Nodine, Joseph Papp, Maria Riva, Jason Robards, Florence Rome, Clara Rotter, Daniel Mayer Selznick, Lauren Bacall, Cy Coleman, Joan Collins, Robert Goulet, Geoffrey Holder, Robert Loggia, Barbara Walters

This film received an Oscar nomination for documentary - feature length.

©Castle Hill Productons, Inc.

2 DAYS IN THE VALLEY

(UNITED ARTISTS) Producers, Jeff Wald, Herb Nanas; Executive Producers, Keith Samples, Tony Amatullo; Director/Screenplay, John Herzfeld; Photography, Oliver Wood; Designer, Catherine Hardwicke; Editors, Jim Miller, Wayne Wahrman; Co-Producer, Jim Burke; Associate Producers, Mindy Marin, Terry Miller, David Gaines; Music, Anthony Marinelli; Costumes, Betsy Heimann; Casting, Mindy Marin, John Papsidera; a Rysher Entertainment presentation of a Redemption production; DTS Digital Stereo; Panavision; Deluxe color; Rated R; 107 minutes; September release

CAST

Dosmo Pizzo	Danny Aiello
Allan Hopper	Greg Cruttwell
Alvin Strayer	Jeff Daniels
Becky Foxx	Teri Hatcher
Susan Parish	Glenne Headly
Roy Foxx	Peter Horton
Audrey Hopper	Marsha Mason
Teddy Peppers	Paul Mazursky
Lee Woods	James Spader
Wes Taylor	Eric Stoltz
Helga Svelgen	Charlize Theron
Detective Creighton	Keith Carradine
Evelyn	Louise Fletcher
Ralph Crupi	Austin Pendleton
Midori	Kathleen Luong
Buck	Michael Jai White
Golfer	Cress Williams
Older Man	Lawrence Tierney
Older Woman	Micole Mercurio
Man at Bar	William Stanton
Driver's Friend	Deborah Benson-Wald
Detective Valenzuela	Ada Maris
Bogey	Coby
Marc the Pitbull	Mark Goldstein

During a 48 hour period ten people's lives intersect following a murder in which one of the hitmen responsible had been set up by his partner to be killed.

Glenne Headly, Greg Cruttwell, Danny Aiello

Charlize Theron, James Spader

Eric Stoltz, Jeff Daniels

Brennan Dyson, Marsha Mason, Deborah Benson-Wald, Charlize Theron, Paul Mazursky

THAT THING YOU DO!

(20TH CENTURY FOX) Producers, Gary Goetzman, Jonathan Demme, Edward Saxon; Director/Screenplay, Tom Hanks; Photography, Tak Fujimoto; Designer, Victor Kempster; Editor, Richard Chew; Costumes, Colleen Atwood; Title song by Adam Schlesinger; a Clinica Estetico production in association with Clavius Base; Dolby Stereo; Deluxe color; Rated PG; 110 minutes; October release

(top) Ethan Embry, Tom Hanks, Steve Zahn;
(bottom) Johnathon Schaech, Liv Tyler, Tom Everett Scott

CAST

Guy Patterson	Tom Everett Scott
Faye Dolan	Liv Tyler
Jimmy	Johnathon Schaech
Lenny	Steve Zahn
The Bass Player	Ethan Embry
Mr. White	Tom Hanks
Tina	Charlize Theron
Lamarr	Obba Babatundé
Chad	Giovanni Ribisi
Horace	Chris Ellis
Sol Siler	Alex Rocco
Del Paxton	Bill Cobbs
Troy Chesterfield	Peter Scolari
Margueritte	Rita Wilson
Uncle Bob	Chris Isaak
Boss Vic Koss	Kevin Pollak
Freddy Fredrickson	Robert Torti
Diane Dane	Chaille Percival
Mr. Patterson	Holmes Osborne, Jr.
Mrs. Patterson	Claudia Stedelin
Darlene Patterson	Dawn Maxey
Villapiano	Jack Milo
Dentist	Keith Neubert
Kitty	Lee Everett
Heckler	Sean Whalen
KJZZ Disc Jockey	Clint Howard
Chrissy Thomkins	Sarah Koskoff
Talent Show M.C.	Mark Brettschneider
Koss' Secretary	Kathleen Kinmont
Polaroid TV Host	Warren Berlinger
Wisconsin Cop	Clive Rosengren
Shades Fan	Brittney Powell
Major Motion Picture Director	Jonathan Demme

and Erika Greene (Major Motion Picture A.D.), Dave Oliver (Rick), Tracy Reiner (Anita), Barry Sobel (Goofball), Mickey Mouse, Goofy (Themselves), Paul Feig (KMPC D.J.), Gedde Watanabe (Play-Tone Photographer), Michael P. Byrne, Dick Corman, Diane McGee (Play-Tone Reporters), Randy Fechter (Play-Tone Tour Manager), Mars Callahan (Disc Master Engineer), Benjamin John Parrillo (Marine Sergeant), Robert Ridgley (Hollywood Showcase Announcer), Marc McClure (Hollywood Showcase Director), Karen Praxel (Hollywood Showcase Script Supervisor), Paulie DiCocco (Hollywood Showcase Floor Manager), Bryan Cranston (Virgil "Gus" Girssom), Charlie Frye (Plate Spinner), Colin Hanks (Page), Elizabeth Hanks (Bored Girl in Dress Shop), Bill Wiley, Cheryl L. Bruton (Pageant Helpers), Heather Hewitt (Sales Lady), Renee Lippin (Beautician), Carol Androsky (Diner Waitress), Ginger Slaughter (Ambassador Waitress), Robert Wisdom (Bobby Washington), Larry Antonino (Scott "Wolfman" Pell), Kennya J. Ramsey, Julie L. Harkness, Darlene Dillinger (Chantrellines), Jennifer York, Bethany Hartf, Kathy Stuber, Cathryne Senescu (Folk Girls), Steve Billington, Andy Duncan, Dave Ryan, Todd Simon, Mike Uhler, Marco Villanova (Legends of Brass), Rick Elias, Ted Kramer, Howard Locke, Don Markese, Paula Nichols, Scott Rogness, Angel Sheppard, Wade Short, Scott Strecker, Jimmy Willis (Play-Tone Band), Thomas Cleo, Ken Empie, Ron Jeffrey, Mike Piccirillo, Chris Wilson (Saturn 5), Barth Beasley, James Leary, Alphonse Mouzon (Blue Spot Trio), Kristie J. Canavan, Bethany Chesser, Tara Schwartz, Melissa Hurley, Cherie Hill, Robin Lindsley Allen (Wisonsin Dancers)

The four young members of a Pennsylvania rock and roll band, The Wonders, find themselves hurled into the show business spotlight after their song "That Thing You Do!" lands on the record charts. This film received an Oscar nomination for its title song.

©*Twentieth Century Fox*

Rita Wilson

Chris Isaak

Johnathon Schaech, Tom Everett Scott, Ethan Embry, Steve Zahn

INFINITY

(FIRST LOOK) Producers, Joel Soisson, Michael Leahy, Patricia Broderick, Matthew Broderick; Co-Producer, Don Phillips; Director, Matthew Broderick; Screenplay, Patricia Broderick; Photography, Toyomichi Kurita; Designer, Bernt Capra; Music, Bruce Broughton; Costumes, Mary Jane Fort; Editors, Elena Maganini, Bill Johnson, Amy Young; Casting, Lisa Bankert; a Neo Motion Pictures production; Dolby Stereo; Color; Rated PG; 119 minutes; October release

Matthew Broderick, Patricia Arquette

CAST

Richard Feynman	Matthew Broderick
Arline Greenbaum	Patricia Arquette
Mel Feynman	Peter Riegert
Tutti Feynman	Dori Brenner
Dr. Hellman	Peter Michael Goetz
Bill Price	Zeljko Ivanek
Gate Guard	Matt Mulhern
Aunt Ruth	Joyce Van Patten
John Wheeler	James LeGros
Young Richard	Jeffrey Force
Harold	David Drew Gallagher
Robert	Raffi Diblasio
David	Joshua Wiener
Abacus Adder	James Hong

and Emerson Tran (Kid), Melissa Delizia (Young Joan), John Hammil, Mary Pat Gleason (Country Doctors), Jack Lindine (Mr. Greenbaum), Helene Moore (Country Nurse #1), Horton Foote, Jr. (Neighborhood Doctor), Mary Kay Wulf (Aunt Rose), Laurence Haddon (Family Doctor), Tom Kurlander (Driver), Mark Burnham, Googie Gress, Joshua Goldin (Passengers), Erich Anderson (Gil), Drew Ebersole, Damion Scheller, Joshua Malina, Demetrius Navarro (Calculator Kids), John Patterson (Stan Ivanek), Cosimo Sherman (Garo), Geoffrey Nauffts (Rob), David Barrera (Chepa), Kelly Wolf (Nurse Kate), Patrick James Clark (Strong Fellow), Kirk Fox (Mechanic), Marianne Muellerleile (Nurse Gracie), Michelle Feynman (Sewing Girl on Train), Kristin Dattilo Hayward (Joan Feynman), Bill Bolender (Isadore Rabi), Corbitt Smith (Henry)

The true story of the relationship between brilliant physicist Richard Feynman and Arline Greenbaum, and how their lives were shattered when she was diagnosed with tuberculosis. This was the first theatrical feature directed by actor Matthew Broderick. The screenwriter, Patricia Broderick, is his mother.

Patricia Arquette

Matthew Broderick

Director Matthew Broderick

STEPHEN KING'S THINNER

(PARAMOUNT) Producers, Richard P. Rubinstein, Mitchell Galin; Executive Producer, Stephen F. Kesten; Director, Tom Holland; Screenplay, Michael McDowell, Tom Holland; Based on the novel by Stephen King; Photography, Kees Van Oostrum; Designer, Laurence Bennett; Costumes, Ha Nguyen; Special Makeup Creator, Greg Cannom; Music, Daniel Licht; a Spelling Films presentation of a Richard P. Rubinstein production; Dolby Stereo; Color; Rated R; 92 minutes; October release

CAST

Billy Halleck	Robert John Burke
Richie Ginelli	Joe Mantegna
Gina Lempke	Kari Wuhrer
Heidi Halleck	Lucinda Jenney
Tadzu Lempke	Michael Constantine
Linda Halleck	Joy Lenz
Prosecutor	Time Winters
Judge Phillips	Howard Erskine
Bailiff	Terrence Garmey
Court Clerk	Randy Jurgensen
Max Duggenfield	Jeff Ware
Mama Ginelli	Antonette Schwartzberg
Gabe Lempke	Terrence Kava
Gypsy Woman	Adriana Delphine
Billy's Secretary	Ruth Miller
Kirk Penschley	Walter Bobbie
Judge Cary Rossington	John Horton
Chief Duncan Hopley	Daniel von Bargen

and Irma St. Paule (Suzanne Lempke), Stephen King (Pharmacist), Sam Freed (Dr. Mike Houston), Elizabeth Franz (Leda Rossington), Patrick Farrelly (Henry Halliwell), Bridget Marks (Ginelli Bar Girl), Mitchell Greenberg, Angela Pietropinto (Clinic Doctors), Michael Walker (Clinic Waiter), Ed Wheeler (Det. Deevers), Peter Maloney (Biff Quigley), Robert Fitch, Sr. (Flash Enders), Sean Hewitt ("Dr." Fander), Josh Holland (Frank Spurton), Allelon Ruggiero (Delivery Boy)

Overweight attorney Billy Halleck accidentally runs down an old gypsy woman, causing the victim's father to place a curse on Halleck that makes him lose weight at an alarming rate.

©*Spelling Films*

Muhammad Ali

Robert John Burke, Joe Mantegna

Muhammad Ali

WHEN WE WERE KINGS

(GRAMERCY) Producers, David Sonenberg, Leon Gast, Taylor Hackford; Executive Producer, David Sonenberg; Director, Leon Gast; Photography, Maryse Alberti, Paul Goldsmith, Kevin Keating, Albert Maysles, Roderick Young; Editors, Leon Gast, Taylor Hackford, Jeffrey Levy-Hinte, Keith Robinson; Co-Producers, Vikram Jayanti, Keith Robinson; a DAS Films presentation; Dolby Stereo; Color; Not rated; 92 minutes; October release. Documentary on the September 25, 1974 boxing match between heavyweight title holder George Foreman and challenger Muhammad Ali.

WITH

Muhammad Ali, George Foreman, Don King, James Brown, B.B. King, Mobutu Sese Seko, Spike Lee, Norman Mailer, George Plimpton, Thomsa Hauser, Malik Bowens, Lloyd Price, The Spinners, The Crusaders, Miriam Makeba.

1996 Academy Award-winner for Best Documentary Feature.

©*Gramercy Pictures*

TREES LOUNGE

(ORION CLASSICS) Producers, Brad Wyman, Chris Hanley; Executive Producers, Julie Silverman Yorn, Nick Wechsler; Co-Producers, Kelley Forsyth, Sarah Vogel; Director/Screenplay, Steve Buscemi; Photography, Lisa Rinzler; Designer, Steven Rosenzweig; Costumes, Mari-An Ceo; Music, Evan Lurie; Editor, Kate Williams; Associate Producer, Christina Larsson; Casting, Walken/Jaffe Casting; a LIVE Entertainment presentation of an Addis-Wechsler and Muse/Wyman production in association with Seneca Falls Productions; Ultra-Stereo; Color; Rated R; 94 minutes; October release

CAST

Tommy Basilio	Steve Buscemi
Debbie	Chloe Sevigny
Mike	Mark Boone Junior
Raymond	Michael Buscemi
Rob	Anthony LaPaglia
Theresa	Elizabeth Bracco
Jerry	Daniel Baldwin
Connie	Carol Kane
Bill	Bronson Dudley
Marie	Eszter Balint
Matthew	Kevin Corrigan
Crystal	Debi Mazar
Sandy	Annette Arnold
Vic	Steven Randazzo
Jackie	Suzanne Shepherd
Stan	Rockets Redglare
George	Michael Imperioli
Larry	Samuel L. Jackson
Uncle Al	Seymour Cassel
Patty	Mimi Rogers
Tony Basilio	Victor Arnold
Johnny	John Ventimiglia
Harry	Joe Lisi
Freddie	Richard Boes
Tina	Brooke Smith
Anna	Carina Finn
Little Boy	Michael Storms
Grandma	Irma St. Paule
Samantha	Daniella Rich

and Marilyn Chris (Josie Basilio), Victor Arnold (Tony Basilio), Christina Gildea (Marie's Mother), Marissa Lanzello (Lisa), Roberta Hanley (Roberta), Larry Guillard, Jr. (James), Io Tillett Wright (Little Girl), Lucian Buscemi (Crystal's Son), Bianca Bakija (Kelly), Charles Newmark (Puck)

Having lost his girlfriend to his former boss, Tommy Basilio, who drowns his sorrow by hanging out at the Trees Lounge, lands a temporary job as an ice cream man, and finds himself becoming attracted to 17-year-old Debbie.

©LIVE Entertainment, Inc.

Bronson Dudley, Steve Buscemi

Elizabeth Bracco, Anthony LaPaglia

Chloe Sevigny

Bronson Dudley, Samuel L. Jackson, Larry Guillard, Jr.

THE CHAMBER

(UNIVERSAL) Producers, John Davis, Brian Grazer, Ron Howard; Executive Producers, David Friendly, Ric Kidney, Karen Kehela; Director, James Foley; Screenplay, William Goldman, Chris Reese; Based on the novel by John Grisham; Photography, Ian Baker; Designer, David Brisbin; Editor, Mark Warner; Costumes, Tracy Tynan; Music, Carter Burwell; Associate Producer, Karen Snow; Casting, Mali Finn; a co-presentation of Imagine Entertainment of a Brian Grazer/Davis Entertainment production; DTS STereo; Panavision; Eastman Color; Rated R; 110 minutes; October release

CAST

Adam Hall	Chris O'Donnell
Sam Cayhall	Gene Hackman
Lee Bowen	Faye Dunaway
E. Garner Goodman	Robert Prosky
Rollie Wedge	Raymond Barry
Sgt. Packer	Bo Jackson
Nora Stark	Lela Rochon
Governor McAllister	David Marshall Grant
Judge Slattery	Nicholas Pryor
Attorney General Roxburgh	Harve Presnell
Wyn Lettner	Richard Bradford
J.B. Gullitt	Greg Goossen
Marvin Kramer	Seth Isler
Ruth Kramer	Millie Perkins
Josh Kramer	Sid Johnson
John Kramer	Blake Johnson
Phelps Bowen	Josef Sommer
Lucas Mann	Leonard Vincent
Ms. Cooley	Bonita Allen
George Nugent	Dick Stilwell
Guard	Gloria Jackson Winters
Joe Lincoln	Greg Elam
Quince Lincoln	Zaquarii Walters
Dr. Anne Biddows	Jane Kaczmarek
Bink	Thom Gossom, Jr.
Gate Attendant	Jana Barraza

and Nick Brett, Curtis Epper, Craig Pinckes (Rally Skinheads), Dan Beene (Lead Sheriff), James Geralden (Newscaster), Michelle Davison (Prof. Burns), Jack Conley (White Guard), Stephanie Bell Flynt (Newscaster on Air), Ruby Wilson (Jessie), Joe Meek (Senate Aide), Anthony Kopczynski, Ken Colquitt, Neil Barton (Visitor's Room Guards), Gilbert Ivan Johnson (Trustee), Jerry Gauny, Ed Siebert, Bob Rummler, Disraeli Ellison, Rod Phillips, Jeff Sanders, Richard T. Munoz, Clee Cottel (Inmates), Ian Brady, Sam Bologna (Deputy Exectioners), Charles Swain (Observation Cell Guard), Tony Scott Sherrom (Governor's Aide)

Young lawyer Adam Hall travels to Mississippi to take on the case of his grandfather, Sam Cayhall, a racist and convicted killer responsible for the bombing murders of two small boys.

©Universal City Studios, Inc.

Gene Hackman, Chris O'Donnell

Lela Rochon, Chris O'Donnell

Chris O'Donnell

Faye Dunaway, Chris O'Donnell

THE LONG KISS GOODNIGHT

(NEW LINE CINEMA) Producers, Renny Harlin, Stephanie Austin, Shane Black; Executive Producers, Steve Tisch, Richard Saperstein, Michael De Luca; Co-Producer, Carla Fry; Director, Renny Harlin; Screenplay, Shane Black; Photography, Guillermo Navarro; Designer, Howard Cummings; Editor, William C. Goldenberg; Costumes, Michael Kaplan; Music, Alan Silvestri; Special Visual Effects, Jeffrey A. Okun; Casting, Mary Vernieu, Ronnie Yeskel; a Forge Production in association with Steve Tisch; Dolby SDDS Stereo; Super 35 Widescreen; Deluxe color; Rated R; 120 minutes; October release

CAST

Samantha Caine (Charly Baltimore)	Geena Davis
Mitch Henessey	Samuel L. Jackson
Caitlin	Yvonne Zima
Timothy	Craig Bierko
Hal	Tom Amandes
Nathan	Brian Cox
Perkins	Patrick Malahide
Luke/Daedalus	David Morse
One-Eyed Jack	Joseph McKenna
Trin	Melina Kanakaredes
Raymond	Dan Warry-Smith
Girls	Kristen Bone, Jennifer Pisana
Man on Bed	Rex Linn
Earl	Alan North
Todd Henessey	Edwin Hodge
Hostage Agent	Bill MacDonald
Alice	Gladys O'Connor
Surveillance Man	Frank Moore
President	G.D. Spradlin
CIA Director	Graham McPherson
Fran Henessey	Sharon Washington
Harry (Perkins' Aide)	Judah Katz
Alley Agent	Robert Thomas
Deer Lick Sentry	John Stead
Teenage Burnouts	Marc Cohen, Chad Donella
Operator	Debra Kirshenbaum
Donlevy Bum Cop	Shawn Doyle
News Anchor	Ken Ryan
Crime Scene Reporter	Craig Eldridge
Helicopter Pilot	Chuck Tamburro
Himself	Larry King

Samantha Caine, suffering from amnesia, hires private detective Mitch Henessey to help her find out her former identity after she is attacked by a crazed assassin.

Geena Davis, Samuel L. Jackson

Geena Davis

Geena Davis, Craig Berko

Samuel L. Jackson

Michael Douglas, Val Kilmer

Val Kilmer

Val Kilmer, John Kani

THE GHOST AND THE DARKNESS

(PARAMOUNT) Producers, Gale Anne Hurd, Paul Radin, A. Kitman Ho; Executive Producers, Michael Douglas, Steven Reuther; Director, Stephen Hopkins; Screenplay, William Goldman; Photography, Vilmos Zsigmond; Designer, Stuart Wurtzel; Editors, Robert Brown, Steve Mirkovich; Co-Producer, Grant Hill; Music, Jerry Goldsmith; Costumes, Ellen Mirojnick; Casting, Mary Selway, Sarah Trevis; a Constellation Films presentation of a Douglas/Reuther production; Dolby Stereo; Panavision; Deluxe color; Rated R; 109 minutes; October release

CAST

Remington . . . . Michael Douglas
Lt. Col. John Patterson . . . . Val Kilmer
Dr. Hawthorne . . . . Bernard Hill
Samuel . . . . John Kani
John Beaumont . . . . Tom Wilkinson
Starling . . . . Brian McCardie
Mahina . . . . Henry Cele
Abdullah . . . . Om Puri
Helena Patterson . . . . Emily Mortimer
Indian Victim . . . . Kurt Egelhof
and Satchu Annamalai, Teddy Reddy, Rakeem Khan (Workers), Jack Devnarain (Nervous Sikh Orderly), Glen Gabela, Richard Nwamba (Orderlies), Nick Lorentz (Photographer), Alex Ferns (Stockton), Kaycey Padayachee (Beaumont's Valet), Giles Masters (Beaumont's Clerk), Patrick and Justin Gifford (Patterson's Son), George Middlekoop (Station Master)

Engineer John Patterson, sent to oversee the building of a railroad bridge in Africa, calls on legendary hunter Remington to help him dispose of two lions who are going on a man-eating rampage. 1996 Academy Award-winner for Best Sound Effects Editing.

©Paramount Pictures

Val Kilmer, Emily Mortimer

Michael Douglas, Bernard Hill

LOOKING FOR RICHARD

(FOX SEARCHLIGHT) Producers, Michael Hadge, Al Pacino; Executive Producer, William Teitler; Director, Al Pacino; Narration Written by Al Pacino, Frederic Kimball; Including scenes from *Richard III* by William Shakespeare; Photography, Robert Leacock; Music, Howard Shore; Line Producer, James Bulleit; Editors, Pasquale Buba, William A. Anderson, Ned Bastille; a Jam production; Dolby Stereo; Color; Rated PG-13; 109 minutes; October release

Kevin Spacey, Al Pacino

CAST

Queen Elizabeth	Penelope Allen
Dorset	Gordon MacDonald
Rivers	Madison Arnold
Grey	Vincent Angell
King Edward	Harris Yulin
Clarence	Alec Baldwin
Richard III	Al Pacino
Prince Edward	Timmy Prairie
Young Prince	Landon Prairie
Hastings	Kevin Conway
Lord Stanley	Larry Bryggman
Buckingham	Kevin Spacey
Margaret	Estelle Parsons
Lady Anne	Winona Ryder
Halberd/Messenger	Phil Parolisi
Murderers	Bruce MacVittie, Paul Guilfoyle
Catesby	Richard Cox
Mistress Shore	Julie Moret
Bishop of Ely	Frederic Kimball
Ratcliffe	Dan von Bargen
Lovel	James Colby
Tyrell	Ira Lewis
Richmond	Aidan Quinn
Messengers	Neal Jones, Luke Toma, Andre Sogliuzzo
Soldier	Marlon Pollick

and F. Murray Abraham, Hayley Barr, Gil Bellows, Don Berry, Nicholas Berry, Robin Berry, Kate Burton, Dominic Chianese, Johann Carlo, Joyce Ebert, Paul Gleason, Esther Gregory, Clare Holman, Linda Iannella Scott, Elaine Kory, Damien Leake, Viveca Lindfors, Judith Malina, Michael Maloney, Jaime Sanchez, David Saltzman, Linda Selman, Ed Setrakian, Kyle Smyth, Heathcote Williams, Kenneth Branagh, Kevin Kline, James Earl Jones, Rosemary Harris, Emrys Jones, Peter Brook, Barbara Everett, Derek Jacobi, John Gielgud, Vanessa Redgrave (The Interviews)

While acting out Shakespeare's Richard III *actor Al Pacino interviews various actors, authorities and audience members on their feelings about and interpretations of the famous play.*

©*Twentieth Century Fox*

Winona Ryder

Aidan Quinn, Al Pacino

Al Pacino

SWINGERS

(MIRAMAX) Producers, Victor Simpkins, Nicole Shay LaLoggia; Executive Producer, Cary Woods; Co-Producer/Screenplay, Jon Favreau; Director/Photography, Doug Liman; Line Producer, Nicole Shay LaLoggia; Designer, Brad Halvorson; Editor, Stephen Mirrione; Costumes, Genevieve Tyrrell; Associate Producers, Bradford L. Schlei, Avram Ludwig; Music, Justin Reinhardt; an Alfred Shay production, presented in association with Independent Pictures; Dolby Stereo; Color; Rated R; 97 minutes; October release

Jon Favreau, Vince Vaughn

CAST

Mike	Jon Favreau
Trent	Vince Vaughn
Rob	Ron Livingston
Sue	Patrick Van Horn
Charles	Alex Desert
Lorraine	Heather Graham
Christy	Deena Martin
Lisa	Katherine Kendall
Nikki	Brooke Langton
Girl with Cigar	Blake Lindsley
Vegas Dealer	Kevin James Kelly
Vegas Waitress	Stephanie Ittleson
$100 Gamblers	Vernon Vaughn, Sheri Rosenblum, Stasea Rosenblum
$5 Winner	Joan Favreau
Peek-a-Boo Girl	Maddie Corman
Girl at Party	Jan Dykstra
Skully	Rio Hackford
Dresden Lounge Act	Marty & Elayne
Derby Band	Big Bad Voodoo Daddy
$5 Gambler	Pamela Shaw
Pit Boss	Tom Alley
Lounge Lizard	Reverend Phil Dixon
Bartender	Ashley M. Rogers
Pink Dot Guy	Mensur Hamud
Party Mystery Guy	Ahmed Ahmed

and Jay Diola, Nicholas Gagliarducci, David Gould, Bill Phillips (Skully's Crew), Eufemia Plimpton, Melinda Starr (Derby Ladies), Samantha Lemole, Jessica Buchman (Dresden Ladies), Gary Aurbach, Brad Halvorson (Derby Doormen), Christopher A. Joyce, Edward Rissien, Jenna Rissien, Mark Smith (Diner Patrons), John Abraham, Rachel Gallaghan, Lisa Guerriero, Thomas Hall, Damiana Kamishin, Curtis Lindersmith, Jennifer Lucero, Pinki Marsolek, Rhonda Martin, Martina Migenes, Paul Mojica, Sam Mollo, Jacob Morris, Michael Scott, Bernard Serrano, Rosalind Smith, Molly Stern, Johnny Walker, Lisa Wolstein (Derby Dancers)

Still hurting from the break-up with his girlfriend, aspiring actor-comedian Mike reluctantly rejoins his buddy Trent on the Los Angeles dating scene.

©Miramax Films

Vince Vaughn, Jon Favreau, Patrick Van Horn

Patrick Van Horn, Vince Vaughn, Jon Favreau, Ron Livingston, Alex Desert

Jon Favreau, Heather Graham

Peter Gallagher, Claire Danes

Laurie Fortier, Claire Danes

Claire Danes, Freddie Prinze, Jr.

Kathy Baker, Claire Danes

Bruce Altman, Peter Gallagher

TO GILLIAN ON HER 37TH BIRTHDAY

(TRIUMPH) Producers, Marykay Powell, David E. Kelley; Director, Michael Pressman; Screenplay, David E. Kelley; Based on the play by Michael Brady; Photography, Tim Suhrstedt; Designer, Linda Pearl; Editor, William Scharf; Music, James Horner; Co-Producer, Terry Morse; Costumes, Deborah L. Scott; Casting, Lynn Stalmaster; a Rastar/David E. Kelly production; Dolby SDDS Stereo; Technicolor; Rated PG-13; 93 minutes; October release

CAST

David Lewis . . . . Peter Gallagher
Gillian Lewis . . . . Michelle Pfeiffer
Rachel Lewis . . . . Claire Danes
Cindy Bayles . . . . Laurie Fortier
Kevin Dollof . . . . Wendy Crewson
Paul Wheeler . . . . Bruce Altman
Esther Wheeler . . . . Kathy Baker
Joey Bost . . . . Freddie Prinze, Jr.
Megan Weeks . . . . Rachel Seidman-Lockamy
Blonde on the Beach . . . . Lori New
Lifeguard . . . . Danny Crook
Paramedic . . . . Todd Haven

Two years after David's wife Gillian died in a boating accident, David's in-laws invite an attractive single woman to Nantucket Island in hopes that she will help David get over his loss. The original Off-Broadway production premiered in 1984 and starred David Rasche (David), Frances Conroy (Kevin), and Sarah Jessica Parker (Rachel).

©Columbia Pictures Industries, Inc.

THE GRASS HARP

(FINE LINE FEATURES) Producers, Charles Matthau, Jerry Tokofsky, John Davis; Executive Producer, John Winfield; Director, Charles Matthau; Screenplay/Co-Producers, Stirling Silliphant, Kirk Ellis; Based on the novel by Truman Capote; Photography, John A. Alonzo; Designer, Paul Sylbert; Costumes, Albert Wolsky; Music, Patrick Williams; Editors, Sidney Levin, Tim O'Meara; a Charles Matthau/Jerry Tokofsky/ John Davis production; Dolby Stereo; Color; Rated PG; 107 minutes; October release

Edward Furlong, Piper Laurie, Walter Matthau

CAST

Dolly Talbo	Piper Laurie
Judge Charlie Cool	Walter Matthau
Verena Talbo	Sissy Spacek
Dr. Morris Ritz	Jack Lemmon
Sister Ida	Mary Steenburgen
Collin Fenwick (teen)	Edward Furlong
Collin Fenwick (child)	Grayson Fricke
Amos Legrand	Roddy McDowall
Catherine Creek	Nell Carter
Reverend Buster	Charles Durning
Riley Henderson	Sean Patrick Flanery
Sheriff Junius Candle	Joe Don Baker
Maude Riordan	Mia Kirshner
Eugene Fenwick	Scott Wilson
Mrs. Buster	Bonnie Bartlett
Little Homer Honey	Adam Crosby
Mrs. Richards	Doris Roberts
Mrs. Peters	Nora Dunfee
Charlie Cool, Jr.	Ray McKinnon
Young Maude	Veronica Lauren
Doc Carter	Danny Nelson
Marcy Wheeler	Rebecca Koon
Martha Cool	Michele Bauer
Barbershop Regular	Charles Matthau
Big Eddie Stover	Alex Van

and Emilie Jacobs (Elizabeth Henderson), Marc McPherson (Hotel Manager), Elizabeth "Boo" Gilder (Snot Nose Date), Brad Bulger (Date), Marty Elcan (Cheap Customer), Richie Dye (Jack Mill), J. Michael McDougal (Ray Oliver), Rosa Tucker (Texaco), Jenjer Vick (Mamie Curtis), Margaret Scarborough (Flo Johnson), Boyd Gaines (Narrator)

After his mother dies young Collin Fenwick is sent to live with his aunts, the strong-willed Verena and the gentle, romantic Dolly.

©*Fine Line Features*

Sissy Spacek, Jack Lemmon

Nell Carter, Walter Matthsu, Piper Laurie, Edward Furlong, Sean Patrick Flanery

PALOOKAVILLE

(SAMUEL GOLDWYN CO.) Producer, Uberto Pasolini; Executive Producer, Lindsay Law; Director, Alan Taylor; Screenplay, David Epstein; Co-Producer, Scott Ferguson; Photography, John Thomas; Designer, Anne Stuhler; Editor, David Leonard; Costumes, Katherine Jane Bryant; Music, Rachel Portman; Casting, Hopkins, Smith, Barden; a Playhouse International Pictures presentation in association with The Samuel Goldwyn Company and Redwave Films; Dolby Stereo; DuArt color; Rated R; 92 minutes; October release

CAST

Jerry	Adam Trese
Russ	Vincent Gallo
Sid	William Forsythe
Ed	Gareth Williams
Betty	Lisa Gay Hamilton
Enid	Bridgit Ryan
Laurie	Kim Dickens
June	Frances McDormand
Mother	Suzanne Shepherd
Chris	Nicole Burdette
Ralph	Robert LuPone
Money Truck Driver	Walter Bryant
Old Man	Douglas Seale
Old Arthur	William Riker
Old Fritz	Nesbitt Blaisdell
Bus Driver	Leonard Jackson
Money Truck Guard	William Duell
Chief of Police	Peter McRobbie
Barney	Stan Tracy
Cop	Gerry Robert
Gangster	Mario Todisco
Sergeant	Paul Austin
Mr. Kott	Sam Coppola
Walt	Jerome Lepage
Ricky	Skylar Lewis

Three friends hope to escape from their dead-end urban lives by pulling off the perfect crime.

©*The Samuel Goldwyn Company*

Vincent Gallo, Adam Trese, William Forsythe

Vincent Gallo, Frances McDormand

Adam Trese, Vincent Gallo, William Forsythe

Adam Trese, Lisa Gay Hamilton

HIGH SCHOOL HIGH

(TRISTAR) Producers, David Zucker, Robert LoCash, Gil Netter; Executive Producer, Sasha Harari; Co-Producer, Patricia Whitcher; Director, Hart Bochner; Screenplay, David Zucker, Robert LoCash, Pat Proft; Photography, Vernon Layton; Designer, Dennis Washington; Editor, James R. Symons; Costumes, Mona May; Music, Ira Newborn; Associate Producer, Jeff Wright; Casting, Elisabeth Leustig; a David Zucker production; Dolby SDDS Stereo; Technicolor; Rated PG-13; 86 minutes; October release

CAST

Richard Clark/Clark's Mother	Jon Lovitz
Victoria Chappell	Tia Carrere
Evelyn Doyle	Louise Fletcher
Griff McReynolds	Mekhi Phifer
Natalie	Malinda Williams
Paco	Guillermo Diaz
Two Bags	Lexie Bigham
Alonzo	Gil Espinoza
Thaddeus Clark	John Neville
Anferny	Brian Hooks
Julie	Natasha Gregson Wagner
DeMarco	Marco Rodriguez
Rhino	Nicholas Worth
Hulk	Eric Allen Kramer
Ms. Wells	Lu Elrod
Miss Foley	Eve Sigall
Mr. Arnott	Michael Nye
Griff's Mom	Joan Ruedelstein
Teacher	McNally Sagal
Operator	Mallory Sandler
Blind Student	Carlos Flores-Recinos
Nurse	Sonya Eddy
African Translator	Adam Otokiti
Viet Translator	Saemi Nakamura
Central American Translator	Marabina Jaimes
Mou Mou/Bartender	Baoan Coleman

and Michelle Jones (Maitre D'), Vernon P. Burton (Cop), Pat Harvey (Anchorwoman), Christian Dyer Mills (Student), Susan Breslau (Thaddeus' Secretary), John Ducey (Student with Paper), Ricky Harris (DJ), Steven Kent (Panhandler), Christopher J. Keene (Faculty Member), Thom Barry (Teacher), Abdul Goznobi (Tourette's Kid), Drew O'Connell (Rookie Cop), Jeff Wright (Security Officer), Shauna Robertson (Little Slut), Kotoko Kawamura (Asian Woman), Ali Hojat (Drama Coach), Charlotte Zucker (Woman Smoking Pipe), Jeremy Breslau, Ben Breslau, Isaac Ardolino (Wellington Students), Io Perry (Moaning Woman), Allen J. Smith (Watch Salesman), Michael W. Williams (Kid in Hallway), Nicole Ann Cohen (Girl in Class), Mina Nims, Rachelle Roderick (Strippers), Mark Swenson (Pizza Guy), Colleen Fitzpatrick (Singer), Stephen Cilurzo (Flowbee Announcer), Danielle Ardolino, Janeane Ardolino, Maureen Ardolino, Andy Lipkis, William Peña, Kim Perry, Francis P. Ruiz, Aaron Zucker, Burton Zucker (Featured Extras)

Comedy spoof in which idealistic Richard Clark accepts an assignment to teach at Marion Barry High, the toughest school in the ghetto.

©TriStar Pictures, Inc.

Natasha Gregson Wagner, Mekhi Phifer, Malinda Williams

Jon Lovitz, Tia Carrere

Tia Carrere, Jon Lovitz, John Neville

Louise Fletcher

GET ON THE BUS

(COLUMBIA) Producers, Reuben Cannon, Bill Borden, Barry Rosenbush; Executive Producer/Director, Spike Lee; Screenplay, Reggie Rock Bythewood; Photography, Elliot Davis; Designer, Ina Mayhew; Editor, Leander T. Sales; Costumes, Sandra Hernandez; Music, Terence Blanchard; Song: "Put Your Heart on the Line" by Kenneth Babyface Edmonds/performed by Michael Jackson; Casting, Reuben Cannon and Associates; a 15 Black Men/40 Acres and a Mule Filmworks production; Dolby SDDS Stereo; Panavision; Color; Rated R; 120 minutes; October release

CAST

Rick	Richard Belzer
Junior	DeAundre Bonds
Flip	Andre Braugher
Evan Thomas, Sr.	Thomas Jefferson Byrd
Jamal	Gabriel Casseus
Craig	Albert Hall
Xavier	Hill Harper
Randall	Harry Lennix
Jay	Bernie Mac
Wendell	Wendell Pierce
Gary	Roger Guenveur Smith
Kyle	Isaiah Washington
Mike	Steve White
Jeremiah	Ossie Davis
George	Charles S. Dutton
Jindal	Joie Lee
Shelly	Kristin Wilson
Jefferson	Frank Clem
Rodney	Bob Orwig
Mitch	Gary Lowery
Sandy	Debra Rogers
Officer Mike	William B. Barillaro
Dr. Cook	Susan Baston
Jamilia	Paula Jai Parker
Gina	Gina Ravera
Ja-Dee	Jadi McCurdy
Doc	Dr. Hosea Brown, III
Khalid	Guy Margo

and Randy Quaid

Drama about a diverse goup of men aboard a bus headed for the Million Man March in Washington D.C. on Oct. 16, 1995.

©Columbia Pictures Industries, Inc.

Harry Lennix, Isaiah Washington

Thomas Jefferson Byrd, DeAundre Bonds

Ossie Davis   Bernie Mac

Charles S. Dutton, Albert Hall

Andre Braugher, Gabriel Casseus, Thomas Jefferson Byrd, Hill Harper, Ossie Davis, Hosea Brown III, Isaiah Washington, DeAundre Bonds, Roger Guenveur Smith, Harry Lennix, Charles S, Dutton, Bernie Mac, Steve White

Andre Braugher, Richard Belzer

Roger Guenveur Smith   Gabriel Casseus

Andre Braugher, Hill Harper

THE ASSOCIATE

(HOLLYWOOD PICTURES) Producers, Frederic Golchan, Patrick Markey, Adam Leipzig; Executive Producers, Ted Field, Scott Kroopf, Robert W. Cort, David Madden; Co-Producers, Réne Gainville, Michael A. Helfant; Director, Donald Petrie; Screenplay, Nick Thiel; Photography, Alex Nepomniaschy; Designer, Andrew Jackness; Editor, Bonnie Koehler; Costumes, April Ferry; Music, Christopher Tyng; Casting, Mary Colquhoun; a Interscope Communications/PolyGram Filmed Entertainment production in association with Frederic Golchan/Rene Gainville; Distributed by Buena Vista Pictures; Dolby Digital Stereo; Technicolor; Rated PG-13; 114 minutes; October release

CAST

Laurel Ayres	Whoopi Goldberg
Sally	Dianne Wiest
Fallon	Eli Wallach
Frank	Tim Daly
Camille	Bebe Neuwirth
Cindy Mason	Lainie Kazan
Aesop Franklin	Austin Pendleton
Walter Manchester	George Martin
Charlie	Kenny Kerr
Bissel	Lee Wilkof
Mrs. Cupchick	Helen Hanft
Plaza Manager	George Morfogen
SEC Agent Thompkins	Zeljko Ivanek
Harry	Miles Chapin
Loan Officer	Jean De Baer
Peabody Club Concierge	Louis Turenne
Detective Templeton	William Hill
Detective Jones	Colleen Camp Wilson
Eddie	Brian Tarantina
Harley Mason	Jerry Hardin
Harley's Associates	John Short, Thomas Wagner
Themselves	Johnny Miller, Donald J. Trump, Sally Jessy Raphael
Dalton	Nicholas Kepros
Executives at Strip Club	Peter McRobbie, Daryl Edwards
Sandy	Allison Janney
Carl Bode	Frederick Rolf

and Larry Gilliard, Jr. (Plaza Bellhop Thomas), Liana Pai (Plaza Concierge Charlotte), Vincent Larseca (Plaza Waiter José), Arthur French (Plaza Men's Room Attendant), Kathleen McClellan (Frank's Girlfriend), Robert Levine (Door Slam Executive), John Rothman (Jogging Track Executive), Jonathan Freeman (Hockey Game Executive), Socorro Santiago (Syntonex Worker), Bernie McInerney (Client at Cutty/Ayres), Katherine Wallach, Leon Addison Brown (Reporters), Judith Calder (Audience Member), Ted Brunetti (Fallon's Messenger), Baxter Harris, Craig Braun (Disgruntled Investors), Rex Robbins, Ira Wheeler (Investors at 21 Club), Boris McGiver, Billy Jaye (Plaza Reporters), Ginny Yang (Funeral Reporter), Joel Blake (Poker Player), Alberto Alejandrino (Maitre D' at Peabody Club), The Roy Gerson Orchestra, featuring Corrine Manning (Fallon Ball Band)

Financial analyst Laurel Ayres finds it difficult to get promoted so she creates a fake business partner, Robert S. Cutty so that clients will take her seriously.

©PolyGram FIlm Productions B.V.

Lainie Kazan, Whoopi Goldberg

Tim Daly, Whoopi Goldberg

Eli Wallach, Bebe Neuwirth

Whoopi Goldberg, Dianne Wiest

LARGER THAN LIFE

(UNITED ARTISTS) Producers, Richard B. Lewis, John Watson, Pen Densham; Execuitve Producers, Wolfgang Glattes, Guy East, Sue Baden-Powell; Director, Howard Franklin; Screenplay, Roy Blount, Jr.; Story, Pen Densham, Garry Williams; Photography, Elliot Davis; Designer, Marcia Hinds-Johnson; Costumes, Jane Robinson; Editor, Sidney Levin; Music, Miles Goodman; Elephant Trainers, Gary Johnson, Kari Johnson; Casting, Gail Levin, Tricia Tomey; DTS Stereo; Deluxe color; Rated PG; 93 minutes; November release

CAST

Jack Corcoran	Bill Murray
Mo Newman	Janeane Garofalo
Tip Tucker	Matthew McConaughey
Hurst	Keith David
Vernon	Pat Hingle
Walter	Jeremy Piven
Luluna	Lois Smith
Mom	Anita Gillette
Terry	Linda Fiorentino
Vera	Tai
Event Coordinator	Jerry Adler
Richie	Richard Alan Baker
Man in Audience	Richie Allan
Pyramid Woman	Kimberly Thornton
Celeste	Maureen Mueller
Matthew	Alex Neiwerth
Party Guest	Alfa-Betty Olsen
Receptionist	Carrie Houk
Trowbridge Bowers	Harve Presnell
Cop	Earl Billings
Outraged Woman	Jeannine Hutchings
Heckler #1	Roy Blount, Jr.
Boy with Ice Cream	Teddy Couch
Boy on Bicycle	Marco Emerson
Wee St. Francis	Tracey Walter
Junkyard Guy	Greg Lewis

and Craig Hawksley, Norman McGowan, Morgan Hatch, Joseph Ribaudo, David Mitchell (Hecklers), Phyllis Shulman (Waitress), Harry Governick (Ticket Man), Rodney Bennett (Incredulous Trucker), Greg Ward (Truckyard Guy), James Gale (Mechanic), Pat Mahoney (Eastbound Trucker), Bob "Dutch" Holland (Insulted Trucker), Darrell Bowen (Bearded Trucker), Marvin Barker (Trucker), Neal Lerner (Makeup Person), Richard Arthur (Assistant Director), Lois Hicks (Truck Stop Waitress), Eugene Johnson (Startled Driver), Margaret Smith (Colorado State Patrolwoman), Joseph Palmas (Priest), Israel Juarbe (Villager), Hector Elias (Local Artisan), Roy Keith (Indian Chief), Ken Jones (Elephant Handler), Jesse D. Goins (Airport Guard), Christopher Darga (Airport Security Head), Dirk Blocker (Airport Security Man), John Hauser (Ring Master), Eugene Johnson (Elephant Trainer)

After inheriting an elephant from his father, Jack Corcoran must take the animal crosscountry to accept one of two offers for the creature to pay off his dad's debts.

©United Artists Pictures, Inc.

Bill Murray, Tai

Bill Murray, Tai, Janeane Garofalo

Bill Murray, Matthew McConaughey

Bill Murray, Lois Smith, Tai, Pat Hingle

Leonardo DiCaprio, Claire Danes

John Leguizamo

Leonardo DiCaprio

Harold Perrineau, Leonardo Di Caprio

WILLIAM SHAKESPEARE'S ROMEO & JULIET

(20TH CENTURY FOX) Producers, Gabriella Martinelli, Baz Luhrmann; Director, Baz Luhrmann; Screenplay, Craig Pearce, Baz Luhrmann; Based on the play by William Shakespeare; Photography, Donald M. McAlpine; Designer, Catherine Martin; Editor, Jill Bilcock; Co-Producer, Martin Brown; Costumes, Kym Barrett; Music, Nellee Hooper, Craig Armstrong, Marius De Vries; Song: "Kissing You (Love Theme From 'Romeo & Juliet')" by Des'ree and Tim Atack/performed by Des'ree; Casting, David Rubin; a Bazmark Production; Dolby Stereo; Panavision; Deluxe color; Rated PG-13; 120 minutes; November release

CAST

Anchorwoman	Edwina Moore
Gregory	Zak Orth
Sampson	Jamie Kennedy
Benvolio	Dash Mihok
Attractive Girl	Lupita Ochoa
Nun	Gloria Silva
Abra	Vincent Laresca
Petruchio	Carlos Martin Manzo Ortalora
Middle Age Occupants	Carolyn Valero, Paco Morayta
Tybalt	John Leguizamo
Kid With Toy Gun	Rodrigo Escandon
Station Mother	Margarita Wynne
Fulgencio Capulet	Paul Sorvino
Ted Montague	Brian Dennehy
Caroline Montague	Christina Pickles
Captain Prince	Vondie Curtis-Hall
Romeo Montague	Leonardo DiCaprio
Dave Paris	Paul Rudd
Balthasar	Jesse Bradford
Apothecary	M. Emmet Walsh
Susan Santandiago	Harriet Harris
Rich Ranchidis	Michael Corbett
Gloria Capulet	Diane Venora
Nurse	Miriam Margolyes
Juliet Capulet	Claire Danes
Peter	Pedro Altamirano
Mercutio	Harold Perrineau
Capulet Bouncer	Mario Cimarro
Diva	Des'ree
OP Officer	Ismael Eguiarte
Father Laurence	Pete Postlethwaite
Altar Boys	Ricardo Barona, Fausto Barona, Alex Newman, Cory Newman
Choir Boy	Quindon Tarver
Post Haste Delivery Man	Jorge Abraham
Sacristan	John Sterlini
Undertaker	Farnesio De Bernal
Post Haste Clerk	Catalina Botello

William Shakespeare's classic story of Romeo and Juliet, two teenagers from warring families who fall in love, updated and set in Verona Beach. Previous film versions were released in 1936 (MGM, starring Leslie Howard and Norma Shearer), 1954 (UA, Laurence Harvey and Susan Shentall), and 1968 (Paramount, Leonard Whiting and Olivia Hussey). This film received an Oscar nomination for art direction.

©*Twentieth Century Fox*

Leonardo DiCaprio

Claire Danes

Diane Venora, Paul Rudd, Paul Sorvino

Annabella Sciorra

Isabella Rossellini

Christopher Walken

THE FUNERAL

(OCTOBER) Producer, Mary Kane; Executive Producers, Michael Chambers, Patrick Panzarella; Co-Producer, Randy Sabusawa; Director, Abel Ferrara; Screenplay, Nicholas St. John; Photography, Ken Kelsch; Music, Joe Delia; Editors, Bill Pankow, Mayin Lo; Associate Producers, Russell Simmons, Jay Cannold, Annabella Sciorra; Designer, Charles Lagola; Casting, Ann Goulder; Dolby Stereo; Color; Rated R; 99 minutes; November release

CAST

Ray Tempio . . . . Christopher Walken
Chez Tempio . . . . Chris Penn
Jean. . . . . Annabella Sciorra
Clara. . . . . Isabella Rossellini
Johnny Tempio . . . . Vincent Gallo
Gaspare . . . . Benicio Del Toro
Helen. . . . . Gretchen Mol
Sali . . . . John Ventimiglia
Ghouly . . . . Paul Hipp
Julius . . . . Victor Argo
Ray Tempio, Sr.. . . . . Gian Di Donna
Sentieri. . . . . Demitri Pryeres
Young Ray . . . . Paul Perri
Young Chez . . . . Gregory Pirelli
Middle Chez . . . . Joey Hannon
Enrico . . . . Robert Miano
Bacco . . . . Frank John Hughes
Murder Witness . . . . Andrew Fiscella
Doctor . . . . Anthony Alessandro
Priest . . . . Robert Castle
Undertaker . . . . Santo Fazio
Crying Kid . . . . Daniel Scarpa
Victor. . . . . Nicholas Decegli
Bridgette . . . . Amber Smith
Union Speaker . . . . Edie Falco
Michael Stein . . . . David Patrick Kelly
Fox . . . . Carrie Slaza
Billy. . . . . Phil Neilson
and Patrick McGaw (The Mechanic), Lance Guerria (Flashback Victim), Doug Crosby (The Florist), Ida Bernadini (Aunt Rosa), John Hoyt (Big John), John Chacha Ciarcia (Cha Cha), Heather Bracken (Liz), Frank Cee (Bartender Frank), Chuck Zito (Zito), Mia Babalis (Mia)

Drama about three racketeering brothers, the Tempios, set in New York City in the 1930s.

©October Films

Chris Penn

MOTHER NIGHT

(FINE LINE FEATURES) Producers, Keith Gordon, Robert B. Weide; Executive Producers, Ruth Vitale, Mark Ordesky, Linda Reisman; Director, Keith Gordon; Screenplay, Robert B. Weide, based on the novel by Kurt Vonnegut; Photography, Tom Richmond; Designer, François Séguin; Editor, Jay Rabinowitz; Music, Michael Convertino; Line Producer, Josette Perrotta; Costumes, Renée April; Casting, Valerie McCaffrey; a Whyaduck production; Dolby Stereo; Fotokem color/black and white; Rated R; 110 minutes; November release

Sheryl Lee, Nick Nolte

CAST

Howard Campbell	Nick Nolte
Helga Noth	Sheryl Lee
George Kraft	Alan Arkin
Dr. Lionel Jones	Bernard Behrens
Epstein's Mother	Anna Berger
Abraham Epstein	Arye Gross
Werner Noth	Norman Rodway
The Black Fuehrer of Harlem	Frankie Faison
Father Keeley	Gerard Parkes
Joseph Goebbels	Zach Grenier
Resi Noth	Kirsten Dunst
Prison Warden	Anthony J. Robinow
Prison Official	Michael McGill
Guard Bernard Liebman	Shimon Aviel
Campbell's Father	Bill Corday
Campbell's Mother	Brownen Mantel
Young Howard Campbell	Brawley Nolte
Major Frank Wirtanen	John Goodman
Old Jewish Man	Louis Strauss
Rudolph Hoess	Richard Zeman
SS Officer	Thomas Hauff
Young German Soldier	Jeff Pufah
Bernard B. O'Hare	David Straithairn
Adolph Eichmann's Voice	Henry Gibson
August Krapptauer	Vlasta Vrana
Violent Man	Michael Moran
TV Reporter	William Haugland
Israeli Vice-Consul (TV)	Joel Miller
Sad Man on Street	Kurt Vonnegut
G-Man	Richard Jutras
Cop	Don Jordan

Awaiting trial as a Nazi war criminal, writer Howard Campbell looks back on how he was coaxed into posing as a Nazi sympathizer in order to spy on the enemy for America.

©Fine Line Features

Alan Arkin

Nick Nolte, Sheryl Lee

Mel Gibson, Rene Russo

Gary Sinise

Mel Gibson

Evan Handler, Liev Schreiber, Donnie Wahlberg

Mel Gibson, Brawley Nolte

RANSOM

(TOUCHSTONE) Producers, Scott Rudin, Brian Grazer, B, Kipling Hagopian; Executive Producer, Todd Hallowell; Director, Ron Howard; Screenplay, Richard Price, Alexander Ignon; Story, Cyril Hume, Richard Maibaum; Photography, Piotr Sobocinski; Designer, Michael Corenblith; Editors, Dan Hanley, Mike Hill; Music, James Horner; Associate Producers, Aldric La'Auli Porter, Louisa Velis; Costumes, Rita Ryack; Co-Producers, Adam Schroeder, Susan Merzbach; Casting, Jane Jenkins, Janet Hirshenson; a Brian Grazer/Scott Rudin production; Distributed by Buena Vista Pictures; Dolby Digital Stereo; Technicolor; Rated R; 121 minutes; November release

Mel Gibson

CAST

Tom Mullen . . . . Mel Gibson
Kate Mullen . . . . Rene Russo
Sean Mullen . . . . Brawley Nolte
Jimmy Shaker . . . . Gary Sinise
Agent Lonnie Hawkins . . . . Delroy Lindo
Maris Connor . . . . Lili Taylor
Clark Barnes . . . . Liev Schreiber
Cubby Barnes . . . . Donnie Wahlberg
Miles Roberts . . . . Evan Handler
Agent Kimba Welch . . . . Nancy Ticotin
Agent Jack Sickler . . . . Michael Gaston
Agent Paul Rhodes . . . . Kevin Neil McCready
Wallace . . . . Paul Guilfoyle
Bob Stone . . . . Allen Bernstein
David Torres . . . . Jose Zuniga
Jackie Brown . . . . Dan Hedaya
Fatima . . . . Iraida Polanco
Roberto . . . . John Ortiz
Man at Party . . . . Mike Hodge
Mayor Barresi . . . . Paul Geier
Woman at Party . . . . Louisa Marie
Guest at Party . . . . Edward Francis Joseph
Reporter Guest . . . . A.J. Benza
Nelson . . . . Peter Anthony Tambakis
Doorman . . . . Tony Hoty
Agent Sam . . . . Daniel May Wong
Agent Dewey . . . . John Short
Technician . . . . Ed Jupp
NYPD/SWAT . . . . Stephen Oates
FBI/SWAT Leader . . . . Gene Harrison
FBI/SWAT Team . . . . Mick O'Rourke, Henry Kingi Jr., Roy Farfel
FBI/SWAT Sniper . . . . Lex D. Geddings
News Reporter . . . . Donna Hanover
News Anchors . . . . Rosanna Scotto, Tony Potts
Newshound . . . . John "Spike" Finnerty
Don Campbell . . . . Todd Hallowell
Bank Manager . . . . Michael Countryman
Agent Levin . . . . Chris Lopata
Agent Lambert . . . . John Richard Hartmann
and Joe Bacino, Carl S. Redding, James Georgiades, Christian Maelen, David Vadim (Cops), Addie O'Donnell, Judy Hudson, Mitzie Pratt, Lynne Redding (Reporters), Anton Evangelista (FBI Agent), Richard Price (Detective #1), Joe Badalucco, Jr. (Liquor Store Cop), Dell Maara (Liquor Store Perp), Tommy Allen (Detective at Kidnap House), John Dorish (Paramedic), Vincent Burns (Detective Doran), Brad Brewer, Darren Brown, Marvin Brown, Glenn King (The Crowtations), Cheryl Howard (Science Fair Coordinator), James Ritz (Science Fair Judge), Anna Marie Wieder (Woman at Science Fair), Joan D. Lowry (Mayor's Wife), Craig Castaldo (Radioman), Teodorina Bello, J.J. Chaback, Lori Tan Chinn (Women on Street), Carl Don, Nathaniel Freeman, Phil Parolisi, Rafael Osorio (Men on Street), Leslie Devlin, Lewis Dodley (Newscasters), John Brian Rogers, Jeffrey Kaufman (ND Cops), Mark Smith (Undercover Cop), Jim Whalen (Detective), Kim Snyder (Kate's Friend), Panicker Upendran (Store Owner)

Lili Taylor

The son of wealthy corporate executive Tom Mullen is kidnapped and held ransom for $2 million dollars. Suggested by the 1956 MGM film Ransom *which starred Glenn Ford and Donna Reed.*

Mel Gibson, Delroy Lindo

Jeff Bridges, Brenda Vaccaro, Barbra Streisand, Mimi Rogers

Barbra Streisand

THE MIRROR HAS TWO FACES

(TRISTAR) Producers, Barbra Streisand, Arnon Milchan; Executive Producer, Cis Corman; Director, Barbra Streisand; Screen Story and Screenplay, Richard LaGravenese; Based on the motion picture *Le Miroir a Deux Faces*, written by André Cayatte and Gérard Oury, and directed by Andre Cayatte; Co-Executive Producer, Ronald Schwary; Photography, Dante Spinotti, Andrzej Bartkowiak; Designer, Tom John; Editor, Jeff Werner; Costumes, Theoni V. Aldredge; Music, Marvin Hamlisch; Love Theme Composed by Barbra Streisand; Song: "I Finally Found Someone" written by Barbra Streisand, Marvin Hamlisch, R.J. Lange, Bryan Adams/performed by Barbra Streisand, Bryan Adams; Casting, Bonnie Finnegan, Todd Thaler; an Arnon Milchan/Barwood Films production, presented in association with Phoenix Pictures; Dolby SDDS Stereo; Technicolor; Rated PG-13; 126 minutes; November release

CAST

Rose Morgan	Barbra Streisand
Gregory Larkin	Jeff Bridges
Hannah Morgan	Lauren Bacall
Henry Fine	George Segal
Claire	Mimi Rogers
Alex	Pierce Brosnan
Doris	Brenda Vaccaro
Barry	Austin Pendleton
Candy	Elle MacPherson
First Student	Ali Marsh
Sara Myers	Leslie Stefanson
Professor	Taina Elg
Felicia	Lucy Avery Brooks
Felicia (Video)	Amber Smith
Claire's Masseur	David Kinzie
Rabbi	Rabbi Howard S. Herman
Reverend	Thomas Hartman
Trevor	Trevor Ristow
Mike (Student)	Brian Schwary
Jill (Student)	Jill Tara Kushner
Randy (Student)	Randy Pearlstein
Stacie (Student)	Stacie Sumter
Taxi Stealer	Cindy Guyer
Taxi Driver	Thomas Saccio
Waiter	Andrew Parks
Jimmy the Waiter	Jimmy Baio
Henry's First Date	Emma Fann
Henry's Second Date	Laura Bailey
Justice of the Peace	Mike Hodge
Gloria	Anne O'Sullivan
Aerobics Instructors	Lisa Wheeler, Kirk Moore
Make-up Artist	Regina Viotto
Hair Colorist	Paul LaBreque
Waiter	Ruggero Comploj
Mr. Jenkins	William Cain
Doorman	Adam LeFevre
Irate Woman	JoAn Mollison
Opera Man	Carlo Scibelli

and Sandi Schroeder, Kiyoko M. Hairston, Ben Weber, Christopher Keys (Students)

Rose Morgan, convinced that she is too unattractive to find a man, finds herself dating Gregory Larkin, who is searching for a relationship free of sex. The original 1958 French film starred Michelle Morgan and Bourvil.This film received Oscar nominations for supporting actress (Lauren Bacall) and song ("I Finally Found Someone").

Lauren Bacall, Barbra Streisand

Jeff Bridges, George Segal, Elle MacPherson

Pierce Brosnan, Barbra Streisand

Jeff Bridges, Barbra Streisand

Lauren Bacall, Jeff Bridges, Barbra Streisand

SET IT OFF

(NEW LINE CINEMA) Producers, Dale Pollock, Oren Koules; Executive Producers, Mary Parent, F. Gary Gray; Director, F. Gary Gray; Screenplay, Kate Lanier, Takashi Bufford; Story, Takashi Bufford; Co-Producers, Takashi Bufford, Allen Alsobrook; Associate Producer, Robert J. Degus; Photography, Marc Reshovsky; Designer, Robb Wilson King; Editor, John Carter; Music, Christopher Young; Costumes, Sylvia Vega Vasquez; Casting, Robi Reed-Humes; a Peak Production; Dolby SDDS Stereo; Super 35 Widescreen; Deluxe color; Rated R; 121 minutes; November release

CAST

Stony	Jada Pinkett
Cleo	Queen Latifah
Frankie	Vivica A. Fox
Tisean	Kimberly Elise
Detective Strode	John C. McGinley
Keith	Blair Underwood
Jajuan	Vincent and Van Baum
Stevie	Chaz Lamar Shepard
Luther	Thom Byrd
Nate	Charlie Robinson
Detective Waller	Ella Joyce
Ms. Wells	Anna Maria Horsford
Ursuala	Samantha MacLachlan
Lorenz	WC
Darnell	Lawrence Calhoun, Jr.
Mr. Zachery	Edmond Schaff
Tanika	Natalie Desselle
Black Sam	Dr. Dre
Bruce	Bruce Williams
Doctor	Gordon Embry
Captain Fredricks	Charles Walker
Nigel	Geoff Callan
Patrice	Roseanna Iversen
Pete Rodney	Jeris Poindexter
Luther's Girlfriend	Tamara Clatterbuck
Waitress	Tonia Rowe
B.B.	Big Daddy Wayne
TV Anchor	Mark Thompson
Bundy	Darryl Gibson
Detective	Twain Tyler
Homeless Man	Walter Robles
Cop	George Fisher
Bank Customer	Brantley Bush

Four women, believing that society will not give them a chance to get ahead financially, become bank robbers.

Queen Latifah, Kimberly Elise, Vivica A. Fox, Jada Pinkett

Blair Underwood

Jada Pinkett, Kimberly Elise, Queen Latifah, Vivica A. Fox

STAR TREK: FIRST CONTACT

(PARAMOUNT) Producer, Rick Berman; Executive Producer, Martin Hornstein; Director, Jonathan Frakes; Screenplay, Brannon Braga, Ronald D. Moore; Story, Rick Berman, Brannon Braga, Ronald D. Moore; Based upon *Star Trek* created by Gene Roddenberry; Photography, Matthew F. Leonetti; Designer, Herman Zimmerman; Editor, John W. Wheeler; Costumes, Deborah Everton; Co-Producer, Peter Lauritson; Visual Effects Supervisor, John Knoll; Music, Jerry Goldsmith; Casting, Junie Lowry-Johnson, Ron Surma; a Rick Berman production; Dolby Stereo; Panavision; Deluxe color; Rated PG-13; 110 minutes; November release

CAST

Capt. Jean-Luc Picard	Patrick Stewart
Cmmdr. William Riker	Jonathan Frakes
Lt. Cmmdr. Data	Brent Spiner
Lt. Cmmdr. Geordi La Forge	LeVar Burton
Lt. Cmmdr. Worf	Michael Dorn
Dr. Beverly C. Crusher	Gates McFadden
Lt. Cmmdr. Deanna Troi	Marina Sirtis
Lily Sloane	Alfre Woodard
Zefram Cochran	James Cromwell
Borg Queen	Alice Krige
Security Officers	Michael Horton, Scott Strozier
Lt. Hawk	Neal McDonough
Eiger	Marnie McPhail
Holographic Doctor	Robert Picardo
Lt. Barclay	Dwight Schultz
Defiant Conn Officer	Adam Scott
Admiral Hayes	Jack Shearer
Porter	Eric Steinberg
Nurse Ogawa	Patti Yasutake
Guards	Victor Bevine, David Cowgill, Scott Haven, Annette Helde
Bartender	C.J. Bau
Ruby	Hillary Hayes
Singer in Nightclub	Julie Morgan
Henchman	Ronald R. Rondell
Nicky the Nose	Don Stark
Vulcan	Cully Fredricksen
Townsperson	Tamara Lee Krinsky

and Don Fischer, J.R. Horsting, Heinrich James, Andrew Palmer, Jon David Weigand, Dan Woren, Robert L. Zachar (Borg)

The crew of the Enterprise follow their enemy, the Borg, back in time to Earth to stop them from preventing the space flight of Zefram Cochrane which resulted in the first contact between humans and beings from another world. The second theatrical film to feature the cast of the syndicated tv series "Star Trek: The Next Generation," following the 1994 Paramount release Star Trek: Generations. This film received an Oscar nomination for makeup.

©Paramount Pictures

Alice Krige, Patrick Stewart

Jonathan Frakes, LeVar Burton

Jonathan Frakes, James Cromwell, LeVar Burton, Marina Sirtis

Alfre Woodard, Brent Spiner, Gates McFadden, Patrick Stewart

Sinbad, Arnold Schwarzenegger

Arnold Schwarzenegger, James Belushi

JINGLE ALL THE WAY

(20TH CENTURY FOX) Producers, Chris Columbus, Mark Radcliffe, Michael Barnathan; Executive Producer, Richard Vane; Director, Brian Levant; Screenplay, Randy Kornfield; Photography, Victor J. Kemper; Designer, Leslie McDonald; Editors, Kent Beyda, Wilton Henderson; Co-Producers, Jennifer Blum, James Mulay; Associate Producer, Paula DuPre' Pesmen; Music, David Newman; Costumes, Jay Hurley; Casting, Judy Taylor; a 1492 Picture; Dolby Digital Stereo; Panavision; Deluxe color; Rated PG; 88 minutes; November release

CAST

Howard Langston	Arnold Schwarzenegger
Myron Larabee	Sinbad
Ted Maltin	Phil Hartman
Liz Langston	Rita Wilson
Officer Hummell	Robert Conrad
DJ	Martin Mull
Jamie Langston	Jake Lloyd
Mall Santa	James Belushi
Johnny	E.J. De La Pena
First Lady	Laraine Newman
Billy	Justin Chapman
President	Harvey Korman
Dementor	Richard Moll
Turbo Man	Daniel Riordan

and Jeff Deist (TV Booster/Puppeteer), Nada Despotovich (Margaret), Ruth Afton Hjelmgren (Single Mother Judy), Caroline Kaiser (Single Mother Mary), Samuel B. Morris (Sensei), Shawn Hamilton (Sensei Assistant), Lewis Dauber (Toy Store Manager), Bill Schoppert (Father at Toy Store), Courtney Goodell (Little Girl at Toy Store), George Fisher (Daring Shopper), Chris Parnell (Toy Store Sales Clerk), Patrick Richwood (Toy Store Co-Worker), Kate McGregor-Stewart (Toy Store Customer), Marcus Toji (Little Boy With Car Remote), Steve Hendrickson, Peter Syvertsen (Fathers on Phones), Mo Collins (Mother on Phone), John Rothman (Mall Toy Store Manager), Christopher Slater, Robert Southgate (Mall Toy Store Employees), Allison Benner, Hayley Benner (Toddlers), Sandra K. Horner (Toddler's Angry Mom), Phyllis Wright, Marvette Knight (Angry Moms), Danny Woodburn (Tony the Elf), Bruce Bohne (Santa at Warehouse Door), Paul "The Giant" Wight (Huge Santa), Ron Gene Browne, Robert Tee Clark, James Riddle, Bill Wilson (Santas in Warehouse), Alan Blumenfeld (Cop at Santa's Warehouse), Traci Christofore (Little Girl Petting Reindeer), Sandy Thomas (Mother in Neighborhood), Martin Ruben (Father in Neighborhood), Nick La Tour (Counterman), Peter Breitmayer (Sparky), Marianne Muellerleile (Tow Truck Driver), Phil Morris (Gale Force), Amy Pietz (Liza Tisch), Judy Slasky (Snoopy), Walter Von Huene (Taxi Driver), Steve Van Wormer (Turbo Man Float Parade Worker), Curtis Armstrong (Chain Smoking Booster), Jim Meskimen (Police Officer at Parade), Martin Valinsky (Police Officer Escorting Myron), Rochelle Vallese (Girl at Parade), Deena Driskill (Barbie), Spencer Klein (Commercial)

On Christmas Eve Howard Langston goes on a desperate search for the Turbo Man action figure he had promised to buy for his son.

©Twentieth Century Fox

Arnold Schwarzenegger, Phil Hartman

Rita Wilson

THE WAR AT HOME

(TOUCHSTONE) Producers, Emilio Estevez, Brad Krevoy, Steve Stabler, James Duff; Executive Producer, Tracie Graham Rice; Co-Producers, Mickey McDermott, Jonathan Brandstein; Co-Executive Producer, Chad Oman; Director, Emilo Estevez; Screenplay, James Duff, based on his play *Homefront*; Photography, Peter Levy; Designer, Eve Cauley; Editor, Craig Bassett; Music, Basil Poledouris; Costumes, Grania Preston; Associate Producers, Jeff Ivers, Peter Richards; Casting, Judy Taylor; an Avatar Entertainment production; Dolby Digital Stereo; Panavision; Technicolor; Rated R; 124 minutes; November release

Martin Sheen, Kathy Bates

CAST

Maurine Collier . . . . Kathy Bates
Bob Collier . . . . Martin Sheen
Karen Collier . . . . Kimberly Williams
Jeremy Collier . . . . Emilio Estevez
Melissa . . . . Carla Gugino
Donald . . . . Corin Nemec
David . . . . Geoffrey Blake
Professor Tracey . . . . Ann Hearn
Private Poe . . . . Marcus H. Nelson
Lieutenant . . . . Michael Wiseman
Coffee House Singer . . . . Jena Kraus
Bus Station Clerk . . . . Chad Morgan
Marjoree . . . . Penny Allen
Brenda . . . . Renee Estevez
Viet Cong . . . . Tuan Tran
Little Girl . . . . Paloma Estevez
and Efrain Briones Jr., Tyler Shea Cone, Harvey L. Cyphers, Christopher Dahlberg, Chris Drewy, Reed Frerichs, Anthony D-Wayne Kitchen, Enoch Lawrence, Joe Lowry, Le'Roy Nellis II, Lee Andrew Pachicano, Jeff D. Richey, Yogi Rise, Octavio O. Sanchez, Derrick Sanders, William Carvell Townsel, Paula A. Watkins (Jeremy's Squad)

Emilio Estevez, Kimberly Williams

Jeremy Collier, back in his hometown after serving in Vietnam, is still haunted by his experiences in battle and cannot find anyone to whom he can turn to heal the pain.

©*Buena Vista Pictures Distribution*

Kathy Bates, Martin Sheen, Emilio Estevez

Billy Bob Thornton, Lucas Black

Dwight Yoakam

Dwight Yoakam, Billy Bob Thornton, John Ritter

J.T. Walsh, Billy Bob Thornton

SLING BLADE

(MIRAMAX) Producers, Brandon Rosser, David L. Bushell; Executive Producer, Larry Meistrich; Director/Screenplay, Billy Bob Thornton; Photography, Barry Markowitz; Editor, Hughes Winborne; Designer, Clark Hunter; Music, Daniel Lanois; Costumes, Douglas Hall; Casting, Sarah Tackett; a Shooting Gallery presentation; Dolby Stereo; Color; Rated R; 134 minutes; November release

CAST

Karl Childers	Billy Bob Thornton
Doyle Hargraves	Dwight Yoakam
Charles Bushman	J.T. Walsh
Vaughan Cunningham	John Ritter
Frank Wheatley	Lucas Black
Linda Wheatley	Natalie Canerday
Jerry Wolridge	James Hampton
Karl's Father	Robert Duvall
Bill Cox	Rick Dial
Scooter Hodges	Brent Briscoe
Melinda	Christy Ward
Marsha Dwiggins	Sarah Boss
Theresa Evans	Kathy Sue Brown
Melvin	Wendell Rafferty
Morris	Col. Bruce Hampton, Ret.
Terence	Vic Chestnutt
Monty Johnson	Mickey Jones
Randy Horsefeathers	Ian Moore
Mrs. Woolridge	Judy Pryor Trice
Bubba Woolridge	Scott Stewart
Sister	Betty Lynn Hall
Frostee Cream	Jim Jarmusch
Preacher	Gary Don Fletcher
Albert	Tim Holder
Freddy	Tom Kagy

and Stacy Barrow (Woolridge Secretary), Jackie Stewart (Walter), Jamie Stewart (Teenage Boy), D.J. Royston (Housekeeper), Lacy Bailey (Karen), Raymond Lewallen (Ticket Agent), Bill Glassock (Voice of Old Man)

Mildly retarded Karl Childers returns to society after spending 25-years in a mental asylum for having killed his mother and her lover with a sling blade. 1996 Academy Award-winner for Best Screenplay Adaptation. The film received an additional nomination for actor (Billy Bob Thornton).

©*Miramax Films*

Billy Bob Thornton

John Ritter, Natalie Canerday, Billy Bob Thornton, Lucas Black

101 DALMATIANS

(WALT DISNEY PICTURES) Producers, John Hughes, Ricardo Mestres; Executive Producer, Edward S. Feldman; Director, Stephen Herek; Screenplay, John Hughes; Based upon the novel *The One Hundred and One Dalmatians* by Dodie Smith; Photography, Adrian Biddle; Designer, Assheton Gorton; Editor, Trudy Ship; Costumes, Anthony Powell, Rosemary Burrows; Music, Michael Kamen; Associate Producer, Rebekah Rudd; Visual Effects Supervisor, Michael Owens; Special Visual Effects and Animation, Industrial Light & Magic; Stunts, Simon Crane; Casting, Celestia Fox, Marcia Ross; a Great Oaks production; Distributed by Buena Vista Pictures; Dolby Digital Stereo; Panavision; Technicolor; Rated G; 103 minutes; November release

CAST

Cruella DeVil	Glenn Close
Roger	Jeff Daniels
Anita	Joely Richardson
Nanny	Joan Plowright
Jasper	Hugh Laurie
Horace	Mark Williams
Skinner	John Shrapnel
Alonzo	Tim McInnerny
Frederick	Hugh Fraser
Herbert	Zohren Weiss
Alan	Mark Haddigan
Police Inspector	Michael Percival
Minister	Neville Phillips
Pensioner with Bulldog	John Evans
Women on Park Bench	Hilda Braid, Margery Mason
Doorman	John Benfield
Police Officers	Andrew Readman, John Peters
Arresting Officer	Bill Stewart
Doctor	Gerald Paris
Veterinarian	Joe Lacey
Television News Reporter	Brian Capron

Dalmatians Pongo and Perdy find their happy household disrupted when their new-born puppies are stolen by fur-loving Cruella DeVil. Remake of the 1961 animated Disney feature One Hundred and One Dalmatians.

©*Disney Enterprises, Inc.*

Glenn Close

Joan Plowright

Joely Richardson, Jeff Daniels

Hugh Laurie, Mark Williams

DAYLIGHT

(UNIVERSAL) Producers, John Davis, Joseph M. Singer, David T. Friendly; Executive Producer, Raffaella De Laurentiis; Director, Rob Cohen; Screenplay, Leslie Bohem; Co-Producer, Hester Hargett; Photography, David Eggby; Designer, Benjamin Fernandez; Editor, Peter Amundson; Music, Randy Edelman; Costumes, Thomas Casterline, Isis Mussenden; Special Effects Supervisor, Kit West; Casting, Margery Simkin; a Davis Entertainment/Joseph M. Singer production; DTS Stereo; Deluxe color; Rated PG-13; 114 minutes; December release

CAST

Kit Latura	Sylvester Stallone
Madelyne Thompson	Amy Brenneman
Roy Nord	Viggo Mortensen
Frank Kraft	Dan Hedaya
Steven Crighton	Jay O. Sanders
Sarah Crighton	Karen Young
Eleanor Trilling	Claire Bloom
Grace	Vanessa Bell Calloway
Mikey	Renoly Santiago
Roger Trilling	Colin Fox
Ashley Crighton	Danielle Harris
Latonya	Trina McGree-Davis
Kadeem	Marcello Thedford
Vincent	Sage Stallone
Boom	Jo Anderson
Chief Dennis Wilson	Mark Rolston
Ms. London	Rosemary Forsyth
Gem Dealer	Luoyong Wang
Norman Bassett	Barry Newman
George Tyrell	Stan Shaw
Grunges	Marc Chadwick, Candace Miller, Lee Oakes
Ms. Doctor	Sakina Jaffrey
Mr. Doctor	Albert Macklin
Cannister Truck Driver	Tony Munafo
Dispatcher	Joseph Ragno
Weller	Nestor Serrano
Police Chief	Harold Bradley
TB Marketing Executive	Stephen Nalewicki
Jonno	John Lees
Father	Robert Sommer
Young Woman	Lenore Lohman

and Mark DeAlessandro, Lisa McCullough (Cops), Penny Crone, Madison, Ed Wheeler, Dan Daily, Stephen James, Isis Mussenden (Reporters)

Kit Latura races against time to save some commuters who have been trapped inside of an underwater tunnel after a devestating explosion has sealed off all exits. This film received an Oscar nomination for sound effects editing.

Amy Brenneman, Sylvester Stallone

Sylvester Stallone

Sylvester Stallone, Amy Brenneman

Sylvester Stallone (c)

Daniel Day-Lewis, Joan Allen

Daniel Day-Lewis

Winona Ryder, Charlayne Woodard

THE CRUCIBLE

(20TH CENTURY FOX) Producers, Robert A. Miller, David V. Picker; Director, Nicholas Hytner; Screenplay, Arthur Miller, based on his play; Photography, Andrew Dunn; Designer, Lilly Kilvert; Editor, Tariq Anwar; Music, George Funton; Costumes, Bob Crowley; Co-Producer, Diana Pokorny; Casting, Donna Isaacson, Daniel Swee; a David V. Picker production; Dolby Stereo; Technicolor; Rated PG-13; 123 minutes; November release

CAST

John Proctor	Daniel Day-Lewis
Abigail Williams	Winona Ryder
Judge Danforth	Paul Scofield
Elizabeth Proctor	Joan Allen
Reverend Parris	Bruce Davison
Reverend Hale	Rob Campbell
Thomas Putnam	Jeffrey Jones
Giles Corey	Peter Vaughan
Mary Warren	Karron Graves
Tituba	Charlayne Woodard
Ann Putnam	Frances Conroy
Rebecca Nurse	Elizabeth Lawrence
Judge Sewall	George Gaynes
Martha Corey	Mary Pat Gleason
Judge Hathorne	Robert Breuler
Betty Parris	Rachael Bella
Ruth Putnam	Ashley Peldon
Francis Nurse	Tom McDermott
Ezekiel Cheever	John Griesemer
Marshal Herrick	Michael Gaston
George Jacobs	William Preston
Goody Osborne	Ruth Maleczech
Goody Good	Sheila Pinkham
Dr. Griggs	Peter Maloney
Mercy Lewis	Kali Rocha
Joanna Preston	Taylor Stanley
Deliverance Fuller	Lian-Marie Holmes
Margaret Kenney	Charlotte Melén
Hannah Brown	Carmella Mulvihill
Deborah Flint	Jessie Kilguss
Rachel Buxton	Simone Marean
Lydia Sheldon	Amee Gray
Sarah Pope	Anna V. Boksenbaum
Esther Wilkens	Mary Reardon
Joseph Proctor	Alexander Streit
Daniel Proctor	Michael McKinstry
Mrs. Griggs	Dorothy Brodesser
Goody Sibber	Dossy Peabody
Goody Barrow	Mara Clark
Goody Bellows	Jane Pulkkinen
Dorcas Bellows	Katrina Nevin
Isaiah Goodkind	Will Lyman
Townswomen	Karen MacDonald, Sheila Ferrini, June Lewin
Goat Owner	Ken Cheeseman
Putnam's Servant	Steven Ochoa

In 1692 a gang of teenage girls accused of witchcraft set off a rash of accusations throughout the town of Salem, bringing several citizens to trial for bonding with the Devil. Previous film version The Witches of Salem/The Crucible *starred Yves Montand and Simone Signoret and was released by Kingsley International in the U.S. in 1958. The original 1953 Broadway production starred Arthur Kennedy and Beatrice Straight. This film received Oscar nomninations for supporting actress (Joan Allen) and screenplay adaptation.*

Robert Breuler, Paul Scofield, George Gaynes

Paul Scofield, Karron Graves

Ashley Peldon, Bruce Davison, Winona Ryder

Elizabeth Lawrence, Daniel Day-Lewis, Mary Pat Gleason

Winona Ryder (c)

Drew Barrymore, Edward Norton

Julia Roberts

Natalie Portman, Gaby Hoffman, Barbara Hollander

EVERYONE SAYS I LOVE YOU

(MIRAMAX) Producer, Robert Greenhut; Executive Producers, Jean Doumanian, J.E. Beaucaire; Co-Executive Producers, Jack Rollins, Charles H. Joffe, Letty Aronson; Director/Screenplay, Woody Allen; Photography, Carlo DiPalma; Designer, Santo Loquasto; Editor, Susan E. Morse; Costumes, Jeffrey Kurland; Co-Producer, Helen Roth; Choreographer, Graciela Daniele; Music Arranger/Conducted, Dick Hyman; Casting, Juliet Taylor; from Sweetland Films; Color; Rated R; 100 minutes; December release

CAST

Bob	Alan Alda
Joe	Woody Allen
Skylar	Drew Barrymore
Scott	Lukas Haas
Steffi	Goldie Hawn
Lane	Gaby Hoffman
DJ	Natasha Lyonne
Holden	Edward Norton
Laura	Natalie Portman
Von	Julia Roberts
Charles Ferry	Tim Roth
Holden's Father	David Ogden Stiers
Nannies	Diva Gray, Ami Almendral, Madeline Balmaceda
Nurse	Vivian Cherry
Old Woman	Tommie Baxter
Homeless Man	Jeff Derocker
Mannequins	Cherylyn Jones, Tina Paul, Vikki Schnurr
Doorman	Kevin Hagan
Frieda	Trude Klein
Himself	Itzhak Perlman
Pianist	Navah Perlman
Claire	Barbara Hollander
Jeffrey Vandermost	John Griffin
Psychiatrist	Waltrudis Buck
Grandpa	Patrick Cranshaw
Cop	Isiah Whitlock
Harry Winston Salesman	Edward Hibbert
Le Cirque Waiter	Frederick Rolf
X-Ray Room Doctor	Timothy Jerome
DJ's Venice Date	Paolo Seganti
Alberto	Andrea Piedimonte
Greg	Robert Knepper
Ken	Billy Crudup
Cab Driver	Robert Khakh
Holden's Mother	Scotty Bloch
Scott's Doctor	Ed Hodson
Bob's Doctor	Michel Moinot
Escaped Convicts	Tony Sirico, Ray Garvey

and Kevin Bogue, Colleen Dunn, Pamela Everett, Susan Misner, Gregory Mitchell, Dana Moore, Troy Myers, Joe Orrach, Michael O'Steen, Tina Paul, Luis Martin Perez, Krissy Richmond (Harry Winston Dancers), Daisy Prince, Linda Maurel-Sithole, Helen Miles, Arlene Martell (Nurses), Rene Ceballos, Ruth Gottschall, Colton Green, Lisa Leguillou, Joe Locarro, Monica McSwain, Jill Nicklaus, Andrew Pacho, Luis Martin Perez, John Selya, Myra Lucretia Taylor, Jo Telford (Hospital Dancers), Gerry Burkhardt, Eileen Casey, Shelley Frankel, Fred C. Mann III, Kathy Sanson, Valda Setterfield, Frank Pietri, Luis Martin Perez (Ghost Dancers), Robert Walker, Devalle Hayes, Damon McCloud (Rap Group), Tommy John, Lindsay Canuel, Richard Cummings, Kristen Pettet, Patrick Lavery, Christy Romano, Jonathan Giordano, Gabriel Millman (Trick-or-Treat Children), Don Correia, Sean Grant, Roland Hayes, Darren Lee, Delphine T. Mantz, Joanne McHugh, John Mineo, Cynthia Onrubia, Luis Martin Perez, Willie Rosario, Nancy Ticotin, Jerome Vivona (Groucho Party Dancers)

A musical-comedy look at the complicated love lives of a well-to-do Manhattan family.

©Miramax FIlms

Goldie Hawn, Alan Alda

Woody Allen, Natasha Lyonne

TIm Roth

Billy Crudup, Natasha Lyonne

Drew Barrymore

Edward Norton, Drew Barrymore, Director Woody Allen

THE SUBSTANCE OF FIRE

(MIRAMAX) Producers, Jon Robin Baitz, Randy Finch, Ron Kastner; Director, Daniel Sullivan; Screenplay, Jon Robin Baitz, based on his play; Co-Producer, Lemore Syvan; Photography, Robert Yeoman; Designer, John Lee Beatty; Editor, Pamela Martin; Music, Joseph Vitarelli; Costumes, Jess Goldstein; Casting, Meg Simon; Dolby Stereo; Technicolor; Rated R; 101 minutes; December release

CAST

Isaac Geldhart	Ron Rifkin
Sarah Geldhart	Sarah Jessica Parker
Martin Geldhart	Timothy Hutton
Aaron Geldhart	Tony Goldwyn
Louis Foukold	Ronny Graham
Val Chenard	Gil Bellows
Gene Byck	Eric Bogosian
Max	Roger Rees
Ms. Barzakian	Elizabeth Franz
Young Isaac Geldhart	Benjamin Ungar
Old Printer	Tom McDermott
Otto the Printer	George Morfogen
Cora Cahn	Lee Grant
Mr. Otani Junior	Andrew Pang
Mr. Otani Senior	Edmund Ikeda
Stewart	John Sullivan
Rachel	Sophia Salguero
Peter	John Patrick Walker
Nurse	Viola Davis
Dr. Bernard Kramer	David S. Howard
Young Martin	Gregory Burke
Mr. Musselblatt	Adolph Green
Mr. Cox	William Cain
New Receptionist	Alec Mapa
Miguel	Edgar Martinez
Book Binder	John Christopher Jones
Mr. McCormack Senior	Dick Latessa
Mr. McCormack Junior	Patrick Page
Rizzoli Book Buyer	Kate Forbes
Esme	Gloria Irizarry
Reena Geldhart	Barbara Eda-Young
Young Book Clerk	Matt McGrath
Dennis the Taylor	Jose Ramon Rosario
Customer with Shoes	William Meisle
Maitre D'	Gina Torres
Martha Hackett	Debra Monk
Rabbi	Rabbi Marc Schneider

A rigid book publisher, haunted by memories of the Holocaust, refuses to publish a book that could save his floundering company, causing his three children to come forward to take over the business. Ron Rifkin and Sarah Jessica Parker repeat their roles from the 1991 Off-Broadway production.

© Miramax Films

Tony Goldwyn, Ron Rifkin, Sarah Jessica Parker

Timothy Hutton

Ron Rifkin, Tony Goldwyn

John Patrick Walker, Tony Goldwyn, Sarah Jessica Parker

THE PREACHER'S WIFE

(TOUCHSTONE/SAMUEL GOLDWYN CO.) Producer, Samuel Goldwyn, Jr.; Executive Producers, Elliot Abbott, Robert Greenhut; Director, Penny Marshall; Screenplay, Nat Mauldin, Allan Scott; Based on a screenplay by Robert E. Sherwood and Leonrado Bercovici, from the novel *The Bishop's Wife* by Robert Nathan; Co-Producers, Debra Martin Chase, Amy Lemisch, Timothy M. Bourne; Photography, Miroslav Ondricek; Designer, Bill Groom; Editors, Stephen A. Rotter, George Bowers; Costumes, Cynthia Flynt; Music, Hans Zimmer; Casting, Paula Herold; a Samuel Goldwyn, Jr. production in association with Parkway Productions and Mundy Lane Entertainment; Dolby Digitial Stereo; Technicolor; Rated PG; 124 minutes; December release

Whitney Houston, Denzel Washington

CAST

Dudley	Denzel Washington
Julia Biggs	Whitney Houston
Rev. Henry Biggs	Courtney B. Vance
Joe Hamilton	Gregory Hines
Marguerite Coleman	Jenifer Lewis
Beverly	Loretta Devine
Jeremiah Biggs	Justin Pierre Edmund
Britsloe	Lionel Richie
Saul Jeffreys	Paul Bates
Osbert	Lex Monson
Hakim	Darvel Davis, Jr.
Billy Eldridge	Willie James Stiggers, Jr.
Anna Eldridge	Marcella Lowery
Mrs. Havergal	Cissy Houston
Teens	Aaron A. McConnaughey, Shyheim Franklin, Taral Hicks, Kennan Scott
Pizza Man	Jernard B. Burks
Robber	Michael Alexander Jackson
Liquor Store Owner	Jaime Tirelli
Arlene Chattan	Shari Headley
Judge	Lizan Mitchell
Bailiff	Robert Colston
Robbie	Victor Williams
Receptionist	Juliehera Destefano
Deborah Paige	Charlotte d'Amboise
Mary Halford	Delores Mitchell

and David Langston Smyrl (Hanley's Waiter), Harsh Nayyar (Christmas Tree Man), Mervyn Warren, Roy Haynes, George Coleman, Ted Dunbar, Jamil Nasser (Jazz Quintet), Helmar Augustus Cooper (Johnson Keeley), St. Cecilia Choir (Hamilton's Carolers), Mary Bond Davis (Bernita), Toukie Smith (Teleprompter Operator), The George Mass Choir & Band: Mozelle Hawkins Allen, Eloise Beasley, Yolanda Beasley-Prime, Cassondra M. Breedlove, Dirk Chaney, Brenda J. Childs, Anthony Dean Copeland, Hayward Cromartie, Betty Cromartie Davis, Valerie Inez Edwards, Kimberly M. Garrett, Rutha Harris, Carolyn Henry, Gary Nuckles-Holt, Teretha G. Houston, Angela L. Jones, Morris Vernon Jones, Rose Merry Jordan, Jacqueline Martin, Betty Matthews, Naguanda Miller, Sharon A. Mitchell, Rev. Corey McGee, Beverly S. Nixon, Krishna Presha, Jacqulyn V. Saunders, Constance Small, Troy L. Sneed Sr., Rev. Lawrence K. Thomas, Ulisa A. Thomas, V. Ranaldo Welcome, Berta J. Williams, Kimberly L. Wright; Musicians: Steven Brown, Rick Carter, Sterling Holloman II, Rev. Kenneth Paden, Dwain L. White (St. Matthew's Choir & Band), Aaron Jordan, Yakin Manassah Jordan (Eldridge Kids), Joshua Jordan (Donkey Nativity Choir), Tiffany Joseph (Shepherd Nativity Choir), Jessica Malloy (Mary Nativity Choir), Amia Hart (Child), Brittany Anderson (Sheep Nativity Choir), Christopher Malloy (Angels Nativity Choir), Andal Fequiere (Joseph), Mark Gilbert, Michael Marshall, Shaun Purefoy (3 Wise Men); Tiffiny Monet Graham, Khalia Hamilton-Montoute (Angels), Marquis Bowen-Wallace, Lakeya Enos (Shepherds), Christine Lameisha Koon (Camel), Anthony Biggham (Lamb), Taleah Enos (Ox), Soul Tempo: Jerry Brunsin, Anthony Burnett, Kevin Mitchell, Phillip Mitchell (4 Painting Singers), Robert Greenhut (Hamilton's Associate)

Whitney Houston, Courtney B. Vance, Justin Pierre Edmund, Jenifer Lewis, Darvel Davis, Jr.

An angel named Dudley comes to the aid of the Reverend Henry Biggs and his family who are hoping to build a new church for their community. Remake of the 1947 RKO-Samuel Goldwyn film The Bishop's Wife *which starred Cary Grant (Dudley), Loretta Young (Julia), and David Niven (Henry).*

Courtney B, Vance, Gregory Hines, Robert Greenhut

Kelly Preston

Cuba Gooding, Jr., Tom Cruise

Tom Cruise, Jonathan Lipnicki

Cuba Gooding, Jr. Regina King

Renee Zellweger, Bonnie Hunt

Rene Zellweger, Tom Cruise

JERRY MAGUIRE

(TRISTAR) Producers, James L. Brooks, Laurence Mark, Richard Sakai, Cameron Crowe; Director/Screenplay, Cameron Crowe; Co-Producers, Bruce S. Pustin, John D. Schofield; Photography, Janusz Kaminski; Designer, Stephen Lineweaver; Editor, Joe Hutshing; Costumes, Betsy Heimann; Music Supervisor, Danny Bramson; Executive for Gracie Films, Bridget Johnson; Casting, Gail Levin; a Gracie Films production; Dolby SDDS Stereo; Technicolor; Rated R; 138 minutes; December release

CAST

Jerry Maguire	Tom Cruise
Rod Tidwell	Cuba Gooding, Jr.
Dorothy Boyd	Renee Zellweger
Avery Bishop	Kelly Preston
Frank Cushman	Jerry O'Connell
Bob Sugar	Jay Mohr
Laurel Boyd	Bonnie Hunt
Marcee Tidwell	Regina King
Ray Boyd	Jonathan Lipnicki
Chad the Nanny	Todd Louiso
Bill Dooler	Mark Pellington
Tyson Tidwell	Jeremy Suarez
Dicky Fox	Jared Jussim
Keith Cushman	Benjamin Kimball Smith
Anne-Louise	Ingrid Beer
Scully	Jann Wenner
Wendy	Nada Despotovich
Bobbi Fallon	Alexandra Wentworth
Tee Pee	Aries Spears
Jan	Kelly Coffield
Alice	Alice Crowe
Women's Group	Larina Adamson, Winnie Holzman, Diana Jordan, Susan Norfleet, Susan Pingleton, Cha-Cha Sandoval, Hynden Walch
Dennis Wilburn	Glenn Frey
Rick (Junior Agent)	Donal Logue
Ben	Tom Gallop
Cleo	Beaumont Bacon
Patricia Logan	Lisa Amsterdam
Kathy Sanders	Angela Goethals
Flight Attendant	Leslie Upson
John Swenson	Rick Johnson
Room Service Waiter	Lightfield Lewis
Jesus of CopyMat	Jerry Cantrell
Steve Remo	Toby Huss
Jesse Remo	Drake Bell
Mrs. Remo	Christina Cavanaugh
Doctor	Russel Lunday
Ethan Valhere	Eric Stoltz
Weepy Athlete	Lamont Johnson
Calvin Nack	Brent Barry
"Baja" Brunard	Rod Tate

and Charlie Cronin, Theo Greenly (Hootie Fans), Danny Rimmer (Sad Autograph Boy), Michael James Johnson (Clark Hodd), Jordan Ross (Art Stallings), Brandon Christianson (Young Golfer), Jerry Ziesmer (Trainer), Kirsten Krueger (Draft Reporter), Shannon Thornton (Pressbox Columnist), Luis Damian, Jesus Alberto Guzman, Juan Arnoldo Morales, Alberto Alfavo (Mariachi Band), Andrea Ferrell, Anthony Natale (Elevator Couple), David Ursin (General Manager), Thomas J. Reilly (Reverend), Reagan Gomez-Preston (Tidwell's Cousin), Jim Moffatt, Leo Zick, Klair Bybee (NFL Guests), Stanley Sessoms (Shower Man), Gale Hilman (Locker Room Athlete), Heather Cheney (Idealized Kissing Wife), Dennis Fitzgerald (Idealized Kissing Husband), Lucy Alexis Liu, Stephanie Vail, Justina Vail, Sam Smith, Ivana Marina, Lisa Rotondi, Lisa Stahl, Emily Procter, Amaryllis Borrego, Stacey Williams, Lauren Parker, Lisa Ann Hadley, Kymberly Kalil, Alison Armitage, Rebecca Rigg, Golde Starger (Former Girlfriends), Roy Firestone, Al Michaels, Dan Dierdorf, Frank Gifford, Mel Kiper, Jeff Lurie, Drew Rosenhaus, Richie Kottie, Tim McDonald, Mike Tirico, Wayne Fontes, Evelyn Fontes, Mike White, Johnnie Morton, Rick Mirer, Drew Bledsoe, Rob Moore, Ki-Jana Carter, Herman Moore, Art Monk, Troy Aikman, Katarina Witt, Dean Biasucci, Warren Moon, Kerry Collins, Erica Sorgi, Tom Friend, Dallas Malloy, Jim Irsay, Meg Irsay (Themselves), Beau Bridges

Having written a document criticizing his company's priorities, top sports agent Jerry Maguire begins to reassess his life, after which he is fired by his agency, but manages to hold on to a single client and a lone, loyal co-worker. Cuba Gooding, Jr. received the 1996 Academy Award for Best Supporting Actor. The film received additional nominations for picture, actor (Tom Cruise), original screenplay and film editing.

Tom Cruise, Renee Zellweger

Jay Mohr

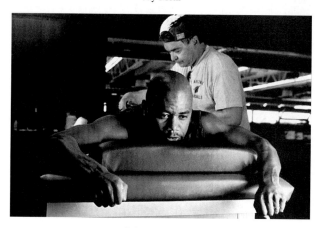

Cuba Gooding, Jr.

Kelly Preston, Laura Dern, Swoosie Kurtz

Laura Dern, Mary Kay Place

Kelly Preston, Laura Dern

Kurtwood Smith, Burt Reynolds, Jeremy Sczepaniak

CITIZEN RUTH

(MIRAMAX) formerly *Precious*; Producers, Cary Woods, Cathy Konrad; Co-Producer, Andrew Stone; Director, Alexander Payne; Screenplay, Alexander Payne, Jim Taylor; Photography, James Glennon; Designer, Jane Ann Stewart; Editor, Kevin Tent; Music, Rolfe Kent; Costumes, Tom McKinley; Associate Producer, Michael Zimbrich; Casting, Lisa Beach; an Independent Pictures production; Dolby Stereo; Color; Rated R; 109 minutes; December release

CAST

Ruth Stoops	Laura Dern
Diane Sieglar	Swoosie Kurtz
Norm Stoney	Kurtwood Smith
Gail Stoney	Mary Kay Place
Rachel	Kelly Preston
Harlan	M.C. Gainey
Dr. Charlie Rollins	Kenneth Mars
Judge Richter	David Graf
Nurse Pat	Kathleen Noone
Jessica Weiss	Tippi Hedren
Blaine Gibbons	Burt Reynolds
Ruth's Lover	Lance Rome
Tony Stoops	Jim Kaal
Arresting Officer	Shea Degan
ER Doctor	Vince Morelli
Kathleen	Marilyn Tipp
Sandy	Lois Nemec
Bail Clerk	Tim Vanderberghe
Matthew Stoney	Sebastian Anzaldo III
Cheryl Stoney	Alicia Witt
Party Dude	Mick McDonald
Norm's Manager	Okley Gibbs
Briana	Roberta Larson
Fran	Pam Carter
Kirk	Steven Wheeldon
Ruth's Mon	Diane Ladd

and Billie Barnhouse-Diekman, John Lapuzza (Clinic Protesters), Susan Stern (Cindy Lindstrom), Jeffrey L. Goos (News Anchor), James Devney (Officer Iverson), Tim Driscoll (Officer Bundy), Caveh Zahedi (Peter), David Hirsch (Man in Motel Lobby), Gail Erwin (Woman in Motel Lobby), Tony Wike (Anecdote-Telling Man), Sherry Josand Fletcher (Helpful Registration Woman), Jim Delmont (Press Conference Reporter), Dennis Grant (Don Mattox), Will Jamieson (Surveillance Guy), Jeremy Sczepaniak (Eric), Delaney Driscoll (Ruth's "Sister"), R.D. "Cuz" O'Connell (Biker), Judith Hart (Sarah Schneider), Joan Pirkle (Dr. Cary Milton), Lorie Obradovich (Receptionist), Joan Hennecke (Nurse), Mike Tourek (Guy Hit by Toilet Lid), Katrina Christensen, John Bell (Ruth's Kids), Jeff "J.J." Johnson, Fred Lovelace, Ed Morehouse, Jim Reinken, Wm. J. "Billy Bob" Muddle (Harlan's Biker Friends).

Paint-sniffing vagrant Ruth Stoops, ordered by the court to abort her latest pregnancy, becomes the subject of a war between a Christian woman's organization fighting abortion and a pro-choice group.

©Miramax Films

ONE FINE DAY

(20TH CENTURY FOX) Producer, Lynda Obst; Executive Producers, Kate Guinzburg, Michelle Pfeiffer; Director, Michael Hoffman; Screenplay, Terrel Seltzer, Ellen Simon; Designer, David Gropman; Editor, Garth Craven; Co-Producer, Mary McLaglen; Music, James Newton Howard; Song: "For the First Time" by Janes Newton Howard, Jud Friedman and Allan Dennis Rich/performed by Kenny Loggins; Costumes, Susie DeSanto; Casting, Lora Kennedy; a Fox 2000 Pictures presentation of a Lynda Obst production in association with Via Rosa Productions; Dolby Stereo; Deluxe color; Rated PG; 108 minutes; December release

Mae Whitman, George Clooney, Michelle Pfeiffer, Alex D. Linz

CAST

Melanie Parker	Michelle Pfeiffer
Jack Taylor	George Clooney
Maggie Taylor	Mae Whitman
Sammy Parker	Alex D. Linz
Lew	Charles Durning
Yates, Jr.	Jon Robin Baitz
Elaine Lieberman	Ellen Greene
Manny Feldstein	Joe Grifasi
Frank Burroughs	Pete Hamill
Evelyn	Anna Maria Horsford
Metro Reporters	Gregory Jbara, Hal Panchansky
Kristen	Sheila Kelley
Yates, Sr.	Barry Kivel
Dr. Martin	Robert Klein
Smith Leland	George Martin
Eddie	Michael Massee
Celia	Amanda Peet
Marla	Bitty Schram
Rita	Holland Taylor
Ruta	Marianne Muellerleile
Vincent Wang	Steven Jang
Rosa	Samantha Cintrón
Doctor	Victor Truro
Jessica	Ashley Greenfield
Mayor Aikens	Sid Armus

and Maggie Wagner, Isabelle Ashland, Jasmin Hartmann (*Daily News* Reporters), Larry Sherman (*Daily News* Visitor), Duke Mooseekian (Foreign Artist Guy), Thomas Schall (Gentleman), Michael Badalucco (Officer Bonomo), Jeanie Van Dam (Old Woman), Kirstin Allen (Pregnant Saleslady), Michael Genet (Press Secretary), Julia Ryder Perce (Lew's Secretary), P.J. Aliseo (Spiderman), Liam Ahern (The Hulk), Jose Rabelo (Museum Guard), Darla Hill (Oribe's Receptionist), Joe Avellar, Jullie Chung (Reporters), Dale Kasman (Lady in the Police Station), Andrew Magarian (Bum in the Police Station), Katherine Argo, Rob Kelly-Buntzen, Brian Cahill (Passerbys), Fred Goehner (Davis), Kuniko Narai (Flower Shop Employee)

A hard-driving newspaper columnist and a career-minded architect are thrown together along with his daughter and her son when the two of them inadvertently swap cellular phones. This film received an Oscar nomination for song ("For the First Time").

©*Twentieth Century Fox*

Holland Taylor   Charles Durning

George Clooncy, Mac Whitman, Alex D. Linz, Michelle Pfeiffer

Michelle Pfeiffer, George Clooney

MARVIN'S ROOM

(MIRAMAX) Producers, Scott Rudin, Jane Rosenthal, Robert De Niro; Executive Producers, Tod Scott Brody, Lori Steinberg; Co-Producers, David Wisnievitz, Bonnie Palef, Adam Schroeder; Director, Jerry Zaks; Screenplay, Scott McPherson, based upon his play; Editor, Jim Clark; Music, Rachel Portman; Costumes, Julie Weiss; Casting, Ilene Starger; a Scott Rudin/Tribeca production; Dolby Stereo; Color; Rated PG-13; 98 minutes; December release

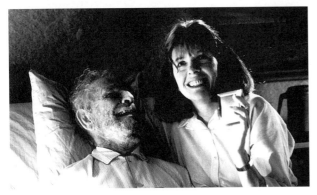

Diane Keaton, Leonardo DiCaprio

CAST

Lee	Meryl Streep
Hank	Leonardo DiCaprio
Bessie	Diane Keaton
Dr. Wally	Robert De Niro
Marvin	Hume Cronyn
Ruth	Gwen Verdon
Charlie	Hal Scardino
Bob	Dan Hedaya
Dr. Charlotte	Margo Martindale
Retirement Home Director	Cynthia Nixon
Amber & Coral	Kelly Ripa
Lance	John Callahan
Beauty Shop Lady	Olga Merediz
Bruno	Joe Lisi
Gas Station Guy	Steve Dumouchel
Janine	Bitty Schramm
Minister	Victor Garber
Novice	Lizabeth MacKay
Nun on Phone	Helen Stenborg
Nun # 3	Sally Parrish

After years of caring for her sickly father and her aunt, Bessie realizes that she herself is ill and turns to her long absent sister, Lee, for help. Based on the 1992 Off-Broadway play that starred Laura Esterman (Bessie), Lisa Emery (Lee), and Mark Rosenthal (Hank). This film received an Oscar nomination for actress (Diane Keaton).

©Miramax Films

Hume Cronyn, Diane Keaton

Diane Keaton, Meryl Streep

Meryl Streep, Leonardo DiCaprio

Hal Scardino, Gwen Verdon

Meryl Streep

Robert De Niro

IN LOVE AND WAR

(NEW LINE CINEMA) Producers, Dimitri Villard, Richard Attenborough; Executive Producer, Sara Risher; Director, Richard Attenborough; Screenplay, Allan Scott, Clancy Sigal, Anna Hamilton Phelan; Screen Story, Allan Scott, Dimitri Villard; Based on the book *Hemingway in Love and War* by Henry S. Villard and James Nagel; Supervising Producer, Chris Kenny; Co-Producer, Diana Hawins; Photography, Roger Pratt; Designer, Stuart Craig; Editor, Lesley Walker; Costumes, Penny Rose; Music, George Fenton; Casting, Jeremy Zimmerman, René Haynes, Clare Walker; a New Line production in association with Dimitri Villard productions; Dolby Stereo; Panavision; Rank color; Rated PG-13; 115 minutes; December release

Sandra Bullock, Chris O'Donnell

CAST

Agnes Von Kurowsky	Sandra Bullock
Ernest Hemingway	Chris O'Donnell
Henry Villard	Mackenzie Astin
Domenico Caracciolo	Emilio Bonucci
Elsie "Mac" MacDonald	Ingrid Lacey
Mabel "Rosie" Rose	Margot Steinberg
Katherine "Gumshoe" De Long	Tara Hugo
Tom Burnside	Colin Stinton
Roberto Zardini	Rocco Quarzell
Jimmy McBride	Ian Kelly
Enrico Biscaglia	Vincenzo Nicoli
Porters	Alan Bennett, Terence Sach
Town Mayor	Caro Croccolo
Italian Child	Gigi Vivan
Grandfather	Giuseppe Bonato
Loretta Cavanaugh	Allegra Di Carpegna
Adele Brown	Diane Witter
Charlotte Anne Miller	Mindy Lee Raskin
Ruth Harper	Tracy Hostmyer
Veta Markley	Kaethe Cherney
Anna Scanlon	Lauren Booth
Elena Crouch	Rebecca Craig
Katherine Smith	Frances Riddelle
Emily Rahn	Wendi Peters
Sonia	Maria Petrucci
Anna Maria	Valeria Fabbri

and Quinto Rolman (Italian Man), Raph Taylor (Francesco), George Rossi (Triage Medic), Todd Curran (Skip Talbot), Matthew Sharp (Joseph Larkin), Nick Brooks (Louis Burton), Tom Goodman-Hill (Houston Kenyon), Doreen Mantle (Emilia), Tim McDonell (Adjutant), Vincenzo Ricotta (Italian Officer), Reno Porcaro (Italian Photographer), Bruno Majean (Alberto Zardini), Joseph Long (Italian Doctor), Bruce Lidington (American Surgeon), Colin Fox (Dr. Hemingway), Kay Hawtrey (Grace Hemingway), Roseline Garland (Carol Hemingway), Evan Smirnow (Leicester Hemingway), Avery Saltzman (*Oak Leaves* Reporter), Rodger Barton (*Sun Times* Reporter), Richard Blackburn (*Tribune* Reporter), Gil Filar, Noah Reid (Boys), Richard Fitzpatrick (Mailman), Philippe Leroy (Count Sergio Caracciolo), Laura Martelli (Isabella Caracciolo), Cyril Taylor (Maitre D'), Milan Rosandic (Waiter)

Mackenzie Astin

The true story of the love affair between young soldier Ernest Hemingway and Agnes Von Kurowsky, the nurse who took care of him after he was wounded in battle during World War I.

©New Line Productions, Inc.

Chris O'Donnell

Chris O'Donnell, Sandra Bullock

GHOSTS OF MISSISSIPPI

(COLUMBIA) Producers, Frederick Zollo, Nicholas Paleologos, Andrew Scheinman, Rob Reiner; Executive Producers, Jeffrey Stott, Charles Newirth; Director, Rob Reiner; Screenplay, Lewis Colick; Photography, John Seale; Designer, Lilly Kilvert; Editor, Robert Leighton; Costumes, Gloria Gresham; Music, Marc Shaiman; Co-Producer, Frank Capra III; Casting, Jane Jenkins, Janet Hirshenson; a Castle Rock Entertainment presentation of a Frederick Zollo production; Dolby SDDS Stereo; Technicolor; Rated PG-13; 131 minutes; December release

CAST

Bobby DeLaughter	Alec Baldwin
Myrlie Evers	Whoopi Goldberg
Byron De La Beckwith	James Woods
Ed Peters	Craig T. Nelson
Peggy Lloyd	Susanna Thompson
Burt DeLaughter	Lucas Black
Drew DeLaughter	Joseph Tello
Claire DeLaughter	Alexa Vega
Charlie Crisco	William H. Macy
Benny Bennett	Lloyd "Benny" Bennett
Darrell Evers	Darrell Evers
Reena Evers	Yolanda King
Van Evers	James Van Evers
Jerry Mitchell	Jerry Levine
Jared Lloyd	Sky Rumph
Clara Mayfield	Margo Martindale
Thelma De La Beckwith	Zoaunne Leroy
Merrida Coxwell	Michael O'Keefe
Jim Kitchens	Bill Smitrovich
Judge Hilburn	Terry O'Quinn

and Rex Linn (Martin Scott), Bill Henderson (Minister), James Pickens, Jr. (Medgar Evers), Virginia Madsen (Dixie DeLaughter), G. Ja'ron Henderson (Darrell age 11), Rae'ven Larrymore Kelly (Reena age 10), Curtis Tyler Haynes (Van age 3), Richard Riehle (Tommy Mayfield), Jim Harley (Delamar Dennis), Bonnie Barlett (Billie DeLaughter), Brock Peters (Walter Williams), Wayne Rogers (Morris Dees), Finn Carter (Cynthia Speetgens), William Howard (Fred Sanders), Diane Ladd (Caroline Moore), Andy Romano (Hardy Lott), Richard Stahl (Judge Hendrick), David Carpenter (Bill Waller), Bill Cobbs (Charlie Evers), Jordan Lund (Deputy), Jerry Hardin (Barney DeLaughter), Ramon Bieri (James Holley), C.R. Doan (Bob Patterson), Katherine Wood (Young Barbara Holder), L.D. Bass, Sr. (Black Man), Monty Thomas (Security Guard), Eliott Keener (Sheriff McMillan), Brandon McKennah (Roy Wilkins), William L. Donald (Waiter at Country Club), Jim Stallings (Hollis Cresswell), Michael Strasser (Bomb Squad Man), Diana Bellamy (Barbara Holder), Rance Howard (Ralph Hargrove), Thomas Kopache (Thorn McIntyre), Frank Hoyt Taylor (Dan Prince), Sarah Hunley (Peggy Morgan), Marilynn Lovell, Jill Andre, Leigh French (Bridge Ladies), James Marshall Wolchok (Press Reporter), John A. Horhn (CNN Reporter), Spencer Garrett, Fenton Lawless, David Armstrong, Michael Hewes, James Homer Best (Reporters), Thomas Barry (Bennie Thompson), Louis E. Armstrong (Louis Armstrong), Ed Bryson, Maggie Wade (Themselves), J.J. Chaback (Assistant D.A.), Keanan K. Evers (Daniel Evers-Everette), Nicole Evers-Everette (Cambi Evers-Everette), Dijon S. Williams (Keanan Evers), Tracey Costello (Assistant D.A.)

Assistant District Attorney Bobby DeLaughter reopens the murder case of Medgar Evers, hoping to bring his killer, Byron De La Beckwith to trial, nearly 31 one years after the event. This film received Oscar nominations for supporting actor (Janes Woods) and make-up.

©Castle Rock Entertainment

Alec Baldwin, Craig T. Nelson

William H. Macy, Lloyd "Benny" Bennett

Yolanda King, Whoopi Goldberg, Darrell Evers

Michael O'Keefe, Bill Smitrovich, James Woods

Drew Barrymore

Skeet Ulrich, Jamie Kennedy, Matthew Lillard

Neve Campbell, Rose McGowan

Courtney Cox, David Arquette

SCREAM

(DIMENSION) Producers, Cary Woods, Cathy Konrad; Executive Producers, Bob Weinstein, Harvey Weinstein, Marianne Maddalena; Co-Executive Producer, Stuart M. Besser; Director, Wes Craven; Screenplay, Kevin Williamson; Co-Producer, Dixie J. Capp; Photography, Mark Irwin; Designer, Bruce Alan Miller; Editor, Patrick Lussier; Music, Marco Beltrami; Special Makeup Effects, Robert Kurtzman, Greg Nicotero, Howard Berger; Casting, Lisa Beach; a Woods Entertainment production; Distributed by Miramax Films; Dolby Stereo; Panavision; Consolidated color; Rated R; 110 minutes; December release

CAST

Dewey Riley	David Arquette
Sidney Prescott	Neve Campbell
Gale Weathers	Courteney Cox
Stuart	Matthew Lillard
Tatum Riley	Rose McGowan
Billy Loomis	Skeet Ulrich
Randy	Jamie Kennedy
Casey Becker	Drew Barrymore
Phone Voice	Roger Jackson
Casey's Father	Kevin Patrick Walls
Casey's Mother	Carla Hatley
Mr. Prescott	Lawrence Hecht
Obnoxious Reporter	Linda Blair
Kenny	W. Earl Brown
Mrs. Tate	Lois Saunders
Principal Himbry	Henry Winkler
Sheriff Burke	Joseph Whipp
Hank Loomis	C.W. Morgan
Mrs. Riley	Frances Lee McCain
Cotton Weary	Liev Schreiber
Reporters	Lisa Beach, Tony Kilbert
Ghost Teens	Troy Bishop, Ryan Kennedy

and Leonora Scelfo (Cheerleader in Bathroom), Nancy Ann Ridder (Girl in Bathroom), Lisa Canning (Mask Reporter), Bonnie Wood (Young Girl), Lucille Bliss (Check-Out Lady), Aurora Draper, Kenny Kwong (Party Teens), Justin Sullivan (Teen on Couch), Kurtis Bedford (Bored Teen), Angela Miller (Girl on Couch)

A mad killer is stalking a small town, using his knowledge of slasher movies to trick his victims and throw the police off his trail.

©Miramax Films

THE EVENING STAR

(PARAMOUNT) Producers, David Kirkpatrick, Polly Platt, Keith Samples; Director, Robert Harling; Screenplay, Robert Harling; Based on the novel by Larry McMurtry; Photography, Don Burgess; Designer, Bruno Rubeo; Editors, Priscilla Nedd-Friendly, David Moritz; Costumes, Renée Ehrlich Kalfus; Music, William Ross; Original *Terms of Endearment* Themes by Michael Gore; Co-Producer, Dennis Bishop; Casting, Jennifer Shull; a co-presentation of Rysher Entertainment of a David Kirkpatrick production; Dolby Stereo; Deluxe color; Rated PG-13; 129 minutes; December release

CAST

Aurora Greenway	Shirley MacLaine
Jerry Bruckner	Bill Paxton
Melanie Horton	Juliette Lewis
Patsy Carpenter	Miranda Richardson
Arthur Cotton	Ben Johnson
Bruce	Scott Wolf
Tommy Horton	George Newbern
Rosie Dunlop	Marion Ross
Teddy Horton	Mackenzie Astin
Hector Scott	Donald Moffat
Ellen	Jennifer Grant
Jane	China Kantner
Garrett Breedlove	Jack Nicholson
Bump	Shawn Taylor Thompson
Henry	Jake Langerud
Dolly	Sharon Bunn
Pascal Ferney	Clement Von Franckenstein
Toni	Antonia Bogdanovich
Jimmie Lee	Jimmie Lee Balthazar
Nurse Susan	Melinda Renna
Dr. Faulkner	Mark Walters
Lola Bruckner	Ann Hardman-Broughton
James	Woody Watson
Billy	Larry Elliott
Joey	Donny Caicedo
Casting Assistant	Connie Cooper
Sitcom Actress Becky	Laura Cayouette
Bernie Steinberg	John McCalmont
Sitcom Dad	John Bennett Perry
Sitcom Mom	Mary Gross
Professor Warwick	Alex Morris

and Will Wallace (Ticket Agent), Kim Terry (Flight Attendant), Eileen Morris (Nurse Margaret), Christopher Ballinger (Bump age 9), Austin Samuel Hembd (Bump age 7), Don Burgess (Stage Manager), Steve Danton (Minister B. Ramsey)

Aurora Greenway believes that she has somehow failed in trying to raise her three grandchildren to amount to something. Sequel to the 1983 Paramount release Terms of Endearment *with Shirley MacLaine and Jack Nicholson repeating their roles from that film. This was the last film appearance of actor Ben Johnson who died on Apr. 8, 1996.*

©*Rysher Entertainment, Inc.*

Juliette Lewis, Shirley MacLaine, George Newbern, Mackenzie Astin

Jack Nicholson, Shirley MacLaine

Bill Paxton, Shirley MacLaine

Miranda Richardson, Shirley MacLaine

MOTHER

(PARAMOUNT) Producers, Scott Rudin, Herb Nanas; Director, Albert Brooks; Screenplay, Albert Brooks, Monica Johnson; Photography, Lajos Koltai; Designer, Charles Rosen; Editor, Harvey Rosenstock; Music, Marc Shaiman; Co-Producers, Barry Berg, Adam Schroeder; Costumes, Judy L. Ruskin; Casting, Deborah Aquila, Jane Shannon Smith; a Scott Rudin production; Dolby Stereo; Deluxe color; Rated PG-13; 104 minutes; December release

Debbie Reynolds, Albert Brooks

CAST

John Henderson	Albert Brooks
Beatrice Henderson	Debbie Reynolds
Jeff Henderson	Rob Morrow
Linda	Lisa Kudrow
Cheryl Henderson	Isabel Glasser
Charles	Peter White
Lawyer	Paul Collins
Karen Henderson	Laura Weekes
Carl	John C. McGinley
TV Installers	Richard Assad, Joey Naber
Donna	Vanessa Williams
Jill Henderson	Danielle Quinn
Josh Henderson	Spencer Klein
Man at Rest Stop	Ernie Brown
Helen	Anne Haney
Alice	Billye Ree Wallace
Waiter	James Gleason
Gap Salesman	Matt Nolan
Pet Store Salesman	Harry Hutchinson
Lingerie Saleslady	Kimiko Gelman
Woman at Gas Station	Rosalind Allen

Having failed at two marriages, science fiction writer John Henderson returns home to straighten out his strained relationship with his mother.

Lisa Kudrow, Albert Brooks

Rob Morrow, Debbie Reynolds, Albert Brooks

Walter Matthau, Ossie Davis

Craig T. Nelson   Amy Irving

Martha Plimpton   Boyd Gaines

I'M NOT RAPPAPORT

(GRAMERCY) Producers, John Penotti, John Starke; Executive Producer, David Sameth; Director/Screenplay, Herb Gardner, based on his play; Photography, Adam Holender; Designer, Mark Friedberg; Editors, Wendey Stanzler, Emily Paine; Music, Gerry Mulligan; Costumes, Jennifer von Mayrhauser; Casting, Lynn Kressel; a Greenstreet production; Dolby Stereo; DuArt color; Rated PG-13; 136 minutes; December release

CAST

Nat Moyer	Walter Matthau
Midge Carter	Ossie Davis
Clara Gelber	Amy Irving
The Cowboy	Craig T. Nelson
Danforth	Boyd Gaines
Laurie	Martha Plimpton
J.C.	Guillermo Diaz
Clara Lemlich	Elina Löwensohn
Feigenbaum	Ron Rifkin
Hannah	Marin Hinkle
Ella Mae Tilden	Nancy Giles
Kamir	Ranjit Chowdhry
Sol	Irwin Corey
Rifka	Mina Bern
Walter	Salem Ludwig
July Carbonelle	Fanni Green
Butcher	Richard Council
Russian Lady	Shirl Bernheim
Harry	Steve Ryan
Gristedes Customers	Alan North, Sidney Armus, Tony Gillan
Boy at Gristedes	York Bergin
Tango Dancer and Partner	Richard Korthaze
Jake	William Preston
Nurse	Becky Ann Baker
Mr. Gunther	Arthur Anderson
3-year-old Cowboy	Michael Angarano
Mother of 3-year-old Cowboy	Jennie Moreau
Bat Kid	Jake Gardner

A pair of New York senior citizens, Nat Moyer, a philosophical Jewish radical, and Midge Carter, a half-blind, black building superintendent, face the pressures and challenges of old age and city life. The original 1985 Off-Broadway and Broadway productions starred Judd Hirsch (Nat) and Cleavon Little (Midge).

©*Gramercy Pictures*

Jonathan Pryce, Madonna

Madonna, Antonio Banderas

Jimmy Nail, Madonna

Antonio Banderas, Madonna

EVITA

(HOLLYWOOD PICTURES) Producers, Robert Stigwood, Alan Parker, Andrew G. Vajna; Director, Alan Parker; Screenplay, Alan Parker, Oliver Stone; Based on the musical play produced on Broadway by Robert Stigwood, in association with David Land; Line Producer, David Wimbury; Photography, Darius Khondji; Designer, Brian Morris; Editor, Gerry Hambling; Music, Andrew Lloyd Webber; Lyrics, Tim Rice; Associate Producer, Lisa Moran; Costumes, Penny Rose; Choreographer, Vincent Paterson; Casting, John & Ros Hubbard; an Andrew G. Vajna presentation of a Cinergi/Robert Stigwood/Dirty Hands production; Dolby Digital Stereo; PLC Widescreen; Technicolor; Rated PG; 134 minutes; December release

CAST

Eva Perón (Evita)	Madonna
Ché	Antonio Banderas
Juan Perón	Jonathan Pryce
Agustín Magaldi	Jimmy Nail
Doña Juana	Victoria Sus
Brother Juan	Julian Littman
Blanca	Olga Meredíz
Elisa	Laura Pallas
Erminda	Julia Worsley
Young Eva	Maria Lujan Hidalgo
Cipriano Reyes	Servando Villamil
Perón's Mistress	Andrea Corr
Domingo Mercante	Peter Polycarpou
Juan Bramuglia	Gary Brooker
Julieta	Mayte Yerro
Carlos	Adrian Collado
Cinema Manager	Gabriel Kraisman

and Martin Drogo (Young Juan), Venesa Weis (Young Blanca), Vernoica Ferrari Risler (Young Elisa), Aldana Garcia Soler (Young Erminda), Domingo Chiofalo (Chivilcoy Priest), Ismael Osorio (Juan Duarte, Sr.), Lidia Leonor Catalano (Estela Grisolía), John Coverdale, Roderick Hart, Ian Hill, Rob Levy, Teddy Peiro, Joe Townsend (Junín Tango Band), Mark Ryan, Gordon Neville, Frederick Warder (Waiters in Junín Bar), Albin Pahernik, Luca Tommassini, Denis Tremblay (Eva's Dance Partners), Eva Vari (Señora Magaldi), Zsanett Farkas (Magaldi Child), Sergio Lerer (Theatre Producer), Mara Bestelli, Monica Lairana, Bettina Menegazzo, Laura Miller (Startlets at Audition), Marcelo Alejandro Auchelli (Huevo), Luis Alday (Emilio Kartulowicz), Luis Boccia (Señor Jabón), Vera Fogwill, Bettina Menegazzo (Zaz Jingle Duo), Alfredo Martin (Col. Aníbal Imbert), Diego Leske, Francisco Napoli, Eduardo Ruderman, Fabian Stratas (Eva's Admirers), David Henry (President Rawson), Fernando Agustin Henin (Eva's Co-Star)

The true story of how Eva Duarte rose from poverty to a position of power as the wife of Argentinian president Juan Perón. The original Broadway production opened in 1979 and starred Patti Lupone (Eva), Mandy Patinkin (Che), and Bob Gunton (Juan Perón). This film received an Academy Award for Best Song: "You Must Love Me." The film received additional nominations for art direction, sound, cinematography and film editing.

©Cinergi Pictures Entertainment Inc. and Cinergi Productions N.V. Inc.

Jonathan Pryce, Madonna, Antonio Banderas

Antonio Banderas, Madonna

Madonna, Jonathan Pryce

Madonna, Jonathan Pryce

John Travolta (c)

Robert Pastorelli, Sparky

Jean Stapleton

Andie MacDowell

MICHAEL

(NEW LINE CINEMA) Producers, Sean Daniel, Nora Ephron, James Jacks; Executive Producers, Delia Ephron, Jonathan D. Krane; Co-Producer, G. Mac Brown; Director, Nora Ephron; Screenplay, Nora Ephron, Delia Ephron, Pete Dexter, Jim Quinlan; Story, Pete Dexter, Jim Quinlan; Photography, John Lindley; Designer, Dan Davis; Editor, Geraldine Peroni; Music, Randy Newman; Song "Heaven Is My Home" by Randy Newman/performed by Randy Newman, Valerie Carter; Costumes, Elizabeth McBride; Casting, Mary Goldberg; a Turner Pictures presentation of an Alphaville production; Dolby SDDS Stereo; Deluxe color; Rated PG; 105 minutes; December release

CAST

Michael	John Travolta
Dorothy Winters	Andie MacDowell
Frank Quinlan	William Hurt
Vartan Malt	Bob Hoskins
Huey Driscoll	Robert Pastorelli
Pansy Milbank	Jean Stapleton
Judge Esther Newberg	Teri Garr
Bruce Craddock	Wallace Langham
Anita	Joey Lauren Adams
Bride	Carla Gugino
Groom	Tom Hodges
Evie	Catherine Lloyd Burns
Italian Waiter	Richard Schiff
Sheriff	Calvin Trillin
Court Bailiff	Don Lee
Tammy	Joann Jansen
Mal	David Harrod
Suzanne	Jane Lanier
Minister	John Hussey

and Margaret Travolta, David Bernstein, Betsy Sokolow, Tracey Doyle (Reporters), Blue Deckert (Joe), Debrah Nunez, Dell Aldrich, Kay Colin (Women), James Harrell, Peyton Park (Old Geezers), Dianne Dreyer (Jennifer), Tim Harrison, Daniel Mimura (Slackers), Mark Nutter (Counterman)

Tabloid reporters Dorothy Winters and Frank Quinlan track down a man who claims to be an angel, hoping to bring him back to Chicago in time for Christmas.

©New Line Cinema

William Hurt

John Travolta

John Travolta, Robert Pastorelli, Andie MacDowell, William Hurt

Courtney Love, Woody Harrelson

Courtney Love

Donna Hanover, Woody Harrelson

Courtney Love, Woody Harrelson

Larry Flynt

THE PEOPLE VS. LARRY FLYNT

(COLUMBIA) Producers, Oliver Stone, Janet Yang, Michael Hausman; Director, Milos Forman; Screenplay, Scott Alexander, Larry Karaszewski; Photography, Philippe Rousselot; Designer, Patrizia Von Brandenstein; Editor, Christopher Tellefsen; Costumes, Theodor Pistek, Arianne Phillips; Music, Thomas Newman; Casting, Francine Maisler; an Ixtlan production, presented in association with Phoenix Pictures; Dolby Stereo; Panavision; Technicolor; Rated R; 130 minutes; December release

CAST

Larry Flynt	Woody Harrelson
Althea Leasure	Courtney Love
Alan Isaacman	Edward Norton
Jimmy Flynt	Brett Harrelson
Ruth Carter Stapleton	Donna Hanover
Charles Keating	James Cromwell
Arlo	Crispin Glover
Chester	Vincent Schiavelli
Miles	Miles Chapin
Simon Leis	James Carville
Jerry Falwell	Richard Paul
Roy Grutman	Burt Neuborne
The Assassin	Jan Triska
10-year-old Larry	Cody Block
8-year-old Jimmy	Ryan Post
Old Hillbilly	Robert Davis
Young Ma Flynt	Kacky Walton
Young Pa Flynt	John Ryan
1st Stripper	Kathleen Kane
Disc Jockey	Greg Roberson
Old Printer	Jim Peck
Trucker	Mike Pniewski
Staffers	Tim Parati, Rick Rogers, Dan Lenzini, David Compton, Gary Lowery
Stills Photographer	Stephen Dupree
Tovah	Rainbeau Mars
News Dealer	Tam Drummond
Ma Flynt	Nancy Lea Owen
Pa Flynt	John Fergus Ryan
Governor Rhodes	Oliver Reed
Jacuzzi Girls	Meresa T. Ferguson, Andrena Fisher
Police Detective	Ken Kidd
Judge Morrissey (Cincinnati Court)	Larry Flynt
Jury Forewoman (Cincinnati Court)	Janie Paris
Court Clerk (Cincinnati Court)	Carl Russell-Woloshin
Rally Singer	Miss Ruby Wilson
Announcer at Rally	Eddie Davis
Ad Sales Guy	Blaine Pickett
Georgia Cops	Kerry White, Joey Hadley
Robert Stapleton	Chris Schadrack

and Mac Pirkle (Georgia Prosecutor), Mark W. Johnson (Georgia Doctor), Doug Bauer (Flynt's Personal Bodyguard), Roberto Roman Ramirez (Bodyguard), Blaine Nashold, M.D. (Dr. Bob), Aurelia Thieree (Cute Receptionist), Scott Winters (Blow Dried Jerk), D'Army Bailey (Judge Thomas Mantke LA Court), Mike McLaren (Lawyer LA Court), Andrew Stahl (Network Lawyer), Michael Detroit (Delorean Attorney), Jaime Jackson (Keating's Secretary), David Dwyer (Federal Marshal), Richard Birdsong, James A. White (Deputy Marshals), Gerry Robert Byrne (Butler), Benjamin Greene, Jr. (Bailiff LA Court), Mary Neal Naylor (Mantke Clerk), Tina M. Bates (Springfield Prison Guard), Evans Donnell, Jay Adams (Divinity Students), Bennett Wood (Dean of Liberty College), Janice Holder (Judge Kirk Roanoke Court), A.V. McDowell (Jury Foreman Roanoke Court), Jim Grimshaw (Chief Justice Rhenquist), James Smith (Justice Marshall), Rand Hopkins (Justice Scalia), Charles M. Crump (Justice Stevens), Pierre Secher (Supreme Court Marshall), Linn Sitler (Svelte Reporter), Mary M. Norman, Jack Shea, Lisa Lax (Reporters), Susan Howe, Michael Davis, Dennis Turner, Patti Hatchett, Ann Marie Hall, Nate Bynum, Paula Haddock, Gary Kraen (Georgia Reporters), Norm MacDonald (Network Reporter), Jeff Johnston (L.A. Reporter), Joey Sulipeck, Jim Palmer (Falwell Reporters), Gene Lyons, Saida Pagan, Jim Hild, Michael Klastorin (DC Reporters), Michelle Robinson (TV Reporter at Supreme Court)

The true story of Hustler *magazine publisher Larry Flynt and his fight for the First Amendment against the Rev. Jerry Falwell. This film received Oscar nominations for actor (Woody Harrelson) and director.*

©Columbia Pictures Industries, Inc.

Edward Norton, Woody Harrelson

Courtney Love

Woody Harrelson, Courtney Love

THE WHOLE WIDE WORLD

(SONY PICTURES CLASSICS) Producers, Carl-Jan Colpaert, Kevin Reidy, Dan Ireland, Vincent D'Onofrio; Executive Producers, Donald Kushner, Peter Locke, Gregory Cascante; Director, Dan Ireland; Screenplay, Michael Scott Myers; Based upon the memoir *One Who Walked Alone* by Novalyne Price Ellis; Photography, Claudio Rocha; Editor, Luis Colina; Music, Hans Zimmer, Harry Gregson-Williams; Designer, John Frick; Costumes, Gail McMullen; Co-Producers, Benjamin Mouton, Michael Scott Myers; Casting, Laurel Smith; from The Kushner Locke Company in cooperation with Cineville; Dolby Stereo; Clairmont-Scope; Color; Rated PG; 105 minutes; December release

VIncent D'Onofrio, Renee Zellweger

CAST

Robert E. Howard	Vincent D'Onofrio
Novalyne Price	Renee Zellweger
Mrs. Howard	Ann Wedgeworth
Dr. Howard	Harve Presnell
Clyde Smith	Benjamin Mouton
Booth Adams	Michael Corbett
Enid	Helen Cates
Woman on Bus	Marion Eaton
Ethel	Leslie Berger
Truett	Chris Shearer
Mammy	Sandy Walper
Mrs. Hemphill	Dell F. Aldrich
Etna Reed Price	Libby Villari
Teacher	Antonia Bodganovich
Mrs. Smith	Elizabeth D'Onforio
Director	Stephen Marshall

True story of the relationship between schoolteacher Novalyne Price and pulp writer, Robert E. Howard, creator of "Conan the Barbarian."

©*Sony Pictures Entertainment, Inc.*

Renee Zellweger

VIncent D'Onofrio

Vincent D'Onofrio, Renee Zellweger

CAUGHT

(SONY PICTURES CLASSICS) Producers, Richard Brick, Irwin Young; Executive Producers, Jim Pedas, Ted Pedas, Bill Durkin, George P. Pelecanos; Director, Robert M. Young; Screenplay, Edward Pomerantz; Photography, Michael Barrow; Designer/Costumes, Hilary Rosenfeld; Editor, Norman Buckley; Music, Chris Botti; Casting, Kimberly Davis; a Cinehaus/DuArt/Circle Films presentation; Color; Rated R; 109 minutes; September release

CAST

Joe	Edward James Olmos
Betty	Maria Conchita Alonso
Nick	Arie Verveen
Danny	Steven Schub
Amy	Bitty Schram
Santiago	Shawn Elliot
Peter	Bernie and Tommy Abbot
Bag Lady	Sandra Kazan
Man in Window	Edward Pomerantz
Crack Dealing Kid	Joseph D'Onofrio
Cops	Angela Ali, Gregory Lichtenson
Fish Dealer	Dominick Oliveri
Big John	Antonio Oliveri
Yacht Salesman	Dick Curry
Yacht Sales Associate	Willo Varsi Hausman

Married couple Joe and Betty give young Nick a job at their Jersey City fish market which leads to an affair between Nick and Betty.

Jean-Claude Van Damme, Natasha Henstridge

Jean-Claude Van Damme, Jean-Hugues Anglade

Edward James Olmos, Arie Verveen

MAXIMUM RISK

(COLUMBIA) Producer, Moshe Diamant; Executive Producer, Roger Birnbaum; Director, Ringo Lam; Screenplay, Larry Ferguson; Photography, Alexander Gruszynski; Designer, Steven Spence; Editor, Bill Pankow; Costumes, Joseph Porro; Music, Robert Folk; Co-Producer, Jason Clark; Action Sequence Choreographer/Stunts, Charles Picerni; Casting, Deborah Brown; a Roger Birnbaum production/Moshe Diamant production; Dolby SDDS Stereo; Super 35 Widescreen; Technicolor; Rated R; 100 minutes; September release

CAST

Alain Moreau/Mikhail Suverov	Jean-Claude Van Damme
Alex Minetti	Natasha Henstridge
Sebastien Thirry	Jean-Hugues Anglade
Ivan Dzasokhov	Zach Grenier
Pellman	Paul Ben-Victor
Loomis	Frank Senger
Red Face	Stefanos Miltsakakis
Davis Hartley	Frank Van Keeken
Kirov	David Hemblen
Chantal	Stephanie Audran
Yuri	Dan Moran
Nicholas	Donald Burda
Morris	Rob Kaman
Martin	Herb Lovelle
Innkeeper	Denis Costanzo
Inspector	Marc Estrada Tournie
Bohemia Bartender	Carlo Rota

abd Joe Pingue, Hugh Thompson (Bohemia Doormen), Gloria Slade (Airline Steward), Jackie Richardson (Large Woman), Ed Sahely (Desk Clerk), Martine Pujol (Cleaning Lady), Albert Schultz (Anderson), Dan Duran (Reporter), Raymond Accolas (Bank Manager), Kedar Brown (Tough Teen), Claire Cellucci (Yuri's Girlfriend), John Bayliss (Kirov's Butler), Henry Gomez (Cab Driver), Louise Naubert (Secretary), Phillip Wotton (Sebastien's Driver), Jean-Pierre Galleri (Paris Police Detective), Stephan Muller (Paris Fireman) John Nelles (Nervous Passenger), John Pearson (Guard Sergeant), Kevin Rushton (Guard), Sharon Bernbaum (Assistant Bank Manager), David Christoffel (Bank Security Guard), Branko Racki (Vladamir), Kamel Krifa (Boris), Brian Jagersky (Tim), Irene Pauzer (Ronnit), Peter Messaline (Ari), Jim Millington (FBI Boss), George Kash (Man in Private Room), David Turner (Inspector #2), Veronique Diehl (Mother Villefranche Apt), Alain Phillip (Morgue Attendant), Christine Manning (Woman in Vault), Jaques Authier (Priest), Charles Drummond (Officer at Bank), Bruno Magnes (Innocent Driver), Danny Lima (Guard #3), Lon E. Katzman, Ed Queffelec (Bodyguards), Ron Van Hart, Brian Kaulback (Ivan's Bodyguards), Eugene Allin (Val), Armin Konn (Petrie), Svetlana Medianik (Club Bohemia Singer), Andrei Smal, Alexander Kanewsky, Mikhael Ziskine, Andrei Denga, Arkadij Kaplan (Club Bohemia Band)

Alain Moreau pretends to be his recently murderered twin brother, investigating his death in the underworld of New York's Little Odessa neighborhood.

Pauly Shore, Stephen Baldwin, William Atherton in *Bio-Dome*
© Metro-Goldwyn-Mayer

BIO-DOME (MGM) Producers, Brad Krevoy, Steve Stabler, Brad Jenkel; Executive Producers, Michael Rotenberg, Jason Blumenthal, Adam Leff, Mitchell Peck; Director, Jason Bloom; Screenplay, Kip Koenig, Scott Marcano; Story, Adam Leff, Mitchell Peck, Jason Blumenthal; Photography, Phedon Papamichael; Designer, Michael Johnston; Music, Andrew Gross; Costumes, Mary Claire Hannan; Co-Producers, Dan Etheridge, Elaine Dysinger; Casting, Rick Montgomery, Dan Parada; a Brad Krevoy/Steve Stabler production, 3 Arts Entertainment and Weasel Productions, presented in association with the Motion Picture Corporation of America; Distributed by MGM/UA; DTS Digital Stereo; Foto-Kem color; Rated PG-13; 95 minutes; January release. CAST: Pauly Shore (Bud Macintosh), Stephen Baldwin (Doyle Johnson), William Atherton (Dr. Noah Faulkner), Kylie Minogue (Petra Von Kant), Joey Adams (Monique), Teresa Hill (Jen), Henry Gibson (William Leaky), Kevin West (T.C. Romulus), Denise Dowse (Olivia Biggs), Dara Tomanovich (Mimi Simkins), Patricia Hearst (Doyle's Mother), Robbie Thibaut, Jr. (Young Doyle), Adam Weisman (Young Bud), Brian Hayes Currie (Guard), Courtney Mizel (Screamer), Butch McCain (Reporter Joachim West), Taylor Negron (Russell), Roger Clinton (Prof. Bloom), Rose McGowan (Denise), Channon Roe (Roach), Trevor St. John (Parker), Jeremy Jordan (Trent), Jack Black, Kyle Gass (Tenacious D), Mark Burton (Guy), Loomis (Drummer), Joe Sib (Singer), Soda Pop (Guitarist), Burdie Cutlas (Bassist), Rene Moreno (Partier), Molly Bryant (Bio-Dome Technician), Ben McCain (Anchor Aries West), Katherine Kousi, Elizabeth Guber, Chloé Hult (Vigilantes), Tucker Smallwood (Gates), Phil Lamarr, Paul Eiding (Assistants), Andy Lucchesi (Swat Guy), Rodger Bumpass (Narrator), Phil Proctor (AXL), Cecile Krevoy (Woman in Bandstand), Jordan Mayerson, Jason Davis (Kid Tourists)

LAWNMOWER MAN 2: BEYOND CYBERSPACE (New Line Cinema) a.k.a. *Lawnmower Man 2: Jobe's War*; Producers, Edward Simons, Keith Fox; Executive Producers, Avram Butch Kaplan, Steve Lane, Peter McRae, Bob Pringle, Clive Turner; Director/Screenplay, Farhad Mann; Story, Farhad Mann, Michael Miner; Photography, Ward Russell; Designer, Ernest H. Roth; Costumes, Deborah Everton; Music,

Matt Frewer in *Lawnmower Man 2*
© New Line Productions

Robert Folk; Editors, James D. Mitchell, Joel Goodman; Special Visual Effects, Cinesite; Casting, Glenn Daniels; an Allied Entertainments co-presentation in association with Fuji Eight Co. Ltd.; Dolby Stereo; Panavision; Consolidated Film Industries Color; U.S.-British-Japanese; Rated PG-13; 93 minutes; January release. CAST: Patrick Bergin (Dr. Benjamin Trace), Matt Frewer (Jobe), Austin O'Brien (Peter), Ely Pouget (Cori), Camille Cooper (Jennifer), Patrick La Brecque (Shawn), Crystal Celeste Grant (Jade), Sean Parhm (Travis), Mathew Valencia (Homeless Kid), Kevin Conway (Walker), Trever O'Brien (Young Peter), Richard Fancy (Senator Greenspan), Ellis Williams (Chief of Security), Castulo Guerra (Guillermo), Molly Shannon (Homeless Lady), Ralph Ahn (Doctor), David Byrd (Judge), Stephanie Menuez (Lawyer), Nancy Chen (Cashier), Amanda Hillwood (News Anchor), Patricia Belcher (Impatient Customer), Gregg Daniel (Trace's Lawyer), Arthur Mendoza (Technician), Dale E. House (Helicopter Pilot), John Benjamin Martin (Henry the Guard), Ayo Adejugbe (Nigerian Businessman), Yoshio Be (Japanese Businessman), Carl Carlsson-Wollbruck (German Businessman), David Gibbs (Pilot), Pamela West (Co-Pilot), Dan Lipe (Security Guard), Kenny Endoso (Train Conductor)

ANGELA (Tree Farm Pictures) Producer, Ron Kastner; Director/Screenplay, Rebecca Miller; Photography, Ellen Kuras; Editor, Melody London; Music, Michael Rohatyn; Designer, Daniel Talpers; Technicolor; Not rated; 103 minutes; January release. CAST: Anna Thomson (Mae), John Ventimiglia (Andrew), Miranda Stuart Rhyne (Angela), Charlotte Blythe (Ellie), Vincent Gallo (Preacher), Ruth Maleczech (Sleepwalker), Hynden Walch (Darlene), Garrett Bemer (Tom), Sara Caitlin Hall (Anne), Henry Stram (Man at Fair), Rodger L. Phillips (Frank), Io Tillet Wright (Sam), Wil McKnight (Greg), Carl Nick Reighn (Fair Attendent), Peter Facinelli (Devil), Jack O'Connell (Man at Bar), Nurith Cohn (Makeover Woman), Constance McCord (The Virgin Mary), Roxanna Stuart (Saleslady)

Miranda Stuart Rhyne in *Angela*
© Tree Farm Pictures

MADAME WANG'S (Film Forum/Independent) Producer, Jack Simmons; Director/Story/Screenplay, Paul Morrissey; Photography, Juan Drago, Jim Tynes; Editors, George Wagner, Michael Nallin; 1981; Color; Not rated; 95 minutes; January release. CAST: Patrick Schoene (Lutz), Christina Indri, William Edgar, Susan Blond, Jimmy Madaus, Virginia Bruce (Madame Wang), Leroy and the Lifters, Phranque, Mentors, Butch, Boneheads.

FORTY-DEUCE (Island Alive/Film Forum) Producer, Jean-Jacques Fourgeaud; Director/Screenplay, Paul Morrissey; Photography, Steven Fierberg; Music, Manu Dibango; Editor, Ken Eluto; 1981; Widescreen; Color; Not rated; 90 minutes; January release. CAST: Kevin Bacon (Ricky), Mark Keyloun (Blow), Orson Bean (Mr. Roper), Harris Laskowy (Augie), Tommy Citera (Crank), Carol Jean Lewis (Coke Dealer), Esai Morales (Mitchell), Susan Blond, John Noonan, Yukio Yamamoto, Meade Roberts (Man in Street), Dave Kris, Rudy de Bellis (Men in Toilet)

Sarita Choudhury in *Fresh Kill*
© Strand Releasing

FRESH KILL (Strand) Producer/Director, Shu Lea Cheang; Co-Producer, Jennifer Fong; Screenplay, Jessica Hagedorn; Photography, Jane Castle; Music, Vernon Reid; Color; Not rated; 80 minutes; January release. CAST: Sarita Choudhury (Shareen Lightfoot), Erin McMurtry (Claire Mayakovsky), Abraham Lim (Jiannbin Lui), Jose Zuniga (Miguel Flores), Laurie Carlos (Mimi Mayakovsky), Will Kempe (Stuart Sterling), Nelini Stamp (Honey Mayakovsky Lightfoot), Rino Thunder (Clayton Lightfoot, Sr.), Ron Vawter (Roger Bailey), Kate Valk (Mother Mary), Robbie McCauley (Nina Simpson), Karen Finley (Bernadette Cherryhome), George C. Wolfe (Cat Lover), Pedro Pietri (Condom Poet), Ching Gonzalez (Man Bathing), Cochise Anderson (Tim), Paul Schulze (Peter Finn), Marlene Forte (Pam Mandel), Ching Valdez Aran (Boss Man), Ryohei Hoshi (Japanese Businessman), Marlies Yearby (Music Executive), James Azor (Rapper), Paul Lynn Williams (Brad), David Ng (Skip), Mario Todisco (Tully), DeWarren Moses (Soap Man), Lou Sumrall (Barry Fox), Nicky Paraiso (Supermarket Manager), Alva Rogers (Woman in Locker), Joel Kovel (Dr. Callahan), Lisa Mayo (Child Psychiatrist), Amber Villenueva (Teru the Psychic), Foo Shen Hsieh (Man with Bullhorn), Lu Yu Liao (Village Matriarch), Chun Yin Hsieh (City Lady), Michael Ringer (Billy Boy), Elaine Tse (Jackie Tan), David Henderson (Jackson), Avis Brown (African Woman), Jessica Hagedorn (Bookseller), Kaja Sehrt (German Tourist)

Hal Stakke in front of Negativeland in Sonic Outlaws

CATWALK (Arrow) Producer, Sug Villa; Fashion Producer, Edie Locke; Executive Producers, Daniel Wolf, Donald Rosenfeld; Directors, Robert Leacock, Milton Moses Ginsberg; Music, Malcolm McLaren; Editor, Milton Moses Ginsberg; Color; Not rated; 95 minutes; February release. Documentary on the fashion industry with Christy Turlington, Naomi Campbell, Kate Moss, Jean-Paul Gaultier, Todd Oldham, Azzedine Alaia, John Galliano, Nino Cerruti, Giorgio Armani, Gianni Versace, Gianfranco Ferre, Valentino, Alberta Ferreti, Karl Lagerfeld.

SONIC OUTLAWS (Film Forum/Independent) Producer/Director, Craig Baldwin; Photography/Editor, Bill Daniel; Color; Not rated; 87 minutes; February release. Documentary about Island Record's lawsuit against guerilla audio artists Negativland, featuring interviews with Negativland, Emergency Broadcast Network, Tape-Beatles, Barbie Liberation Organization.

THE SHOT (Bread & Water Prods.) Producers, Jude Horowitz, Sherrie Rose; Director/Screenplay, Dan Bell, based on his play; Photography, Alan Caudillo; Editor, Kevin Greutert; Music, Dan Sonis; Ultra-Stereo; Foto-Kem color; Not rated; 84 minutes; February release. CAST: Dan Bell (Dern Reel), Michael Rivkin (Patrick St. Patrick), Jude Horowitz (Anna), Michael DeLuise (Bob Mann), Mo Gaffney (Sheila Ricks), Jack Kehler (Det. Markinson), Ted Raimi (Det. Corelli), Vincent Ward (Smith), Bob Dickman (Metaphor Man), Tracy Arnold (Sissy Mayron), Lee Tergesen (Doughnut), Dana Carvey (Himself)

Whoopi Goldberg, Theodore Rex in *Theodore Rex*
© New Line Productions

THEODORE REX (New Line Cinema) Producers, Richard Abramson, Sue Baden-Powell; Executive Producer, Stefano Ferrari; Director/Screenplay, Jonathan Betuel; Photography, David Tattersall; Editors, Rick Shaine, Steve Mirkovich; Music, Robert Folk; Designer, Walter Martishius; Costumes, Mary Voft; Dinosaurs Creator, Criswell Prods.; Visual Effects Supervisor, Robert Habros; Casting, Elisabeth Leustig; a Shooting Star Entertainment production presented in association with J&M Entertainment; Dolby Stereo; Color; Rated PG; 91 minutes; February release. CAST: Whoopi Goldberg (Katie Coltrane), Armin Mueller-Stahl (Dr. Edgar Kane), Juliet Landau (Dr. Shade), Bud Cort (Splinter), Stephen McHattie (Edge), Richard Roundtree (Commissioner Lynch), George Newbern (Voice of Theodore Rex), Carol Kane (Voice of Molly Rex), Jack Riley (Alaric), Peter Mackenzie (Alex Summers), Joe Dallesandro (Rogan), Tony T. Johnson (Sebastian), Susie Coelho (Dr. Armitraj), Peter Kwon (Toymaker), Robert Martin Robinson (Knife), Edith Diaz (Ella), Queen Kong (Meanest Woman Truck Driver), William Boyett (Desk Sergeant), Marius Mazmanian (Butler), Noon Orsatti (Adam), Hilary Shepard (Sarah Jiminez), Elisabeth Galasso (New Eden Secretary), Michael Sharrett (New Eden Volunteer), Jan Rabson (Voice of Tina Rex), Charles Chiodo (Voice of Guy in the Bag), Lynne Larsen, Patricia Healy, Kristen Trucksess (Reporters), Gregory H. Alpert, Al Eisenmann II, Clyde "C.K." Johnson, Brad Wilson (Grid Police Officers), Bobby McGee, Gregory Synstelien (Grid Police Rookies)

HEADLESS BODY IN TOPLESS BAR (Northern Arts) Producers, Charles Weinberger, Rustam Branaman, Stephen Falick; Executive Producers, Tom Breznahan, Sean Gavigan, Boyd Willat; Director, James Bruce; Screenplay/Co-Producer, Peter Koper; Photography, Kevin Morrisey; Editor, Robert Barrere; Music, Charles Barnett; Designer, Gustav Alsina; Costumes, Natasha Landau; a Boyd Willat production; Color; Not rated; 101 minutes; February release. CAST: Raymond J. Barry (The Man), Jennifer MacDonald (Candy), Rustam Branaman (Vic), Taylor Nichols (Danny), David Selby (Bradford Lumpkin), Paul Williams (Carl Levin), April Grace (Letita Jackson), Biff Yeager (Joe)

Chance, Kevin Chevalia in *Homeward Bound II*
© The Walt Disney Company

HOMEWARD BOUND II: LOST IN SAN FRANCISCO (Walt Disney Pictures) Producer, Barry Jossen; Director, David R. Ellis; Screenplay, Chris Hauty, Julie Hickson; Based upon characters from the book *The Incredible Journey* by Sheila Burnford; Photography, Jack Conroy; Designer, Michael Bolton; Editors, Peter E. Berger, Michael A. Stevenson; Music, Bruce Broughton; Co-Producers, James Pentecost, Justis Greene; Animal Coordinator, Gary Gero; Casting, Megan McConnell; Distributed by Buena Vista Pictures; Dolby Digital Stereo; Clairmont-scope; Technicolor; Rated G; 89 minutes; March release. ANIMAL CHARACTER VOICES: Michael J. Fox (Chance), Sally Field (Sassy), Ralph Waite (Shadow), Al Michaels (Sparky Michaels), Tommy LaSorda (Lucky LaSorda), Bob Uecker (Trixie Uecker), Tress MacNeille (French Poodle), Jon Polito (Ashcan), Adam Goldberg (Pete), Sinbad (Riley), Carla Gugino (Delilah), Tisha Campbell (Sledge), Stephen Tobolowsky (Bando), Ross Malinger (Spike), Michael Bell (Stokey); CAST: Veronica Lauren (Hope), Kevin Chevalia (Jamie), Robert Hays (Bob), Kim Greist (Laura), Benj Thall (Peter), Kristina Lewis (Stacey), Adrienne Carter (Tough Girl), Deryl Hayes (Skycap), Gary Jones, Jeff Chivers (Baggage Handlers), Robin Douglas (Airport Worker), Ernie Prentice (Poodle Owner), Michael Rispoli (Jack), Max Perlich (Ralph), Ed Hong-Louie (Fish Seller), Keegan MacIntosh (Tucker), Sandra Ferens (Tucker's Mom), Hrothgar Mathews (Animal Control Officer), Andrew Airlie (Tucker's Dad), Rhys Huber (Boy), Nathaniel De Veaux (Fire Captain), William Sasso (Pizza Boy), Tom Wagner (Truck Driver)

Valentina Vargas, Doug Bradley in *Hellraiser: Bloodline*
© Dimension Films

HELLRAISER: BLOODLINE (Dimension) Producer, Nancy Rae Stone; Executive Producers, Clive Barker, Paul Rich, C. Casey Bennett; Director, Alan Smithee; Screenplay, Peter Atkins; Photography, Gary Lively; Designer, Ivo Cristante; Music, Daniel Licht; Editors, Rod Dean, Randolph K. Bricker, Jim Prior; Costumes, Eileen Kennedy; Makeup Effects Creator/Designer, Gary Tunnicliffe; Casting, Anrea Stone, Laurel Smith; a Dimension Films/Trans Atlantic Entertainment presentation in

association with Clive Barker; Distributed by Miramax Films; Dolby Stereo; CFI color; Rated R; 85 minutes; March release. CAST: Bruce Ramsay (Phillip/John/Paul), Valentina Vargas (Angelique), Doug Bradley (Pinhead), Charlotte Chatton (Genevieve), Adam Scott (Jacques), Kim Myers (Bobbi), Mickey Cottrell (Duc De L'Isle), Louis Turenne (Auguste), Courtland Mead (Jack), Louis Mustillo (Sharpe), Jody St. Michael (The Beast), Paul Perri (Edwards), Pat Skipper (Carducci), Christine Harnos (Rimmer), Wren Brown (Parker), Tom Dugan (Chamberlain), Michael Polish, Mark Polish (Twins), Jimmy Schuelke, David Schuelke (Security Guards)

Antonio Banderas, Melanie Griffith, Antonio Banderas, Daryl Hannah in *Two Much*
© Interscope Communications, Inc.

TWO MUCH (Touchstone) Producer, Cristina Huete; Executive Producers, Ted Field, Adam Leipzig, Robert W. Cort; Director, Fernando Trueba; Screenplay, Fernando & David Trueba; Based on the novel by Donald E. Westlake; Photography, Jose Luis Alcaine; Music, Michel Camilo; Designer, Juan Botella; Costumes, Lala Huete; Associate Producers, Fernando Garcillan, Paul Diamond; Casting, Johanna Ray, Elaine J. Huzzar; Presented in association with Interscope Communications and PolyGram Filmed Entertainment; an Andres Vicente Gomez production in association with Lolafilms/Sogetel/Fernando Trueba P.C.; Distributed by Buena Vista Pictures; Dolby Digital Stereo; Panavision; Technicolor; Rated PG-13; 118 minutes; March release. CAST: Antonio Banderas (Art Dodge), Melanie Griffith (Betty Kerner), Daryl Hannah (Liz Kerner), Danny Aiello (Gene Palletto), Joan Cusack (Gloria Fletcher), Eli Wallach (Sheldon Dodge), Gabino Diego (Manny), Austin Pendleton (Dr. Huffeyer), Allan Rich (Rev. Larrabee), Vincent Schiavelli (Sommelier), Phil Leeds, Sid Raymond, Louis Seeger Crume (Lincoln Brigade), Jeff Moldovan, Joe Hess (Goons), Theodora Castellanos (Conchita), Genevieve Chase (Mrs. Doyle), Marcella Vitalainai Aitken (Mrs. Palletto), Ellen Jacoby (Waitress), Santiago Segura, Gabriel Traversari (Paparazzi), Rosa Jimenez (Maria), Katrina Flett (University Student), George Kapetan (Tailor), Don McArt (Funeral Priest), Levis Mora-Arriaga, Jose Mora-Arriaga, David Mora-Arriaga (Mariachis)

"Ed," Matt LeBlanc in *Ed*
© Universal City Studios, Inc.

Dirk Shafer, Phil Donahue in *Man of the Year*
© Seventh Art Releasing

ED (Universal) Producer, Rosalie Swedlin; Executive Producers, Bill Finnegan, Bill Couturié, Brad Epstein; Director, Bill Couturié; Screenplay, David Mickey Rose; Story, Ken Richards, Janus Cercone; Photography, Aln Caso; Designer, Curtis A. Schnell; Editor, Robert K. Lambert; Costumes, Robin Lewis; Music, Stephen D. Endelman; "Ed" Special Makeup Creators, Dave Nelson, Norman Tempia, Animated Engineering; Casting, Shari Rhodes, Joseph Middleton; a Longview Entertainment production; DTS Stereo; Deluxe color; Rated PG; 94 minutes; March release. CAST: Matt LeBlanc (Jack Cooper), Jayne Brook (Lydia), Jack Warden (Chubb), Bill Cobbs (Tippet), Patrick Kerr (Kirby Woods), Doren Fein (Liz), Charlie Schlatter (Buddy Halsten), Carl Anthony Payne II (Stats Jefferson), James Caviezel (Dizzy Anderson), Mike McGlone (Oliver Barnett), Zack Ward (Dusty Richards), Phillip Bruns (Clarence), Curt Kaplan (Randall "Zonk" Cszonka), Valente Rodriguez (Jesus Rodriguez), Jay Caputo, Denise Cheshire (Ed Sullivan), Gene Ross (Red), Paul Hewitt (Bucky), Sage Allen (Cooper's Mother), Stan Ivar (Cooper's Father), Jim O'Heir (Art), Rick Johnson (Kurt "Crush" Bunyon), Leonard Kelly-Young (Customer Joe), Troy Evans (Bus Driver), Richard Gant (Umpire—Sharks Game), Bill Capizzi (Farley), Steve Eastin (Sharks' Manager), K.C. Corkery (Little Boy—banana toss), Jaquita Green (Little Girl), Ken Zavayna (Peanut Man), Kevin Kraft (Shortstop), Brad Hunt (Carnie), Mark Cassella (Security Guard), Joe Bucaro, Noon Orsatti (Goons), John-Clay Scott (Banana Truck Driver), Jessica Pennington (Nurse Rosa Cays), Tommy Lasorda (Himself), Mitchell Ryan (Abe Woods), Macka Foley (Umpire—Championship Game), Michael Chieffo (Dr. Joseph Middleton), Gary Hecker (Voice of Ed Sullivan)

Charlie, David, Itchy in *All Dogs Go to Heaven 2*
© Metro-Goldwyn-Mayer Animation, Inc.

MAN OF THE YEAR (Seventh Art Releasing) Producer, Matt Keener; Executive Producer, Christian Moeyaert; Director/Screenplay, Dirk Shafer; Photography, Stephen Timberlake; Designer, Michael Mueller; Editors, Barry Silver, Ken Solomon; from Artisan Productions; Color; Not rated; 87 minutes; March release. Mock documentary about director

Shafer's experiences as a Playgirl model, featuring Dirk Shafer, Thom Collins, Deidra Shafer, Fabio (Themselves), Claudette Sutherland (Tammy Shafer), Michael Ornstein (Mike Miller), Cal Bartlett (Ken Shafer), Mary Stein (Angela Lucassey), Beth Broderick (Kelly Bound), Cynthia Szigeti (Betty Levy), Dennis Bailey (Howie Diadone), Charles Sloane (Ed, the Photographer), Patricia Domiano (Ballroom Dancer), Dawn Christie (Woman Exercising), Phyllis Franklin (Dr. Marsha Demarky), Bill Brochtrup (Pledge Cartwright), Lu Leonrad (Dee Dee Sweatman), Rhonda Dotson (Lady La Flame), Paul Fow (Rex Chandler), Fort Atkinson (Buck Hallren), Felix Montano (Jimmy Morgan), Michael Mueller, Kevin Bandy, Brett Sylver (Act Outs), Vivian Paxton (Herself/Chris), Joe Fusco (Act Out Stage Manager), Merri Biechler (Leslie Dameron), Mindy Sterling (Cindee)

Raoul O'Connell, Jaie Laplante, Michael Gunther in *Frisk*
© Strand Releasing

ALL DOGS GO TO HEAVEN 2 (MGM) Producers, Paul Sabella, Jonathan Dern, Kelly Ward, Mark Young; Directors, Paul Sabella, Larry Leker; Screenplay, Arne Olsen, Kelly Ward, Mark Young; Story, Mark Young, Kelly Ward; Art Director, Deane Taylor; Music, Mark Watters; Songs, Barry Mann, Cynthia Weil; Animation Director, Todd Waterman; Directing Animator, David Feiss; Sequence Director, Paul Schibli; Supervising Editors, Michael Bradley, Thomas V. Moss; an MGM Family Entertainment presentation of a Metro-Goldwyn-Mayer Animation production; Distributed by MGM/UA; DTS Stereo; Deluxe color; Rated G; 84 minutes; March release. VOICE CAST: Charlie Sheen (Charlie Barkin), Sheena Easton (Sasha La Fleur), Dom DeLuise (Itchy Itchiford), Ernest Borgnine (Carface), George Hearn (Red), Bebe Neuwirth (Anabelle), Adam Wylie (David), Hamilton Camp (Chihuahua), Steve Mackall (Short Customs Dog), Dan Castellaneta (Tall Customs Dog/Angel Dog #1), Tony Jay (Reginald), Jim Cummings (Jingles), Wallace Shawn (Labradour MC), Kevin Michael Richardson (St. Bernard/Officer Andrews), Pat Corley (Officer McDowell), Marabina Jaimes (Officer Reyes), Bobby DiCicco (Thom), Annette Helde (Claire), Maurice La Marche (Lost & Found Officer)

FRISK (Strand) Producers, Marcus Hu, Jon Gerrans; Director/Editor, Todd Verow; Screenplay, James Dwyer, George LaVoo, Todd Verow; Based on the novel by Dennis Cooper; Executive Producer, George LaVoo; Co-Producer, Richard Huggard; Photography, Greg Watkins; Designer, Jennifer Graber; an Industrial Eye production; Color; Not rated; 83 minutes; March release. CAST: Michael Gunther (Dennis), Craig Chester (Henry), Parker Posey (Ferguson), Alexis Arquette (The Punk), Jaie Laplante (Julian), James Lyons (Gypsy Pete/Pete), Raoul O'Connell (Kevin), Michael Stock (Uhrs), Michael Waite (Gary), Alyssa Wendt (Susan), Mark Ewert (Young Dennis/Jan—Victim #1/Young Boy in Park—Victim #4), Dustin Schell (Snuff Photographer), Michael Wilson, Paul B. Riley, Donald Mosner, James Mackay, Brook Dillon, Kimberly MacInnis, Edward Zold, Sean Bumgarner, Kari Birmingham, Joseph Smith (Party Goers), Todd Verow (Blond Man in Bathroom), Bonnie Dickenson (Blond Party Girl), David Webb (Married John), Michael Waite (Gary), Frankie Payne (Uhrs' Porn Co-Star), Mark Miller, B.J. Calnor, Howard Pope, Terry S. Seiler, Kevin Masters, Robin Gurney (Porn Actors), Joan Jett Black (Silver), Timothy Innes (Warren), Eric Sapp (Sampson), Roberto Friedman (Bartender), Peter Searls (Finn), Dennis Cooper (Man in Hall), Eric Dekker (John—Victim #2), Mark Finch (Newscaster), Michael Now (Shop Clerk), Daniel Boyle (Boy on Train)

Eric Schaeffer, Sarah Jessica Parker in *If Lucy Fell*
© TriStar Pictures

Isabel Gillies, Annie Golden in *One Way Out*
© Arrow Releasing Inc.

IF LUCY FELL (TriStar) Producers, Brad Krevoy, Steve Stabler, Brad Jenkel; Director/Screenplay, Eric Schaeffer; Story, Eric Schaeffer, Tony Spiridakis; Co-Producers, Terence Michael, Deborah Ridpath, Eric Schaeffer; Photography, Ron Fortunato; Designer, Ginger Tougas; Editor, Susan Graef; Music, Charlton Pettus, Amanda Kravat; Costumes, Ane Crabtree; Songs Performed by Marry Me Jane; Line Producer, Adam Brightman; Casting, Sheila Jaffe, Georgianne Walken; a Motion Picture Corporation of America Production in association with Brad Krevoy and Steve Stabler; Dolby Stereo; Technicolor; Rated R; 93 minutes; March release. CAST: Sarah Jessica Parker (Lucy Ackerman), Eric Schaeffer (Joe MacGonaughgill), Ben Stiller (Bwick Elias), Elle MacPherson (Jane Linquist), James Rebhorn (Simon Ackerman), Robert John Burke (Handsome Man), David Thornton (Ted), Bill Sage (Dick), Dominic Chianese (Al), Scarlett Johansson (Emily), Michael Storms (Sam), Jason Myers (Billy), Emily Hart (Eddy), Paul Greco (Rene), Mujibur Rahman, Sirajul Islam (Countermen), Ben Lin (Chinese Messenger), Alice Spivak (Elegant Middle-Aged Woman), Lisa Gerstein (Saleswoman), Molly Schulman (Kid), Peter Walker (Bag Man), Brad Jenkel (Neighbor), Brian Keane (Man in Gallery)

SWEET NOTHING (Independent/Film Forum) Producers, Rick Bowman, Gary Winick; Director, Gary Winick; Screenplay, Lee Drysdale; Photography, Makoto Watanabe; Editor, Niels Mueller; Music, Amy Tapper; Costumes, Franne Lee; 1993; Dolby Stereo; Color; Rated R; 90 minutes; March release. CAST: Michael Imperioli (Angel), Mira Sorvino (Monika), Paul Calderon (Raymond), Billie Neal (Rio), Brian Tarantina (Dee Dee), Patrick Breen (Greg), Lisa Langford (Edna), Richard Bright (Jack the Cop), Chuck Cooper (Mark the Cop), Maria Tucci (Monika's Mother), Sean Marquette (Young Richie), Christopher Marquette (Richie), Michelle Casey (Annie), Carlos Yensi (Jose)

ONE WAY OUT (Arrow) Producers, Thomas Gallo, Kevin Lynn; Executive Producers, Dennis Friedland, Jason Blum; Co-Producers, John Bertholon, Dick Fisher, Marisa Polvino; Director, Kevin Lynn; Screenplay, Jeff Monahan; Photography, Dick Fisher; Designer, Mark Coehlo; Music, Sean Murray; Costumes, Melissa Toth; Editors, Dick Fisher, Kevin Lynn; Casting, Donna DeSeta, David Cady; Color; Rated R; 95 minutes; March release. CAST: Isabel Gillies (Betsy Cavanaugh), Jack Gwaltney (Frank Damico), Jeff Monahan (Bobby), Annie Golden (Eve Petrone), Robert Turano (Snooky Damico), Michael Ironside (Walt)

FROM THE JOURNALS OF JEAN SEBERG (Planet Pictures) Director/Screenplay/Editor, Mark Rappaport; Photography, Mark Daniels; from Couch Potato Productions; Color/black and white; Not rated; 97 minutes; March release. CAST: Mary Beth Hurt (Jean Seberg), in a fictional autobiography of the life of the actress.

TARANTELLA (Tara) Producer, George LaVoo; Director, Helen De Michiel; Screenplay, Helen De Michiel, Richard Hoblock; Photography, Teodoro Maniaci; Designer, Diane Lederman; Creator & Director of Puppetry, Sandy Spieler; Editor, Richard Gordon; Music, Norman Noll; an ITVS presentation; Color; Not rated; 84 minutes; March release. CAST: Mira Sorvino (Diana di Sorella), Rose Gregorio (Pina de Nora), Matthew Lillard (Matt), Frank Pellegrino (Lou), Stephen Spinella (Frank), Antonia Rey (Grandmother), Melissa Maxwell (Young Diana), Maryann Urbano (Mother), James Georgiades (Bartender), Magda Lang, Sean Baldwin (Home Buyer Couple), Derek Contreras, A.J. Lopez (Home Buyer Young Men)

MYSTERY SCIENCE THEATER 3000: THE MOVIE (Gramercy) Producer/Director, Jim Mallon; Screenplay, Michael J. Nelson, Trace Beaulieu, Jim Mallon, Kevin Murphy, Mary Jo Pehl, Paul Chaplin, Bridget Jones; Photography, Jeff Stonehouse; Designer, Jef Maynard; Editor, Bill Johnson; Music, Billy Barber; Costumes, Linda Froiland; a Best Brains production; Dolby Stereo; Color; Rated PG-13 ; 73 minutes; April release. CAST: Trace Beaulieu (Dr. Forrester/Crow T. Robot), Michael J. Nelson (Mike Nelson), Jim Mallon (Gypsy), Kevin Murphy (Tom Servo), John Brady (Benkitnorf); *This Island Earth* a 1954 Universal release, features Jeff Morrow, Rex Reason, Faith Domergue, Russell Johnson, Lance Fuller and Douglas Spencer.

Mira Sorvino, Michael Imperioli in *Sweet Nothing*
© Film Forum

Mary Beth Hurt in *From the Journals of Jean Seberg*
© Planet Pictures

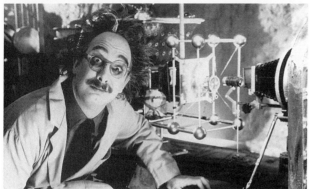

Trace Beaulieu in *Mystery Science Theatre 3000*
© Gramercy Pictures

Jennifer Connelly, Antonio Banderas in *Of Love and Shadows*
© Miramax Films

CELTIC PRIDE (Hollywood Pictures) Producer, Roger Birnbaum; Executive Producers, Judd Apatow, Charles J.D. Schlissel, Jonathan Glickman; Director, Tom De Cerchio; Screenplay, Judd Apatow; Story, Judd Apatow, Colin Quinn; Photography, Oliver Wood; Designer, Stephen Marsh; Editor, Hubert De La Bouillerie; Costumes, Mary Claire Hannan; Music, Basil Poledouris; Casting, Ferne Cassel; a Roger Birnbaum production, presented in association with Caravan Pictures; Distributed by Buena Vista Pictures; Dolby Digital Stereo; Technicolor; Rated PG-13; 91 minutes; April release. CAST: Damon Wayans (Lewis Scott), Daniel Stern (Mike O'Hara), Dan Aykroyd (Jimmy Flaherty), Gail O'Grady (Carol), Adam Hendershott (Tommy), Paul Guilfoyle (Kevin O'Grady), Deion Sanders, Bill Walton, Larry Bird, Marv Albert, Bob Cousy (Themselves), Christopher McDonald (Coach Kimball), Gus Williams (Derrick Lake), Ted Rooney (Tony Sheppard), Vladimir Cuk (Lurch), Keith Gibbs (Terry Kirby), Joe Mingle (Referee), Peter A. Hulne (Pat Fitzsimmons), Patrick Hulne (Tim Fitzsimmons), Will Lyman (Rich Man), Darrell Hammond (Chris McCarthy), Colton Russo (Josh), Ed "The Machine" Regine (Ralph), Bill McDonald (Mr. Tanner), Belle McDonald (Mrs. Tanner), Charles Broderick (Drunken Fan), Jeffrey Ross (Car Theft Victim), Scott Lawrence (Ted Hennison), Steve Sweeney (Nick), Tony V. (Cabbie), Mary Klug (Grandma), Charlie Haugk (John 3:16 Guy), Andy Jick (Boston Garden Announcer), Connie Perry (Suzy), Curt Frisk (Big Jim Fulton), James Dickinson (Basketball Player), George MacDonald (Reporter), Charles Porter (Bartender), Ed Logan (Program Seller), Robert M. Curcuro (Bobby), Nicole Brathwaite (Kid in Gym), Michael Biase (Bar Patron), Kevin Benton (Security Guard), Maryanne Di Modica (Waitress), Bob Haggerty (Man in Bathroom)

THE DEMOLITIONIST (Planet/A-Pix) Producer, Donald P. Borchers; Executive Producers, Robert E. Baruc, John Fremes; Director, Robert Kurtzman; Screenplay, Brian DiMuccio, Dino Vindeni; Story, Robert and Anne Kurtzman; Photography, Marcus Hahn; Designer, Charley Cabrera; Editor, Paolo Mazzucato; Makeup, K.N.B. Efx Group Inc.; an A-Pix Entertainment & Le Monde Entertainment presentation; Color; Rated R; 95 minutes; May release. CAST: Nicole Eggert (Alyssa—The Demolitionist), Bruce Abbott (Prof. Jack Crowley), Susan Tyrrell

(Mayor), Peter Jason (Higgins), Sarah Douglas (Surgeon), Andras Jones (Daniel), Heather Lagenkamp (Christy Caruthers), David Anthony Marshall (One Eye), Jack Nance (Father McKenzie), Josef Pilato (Boxer), Tom Savini (Roland), Nils Allen Stewart (Hammerhead), Richard Grieco (Mad Dog), James Mongold (Arlis), Danny Hicks (Krutchfield), Joelle Sailers (Biker Slut), Paul Munoz (Skin), Michael Maranda (Otto), Richard French (J.C.)

OF LOVE AND SHADOWS (Miramax) Producers, Richard Goodwin, Betty Kaplan, Paul F. Mayersohn; Executive Producers, Ernst Goldschmidt, Isidro Miguel, Herve Hachuel; Director, Betty Kaplan; Screenplay, Donald Freed; Based on the novel by Isabel Allende; Photography, Felix Monti; Editors, Kathryn Himoff, Bill Butler; Music, Jose Nieto; Art Director, Abel Faccello; a Betka Film Ltd. production; Spanish-Argentinian, 1994; Color; Rated R; 109 minutes; May release. CAST: Jennifer Connelly (Irene), Antonio Banderas (Francisco), Stefania Sandrelli (Beatriz), Camilo Gallardo (Gustavo), Patricio Contreras (Mario), Susana Cortinez (Rosa), Diego Wallraff (Jose), Jorge Rivera Lopez (Prof. Leal), Angela Ragno (Hilda Leal), Alejandro Toccalino (Guard at Roadblock), Alfredo Martin (Surgeon), Anita Lesa (Evangelina), Carmen Renard (The Rich Widow), Cesar Parlani (Reverend), Claudio Ciacci (Comandant Ramirez)

THE ARRIVAL (Orion) Producers, Thomas G. Smith, Jim Steele; Executive Producers, Ted Field, Robert W. Cort; Co-Producer, Cyrus Yavner; Director/Screenplay, David Twohy; Photography, Hiro Narita; Designer, Michael Novotny; Editor, Martin Hunter; Music, Arthur Kempel; Visual Effects Producer, Charles L. Finance; Costumes, Mayes C. Rubeo; Associate Producer, Lorenzo O'Brien, David Tripet; Casting, Mary Jo Slater, Steven Brooksbank; a Live Entertainment presentation a Steelwork Films and Thomas G. Smith production; Dolby Digital Stereo; Panavision; Color; Rated PG-13; 109 minutes; May release. CAST: Charlie Sheen (Zane Ziminski), Ron Silver (Gordian), Lindsay Crouse (Ilana Green), Teri Polo (Char), Richard Schiff (Calvin), Tony T. Johnson (Kiki), Leon Rippy, Buddy Joe Hooker (DODs)

Dan Aykroyd, Damon Wayans, Daniel Stern in *Celtic Pride*
© Hollywood Pictures Company

Charlie Sheen, Teri Polo in *The Arrival*
© LIVE Entertainment, Inc.

Missy Crider, Scott Caan in *A Boy Called Hate*
© Dove Pictures

A BOY CALLED HATE (Dove Entertainment) Producer, Steve Nicolaides; Executive Producers, Tom Rowe, Tony Allard, Marjorie Skouras; Director/Screenplay, Mitch Marcus; Photography, Paul Holahan; Editor, Michael Ruscio; Music, Pray for Rain; Designer, Caryn Marcus; a Nickel/Pacific Motion Pictures production; Dolby Stereo; Color;Rated R; 95 minutes; May release. CAST: Scott Caan (Steve/Hate), Missy Crider (Cindy), James Caan (Jim), Elliott Gould (Richard), Adam Beach (Billy Little Plume)

THE HAUNTED WORLD OF EDWARD D. WOOD JR. (Wood-Thomas Pictures) Producers, Crawford John Thomas, Brett Thompson, Wade Williams; Director/Screenplay/Editor, Brett Thompson; Photography, David Miller; Music, Louis Febre; Color/black and white; Not rated; 110 minutes; May release. Documentary on filmmaker Edward D. Wood Jr. featuring with Maila Nurmi (Vampira), Dolores Fuller, Conrad Brooks, Loretta King, Rev. Dr. Lynn Lemon, Bela Lugosi Jr., Paul Marco, Lyle Talbot, Mona McKinnon, Norma McCarty, Michael McCarty, Joe Robertson, Harry Thomas, Crawford John Thomas, Joe Robertson, Gregory Walcott, David Ward, Toni Griffin, John Faiola.

Rick Gianasi, Brick Bronsky in *Sgt. Kabukiman N.Y.P.D.*
© Troma

SGT. KABUKIMAN N.Y.P.D. (Troma) Producers/Directors, Michael Herz, Lloyd Kaufman; Screenplay, Lloyd Kaufman, Andrew Osborne, Jeffrey W. Sass, Robert Coffey, Cliff Hahn; Photography, Bob Williams; Music, Bob Mithoff, inspired by Puccini's *Madame Butterfly;* Editors, Ian Slater, Peter Novak; Color; Not rated; 104 minutes; May release. CAST: Rick Gianasi (Harry Griswold/Sgt. Kabukiman), Susan Byun (Lotus), Bill Weeden (Reginald Stuart), Thomas Crnkovich (Rembrandt), Larry Robinson (Reverend Snipes), Noble Lee Lester (Capt. Bender), Brick Bronsky (Jughead), Pamela Alster (Connie LaRosa), Shaler McClure (Felicia), Daniel Boone (Toyota)

THE GATE OF HEAVENLY PEACE (Long Bow Group) Producers, Richard Gordon, Carma Hinton, Peter Kovler, Orville Schell, Lise Yasui; Directors, Richard Gordon, Carma Hinton; Screenplay, Geremie Barme, John Crowley; Photography, Richard Gordon; Editors, David Carnochan, Charles Phred Churchill; Music, Mark Pevsner; Narrator, Deborah Amos; Dolby Stereo; Color; Not rated; 190 minutes; May release. Documentary on the events leading to the uprising at Tianamen Square in June of 1989.

A MODERN AFFAIR (Tara) Producers, Melanie Webber, Jennifer Wilkinson, Vern Oakley; Executive Producer, Marc Bailin; Director, Vern Oakley; Screenplay, Paul Zimmerman; Story, Vern Oakley, Paul Zimmerman; Photography, Rex Nicholson; Editor, Suzanne Pillsbury; Music, Jan Hammer; Designer, Cathy T. Marshall; Costumes, Gayle Alden Robbins; Casting, Bernard Telsey; Color; Not rated; 90 minutes; May release. CAST: Lisa Eichhorn (Grace Rhodes), Stanley Tucci (Peter Kessler), Caroline Aaron (Elaine), Mary Jo Salerno (Lindsay), Tammy Grimes (Dr. Greshem), Wesley Addy (Ed Rhodes), Robert Joy (Ernest Pohlsab), Cynthia Martells (Ellen), Robert LuPone (Ben), J. Smith-Cameron (Diane), Vincent Young (Tony), Len Stanger (Older Executive), Jon Huberth, Jim Lavin, Claywood Sempliner (Suits), Gary Lahti (Jerry)

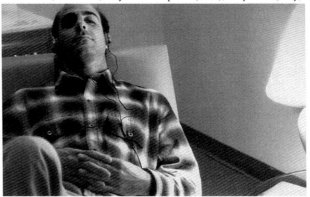

Stanley Tucci in *A Modern Affair*
© Tara Releasing

BARB WIRE (Gramercy) Producers, Brad Wyman, Mike Richardson, Todd Moyer; Executive Producer, Peter Heller; Director, David Hogan; Screenplay Chuck Pfarrer, Ilene Chaiken; Story, Ilene Chaiken; Photography, Rick Bota; Designer, Jean-Philippe Carp; Editor, Peter Schink; Costumes, Rosanna Norton; Music, Michel Colombier; Casting, Rick Montgomery, Dan Parada; a PolyGram Filmed Entertainment presentation of a Propaganda Films/Dark Horse Entertainment production; Dolby Stereo; Technicolor; Rated R; 90 minutes; May release. CAST: Pamela Anderson Lee (Barb Wire), Temuera Morrison (Axel Hood), Victoria Rowell (Cora D), Jack Noseworthy (Charlie Kopetski), Xander Berkeley (Alexander Willis), Steve Railsback (Col. Pryzer), Udo Kier (Curly), Rosey Brown (Big Fatso), Tony Bill (Foster), Clint Howard (Schmitz), Tiny "Zeus" Lister (Bouncer), Amir Aboulela (Patron), Adriana Alexander (Redhead), Miles Dougal, David Andriole (Goons), Vanessa Lee Asher (Emily), Ron Balicki, Diana Lee Insanto (Customs Agents), Jennifer Banko (Spike), Candace Camille Bender (Dancer), Alex Bookston (Man in White Suit), Gil Borgos (Old Man), Marc Collver (Mann), Tina Coté, Rene Stahl (Women in Bar), Vinnie Curto (Aide to Pryzer), Shelly Desai (Sharif), Ken Forsgren (Greaseball), Darrel Heath (Soldier—Flashback), Neil Hunt (Weasel), Henry Kingi (Moe), Tiffany Lawrence (Security Guard), Marshall Manesh (Sheik), John Paxton (Smooth), Pee Wee Piemonte (Frick), Mary Anna Reyes (Woman in Torture Room), Jeffrey Dean Rosenthal (Bald Man), Loren Rubin (Krebs), Michael Russo (Santo), Joe Sagal (Fred the Bartender), Diane Shay (Stripper in Dressing Room), Harvey Shield (Dad), Nils Allen Stewart (Jack), Teo (Disc Jockey), Patti Tippo (Mom), Dominique Vandenberg (Frack), Al Wan (China), Diane Warshay (Maria), Nicholas Worth (Reuben), Jack Wright (Package Check Guy), Salvator Xuereb (Young Soldier)

Pamela Anderson Lee in *Barb Wire*
© Gramercy Pictures

WILD BILL: HOLLYWOOD MAVERICK (Will Bill/Turner) Producer, Kenneth A. Carlson; Executive Producer, William A. Wellman Jr.; Director/Screenplay, Todd Robinson; Photography, Theodor M. Angell, Christian Sebaldt; Editor, Leslie Jones; Music, David Bell; Narrator, Alec Baldwin; a Coyote Film Group production, presented in association with Carlson Films; Dolby Stereo; Foto-Kem color; Not rated; 94 minutes; May release. Documentary on director William A. Wellman (1896-1975) featuring Mike Connors, Clint Eastwood, John Gallagher, James Garner, Darryl Hickman, Arthur Hiller, Tab Hunter, Howard W. Koch, Tom Laughlin, Burgess Meredith, Robert Mitchum, Harry Morgan, Gregory Peck, Sidney Poitier, Nancy Reagan, Robert Redford, Buddy Rogers, Martin Scorsese, Tony Scott, Robert Stack, Frank Thompson, Michael Wayne, Dorothy Wellman, William Wellman Jr., James Whitmore, Richard Widmark, Robert Wise, Jane Wyman.

PAINTED HERO (Legacy) Producers, Jeff G. Waxman, Richard C. Weinman, Terry Benedict, Peter Greene; Director, Terry Benedict; Screenplay, Terry Benedict, Stan Bertheaud; Photography, David Bridges; Editors, Jeff Wood, Gary McLaughlin; Music, Rick Marotta; Casting, Melissa Skoff; an Americana Images Inc. presentation of a Sound Shore production; Ultra-Stereo; Color; Rated R; 105 minutes; May release. CAST: Dwight Yoakam (Virgil Kidder), Michelle Joyner (Kaitlin), Bo Hopkins (Brownie), John Getz (Sheriff Gil Acuff), Kiersten Warren (Teresa), Cindy Pickett (Sadie), Walt Goggins (Roddy),

TOLLBOOTH (TransAtlantic Entertainment) Producer, Steven J. Wolfe; Executive Producers, Herschel Weingrod, Robert M. Bennett, Paul Rich, Rena Ronson; Director/Screenplay, Salomé Breziner; Photography, Henry Vargas; Editor, Peter Teschner; Music, Adam Gorgoni; Designer, Brendan Barry; a Roadkill Films production in association with Sneak Preview productions, 1994; Color; Rated R; 108 minutes; June release. CAST: Fairuza Balk (Doris), Lenny Von Dohlen (Jack), Will Patton (Dash), Louise Fletcher (Lillian), Seymour Cassel (Larry/Leon), James Wilder (Vic), William Katt (Waggy)

THE SEARCH FOR ONE-EYE JIMMY (Northern Arts) Producers, Lisa Bruce, Robert Nickson; Director/Screenplay, Sam Henry Kass; Photography, Charles Levey; Designer, Ray Recht; Editor, Mark Jurgens; Music, William Bloom; Casting, Marcia Shulman; a Cabin Fever Entertainment presentation; Color; Rated R; 82 minutes; June release. CAST: Nick Turturro (Junior), Steve Buscemi (Ed Hoyt), Michael Badalucco (Joe Head), Ray "Boom Boom" Mancini (Lefty), Holt McCallany (Les), Anne Meara (Holly Hoyt), John Turturro (Disco Bean), Samuel L. Jackson (Colonel Ron), Jennifer Beals (Ellen), Tony Sirico (The Snake), Aida Turturro (Madame Esther), Wayne Maugans (Tommy Hoyt), Pat McNamara (Harold Hoyt), Joe Siravo (Father Julio), Adam Lefevre (Detective), Sam Rockwell ("One-Eye" Jimmy)

Nick Turturro in *The Search for One-Eye Jimmy*
© Northern Arts

A PERFECT CANDIDATE (Seventh Art) Producers/Directors, R.J. Cutler, David Van Taylor; Co-Producers, Dan Partland, Ted Skillman; Photography, Nicholas Doob; Editor, Mona Davis; Color; Not rated; 105 minutes; June release. Documentary about the campaign for the Virginia Senate between Oliver North and incumbent Democrat Chuck Robb, featuring Don Baker, Mark Goodin, Charles S. Robb, and Oliver L. North.

DESOLATION ANGELS (McCann & Co. Films) Producers, Tim McCann, Steven Olivieri; Director/Screenplay/Editor, Tim McCann; Photography, Matthew Howe; Designer, Larry O'Neil; Music, Drew Stiles; Presented by Jonathan Demme, Barbet Schroeder in association with Fabiano Canosa; Color; Not rated; 90 minutes; June release. CAST: Michael Rodrick (Nick), Jennifer Thomas (Mary), Peter Bassett (Sid), Shannon Gold (Ralph), Mike Alpert (Hank), Cheryl Clifford (Donna), Linda Moran (Sarah), Frank Olivier (Otis), Glen Schuld (Jerry), Virginia D'Ruc (Mrs. Cain), Robert Bryson (Jackson), Quentin Crisp (Beggar)

Oliver North, G. Gordon Liddy in *A Perfect Candidate*
© Seventh Art Releasing

Jennifer Thomas, Peter Bassett in *Desolation Angels*
©McCann & Co.

Francis Capra, Shaquille O'Neal in *Kazaam*
© Interscope Communications, Inc.

KAZAAM (Touchstone) Producers, Scott Kroopf, Paul M. Glaser, Bob Engelman; Executive Producers, Ted Field, Robert W. Cort, Leonard Armato, Shaquille O'Neal; Director/Story, Paul M. Glaser; Screenplay, Christian Ford, Roger Soffer; Co-Executive Producers, Michael A. Helfant, Beth Maloney Jelin, Bruce Binkow; Photography, Charles Minsky; Designer, Donald Burt; Editor, Michael E. Polakow; Visual Effects Supervisor, Charles Gibson; Costumes, Hope Hanafin; Music, Christopher Tyng; Casting, Dianne Crittenden; an Interscope Communications/PolyGram Filmed Entertainment production; Distributed by Buena Vista Pictures; Dolby Digital Stereo; Technicolor; Rated PG; 93 minutes; July release. CAST: Shaquille O'Neal (Kazaam), Francis Capra (Max), Ally Walker (Alice), Marshall Manesh (Malik), James Acheson (Nick), Fawn Reed (Asia Moon), John Costelloe (Travis), JoAne Hart (Mrs. Duke), Brandon Durand (Vasquez), Wade J. Robson (Elito), Jake Glaser (Jake), Efren Ramirez (Carlos), Jonathan Carrasco (Z-Dog), Jesse Perez (Vasquez's Sidekick), Todd Sible (Engineer Ed), Juan "Rambo" Reynoso (Hassem), Anthony Ferar (El-Baz), Randall Bosley (Foad), Steve Barr (Sam), Deidra "Spin" Roper (Spinderella), Kashi Barrett, Eboni Parson, Iris Burruss (KEI), Shawntae Harris (Da Brat), Nicole Jackson (Da Brat's Assistant), Altameza Reeves, Sandra Chriss, Shana Renee (The Kazettes), Davidson King (Rasta Singer), Deborah Rennard (Malik's Dinner Mate), Kelly Duncan (Cindi), Bob Clendenin (Stage Manager), Eugene McCarthy, Jeffrey Paul Johnson (Kitchen Workers), Brad Wilson (Club Curmudgeon), Miguel Escobar, Hector Jimenez (Additional Gang Kids), Michael Wajacs (Truck Driver), Rory Leidelmeyer (Bouncer), Charles E. Bennett (Roadie), Larry Clardy (Fireman)

THE POMPATUS OF LOVE (CFP) Producers, D.J. Paul, Jon Resnik; Director, Richard Schenkman; Screenplay/Co-Producers, Jon Cryer, Adam Oliensis, Richard Schenkman; Photography, Russell Lee Fine; Designer, Michael Krantz; Editor, Dan Rosen; Costumes, Carlyn Grifel; Music, John Hill; Casting, Judy Henderson & Assocs.; an In Pictures in association with BMG Independents presentation; Stereo; Color; Not rated; 99 minutes; July release. CAST: Jon Cryer (Mark), Tim Guinee (Runyon), Adam Oliensis (Phil), Adrian Pasdar (Josh), Mia Sara (Cynthia), Kristin Scott Thomas (Caroline), Arabella Field (Lori), Paige Turco (Gina), Dana Wheeler-Nicholson (Kathryn), Kristen Wilson (Tasha), Charlie Murphy (Saxophone Man), Liana Pai (Ting), Jim Turner (Dick Spellman), Rene Props (Flynn), Michael McKean, Fisher Stevens (Sitcom Stars), Jennifer Tilly (Tarzaan), Roscoe Lee Browne (Leonard Folder)

Jenny Shmizu, Angelina Jolie in *Foxfire*
© Rysher Entertainment

FOXFIRE (Samuel Goldwyn Co.) Producers, Jeffrey Lurie, John Bard Manulis, John P. Marsh; Director, Annette Haywood-Carter; Screenplay, Elizabeth White; Based on the book by Joyce Carol Oates; Executive Producers, Paige Simpson, Mike Figgis, Laura Friedman; Photography, Newton Thomas Sigel; Designer, John Myhre; Editor, Louise Innes; Music, Michel Colombier; Costumes, Laura Goldsmith; Co-Producer, Marc S. Fischer; a Rysher Entertainment presentation in association with Chestnut Hill Productions and Red Mullet Productions; Dolby; Super 35 Widescreen; Color; Rated R; 102 minutes; August release. CAST: Hedy Burress (Maddy Wirtz), Angelina Jolie (Legs Sadovsky), Jenny Lewis (Rita Faldes), Jenny Shimizu (Goldie Goldman), Sarah Rosenberg (Violet Kahn), Peter Facinelli (Ethan Bixby), Dash Mihok (Dana Taylor), Michelle Brookhurst (Cindy), Elden Ratliff (Bobby), Cathy Moriarty (Martha Wirtz), Richard Beymer (Mr. Parks), Fran Bennett (Judge Holifield), John Diehl (Mr. Buttinger), Chris Mulkey (Dan Goldman), Jay Acovone (Chuck), Arwen Carter (Leaflet Girl), Ever Carradine (Girl in Printshop), Maria Celedonio (Zoe), Raissa Fleming (Rita's Mom), T.J. Galash (Teenage Boy), Scott Gallegos, Jason Wilhite (Jock Friends), Kaci Garcia (Rita's Younger Sister), Wesley Johnson (Tom), Rick Jones (Security Guard), Joel Moore (First Geek), Betty Moyer (Violet's Mother), Barbara Niven (Goldie's Stepmother), Steven Clark Pachoso (Cop), Stuart Regen (Art Teacher), Lori Rogers (First Year Girl), Burl Ross (Mr. Penn), Shiloh Strong (Steve), Rasa Yurchis (Street Junkie)

Adam Oliensis, Tim Guinee, Jon Cryer, Adrian Pasdar in
The Pompatus of Love © CFP

Jermaine "Huggy" Hopkins in *Phat Beach*
© Live Entertainment, Inc.

Jessica Lundy, Alex McKenna, Tom Arnold, Bug Hall in *The Stupids*
© New Line Productions, Inc.

PHAT BEACH (Orion) Producer, Cleveland O'Neal; Executive Producer, Michael Schultz; Co-Producers, Brian E. O'Neal, Juanita Diana; Director, Doug Ellin; Screenplay, Doug Ellin, Brian E. O'Neal, Ben Morris; Story, Cleveland O'Neal, Brian E. O'Neal; Photography, Jim Lebovitz, Jurgen Baum; Editors, Richard Nord, Jeremy Craig Kasten; Music, Paul Stewart, Gary Meals; Designers, Terri Schaetzle, Colleen Devine; Costumes, Mona Thalheimer; Casting, Connection III; a Live Entertainment and Connection III Entertainment presentation; Dolby Stereo; Color; Rated R; 99 minutes; August release. CAST: Jermaine "Huggy" Hopkins (Benny King), Brian Hooks (Durrel Jackson), Gregg D. Vance (Mikey Z), Claudia Kaleem (Candace Williams), Erick Fleeks (Carl King), Alma Collins (Janet King), Candice Merideth (Tasha King), Sabrina De Pina (Tanya Watkins), Jennifer Lucienne (Denise Marie), Coolio (Himself), Tre Black (Emcee), Tiny "Zeus" Lister, Jr., Y?N-VEE

Vincent Perez, Mia Kirshner in *The Crow: City of Angels*
© Dimension Films

THE STUPIDS (New Line Cinema) Producer, Leslie Belzberg; Director, John Landis; Screenplay, Brent Forrester; Based on characters created by James Marshall, Harry Allard; Photography, Manfred Guthe; Designer, Phil Dagort; Editor, Dale Beldin; Costumes, Deborah Nadoolman; Music, Christopher Stone; Casting, Amy Lippens; a Savoy Pictures presentation in association with Rank Film Distributors of a Landis/Belzberg Film; Dolby Stereo; Color; Rated PG; 94 minutes; August release. CAST: Tom Arnold (Stanley Stupid), Jessica Lundy (Joan Stupid), Bug Hall (Buster Stupid), Alex McKenna (Petunia Stupid), Scott Kraft (Policeman), Victor Ertmanis, Earl Williams (Garbagemen), George Chiang, Arthur Eng (Chinese Waiters), Max Landis (Graffiti Artist), Carol Ng (Jade Palace Hostess), Jennifer Dean (Meter Maid), Mark Metcalf (Colonel), Mark Keeslar (Lieutenant), Garry Robbins (Extremely Tall Guy), Nicu Branzea, Richard Crook (Arms Buyers), Gurinder Chadha (Reporters), Jeremy Ratchford (Soldier), John Stoneham, Jr. (Green

Alien), Ken Quinn (Orange Alien), Gillian Vanderburgh (Alien Stewardess), Harvey Atkin (Deli Guy), David Cronenberg (Postal Supervisor), Markus Parilo (Special Forces Guy), Costa Gavras (Gas Station Guy), MIF (Explosive Guy), Walter Alza (Taxi Driver), Robert Wise (Stanley's Neighbor), Christopher Lee (Evil Sender), Frankie Faison (The Lloyd), Mo Kelso (Airbag Woman), Sherry Miller (Anchorwoman), Bob Keeshan (Charles Sender), Jeff Clarke (Delivery Guy), Atom Egoyan (TV Studio Guard), Wendy Hopkins (TV Assistant Director), Jacqueline McLeod (Make-Up Woman), Jenny McCarthy (Glamorous Actress), David Ferry (Late Night Show Host), Norman Jewison (TV Director), Frederic Devancker (French Chef), Rolanda Watts (Talk Show Hostess); Gillo Pontecorvo, Nicholas Rice, Julie Champnella (Talk Show Guests), Philip Akin, Kevin Conway (Henchmen), Carol Anderson (Checkpoint Guard), Rick Avery (Bad Guy), Fiona Highet, Phillip Jarret, Jim Amross, Wayne Ward (Cops), Michael Bell (Voices of Xylophone & Kitty)

Kevin Pollack, Christopher McDonald, Jamie Lee Curtis, Sheila McCarthy in House Arrest
© Rysher Entertainment, Inc.

THE CROW: CITY OF ANGELS (Miramax) Producers, Edward R. Pressman, Jeff Most; Executive Producers, Bob Weinstein, Harvey Weinstein, Alessandro Camon; Co-Producer, Michael Flynn; Director, Tim Pope; Screenplay, David S. Goyer; Based on the comic book series and comic strip by James O. Barr; Photography, Jean Yves Escoffier; Designer, Alex McDowell; Editors, Michael N. Knue, Anthony Redman; Costumes, Kirsten Everberg; Music, Graeme Revell; Visual Effects Supervisor, Roger Dorney; Casting, Lora Kennedy; a Miramax/Dimension Films presentation of an Edward R. Pressman production in association with Jeff Most productions; Dolby Stereo; Color; Rated R; 84 minutes; August release. CAST: Vincent Perez (Ashe), Mia Kirshner (Sarah), Richard Brooks (Judah), Iggy Pop (Curve), Thomas Jane (Nemo), Vincent Castellanos (Spider Monkey), Thuy Trang (Kali), Eric Acosta (Danny), Ian Dury (Noah), Tracey Ellis (Sybil), Beverley Mitchell (Grace), Aaron Thell Smith (Tattoo Customer), Alan Gelfant (Bassett), Shelly Desai (Hindu), Holley Chant (Holly Daze), Kerry Rossall (Zeke), Reynaldo Duran (Priest), Danny Verduzco (Boy in Church), Maria Julia Moran (Old Lady in Church)

HOUSE ARREST (MGM) Producer, Judith A. Polone, Harry Winer; Executive Producer, Keith Samples; Director, Harry Winer; Screenplay, Michael Hitchcock; Photography, Ueli Steiger; Designer, Peter Jamison; Editor, Ronald Roose; Associate Producer, Laura Friedman; Co-Producer, Carroll Newman; Music, Bruce Broughton; Costumes, Hope Hanafin; Casting, Wendy Kurtzman; a Rysher Entertainment presentation; Digital DTS Stereo; Deluxe color; Rated PG; 108 minutes; August release. CAST: Kyle Howard (Grover Beindorf), Russel Harper (T.J. Krupp), Jamie Lee Curtis (Janet Beindorf), Kevin Pollak (Ned Beindorf), Amy Sakasitz (Stacy Beindorf), Mooky Arizona (Matt Finley), Caroline Aaron (Louise Finley), Alex Seitz (Jimmy), Josh Wolford (Teddy), Wallace Shawn (Vic Finley), Jennifer Love Hewitt (Brooke Figler), Patrika Darbo (Cafeteria Cashier), Ray Walston (Chief Rocco), Christopher McDonald (Donald Krupp), Colleen Camp (Mrs. Burtis), Sheila McCarthy (Gwenna Krupp), Jennifer Tilly (Cindy Figler), K. Todd Freeman (Officer Davis), Daniel Roebuck (Officer Brickowski), Ben Stein (Ralph Doyle), Michael Hitchcock (Cop), Rosie Winer (Flower Girl), Jessica Frank (Jr. Bridesmaid)

Mario Van Peebles (r) in *Solo*.
© Columbia Pictures Industries, Inc.

Zachary Taylor, Kris Park in *Camp Stories*
© Artistic License

SOLO (Triumph Films) Producers, Joseph Newton Cohen, John Flock; Director, Norberto Barba; Screenplay, David Corley; Based on the novel *Weapon* by Robert Mason; Photography, Christopher Walling; Designer, Markus Canter; Co-Producers, Jose Ludlow, Gina Resnick; Music, Christopher Franke; Editor, Scott Conrad; Fight Choreographer, Tom Muzila; Casting, Karen Rea; an Orpheus Films-John Flock Production in association with Van Peebles Films; Dolby SDDS Stereo; Super 35 Widescreen; Technicolor; Rated PG-13; 93 minutes; August release. CAST: Mario Van Peebles (Solo), Bary Corbin (Gen. Clyde Haynes), William Sadler (Col. Madden), Jaime Gomez (Lorenzo), Damian Bechir (Rio), Seidy Lopez (Agela), Abraham Verduzco (Miguel), Joaquin Garrido (Vasquez), William Wallace (Mr. Thompson), Adrien Brody (Bill Stewart), Brent Schaefer (Communications Officer), Lucas Dudley (Heimsman), Christopher Michael (Flight Deck Officer), Rafael Velasco (Justos), Abel Woolrich (Lazaro), Fernecio De Bernal (Father Cerna), Socorro Avelar (Abuelita), Alvaro Carcano, Carlos Quintero (Elders), William Ungerman (Bayne), Greg Collins (Scanion), Randy Reyes (Locke), Sid Belk (Pierson), Kevin Cole (Hawkins), Charlie Tuitavuki (Stone), Norberto Barba (Rebel Soldier), John Flock (Lab Tech), Juliano Buccio (Rebel in Church)

TALES FROM THE CRYPT PRESENTS BORDELLO OF BLOOD (Universal) Producer/Director, Gilbert Adler; Screenplay, AL Katz, Gilbert Adler; Story, Bob Gale, Robert Zemeckis; Based on "Tales From the Crypt" comic books originally published by William M. Gaines; Executive Producers, Richard Donner, David Giler, Walter Hill, Joel Silver, Robert Zemeckis; Photography, Tom Priestley; Designer, Gregory Melton; Editor, Stephen Lovejoy; Music, Chris Boardman, Danny Elfman; Co-Producers, AL Katz, Alexander Collett; Costumes, Trish Keating; Additional Prosthetic Effects Designer/Creator, Todd Masters Company; Casting, Victoria Burrows; DTS Stereo; Deluxe color; Rated R; 87 minutes; August release. CAST: John Kassir (Voice of the Crypt Keeper), Dennis Miller (Rafe Guttman), Erika Eleniak (Katherine Verdoux), Angie Everhart (Lilith), Chris Sarandon (Reverend Current), Corey Feldman (Caleb Verdoux), Aubrey Morris (McCutcheon), Phil

Fondacaro (Vincent Prather), William Sadler (Mummy), Ciara Hunter (Tamara), Leslie Ann Phillips (Patrice), Juliet Reagh (Tallulah), Eli Gabay (Miguel), Matt Hill (Reggie), Eric Keenleyside (Noonan), Kim Kondrashoff (Jenkins), Robert Paul Munic (Zeke), Gary Starr (Jed), Robin Douglas (Louise), Dorian "Joe" Clark (Jonas), Ravinder Toor (Bartender), Robert Rozen (Rabbi Goldman), Jen Jasey (Woman), Heather Hanson (Babe), Sibel Thrasher, Tom Pickett, Topaz Hasfal, Lovie Eli (Gospel Singers), Korrine St. Onge, Claire Marie Harvey, Lyne Hachey, Sheena Galloway, Kikka Ferguson, Melody Cherpaw (Bordello Vampires), Sheila Mills (Bride of Frankenstein), Natalie Ross, Angela Nesbitt-Dufort (Dancers), Gloria Roy, Maria Marhoffer-Bains (Waitress), Whoopi Goldberg

SYNTHETHIC PLEASURES (Caipirinha Prods.) Producer, George Gund III; Director/Screenplay, Iara Lee; Photography, Marcus Hahn, Kramer Morgenthau, Toshifumi Furusawa; Editors, Andreas Troeger, Stacia Thompson; Dolby Stereo; Color; Not rated; 83 minutes; August release. Documentary looks at various technologies and their influence on creating an artificial reality in our culture, featuring John Perry Barlow, Jeffrey Baxter, Scott Bukatman, Robert Ettinger, Scott Frazier, Robert Gurland, Michio Kaku, Jaron Lanier, Timothy Leary, Max More, Orlan, Lisa Palac, Ed Regis, Howard Rheingold, Steve Roberts, R.U. Sirius

CAMP STORIES (Artistic License) Producers, Robin O'Hara, Scott Macaulay; Director/Screenplay, Herbert Beigel; Photography, Paul Gibson; Designer, Deena Sidney; Editor, Meg Reticker; Music, Roy Nathanson; Casting, Hopkins, Smith & Barden Associates; a Forensic Films production; Color; Not rated; 99 minutes; August release. CAST: Jerry Stiller (Schlomo), Paul Sand (Moishe), Zachary Taylor (Young David), Kris Park (Young Paul), Ted Marcoux (Chaim), Talia Balsam (Mary), Susan Vanech (Sally), Brett Barsky (Malcolm), Jason Biggs (Abby), Andrew Barlow (Milty), Ben Shenkman (Yehudah), Richard Council (Older Paul), Scott Cohen (Schnair), Susan Bruce (Sarah), Elliott Gould (Older David)

Angie Everhart, Dennis Miller in *Bordello of Blood*
© Universal City Studios, Inc.

Jennifer Tilly, John Savage in *American Strays*
© Unapix Films

Keanu Reeves, Cameron Diaz in *Feeling Minnesota*
© Fine Line Features

Damien Wayne Echols in *Paradise Lost*
© Home Box Office

AMERICAN STRAYS (Unapix) Producers, Rod Dean, Kirk Hassig, Douglas Textor; Executive Producer, Frank Agrama; Director/Screenplay, Michael Covert; Executive in Charge of Production, Norman Siderow; Photography, Sean Mutarevic; Designer, Paul Holt; Music, John Graham; Editor, Rod Dean; from Canned Pictures; Color; Rated R; 93 minutes; September release. CAST: Jennifer Tilly (Patty Mae), Eric Roberts (Martin), John Savage (Dwayne), Luke Perry (Johnny), Carol Kane (Helen), Joe Viterelli (Gene), James Russo (Harv), Vonte Sweet (Mondo), Sam Jones (Exterminator), Brion James (Otis), Toni Kalem (Alice), Melora Walters (Cindy), Scott Plank (Sonny), Anthony Lee (Omar), Stephanie Cushna (Johnny's Girlfriend), Stace Williamson (Johnny's Brother), Luana Anders (Martha), Robert Fields (Harry), Jack Kehler (Walker), Charles Bailey-Gates (Bob), Tom Eliot (Timmy), Will Rothhaar (Jordan), Jessica Perelman (Daphne), Mike Horse (Lead Cop), Patrick Warburton, Mike Kaliski, Leland Crooke (Cops)

FEELING MINNESOTA (Fine Line Features) Producers, Danny DeVito, Michael Shamberg, Stacey Sher; Executive Producer, Erwin Stoff; Co-Producer, Eric McLeod; Director/Screenplay, Steven Baigelman; Photography, Walt Lloyd; Designer, Naomi Shohan; Costumes, Eugenie Bafaloukos; Editor, Martin Walsh; Casting, Francine Maisler; Music, Los Lobos; a Jersey Films production; Dolby SDDS Stereo; Super 35 Widescreen; Color; Rated R; 99 minutes; September release. CAST: Keanu Reeves (Jjaks), Vincent D'Onofrio (Sam), Cameron Diaz (Freddie), Delroy Lindo (Red), Courtney Love (Rhonda the Waitress), Tuesday Weld (Nora), Dan Aykroyd (Ben), Levon Helm (Bible Salesman), Drew DesMarais (Young Jjaks), Aaron Michael Metchik (Young Sam), Russell Konstans (Joseph), David Alan Smith (Lloyd), Bill Schoppert (Minister), Steve Ghizoni (Wedding Band Singer), Jack Walsh (Gas Station Bob), Buffy Sedlachek (Gas Station Attendant), Paul Smith (Horse Driver), Bill Vergis, Scott Clemens (Horse Thieves), Michael Rispoli (Manager, Suburban Motel), Arabella Field (Manger's Wife), Peter Syvertsen, John Carroll Lynch (Cops), Ollie Osterberg (Man on Phone), Max Perlich (Clerk at Saddlebrook Motel), Dale Dunham (Manager at Saddlebrook Motel)

CURDLED (Miramax) Producers, John Maass, Raul Puig; Executive Producer, Quentin Tarantino; Director, Reb Braddock; Screenplay, John Maass, Reb Braddock; Photography, Steven Bernstein; Designer, Sherman Williams; Editor, Mallory Gottlieb; Music, Joseph Julian Gonzalez; Costumes, Beverly Nelson Safier; Casting, Yvonne Casas; a Band Apart and Tinderbox Films production; Dolby Stereo; Deluxe Color; Rated R; 94 minutes; September release. CAST: Angela Jones (Gabriela), William Baldwin (Paul Guell), Bruce Ramsay (Eduardo), Lois Chiles (Katrina Brandt), Barry Corbin (Lodger), Mel Gorham (Elena), Daisy Fuentes (Clara), Carmen Lopez (Lourdes), Vivienne Sandaydiego (Eva), Caridad Ravelo (Joan), Sandra Thigpen (Grace), Kelly Preston (Kelly Hogue), Lupita Ferrer (Marie Clement), Sabrina Cowan (Red Haired Waitress), Charles J. Tucker (Sam the Barback), Alyssa Tacher (Young Gabriela), Nattacha Amador (Young Gabriela's Mother), Therese Marie Guitierez (P.F.C.S. Spokesmaid), Jay Amor (Falling Man)

PARADISE LOST: THE CHILD MURDERS AT ROBIN HOOD HILLS (Home Box Office) Producers/Directors/Editors, Joe Berlinger, Bruce Sinofsky; Photography, Robert Richman; Executive Producer, Sheila Nevins; Music, Metallica; from Creative Thinking International, Ltd.; Color; Not rated; 150 minutes. Documentary on the murder of three 8-year-old boys in Arkansas, and the subsequent trial of three teenagers accused of the crimes. This film originally premiered on HBO in July of 1996.

THE LEOPARD SON (Discovery Channel Pictures) Producers, Hugo Van Lawick, Tim Cowling; Director, Hugo Van Lawick; Executive in Charge of Production, Denise Baddour; Executive Producer, Tim Cowling; Screenplay, Michael Olmert; Editors, Mark Fletcher, Gerrit Netten; Associate Producers, Evert Van Den Bos, Edith Brinkers; Music, Stewart Copeland; a co-presentation of Nature Conservation Films; Dolby Digital Stereo; Color; Rated G; 84 minutes; September release. Documentary follows the early years in the life of a leopard in Africa's Serengeti Plain; narrated by John Gielgud (voice of Hugo Van Lawick).

Angela Jones, William Baldwin in *Curdled*
© Miramax Films

Leopard Mother in *The Leopard Son*
©The Discovery Channel

Martin Sheen, Moira Kelly in *Entertaining Angels*
© Paulist Pictures

ENTERTAINING ANGELS: THE DOROTHY DAY STORY (Paulist Pictures) Producer, Ellwood E. Keiser; Co-Producers, Peter Burrell, Chris Donahue; Director, Michael Ray Rhodes; Screenplay, John Wells; Photography, Michael Fash; Designer, Charles Rosen; Editors, George Folsey, Jr., Geoffrey Rowland; Music, Bill Conti, Ashley Irwin; Casting, Caro Jones; Dolby Stereo; Color; Rated PG-13; 110 minutes; September release. CAST: Moira Kelly (Dorothy Day), Martin Sheen (Peter Maurin), Lenny Von Dohlen (Forster Battingham), Heather Graham (Maggie), Paul Lieber (Mike Gold), Geoffrey Blake (Floyd Dell), James Lancaster (Eugene O'Neill), Boyd Kestner (Lionel Moise), Tracey Walter (Joe Bennett), Allyce Beasley (Frankie), Melinda Dillon (Sister Aloysius), Brian Keith (The Cardinal)

KIDS OF SURVIVAL: THE ART AND LIFE OF TIM ROLLINS & K.O.S. (Geller/Goldfine) Producers/Directors/Photography, Daniel Geller, Dayna Goldfine; Photography, Daniel Geller; Editors, Elizabeth Finlayson, Daniel Geller, Eve Goldberg, Dayna Goldfine; Music, Todd Boekelheide; Color; Not rated; 87 minutes; September release. Documentary on artist-teacher Tim Rollins and his unique workshop for inner-city youths.

THE BIG SQUEEZE (First Look Pictures) formerly *Body of a Woman*; Producers, Zane W. Levitt, Mark Yellen, Liz McDermott; Director/Screenplay, Marcus De Leon; Photography, Jacques Haitkin; Designer, J. Rae Fox; Editor, Sonny Baskin; Music, Mark Mothersbaugh; Costumes, Charmain Schreiner; Casting, Laura Schiff; a Zeta Entertainment production; Dolby Digital Stereo; Color; Rated R; 98 minutes; September release. CAST: Lara Flynn Boyle (Tanya), Peter Dobson (Benny O'Malley), Danny Nucci (Jesse), Luca Bercovici (Henry), Teresa Dispina (Cece), Michael Chieffo (Inspector), Sam Vlahos (Father Sanchez), Valente Rodriguez (Father Arias), Bert Santos (Manny), Raye Birk (Contractor), Angelina Estrada (Mother Dolores), Janet MacLachlan (Bank Manager), Demetrius Navarro (Young Man), Marita De Leon (Young Woman), Tony Genaro (Older Man), Gary Paul (Mechanic), Laura Ceron (Letter Carrier)

Peter Dobson, Danny Nucci, Lara Flynn Boyle in *The Big Squeeze*
© First Look Pictures

CRIMINALS (Reality Prods.) Producers, Elinor Bunin, Joseph Strick; Director, Joseph Strick; Photography, Joseph Strick, Peter Skuts; Editor, Ruth Cullen; Narration, C.K. Williams; Narrator, Louise Smith; Color; Not rated; 75 minutes; September release. Documentary featuring various district attorney interviews with criminals and surveillance camera footage of robberies.

UNCONDITIONAL LOVE (Prodigy) Producer/Director, Arthur Bjorn Egeli; Executive Producer, David Ellsworth; Screenplay, Arthur Bjorn Egeli, Ian Bowater; Photography, Teresa Medina; Editor, Barbara Boguski; Music, Michael Errington; Dolby Stereo; Colorlab color; Not rated; 85 minutes; September release. CAST: Pablo Bryant (Steven Buchanan), Aleksandra Kaniak (Mary Chambers), Isabelle Dahlin (Melissa Gardner), David Ellsworth (Robert Hoffman), Jessica Brytn Flannery (Theresa), Joe Estevez (Ron Chambers), Hal Streit (Hal Wilson), Adrienne Newberg (Anne Melon)

Halle Berry, Peter Greene in *The Rich Man's Wife*
© Hollywood Pictures Company

FREEBIRD...THE MOVIE (Cabin Fever) Producer/Director, Jeff G. Waxman; Screenplay, Sanford Santacroce; Executive Producers, Tom Molito, Judy Van Zant Jenness; Editor, Dave De La Parra; Presented in association with Freebird Film Productions, Inc.; DTS Stereo; Color; Rated PG; 105 minutes; September release. Concert film of Lynyrd Skynyrd featuring Allen Collins, Steve Gaines, Billy Powell, Artimus Pyle, Gary Rossington, Ronnie Van Zant, Leon Wilkeson, Jojo Billingsley, Cassie Gaines, Leslie Hawkins.

LOSER (Edge Cinema) Producer, Peter Baxter; Executive Producers, Jonathan Chaus, Tina Kuykendall; Director/Screenplay, Kirk Harris; Photography, Kent Wakeford; Editor, Adam Pertofsky; a Don't Count Me Out production; Dolby Stereo; Color; Not rated; 85 minutes; September release. CAST: Kirk Harris, Jonathan Chaus, Norman Saleet, Peta Wilson, Jack Rubio, Kim Antepenko, David Michael.

THE RICH MAN'S WIFE (Hollywood Pictures) Producers, Roger Birnbaum, Julie Bergman Sender; Executive Producer, Jennifer Ogden; Director/Screenplay, Amy Holden Jones; Photography, Haskell Wexler; Designer, Jeannine Oppewall; Editor, Wendy Greene Bricmont; Music, John Frizzell, James Newton Howard; Casting, Nancy Klopper; Presented in association with Caravan Pictures; Distributed by Buena Vista Pictures; Dolby Digital Stereo; Technicolor; Rated R; 95 minutes; September release. CAST: Halle Berry (Josie Potenza), Christopher McDonald (Tony Potenza), Clive Owen (Jake Golden), Peter Greene (Cole), Charles Hallahan (Dan Fredricks), Frankie Faison (Ron Lewis), Clea Lewis (Nora Golden), Loyda Ramos (Grace), William Crossett (Cab Driver), Eddie Francis (Bartender), Lou Di Maggio, Alexandra Hedison (Party Guests), John Paragon (Maitre D'), Marc Shelton (Instateller Man), Kelly Jo Minter (Cursing Hooker), Allan Rich (Bill Adolphe), Marc Lynn (Police Photographer), Zoaunne Le Roy (Gray-Haired Waitress), Greg Serano, Michelle Bonilla, Rolando Molina (Gangbangers), Valente Rodriguez (Freeway Driver), Michael Marich (Williams), Suzanne Michaels, Bruce Wright (Newscasters), Angela Nogaro (Receptionist)

Michael DeLorenzo, Anthony Quinn in *Somebody To Love*
© Legacy

Karl Giant, Michael Albanese in *Sleepover*
© Artistic License Films

SOMEBODY TO LOVE (Legacy) Producer, Lila Cazes; Director, Alexandre Rockwell; Screenplay, Alexandre Rockwell, Sergei Bodrov; Co-Executive Producer, Marie Cantin; Photography, Bob Yeoman; Designer, J. Rae Fox; Editor, Elena Maganini; Costumes, Alexandra Welker; Music, Mader; Casting, Georgianne Walken, Sheila Jaffee; a Lumiere Pictures release; French, 1995; Dolby Stereo; Color; Rated R; 103 minutes; September release. CAST: Rosie Perez (Mercedes), Harvey Keitel (Harry Harrelson), Michael DeLorenzo (Ernesto), Stanley Tucci (George), Steve Buscemi (Jackie), Steve Randazzo (Nick), Gerardo (Armando), Paul Herman (Pinky), Anthony Quinn (Emilio), Angel Aviles (Pregnant Taxi Dancer), Lorelei Leslie (Blonde Taxi Dancer), Sam Fuller (Sam Silverman), Quentin Tarantino (Bartender)

GLORY DAZE (Seventh Art Releasing) Producers, Aaron M. Weinberg, William R. Woodward, Chris Moore; Executive Producers, Michael S. Bloom, William P. O'Reilly; Director/Screenplay, Rich Wilkes; Photography, Christopher Taylor; Designer, Alfred Sole; Editor, Richard Candib; Casting, Felicia Fasano; a Fusion Studios, Inc./Woodward Productions/Weiny Bro Productions presentation; Dolby Stereo; Color; Not rated; 104 minutes; September release. CAST: Ben Affleck (Jack), Sam Rockwell (Rob), Megan Ward (Joannie), French Stewart (Dennis), Vien Hong (Slosh), Vinne DeRamus (Mickey), Kristen Bauer (Dina), Alyssa Milano (Chelsea), John Rhys-Davies (Luther), Lance Wilson-White (Stew), Mary Woronov (Joannie's Mom), Tegan West (Doc), Matthew McConaughey (Rental Truck Guy), Sean Whalen (Flunky), Christine Klotz (Graduation Woman), Christopher Slater (Crazy), Elizabeth Ruscio (Jack's Mom), Spalding Gray (Jack's Dad), Brendan Fraser (Doug), Leah Remini (Theresa), Jay Lacopo (The Bus Driver), Bob Libman (Chancellor Bob), Matthey Hennesey, Soren Ray (Wise Guys on Cliff), Michael Stephen Ferrari (Dina's Boyfriend), Matt Damon (Edgar Pudwhacker), Jacobi Wynne, Shane Matthews, Dan Ryan (Young Guys), Alfred Sole (Abusive Fisherman)

TRUE AMERICAN (Independent) Director/Screenplay, Paul Roberts; No other credits available ; Color; Not rated; 95 minutes; October release. CAST: Dwight Martin, Juvencio Gonzalez, Jr., Gernet Miller.

STREET CORNER JUSTICE (Sunset Films Intl.) Producers, Jack Brown, Chuck Bail; Executive Producers, Jack Brown, Chuck Bail, Steve Restivo, Joe Restivo; Director, Chuck Bail; Screenplay, Stan Berkowitz, Gary Kent, Chuck Bail; Photography, Doug O'Neons, David Golia; Music, K. Alexander Wilkinson; Editor, W. Peter Miller; produced in association with Street City Films; Color; Rated R; 102 minutes; October release. CAST: Marc Singer (Mike Justus), Steve Railsback (Ryan Freeborn), Kim Lankford (Jenny Connor), Willie Gee (Beverly Leech), "Tiny" Lister, Jr. (Angel Aikens), Soon-Teck Oh (Kwong Chuck Lee)

SLEEPOVER (Artistic License) Producer/Editor, Jim McNally; Director, John Sullivan; Photography, Joaquin Baca-Asay; Music, Jeff Buckley; Associate Producers, Simon Allen, Betsy Millburn; a Leo Films in association with JSP Inc. and Steve Austin Films presentation; Color; Not rated; 88 minutes; October release. CAST: Karl Giant (Sean), Michael Albanese (Mark), Heather Casey (Brooke), Megan Shand (Megan), Shannon Barry (Anne). Ken Miles

CALLING THE GHOSTS: A STORY ABOUT RAPE, WAR AND WOMEN (Independent) Producer, Mandy Jacobson; Executive Producers, Anita Saewitz, Maury Solomon, Julia Ormond; Director/Screenplay, Mandy Jacobson, Karmen Jelinic; Color; Not rated; 63 minutes; October release. Documentary on the International War Crimes Tribunal and the accusations towards Serb soldiers of the rape of several Muslim women.

I SHOT A MAN IN VEGAS (Arrow) Producers, Alec Choches, Molly Mayeux, Scott Moore; Executive Producers, Terence Michael, Adam Gainsburg; Director/Screenplay, Keoni Waxman; Photography, Steven Finestone; Editor, Ken Blackwell; Costumes, Mari-An Ceo; Music, Shark; Color; Not rated; 80 minutes; October release. CAST: John Stockwell (Grant), Janeane Garofalo (Gale), Brian Drillinger (Martin), David Cubitt (Johnny), Noelle Lippman (Amy), Ele Keats (Hippie Chick), Todd Cole (Nick), Patrick J. Statham, Ellen S. Statham, Tyler Patton (Cops), Craig Wasson (Radio Caller)

French Stewart, Ben Affleck, Sam Rockwell, Vien Hong, Megan Ward, Alyssa Milano, Vinnie DeRamus in *Glory Days* © Seventh Art Releasing

John Stockwell in *I Shot A Man in Vegas*
© Arrow Releasing

Joshua Jackson, Vincent A. LaRusso in *D3: The Mighty Ducks*
© Disney Enterprises, Inc.

D3: THE MIGHTY DUCKS (Walt Disney Pictures) Producers, Jordan Kerner, Jon Avnet; Executive Producers, Steven Brill, C. Tad Devlin; Director, Robert Lieberman; Screenplay, Steven Brill, Jim Burnstein; Story, Kenneth Johnson, Jim Burnstein; Photography, David Hennings; Designer, Stephen Storer; Editors, Patrick Lussier, Colleen Halsey; Costumes, Kimberly A. Tillman; Music, J.A.C. Redford; Casting, Judy Taylor; an Avnet/Kerner production; Distributed by Buena Vista Pictures; Dolby Digital Stereo; Technicolor; Rated PG; 104 minutes; October release. CAST: Emilio Estevez (Gordon Bombay), Jeffrey Nordling (Coach Orion), David Selby (Dean Buckley), Heidi Kling (Casey), Joshua Jackson (Charlie), Joss Ackland (Hans), Elden Ryan Ratliff (Fulton), Shaun Weiss (Goldberg), Vincent A. LaRusso (Banks), Matt Doherty (Averman), Garette Ratliff Henson (Guy), Marguerite Moreau (Connie), Michael Cudlitz (Cole), Christopher Orr (Rick), Aaron Lohr (Portman), Ty O'Neal (Dwayne), Kenan Thompson (Russ), Mike Vitar (Luis), Colombe Jacobsen (Julie), Justin Wong (Ken), Scott Whyte (Scott), Margot Finley (Linda), Lynn Phillip Seibel (Tom Riley), Benjamin Salisbury (Josh), Eliza Coyle (Angela Delaney), James Craven (Mr. Barber), Claudia Wilkins (Mrs. Madigan) Melissa Keller (Mindy), Samantha Harris (Cindy), Jack White (Coach Wilson), Steven Brill (Arcade Attendant), Mary Brill (Jeannie), Jeannette Kerner, Herbert Brill (Board Members), Mike Kelly (Referee), Claire Bednarski (Gabriella), Jerry Kerner, Bert Sandberg (Customers at Mickey's Diner)

FREEWAY (Roxie/Republic) Producers, Brad Wyman, Chris Hanley, Muse Productions; Executive Producers, Oliver Stone, Dan Halsted, Richard Rutowski; Co-Producers, Marc Ezralow, Adam J. Merims; Director/Screenplay, Matthew Bright; Photography, John Thomas; Designer, Pam Warner; Costumes, Merrie Lawson; Music, Danny Elfman; Editor, Maysie Hoy; a Republic Pictures, Kushner-Locke and Samuel Hadida, in association with August Entertainment and Davis Films presentation of an Illusion Entertainment Group and Muse/Wyman Production; Dolby Stereo; Color; Rated R; 91 minutes; October release. CAST: Kiefer Sutherland (Bob Wolverton), Reese Witherspoon

Reese Witherspoon, Kiefer Sutherland in *Freeway*
© The Kushner-Locke Company

(Vanessa), Brooke Shields (Mimi Wolverton), Wolgang Bodison (Detective Breer), Dan Hedaya (Detective Wallace), Amanda Plummer (Ramona—Vanessa's Mother), Michael T. Weiss (Larry—Vanessa's Stepdad), Bokeem Woodbine (Chopper), Brittany Murphy (Rhonda), Sidney Lassick (Norman), Kitty Fox (Grandma)

GET OVER IT (Strand) Producer/Director/Screenplay/Photography/Editor, Nick Katsapetses; a Verging Production presentation; Black and white; Not rated; 78 minutes; October release. CAST: Christian Canterbury (Spencer), Deborah Cordell (Pam), Nick Katsapetses (Derek), David McCrea (Robert), Carrie Morgan (Sarah), Troy Morgan (Steven), Steven Sorensen (Michael), Alison Jean Trotta (Elisha), Kara Tsiaperas (Christine)

YOU'LL NEVER MAKE LOVE IN THIS TOWN AGAIN (Dove Entertainment) Producer/Director/Screenplay, Michael Viner; Based on the book by Robin, Liza, Linda and Tiffany, as told to Joanne Parrent; Photography, Eric Bakke, Chip Goebert; Editor, Tony Nassour; Color; Not rated; 82 minutes; October release. Documentary looks at the lives of some high-priced call girls, with Robin, Liza, Linda, Tiffany.

NORMAL LIFE (Fine Line) Producers, Richard Maynard, John Saviano; Co-Producer, Steven A. Jones; Director, John McNaughton; Screenplay, Peg Haller, Bob Schneider; Photography, Jean De Segonzac; Editor, Elena Maganini; Designer, Rick Paul; Costumes, Jacqueline St. Anne; Astro color; Not rated; 101 minutes; October release. CAST: Ashley Judd (Pam Anderson), Luke Perry (Chris Anderson), Bruce Young (Agent Parker), Jim True (Mike Anderson), Dawn Maxey (Eva), Penelope Milford (Adele Anderson), Tom Towles (Frank Anderson)

Ashley Judd, Luke Perry in *Normal Life*
© Fine Line Features

NOT BAD FOR A GIRL (Horizon) Producer/Director/Screenplay, Dr. Lisa Rose Apramian, Ph. D.; Executive Producer, Tina Silvey; Editor, Kyle C. Kyle; a Spitshine Production; Color; Not rated; 90 minutes; October release. Documentary on all-female bands in alternative rock music, featuring Courtney Love and Hole, Kat Bjelland and Babes in Toyland, Becky Wreck and Lunachicks, Donita Sparks and L7, Joan Jett, Mudwimin, Lesley Rankine, Jula Bell, Gilly Hanner, Choptank, Gunk, Chicken Milk, Cheesecake, Erika Reinstein, Anne Stanley, Rock 'n' Roll High School.

MERCY (Unapix) Producers, Rolfe Kent, Rocky Collins, Richard Shepard; Executive Producer, Jennifer L. Pearlman; Director/Screenplay, Richard Shepard; Photography, Sarah Cawley; Designer, Anne Ross; Editor, Adam Lichtenstein; Music, Rolfe Kent; Costumes, Leonardo Iturregui; from Injosho Films in association with Elevator Pictures; Ultra Stereo; Color; Not rated; 85 minutes; November release. CAST: John Rubinstein (Frank Kramer), Amber Kain (Ruby), Sam Rockwell (Matty), Jane Lanier (Carol), Novella Nelson (Angela), Phil Brock (Phil Kline), Rhea Silver-Smith (Nicole), Christopher J. Quinn (Joey), Kevin Joseph (Livingston), Maura Tierney (Simonett), Mark Mullin (Mr. Funbags the Clown), Flottila DeBarge (Transvestite Hooker), Rick Gomez (Peter), Robert Shepard (Cab Driver), Ajay Mehta (Wendell), Dan Atkins (Wendell), Judy Goldschmidt, Joe Donahue, Billy Lux

Courtney Love in *Not Bad For A Girl*
© Horizon Unlimited

Dan Futterman, Susan Floyd in *Breathing Room*
© Holiday Pictures Group

MAN WITH A PLAN (Bellwether Films) Producer/Director/Screenplay/Editor, John O'Brien; Photography, Richard Morse, John O'Brien; DuArt Color; Not rated; 90 minutes; November release. CAST: Fred Tuttle, Bill Blachly, Joe Tuttle, Bryan Pfeiffer, Bruce Lyndes, Jim Wallace, Tom Blachly, Kermit Glines, Euclid Farnham, Priscilla Farnham, Edgar Dodge, Barbara Kohn (Themselves).

BREATHING ROOM (Arrow) Producer, Tim Perell; Executive Producer, Jack Edward Barron; Director, Jon Sherman; Screenplay, Tom Hughes, Jon Sherman; Story, Tom Hughes; Photography, Jim Denault; Music, Pat Irwin; Editor, Sabine Hoffman; Designer, Sharon Lomofsky; Costumes, Sara Jane Slotnick; Casting, Gabriela Leff, Marcia DeBonis; a Eureka Pictures production; Color; Not rated; 90 minutes; November release. CAST: Susan Floyd (Kathy), Dan Futterman (David), David Thornton (Brian), Amy Hohn (Cousin Judy), Rod McLachlan (Cousin Andy), Nadia Dajani (Claire), Saverio Guerra (Tony), Stryker Hardwicke (Larry), Maribel Vasquez (Madame Vasquez), Juanita Suarez (Madame Suarez), Dmitriy Tsybulskiy (Vladimir), Vitaly Blokhin (Mikhail), Edie Falco (Marcy), Marin Hinkle (Larissa), Kim Chan (Meditation Teacher), Shifra Lerer (Kathy's Grandmother), Peg Small (David's Mother), Rex Robbins (David's Father), Andre Blake (Keith), Paul Giamatti (George), Robin Held (Waitress), Joanna Chang (Cashier), Jianzhung Gu (Grocer), Bernadette Lee (Club Girl in Bathroom), Arthur Halpern (Larry II), Adam Strider (Larry III), Jennifer Lovatt (Larry IV), Greg Luedtke (Tree Salesman), Dino Stamatopoulos (Jersey Rocker), Cynthia Halpern (Jersey Girl), Shanon Shen (Knock-Knock Joke Student), Rafael Perez (Knock-Knock Joke Encourager), Arshad Javaid (Cab Driver), Yuliya Blokhin (Mrs. Cherkin the Babka Lady), Fred Lin Sye (Mr. Lin the Crazy Man)

MAD DOG TIME (United Artists) formerly *Trigger Happy*; Producer, Judith Rutherford James; Executive Producers, Stephan Manpearl, Len Shapiro; Director/Screenplay/Co-Producer, Larry Bishop; Photography, Frank Byers; Designer, Dina Lipton; Editor, Norman Hollyn; Music, Earl Rose; Costumes, Ileane Meltzer; Casting, Amy Lieberman; a Dreyfuss/James production, in association with Skylight Films;

Distributed by MGM/UA; DTS Digital Stereo; Deluxe color; Rated R; 92 minutes; November release. CAST: Michael J. Pollard (Red Nash), Henry Silva (Sleepy Joe Carlisle), Gabriel Byrne (Ben London), Jeff Goldblum (Mickey Holliday), Ellen Barkin (Rita Everly), Gregory Hines (Jules Flamingo), Angie Everhart (Gabriella), Kyle MacLachlan (Jake Parker), Billy Idol (Lee Turner), Juan Fernandez (Davis), Billy Drago (Wells), Christopher Jones ("Nicholas Falco"), Richard Dreyfuss (Vic), Burt Reynolds ("Wacky" Jacky Jackson), Real Andrews (Clarke), Jon Ingrassia (Young), Paul Anka (Danny Marks), Larry Bishop (Nick), Rob Reiner (Albert the Chauffeur), Diane Lane (Grace), Joey Bishop (Mr. Gottlieb), Richard Pryor (Jimmy the Grave Digger)

THE DARIEN GAP (Northern Arts) Producers, Jim Taylor Brad Anderson; Director/Screenplay, Editor, Brad Anderson; Photography, Peter Krieger; Music, Gareth Kear; a Nomad Films presentation in association with Robbins Entertainment Group; Color; Not rated; 92 minutes; November release. CAST: Lyn Vaus (Lyn Vaus), Sandi Carroll (Polly Joy)

TROMEO & JULIET (Troma Team) Producers, Lloyd Kaufman, Michael Herz; Executive Producers, Daniel Laikind, Robert Schiller, Grant Quasha; Co-Producers, Jonathan Foster, Robert Hersov; Director, Lloyd Kaufman; Screenplay, James Gunn, Lloyd Kaufman; Based on the play *Romeo & Juliet* by William Shakespeare; Photography, Brendan Flynt; Editor, Frank Reynolds; Music, Willie Wiseley; Designer, Roshelle Berliner; Special Makeup Effects Designer, Callie French; Associate Producer/Casting, Andrew Weiner; Color; Not rated ; 102 minutes; November release. CAST: Will Keenan (Tromeo Que), Jane Jensen (Juliet Capulet), Debbi Rochon (Ness), Valentine Miele (Murray Martini), Patrick Connor (Tyrone Capulet), Stephen Blackehart (Benny Que), Sean Gunn (Sammy Capulet), Maximillian Shaun (Cappy Capulet), Steve Gibbons (London Arbuckle), Lemmy (Ness), Flip Brown (Father Lawrence), Earl McKoy (Monty Que), Gene Terinoni (Det. Ernie Scalus), Wendy Adams (Ingrid Capulet), Tamara Craig Thomas (Georgie Capulet)

Frd Turtle in *ManWith a Plan*
© Bellwether Films

Ellen Barkin, Gabriel Byrne, Jeff Goldblum in *Mad Dog Time*
© United Artists Pictures

Jennifer Connelly, Edward Atterton, Jim True in *Far Harbor*
© Castle Hill Productions

FAR HARBOR (Castle Hill) Producer, Gigi De Pourtales Davis; Executive Producers, John Huddles, Gary Huddles, John Wolstenholme; Director/Screenplay, John Huddles; Co-Producer, Laura Barnett; Photography, Tami Reiker; Designer, Maggie Martin; Costumes, Erin Folsey; Music, Christopher Tyng, Keola Beamer; Editors, Wilton Henderson, Margaret Guinee, Janice Keuhnelian; Associate Producers, Colleen Hahn, Sarah Porter; Casting, Mikie Heilbrun, Lisa Essary; a Far Harbor Films and Huddles-Lauren-Cinematics presentation; Color; Not rated; 101 minutes; November release. CAST: Edward Atterton (Frick), Jennifer Connelly (Ellie), Dan Futterman (Brad), Marcia Gay Harden (Arabella), Andrew Lauren (Trey), George Newbern (Jordan), Tracee Ellis Ross (Kiki), Jim True (Ryland)

PARALLEL SONS (CG/Black Brook Films) Producers, James Spione, Nancy Larsen; Director/Screenplay, John G. Young; Photography, Matthew Howe; Editors, John G. Young, James Spione; Music, E.D. Menasche; Color; Not rated; 92 minutes; November release. CAST: Gabriel Mick (Seth Carlson), Laurence Mason (Knowledge Johnson), Murphy Guyer (Sheriff Mott), Graham Alex Johnson (Peter Carlson), Heather Gottlieb (Kristen Mott), Maureen Shannon (Francine), Josh Hopkins (Marty), Julia Weldon (Sally Carlson)

Hype
© CFP Distribution

HYPE! (CFP) Producer, Steven Helvey; Co-Producers, Lisa Dutton, Pete Vogt; Director, Doug Pray; Narrative Structure, Brian Levy; Editors, Earl Ghaffari, Doug Pray, Joan Zapata; Photography, Robert Bennett; a Helvey/Pray Productions presentation; DTS Stereo; Color; Not rated; 84 minutes; November release. Rock documentary featuring Ledge Morrisette, Dave Crider, John Mortenson, Aaron Roeder (The Mono Men), Charles Peterson, Art Chantry, Jack Endino; Chris Eckman, Carla Torgerson (The Walkabouts); Nils Bernstein, Steve Fisk, Dawn Anderson; Matt Cameron, Kim Thayil (Soundgarden); Kim Warnick, Kurt Bloch, Lulu Gargiulo (The Fastbacks); Calvin Johnson; Van Conner, Barrett Martin (Screaming Trees); Buzz Osborne, Dale Crover (The Melvins); Don Blackstone, Matt Wright, Tom Price, Joe Newton (Gas Huffer); Mark Arm, Steve Turner (Mudhoney); Jim Sangster, Tad Hutchison, Scott MacCaughey (The Young Fresh Fellows); Leighton Beezer, Martin Rushent, Conrad Uno; Ron Heathman, Eddie Spaghetti, Dan Siegel (The Supersuckers); Daniel House; Kurt Danielson, Tad Doyle (Tad); Jonathan Poneman, Bruce Pavitt, Megan Jasper, Susan Silver, Susie Tennant; Eddie Vedder (Pearl Jam); Blake Wright; Rob Skinner, Peter Litwin, David Brooks, Jeff Lorien (Coffin Break); Selene Vigil, Elizabeth Davis, Valerie Agnew (7 Year Bitch); Mike Vraney; John Atkins, Wade Neal (Seaweed); Frank Harlan.

SANTA WITH MUSCLES (Legacy) Producer, Brian Shuster; Executive Producers, Harry Shuster, Jordan Belfort, Danny Porush; Director, John Murlowski; Screenplay, Jonathan Bond, Fred Mata, Dorrie Krum Raymond; Photography, Michael Gfelner; Desinger, Chuck Conner; Editors, William Marrinson, Stephen R. Myers; Music, James Covell; Casting, Tom McSweeney; a Hit Entertainment Inc. in association with Cabin Fever Entertainment, Inc. presentation; Color; Rated PG; 97 minutes; November release. CAST: Hulk Hogan (Blake Thorne), Don Stark (Lenny), Robin Curtis (Leslie), Garrett Morris (Clayton), Aria Noelle Curzon (Elizabeth), Adam Wylie (Taylor), Mila Kunis (Sarah), Jennifer Paz (Helen Chu), Clint Howard (Hinkley), William Newman (Chas), Robert Apisa (Franco), Pierre Dulat (Pierre), Steve Valentine (Dr. Blight), Ed Begley, Jr. (Ebner Frost), Kai Ephron (Dr. Vlal), Diane Robin (Dr. Watt), Kevin West (Dr. Flint), Ed Donno (Mr. Rapini), Andre Jamal Kinney (Steven), Brentley Shuster (Girl), Troy Robinson (Baldie), Pete Apisa (Nose Ring), Brenda Song (Susan), Malone Brinton (Brat Kid), Bridget Michelle (Mall Manager), Ed Leslie (Sumo Lab Assist.), Blake Shuster (Boy in Corridor)

DEAR GOD (Paramount) Producer, Steve Tisch; Executive Producer, Mario Iscovich; Director, Garry Marshall; Screenplay, Warren Leight, Ed Kaplan; Photography, Charles Minsky; Designer, Albert Brenner; Editor, Debra Neil-Fisher; Music, Jeremy Lubbock, James Patrick Dunne; a Steve Tisch production, in association with Rysher Entertainment; Dolby Stereo; Color; Rated PG; 110 minutes; November release. CAST: Greg Kinnear (Tom Turner), Laurie Metcalf (Rebecca Frazen), Tim Conway (Herman Dooly), Roscoe Lee Browne (Idris Abraham), Jon Seda (Handsome), Anna Maria Horsford (Lucille), Hector Elizondo (Vladek Vidov), Maria Pitillo (Gloria McKinney), Seth Mumy (Joey), Donal Logue (Webster), John Pinette (Junior), Timothy Stack (Cousin Guy), Felix A. Pire (Ramon), Isadora O'Boto (Hot Mary), Kathleen Marshall (Whispering Wendy), Deborah Benson-Wald (Juanita), Odette Yustman (Angela), Ellen Cleghorne (Marguerite), Curtis Williams (Marguerite's Son), Jack Sheldon (White Beard), Coolio (Gerard), Rue McClanahan (Mom Turner), Nancy Marchand (Federal Judge), Sam McMurray (Federal Prosecutor), Jack Klugman (Jemi)

ADRENALIN: FEAR THE RUSH (Legacy) Producers, Tom Karnowski, Gary Schmoeller; Executive Producers, Barr B. Potter, Paul Rosenblum; Co-Producer, Mark Scoon; Director/Screenplay, Albert Pyun; Photography, George Mooradian; Art Director, Nenad Pecur; Costumes, Shelly Boies; Special Makeup Design, Maureen Schlenz; Special Effects, John McLeod; Editor, Ken Morrisey; Music, Tony Riparetti; a Largo Entertainment Inc., in association with Filmwerks presentation; Dolby Stereo; Color; Rated R; 77 minutes; December release. CAST: Christopher Lambert (Lemieux), Natasha Henstridge (Delon), Norbert Weisser (Cuzo), Elizabeth Barondes (Wocek), Xavier Declie (Volker), Craig Davis (Suspect), Nicholas Guest (Rennard), Andrew Divoff (Sterns), Jon Epstein (Waxman)

FIRE ON THE MOUNTAIN (First Run Features) Producers/Directors, Beth Gage, George Gage; Screenplay, Beth Gage; Narrator, Steve Kanaly; Music, Todd Barton; Editors, Scott Conrad, Krysia Carter; Documentary about America's 10th· Mountain Division, a ski patrol formed during World War II as a defensive team against possible enemy invasion of the country's mountain regions, featuring Fritz Benedict, Bill Bowerman, David Brower, Bill Hackett, Bob Lewis, Lt. Gen. John Hay, John Jay, Dev Jennings, Steve Knowlton, Morely Nelson, Robert Parker, Paul Petzoldt, Friedl Pfeifer, Peter Seibert.

Norbert Weisser, Christopher Lambert, Natasha Henstridge in *Adrenalin: Fear the Rush*
© Largo Entertainment, Inc.

Helen Mirren in *Losing Chase*
© CFP Distribution

LOSING CHASE (CFP) Producer, Milton Justice; Executive Producer, Kyra Sedgwick; Director, Kevin Bacon; Screenplay, Anne Meredith; Photography, Dick Quinlan; Editor, Alan Baumgarten; Music, Michael Bacon; Designer, Lindsey Hermer-Bell; Casting, Tina Gerussi; a Showtime presentation in association with Hallmark Entertainment; Ultra-Stereo; Color; Rated R; 92 minutes; December release. CAST: Helen Mirren (Chase Philips), Kyra Sedgwick (Elizabeth Cole), Beau Bridges (Richard Philips), Michael Yarmush (Little Richard), Lucas Denton (Jason Philips), Elva Mai Hoover (Margaret Thompson), Nancy Beatty (Cynthia Porter), Rino Romano (Bartender), Simon Reynolds (Instructor), B.J. McLellan (Winston), Bunty Webb (Housekeeper), Kate Hennig (Katherine), Cheryl Swarts (Nurse), Ron Gabriel (Jack). (This film originally premiered on Showtime in August, 1996).

BEAVIS AND BUTT-HEAD DO AMERICA (Paramount) Producer, Abby Terkuhle; Co-Producer, John Andrews; Director, Mike Judge; Screenplay, Mike Judge, Joe Stillman; Based on the MTV series "Beavis and Butt-Head" created by Mike Judge; Line Producer, Winnie Chaffee; Animation Director, Yvette Kaplan; Music, John Frizzell; Art Director, Jeff Buckland; Editors, Terry Kelley, Gunter Glinka, Neil Lawrence; Executive Producers, David Gale, Van Toffler; Song: "Two Cool Guys (Theme from *Beavis and Butt-Head Do America*)" by Isaac Hayes, Mike Judge/performed by Isaac Hayes; an MTV Production, presented in association with Geffen Pictures; Dolby Stereo; Color; Rated PG-13; 80 minutes; December release. VOICE CAST: Mike Judge (Beavis/Butt-Head/Tom Anderson—Old Guy With Camper/Van Driessen—Hippie Teacher/Principal McVicker), Robert Stack (Agent Flemming), Cloris Leachman (Old Woman on Plane and Bus), Jacqueline Barba (Agent Hurly), Pamela Blair (Flight Attendant/White House Tour Guide), Eric Bogosian (Ranger at Old Faithful/Press Secretary/Lieutenant at Strategic Air Command), Kristofor Brown (Man on Plane/Man in Confession Booth #2/Old Guy/Jim), Tony Darling (Motley Crue Roadie #2/Tourist Man), John Doman (Airplane Captain/White House Representative), Francis DuMaurier (French Dignitary), Jim Flaherty (Petrified Forest Recording), Tim Guinee (Hoover Guide/ATF Agent), "Earl Hofert"/David Letterman (Motley Crue Roadie #1), Toby Huss (TV

Thief #2/Concierge/Bellboy/Male TV Reporter), Sam Johnson (Limo Driver/TV Thief #1/Man in Confession Booth #1/Petrified Forest Ranger), Richard Linklater (Tour Bus Driver), Rosemary McNamara (Flight Attendant #2), Harsh Nayyar (Indian Dignitary), Karen Phillips (Announcer in Capitol), Dale Reeves (President Clinton), Mike Ruschak (Hoover Technician/General at Strategic Air Command), Gail Thomas (Flight Attendant #3), Bruce Willis, Demi Moore (Additional Voices)

MESSAGE TO LOVE: THE ISLE OF WIGHT FESTIVAL (Strand) Producer/Director, Murray Lerner; Executive Producers, Geoff Kempin, Rocky Oldham, Malcolm Gerrie, Avril MacRory; Photography, Andy Carchrae, Jack Hazan, Nic Knowland, Norman Langley, Murray Lerner, Richard Stanley, Charles Stewart, Mike Whittaker; Editors, Einar Westerlund, Stan Warnow, Greg Sheldon, Howard Alk; a Castle Music Pictures presentation in association with Initial Film and Television and the BBC; Dolby Stereo; Color; Not rated; 128 minutes; December release. Documentary on the 1970 rock concert on the Isle of Wight, featuring Jimi Hendrix, The Who, Free, Taste, Tiny Tim, John Sebastian, Donovan, Ten Years After, The Doors, The Moody Blues, Kris Kristofferson, Joni Mitchell, Miles Davis, Leonard Cohen, Emerson Lake & Palmer, Joan Baez, Jethro Tull.

BIG BULLY (Morgan Creek) Producers, Lee Rich, Gary Foster; Executive Producers, Gary Barber, Dylan Sellers; Director, Steve Miner; Screenplay, Mark Steven Johnson; Photography, Daryn Okada; Designer, Ian Thomas; Editor, Marshall Harvey; Music, David Newman; Casting, Ferne Cassel, Michelle Allen; a James G. Robinson presentation of a Morgan Creek production in association with Lee Rich Productions; Distributed by WB; Dolby Stereo; Technicolor; Rated PG; 97 minutes; January release. CAST: Rick Moranis (David Leary), Tom Arnold (Rosco

Fire on the Mountain
© First Run Features

Beavis, Butt-head in *Beavis and Butt-head Do America*
© MTV Networks

Bigger—"Fang"), Julianne Phillips (Victoria), Carol Kane (Faith), Jeffrey Tambor (Art), Curtis Armstrong (Clark), Faith Prince (Betty), Tony Pierce (Ulf), Don Knotts (Principal Kokelar), Blake Bashoff (Ben), Cody McMains (Kirby), Harry Waters, Jr. (Alan), Stuart Pankin (Gerry), Justin Jon Ross (Young David), Michael Zwiener (Young Fang), Tiffany Foster (Young Victoria), Matthew Slowik (Young Ulf), C.J. Grayson (Young Alan), Grant Hoover (Young Gerry), Bill Dow (David's Father), Susan Bain (David's Mother), Christine Willes (Teacher—1970), Ingrid Torrance (Fourth Grade Teacher), Tyler Van Blankenstein (Freckle Faced Kid), Doug Abrahams (Guard), Lillian Carlson (Old Woman), Matt Hill (Teenager), Kate Twa (Shop Clerk), Norma MacMillan (Mrs. Rumpert), Eryn Collins, Gregory Smith (Kids), Tegan Moss (Girl in Class), Lois Dellar, Alf Humphreys (Teachers), Claire Riley (Sympathetic Teacher), Brent Morrison (Stookie), Alexander Pollock (Corky), Kyle Labine (Stevie), Zachary Webb (Kyle), Eric Pospisil (Bobby), Miriam Smith (Crying Teacher), Colum Cantillon (Paul), Dawn Stofer (Secretary), Dawn Stofer (Secretary), Steven Taylor, Justin Goodrich, Anthony Pavlokovic (Hallway Kids), Andrew Wheeler (Soldier), James Sherry, Tommy Anderson (Delinquents), Tina Klassen (Korean Lady in Bookstore), Tamara Stanners (Connie), Helena Yea, Ray Fairchild (Connie TV Guests)

TWISTER (Amblin Entertainment) Producers, Kathleen Kennedy, Ian Bryce, Michael Crichton; Executive Producers, Steven Spielberg, Walter Parkes, Laurie MacDonald, Gerald R. Molen; Director, Jan De Bont; Screenplay, Michael Crichton, Anne-Marie Martin; Photography, Jack N. Green; Designer, Joseph Nemec III; Editor, Michael Kahn; Music, Mark Mancina; Special Effects Supervisor, John Frazier; Special Visual Effects and Animation, Industrial Light & Magic; Stunts, Mic Rogers; an Amblin Entertainment production; Distributed by WB/Universal; Dolby DTS Stereo; Panavision; Technicolor; Rated PG-13; 114 minutes; May release. CAST: Helen Hunt (Jo), Bill Paxton (Bill), Jami Gertz (Melissa), Cary Elwes (Jonas), Lois Smith (Aunt Meg), Philip Seymour Hoffman (Dusty), Alan Ruck (Rabbit), Sean Whalen (Sanders), Scott Thomson (Preacher), Todd Field (Beltzer), Joey Slotnick (Joey), Wendle Josepher (Haynes), Jeremy Davies (Laurence), Zach Grenier (Eddie), Gregory Sporleder (Willie), Patrick Fischler (The Communicator), Nicholas Sadler (Kubrick), Ben Weber (Stanley), Anthony Rapp (Tony), Eric LaRay Harvey (Eric), Abraham Benrubi (Bubba), Jake Busey (Mobile Lab Technician), Melanie Hoopes (Patty), J. Dean Lindsay (Dean), Dan Kelpine (Diner Mechanic), Sharonlyn Morrow (Waitress), Richard Lineback (Father), Rusty Schwimmer (Mother), Alexa Vega (Jo—5 years old), Taylor Gilbert (NSSL Scientist—Bryce), Bruce Wright (NSSL Scientist—Murphy), Gary England, Jeff Lazalier, Rick Mitchell (TV Meteorologists), John Thomas Rhyne (Paramedic), Paul Douglas (Bodger), Samantha McDonald, Jennifer L. Hamilton (Drive-In Girls), Anneke De Bont (Farm Girl)

ERASER (Arnold Kopelson Prods.) Producers, Arnold Kopelson, Anne Kopelson; Director, Charles Russell; Screenplay, Tony Puryear, Walon Green; Story, Tony Puryear, Walon Green, Michael S. Chernuchin; Executive Producers, Michael Tadross, Charles Russell; Photography, Adam Greenberg; Designer, Bill Kenney; Editor, Michael Tronick; Co-Producers, Stephen Brown, Caroline Pham; Music, Alan Silvestri; Costumes, Richard Bruno; Casting, Bonnie Timmermann; an Arnold Kopelson production, distributed by WB; Dolby Stereo; Panavision; Technicolor; Rated R; 115 minutes; June release. CAST: Arnold Schwarzenegger (Eraser), James Caan (Deguerin), Vanessa Williams (Lee), James Coburn (Beller), Robert Pastorelli (Johnny C.), James Cromwell (Donahue), Danny Nucci (Monroe), Andy Romano (Harper), Nick Chinlund (Calderon), Michael Papajohn (Schiff), Joe Viterelli (Tony), Mark Rolston (J. Scar), John Slattery (Corman), Robert Miranda (Frediano), Roma Maffia (Claire), Tony Longo (Little Mike), Gerry Becker (Morehart), John Snyder (Sal), Melora Walters (Darleen), Olek Krupa (Sergei), Cylk Cozart (Darryl), K. Todd Freeman (Dutton), Rocco Sisto (Pauley), Gerald Berns (Young Agent), Steve Ford (Knoland), Ismael "East" Carlo (Priest), Thomas J. Huff (Somes), Rick Batalla (Bartender), Michael Gregory (Leiman), Patrick Kilpatrick (Haggerty), James Short (Crane Sniper), A.J. Nay (Sniper #2), Camryn Manheim (Nurse), Skipp Sudduth (Watch Commander), Anthony Fusco, Gregory McKinney (Witsec Ops), Craig Barnett (Clerk), Corey Joshua Taylor (Officer), Rick Marzan (Crawford), Brian Libby, Dan Wynands (Perimeter Guys), David Wolos-Fonteno (Security Official), Sonny H. King, Edward Rote (Security Guards) Michael Cameron (Gate Guard), Tim Colceri, Dieter R. Trippel (Lobby Guards), Matthew Mahaney (Vault Guard), Denis Forest (Technician), Christopher Mankiewicz (Zoo Guard), Michael Stone (Zoo Killer), Kevin Fry, Sam Scarber (Dock Guards), Richie Varga (Secretary), Diana Morgan, Ben Shenkman, Dominic Marcus (Reporters), Pat Collins (Anchorman), Dorin Seymour (Attorney), Clayton Landey (Witsec Agent), Terry Beeman, Michael Gregory Cong, Sebastian LaCause (Dancers), Frank Minitolo (Paramedic), Charles Chiquete (Officer Worker #1), Glenndon Chatman (Glenndon), Camille Winbush (Camille), Vic Polizos (Hannon), James Clark (Locomotive Engineer), David Bilson, Al Cerullo, Rick Shuster (Pilots)

JOE'S APARTMENT (Geffen Pictures) Producers, Diana Phillips, Bonni Lee; Executive Producers, Abby Terkuhle, Judith McGrath, Griffin Dunne; Director/Screenplay, John Payson; Based on the MTV short film; Photography, Peter Deming; Designer, Carol Spier; Editor, Peter Frank; Music, Carter Burwell; an MTV production; Distributed by WB; Dolby Stereo; Color; Rated PG-13; 80 minutes; July release. CAST: Jerry O'Connell (Joe), Megan Ward (Lily), Billy West (Voice of Ralph Roach), Reginald Hudlin (Voice of Rodney Roach), Jim Turner (Walter), Robert Vaughn (Senator Dougherty), Don Ho (Alberto Bianco), Jim Sterling (Jesus Bianco), Shiek Mahmud-Bey (Vlad Bianco), David Huddleston (P.J. Smith), Frank Bello, Lord Kayson, Alejandro Molina (Stick-Up Men), Wayman Ezell, Vincent Pastore (Apartment Brokers), Rose Kimmel (Mrs. Grotowski), Cynthia Nielson (Dangling Woman), Tracy Vilar, John Palomino, Willi One Blood, William Preston, Michael Mandell, Roy Davis (Complaint Handlers), Edward Rosado (Boy at Play), Desiree Casado (Girl at Play), Salvatore Piro (Sal), Peter Yoshida (Zipp Copy Customer), Stewart Russell (Zipp Copy Manager), Rae C. Wright (Movie Goer), Toukie Smith (Head Usher), Tommy Hollis (Boss Plumber), Scott "Bam Bam" Bigelow (Boss Construction), Christopher Durang (Boss Clergy), Dale Goodson (Boss Clown), Patricia O'Connell (Ms. Featherstone), Fanni Green, Peg Healey (Counsel Members), Cristina Martinez, Jonathan Spencer, Jens Jurgenson, Hollis Yungblut (Boss Hog Band Members), Nick Zedd, Solange Monnier (Pizza Couple), Paul Bartel (NEA Scout), Richard "Moby" Hall (Club DeeJay), William Wegman (Distinguished Gentleman), Glenn Kubota (Lab Manager), Rick Aviles, Vebe Borge, Owen Burke, Dave Chappelle, Godfrey Danchimah, Kenan Moran, Jennie Moreau, Tim Blake Nelson, Mark Rosenthal, James Stauffer, Jim Sterling, John Terelle, Kevin Weist, Geoffrey Whelan, B.D. Wong (Voices of Roaches)

CARPOOL (Regency Enterprises) Producers, Arnon Milchan, Michael Nathanson; Executive Producer, Fitch Cady; Director, Arthur Hiller; Screenplay, Don Rhymer; Photography, David M. Walsh; Designer, James D. Vance; Editors, William Reynolds, L. James Langlois; Music, John Debney; Costumes, Trish Keating; Casting, Lynn Stalmaster; an Arnon Milchan production; Distributed by WB; Dolby Stereo; Technicolor; Rated PG; 119 minutes; August release. CAST: Tom Arnold (Franklin Laszlo), David Paymer (Daniel Miller), Rhea Perlman (Martha), Rod Steiger (Mr. Hammerman), Kim Coates (Det. Erdman), Rachael Leigh Cook (Kayla), Micah Gardener (Bucky Miller), Jordan Blake Warkol (Travis), Colleen Rennison (Chelsea), Ian Tracey (Meil), John Tench (Jerry), Stellina Rusich (Mrs. Miller), David Kaye (Scott Lewis), Obba Babatunde (Jeffery), Alan Van Sprang (Kirk), Seamus (Mr. Kupek), Betty Linde (Edith), Shawn MacDonald (Todd), Brian Arnold (News Anchor), Wren Robertz (Jeep Owner), Dolores Drake (Bonnie), Victor Favrin (Carlos), Patti Allan (Wax Lips), Michael Tiernan (Road Block Cops), Michael Dobson, Myron Pechet (Workers), Nathaniel Deveaux (Mall Cop), Justin Wilkie (Keith), Dave "Squatch" Ward (Erno), Tatiana Checkova (Alexandra), Hiro Hauata (Jake the Fire Eater), Alexis Ioannidis (Lydia the Human Globe), Jeremy Radick (The Dog Faced Boy), Mary McDonald (Bearded Woman), Rick Poltaruk (Strong Man), Larry Musser (Travis' Dad), Victor Magnussen (Hammerman's Assistant), Jewel Staite (Soap Opera Actress), Jack Thomas (Tow Truck Driver), William Bauer (Bank Security Guard), Julie Arnold (Hairstylist), Kay Arnold (Hair Dryer Woman), Steve Billnitzer (SWAT Team Guy), Jonathan Walker (SWAT Team Guy), Judy Kovar (Kayla's Mom), Edie McClurg, Kathleen Freeman, Miriam Flynn (Voice of Franklin's Mom)

THE GLIMMER MAN (Seagal/Nasso) Producers, Steven Seagal, Julius R. Nasso; Executive Producer, Michael Rachmil; Director, John Gray; Screenplay, Kevin Brodbin; Photography, Rick Bota; Designer, William Sandell; Editor, Donn Cambern; Music, Trevor Rabin; Costumes, Luke Reichle; Casting, Debi Manwiller; Distributed by WB; Dolby SDDS Stereo; Technicolor; Rated R; 92 minutes; October release. CAST: Steven Seagal (Jack Cole), Keenen Ivory Wayans (Jim Campbell), Bob Gunton (Frank Deverell), Brian Cox (Mr. Smith), John M. Jackson (Donald), Michelle Johnson (Jessica), Stephen Tobolowsky (Christopher Maynard), Peter Jason (Millie's Father), Ryan Cutrona (Capt. Harris), Richard Gant (Det. Roden), Johnny Strong (Johnny Deverell), Robert Mailhouse (Smith's Bodyguard), Jesse Stock (Cole's Son), Alexa Vega (Cole's Daughter), Nikki Cox (Millie), Wendy Robie (Melanie Sardes), Harris Laskawy (Coroner), Dennis Cockrum (Det. Tom Farrell), Blake Lindsley (School Teacher), John Bluto (Hotel Desk Clerk), Sid Conrad (Cemetery Priest), George Fisher (Misha), Michael Bryan French, Victor Ivanov (Russian Detectives), Stephen Mills (Hostage Priest), Bibi Osterwald (Woman in Ovington Arms), George Couts (Ghetto Kid), Susan Reno (Mrs. Roslov), Freda Foh Shen (Polygram Technician), Richard Tanner (Lento's Maitre 'D), Paul Raci, Kevin White (Internal Affairs Agents), Ellis E. Williams (Brother Gaglio), Mireille Fournier (Sister Rose), Patricia Carraway (Detective), Paige Rowland (Hostess), Fritz Coleman (Himself), Albert Wong (Mr. Lee), Nancy Yee (Mae Lee), John P. Gulino (Task Force Lawyer), Stacy Studen (NY Detective)

BAD MOON (Morgan Creek) Producer, James G. Robinson; Executive Producers, Gary Barber, Bill Todman, Jr.; Director/Screenplay, Eric Red; Based on the novel *Tor* by Wayne Smith; Photography, Jan Kiesser; Designers, Richard Paris, Linda Del Rosario; Editor, C. Timothy O'Meara; Co-Producer, Jacobus Rose; Music, Daniel Licht; Special Makeup Effects Supervisor, Steve Johnson; Casting, Michelle Allen, Tori Herald; a James G. Robinson presentation of a Morgan Creek Production; Distributed by WB; Dolby Stereo; Clairmont-Scope; Color; Rated R; 80 minutes; November release. CAST: Mariel Hemingway (Janet), Michael Pare (Ted Harrison), Mason Gamble (Brett), Ken Pogue (Sheriff Jenson), Hrothgar Mathews (Flopsy), Johanna Marlowe Lebovitz (Marjorie), Gavin Buhr (Forest Ranger), Julia Montgomery Brown (Reporter), Primo (Thor), Ken Kirzinger (The Werewolf)

TWO IF BY SEA (Morgan Creek) Producer, James G. Robinson; Executive Producers, Gary Barber, Bill Todman, Jr.; Co-Producer, Michael MacDonald; Director, Bill Bennett; Screenplay, Denis Leary, Mike Armstrong; Story, Denis Leary, Mike Armstrong, Ann Lembeck; Photography, Andrew Lesnie; Designer, David Chapman; Editor, Bruce Green; Music, Nick Glennie-Smith, Paddy Moloney of the Chieftans; a James G. Robinson presentation of a Morgan Creek production; Distributed by WB; Dolby Stereo; Color; Rated R; 96 minutes; January release. CAST: Denis Leary (Frank), Sandra Bullock (Roz), Stephen Dillane (Evan Marsh), Yaphet Kotto (O'Malley), Mike Starr (Fitzie), Jonathan Tucker (Todd), Wayne Robson (Beano), Michael Badalucco (Quinn), Lenny Clarke (Kelly), Jonny Fido (Burke), Don Gavin (Sully), Shaun R. Clark (Sweeney), Markus Parilo (Peters), John Friesen (Sheriff Horn), Ian White (Jim Kellerher), Jane Moffat (Marcy Kellerher), Geoffrey McLean (Crew Member), Sean Runnette (Marty), Richard Fitzpatrick (FBI Chief), Ferne Downey (Mercedes Owner), Philip Williams (Man with Phones), Katya Ladan (Older Woman), Lorne Cossette (Older Man), John Fulton (Driver), Angela Moore (Nanny), Kay Hawtrey (Lady with Dog), Claire Rankin, Michael Risley (Reporters), Martha Irving (Duty Manager), Leslie Boyd (Video Woman), Dennis O'Connor (Cop on Scene), Joseph Di Mambro, Tracy Jones (Cops), Sandi Ross (Conductor), Chris Benson (Local Cop), Julia Montgomery Brown (Beautiful Woman), Gary Vermeir (Buyer)

DIABOLIQUE (Morgan Creek) Producers, Marvin Worth, James G. Robinson; Executive Producers, Gary Barber, Bill Todman, Jr., Jerry Offsay, Chuck Binder; Director, Jeremiah Chechik; Screenplay, Don Roos; Based upon the film *Les Diaboliques* by Henri Georges Clouzot, and upon the novel *Celle Qui N'etait Plus* by Pierre Boileau and Thomas Narcejac; Photography, Peter James; Designer, Leslie Dilley; Editor, Carol Littleton; Co-Producer, Gary Daigler; a James G. Robinson presentation of a Morgan Creek production in association with Marvin Worth Productions; Distributed by WB; Dolby Stereo; Technicolor; Rated R; 107 minutes; March release. CAST: Sharon Stone (Nicole Horner), Isabelle Adjani (Mia Baran), Chazz Palminteri (Guy Baran), Kathy Bates (Shirley Vogel), Spalding Gray (Simon Veatch), Shirley Knight (Edie Danziger), Allen Garfield (Leo Katzman), Adam Hann-Byrd (Erik Pretzer), Donal Logue, Jeffrey Abrams (Video Photographers), Diana Bellamy (Ms. Vawze), Clea Lewis (Lisa Campos), O'Neal Compton (Irv Danziger), Bingo O'Malley (Gannon), Stephen Liska (PHP Officer), Jim Kisicki (Rear-ender), Kevin Vinay (Desantis), Cory Pattak (Nunez), Kate Young (Phot Shop Clerk), Sophia Salguero (Maid), Hank Stohl (Morgue Cop), Zachary Mott (Howie), Jesse Sky Ross (Hall Monitor)

BOGUS (Regency Enterprises) Producers, Norman Jewison, Arnon Milchan, Jeff Rothberg; Executive Producers, Michael Nathanson, Patrick Markey, Gayle Fraser-Baigelman; Director, Norman Jewison; Screenplay, Alvin Sargent; Story, Jeff Rothberg, Francis X. McCarthy; Photography, David Watkin; Designer, Ken Adam; Editor, Stephen Rivkin; Music, Marc Shaiman; Costumes, Ruth Myers; Associate Producer, Michael Jewison; Casting, Howard Feuer; a Yorktown/New Regency production; Distributed by WB; Dolby Digital Stereo; Technicolor; Rated PG; 111 minutes; September release. CAST: Whoopi Goldberg (Harriet), Gerard Depardieu (Bogus), Haley Joel Osment (Albert), Andea Martin (Penny), Nancy Travis (Lorraine), Denis Mercier (Antoine), Ute Lemper (Babette), Sheryl Lee Ralph (Ruthie), Barbara Hamilton (Mrs. Patridge), Al Waxman (School Principal), Elizabeth Harpur (Ellen), Fiona Reid (School Teacher), Kevin Jackson (Bob Morrison), Richard Portnow (M. Clay Thrasher), Mo Gaffney (Travellers Aide—New Jersey), Sara Peery (Travellers Aide—Las Vegas), Cynthia Mace (Flight Attendant), Don Francks (Dr. Surprise), Justine Johnston (Woman in Plane), Frank Medrano (Man in Plane), Philip Williams (Airport Cop), Jackie Richardson (Babysitter), Quancetta Hamilton (Meter Maid), Jared Durand, Michael Vollans (Boys in Playground), D. Ruby Son, Michael Ho, Fielding Horan (Kids in Classroom), Dina Morrone (Mom at Party), Stuart Hughes (Airline Agent), Stan Coles (Mr. Franklin), Yetunde Alabi (Harriet—Age 7), Jennifer Pisana (Lorraine—Age 7), Michael R. Sousa (Strongman), Yvan Labelle (Little Person), Damon D'Oliveira (Office Worker), Csaba McZala (Traffic Officer), Muguette Moreau (Assistant to Dr. Surprise), Tabitha Lupien (Girl at Party),

Nicolette Hazenwinkel (Wirewalker), Doug Gilmore (Surprise Guest), Rebekah Abou-Keer, Kenner Ames, Shelley Bianchi, Heather Braaten, Roger Clown, David Dunlop, Alexei Fateyev, Vince Fera, Joe Gladman, Theresa Fung, Orville Heyn, Peter Jarvis, Lisa Rnee Knight, Gigi De Leon, Kelly McIntosh, Jennifer Podemski, Simmi Raymond, Sonny Tran, Jason Twardowski (Circus Characters)

THE PROPRIETOR (Merchant Ivory Productions) Producers, Humbert Balsan, Donald Rosenfeld; Executive Producers, Paul Bradley, Osman Eralp; Director, Ismail Merchant; Screenplay, Jean-Marie Besset, George Trow; Photography, Larry Pizer; Editor, William Webb; Music, Richard Robbins; Designers, Bruno Santini, Kevin Thompson; Costumes, Anne de Laugardiere, Abigail Murray; Casting, Frederique Moidon; a Merchant Ivory presentation; Distributed by WB; Dolby Stereo; Super 35 Widescreen; Color; Rated R; 113 minutes; October release. CAST: Jeanne Moreau (Adrienne Mark), Sean Young (Virginia Kelly), Sam Waterston (Harry Bancroft), Christopher Cazenove (Elliott Spencer), Nell Carter (Milly), Jean-Pierre Aumont (Franz), Austin Pendleton (Willy Kunst), Charlotte De Turckheim (Judith Mark), Pierre Vaneck (Raymond T.K.), Marc Tissot (Patrice Legendre), Josh Hamilton (William O'Hara), Joanna Adler (F. Freemder), James Naughton, J. Smith-Cameron (Texans), Michael Bergin (Bobby), John Dalton (Emilio), Jack Koenig (Apt. Doorman), Panther, Bull, Kim Gilmore, Falcon (Guardian Angels), Joan Audiberti, Katherine Argo (French Ladies), Judy Alanna (Woman in Park), Hubert St. Macary (Taxi Driver), Diane Nignan (Pedestrian), Guillemette Grovon (Suzanne T.K.), Cherif Ezzeldin, Valerie Toledano (French Couple) Jorg Schnass, Paula Klein (German Couple), Suzanna Pattoni (Concierge), Alain Rimoux (Notaire), Humbert Balsan (Maitre Vicks), Donald Rosenfeld (Maitre Ertaud), Frank De La Personne (TV Moderator), Gilles Arbona (Politician), Henri Garein (Interviwer), Jeanne-Marie Darblay (Journalist), Catherine Kinley (*Entertainment Tonight* Presenter), Marjolaine De Graeve (Young Adrienne), Carole Franck, Azmine Jaffer (Shop Assistants), Brigitte Catillon (Aristocratic Lady), Jean-Yves Dubois (Fan-Fan), Herve Briaux (Aristocratic Man), Sophie Camus (Gril in the Nightmare), Eric Ruf (Theodore), Elodie Bouchez (Young Girl), Judith Remy (Nadine), Wade Childress (Ben), Thomas Tomazewski (Frank)

THE SUNCHASER (Regency Enterprises) Producers, Arnon Milchan, Michael Cimino, Larry Spiegel, Judy Goldstein, Joseph S. Vecchio; Executive Producers, Michael Nathanson, Joseph M. Caracciolo; Director, Michael Cimino; Screenplay, Charles Leavitt; Photography, Doug Milsome; Designer, Victoria Paul; Editor, Joe D'Augustine; Music, Maurice Jarre; Casting, Terry Liebling; a Regency Enterprises presentation of an Arnon Milchan/Vecchio-Appledown production; Dolby Stereo; Panavision; Technicolor; Rated R; 122 minutes; October release. CAST: Woody Harrelson (Dr. Michael Reynolds), Jon Seda (Brandon "Blue" Monroe), Anne Bancroft (Dr. Renata Baumbauer), Alexandra Tydings (Victoria Reynolds), Matt Mulhern (Dr. Chip Byrnes), Talisa Soto (Navajo Woman), Richard Bauer (Dr. Bradford), Victor Aaron (Webster Skyhorse), Lawrence Pressman (A.I.C. Collier), Michael O'Neill (Agent Moreland), Harry Carey, Jr. (Cashier), Carmen Dell'Orefice (Arabella), Brooke Ashley (Calantha), Andrea Roth (Head Nurse), Bob Minor (Deputy Lynch), Sal Landi (2nd Deputy), Harper Roisman (Mr. Vogel), Kelly Perine, Andrew Mark Berman (Fellows in Oncology), Kirsten Getchell (Sally), Emil Alexander (Walter), John Christian Graas (Young Michael), Christopher Kennedy Masterson (Jimmy), Antwon Tanner (Smokes), Pam Morton (Herself), Linda M. Duenas (Waitress), Tony Epper (Hay Hauler), Mickey Jones (Fuzzy), Gregory Scott Cummins (2nd Biker), Douglas B. Hall, Dan P. Pastre (State Troopers), Elaine Kagan (Pretty Woman), Robert M. Zajonc (FBI Pilot), Jeri Arredondo (Pharmacist), Brian Bossetta (Security Guard), Cynthia Allison (CNN Reporter), Carolyn Tomlin (Hospital Spokesperson), Brian K. Francis (Navajo Boy), Alan Keller, Brett Harrelson (Highway Patrol Officers), Zoe Trilling (Mini-Mart Cashier), Betty Carvalho (Rosa), Matthew Abe, Eugene Boggs (Surgeons), Philip Zachary (Disc Jockey), David Green (First Inmate), Askia Won-Ling Jacob (UCLA Student), Robert Downey (Telephone Voices)

EXECUTIVE DECISION (Silver Pictures) Producer, Joel Silver; Executive Producer, Steve Perry; Co-Producer, Karyn Fields; Director, Stuart Baird; Screenplay, Jim Thomas, John Thomas; Photography, Alex Thomson; Designer, Terence Marsh; Editors, Dallas Puett, Frank J. Urioste, Stuart Baird; Music, Jerry Goldsmith; Costumes, Louise Frogley; Casting, Amanda Mackey Johnson, Cathy Sandrich; Visual Effects Supervisor, Peter Donen; a Silver Pictures production distributed by WB; Dolby SDDS Stereo; Panavision; Technicolor; Rated R; 132 minutes; March release. CAST: Kurt Russell (David Grant), Steven Seagal (Lt. Col. Austin Travis), Halle Berry (Jean), John Leguizamo (Rat), Oliver Platt (Cahill), Joe Morton (Cappy), David Buchet (Nagi Hassan), B.D. Wong (Louie), Len Cariou (Sec. of Defense Charles White), Whip Hubley (Baker), Andreas Katsulas (Jaffa), Mary Ellen Trainor (Allison), Marla Maples Trump (Nancy), J.T. Walsh (Sen. Mavros), Ingo Neuhas (Doc), William James Jones (Catman), Paul Collins (Nelson), Nicholas Pryor (Sec. of State Jack Douglas), Stanley Grover

(Gen. Price), Eugene Roche (Adm. Lewis), Ken Jenkins (Gen. Wood), Charles Hallahan (Gen. Sarlow), Dey Young (Gail), Richard Riehle (Air Marshal), Robert Apisa (Demou), Granville Hatcher (Ahmed), Chris Maher (Kahlil), Jay Tavare, Ahmed Ahmed, Shaun Toub, Majed Ibrahim, Jon Huertas, Joey Naber (Terrorists), Ray Baker (747 Capt.), Michael Milhoan (747 1st Officer), Julie Wright, Sunni Boswell (Flight Attendants), Gregg Artz, Will Schaub (Assts. to Sen. Mavros), Yvonne Zima (Little Girl), Marianne Muellerleile (Diabetic Woman), Brad Blaisdell (Beckings Institute Aide), Don Fischer (Remora Pilot), John Rixey Moore (Flight Instructor), Warren Munson (American Ambassador), Lance August (American Embassy Duty Officer), Maggie Egan (CNN Reporter), James Victor (Spider), Tim Kelleher (Bulldog), David Birznieks, Paul Bollen (Fire Fighters), Nick Jameson (London Maitre 'D), Juan Fernandez (London Bomber), Todd Jeffries (Collins), Joe Cook, Ilia Volokh (Chechens), Blaire Valk (Yugoslavian Girl), Joseph Makkar (Arab Co-Pilot), Damon Lee (Translator), Jayne Walter (London Hostess), Robert Londberg (Diamond Smuggler), Edmond Brown (FBI Agent), Michelle Boudreau (Party Girl), Kurt Kohler (MP)

A TIME TO KILL (Regency Enterprises) Producers, Arnon Milchan, Michael Nathanson, Hunt Lowry, John Grisham; Director, Joel Schumacher; Screenplay, Akiva Goldsman; Based on the novel by John Grisham; Photography, Peter Menzies, Jr.; Designer, Larry Fulton; Editor, William Steinkamp; Music, Elliot Goldenthal; Costumes, Ingrid Ferrin; Casting, Mali Finn; a Regency Enterprises presentation of an Arnon Milchan production, distributed by WB; Dolby SDDS Stereo; Panavision; Technicolor; Rated R; 149 minutes; July release. CAST: Matthew McConaughey (Jake Brigance), Sandra Bullock (Ellen Roark), Samuel L. Jackson (Carl Lee Hailey), Kevin Spacey (Rufus Buckley), Oliver Platt (Harry Rex Vonner), Charles S. Dutton (Sheriff Ozzie Walls), Brenda Fricker (Ethel Twitty), Donald Sutherland (Lucien Wilbanks), Kiefer Sutherland (Freddie Cobb), Patrick McGoohan (Judge Omar Noose), Ashley Judd (Carla Brigance), Tonea Stewart (Gwen Hailey), Raeven Larrymore Kelly (Tonya Hailey), Darrin Mitchell (Skip Hailey), LaConte McGrew (Slim Hailey), Devin Lloyd (Willie Hailey), John Diehl (Tim Nunley), Chris Cooper (Deputy Looney), Nicky Katt (Billy Ray Cobb), Doug Hutchison (Pete Willard), Kurtwood Smith (Stump Sisson), Tim Parati (Winston), Mark Whitman Johnson (Deputy Hastings), Beth Grant (Cora Cobb), Joe Seneca (Rev. Isaiah Street), Anthony Heald (Dr. Rodeheaver), Thomas Merdis (Rev. Ollie Agee), Alexandra Kyle (Hannah Brigance), Terry Loughlin (Jury Foreman), Andy Stahl (Reluctant Juror), Joe Bullen (Joe Frank Perryman), Lorraine Middleton (Blonde Juror), Graham Timbes (Juror), Jonathan Hadary (Norman Reinfield), Benjamin Mouton (Klan Bomber), Byron Jennings (Brent Musgrove), Patrick Sutton (Militant Teenager), Greg Lauren (Taylor), Danny Nelson (Bud Twitty), Mike Pniewski (Deputy Tatum), Elizabeth Omilami (Woman Angy at Klan), Lukas Cain (Looney's Son), Stacy Rae Toyon (Looney's Wife), Wayne deHart (Claude), Helen E. Floyd (Waitress at Claude's), David Brian Williams (Customer at Claude's), Octavia Spencer (Roark's Nurse), Rebecca Koon (Dell), James M. Crumley, Jr. (Guardsman Mackenvale), Jim Ritchie (Tom Hardy), Perry Ritchie (Sarah Hardy), Mike McLaren (Administrator at Whitfield), Timothy F. Monich (Rev. Fink), Leonard Thomas (Man in Lumberyard), Brance H. Beamon (Noose's Butler), Mildred J. Gilbreath (Noose's Housekeeper), Will Crapps (Minister), David U. Hodges (Bailiff), Maggie Wage Dixon (T.V. Anchor), Russell Hambline (Old Man Bates), Robert Chapman (Young Fisherman), Robert R. Bell, Jr. (Fisherman), Tommy McCullough (Old Fisherman), Ryk St. Vincent (Deputy), Bettina Rose (Buckley's Secretary), Linda Calvin Johnson (Sugar), Terrance Freeman (Court Deputy), Alice Julius-Scott (NAACP Woman), Dr. William Truly, Jr., Walter L. Hutchins (NAACP Men), Jerry Hunt (Electrical Company Worker), Howard Ballou (Reporter with Hastings), Todd Demers, Sherri Hilton (Reporters with Jake), Stephanie Strickland, Kim Hendrix, Rob Jay (Reporters with Buckley), Steve Coulter (Klansman), Jackie Stewart (Fire Chief), Rosebud Dixon-Green (Woman at Rally), M. Emmet Walsh

TIN CUP (Regency Enterprises) Producers, Gary Foster, David Lester; Executive Producer, Arnon Milchan; Director, Ron Shelton; Screenplay, John Norville, Ron Shelton; Photography, Russell Boyd; Designer, James Bissell; Editors, Paul Seydor, Kimberly Ray; Music, William Ross; Associate Producers, Karin Freud, Kellie Davis; Costumes, Carol Oditz; Casting, Victoria Thomas, Ed Johnston; a Regency Enterprises presentation of a Gary Foster production, distributed by WB; Dolby SDDS Stereo; Panavision; Technicolor; Rated R; 133 minutes; August release. CAST: Kevin Costner (Roy "Tin Cup" McAvoy), Rene Russo (Dr. Molly Griswold), Don Johnson (David Simms), Cheech Marin (Romeo Posar), Linda Hart (Doreen), Dennis Burkley (Earl), Rex Linn (Dewey), Lou Myers (Clint), Richard Lineback (Curt), George Perez (Jose), Mickey Jones (Turk), Michael Milhoan (Boone), Gary McCord, Craig Stadler, Peter Jacobsen (Themselves), Jim Nantz, Ken Venturi, Ben Wright (CBS Announcers), Frank Chirkinian (CBS Coordinating Producer), Lance Barrow (CBS Director), Brian Hammons, Mike Ritz (Golf Channel Announcers), Peter Kostis (Golf Channel Reporter), Jimmy Roberts (ESPN Reporter), George Michael (Host of *The Sports*

Machine), Kris Ancira (Golden Tassel Dancer), Sharyn McCreedy (Golden Tassel Waitress), Gregory Avellone (Man Behind the Ropes), Kevin Wilson (Mickelson's Caddie), Susan Cabral (Patient in Exit Room), Del Roy (Local Qualifier Starter), Sanford Gibbons (Local Qualifier Official), Irina Gasanova (19th Hole Waitress), Bill Caplan (U.S. Open Starter), Sharon Costner, Bill Costner (Grandparents with Dog), Joe Costner (Grandchild), Rob Harris (Simms' Agent), Nick Kiriazis, Tom Todoroff, Frederick Lewis, Jess King (Guys at Bar), Harold Herthum (Bartender), Allan Malamuid (U.S. Open Reporter), Melissa Young (Beautiful Blonde), Steven "Sven" Lewison (Simms' Caddie), Brad Britton (Jacobsen's Caddie), Corey Pavin, Phil Mickelson, Fred Couples, Jerry Pate, Lee Janzen, Billy Mayfair, Steve Elkington, John Cook, Andrew Magee, David Ogrin, John Mahaffey, Jeff Maggert, D.A. Weibring, Blaine McCallister, Tom Purtzer, Bruce Lietzke, Tommy Armour III, Gregory Buff White, Mike Standly, Jim McLean, Howard Twitty, Amy Alcott (PGA Tour Golfers)

SURVIVING PICASSO (Merchant Ivory/Wolper) Producers, Ismail Merchant, David L. Wolper; Executive Producers, Donald Rosenfeld, Paul Bradley; Director, James Ivory; Screenplay, Ruth Prawer Jhabvala; Based on the book *Picasso: Creator and Destroyer* by Arianna Stassinopoulos Huffington; Photography, Tony Pierce-Roberts; Designer, Luciana Arrighi; Editor, Andrew Marcus; Co-Producer, Humbert Balsan; Music, Richard Robbins; Costumes, Carol Ramsey; Casting, Celestia Fox (London), Joanna Merlin (New York); a Merchant Ivory/Wolper production of a James Ivory Film, distributed by WB; Dolby Stereo; Technicolor; Rated R; 125 minutes; September release. CAST: Anthony Hopkins (Pablo Picasso), Natasha McElhone (Francoise), Julianne Moore (Dora Maar), Joss Ackland (Matisse), Peter Eyre (Sabartes), Jane Lapotaire (Olga Piccaso), Joseph Maher (Kahnweiler), Bob Peck (Father), Diane Venora (Jacqueline), Joan Plowright (Grandmother), Tom Fisher (German Officer), Andreas Wisniewski (German Soldier), Allegra Di Capegna (Genevieve), Nigel Whitney (Pierre), Leon Lissek (Testicle), Hamish McColl (Torso), Judith Sharp (Peachy), Rose English (Plummy), Celia Hewitt (Stage Directions), Agapi Stassinopoulos (Ines), Andrew Litvack (American Officer Presenting a Dagger), Seth Rubin (GI Presenting a Cowboy Hat), Valerie Toledano (Maid), Peter Gerety (Marcel), Susannah Harker (Marie-Therese), Laura Aikman (Maya), Sevilla Delofski (Waiting Woman), David Sterne (Waiting Man), Dennis Boutsikaris (Kootz), Cengiz Kahn (Man without a Match), Jean-Gabriel Nordmann, Laurent Schwaar, Scott Thrun, Marc Tissot (Reporters), Damien Brun (Claude, age 2), Andrea Nagy (Olga as Ballerina), Vernon Dobtcheff (Diaghilev), Dominic West (Paulo Picasso), Anthony Milner (Police Commissioner), Sandor Eles, Olegario Fedoro, Brigitte Kahn, Bruno Pasquier-Desvignes, Gwen Reed, Georgio Serafini (Party Guests), Alexi Jawdokimov (Commissar), Boris Isarov (Translator), Stefan Gryff (Drunken Comrade), Olivier Galfione (Priest), Valentina Yukunina (Lydia), Jacques Pratoussy (Man Servant), Joe Gecks (Claude Picasso, age 7), Alex Pooley (Paloma Picasso, age 5), Debbie Cusmans, Beth Lawson (Jugglers), Mike Bonfield, John Lawson, Kevin Toomey, Mathew Ware (Clowns), Nicola Christian (Snake Woman), Lean Whitney (Poodle Woman), Charotte Balthorpe (Trapeze Artist), Marc Monnet (Matador)

MICHAEL COLLINS (Geffen Pictures) Producer, Stephen Woolley; Director/Screenplay, Neil Jordan; Co-Producer, Redmond Morris; Photography, Chris Menges; Designer, Anthony Pratt; Editors, J. Patrick Duffner, Tony Lawson; Music, Elliot Goldenthal; Costumes, Sandy Powell; Casting, Susie Figgis; a Geffen Pictures presentation of a Stephen Woolley production, distributed by WB; U.S.-Irish; Dolby SDDS Stereo; Technicolor; Rated R: 132 minutes; October release. CAST: Liam Neeson (Michael Collins), Aidan Quinn (Harry Boland), Stephen Rea (Ned Broy), Alan Rickman (Eamon De Valera), Julia Roberts (Kitty Kiernan), Ian Hart (Joe O'Reilly), Richard Ingram (British Officer), John Kenny (Patrick Pearse), Roman McCairbe (Thomas McDonagh), Ger O'Leary (Thomas Clarke), Michael Dwyer (James Connolly), Martin Murphy (Capt. Lee-Wilson), Sean McGinley (Smith), Gary Whelan (Hoey), Frank O'Sullivan (Kavanagh), Frank Laverty (Sean McKeoin), Owen O'Neill (Rory O'Connor), Stuart Graham (Tom Cullen), Brendan Gleeson (Liam Tobin), Gerard McSorley (Austin Stack), Owen Roe (Arthur Griffith), Paul Bennett (Cosgrave), Claude Clancy (Vaughan's Hotel Clerk), Paul Hickey (Dublin Castle Soldier), Tom Murphy (Vinny Byrne), David Gorry (Charlie Dalton), Gary Lydon, David Wilmot (Squad Youths), Joe Hanley, Colm Coogan (Squad Men), Aiden Grennell (Chaplain at Lincoln Jail), Dave Seymour (Lincoln Taxi Driver), Ian McElhinney (Belfast Detective), Tony Clarin (Soldier at Station), Charles Dance (Soames), Luke Hayden (McCrae), Gary Powell, Max Hafler (Black and Tans on Larry), Laura Brennan (Rosie), Aidan Kelly (Gresham Hotel Bellboy), Jim Isherwood (Man following Broy), Michael James Ford (Black and Tan), Mal Whyte (Officer in Bath), Martin Phillips (Officer in Bed), Aisling O'Sullivan (Girl in Bed), Malcolm Douglas (Officer in Park), Brian "Joker" Mulvey (Croke Park Hurler), Frank Patterson (Tenor in Restaurant), Peter O'Brien (Pianist in Restaurant), Mike McCabe (Journalist), Vnnie McCabe (Speaker in the Dail), Alan Stanford (Vice-Consul McCready), Gary Paul Mullen (Young Gunman), Barry Barnes (Free State

Soldier), Denis Conway, Don Wycherley (Republicans), Paraic Breathnach (Santry the Blacksmith), Jonathan Rhys Myers (Collins' Assassin)

SLEEPERS (PolyGram Filmed Entertainment) Producers, Barry Levinson, Steve Golin; Executive Producer, Peter Giuliano; Director/Screenplay, Barry Levinson; Co-Producer/Based on the book by Lorenzo Carcaterra; Photography, Michael Ballhaus; Designer, Kristi Zea; Editor, Stu Linder; Costumes, Gloria Gresham; Music, John Williams; Casting, Louis DiGiaimo; a PolyGram Filmed Entertainment presentation of a Propaganda Films/Baltimore Pictures production, distributed by WB; Dolby Stereo; Super 35 Widescreen; Technicolor; Rated R; 147 minutes; October release. CAST: Kevin Bacon (Nokes), Billy Crudup (Tommy), Robert De Niro (Father Bobby), Ron Eldard (John), Minnie Driver (Carol), Vittorio Gassman (King Benny), Dustin Hoffman (Danny Snyder), Terry Kinney (Ferguson), Bruno Kirby (Shakes' Father), Frank Medrano (Fat Mancho), Jason Patric (Shakes), Joe Perrino (Young Shakes), Brad Pitt (Michael), Brad Renfro (Young Michael), Jonathan Tucker (Young Tommy), Geoffrey Wigdor (Young John), Peter Appel (Boyfriend), Joe Attanasio, Rose Caiola (Jurors), Gerry Becker (Forensics Expert), Casandra Brooks (Young John's Mother), William Butler (Juanito), Eugene Byrd (Rizzo), Pasquale Cajano (Superintendent), Robert W. Castle, Father Peter Mahoney (Priests), John DiBenedetto (Tony), Jeffrey Donovan (Addison), Drew Eliot, Reuben Larry Elliott (Businessmen), George Georgiadis (Hot Dog Vendor), Marco Greco (Waiter), Saverio Guerra, Larry Romano (Men), Don Hewitt (James Caldwell), Ben Hammer (Judge Weisman), Paul Herman (Court Bailiff), Frank Inzerillo (Hanging Man), Lennie Loftin (Styler), Chuck Lewis Low (Dance Judge), Ruth Maeczech (Women at Subway Station), Juan Maria, Jr. (Davy), Daniel Mastrogiorgio (Nick Davenport), Mary McCann (Sister Carolyn), Pat McNamara (Guard), Peter McRobbie (Lawyer), Conrad Meertins, Jr. (Inmate #2), Gina Menza (Jury Foreman), Dash Mihok (K.C.), Michael P. Moran (Judge #1), Rocco Masacchia (Salvatore), Mick O'Rourke (Man in Tub), Carmine Parisi (King Benny's Boy), James Pickens, Jr. (Marlboro), Wendell Pierce (Little Caesar), Salvatore Paul Piro (Mimi), Monica Polito (Young Carol), Angela Marie (Shakes' Mother), Sean Patrick Reilly (Young King Benny), Peter Rini (Frank Magcolco), Gayle Scott (Confessional Woman), Tom Signorelli (Confessional Man), Henry Stram (Prison Doctor), Ralph Tabakin (Warden), Mary Testa (Nun), Jenique Torres (Davy's Sister), Patrick Tull (Jerry the Bartender), Aida Turturro (Mrs. Salinas), Joseph Urla (Carson)

SPACE JAM (Ivan Reitman/David Falk-Ken Ross Production) Producers, Ivan Reitman, Joe Medjuck, Daniel Goldberg; Executive Producers, David Falk, Ken Ross; Director, Joe Pytka; Screenplay, Leo Benvenuti, Steve Rudnick, Timothy Harris, Herschel Weingrod; Co-Producers, Gordon Webb, Sheldon Kahn, Curtis Polk; Photography, Michael Chapman; Designer, Geoffrey Kirkland; Editor, Sheldon Kahn; Music, James Newton Howard; Live Action/Animation Visual Effects, Ed Jones; Animation Producers, Ron Tippe, Jery Rees, Steven Paul Leiva; Costumes, Marlene Stewart; Directors of Animation, Bruce W. Smith, Tony Cervone; Casting, Jane Jenkins, Janet Hirshenson; an Ivan Reitman/David Falk-Ken Ross production, distributed by WB; Dolby SDDS Stereo; Technicolor; Rated PG; 87 minutes; November release. CAST: Michael Jordan, Larry Bird, Bill Murray, Charles Barkley, Patrick Ewing, Muggsy Bogues, Larry Johnson, Shawn Bradley, Ahmad Rashad, Del Harris, Vlade Divac, Cedric Ceballos, Jim Rome, Paul Westphal, Danny Ainge, Alonzo Mourning, A.C. Green, Charles Oakley, Derek Harper, Jeff Malone, Anthony Miller, Sharone Wright (Themselves), Wayne Knight (Stan Podolak), Theresa Randle (Juanita Jordan), Manner "Mooky" Washington (Jeffery Jordan), Eric Gordon (Marcus Jordan), Penny Bae Bridges (Jasmine Jordan), Brandon Hammond (Michael Jordan—10 years old), Bebe Drake (Jordan Housekeeper), Patricia Heaton, Dan Castellaneta (Fans), Linda Lutz (Seer), Nicky McCrimmon (Basketball Girl), Kelly Vint (Little League Girl), William G. Schilling (Golfer), Albert Hague (Psychiatrist), Michael Alaimo (Doctor), James O'Donnell (NBA Referee), David Ursin (Charlotte Coach), Douglas Robert Jackson (Commissioner), Rosey Brown (Umpire), Brad Henke (Stars Catcher), Connie Ray (Owner's Girlfriend), John Roselius (Baron's Manager), Joe Bays (Baron's Coach), Charles Hoyes (Baron's Catcher), Luke Torres, Steven Shenbaum, Bean Miller (Players); VOICES: Billy West (Bugs Bunny/Elmer Fudd), Dee Bradley Baker (Daffy Duck/Tazmanian Devil/Bull), Danny DeVito (Swackhammer), Bob Bergen (Bert/Herbie/Marvin the Martian/Porky Pig/Tweety), Bill Farmer (Sylvester/Yosemite Sam/Foghorn Leghorn), June Foray (Granny), Maurice LaMarche (Pepe Le Pew), Kath Soucie (Lola Bunny), Jocelyn Blue (Nerdluck POUND), Charity James (Nerdluck BLANKO), June Melby (Nerdluck BANG), Catherine Reitman (Nerdluck BUPKUS), Colleen Wainwright (Nerdluck NAWT/Sniffles), Dorian Harewood (Monstar BUPKUS), Joey Camen (Monstar BANG), TK Carter (Monstar NAWT), M. Darnell Suttles (Monstar POUND), Steve Kehela (Monstar BLANKO/Announcer), Frank W. Welker (Charles the Dog)

MARS ATTACKS! (Tim Burton) Producers, Tim Burton, Larry Franco; Director, Tim Burton; Screen Story/Screenplay, Jonathan Gems; Based on the Topps trading cards; Photography, Peter Suschitzky; Designer, Wynn Thomas; Music, Danny Elfman; Editor, Chris Lebenzon; Visual Effects Supervisors, James Mitchell, Michael Fink, David Andews; Martian Visual Effects and Animation, Industrial Light & Magic; Costumes, Colleen Atwood; Casting, Victoria Thomas, Jeanne McCarthy, Matthew Barry; Distributed by WB; Dolby Digital Stereo; Panavision; Technicolor; Rated PG-13; 103 minutes; December release. CAST: Jack Nicholson (President Dale/Art Land), Glenn Close (Marsha Dale), Annette Bening (Barbara Land), Pierce Brosnan (Donald Kessler), Danny DeVito (Rude Gambler), Martin Short (Jerry Ross), Sarah Jessica Parker (Nathalie Lake), Michael J. Fox (Jason Stone), Rod Steiger (General Decker), Tom Jones (Himself), Lukas Haas (Richie Norris), Natalie Portman (Taffy Dale), Jim Brown (Byron Williams), Lisa Marie (Martian Girl), Sylvia Sidney (Grandma Norris), Paul Winfield (General Casey), Pam Grier (Louise Williams), Jack Black (Billy Glenn Norris), Janice Rivera (Cindy), Ray J (Cedric), Brandon Hammond (Neville), Joe Don Baker (Glenn Norris), O-Lan Jones (Sue Ann Norris), Christina Applegate (Sharona), Brian Haley (Mitch), Jerzy Skolimowski (Dr. Zeigler), Timi Prulhiere (Tour Guide), Barbet Schroeder (French President), Chi Hoang Cai (Mr. Lee), Tom Bush (Hillbilly), Joseph Maher (Decorator), Gloria M. Malgarini, Betty Bunch, Gloria Hoffmann (Nuns), Willie Garson (Corporate Guy), John Roselius (GNN Boss), Michael Reilly Burke, Valerie Wildman, Richard Irving (GNN Reporters), Jonathan Emerson (Newscaster), Tamara "Gingir" Curry, Rebecca Broussard (Hookers), Vinny Argiro (Casino Manager), Steve Valentine (TV Director), Coco Leigh (Journalist), Jeffrey King (Nasa Tech), Enrique Castillo (Hispanic Colonel), Don LaMoth (Colonel #2), C. Wayne Owens, Joseph Patrick Moynihan (Strangers), Roger Peterson (Colonel), John Finnegan (Speaker of the House), Ed Lambert (Morose Old Guy), John Gray (Incredibly Old Guy), Gregg Daniel (Lab Technician), J. Kenneth Campbell, Jeanne Mori (Doctors), Rance Howard (Texan Investor), Richard Assad (Saudi Investor), Velletta Carlson (Elderoly Slots Lady), Kevin Mangan (Trailer Lover), Rebeca Silva (Hispanic Woman), Josh Weinstein (Hippie), Julian Barnes (White House Waiter), Ken Thomas (White House Photographer), Darelle Porter Holden, Cristi Black, Sharon Hendrix (Tom Jones Backup Singers), Frank W. Welker (Various Martian Voice Overs), Poppy (Poppy)

MY FELLOW AMERICANS (Peters Entertainment/Storyline Entertainment) Producer, Jon Peters; Director, Peter Segal; Screenplay, E. Jack Kaplan, Richard Chapman, Peter Tolan; Story, E. Jack Kaplan, Richard Chapman; Executive Producers, Craig Zadan, Neil Memo, Tracy Barone; Photography, Julio Macat; Designer, James Bissell; Editor, William Kerr; Co-Producers, Jean Higgins, Michael Ewing; Music, William Ross; Costumes, Betsy Cox; Casting, Karen Rea; a Peters Entertainment production in association with Storyline Entertainment, distributed by WB; Dolby SDDS Stereo; Technicolor; Rated PG-13; 101 minutes; December release. CAST: Jack Lemmon (Russell P. Kramer), James Garner (Matt Douglas), Dan Aykroyd (William Haney), John Heard (Ted Matthews), Wilford Brimley (Joe Hollis), Lauren Bacall (Margaret Kramer), Sela Ward (Kaye Griffin), Everett McGill (Col. Paul Tanner), Bradley Whitford (Carl Witnaur), James Rebhorn (Charlie Reynolds), Esther Rolle (Rita), Conchata Ferrell (Truck Driver), Jack Kehler (Wayne), Connie Ray (Genny), Tom Everett (Wilkerson), Mark Lowenthal (Caldwell), Jeff Yagher (Dorothy/Lt. Ralph Fleming), Edwin Newman (Himself), Lynn Clark (Chrissy Kramer), Leigh Rose (Katherine Douglas), Mihoko Tokoro (Japanese Singer), Ken Enomoto (Hiroshi Ashino), Gunnar Peterson (Bruce), Scott Burkholder (Greg), Wayne Duvall (Chet), Jack Garner (Pres. Haney's Caddy), Gene Bolande (Injured Golf Spectator), Francesca Rollins, Paul Feig (Reporters), Cathy Ladman (Reynolds' Secretary), Tom Wright (Jim), Dana Gould (Sandwich Guy at Book Convention), Scott Hoxby (Man with Subpoena), Jonathan Osser (Kramer's Grandson), Mitch Braswell (Marine One Pilot), Art Booth (Marine One Co-Pilot), Steve Carlisle (Man in Train Station Bathroom), Todd McDurmont (Elvis), Madison Wellington (Tina), David "Skippy" Malloy (Will), Jennifer L. Jones (Fran), Rob Roy Fitzgerald (Dean), Jennifer Austin (Marilyn Monroe), Bobby Bass, Steve Chambers, Jimmy Nickerson (NSA Hit Men), Cara Gooden (Truck Stop Girl), Matt Zboyovski (Truck Stop Boy), Michael Pena (Ernesto), Alex Joganic (Kevin), Ocie Pouncie (Man in Diner), Neva Howell (Charlene—Budget Agent), Sheri Mann Stewart (Sandy—Budget Agent), Peter Penuel (Man in Parade), John O'Leary (Caretaker Ben), Leighanne Wallace (Witnaur's Girlfriend), Rick Hall (White House Guard), Eric Siegel (Pres. Haney's Aide), Ann Cusack (White House Tour Guide), Jean Speegle Howard (Asthmatic Woman on Tour), Dorothy Lucey (News Anchor), Jeff Mandon, James Bissell, Shawn D. Woodyard (Secret Service Agents), Stephen Wedan, Tom Sean Foley (Mounted Police), Michael Russo (White House Sharpshooter), Chris Kriesa (Agent Kopeck), William Kerr (V.P. Matthews' Make-Up Man), Peter Segal (TV Technician)

TOP 100 BOX OFFICE FILMS OF 1996

1. Independence Day (20th/Jul) $303,140,000

2. Twister (May) $238,990,000

3. Mission Impossible (Par/May) $179,000,000

4. Jerry Maguire (TriS/Dec) $153,660,000

5. Ransom (BV/Nov) $136,460,000

6. 101 Dalmatians (BV/Nov) $135,920,000

7. The Rock (BV/Jun) $133,980,000

8. The Nutty Professor (Univ/Jun) $128,270,000

9. The Birdcage (UA/Mar) $123,900,000

10. A Time to Kill (Jul) $108,100,000

26. Executive Decision (Mar) $56,200,000

27. Primal Fear (Par/Apr) $55,980,000

28. Tin Cup (Aug). $53,420,000

29. Sleepers (Oct). $53,270,000

30. Up Close & Personal (BV/Mar) $51,100,000

31. Dragonheart (Univ/May) $50,440,000

32. Evita (BV/Dec) $49,490,000

33. The Preacher's Wife (BV/Dec). $48,100,000

34. Wm Shakespeare's Romeo & Juliet (20th/Nov) $46,300,000

35. One Fine Day (20th/Dec) $46,120,000

36. The Mirror Has Two Faces (TriS/Nov). $41,270,000

37. The Ghost and the Darkness (Par/Oct) $38,570,000

38. Happy Gilmore (Univ/Feb) $38,470,000

39. Mars Attacks! (Dec) $37,690,000

40. Set It Off (NLC/Nov) $36,100,000

41. Shine (FL/Nov) $35,140,000

42. A Thin Line Between Love and Hate (NLC/Apr) $34,900,000

43. The Truth About Cats and Dogs (20th/Apr). $34,100,000

44. The Long Kiss Goodnight (NLC/Oct) $33,450,000

45. Muppet Treasure Island (BV/Feb). $33,200,000

46. Striptease(Col/Jun) $32,780,000

47. Daylight (Univ/Dec) $32,770,000

48. Matilda (TriS/Aug) $32,740,000

49. Black Sheep (Par/Feb) $32,280,000

50. Homeward Bound II (BV/Mar) $31,480,000

Will Smith in *Independence Day* © Twentieth Century Fox

11. The First Wives Club (Par/Sep) $105,240,000

12. Phenomenon (BV/Jul) $104,620,000

13. Scream (Mir/Dec). $103,100,000

14. Eraser (Jun) $100,200,000

15. The Hunchback of Notre Dame (BV/Jun) $100,130,000

16. Michael (NLC/Dec) $94,300,000

17. Star Trek: First Contact (Par/Nov) $91,930,000

18. Space Jam (Nov) $90,450,000

19. The English Patient (Mir/Nov). $78,100,000

20. Broken Arrow (20th/Feb) $68,990,000

21. Beavis & Butt-Head Do America (Par/Dec) $62,540,000

22. Jingle All the Way (20th/Nov) $60,480,000

23. The Cable Guy (Col/Jun) $60,170,000

24. Courage Under Fire (20th/Jul). $59,100,000

25. Jack (BV/Aug) $58,630,000

Leonardo DiCaprio, Claire Danes in *William Shakespeare's Romeo & Juliet* © Twentieth Century Fox

Ethan Embry, Steve Zahn, Johnathon Schaech, Tom Everett Scott in
That Thing You Do! ©Twentieth Century Fox

51. Eddie (BV/May) $31,100,000

52. Rumble in the Bronx (NLC/Feb) $29,820,000

53. Sgt. Bilko (Univ/Mar) $29,500,000

54. James and the Giant Peach (BV/Apr) $28,930,000

55. The Island of Dr. Moreau (NLC/Aug) $27,690,000

56. Harriet the Spy (Par/Jul) $26,470,000

57. Eye for an Eye (Par/Jan) $26,460,000

58. First Kid (BV/Aug) $26,430,000

59. Spy Hard (BV/May) $26,100,000

60. That Thing You Do! (20th/Oct) $25,790,000

61. From Dusk Till Dawn (Mir/Jan) $25,670,000

62. Escape From L.A. (Par/Aug) $25,370,000

63. Down Periscope (20th/Mar) $24,830,000

64. The Craft (Col/May) $24,770,000

65. Fly Away Home (Col/Sep) $24,550,000

66. Sling Blade (Mir/Nov) $24,490,000

67. Fargo (Gram/Mar) $24,410,000

68. Kingpin (MGM/Jul) $24,100,000

69. My Fellow Americans (Dec) $22,250,000

70. Emma (Mir/Aug) $22,110,000

71. The Juror (Col/Feb) $22,100,000

72. D3: The Mighty Ducks (BV/Oct) $21,840,000

73. Bulletproof (Univ/Sep) $21,200,000

74. High School High (TriS/Oct) $21,000,000

75. The Glimmer Man (Oct) $20,410,000

76. The Quest (Univ/Apr) $20,200,000

77. City Hall (Col/Feb) $20,140,000

78. The People vs. Larry Flynt (Col/Dec) $20,100,000

79. Chain Reaction (20th/Aug) $19,800,000

80. Flipper (Univ/May) $19,850,000

81. Don't Be a Menace to South Central (NLC/Jan) $19,680,000

82. Fear (Univ/Apr) $19,430,000

83. Bed of Roses (NLC/Jan) $18,980,000

84. Kazaam (BV/Jul) $18,890,000

85. Mother (Par/Dec) $18,740,000

86. Multiplicity (Col/Jul) $18,650,000

87. Oliver & Company (BV/Mar reissue) $18,400,000

88. Last Man Standing (NLC/Sep) $18,120,000

89. The Fan (TriS/Aug) $17,800,000

Madonna in *Evita* ©Cinergi Pictures Entertainment, Inc.

90. A Very Brady Sequel (Par/Aug) $17,700,000

91. The Crow: City of Angels (Mir/Aug) $17,620,000

92. Extreme Measures (Col/Sep) $17,320,000

93. The Phantom (Par/Jun) $17,310,000

94. Diabolique (Mar) $17,110,000

95. Fled (MGM/Jul) $16,980,000

96. The Frighteners (Univ/Jul) $16,560,000

97. Trainspotting (Mir/Jul) $16,520,000

98. Supercop (NLC/Jul) $16,100,000

99. The Adventures of Pinocchio (NLC/Jul) $15,390,000

100. Stephen King's Thinner(Par/Oct) $15,200,000

PROMISING NEW ACTORS OF 1996

JENNIFER ANISTON
(She's the One)

ETHAN EMBRY
(White Squall, That Thing You Do!)

MATTHEW McCONAUGHEY
(A Time to Kill, Larger Than Life, Lone Star)

ANNE HECHE
(The Juror, Walking & Talking)

EWAN McGREGOR
(Trainspotting, Emma)

NATALIE PORTMAN
(Beautiful Girls, Mars Attacks!)

CHLOE SEVIGNY
(Trees Lounge)

EDWARD NORTON
(Primal Fear, Everyone Says I Love You, The People vs. Larry Flynt)

TOM EVERETT SCOTT
(That Thing You Do!)

EMILY WATSON
(Breaking the Waves)

RENEE ZELLWEGER
(Jerry Maguire, The Whole Wide World)

VINCE VAUGHN
(Swingers, The Lost World)

Ralph Fiennes, Kristin Scott Thomas

Ralph Fiennes, Kristin Scott Thomas

Willem Dafoe

Colin Firth, Kristin Scott Thomas

ACADEMY AWARD WINNER FOR BEST PICTURE OF 1996

THE ENGLISH PATIENT

(MIRAMAX) Producer, Saul Zaentz; Executive Producers, Bob Weinstein, Harvey Weinstein, Scott Greenstein; Director/Screenplay, Anthony Minghella; Based on the novel by Michael Ondaatje; Photography, John Seale; Designer, Stuart Craig; Music, Gabriel Yared; Associate Producers, Paul Zaentz, Steve Andrews; Line Producer, Alessandro von Normann; Costumes, Ann Roth; Editor, Walter Murch; Casting, Michelle Guish, David Rubin; a Saul Zaentz production; Dolby Digital Stereo; Color; Rated R; 159 minutes; November release

CAST

Count Laszlo de Almasy	Ralph Fiennes
Hana	Juliette Binoche
Caravaggio	Willem Dafoe
Katherine Clifton	Kristin Scott Thomas
Kip	Naveen Andrews
Geoffrey Clifton	Colin Firth
Madox	Julian Wadham
Hardy	Kevin Whately
Fenelon-Barnes	Clive Merrison
D'Agostino	Nino Castelnuovo
Fouad	Hichem Rostom
Bermann	Peter Ruhring
Oliver	Geordie Johnson
Mary	Torri Higginson
Jan	Lisa Repo-Martell
Rupert Douglas	Raymond Coulthard
Corporal Dade	Philip Whitchurch
Spalding	Lee Ross
Beach Interrogation Officer	Anthony Smee
Young Canadian Soldier	Matthew Ferguson
Kiss Me Soldier	Jason Done
Sergeant, Desert Train	Roger Morlidge
Private, Desert Train	Simon Sherlock
Interrogation Room Soldiers	Sebastian Schipper, Fritz Eggert
Araba Nurse	Sonia Mankai
AIcha	Rim Turki
Officer in Square	Sebastian Rudolph
Interpreter in Square	Thoraya Sehill
Woman with Baby in Square	Sondess Belhassen
Officer, El Taj	Dominic Mafham
Corpora, El Taj	Gregor Truter
Bedouin Doctor	Salah Miled
Ancient Arab	Abdellatif Hamrouni
Kamal	Samy Azaiez
Al Auf	Habib Chetoui
Officer's Wife	Phillipa Day
Amanda Walker	Amanda Walker
Sir Ronnie Hampton	Paul Kant

While being attended by a lone nurse at an Italian monastery facially disfigured Count Almasy thinks back on his relationship with married Katherine Clifton.

1996 Academy Award Winner for Best Picture, Director, Supporting Actress (Binoche), Art Direction, Cinematography, Costume Design, Film Editing, Sound and Original Dramatic Score. The film received additional nominations for actor (Fiennes), actress (Scott Thomas) and adapted screenplay

Ralph Fiennes, Kristin Scott Thomas

Juliette Binoche

Naveen Andrews, Juliette Binoche

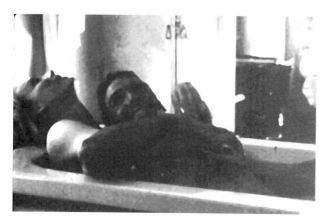

Kristin Scott Thomas, Ralph Fiennes

Kristin Scott Thomas

GEOFFREY RUSH
in *Shine*
© Fine Line Features.
ACADEMY AWARD FOR BEST ACTOR OF 1996

FRANCES McDORMAND
in *Fargo*
© Gramercy Pictures
ACADEMY AWARD FOR BEST ACTRESS OF 1996

CUBA GOODING, JR.
in *Jerry Maguire*
© TriStar Pictures
ACADEMY AWARD FOR BEST SUPPORTING ACTOR OF 1996

JULIETTE BINOCHE
in *The English Patient*
© Miramax Films
ACADEMY AWARD FOR BEST SUPPORTING ACTRESS OF 1996

ACADEMY AWARD NOMINEES FOR BEST ACTOR

Tom Cruise in *Jerry Maguire*

Ralph Fiennes in *The English Patient*

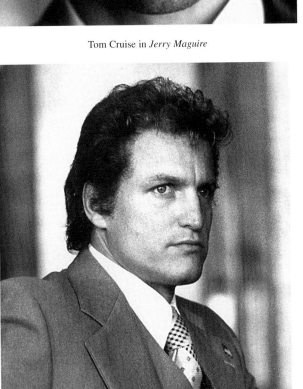

Woody Harrelson in *The People vs. Larry Flynt*

Billy Bob Thornton in *Sling Blade*

ACADEMY AWARD NOMINEES FOR BEST ACTRESS

Brenda Blethlyn in *Secrets & Lies*

Diane Keaton in *Marvin's Room*

Kristin Scott Thomas in *The English Patient*

Emily Watson in *Breaking the Waves*

ACADEMY AWARD NOMINEES FOR BEST SUPPORTING ACTOR

William H. Macy in *Fargo*

Armin Mueller-Stahl in *Shine*

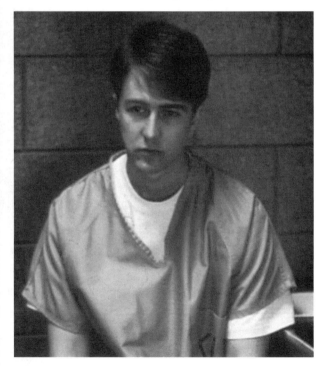

Edward Norton in *Primal Fear*

James Woods in *Ghosts of Mississippi*

ACADEMY AWARD NOMINEES FOR BEST SUPPORTING ACTRESS

Joan Allen in *The Crucible*

Lauren Bacall in *The Mirror Has Two Faces*

Barbara Hersey in *The Portrait of a Lady*

Marianne Jean-Baptiste in *Secrets & Lies*

Zdenek Sverak, Andrej Chalimon

Zdenek Sverak, Andrej Chalimon

Zdenek Sverak, Libuse Safrankova

KOLYA

(MIRAMAX) Producers, Eric Abraham, Jan Sverak; Director, Jan Sverak; Screenplay, Zdenek Sverak; Based on a story by Pavel Taussig; Photography, Vladimir Smutny; Music, Ondrej Soukop; Editor, Alois Fisarek; Designer, Milos Kohout; Costumes, Katerina Holla; Casting, Sona Tichackova; Czech; Dolby Stereo; Color; Rated PG-13; 110 minutes; January, 1997 release

CAST

Frantisek Louka	Zdenek Sverak
Kolya	Andrej Chalimon
Klara	Libuse Safrankova
Mr. Broz	Onrez Vetchy
Mother	Stella Zazvorkova
Mr. Houdek	Ladislav Smoljak
Nadezda	Irena Livanova
Aunt Tamara	Lilian Mankina
Pasha	Petra Spalova
Mrs. Brozova	Nella Boudova
Capt. Pokorny	Rene Pribyl
Capt. Novotny	Miroslav Taborsky
Mrs. Bustikova	Slavka Budinova
Uncle Ruzicka	Jiri Sovak
Mr. Musil (Organist)	Karel Hermanek

After agreeing to marry a woman to guarantee her Czech citizenship, Frantisek Loukas is abandoned by her and left with the resonsibility of taking care of her 5-year-old Russian son who doesn't speak a word of Czech.

© Miramax Films

ACADEMY AWARD FOR BEST FOREIGN LANGUAGE FILM OF 1996

212

FRENCH TWIST

(MIRAMAX ZÖE) Executive Producer, Pierre Grunstein; Director/Screenplay, Josiane Balasko; Adaptation , Telsche Boorman, Josiane Balasko; Photography, Gerard De Battista; Editor, Claudine Merlin; Costumes, Fabienne Katany; Designers, Claude Parnet, Bernard Prim; a Renn productions/TF1 Films production/Les Films Flam co-production, with the participation of Canal+; French, 1995; Dolby Stereo; Color; Rated R; 100 minutes; January release

CAST

Loli	Victoria Abril
Marijo	Josiane Balasko
Laurent	Alain Chabat
Antoine	Ticky Holgado
Diego, the Young Man	Miguel Bose
Dany	Catherine Hiegel
The Prostitute	Catherine Samie
Sophia, the Boss	Catherine Lachens
Solange	Michele Bernier
Dorothy Crumble	Tolache Boorman
Emily Crumble/Vero	Veronique Barrault
Ingrid	Sylvie Audcoeur
Cristelle	Maureen Diot

Loli, a scorned housewife, finds out that her husband has been cheating on her and takes up with another woman.

© Miramax Films

Josiane Balasko, Victoria Abril, Alan Chabat

Victoria Abril, Alain Chabat

Victoria Abril

Victoria Abril, Alain Chabat, Josiane Balasko

SCREAMERS

(TRIUMPH) Producers, Tom Berry, Franco Battista; Executive Producer, Charles W. Fries; Director, Christian Duguay; Screenplay, Dan O'Bannon, Miguel Tejada-Flores; Based upon the short story *Second Variety* by Philip K. Dick; Photography, Rodney Gibbons; Designer, Perri Gorrara; Music, Normand Corbeil; Supervising Producer, Antony I. Ginnane; Co-Executive Producers, Josée Bernard, Masao Takiyama; Associate Producer, Stefan Wodoslawsky; Digital Effects Supervisor, Richard Ostiguy; Visual Effects Supervisor, Ernest Farino; Editor, Yves Langlois; Casting, Mary Margiotta, Karen Margiotta, Lucie Robitaille; an Allegro Films production, presented in association with Fuji Eight Co. Ltd. and Fries Film Company; Canadian-Japanese-U.S., 1995; Dolby SDDS Stereo; Color; Rated R; 107 minutes; January release

CAST

Col. Hendricksson	Peter Weller
Becker	Roy Dupuis
Jessica	Jennifer Rubin
Ace	Andy Lauer
Ross	Charles Powell
Elbarak	Ron White
David	Michael Caloz
Landowska	Liliana Komorowska
Leone	Jason Cavalier
Corp. McDonald	Leni Parker
NEB Soldier	Sylvain Masse
Secretary Green	Bruce Boa
Technician	Tom Berry
Screamers Crawl Narration	Henry Ramer

On a futuristic war torn planet, Col. Hendricksson attempts to negotiate peace while battling a race of man-made killing devices called Screamers, created to destroy the enemy.

© Tristar Pictures, Inc.

Andy Lauer, Charles Powell

Jennifer Rubin, Peter Weller

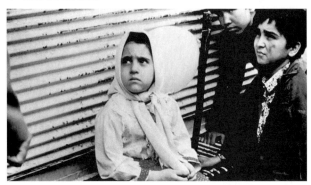

Aida Mohammadkhani, Mohsen Kalifi

Aida Mohammadkhani, Fereshteh Sadr Orfani

THE WHITE BALLOON

(OCTOBER) Director/Editor/Set Designer, Jafar Panahi; Screenplay, Abbas Kiarostami; Based on an idea by Jafar Panahi, Parviz Shahbazi; Photography, Farzad Jowdat; from Ferdos Films; Iranian/Farsi, 1995; Color; Not rated; 85 minutes; January release

CAST

Razieh	Aida Mohammadkhani
Ali	Mohsen Kalifi
Mother	Fereshteh Sadr Orfani
Old Woman	Anna Bourkowska
Soldier	Mohammad Shahani
Tailor	Mohammad Bahktiari

In Tehran a seven-year-old girl sets off to the pet shop to buy a goldfish but loses the bank note she begged her mother for on the way to the store.

© October Films

ANGELS & INSECTS

(SAMUEL GOLDWYN CO.) Producers, Joyce Herlihy, Belinda Haas; Executive Producer, Lindsay Law; Director, Philip Haas; Screenplay, Belinda Haas, Philip Haas; Based on the novella *Morpho Eugenia* by A.S. Byatt; Photography, Bernard Zitzermann; Designer, Jennifer Kernke; Costumes, Paul Brown; Music, Alexander Balanescu; Editor, Belinda Haas; Casting, Celestia Fox; a Playhouse International Pictures presentation; British-U.S., 1995; Color; Not rated; 116 minutes; January release

CAST

William Anderson	Mark Rylance
Matty Crompton	Kristin Scott Thomas
Eugenia Alabaster	Patsy Kensit
Sir Harald Alabaster	Jeremy Kemp
Edgar Alabaster	Douglas Henshall
Rowena Alabaster	Saskia Wickham
Robin Swinnerton	Chris Larkin
Lady Alabaster	Annette Badland
Lady Alabaster's Maid	Lindsay Thomas
Margaret Alabaster	Michelle Sylvester
Elaine Alabaster	Clare Lovell
Edith Alabaster	Jenny Lovell
Miss Mead	Anna Massey
Alice Alabaster	Oona Haas
Guy Alabaster	Angus Hodder
Nurse	Margery Golder
Tom	Paul Ready
Martha	Naomi Gudge
Ralph Blackwood	John Jenkins
Arthur	John Veasey
Amy	Clare Redman

and Jack Turney, Elizabeth Turney (Newborn Twins), Nicky Turney (Wetnurse), Alice Maitland, Hannah Maitland (Six-Month-Old Twins), Vita Haas (Rodger Edgar, one-year-old), Pam Smitham (Midwife), Brett Harris (Stable Lad)

After losing the specimens he obtained on his journey to South America, naturalist William Anderson is invited to stay at the Alabaster estate where he falls in love with the owner's daughter Eugenia.

This film received an Oscar nomination for costume design.

© The Samuel Goldwyn Company

Mark Rylance, Kristin Scott Thomas

Patsy Kensit

Kristin Scott Thomas, Patsy Kensit, Mark Rylance, Jeremy Kemp

A MIDWINTER'S TALE

(SONY PICTURES CLASSICS) a.k.a. *In the Bleak Midwinter*; Producer, David Barron; Director/Screenplay, Kenneth Branagh; Photography, Roger Lanser; Designer, Tim Harvey; Music, Jimmy Yuill; Costumes, Caroline Harris; Editor, Neil Farrell; from Castle Rock Entertainment; British, 1995; Dolby Digital Stereo; Black and white; Rated R; 98 minutes; February release

Jennifer Saunders, Joan Collins

CAST

Joe Harper	Michael Maloney
Henry Wakefield	Richard Briers
Vernon Spatch	Mark Hadfield
Tom Newman	Nicholas Farrell
Carnforth Greville	Gerard Horan
Terry Du Bois	John Sessions
Fadge	Celia Imrie
Molly	Hetta Charnley
Nina	Julia Sawalha
Margaretta D'Arcy	Joan Collins
Nancy Crawford	Jennifer Saunders
Mortimer	Robert Hines
Tim	James D. White
Mrs. Branch	Ann Davies
Nina's Father	Edward Dewesbury
Tap Dancer	Allie Byrne
Young Actor	Adrian Scarborough
Ventriloquist	Brian Petifer
Scotsman	Patrick Doyle
Mule Train Man	Shaun Prendergast
Audience Member	Carol Starks

Struggling actor Joe Harper decides to prove his worth by directing a low budget production of Hamlet *with a cast of six.*

© Castle Rock Entertainment

Michael Maloney, Director Kenneth Branagh

Richard Briers, Gerard Horan, Nicholas Farrell, Hetta Charnley, Michael Maloney, John Sessions, Julia Sawalha, Mark Hadfield, Celia Imrie

HATE (LA HAINE)

(GRAMERCY) Producer, Christophe Rossignon; Director/Screenplay, Mathieu Kassovitz; Photography, Pierre Aim; Editors, Mathieu Kassovitz, Scott Stevenson; Art Director, Giuseppe Ponturo; Costumes, Virginie Montel; from Lazennec Productions in association with Le Studio Canal+, La Sept Cinema and Kasso Inc. with the participation of Canal+ Cofimage 6 and Studio Images; Presented by Jodie Foster and Egg Pictures; French, 1995; Dolby Stereo; Black and white; Not rated; 95 minutes; February release

CAST

Vinz	Vincent Cassel
Hubert	Hubert Kounde
Saïd	Saïd Taghmaoui
Samir	Karim Belkhadra
Darty	Edouard Montoute
Asterix	Francois Levantal
Santo	Solo Dicko
Inspecteur "Notre Dame"	Marc Duret
Sarah	Heloise Rauth
Grand-mère Vinz	Rywka Wajsbrot
Monsieur Toilettes	Tadek Lokcinski
Nordine	Choukri Gabteni
Sam	Nabil Ben Mhamed
Mere Hubert	Felicite Wouassi
Soeur Hubert	Fatou Thioune

and Zinedine Soualem, Bernie Bonvoisin, Cyril Ancelin (Policiers Civils), Karine Viard, Julie Mauduech (Filles Galarie)

Following a riot three friends find a gun left behind by the Paris Police Department.

© Gramercy Pictures

Vincent Cassel, Said Taghmaoui, Hubert Kounde

Vincent Cassel

THE YOUNG POISONER'S HANDBOOK

(CINEPIX FILM PROPERTIES) Producer, Sam Taylor; Executive Producers, Caroline Hewitt, Eric Stonestrom; Associate Producer, David Redman; Co-Producers, Carole Scotta (France), Rainer Kolmel (Germany); Director, Benjamin Ross; Screenplay, Jeff Rawle, Benjamin Ross; Photography, Hubert Taczanowski; Designer, Maria Djurkovic; Costumes, Stewart Meachem; Editor, Anne Sopel; Casting, Michelle Guish; a Mass productions film in co-production with Kinowelt and Haut et Court Film with the participation of the Bavarian Film Fund, British Screen, Eurimages and Pandora; British-French-German, 1995; Metrocolor; Not rated; 99 minutes; February release

CAST

Graham	Hugh O'Conor
Dr. Zeigler	Antony Sher
Molly	Ruth Sheen
Fred	Roger Lloyd Pack
Winnie	Charlotte Coleman
Dennis	Paul Stacey
Sue	Samantha Edmonds
Aunt Panty	Vilma Hollingbery
Uncle Jack	Frank Mills
Berridge	Charlie Creed-Miles
Ray	Arthur Cox
Nathan	John Thomson
Debra	Jean Warren
John	Simon Kunz
Billy	Frank Coda
Simon	Tim Potter
Edna	Hazel Douglas
Geoff	Roger Frost

and Norman Caro (Mr. Goez), Dorothea Alexander (Mrs. Goez), Robert Demeger (Mr. Dexter), Jack Deam (Mick), Peter Pacey (Dickie Boone), Rupert Farley (Nurse Trent), Malcolm Sinclair (Dr. Triefus), John Abbott (Chairman), Cate Fowler (Social Services Lady), Frank Baker (Placement Officer), David Saville (Chief Medical Inspector), Mark Gordon (Vicar)

Black comedy about a disturbed fourteen year old boy who spends his time experimenting with toxic substances to use on his relatives.

© CFP Distribution

Samantha Edmonds, Hugh O'Conor

Hugh O'Conor, Roger Lloyd Pack, Charlotte Coleman

Jackie Chan

Jackie Chan

Jackie Chan

Jackie Chan

Jackie Chan

RUMBLE IN THE BRONX

(NEW LINE CINEMA) Producer, Barbie Tung; Executive Producer, Leonard Ho; Co-Producer, Roberta Chow; Director, Stanley Tong; Screenplay, Edward Tang, Fibe Ma; Photography, Jingle Ma; Designer, Oliver Wong; Editors, Michael Duthie, Peter Cheung; Music, J. Peter Robinson; a Raymond Chow/Golden Harvest Production; Hong Kong/Mandarin—dubbed in English; Dolby Stereo; Technovision; Color; Rated R; 89 minutes; February release

CAST

Keung	Jackie Chan
Elaine	Anita Mui
Nancy	Francoise Yip
Uncle Bill	Bill Tung
Tony	Marc Akerstream
Angelo	Garvin Cros
Danny	Morgan Lam
White Tiger	Kris Lord
Whitney	Carrie Cain Sparks

and Alien Sit, Chan Man Ching, Fred Andrucci, Mark Antoniuk, Lauro Chartrand, Chris Franco, Lance Gibson, David Hooper, Kathy Hubble, Terrance Leigh, Dean McKenzie, Kimani Ray Smith, Lisa Stevens (Tony's Gang Members), Richard Faraci, Mark Fielding, Terry Howsen, Jordan Lennox, Gabriel Ostevic, John Sampson, Owen Walstrom (White Tiger's Gang Members), Guyle Frazier, David Fredericks, Gary Wong (Police Officers)

Keung comes to the South Bronx to attend his uncle's wedding and finds himself doing battle with a ruthless motorcycle gang.

Margot Frank, Otto Frank, Anne Frank

Anne Frank

Anne Frank

ANNE FRANK REMEMBERED

(SONY PICTURES CLASSICS) Producer/Director/Screenplay, Jon Blair; Photography, Barry Ackroyd; Editor, Karen Steininger; Music, Carl Davis; Narrator, Kenneth Branagh; Excerpts from *The Diary of Anne Frank* read by Glenn Close; Associate Producer, Wouter Van Der Sluis; a Jon Blair Film Company production in cooperation with the Anne Frank House Amsterdam and in association with the BBC and the Disney Channel; British, 1995; Dolby Stereo; Color/Black and white; Rated PG; 122 minutes; February release. Documentary on Anne Frank and her family who hid in an attic from the Nazis for over two years.

Academy Award Winner for Best Feature Documentary, 1995.

© Sony Pictures Entertainment, Inc.

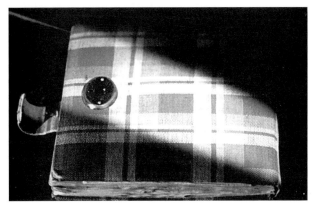

The Dairy

Margot Frank, Anne Frank

THE FLOWER OF MY SECRET

(SONY PICTURES CLASSICS) Executive Producer, Agustin Almodovar; Director/Screenplay, Pedro Almodovar; Photography, Affonso Beato; Editor, Jose Salcedo; Music, Alberto Iglesias; Director of Production, Esther Garcia; an El Deseo SA—CIBY 2000 co-production; Spanish-French, 1995; Dolby Stereo; Color; Rated R; 100 minutes; March release

CAST

Leo	Marisa Paredes
Angel	Juan Echanove
Paco	Imanol Arias
Betty	Carmen Elias
Rosa	Rossy De Palma
Mother	Chus Lampreave
Antonio	Joaquin Cortes
Blanca	Manuela Vargas
Manuela	Kiti Manver
Doctor A	Jordi Molla
Doctor B	Nancho Novo
Alicia	Gloria Munoz
Tomas	Juan Jose Otegui
Junkie	Jose Palau

and Abraham Garcia (Bartender), Marisol Muriel (Dancer), Alicia Agut, Maria Teresa Ibanez (Neighbors)

A woman who has a secret life as the author of romance novels begins to believe that her husband no longer loves her.

© Sony Pictures Entertainment

Rossy de Palma, Chus Lampreave

Valerie Chow, Tony Leung Chiu-Wai

Faye Wang

Joaquin Cortes, Marisa Paredes

CHUNGKING EXPRESS

(MIRAMAX) Producer, Chan Yi-Kan; Executive Producer, Chan Pui-Wah; Director/Screenplay, Wong Kar-Wai; Photography, Christopher Doyle; Music, Frankie Chan, Roel A. Garcia, Michael Calasso; Editors, William Chang, Hai Kit-Wai, Kwong Chi-Leung; Art Director, William Chang; a Jet Tone Production Co. Ltd/a Rolling Thunder release; Hong Kong, 1994; Color; Rated PG-13; 103 minutes; March release

CAST

Drug Dealer	Brigitte Lin Chin-Hsia
He Quiwu, Cop 223	Takeshi Kaneshiro
Cop 663	Tony Leung Chiu-Wai
Faye	Faye Wang
Air Hostess	Valerie Chow

A two part romantic drama taking place in a modern housing development and an all-night fast food stand.

© Miramax Films

LAND AND FREEDOM

(GRAMERCY) Producer, Rebecca O'Brien; Executive Producers, Sally Hibbin, Gerardo Herrero, Ulrich Felsberg; Director, Ken Loach; Screenplay, Jim Allen; Photography, Barry Ackroyd; Designer, Martin Johnson; Music, George Fenton; Associate Producer, Marta Esteban; Costumes, Ana Alvargonzalez; a British Screen with the participation of the European Co-Production Fund (UK), Television Española, Canal+ (Spain), BBC Films, Degeto and ARD and Filmstiftung Nororhein-Westfallen and the support of BIM Distribuzione, Diaphana and the Eurimages Fund of the Council of Europe presentation of a Parallax Pictures, Messidor Films and Road Movies Driite Produktionen production; British-Spanish-German-U.S., 1995; Dolby Stereo; Color; Not rated; 109 minutes; March release

CAST

David	Ian Hart
Blanca	Rosana Pastor
Maite	Iciar Bollain
Lawrence	Tom Gilroy
Vidal	Marc Martinez
Bernard	Frederic Pierrot
Kim	Suzanne Maddock
Dot	Mandy Walsh
Speaker at Meeting	Miguel Cabrillana
Kitty	Angela Clarke
Barracks Officer	Rafael Diaz
Nationalist Officer	Felicio Pellicer
Priest	Ricard Arilla
Salas	Jordi Dauder

and Pep Molina (Concierge), Enriqueta Ferre (Old Woman), Asuncion Royo (Casado) Francesc Orella, Phil O'Brien, Dave Seddon (Ambulance Man), Andres Aladren, Raffaele Cantatore, Paul Laverty, Eoin McCarthy, Roca, Sergi Calleja, Pascal Demolon, Josep Magem, Jürgen Müller, Emilia Samper (The Militia), Neus Agullo, Pep Cortes (Blanca's Parents)

In 1936, David leaves Liverpool to join an international divisino of the Republican Militia to fight Fascism in Spain.

© Gramercy Pictures

Rosana Pastor, Ian Hart

Ian Hart

JACK & SARAH

(GRAMERCY) Producers, Pippa Cross, Simon Channing-Williams, Janette Day; Director/Screenplay, Tim Sullivan; Photography, Jean-Yves Escoffier; Designer, Christopher J. Bradshaw; Editor, Lesley Walker; Music, Simon Boswell; Costumes, Dany Everett; Casting, Simone Reynolds; British-French, 1995; Color; Rated R; 110 minutes; March release

CAST

Jack	Richard E. Grant
Amy	Samantha Mathis
Margaret	Judi Dench
William	Ian McKellen
Anna	Cherie Lunghi
Phil	Eileen Atkins
Sarah	Imogen Stubbs
Michael	David Swift
Alain	Laurent Grevill
Pamela	Kate Hardie
Sarah—Baby	Bianca and Sophia Lee
Sarah—Toddler	Sophia Sullivan
Nathaniel	Niven Boyd

and Tracy Thorne (Susan), Lorraine Ashbourne (Jackie), Deborah Findlay (Miss Cartwright), Claire Toeman (Health Visitor), Geff Francis (Rob), Matyelok Gibbs (Physiotherapist), Michael McStay (Security Man), James Bannon (City Boy), David J. Nicholas (Delivery Man), Susie McKenna (Paramedic), Keith Bartlett (Taxi Driver), John Grillo (Landlord), Richard Leaf (Stoned Man), Andrew Read (Office Boy), Raymond Brodie (Office Party Guest)

A selfish lawyer must take on the responsibility of raising his new baby daughter after his wife dies in childbirth.

© Gramercy Pictures

Richard E. Grant, Sophia Sullivan, Samantha Mathis

Judi Dench, Eileen Atkins, Ian McKellen

Charlotte Gainsbourg, Ralph Nossek, William Hurt

Elle Macpherson

Josephine Serre, Charlotte Gainsbourg

Charlotte Gainsbourg, Joan Plowright

JANE EYRE

(MIRAMAX) Producer, Dyson Lovell; Co-Executive Producers, Harvey Weinstein, Bob Weinstein; Director, Franco Zeffirelli; Screenplay, Hugh Whitemore, Franco Zeffirelli; Based on the novel by Charlotte Bronte; Co-Producers, Giovannella Zannoni, Jean Francois Lepetit; Photography, David Watkin; Designer, Roger Hall; Costumes, Jenny Beavan; Music, Alessio Vlad, Claudio Capponi; Editor, Richard Marden; Casting, Noel Davis; a Rochester Films Ltd./Cineritmo S.R.I./Flach Film, Mediaset and R.C.S. Editori S.P.A./Dyson Lovell/Riccardo Tozzi production; French-Iltalian-British-U.S.; Dolby Digital Stereo; Color; Rated PG; 117 minutes; April release

CAST

Edward Rochester	William Hurt
Jane Eyre	Charlotte Gainsbourg
Mrs. Fairfax	Joan Plowright
Young Jane	Anna Paquin
Miss Scatcherd	Geraldine Chaplin
Grace Poole	Billie Whitelaw
Bertha	Maria Schneider
Mrs. Reed	Fiona Shaw
Blanche Ingram	Elle MacPherson
Mr. Brocklehurst	John Wood
Miss Temple	Amanda Root
St. John Rivers	Samuel West
Adele	Josephine Serre
Helen Burns	Leanne Rowe
Mason	Edward De Souza
Mary Rivers	Charlotte Attenborough
John Reed	Nic Knight
Eliza Reed	Nicola Howard
Georgiana Reed	Sasha Graff
John	Richard Warwick
Leah	Judith Parker
Henry Eshton	Simon Beresford
Frederick Lynn	Chris Larkin
Lady Ingram	Miranda Forbes
Lady Lynn	Ann Queensberry
Lady Eshton	Sheila Burrell

and Sara Stevens (Amy Eshton), Orine Messina (Louisa Eshton), Marissa Dunlop (Mary Ingram), Julian Fellowes (Colonel Dent), Barry Martin (Sir George Lynn), Walter Sparrow (Lord Eshton), Steffan Boje (Party Guest), Golda Broderick (Mrs. Bennett), John Tranter (Dr. Carter), Ralph Nossek (Rev. Wood), Peter Woodthorpe (Briggs)

Orphaned Jane Eyre travels to the remote Thornfield Hall to serve as teacher to Adele and falls under the spell of the estate's brooding, mysterious owner Edward Rochester. Previous film versions include the 1944 20th Century Fox release starring Joan Fontaine and Orson Welles.

© Miramax Films

MA SAISON PRÉFÉRÉE (MY FAVORITE SEASON)

(FILMOPOLIS) Producer, Alain Sarde; Director, André Téchiné; Photography, Thierry Arbogast; Designer, Carlos Conti; Costumes, Claire Fraisse; Editor, Remy Attal; Music, Philippe Sarde; French, 1993; Dolby Stereo;Panavision; Color; Not rated; 124 minutes; April release

CAST

Emilie	Catherine Deneuve
Antoine	Daniel Auteuil
Berthe	Marthe Villalonga
Bruno	Jean-Pierre Bouvier
Anne	Chiara Mastroianni
Khadija	Carmen Chaplin
Lucien	Anthony Prada
The Cemetery Man	Jacques Nolot

A brother and sister, having reached middle age, must cope with the seriousness of their mother's illness.

© Filmopolis Pictures Inc.

Michel Serrault, Emmanuelle Beart

AUGUST

(SAMUEL GOLDWYN CO.) Producers, June Wyndham Davies, Pippa Cross; Executive Producers, Steve Morrison, Guy East; Director/Music, Anthony Hopkins; Screenplay, Julian Mitchell; Based on the play *Uncle Vanya* by Anton Chekov; Co-Producer, Janette Day; Photography, Robin Vidgeon; Designer, Eileen Diss; Editor, Edward Mansell; Costumes, Dany Everett; Line Producer, Craig McNeil; a Majestic Films/Newcomm and Granada presentation; British; Dolby Stereo; Color; Not rated; 90 minutes; April release

CAST

Ieuan Davies	Anthony Hopkins
Helen	Kate Burton
Prof. Alexander Blathwaite	Leslie Phillips
Dr. Lloyd	Gawn Grainger
Sian	Rhian Morgan
Prosser	Hugh Lloyd
Mair Davies	Rhoda Lewis
Gwen	Menna Trussler

In this interpretation of Uncle Vanya, *set in Wales, various visitors descend on the Davies household where they are tormented by unrequited passions and relationships that shall never be fulfilled.*

© The Samuel Goldwyn Company

Catherine Deneuve, Daniel Auteuil

NELLY AND MONSIEUR ARNAUD

(ARTIFICIAL EYE) Producer, Alain Sarde; Director, Claude Sautet; Screenplay, Claude Sautet, Jacques Fieschi, Yves Ulmann; Photography, Jean-François Brown; Costumes, Catherine Bouchard, Marie Piazzola; Editor, Jacqueline Thiedot; a Les Films Alain Sarde/TF1 Films Production/Cecchi Gori Tiger Group Cinematografica SRL/Prokino Filmproduktion GMBH production; French-Italian-German, 1995; Color; Not rated; 106 minutes; April release

CAST

Nelly	Emmanuelle Beart
Monsieur Arnaud	Michel Serrault
Vincent	Jean-Hugues Anglade
Jacqueline	Claire Nadeau
Lucie	Françoise Brion
Isabelle	Michèle Laroque
Dollabella	Michael Lonsdale
Jérôme	Charles Berling
Christophe	Jean-Pierre Lorit
Taieb	Michel Albertini
Marianne	Coraly Zahonero
Laurence	Graziella Delerm
Jean-Marc	Olivier Pajot

Elderly Monsieur Arnaud invites 25-year-old Nelly to work for him typing his memoirs and finds that he has become infatuated with her.

© Artificial Eye Film Co.

Anthony Hopkins, Gawn Grainger

THE MONSTER

(CFP) Producers, Roberto Benigni, Yves Attal; Executive Producer, Elda Ferri; Director, Roberto Benigni; Screenplay, Roberto Benigni, Vincenzo Cerami, Michel Blanc; Photography, Carlo Di Palma; Costumes, Danilo Donati; Art Director, Giantilo Burchiellaro; Music, Evan Lurie; Editor, Nino Baragli; Supervising Producer, Alessandro Calosci; from Iris Films/ UGC Images/ LaSEPT Cinema/ Sofia Sofinergie 3/ Melampo Cinematographica with the participation of Canal+; Italian-French,1994; Color; Not rated; 112 minutes; April release

CAST

Loris	Roberto Benigni
Detective Jessica Rosetti	Nicoletta Braschi
Taccone, the Psychiatrist	Michel Blanc
Loris' Landlord	Jean-Claude Brialy
Taccone's Wife	Dominique Lavanant
The Chinese Teacher	Franco Mescollini
Pascucci	Ivano Marescotti
Frustalupi, The Chief of Police	Laurent Spielvogel
Loris' Neighbor	Massimo Girotti

A mischievous con man, Loris, is mistaken for a serial killer known as "the Monster."

© CFP Distribution

Roberto Benigni, Michel Blanc

Roberto Benigni

Peter Outerbridge, Russell Crowe

Bruce Boa, Sara McMillan, Christine Hirt

FOR THE MOMENT

(JOHN AARON RELEASING) Producers, Aaron Kim Johnston, Jack Clements; Director/Screenplay, Aaron Kim Johnston; Co-Producers, Joe MacDonald, Ches Yetman; Photography, Ian Elkin; Music, Victor Davies; Editor, Rita Roy; Designer, Andrew Deskin; a co-production with the National Film Board of Canada; Canadian; Dolby Stereo; Color; Rated PG-13; 120 minutes; April release

CAST

Lachlan	Russell Crowe
Lill	Christianne Hirt
Betsy	Wanda Cannon
Zeek	Scott Kraft
Johnny	Peter Outerbridge
Kate	Sara McMillan
Mr. Anderson	Bruce Boa
Marion	Katelynd Johnston
Charlie	Tyler Woods
Dipper	John Bekavac
Scotty	Robert G. Slade
Dennis	Kelly Proctor
Anne	Roxanne Boulianne

and David Warburton (Commander Levin), Ari Cohen (Cecil), Glen Thompson (Nigel), Guy Stewart (Richard), Grant Dilworth (Navigation Instructor), Curtis Sali, Sean Bowie (Dipper's Cronies), Alistair Abell (Airman #1), Riel Lanlois (Frenchie), Clement Nelson (Black Dancer), David Cowie (Controller), Steve James Young (New Zealander)

During the 1940s young Australian flyer Lachlan falls in love with married Lill, while flight instructor Zeek pursues the outgoing Betsy.

© Twentieth Century Fox

CEMETERY MAN

(OCTOBER) Producers, Tilde Corsi, Gianni Romoli, Michele Soavi; Executive Producers, Conchita Airoldi, Dino Di Dionisio; Director, Michele Soavi; Screenplay, Gianni Romoli; Based on the "Dylan Dog" novel *Dellamorte Dellamore* by Tiziano Sclavi; Photography, Mauro Marchetti; Costumes, Maurizio Millenotti; Set Designer, Antonello Geleng; Editor, Franco Fraticelli; Music, Manuel De Sica; Makeup, Gino Zamprioli; Mechanical Special Effects, Sergio Stivaletti; from Audifilm-Urania Film-KG Productions-Le Studio Canal+ and Bibo TV ET Film Productions; Italian-French-U.S., 1995; Dolby Stereo; Color; Rated R; 100 minutes; April release

CAST

Francesco Dellamorte	Rupert Everett
Gnaghi	Francois Hadji-Lazaro
The Three "She"	Anna Falchi
Mayor Scanarotti	Stefano Masciarelli
Foreign Marshal	Mickey Knox
Doctor Verseci	Clive Riche
Valentina	Fabiana Formica
Thin Girl	Katja Anton
Miss Chiaromondo	Claudia Lawrence
Franco	Anton Alexander
Magda	Barbara Cupisti
Claudio	Alessandro Zamatto
New Mayor Civardi	Pietro Genuardi

and Maurizio Romoli (Hospital Doctor) Patrizia Punzo (Claudio's Mother), Renato Donis (Husband of "She"), Elio Cesari (Nun), Vito Passeri (Ghighi), Stefano de Tomassi, Simone Ervini, Flavio Marti, Daniele Mezzoprete (Boy Scouts), Sandro Prati, Fabio Alberici, Tiziano Nardoni, Gianluca Gennaro (Boys on Square), Marco Fiorentini (Photographer), Mariaelena Fresu (Hospital Sister), Francesca Gamba (Hospital Nurse), Maddalena Ischiale (Stanza Franco Nurse), Micha Kopman (2nd Returner), Fiorenzo Marsili (Returning Priest), Rinaldo Zamperla (Cyclist)

Dellamorte, the watchman at the Buffalora Cemetery, finds that he must kill the corpses a second time when they begin rising from the dead.

© October Films

Francois Hadji-Lazaro, Rupert Everett

Anna Falchi, Rupert Everett

CAPTIVES

(MIRAMAX) Producer, David M. Thompson; Executive Producers, Anant Singh, Mark Shivas; Director, Angela Pope; Screenplay, Frank Deasy; Photography, Remi Adefarasin; Designer, Stuart Walker; Editor, Dave King; Music, Colin Towns; Associate Producer, Ian Hopkins; Costumes, Odile Dicks-Mireaux; Casting, Gail Stevens; a BBC Films and Distant Horizon production; British-U.S., 1995; Dolby Stereo; Color; Rated R; 99 minutes; May release

CAST

Philip Chaney	Tim Roth
Rachel Clifford	Julia Ormond
Lenny	Keith Allen
Sue	Siobhan Redmond
Simon	Peter Capaldi
Towler	Colin Salmon
Sexton	Richard Hawley
Maggie	Annette Badland
Harold	Jeff Nuttall
Dr. Hockley	Kenneth Cope
Surgery Officer	Bill Moody
Katie	Christina Collingridge
Dental Nurse	Victoria Scarborough
Blackie	Anthony Kernan

and Aedin Moloney (Supermarket Checker), Tricia Thorns (Prison Receptionist), Cathy Murphy (Companion), Mark Strong (Kenny), Sandra James-Young (Angie), Sharon Hines (Melissa), Julian Maud (Newsreader), Tony Curran (Spider), James Hooton (Trustee Prisoner), Steven Swinscoe, David MacCreedy, Douglas McFerran (Officers), Catherine Sanderson (Coffee-shop Waitress), Michael L. Blair (Hare Krishna Man), Joe Tucker (Con), Shaheen Khan (Estate Agent), Shend (Gus), Gilbert Martin (Bulldog Officer), David Hounslow (Detective)

Rachel takes a job as a prison dentist where she is seduced by Philip who is nearing the end of a ten year sentence.

© Miramax Films

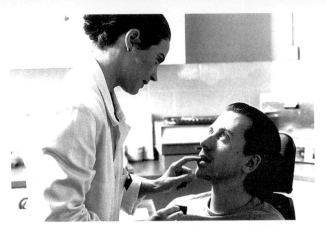

Julia Ormond, Tim Roth

Julia Ormond

BUTTERFLY KISS

(CFP) Producer, Julie Baines; Director, Michael Winterbottom; Screenplay, Frank Cottrell Boyce; Photography, Seamus McGarvey; Editor, Trevor Waite; Music, John Harle; Associate Producer, Sarah Daniel; Art Director, Rupert Miles; Costumes, Rachael Fleming; a British Screen and The Merseyside Film Production Fund presentation; British; Dolby Sterero; Color; Not rated; 88 minutes; May release

CAST

Eunice	Amanda Plummer
Miriam	Saskia Reeves
Wendy	Kathy Jamieson
Eric	Des McAleer
Danielle	Lisa Jane Riley
Elsie	Freda Dowie
Ella	Paula Tilbrook
Tony	Fine Time Fontayne
Waitresses	Elizabeth McGrath, Shirley Vaughan
Angela	Joanne Cook

and Paul Bown (Gary), Emily Aston (Katie), Ricky Tomlinson (Robert), Katy Murphy (Judith), Adele Lawson (Wife), Jeffrey Longmore (Husband), Suzy Yannis (Motel Receptionist), Julie Walker (Shop Assistant), Kelly (Kelly)

Miriam, a sales clerk, takes an interest in a dangerous, deeply disturbed woman name Eunice who shows up at a service station searching for someone named Judith.

© CFP Distribution

Amanda Plummer

Amanda Plummer, Saskia Reeves

SOMEONE ELSE'S AMERICA

(OCTOBER) Producers, Antoine De Clermont-Tonnerre, David Rose, Helga Bähr; Director, Goran Paskaljevic; Screenplay, Gordan Mihic; Photography, Yorgos Arvanitis; Art Director, Wolf Seesselberg; Editor, William Diver; Costumes, Charlotte Holdich; Music, Andrew Dickson; Co-Producers, Gabrielle Tana, Johanna Baldwin; a co-production between MACT Productions, Intinsica Films, Lichtblick Filmproduktion, Stefi 2, in association with Pandora Cinema; French-British-Greek; Dolby Stereo; Color; Rated R; 96 minutes; May release

CAST

Alonso	Tom Conti
Bayo	Miki Manojlovic
Alonso's Mother	Maria Casares
Bayo's Mother	Zorka Manojlovic
Luka	Sergej Trifunovic
Panchito	Jose Ramon Rosario
Guide	Lanny Flaherty
Greek Agent	Michalis Yannatos
Foreman	Michael Willis
Doctor	Predrrag Ejdus
Chinese Girl	Chia-Ching Niu
Savka	Andjela Stojkovic
Pepo	Lazar Kalmic
Alfisi	Ananda Ellis

and John Norman Thomas (Alfisi's Brother), Jonathon Peck (Sam), Yan Shi (Chou), Miou (Japanese Girl), Anibal Lleras (Philipino), Ai Ya (Chinese Grandma), Shuain Hui (Chinese Grandpa), Loi Gao Li (Chinese Musician), Dominique Lasaki, Robert Franz, Juan Rodriguez Vila (Flamenco Group)

Two immigrants, Alonso from Spain, and Bayo from Montenegro, form an unlikely friendship while living in a crowded section of Brooklyn.

© October Films

Sonia Braga

Michael Gambon

Miki Manojlovic, Tom Conti

Sergej Trifunovic, Zorka Manojlovic

TWO DEATHS

(CASTLE HILL) Producers, Carolyn Montagu, Luc Roeg; Executive Producers, Allan Scott, Jonathon Olsberg, Mark Shivas; Director, Nicolas Roeg; Screenplay, Allan Scott; Photography, Witold Stok; Designer, Don Taylor; Editor, Tony Lawson; Music, Hans Zimmer; Costumes, Elizabeth Waller; Casting, Celestia Fox; British, 1995; Color; Rated R; 102 minutes; May release

CAST

Dr. Daniel Pavenic	Michael Gambon
Ana Puscasu	Sonia Braga
George Bucsan	Patrick Malahide
Carl Dalakiss	Ion Caramitru
Marius Vernescu	Nicholas Grace
Cinca	John Shrapnel
Lieutenant	Ravil Isyanov
Elena	Sevilla Delofski
Leon	Matthew Terdre
Young Ana	Lisa Orgolini
Young Pavenic	Niall Refoy
Cora Bucsan	Amanda Royle
Roberto Constantin	Karl Tessler
Captain Jorgu	Andrew Tiernan
Colonel George Lapadus	Rade Serbedzija
Marta	Laura Davenport

At his annual dinner for his former classmates, Dr. Pavenic talks of his obsession with his beautiful housekeeper, Ana, as a student uprising takes place outside.

© Castle Hill Productions

COLD COMFORT FARM

(GRAMERCY) Producer, Alison Gilby; Director, John Schlesinger; Screenplay, Malcolm Bradbury; Based on the novel by Stella Gibbons; Executive Producers, Richard Broke (BBC), Antony Root (Thames Intl.); Photography, Chris Seager; Designer, Malcolm Thornton; Editor, Mark Day; Music, Robert Lockhart; Costumes, Amy Roberts; Hair/Makeup, Dorka Nieradzik; Associate Producer, Joanna Gueritz; Casting, Noel Davis; presented in association with BBC Films and Thames International; British, 1995; Dolby Stereo; Rank color; Rated PG; 95 minutes; May release

CAST

Judith Starkadder	Eileen Atkins
Flora Poste	Kate Beckinsale
Ada Doom	Sheila Burrell
Mybug	Stephen Fry
Adam Lambsbreath	Freddie Jones
Mrs. Smiling	Joanna Lumley
Amos Starkadder	Ian McKellen
Mrs. Beetle	Miriam Margolyes
Seth	Rufus Sewell
Reuben	Ivan Kaye
Urk	Jeremy Peters
Elfine	Maria Miles
Charles Fairford	Christopher Bowen
Meriam Beetle	Louise Rea
Rennet	Sophie Revell
Dick Hawk-Monitor	Rupert Penry-Jones
Mrs. Hawk-Monitor	Angela Thorne
Mr. Hawk-Monitor	Tim Myers
Earl P. Neck	Harry Ditson
Sneller	Trevor Baxter
Dr. Adolf Mudel	Frederick Jaeger
Aunt Gwen	Pat Keen

and Robert James (Mr. McKnag), William Masson (Bikki), Susannah Morley (Mrs. Murther), Richard Bebb (Hawk-Monitor Butler), William Osborne (Coiffeur), Basil Hoskins (Couturier), Allison Roberts (Girl in Hayloft), Ninka Scott (Tea Shop Waitress), Myfanwy Hill (Young Ada Doom)

Facing financial difficulties sophisticated Flora Poste receives an offer from some distant relatives to stay at Cold Comfort Farm a ramshackle place populated by some rather weird residents

© Gramercy Pictures.

(rear) Rufus Sewell, Kate Beckinsale, Eileen Atkins, Ivan Kaye, Jeremy Peters; (front) Sophie Revell, Louise Rea, Maria Miles

Eileen Atkins   Ian McKellen

Kate Beckinsale, Joanna Lumley

Rufus Sewell, Kate Beckinsale

THE HORSEMAN ON THE ROOF

(MIRAMAX ZOË) Producer, Rene Cleitman; Executive Producer, Bernard Bouix; Director, Jean-Paul Rappeneau; Screenplay Adaptation, Jean-Paul Rappeneau, Nina Companeez, Jean-Claude Carriere; Based on the novel by Jean Giono; Photography, Thierry Arbogast; Art Director, Ezio Frigerio; Costumes, Franca Squarciapino; Music, Jean-Claude Petit; Editor, Noelle Boisson; a Rene Cleitman presentation of a Hachette Premiere production; French, 1995; Dolby DTS Stereo; Super 35 Widescreen; Color; Rated R; 132 minutes; May release

CAST

Pauline de Theus	Juliette Binoche
Angelo Pardi	Olivier Martinez
Mr. Peyrolle	Pierre Arditi
The Doctor	Francois Cluzet
The Peddler	Jean Yanne
Maggionari	Claudio Amendola
Guiseppe	Carlo Cecchi
Madame Peyrolle	Christiane Cohendy
The Old Man	Jacques Sereys
Mrs. Barthelemy	Nathalie Krebs
Carla	Laura Marinoni
The Farm Woman	Elizabeth Margoni
Mrs. Rigoard	Yolande Moreau
Mr. Barthelemy	Christophe Odent
Brigadier Maugin	Herve Pierre
Attorney Rigoard	Daniel Russo
Franz, the Leader	Richard Sammel
Alexandre Petit, The Merchant	Jean-Marie Winling
Laurent de Theus	Paul Freeman
Giacomo	Paul Chevillard
Police Superintendent	Gerard Depardieu

and Patrick Medioni, Philppe Guegan, Jean-Francois Pages (The Austrian Agents), Carlos Moreno, Jean-Claude Dumas, Jean-Paul Journot (Harvesters), Georges Neri (The Old Harvester), Viginie Matheron (The Sick Maid), Cristophe Le Masne (Martial, the Valet), Gerard Lacombe (The Patron), Didier Bourguignon (Man fightning Cholera), Antonin Lebas-Joly (Edmond, the Little Boy), Azur Guillier (Camille, the Little Girl), Rene-Andre Fernandez, Jacques Pater (Militia Men), Robert Lucibello (Man with an Apron), Viviane Cayol (The Sick Woman), Claire Massabo (Mrs. Terrasson), Celita Villar (Woman at Window), Bruno Cecillon (The Bourgeois), Frederique Ruchaud (Mrs. Marguerite), Jocelyne Carmichael (The Shrew), Gerard Bayle (The Forge Owner), Desire Saorin, Gerard Dubouche (Blacksmiths), Alexis Nitzer (Hysterical Man), Alex Nitzer (Excited Man), Serge Pauthe (Police Employee).

In 1832 France, Italian cavalry officer Angelo Pardi, on the run from Austrian spies, meets and falls in love with Pauline de Theus.

© Miramax Zoe Films

Olivier Martinez

Juliette Binoche

Olivier Martinez (c)

Olivier Martinez, Juliette Binoche

STEALING BEAUTY

(FOX SEARCHLIGHT) Producer, Jeremy Thomas; Director/Story, Bernardo Bertolucci; Screenplay, Susan Minot; Photography, Darius Khondji; Designer, Gianni Silvestri; Costumes, Louise St. Jernsward, Giorgio Armani; Editor, Pietro Scalia; Music, Richard Hartley; Associate Producer, Chris Auty; Casting, Howard Feuer, Celestia Fox; a Recorded Picture Company and UGC Images presentation; French-Italian-British; Dolby Stereo; Super 35 Widescreen; Color; Rated R; 119 minutes; June release

CAST

Alex Parrish	Jeremy Irons
Lucy Harmon	Liv Tyler
Diana Grayson	Sinead Cusack
M. Guillaume	Jean Marais
Ian Grayson	Donal McCann
Richard Reed	D.W. Moffett
Noemi	Stefania Sandrelli
Carlo Lisca	Carlo Cecchi
Miranda Fox	Rachel Weisz
Christopher Fox	Joseph Fiennes
Gregory	Jason Flemyng
Chiarella Donati	Anna Maria Gherardi
Osvaldo Donati	Ignazio Oliva
Michele Lisca	Francesco Siciliano
Lieutenant	Leonardo Treviglio
Daisy Grayson	Rebecca Valpy
Marta	Alessandra Vanzi
Nicolo Donati	Roberto Zibetti

19-year-old Lucy Harmon arrives at a villa in Tuscany hoping to renew an acquaintance with a young boy she'd met four years earlier and to decipher her mother's diary.

© Twentieth Century Fox

Jeremy Irons, Liv Tyler

Jason Flemyng, Liv Tyler

MAYBE...MAYBE NOT

(ORION CLASSICS) Producer, Bernd Eichinger; Executive Producers, Martin Moszkowicz, Molly von Furstenberg, Harry Kugler, Elvira Senft; Director/Screenplay, Sonke Wortmann; Based on the comic books by Ralf Konig; Photography, Gernot Roll; Designer, Monika Bauert; Costumes, Katharina von Martius; Editor, Ueli Christen; Music, Torsten Breuer; Songs, Palast Orchester; Vocalist, Max Raabe; a LIVE Entertainment presentation; German, 1995; Color; Rated R; 93 minutes; June release

CAST

Axel	Til Schweiger
Doro	Katja Riemann
Norbert	Joachim Krol
Waltraud	Rufus Beck
Elke	Antonia Lang
Horst	Armin Rohde

After being thrown out by his girlfriend for cheating on her Axel takes up residence with Norbert, an acquaintence who has a crush on Axel.

© LIVE Entertainment, Inc.

Katja Riemann, Joachim Krol, Til Schweiger

THE FRIGHTENERS

(UNIVERSAL) Producers, Jamie Selkirk, Peter Jackson; Executive Producer, Robert Zemeckis; Director, Peter Jackson; Screenplay, Fran Walsh, Peter Jackson; Photography, Alun Bollinger, John Blick; Designer, Grant Major; Editor, Jamie Selkirk; Music, Danny Elfman; Digital Effects Producer, Charlie McClellan; Creature and Miniature Effects, Richard Taylor; Judge Make-Up Design, Rick Baker; Associate Producer, Fran Walsh; Co-Producer, Tim Sanders; Casting, Victoria Burrows; a Wingnut Films production; New Zealand - U.S.; Dolby DTS Stereo; Super 35 widescreen; Eastman color; Rated R; 109 minutes; July release

CAST

Frank Bannister	Michael J. Fox
Lucy Lynskey	Trini Alvarado
Ray Lynskey	Peter Dobson
The Judge	John Astin
Milton Dammers	Jeffrey Combs
Patricia Bradley	Dee Wallace Stone
Johnny Bartlett	Jake Busey
Cyrus	Chi McBride
Stuart	Jim Fyfe
Sheriff Perry	Troy Evans
Old Lady Bradley	Julianna McCarthy
Hiles	R. Lee Ermey
Madga Rees-Jones	Elizabeth Hawthorne
Debra Bannister	Angela Bloomfield
Harry Sinclair	Desmond Kelly
Steve Bayliss	Jonathan Blick
Bryce Campbell	John Leigh
Young Patricia	Nicola Cliff
Dr. Kamins	Ken Blackburn
Museum Curator	Stuart Devenie
TV Presenter	Genevieve Westcott
Doctor	KC Kelly

and Todd Rippon, John Sumner, Michael Robinson, Jim McLarty, Anthony Ray Parker, Paul Yates, Melanie Lynskey (Deputies), Leslie Wing (Mrs. Waterhouse), Leslie Klein (Maid), Frank Edwards (Resuscitating Man), Alan O'Leary (The Waiter), Danny Lineham (Barry), Charlie McClellan (Reporter), William Pomeroy (Jacob Platz), George Port (Orderly), Billy Jackson (Baby in Bouncer), Sophie Watkins, Taea Hartwell, Max Grover, George Grover (Nursery Babies), Tony Hopkins, Lewis Martin (Hospital Patients), Clay Nelson, Robert McNeill, Matthew Chamberlain (Passerby), Vivienne Kaplan, Liz Mullane (Nuns)

Psychic swindler Frank Bannister comes to realize that the series of inexplicable deaths occuring in a small town are the work of a deadly poltergeist.

© Universal City Studios, Inc.

Jim Fyfe, Michael J. Fox

Jeffrey Combs

Peter Dobson, Trini Alvarado

Dee Wallace Stone

231

Jonny Lee Miller, Ewan McGregor, Kevin McKidd, Ewen Bremner

Ewan McGregor

Ewan McGregor

Kelly Macdonald, Ewan McGregor

TRAINSPOTTING

(MIRAMAX) Producer, Andrew MacDonald; Director, Danny Boyle; Screenplay, John Hodge; Based on the novel by Irvine Welsh; Photography, Brian Tufano; Editor, Masahiro Hirakubo; Designer, Kave Quinn; Costumes, Rachel Fleming; Casting, Gail Stevens, Andy Pryor; a Channel Four Films presentation of a Figment Film in association with the Noel Gay Motion Picture Company; British; Dolby Stereo; Rank color; Rated R; 94 minutes; July release

CAST

Renton	Ewan McGregor
Spud	Ewen Bremner
Sick Boy	Jonny Lee Miller
Tommy	Kevin McKidd
Begbie	Robert Carlyle
Diane	Kelly MacDonald
Swanney	Peter Mullan
Mr. Renton	James Cosmo
Mrs. Renton	Eileen Nicholas
Allison	Susan Vidler
Lizzy	Pauline Lynch
Gail	Shirley Henderson
Mikey	Irvine Welsh
Game Show Host	Dale Winton
Dealer	Keith Allen
Andreas	Kevin Allen

Mark Renton and his friends spend their time shooting up drugs, waiting for their next fix, and facing a meaningless, hedonistic existence in Edinburgh, Scotland.

The film received an Oscar nomination for adapted screenplay.

© Miramax Films

Ewan McGregor, Jonny Lee Miller

Kevin McKidd, Ewen Bremner

Ewan McGregor

THE VISITORS

(MIRAMAX ZOË) Producer, Alain Terzian; Director, Jean-Marie Poiré; Screenplay, Christian Clavier, Jean-Marie Poiré; Photography, Jean-Yves Le Mener; Editor, Catherine Kelber; Art Director, Hugues Tissandier; Costumes, Catherine Leterrier; Music, Eric Levi; a co-production of Gaumont/France 3 Cinema/Alpilles Productions/Amigo Productions; French, 1993; Widescreen Color; Rated R; 106 minutes; July release

CAST

Godefroy	Jean Reno
Jacquouille/Jacquart	Christian Clavier
Frenegonde/Beatrice	Valerie Lemercier
Ginette	Marie-Anne Chazel
Jean-Pierre	Christian Bujeau
Fabienne Morlot	Isabelle Nanty
Edgar Bernay	Gerard Sety
Louis VI	Didier Pain
Marechal des Logis Gibon	Jean-Paul Muel
Jacqueline	Arielle Semenoff
Edouard Bernay	Michel Peyrelon
The Wizard/Mr. Ferdinand	Pierre Vial
The Priest	Francois Lalande
The Boarder	Didier Benureau\
Freddy	Frederic Baptiste
Sergent-Chef Morlet	Pierre Aussedat

Hoping to break a spell cast by a vengeful witch, Godefroy, a knight in 1123 France, finds himself and his faithful squire Jacquouille, accidentally transported to the Twentieth Century.

© Miramax Zoe

Jean Reno, Christian Clavier

Jean Reno

Valerie Lemercier

Christian Clavier, Jean Reno

234

CELESTIAL CLOCKWORK

(OCTOBER) Producer/Director, Fina Torres; Executive Producer, Gerard Costa; Screenplay, Fina Torres, Daniel Odier, Blanca Strepponi, Telsche Boorman, Yves Delaubre, Chantal Pelletier; Photography, Ricardo Aronovich; Designers, Claire Dague, Sandi Jelambi; Editors, Christiane Lack, Catherine Trouillet; Music, Alma Rosa Castellanos, Francois Farrugia, Michel Musseau; a co-production of Miralta Films-Mistral Films/Pandorados C.A./I.N.H.-Paradise Films/Club D'Investissement Media/Bastille Films; French-Venezuelan-Belgian-Spanish; Dolby Stereo; Color; Not rated; 85 minutes; July release

CAST

Ana	Ariadna Gil
Celeste	Arielle Dombasle
Alcanie	Evelyne Didi
Armand	Frederic Longbois
Italo	Lluis Homar
Tina	Chantal Aimee
Lucila	Alma Rosa Castellanos
Gaby	Dominique Abel
Toutou	Hidegar Garcia Madriz
Claude	Oliver Granier
Grigorieff	Michel Debrane
Mariano	Pedro Del Llano
Pierre-Jean	Didier Azoulay
Herve	Philippe Beautier

Ana abruptly exits her wedding ceremony to pursue her life long dream of becoming an opera singer.

© October Films

Frederic Longbois, Ariadna Gil

Frederick Weller, Guillermo Diaz

Duane Boutte (c)

Arielle Dombasle

STONEWALL

(STRAND) Producer, Christine Vachon; BBC Producer, Ruth Caleb; Executive Producers, George Faber, Anthony Wall; Director, Nigel Finch; Screenplay, Rikki Beadle Blair; Based on the book by Martin Duberman; Photography, Chris Seager; Designer, Therese DePrez; Musc, Michael Kamen, Stephen McGlaughlin; Casting, Billy Hopkins, Suzanne Smith, Kerry Barden; a BBC Films and Arena NY presentation; British-U.S.; Dolby Stereo; Color; Not rated; 93 minutes; July release

CAST

LaMiranda	Guillermo Diaz
Matty Dean	Frederick Weller
Ethan	Brendan Corbalis
Bostonia	Duane Boutté
Skinny Vinnie	Bruce MacVittie
Burt	Peter Ratray
Helen Wheels	Dwight Ewell
Princess Ernestine	Michael McElroy
Vito	Luis Guzman
Randy	Jose Zuniga

and Matthew Faber, Tim Artz, Isaiah Washington, Joey Dedio, Candis Cayne, David Drumgold, Keith Levy, Margaret Gibson, Fenton Lawless, Vincent Capone, George Rafferty, Joe Mosso, Nicole Parker, Stan Tracy, Chuck Pfeifer, Gerry Becker, Aida Turturro, Emanuel Xuereb, Doug Barron, John Ventimiglia, Peter Davies, Ronnie Pincus, and Gabriel Mick

On the eve of the 1969 Stonewall riots, Matty Dean arrives in New York and begins a relationship with drag queen LaMiranda.

© Strand Releasing

THE ADVENTURES OF PINOCCHIO

(NEW LINE CINEMA) Producers, Raju Patel, Jeffrey Sneller; Executive Producers, Sharad Patel, Peter Locke, Donald Kushner; Director, Steve Barron; Screenplay, Sherry Mills, Steve Barron, Tom Benedek, Barry Berman; Based on the novel by Carlo Collodi; Co-Executive Producer, Lawrence Mortorff; Co-Producers, Michael MacDonald, Tim Hampton; Photography, Juan Ruiz Anchia; Designer, Allan Cameron; Editor, Sean Barton; Costumes, Maurizio Millenotti; Music, Rachel Portman; Pinochio and Animatronic Creatures, Jim Henson's Creature Shop; Visual Effects Supervisor, Angus Bickerton; Casting, Annette Benson, Irene Lamb; a co-production of Allied Pinocchio Productions Ltd./Davis Films/Deiter Geissler Filmproduktion GmbH in association with Alta Vista Film GmbH and bibo film productions GmbH; a co-presentation of Savoy Pictures; British-French-German; Dolby Stereo; Panavision; Color; Rated G; 96 minutes; July release

CAST

Geppetto	Martin Landau
Pinocchio	Jonathan Taylor Thomas
Leona	Genevieve Bujold
Lorenzini	Udo Kier
Felinet	Bebe Neuwirth
Volpe	Rob Schneider
Lampwick	Corey Carrier
Baker	Marcello Magni
Baker's Wife	Dawn French
Saleo	Richard Claxton
Tino	Griff Rhys Jones
Schoolmaster	John Sessions
Magistrate	Jean-Claude Drouot
Foreman	Jean-Claude Dreyfus
Henchmen	Teco Celio, Wilfred Benaiche
Zito	Erik Averlont
Voice of Pepe the Cricket	David Doyle
Luigi	Vladimir Koval
Lampwick's Mother	Daniela Tolkein

and Anita Zagaria (Luigi's Wife), Lilian Malkina (Woman in Laundry), Vaclav Vydra (Infantino Father), Petr Bednar (Growling Father), Stefan Weclawek (Infantino), Zdének Podhursk´y, Jirí Kvasnicka (Cabineers), Gorden Lovitt (Big One Attendant), Jan Slovák (Butler), Dean Cook (Boy with Red Ball), Joe Swash (Fighting Boy), Oliver Barron, Jake Court, Luke DeLeon, Kevin Dorsey, Thomas Orange, Sean Woodward (Boys), Jirí Patocka (Man with Donkey), Lida Vlaskova (Woman in Bakery)

Lonely puppetmaker Geppetto carves a wooden boy from a treetrunk who magically springs to life. Previous film version was released by Walt Disney— RKO in 1940.

© New Line Productions, Inc.

Martin Landau, Pinocchio

Pinocchio (top), Jonathan Taylor Thomas (bottom)

Martin Landau, Jonathan Taylor Thomas

236

FLIRT

(CFP) Producer, Ted Hope; Executive Producers, Reinhard Brundig, Satoru Iseki, Jerome Brownstein; Director/Screenplay, Hal Hartley; Photography, Michael Spiller; Music, Ned Rifle, Jeff Taylor; Designer, Steven Rosenzweig; Casting, Billy Hopkins, Suzanne Smith; a True Fiction/Pandora Film/Nippon Film Development and Finance co-production with the support of Filmboard Berlin-Brandenburg Gmbh; U.S.-German-Japanese; Color; Not rated; 85 minutes; August release

CAST

New York

Bill . . . . Bill Sage
Walter . . . . Martin Donovan
Emily, Bill's Girlfriend . . . . Parker Posey
Michael, Bill's Friend . . . . Michael Imperioli
Bartender . . . . Holt McCallany
Dr. Clint . . . . Karen Sillas
Nurse . . . . Erica Gimpel
and Lianna Pai (Woman at Phone Booth), Hannah Sullivan (Trish-Waitress), Harold Perrineau, Robert John Burke, Paul Austin (Men's Room Men), Jose Zuniga (Cab Driver), Patricia Scanlon (Woman at Bar)

Berlin

Dwight . . . . Dwight Ewell
Greta, Werner's Wife . . . . Geno Lechner
Doctor . . . . Peter Fitz
Johan, Dwight's Boyfriend . . . . Dominik Bender
Elisabeth, Dwight's Friend . . . . Susanna Simon
Simon(e), Fashion Stylist . . . . Boris Aljinovic
and Maria Schrader (Woman at Phone Booth), Elina Löwensohn (Nurse), Nils Brück (Tom), Sebastian Koch (Dick), Frank Schendler (Harry), Hans Martin Stier, Lars Rudolph, Jörg Biester (Laborers), Gerhard Severin (Mac, the Bartender), Sabine Svoboda (Barkeeper), Susie Bick (Model), Amina Gusner (Photographer), Stefan Kolosko (Assistant), Jakob Klaffke (Werner), Bano Dost (Neighbor), Hasan Ali Mete (Man)

Tokyo

Miho . . . . Miho Nikaidoh
Naomi, Miho's Friend . . . . Kumiko Ishizuka
Yuki, Ozu's Wife . . . . Chikako Hara
Mr. Ozu . . . . Toshizo Fujiwara
and Meikyoh Yamada (Mochi, Policeman), Mansaku Ikeuchi (Tomo, Younger Policeman), Yutaka Matsushige (Doctor), Tomoko Fujita (Nurse), Eri Yu, Yuri Aso, Natsumi Mizuno (Jailbirds), Hal Hartley (Hal, Miho's Boyfriend), Masatoshi Nagase (Hal's Assistant)

The same story is told in three different locations in three different ways as three couples question their relationships as one of the partners heads off on a trip for an extended period of time.

© CFP Distribution

Tran Nu Yen Khe, Tony Leung Chiu Wai

Bill Sage, Martin Donovan

Maria Schrader, Dwight Ewell

CYCLO

(CFP) Producer, Christophe Rossignon; Director/Screenplay, Tran Anh Hung; Dialogue, Nguyen Trung Bing, Tran Anh Hung; Photography, Benoit Delhomme; Art Director, Benoit Barouh; Costumes, Henriette Raz; Editors, Nicole Dedieu, Claude Ronzeau; a Les Productions Lazennec presentation; Vietnamese; Color; Not rated; 120 minutes; August release

CAST

The Cyclo . . . . Le Van Loc
The Poet . . . . Tony Leung-Chiu Wai
The Sister . . . . Tran Nu Yen Khe
The Madam . . . . Nguyen Nhu Quynh
Tooth . . . . Nguyen Hoang Phuc
Knife . . . . Ngo Vu Quang Hai
The Happy Woman . . . . Nguyen Tuyet Ngan
The Sad Woman . . . . Doan Viet Ha
The Crazy Son . . . . Bjuhoang Huy
The Cyclo's Friend . . . . Vo Vinh Phuc
and Le Dinh Huy (The Grandfather), Pham Ngoc Lieu (The Little Sister), Le Tuan Anh (The Handcuff Man), Le Cong Tuan Anh (The Drunken Dancer), Nguyen Van Day (The Lullaby Man), Biu Thi Mingh Duc (The Poet's Mother), Trinh Thinh (The Foot Fetishist), Nguyen Dinh Tho (The Poet's Father), Nguyen Viet Thang (The Cocaine Policeman)

In order to pay for the bicycle that has been stolen from him, a young cyclo finds himself coerced into finding work in the city's underworld.

© CFP Distribution

RENDEZVOUS IN PARIS

(ARTIFICIAL EYE) Producer, Francoise Etchegarary; Director/Screenplay, Eric Rohmer; Photography, Diane Baratier; Editor, Mary Stephen; Music, Sebastien Erms; a Compagnie Eric Rohmer Production with the participation of Canal+; French; Color; Not rated; 100 minutes; August release

CAST

The Seven O'Clock Rendezvous

Esther . . . . Clara Bellar
Horace . . . . Antoine Basler
The Flirt . . . . Mathias Megard
and Judith Chancel (Aricie), Malcolm Conrath (Felix), Cecile Pares (Hermione), Olivier Poujol (The Waiter)

The Benches of Paris

The Woman . . . . Aurore Rauscher
The Man . . . . Serge Renko

Mother and Child

The Painter . . . . Michael Kraft
The Young Woman . . . . Benedicte Loyen
The Swedish Woman . . . . Veronika Johansson

Three different tales of love set in Paris: a woman suspecting her lover of cheating on her confronts him; a professor is lured into an affair with a woman who is hoping to leave her fiancee; while on a trip with his date to the Picasso Museum a painter falls in love with another woman.

©Artificial Eye Film Company Inc.

Aurore Rauscher, Serge Renko

Clara Bellar

Benedicte Loyen

Bernard Hill, John Hannah

MADAGASCAR SKIN

(INTERNATIONAL FILM CIRCUIT) Producer, Julie Baines; Executive Producer, Ben Gibson; Director/Screenplay, Chris Newby; Photography, Oliver Curtis; Designer, Paul Cross; Editors, Chris Newby, Annabel Ware; Costumes, Annie Symons; Casting, Simone Ireland; British; Color; Not rated; 93 minutes; August release

CAST

Flint . . . . Bernard Hill
Harry . . . . John Hannah
Adonis . . . . Mark Anthony
Lovers . . . . Mark Pettit, Danny Earl
Thugs . . . . Robin Neath, Simon Bennett, Matthew Davies
Sailor . . . . Alex Hooper
Little Girls . . . . Alex Symons-Sutcliffe, Virginia Davies
Black Bikini Woman . . . . Susan Harries
Crab Hunters . . . . George Thomas, Sarah Thomas
Old Man . . . . William Burke

A young gay man, scorned because of the birthmark that mars his face, rescues a facially scarred man who is buried in the sand up to his neck and finds himself becoming attracted to him.

© Intl. Film Circuit

Joe McFadden, Laura Fraser

Kevin McKidd

Iain Robertson

SMALL FACES

(OCTOBER) Producers, Billy MacKinnon, Steve Clar-Hall; Executive Producers, Mark Shivas, Andrea Calderwood; Director, Gillies MacKinnon; Screenplay, Gillies MacKinnon, Billy MacKinnon; Photography, John De Borman; Designer, Zoe MacLeod; Music, John Zeane; Editor, Scott Thomas; Costumes, Kate Carin; Casting, Hayley Murt, Pat Harkins;a BBC Films in association with the Glasgow Film Fund presentation of a Billy MacKinney/Skyline production; Scottish-British, 1995; Dolby Stereo; Color; Rated R; 108 minutes; August release

CAST

Lex MacLean	Iain Robertson
Alan MacLean	Joseph McFadden
Bobby MacLean	J.S. Duffy
Joanne MacGowan	Laura Fraser
Charlie Sloan	Garry Sweeney
Lorna MacLean	Clare Higgins
Malky Johnson	Kevin McKidd
Gorbals	Mark McConnochie
Welch	Steven Singleton
Fabio	David Walker
Uncle Andrew	Ian McElhinney
Jake	Paul Doonan
Dowd	Colin Semple
Doug	Colin McCredie

and Debbie Welch (Rebecca), Eilidh McCormack (Alice), Monica Brady (Aunt), Elizabeth McGregor (Mrs. MacGowan), Andy Gray (Tactless Man), Louise O'Kane (Polly), Lisa McIntosh (Patty), Kirsty Mitchell (Maggie), Sheila Greer Smith (Assistant), Karen McColl (Helen), Karen Murphy (Maria), Carmen Pieraccini (Jeannie), Rab Christie (Talker), Allan Atkins (Boy with Scar), Tom Gallacher (Davie), Joanne Reilly (Barbara), Matt Costello (Shuggy)

In 1968 Glasgow, 13-year-old Lex is torn between the influence of his older brothers: Alan, an aspiring artist hoping to get into art school, and Bobby, who heads a local gang of young thugs.

© October Films

J.S. Duffy, Iain Robertson

239

KANSAS CITY

(FINE LINE FEATURES) Producer/Director, Robert Altman; Screenplay, Robert Altman, Frank Barhydt; Photography, Oliver Stapleton; Designer, Stephen Altman; Editor, Geraldine Peroni; Costumes, Dona Granata; Music, Hal Willner; Co-Producers, Matthew Seig, David Thomas; Executive Producer, Scott Bushnell; Associate Producer, James McLindon; Casting, Elisabeth Leustig; a Sandcastle 5/Ciby 2000 co-production; U.S.-French; Dolby SDDS Stereo; CFI color; Rated R; 115 minutes; August release

CAST

Blondie O'Hara . . . . Jennifer Jason Leigh
Carolyn Stilton . . . . Miranda Richardson
Seldom Seen . . . . Harry Belafonte
Henry Stilton . . . . Michael Murphy
Johnny O'Hara . . . . Dermot Mulroney
Johnny Flynn . . . . Steve Buscemi
Babe Flynn . . . . Brooke Smith
Nettie Bolt . . . . Jane Adams
Addie Parker . . . . Jeff Feringa
Sheepshan Red . . . . A.C. Smith
"Blue" Green . . . . Martin Martin
Charlie Parker . . . . Albert J. Burnes
Pearl Cummings . . . . Ajia Mignon Johnson
Rally Speaker. . . . . Tim Snay
Rose . . . . Tawanna Benbow
Governor Park . . . . Cal Pritner
Tom Pendergast . . . . Jerry Fornelli
Jackie Ciro. . . . . Michael Ornstein
Charlie Gargotta . . . . Michael Garozzo
John Lazia . . . . Joe Digirolamo
Gas Station Attendant. John Durbin
Hey Hey Club Hostess. . . . . Gina Belafonte
Telegraph Operator. . . . . Nancy Marcy
Train Station Agent. . . . . Buck Baker
Mrs. Bruce . . . . Dorothy Kemp-Clark
and Edward Pennington (Governor Park's Butler), Robert Elliott, Marlon Hoffman, Patrick Oldani, Philip Trovato (Lazia Men); Hey Hey Club Musicians: James Carter, Craig Handy, David Murray, Joshua Redman (Tenor Saxophone), Jesse Davis, David "Fathead" Newman, Jr. (Alto Saxophone), Don Byron (Clarinet/Baritone Saxophone), Olu Dara, Nicholas Payton, James Zollar (Trumpet), Curtis Fowlkes, Clark Gayton (Trombone), Victor Lewis (Drums), Geri Allen, Cyrus Chestnut (Piano), Ron Carter, Christian McBride, Tyrone Clarke (Bass), Russell Malone, Mark Whitfield (Guitar), Kevin Mahogany (Vocalist)

After Johnny is captured by gangster and club owner Seldom Seen in retaliation for robbing one of his favored customers, Johnny's wife Blondie kidnaps the wealthy Carolyn Stilton hoping to use her as a swap for her husband's life.

Harry Belafonte

Steve Buscemi

Miranda Richardson, Jennifer Jason Leigh

Jennifer Jason Leigh, Miranda Richardson

BROTHER OF SLEEP

(SONY PICTURES CLASSICS) Director/Photography, Joseph Vilsmaier; Screenplay, Robert Schneider; Based on his novel; Dramaturgy, Jürgen Büscher; Designer, Rolf Zehetbauer; Costumes, Ute Hofinger; Music, Norbert J. Schneider, Hubert von Goisern; a production of Perathon Film/B.A. Film/Kuchenreuther Filmproduktion/Iduna Filmprodukution/DOR-Film (in collaboration with the Austrian Film Institute and ORF); German; Dolby DTS Stereo; Cinemascope; Color; Rated R; 127 minutes; September release

CAST

Elias Johannes Alder .... André Eisermann
Elsbeth .... Dana Vávrová
Peter .... Ben Becker
Bruga .... Angelika Bartsch
Nulf .... Michael Mendl
Nulf's Wife .... Eva Mattes
Seff .... Peter Franke
Seff's Wife .... Michaela Rosen
Lukas .... Detlef Bothe
and Jochen Nickel (Michael, the Charcoal Burner), Jürgen Schornagel (Curate Benzer), Paulus Manker (Oskar), Lena Stolze (Oskar's Wife), Heinz Emigholz (Haintz), Martin Heesch (Paul), Gilbert von Sohlern (Albert), Birge Schade (Franziska) Nadine Neumann (Magdalena), Regina Fritsch (Midwife), Ingo Naujoks (Sgt. Hirsch), Herbert Knaup (Choirmaster Goller), Conradin Blum (Elias—as a Child), Daniel Lins (Peter—as a Child), Michaela Pfeiffer (Philipp—as a Child), Robert Studer (Fritz—as a Child), Florian Wostry (Lukas—as a Child), Peter Füschl (Paul—as a Child), Ralph Sauerwein (Albert—as a Child), Natalie Winkel (Franziska—as a Child), Theresa Longoni (Girl), Robert Schneider (Girl), Janina (Anna—9 years), Josefina (Anna—2 years)

In a remote Alpine village at the turn of the 19th Century musical genius Elias Johannes Alder finds himself bound physically and spiritually to his friend Peter's sister Elsbeth.

© Sony Pictures Entertainment

André Eisermann, Dana Vávrová

André Eisermann, Ben Becker

THREE LIVES AND ONLY ONE DEATH

(NEW YORKER) Producer, Paulo Branco; Director, Raul Ruiz; Screenplay, Raul Ruiz, Pascal Bonitzer; Photography, Laurent Machuel; Music, Jorge Arriagada; Editor, Rodolfo Wedeles; a co-production of Gemini Films (France), La Sept Cinema (France), Madragoa Filmes (Portugal), with the participation of Canal Plus and of Centre National de la Cinématographie and the support of Le Groupement National des Cinémas de Recherche; French-Portuguese; Color; Not Rated; 123 minutes; September release

CAST

Mateo Strano/Georges Vickers/The Butler/
Luc Allamand .... Marcello Mastroianni
Tania .... Anna Galiena
Maria .... Marisa Paredes
Martin .... Melvil Poupaud
Cécile .... Chiara Mastroianni
Hélène .... Arielle Dombasle
André .... Féodor Atkine
Mario .... Jean-Yves Gautier
Tania's Husband .... Jacques Pieiller
The Narrator .... Pierre Bellemare
Luca .... Smain
Beggars .... Lou Castel, Roland Topor, Jacques Delpi
Antoine José .... Jean Badin
Mrs. Vickers .... Monique Melinand
Carlito .... Bastien Vincent
Four stories of multiple personalities involving: Mateo Strano, a traveling salesman; Georges, a professor of "negative" anthropology; the butler at a mansion inherited by a young couple; and Luc Allamand, a successful businessman visited by his family.

©New Yorker Films

Marcello Mastroianni, Marisa Paredes

Marecello Mastroianni, Melvin Poupard, Chiara Mastroianni

Marianne Jean-Baptiste, Brenda Blethyn

Elizabeth Berrington, Timothy Spall, Marianne Jean-Baptiste, Brenda Blethyn, Phyllis Logan, Claire Rushbrook, Lee Ross

SECRETS & LIES

(OCTOBER) Producer, Simon Channing-Williams; Director/Screenplay, Mike Leigh; Photography, Dick Pope; Music, Andrew Dickson; Editor, John Gregory; Designer, Alison Chitty; Costumes, Maria Price; Casting, Stern and Parriss; a Ciby 2000 and Thin Man Films production, in association with Channel Four Films; British; Dolby Stereo; Color; Rated R; 142 minutes; September release

CAST

Maurice	Timothy Spall
Monica	Phyllis Logan
Cynthia	Brenda Blethyn
Roxanne	Claire Rushbrook
Hortense	Marianne Jean-Baptiste
Jane	Elizabeth Berrington
Dionne	Michele Austin
Paul	Lee Ross
Social Worker	Lesley Manville
Stuart	Ron Cook
Girl with Scar	Emma Amos
Hortense's Brothers	Brian Boyell, Trevor Laird
Hortense's Sister-in-Law	Clare Perkins
Hortense's Nephew	Elias Perkins McCook
Senior Optometrist	June Mitchell
Junior Optician	Janice Acquah
Girl in Optician's	Keeley Flanders
First Bride	Hannah Davis
First Bride's Father	Terence Harvey
Second Bride	Kate O'Malley
Groom	Joe Tucker
Vicar	Richard Syms
Best Man	Grant Masters
Mother in Family Group	Annie Hayes
Grandmother	Jean Ainslie
Teenage Son	Daniel Smith
Nurse	Lucy Sheen
Young Mother	Frances Ruffelle
Baby	Felix Manley
Potential Husband	Nitin Chandra Ganatra
Conjuror	Metin Marlow
Raunchy Women	Amanda Crossley, Su Elliot, Di Sherlock
Triplets	Alex Squires, Lauren Squires, Sade Squires
Little Boy	Dominic Curran
Men in Suits	Stephen Churchett, David Neilson, Peter Stockbridge, Peter Waddington
Graduate	Rachel Lewis
Grinning Husband	Paul Trussell
Uneasy Woman	Denise Orita
Elderly Lady	Margery Withers
Daughter	Theresa Watson
Laughing Man	Gordon Winter
Fiance	Jonathan Coyne

and Bonzo (Dog), Texas (Cat), Peter Wight (Father in Family Group), Gary McDonald (Boxer), Alison Steadman (Dog Owner), Liz Smith (Cat Owner), Sheila Kelley (Fertile Mother), Angela Curran (Little Boy's Mother), Linda Beckett (Pin Up Housewife), Philip Davis (Man in Suits), Wendy Nottingham (Glum Wife), Anthony O'Donnell (Uneasy Man), Ruth Sheen (Laughing Woman), Mia Soteriou (Fiancee)

A white, working-class, single mother is confronted by the grown-up, black daughter she gave up for adoption. The film received Oscar nominations for picture, actress (Brenda Blethyn), supporting actress (Marianne Jean-Baptiste), director and original screenplay.

Brenda Blethyn, Claire Rushbrook

Timothy Spall

JUDE

(GRAMERCY) Producer, Andrew Eaton; Director, Michael Winterbottom; Executive Producers, Stewart Till, Mark Shivas; Screenplay, Hossein Amini; Based on the novel Jude the Obscure by Thomas Hardy; Photography, Eduardo Serra; Editor, Trevor White; Designer, Joseph Bennett; Costumes, Janty Yates; Music, Adrian Johnston; Casting, Simone Ireland, Vanessa Pereira; a PolyGram Filmed Entertainment presentation in association with BBC Films of a Revolution Films production; British; Dolby Stereo; Color; Rated R; 123 minutes; October release

Kate Winslet, Christopher Eccleston

CAST

Jude Fawley	Christopher Eccleston
Sue Bridehead	Kate Winslet
Phillotson	Liam Cunningham
Arabella	Rachel Griffiths
Aunt Drusilla	June Whitfield
Little Jude	Ross Colvin Turnbull
Jude as a Boy	James Daley
Farmer Troutham	Berwick Kaler
Stonemasons	Sean McKenzie, Richard Albrecht
Anny	Caitlin Bossley
Sarah	Emma Turner
Shopkeeper	Lorraine Hilton
Uncle Joe	James Nesbitt
Tinker Taylor	Mark Lambert
Uncle Jim	Paul Brown
Gypsy Saleswoman	Amanda Ryan
Curator	Vernon Dobtcheff
Drunken Undergraduate	David Tennant
Punter	Darren Tighe
Mr. Willis	Paul Copley
Mr. Biles	Ken Jones
Auctioneer	Roger Ashton Griffiths

and Raymond Ross (Old Man), Freda Dowie (Elderly Landlady), Dexter Fletcher (Priest), Moray Hunter (Politician), Adrian Bower (Blacksmith), Kerry Shale (Showman), Billie Dee Roberts (Little Sister), Chantel Neary (Baby), James Scanlon (Newborn Baby)

In 19th Century England, stone mason Jude Fawley, longing to attend university, moves to Christminster where he falls fatally in love with his cousin Sue Bridehead.

James Daley, Liam Cunningham

Kate Winslet, Christopher Eccleston

MICROCOSMOS

(MIRAMAX) Producers, Galatee Films, Jacques Perrin, Christophe Barratier, Yvette Mallet; Executive Producers, Michel Faure, Philippe Gautier, Andre Lazare, Patrick Lancelot; Directors, Claude Nuridsany, Marie Perennou; Photography, Claude Nuridsany, Marie Perennou, Hughes Ryffel, Thierry Machado; Editors, Marie-Josephe Yoyotte, Florence Ricard; Music, Bruno Coulais; a co-production of Galatee Films/France 2 Cinema/BAC Films/Delta Images/Les Productions J&H/Romande/Urania Films; French-Swiss-Italian; Dolby Digital Stereo; Color; Rated R; 77 minutes; October release. Documentary on the insect world, narrated by Kristin Scott Thomas.

BEAUTIFUL THING

(SONY PICTURES CLASSICS) Producers, Tony Garnett, Bill Shapter; Director, Hettie MacDonald; Screenplay, Jonathan Harvey, based on his play; Photography, Chris Seager; Designer, Mark Stevenson; Editor, Don Fairservice; Costumes, Pam Tait; Songs performed by Cass Elliott; Casting, Gail Stevens, Andy Pryor; a Channel Four Films presentation of a World Production; British; Color; Rated R; 89 minutes; October release

CAST

Jamie Gangel	Glen Berry
Sandra Gangel	Linda Henry
Ste Pearce	Scott Neal
Leah	Tameka Empson
Tony	Ben Daniels
Rose	Jeillo Edwards
Marlene	Anna Karen
Trevor Pearce	Daniel Bowers
Ronnie Pearce	Garry Cooper
Louise	Sophie Stanton
Gina	Julie Smith
Ryan McBride	Steven Martin
Kelly	Catherine Sanderson
Claire	Liane Ware
Rodney Barr	John Benfield
Betty	Marlene Sidaway
Jayson	Andrew Fraser
Lenny	John Savage

and Davyd Harries (Brewery Official), Beth Goddard (Brewery Official), Martin Walsh (Bennett), Dave Lynn (Drag Performer), Meera Syal (Miss Chauan), Ozdemir Mamodeally (Slasher)

Taking refuge from the beatings given him by his father and brother young Ste spends time with his next door neighbors, gradually discovering the feelings his fellow schoolmate, Jamie, has for him.

© Sony Pictures Entertainment Inc.

Linda Henry, Ben Daniels

Tameka Empson, Linda Henry

Glen Berry, Scott Neal

TWELFTH NIGHT
OR WHAT YOU WILL

(FINE LINE FEATURES) Producers, Stephen Evans, David Parfitt; Executive Producers, Greg Smith, Ruth Vitale, Jonathan Weisgal, Ileen Maisel; Director/Screenplay, Trevor Nunn; Based on the play by William Shakespeare; Photography, Clive Tickner; Designer, Sophie Becher; Editor, Peter Boyle; Line Producer, Mark Cooper; Costumes, John Bright; Music, Shaun Davey; Casting, Carl Proctor Associates; a Summit Entertainment N.V., Circus Films and BBC Films presentation of a Renaissance Films production; British; Dolby Stereo; Technicolor; Rated PG; 134 minutes; October release

CAST

Viola	Imogen Stubbs
Sebastian	Steven Mackintosh
Antonio	Nicholas Farrell
Captain	Sid Livingstone
Feste	Ben Kingsley
Priest	James Walker
Olivia	Helena Bonham Carter
Malvolio	Nigel Hawthorne
Sir Toby Belch	Mel Smith
Maria	Imelda Staunton
Orsino	Toby Stephens
Valentine	Alan Mitchell
Fabian	Peter Gunn
Sir Andrew Aguecheek	Richard E. Grant
First Officer	Timothy Bentinck
Second Officer	Rod Culbertson
Gardener	Jeff Hall

Posing as a man after surviving a shipwreck, Viola is shocked to find that Olivia has fallen in love with her.

Helena Bonham Carter, Imogen Stubbs, Toby Stephans

Helena Bonham Carter

Ben Kingsley

Nigel Hawthorne

Imogeb Stubbs, Helena Bonham Carter

Bernard Giraudeau, Fanny Ardent

Charles Berling, Judith Godreche

RIDICULE

(MIRAMAX ZOË) Producers, Gilles Legrand, Frederic Brillion, Philippe Carcassonne; Director, Patrice Leconte; Screenplay, Remi Waterhouse, Michel Fessler, Eric Vicaut; Photography, Thierry Arbogast; Designer, Ivan Maussion; Editor, Joelle Hache; Music, Antoine Duhamel; Costumes, Christian Gasc; French; Dolby Stereo; Panavision; Color; Rated R; 102 minutes; November release

CAST

Gregoire Ponceludon de Malavoy	Charles Berling
Marquis de Bellegarde	Jean Rochefort
Madame de Blayac	Fanny Ardant
Mathilde de Bellegarde	Judith Godreche
Abbot de Vilecourt	Bernard Giraudeau
Monsieur de Montalier	Bernard Dheran
Knight de Milletail	Carlo Brandt
Abbot de l'Epee	Jacques Mathou
Louis XVI	Urbain Cancelier
Baron de Malenval	Albert Delpy
Paul	Bruno Zanardi
Charlotte	Marie Pillet
Colonel de Chevernoy	Jacques Roman
Baron de Malenval	Philippe Magnan
The Notary	Maurice Chevit
Maurepas	Jacques-Francois Zeller
Victor	Gerard Hardy
Duke de Guines	Marc Berman
The Genealogist	Philippe Du Jannerand
Monsignor d'Artimont	Claude Dereppe
Baroness de Boisjoli	Isabelle Spade
Baroness d'Oberkirchner	Isabelle Petit-Jacques
Countess de Blancfagot	Nathalie Mann
Viscount du Closlabbe	Etienne Draber
Knight de St. Tronchain	Fabrice Eberhard

and Stephane Fourmond (Marquis de Carmes), Jean-Jacques Le Vessier (Viscount de Sabran), Lucien Pascal (Monsieur de Blayac), Nicolas Chagrin (Lord Bolingbroke), Fabien Behar (Secretary to the King), Mirabelle Kirkland (Marie-Antoinette), Marie Llano (Leonard's Mother), Antonin Lebas Joly (Leonard), Didier Abot (Priest), Julien Bukowski (Gentleman), Jose Fumanal (Officer in Duel), Sylvie Herbert (Ponceludon's Mother), Alain Hocine (Le Player), Clementine Buxtorf (The Sister), Boris Napes (The Painter), Gerard Sergue (The Thief), Laurent Valo (Simon), Claire Garguier (Therese), Marine Guez (The Singer)

Gregoire Ponceludon de Malavoy arrives at the court of King Louis XVI in hopes of persuading him to finance a swamp drainage project but discovers that he must play certain games with the shallow members of the court to achieve his goal. The film received an Oscar nomination for best foreign language film of 1996.

©Miramax Zoe

Charles Berling, Fanny Ardant

Charles Berling

BREAKING THE WAVES

(OCTOBER) Producers, Vibeke Windeløv, Peter Aalbæk Jensen; Executive Producer, Lars Jonsson; Director, Lars Von Trier; Screenplay, Lars Von Trier, Peter Asmussen; Photography, Robby Müller; Art Director, Karl Juliusson; Costumes, Manon Rasmussen; Editor, Anders Refn; Co-Producers, Axel Helgeland, Peter Van Vogelpoel, Rob Langestraat, Marianne Slot; Casting, Joyce Nettles; a co-production with Trust Film Svab, Liberator Productions S.A.R.L., Argus Film Produktie, Northern Lights A/S, SVT Drama Stockholm, Nordic Film & TV Fund, La SEPT Cinéma, VPRO Television, Media Investment Club; Danish-Swedish-Norwegian-Finnish; Dolby Stereo; Color; Rated R; 156 minutes; November release

Emily Watson, Stellan Skarsgård

CAST

Bess	Emily Watson
Jan	Stellan Skarsgard
Dodo	Katrin Cartlidge
Terry	Jean-Marc Barr
Man on the Trawler	Udo Kier
Doctor Richardson	Adrian Rawlins
The Minister	Jonathan Hackett
Bess' Mother	Sandra Voe
Pits	Mikkel Gaup
Pim	Roef Ragas
Grandfather	Phil McCall
Chairman	Robert Robertson
An Elder	Desmond Reilly
Sybilla	Sarah Grudgeon
Coroner	Finlay Welsh
Glasgow Doctor	David Gallacher
Man on Bus	Ray Jeffries
Man at Lighthouse	Owen Kavanagh
Man on Boat	Bob Dogherty
Young Sailor	David Bateson

and Callum Cuthbertson (Radio Operator), Gavin Mitchell, Brian Smith (Police Officers), Iain Agnew, Charles Kearney, Steven Leach (Praying Men), Dorte Rømer (Nurse), Anthony O'Donnell, John Wark (Boys), Ronnie McKellaig (Precentor)

After Bess's husband Jan is bedridden by an oil-rigging accident he encourages her to go on with her life and to fulfill both their sexual needs in a bizarre manner. This film received an Oscar nomination for actress (Emily Watson).

© October Films

Emily Watson, Katrin Cartlidge

Stellan Skarsgård, Emily Watson

Katrin Cartlidge, Emily Watson

Geoffrey Rush

Lynn Redgrave, Geoffrey Rush

John Gielgud, Noah Taylor

SHINE

(FINE LINE FEATURES) Producer, Jane Scott; Director/Story, Scott Hicks; Screenplay, Jan Sardi; Photography, Geoffrey Simpson; Editor, Pip Karmel; Music, David Hirschfelder; Designer, Vicki Niehus; Costumes, Louise Wakefield; Casting, Liz Mullinar Casting (Australia), Sharon Howard Field (USA), Karen Lindsay-Stewart (UK); an Australian Film Finance Corporation in association with Pandora Cinema / South Australian Film Corporation / British Broadcasting Corporation / Film Victoria presentation of a Momentum Films production; Australian; Dolby Stereo; Color; Rated PG-13 ; 105 minutes; November release

Armin Mueller-Stahl, Noah Taylor

CAST

Peter Helfgott	Armin Mueller-Stahl
David Helfgott as an Adolescent	Noah Taylor
David Helfgott an Adult	Geoffrey Rush
Gillian	Lynn Redgrave
Katharine Susannah Prichard	Googie Withers
Sylvia	Sonia Todd
Ben Rosen	Nicholas Bell
Cecil Parkes	John Gielgud
David as a Child	Alex Rafalowicz
Tony	Justin Braine
Sam	Chris Haywood
Eisteddfod Presenter	Gordon Poole
Suzie as a Child	Danielle Cox
Margaret	Rebecca Gooden
Rachel	Marta Kaczmarek
Jim Minogue	John Cousins
State Champion Announcer	Paul Linkson
Isaac Stern	Randall Berger
Boy Next Door	Ian Welbourn
Louise as a Baby	Kelly Bottrill
Rabbi	Beverley Vaughan
Synagogue Secretary	Phyllis Burford
Society Hostess	Daphne Grey
Soviet Society Secretary	Edwin Hodgeman
Sonia	Maria Dafnero
Postman	Reis Porter
Roger Woodward (Younger)	Stephen Sheehan
Announcer	Brenton Whittle
Suzie as a Teenager	Marianna Doherty
Louise as a Child	Camilla James
Viney	David King
Registrar	Danny Davies
Sarah	Helen Dowell
Muriel	Louise Dorling
Student	Sean Carlsen
Ashley	Richard Hansell
Robert	Robert Hands
Ray	Marc Warren
RCOM Conductor	Neil Thomson
Suzie as an Adult	Joey Kennedy
Nurse	Ellen Cressey
Beryl Alcott	Beverley Dunn
Bar Customer	Andy Seymour
Jessica	Ella Scott Lynch
Rowan	Jethro Heysen-Hicks
Roger Woodward (Older)	John Martin
Celebrant	Bill Boyley

and Teres La Rocca, Lindsey Day, Grant Doyle (Opera Singers), Leah Jennings, Kathy Monaghan, Mark Lawrence, Gordon Coombes, Luke Dollman, Margaret Stone, Tom Craig, Helen Ayres (Musicians), Suzi Jarratt, Samantha McDonald (Vocalist)

Noah Taylor

David Helfgott looks back on his childhood when his father pushed him relentlessly to become a piano virtuoso, eventually driving him to a nervous breakdown. Geoffrey Rush received the Academy Award for Best Actor of 1996. The film received additional nominations for picture, supporting actor (Armin Mueller-Stahl), director, film editing, musical score-dramatic and original screenplay.

Geoffrey Rush

JOSEPH CONRAD'S THE SECRET AGENT

(FOX SEARCHLIGHT) Producer, Norma Heyman; Executive Producer, Bob Hoskins; Director/Screenplay, Christopher Hampton; Based on the novel by Joseph Conrad; Photography, Denis Lenoir; Designer, Caroline Amies; Editor, George Akers; Music, Philip Glass; Co-Producer, Joyce Herlihy; Costumes, Anushia Nieradzik; a Heyman/Hoskins production in association with Capitol Films; British; Dolby Stereo; Color; Rated R; 95 minutes; November release

CAST

Adolf Virloc	Bob Hoskins
Winnie Virloc	Patricia Arquette
Ossipon	Gerard Depardieu
Chief Inspector Heat	Jim Broadbent
Stevie	Christian Bale
The Professor	Robin Williams
Vladimir	Eddie Izzard
Winnie's Mother	Elizabeth Spriggs
The Driver	Peter Vaughan
The Assistant Commissioner	Julian Wadham
Michaelis	Roger Hammond
Yundt	Ralph Nossek
Ticket Clerk	Neville Phillips

Secret Agent Adolf Verloc is asked by the police to betray the members of the anarchist group he has infiltrated. He winds up enlisting his simple-minded brother-in-law Stevie to participate in a terrorist act with disastrous results.

Bob Hoskins, Patricia Arquette

Christian Bale

Daniel Auteuil, Catherine Deneuve

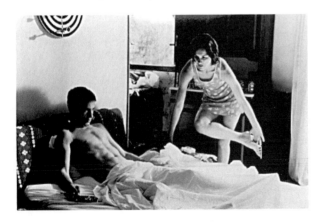

Benoit Magimel, Laurence Cote

LES VOLEURS (THIEVES)

(SONY PICTURES CLASSICS) Producer, Alain Sarde; Director, Andre Techine; Screenplay, Andre Techine, Gilles Taurand, Michel Alexandre, Pascal Bonitzer; Photography, Jeanne Lapoirie; Music, Philippe Sarde; Editor, Martine Giordano; Designer, Ze Branco; Costumes, Elisabeth Tavernier; Casting, Michel Nasri; a co-production of Les Films/Alain Sarde/TFI Films production/Rhone Alpen Cinema/D.A. Films; French; Dolby Stereo; Color; Rated R; 117 minutes; December release

CAST

Marie	Catherine Deneuve
Alex	Daniel Auteuil
Juliette	Laurence Côte
Jimmy	Benoit Magimel
Mireille	Fabienne Babe
Ivan	Didier Bezace
Justin	Julien Riviere
Victor	Ivan Desny
Fred	Pierre Perez
Regis	Regis Betoule
Nabil	Naguime Bendidi
Lucien	Didier Raymond

Marie, a philosophy professor, and Alex, a detective, both embark on separate affairs with young Juliette whom the latter had arrested for shoplifting.

© Sony Pictures Entertainment

Virginie Ledoyen, Jaqueline Bisset

Isabelle Huppert, Sandrine Bonnaire

LA CÉRÉMONIE

(NEW YORKER) Producer, Marin Karmitz; Director, Claude Chabrol; Screenplay, Claude Chabrol, Caroline Eliacheff; Based on the novel *A Judgement in Stone* by Ruth Rendell; Photography, Bernard Zitzermann; Costumes, Corinne Jorry; Set Decorator, Daniel Mercier; Editor, Monqieu Fardoulis; Music, Mathieu Chabrol; a co-production with MK2 Productions S.A., France 3 Cinéma, Prokino Filmproduktion GMBH, OLGA Film, Z.D.F., with the participation of Canal+ and Centre National de la Cinématographie; French, 1995; Color; Not Rated; 111 minutes; December release

CAST

Sophie	Sandrine Bonnaire
Jeanne	Isabelle Huppert
Catherine	Jacqueline Bisset
Georges	Jean-Pierre Cassel
Melinda	Virginie Ledoyen
Gilles	Valentin Merlet

Postmistress Jeanne, a dangerous woman with a hatred for the upper class, influences Sophie, the housekeeper at the Lelievre chateau, to turn against her employers.

© New Yorker Films

THE PORTRAIT OF A LADY

(GRAMERCY) Producers, Monty Montgomery, Steve Golin; Director, Jane Campion; Screenplay, Laura Jones; Based on the novel by Henry James; Co-Producer, Ann Wingate; Photography, Stuart Dryburgh; Designer/Costumes, Janet Patterson; Editor, Veronika Jenet; Music, Wojiech Kilar; from Propaganda Films; British; Dolby Stereo; Super 35 Widescreen; Technicolor; Rated PG-13; 144 minutes; December release

CAST

Isabel Archer	Nicole Kidman
Gilbert Osmond	John Malkovich
Madame Serena Merle	Barbara Hershey
Henrietta Stackpole	Mary-Louise Parker
Ralph Touchett	Martin Donovan
Mrs. Touchett	Shelley Winters
Lord Warburton	Richard E. Grant
Countess Gemini	Shelley Duvall
Edward Rosier	Christian Bale
Caspar Goodwood	Viggo Mortensen
Pansy Osmond	Valentina Cervi
Mr. Touchett	John Gielgud
Bob Bantling	Roger Ashton-Griffiths

and Catherine Zago (Mother Superior), Alessandra Vanzi (Nun #2), Katie Campbell (Miss Molyneaux #1), Katherine Anne Porter (Miss Molyneaux #2), Eddy Seager (Strongman's Spruiker), Pat Roach (Strongman), Emanuelle Carucci Viterbi (Roccanera Butler), Francesca Bartellini (Isabel's Maid), Achille Brugnini (Footman at Ballroom)

Isabel Archer, having received a large inheritance from an Uncle, is led into an unfortunate marriage to a self-serving dillettante, Gilbert Osmond. The film received Oscar nominations for supporting actress (Barbara Hershey) and costume design.

John Malkovich, Nicole Kidman

Barbara Hershey, John Malkovich

Kenneth Branagh, Julie Christie

HAMLET

(COLUMBIA) Producer, David Barron; Director/Adaptation, Kenneth Branagh; Based on the play by William Shakespeare; Photography, Alex Thomson; Designer, Tim Harvey; Editor, Neil Farrell; Costumes, Alex Byrne; Music, Patrick Doyle; Casting, Vanessa Pereira, Simone Ireland; a Castle Rock Entertainment presentation; British-U.S.; SDDS Digital Stereo; Panavision Super 70; Technicolor; Rated PG-13; 239 minutes; December release

CAST

Hamlet	Kenneth Branagh
Gertrude	Julie Christie
First Gravedigger	Billy Crystal
Reynaldo	Gerard Depardieu
Player King	Charlton Heston
Claudius	Derek Jacobi
Marcellus	Jack Lemmon
Fortinbras	Rufus Sewell
Osric	Robin Williams
Ophelia	Kate Winslet
English Ambassador	Richard Attenborough
Ghost	Brian Blessed
Polonius	Richard Briers
Hecuba	Judi Dench
Guildenstern	Reece Dinsdale
Horatio	Nicholas Farrell
Priam	John Gielgud
Player Queen	Rosemary Harris
Laertes	Michael Maloney
Old Norway	John Mills
Rosencrantz	Timothy Spall
Attendants to Claudius	Riz Abbasi, David Blair, Peter Bygott
Priest	Michael Bryant
Stage Manager	Charles Daish
Yorich	Ken Dodd
Attendants to Gertrude	Angela Douglas, Rowena King, Sarah Lam
Lucianus	Rob Edwards
Francisco	Ray Fearon
Doctor	Yvonne Gidden
Cornelius	Ravil Isyanov
Fortinbras's Captain	Jeffery Kissoon
Barnardo	Ian McElhinney
Fortinbras's General	Duke of Marlborough
Sailors	Jimi Mistry, David Yip
Prologue	Sian Radinger
Prostitute	Melanie Ramsay
Second Gravedigger	Simon Russell Beale
Young Lord	Andrew Schofield
Young Hamlet	Tom Szekeres
First Player	Ben Thom
Voltemand	Don Warrington
Second Player	Perdita Weeks

Hamlet, Prince of Denmark, plots his revenge on King Claudius who has wed his mother, Gertrude, shortly after the death of Hamlet's father, whom the Prince suspects Claudius has murdered. Previous film versions of the play include those starring Laurence Olivier (1948), Richard Burton (1964), Nicol Williamson (1969), and Mel Gibson (1990). The film received Oscar nominations for art direction, costume design, musical score- dramatic, and adapted screenplay.

© Castle Rock Entertainment

Nicholas Farrell, Kenneth Branagh, Jack Lemmon

Derek Jacobi, Kenneth Branagh, Julie Christie

Michael Maloney, Richard Briers, Kate Winslet

Rosemary Harris, Charlton Heston

Gerard Depardieu

Billy Crystal

SOME MOTHER'S SON

(COLUMBIA) Producers, Jim Sheridan, Arthur Lappin, Edward Burke; Director, Terry George; Screenplay, Terry George, Jim Sheridan; Photography, Geoffrey Simpson; Designer, David Wilson; Costumes, Joan Bergin; Editor, Craig McKay; Associate Producer, Helen Mirren; Music, Bill Whelan; Casting, Nuala Moiselle; a Castle Rock Entertainment presentation of a Hell's Kitchen production; Irish-British-U.S.; Dolby Stereo; Technicolor; Rated R; 112 minutes; December release

CAST

Kathleen Quigley	Helen Mirren
Annie Higgins	Fionnula Flanagan
Gerard Quigley	Aidan Gillen
Frank Higgins	David O'Hara
Bobby Sands	John Lynch
Farnsworth	Tom Hollander
Harrington	Tim Woodward
Danny Boyle	Ciaran Hinds
Alice Quigley	Geraldine O'Rawe
Fr. Daly	Gerard McSorley
Inspector McPeake	Dan Gordon
Theresa Higgins	Grainne Delany
Liam Quigley	Ciaran Fitzgerald
Government Minister	Robert Lang
Young Turk	Stephen Hogan
SAS Leader	Peter Howitt
British Captain	Bosco Hogan
Jimmy Higgins	Jimmy Keogh

nd John Kavanagh (Cardinal), Oliver Maguire (Frank Maguire), Doreen Keogh (Mother Superior), Anna Megan (Rosie Quigley), Hugh O'Donnell (Paddy), John Higgins (John Deegan), Joan Sheehy, Jennifer Gibney (Women Searchers), Mal Whyte (Barrister), Alan Barry (Judge), Barry Cassin (Prosecutor), Brian Mallon (Prison Officer Jones), Sean Lawlor (Platoon Leader), Michael Sherrie (Assistant Governor), James Hickey (Young Son), Karen Carlisle (Prisoner's Girlfriend), Fiona Higgins (Prisoner's Sister), Jer O'Leary, Tim McDonnell (Hunger Strikers), Tony Flynn (Cyclist), Liam Byrne (Prisoner Murphy), Pat Mulryan (IRA Man #1), Valerie Roe (Girl in Farnsworth's Office), Deirdre McAliskey (Woman in Court), Michael F. Sullivan (Prison Officer Davis), Robert Taylor (Election Agent), Kate Perry (Prison Officer's Widow), Anthony Brophy (Prisoner's Leader), Mickey McEneaney, Paddy McEneaney, Gene Berrills (The Merry Macs), Ronan O'Donoghue, Richard Neilson (Radio Announcers)

The true story of the 1981 hunger strike of 21 IRA prisoners led by Bobby Sands, as told from the point of view of the mother of one of the young men.

© Castle Rock Entertainment

Helen Mirren, Fionnula Flanagan

Aiden Gillen, David O'Hara

Helen Mirren, Aiden Gillen

Aidan Gillen, John Lynch

Roujin-Z
© Central Park Media

Jane Birkin, Mathieu Carriére in
Egon Schiele

ROUJIN-Z (Kit Parker Films) Producer, Yoshiaki Motoya; Director, Toshiaki Honatni; Original Work/Screenplay/Mechanical Design, Katsuhiro Otomo; Based on his original story with script adapation by George Roubicek; Photography, Hideo Okazaki; Art Design, Satoshi Kon; Animation Director, Fumio Iida; Music, Bun Itakura; from Tokyo Theatres Co Inc./The Television Inc./Movic Co Ltd./TV Asahi; Japanese; Color; Rated PG-13; 80 minutes; January release. VOICE CAST: Allan Wenger (Terada), Toni Barry (Haruko), Barbara Barnes (Nobuko), Adam Henderson (Maeda), Jana Carpenter (Norie), Ian Thompson (Takazawa), John Jay Fitzgerald (Hasegawa), Nicolette McKenzie (Haru), Sean Barrett, Blain Fairman, Nigel Anthony (Aches)

EDEN VALLEY (M.D. WAX/COURIER FILMS) Producers/Directors /Screenplay/Photography, Richard Grassick, Ellen Hare, Sirkka Liisa Konttinen, Murray Martin, Pat McCarthy, Lorna Powell, Pete Roberts; from the Amber Production Team in association with Channel 4, NDR, ARTE, Northern Arts; British, 1994; Color; Not rated; 95 minutes; January release. CAST: Brian Hogg (Hoggy), Darrell Bell (Billy), Mike Elliott (Danker), Jimmy Killeen (Probation Officer), Wayne Buck, Kevin Buck (Young Lads), John Middleton, Charlie Hardwick, Katja Roberts (Townies), Mo Harrold (Mother), Art Davies (Boyfriend), Bill Speed (Auctioneer), Amber Styles (Woman in Underpass)

HALFMOON (First Run Features) Directors/Producers/Screenplay, Frieder Schlaich, Irene von Alberti; Photography, Volker Tittel; Editors, Magdolna Rokop, Margarete Rose; Music, Roman Bunka; Art Director, Harald Turzer; Costumes, Anne Schlaich; Produced for Filmgalerie 451 in association with Filmforderung Baden-Wurtemberg, Hamburger Filmburo, Filmburo NW; German; Dolby Stereo; Color; Not rated; 90 minutes; January release. CAST: Samir Guesmi (Lachen), Khaled Ksouri (Idir), Sondos Belhassen (Girl), Veronica Quilligan (Woman), Sam Cox (Man), Said Zakir (Allal), Mohammed Belfquih (Old Man), Paul Bowles (Narrator)

THE SEXUAL LIFE OF THE BELGIANS (First Run Features) Producer/Director/Screenplay, Jan Bucquoy; Executive Producer, Francoise Hoste; Photography, Michel Baudour; Designer, Nathalie Andre; Editor, Matyas Veress; a Transatlantic Films production; Belgian; Agfacolor; Not rated; 80 minutes; January release. CAST: Jean-Henri Compere (Jan Bucquoy), Noe Francq (Jan as a Child), Isabelle Legros (Noella Bucquoy), Sophie Schneider (Therese), Pascale Binneri (Ariane Bucquoy), Michele Shor (Aunt Martha), Dorothee Capelluto (Mia)

EGON SCHIELE: EXCESS AND PUNISHMENT (Independent/Film Forum) Producer, Dieter Giessler; Director/Screenplay, Herbert Vesely; Photography, Rudolf Blahacek; Music, Brian Eno, Anton von Webern, Felix Mendelssohn-Bartholdy; German-Austrian, 1980; Color; Not rated; 90 minutes; January release. CAST: Mathieu Carriérc (Egon Schiclc), Jane Birkin (Vally), Christine Kaufmann (Edith), Marcel Ophuls (Dr. Stovel), Nina Fallenstein (Runaway)

VUKOVAR (Tara) Producer, Danka Muzdeka Mandzuka; Director, Boro Draskovic; Screenplay, Maja Draskovic, Boro Draskovic; Photography, Aleksandar Petkovic; Editor, Snezana Ivanovic; Executive Producer, Steven North; Art Director, Miodrag Maric; Serbo-Croatian; Color; Not rated; 94 minutes; February release. CAST: Mirjana Jokovic (Anna), Boris Isakovic (Toma), Monica Romic (Ratka), Nebojsa Glogovac (Fadil), Svetlana Bojkovic (Vilma), Predrag Ejdus (Stjepan), Dusica Zegarac (Vera), Mihajlo Janketic (Dusan)

HEIDI FLEISS HOLLYWOOD MADAM (Lafayette) Producer/Director, Nick Broomfield; Co-Producers, Jamie Ader-Brown, Kahane Corn; Photography, Paul Kloss; Editor, S.J. Bloom; Music, David Bergeaud; Produced in association with In Pictures/Canadian Broadcasting Corp./Cinemax/Westdeutscher Rundfunk Köln; British-Canadian-German; Color; Not rated; 107 minutes; February release. Documentary on Heidi Fleiss who ran a call-girl operation from Beverly Hills, with appearances by Heidi Fleiss, Ivan Nagy, Madam Alex, Victoria Sellers, Cookie, Daryl Gates, L'Hua Reid

Agathe Cornez, Jean-Henri Compere in *The Sexual Life of the Belgians*
© First Run Features

Heidi Fleiss in *Heidi Fleiss: Hollywood Madam*
© Lafayette

Leon Schuster, John Matshikiza in *Yankee Zulu*
© CFP Distribution

YANKEE ZULU (CFP) Producer, Andre Scholtz; Executive Producer, Edgar Bold; Co-Producers, Leon Schuster, Carl Fischer; Director, Gray Hofmeyer; Screenplay, Leon Schuster, Gray Hofmeyer; Story, Leon Schuster; Photography, James Robb; Designers, Jon Jon Lambon, Robert van de Coolwijk; Music, Stanislas Syrewicz; Editors, Johan Lategan, Tiny Laubscher, Gerri Van Wyk, Alastair Henderson; a Toron Screen Corporation/Koukus Troika production; South African; Color; Rated PG; 87 minutes; February release. CAST: Leon Schuster (Rhino Labushchange), John Matshikiza (Zulu Rakabela), Wilson Dunster (Diehard), Terri Treas (Rowena), Michelle Bowes (Tienkie)

TARGET (Filmopolis) Director, Sandip Ray; Screenplay, Satyajit Ray; Based on the novel *Manusher Juddha* by Prafulla Roy; Photography, Barun Raha; Editor, Dulal Dutt; Indian, 1995; Color; Not rated; 122 minutes; February release. CAST: Om Puri (Bharosa), Mohan Agashe (Singh), Champa Islam (Bijri), Anjan Srivastava (Choubey), Jhanesh Mukherjee (Rampear), Baroon Chakraborty (Chaupatial)

Caridad Ravelo, Y Luisito Marti in *Nueba Yol*
© Kit Parker Films

NUEBA YOL (Kit Parker Films) Producers, Carlota Carretero, Joseph Medina; Producer/Director/Screenplay, Angel Muniz; Photography, Christopher Norr; Editor, Robinson Perez; Music, Pengbian Sang; Color; Not rated; 104 minutes; February release. CAST: Luisito Marti (Balbuena), Caridad Ravelo (Nancy), Rafael Villalona (Pedro), Raul Carbonell (Fellito), Joel Garcia (Pancho), Alfonso Zayas (Chef)

SHOPPING (Concorde-New Horizons) Producer, Jeremy Bolt; Director/Screenplay, Paul Anderson; Photography, Tony Imi; Designer, Max Gottlieb; Editor, David Stiven; Music, Barrington Pheloung; Casting, Jane Frisby; British; Color; Rated R; 87 minutes; February release. CAST: Sadie Frost (Jo), Jude Law (Billy), Sean Pertwee (Tommy), Fraser James (Be Bop), Sean Bean (Venning), Marianne Faithful (Bev), Jonathan Pryce (Conway), Danny Newman (Monkey), Lee Whitlock (Pony), Ralph Ineson (Dix), Eammon Walker (Peters)

CROWS (New Yorker) Director/Screenplay, Dorota Kedzierzawska; Photography, Arthur Reinhart; Set Designer, Magdalena Kujszczuk; Editors, Dorota Kedzierzawska, Arthur Reinhart; Music, Wiodek Pawlik; from Studio Filowe "Oko" and Telewizja Polska (Polish Television TVP); Polish; Color; Not rated; 66 minutes; March release. CAST: Karolina Ostronzna (Wrona), Kasia Szczepanik (Malenstwo), Malgorzata Hajewska (Matka Wrony), Anna Prucnal (Nauczycielka), Ewa Bukowska (Matka Malenstwa), Krzysztof Grabarczyk (Ojciec Malenstwa), Agneiszka Pilaszewska (Matka Piotrusia), Antoni Majak (Starszy Pan), Paul Verkade (Cudzoziemiec), Bartek Topa (Policjant), Marek Bukowski (Pan Mlody), Katarzyna Gajewska (Piekareczka), Kazimierz Rabsky (Mezczyzna)

Danny Newman, Sadie Frost, Jude Law, Fraser James in *Shopping*
© New Horizons Pictures

THE STAR MAKER (Miramax) Producers, Vittorio & Rita Cecchi Gori; Executive Producer, Mario Cotone; Director/Story, Giuseppe Tornatore; Screenplay, Giuseppe Tornatore, Fabio Rinaudo; Photography, Dante Spinotti; Designer, Francesco Bronzi; Costumes, Beatrice Bordone; Editor, Massimo Quaglia; Music, Ennio Morricone; a Mario & Vittorio Cecchi Gori presentation; Italian, 1995; Dolby Digital Stereo; Panavision; Color; Rated R; 113 minutes; March release. CAST: Sergio Castellitto (Joe Morelli), Tiziana Lodato (Beata), Franco Scaldati (Brigadiere Mastropaolo), Leopoldo Trieste (Mute), Clelia Rondinella (Anna's Mother), Tano Cimarosa (Grandpa Bordonaro), Nicola DiPinto (Communal Functionary), Constantino Carrozza (The Collector), Jane Alexander (Princess), Tony Sperandeo (1st Baldalamenti), Leo Gullotta (Vito), Luigi Maria Burruano (Flirtatious Client), Carmelo Di Mazzarelli (Old Man in Wheelchair), Marzio Onorato (Architect Panebianco), Antonella Attili (Nurse), Domenico Dolce (Peasant on Bus), Stefano Gabana (Photographer on Bus), Maria Rosa Parrello (Santina), Rita Lia (Pinuccia), Vincent Navarra (Shepherd), Alessandro Guarrera (Clapboard Kid), Spiro Scimone, Francesco Serameli (Nasca Brothers), Tony Palazzo (Pio Li Fusi), Mimmo Gennaro, Emilio Scimone (Mafioso), Massimo Pupella (Bordonaro Jr.), Giorgio Guerrieri (Cinema Cashier), Salvatore Billa (Prince), Peppino Tornatore (Dottore Mistretta), Filippo Tarantino (2nd Badalamenti), Onofrio Ducato (Mafia Boss Realzisa), Paolo Noto (Zu' Leonardo)

Clelia Rondinella, Sergio Castellito in *The Star Maker*
© Miramax Films

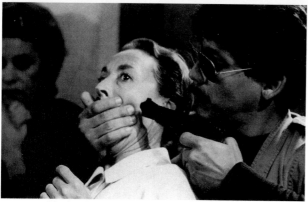
Vernica Oddo, Mirta Ibarra in *Knocks at My Door*
© International Film Circuit

KNOCKS AT MY DOOR (International Film Circuit) Producer/Director, Alejandro Saderman; Executive Producer, Antonio Lierandi; Screenplay, Juan Carlos Gene; Photography, Adriano Moreno; Music, Julio D'Escrivan; Editor, Claudia Uribe; Venezuelan, 1993; Color; Not rated; 105 minutes; March release. CAST: Vernica Oddo (Sister Ana), Elba Escobar (Sister Ursula), Juan Carlos Gene (Mayor), Jose Antonio Rodriguez (Monsignor), Frank Spano (Pablo, the Fugitive), Ana Castell (Severa, the Widow), Mirta Ibarra (Amanda, the Nasty Neighbor), Eduardo Gil (Father Emilio), Dimas Gonzalez (Captain Torres)

INSTITUTE BENJAMENTA (Zeitgeist) Producers, Keith Griffiths, Janine Marmont; Director, The Brothers Quay; Screenplay, Alan Passes, The Brothers Quay; Based on the novella *Jakob von Gunten* and other texts by Robert Walser; Photography, Nic Knowland; Editor, Larry Sider; Designer, Jennifer Kernke; Music, Lech Jankowski; a Koninck production; British; Color; Not rated; 105 minutes; March release. CAST: Alice Krige (Lisa Benjamenta), Gottfried John (Herr Benjamenta), Mark Rylance (Jakob von Gunten), Daniel Smith (Kraus)

Alice Krige in *Institute Benjamenta*
©Zeitgeist

ALL THINGS FAIR (PFM) Producer, Per Holst; Director/Screenplay/Editor, Bo Widerberg; Photography, Morten Bruus; Designer, Palle Arestrup; a Per Holst Film Production; Swedish-Danish, 1995; Dolby Stereo; Color; Not rated; 128 minutes; March release. CAST: Johan Widerberg (Stig), Marika Lagercrantz (Viola), Tomas von Bromssen (Frank), Karin Huldt (Lisbet), Bjorn Kjellman (Sigge), Kenneth Milldoff (Stig's Father), Nina Gunke (Stig's Mother), Jossi Sabbah (Isse), Linus Eriksson (Peter), Magnus Andersson ("Sleepy"), Frida Lindholm (Olga)

LITTLE INDIAN, BIG CITY (Touchstone) Producers, Louis Becker, Thierry Lhermitte; Director, Hervé Palud; Screenplay, Hervé Palud, Igor Aptekman; Adapted for the screen by Hervé Palud, Thierry Lhermitte, Philippe Bruneau; Photography, Fabio Conversi; Designer, Ivan Maussion; Editor, Roland Baubeau; Costumes, Martine Rapin; Casting, Mamade, Carlos Reyes; an Ice Films/TF1 Films production with the participation of Canal+ and Procirep; Distributed by Buena Vista Pictures; French (dubbed in English), 1994; Dolby Stereo; Technicolor; Rated PG; 90 minutes; March release. CAST: Thierry Lhermitte (Stephan Marchado), Patrick Timsit (Richard), Ludwig Briand (Mimi-Siku), Miou Miou (Patricia), Arielle Dombasle (Charlotte), Sonia Vollereaux (Marie), Tolsty (Pavel), Jackie Berroyer (Jonavisky), Marc De Jonge (Rossberg), Louba Guertchikoff (Mrs. Godette), Philippe Bruneau (Mr. Marshal), Dominique Besnehard (Master Dong), Cheik Doukoure (Mr. Bonaventure), Marie-Charlotte Leclaire (Rossberg's Secretary), Olga Jirouskova (Sonia Koutchnoukov), Chick Ortega (Russian), Paco Portero (The Snake Man), Sonia Lezinska (Stewardess), Marc Brunet, Olivier Hemon (Policemen), Thierry Desroses (Customs Officer), Katia Weitzenbock (Miss Van Hodden), Feliciano Tello Rossi (Chief Mouloukou), Maurice Illouz (Man in Airplane), Suzy Marquis (Woman in Building), Carlos Reyes (Mailman in the Amazon), Richard Holzle (Man with Canoe), Christian Roy (Missile Technician), Jean-Pierre Richette (Man at the Red Light), Pauline Pinsolle (Sophie), Stanley Zana (Jonathan), Gaston Dolle (Benjamin)

Ludwig Briand in *Little Indian, Big City*
© Ice Films- TFI Films

NEUROSIA: 50 YEARS OF PERVERSITY (First Run Features) Producer/Director, Rosa von Praunheim; Screenplay, Valentin Passoni; Photography, Lorenz Haarmann; Editor, Mike Shepard; Music, Alexander Kraut; Art Director, Volker Marz; German; Color; Not rated; 89 minutes; April release. CAST: Desiree Nick, Lotti Huber, Evelyn Kunneke, Luzi Kryn, Eva Ebner, Friedrich Steinhauer, Gertrud Mischwitzky, Ichgola Androgyn

RUDE (Alliance) Producers, Damon D'Oliveira, Karen A. King; Director/Screenplay, Clement Virgo; Photography, Barry Stone; Editor, Susan Maggi; Music, Aaron Davis; from KJM3 Entertainment Group; Canadian; Color; Not rated; 89 minutes; April release. CAST: Maurice Dean Wint (The General), Rachael Crawford (Maxine), Clark Johnson (Reece), Richard Chevoileau (Jordan), Sharon M. Lewis (Rude), Melanie Nicholls-King (Jessica), Stephen Shellen (Yankee), Ashley Brown (Johnny), Gordon Michael Volvett, Dayo Ade, Dean Marshal, Andy Marshall, Falconer Abraham, Junior Williams, Andrew Moodie, Nicole Parker, Michael Greyeyes, Ramiah Hylton, Xuan Fraser, Thomas Mitchell, Joel Gordon, Danny Ho

2 FRIENDS (Milestone Films) Producer, Jan Chapman; Director, Jane Campion; Screenplay, Helen Garner; Photography, Julian Penney; Music, Martin Armiger; Editor, Bill Russo; Australian, 1986; Color; Not rated; 76 minutes; April release. CAST: Emma Coles (Louise), Kris Bidenko (Kelly), Kris McQuade (Janet), Stephen Leeder (Jim), Debra May (Chris)

IN A STRANGE CITY (Filmopolis) Producer, Li-kong Hsu; Director/Editor, Chi Yin; Screenplay, Wen-tsai Dai, Chi Yin; Photography, Suki Medencevic; Music, Paul McCarty; a Central Motion Picture presentation; Taiwanese; Color; Not rated; 100 minutes; April release. CAST: Kuei-mei Yang (Jane Yu), Winston Chao (Xiang Guo-chien), Angela Chang (Nan-nan), Guo-Chu Chang (Lao Kai)

Oliver Milburn in *Loaded*
© Miramax Films

GHOST IN THE SHELL (Manga Entertainment) Producers, Yoshimasa Mizuo, Shigeru Watanabe, Ken Iyadomi, Mitsunisu Ishikawa; Director/Screenplay, Kazunori Ito; Original Story and Comic, Masamune Shirow; Animation Director, Toshiluko Nishikubo; Designer, Takashi Watanabe; Character Design, Keisuke Okiura; Japanese; Dolby Stereo; Color; Not rated; 82 minutes; April release. Animated

LOADED (Miramax) Producers, David Hazlett, Caroline Hewitt, Bridget Ikin, John Maynard; Executive Producer, Ben Gibson; Director/Screenplay, Anna Campion; Photography, Alan Almond; Designer, Alistair Kay; Editor, John Gilbert; Music, Simon Fisher Turner; Costumes, Stewart Meacham; Casting, John & Ros Hubbard; British-New Zealand, 1994; Dolby Digital Sound; Color; Rated R ; 105 minutes; April release. CAST: Oliver Milburn (Neil), Nick Patrick (Giles), Catherine McCormick (Rose), Thandie Newton (Zita), Mathew Eggleton (Lionel), Danny Cunningham (Lance), Biddy Hodson (Charlotte), Dearbhla Molloy (Ava), Caleb Lloyd (Young Neil), Joe Gecks (Brother on Bike), Bridget Brammall (Shop Assistant), Tom Welsh (Skinhead)

MADAME BUTTERFLY (Sony Classical) Producers, Daniel Toscan Du Plantier, Pierre-Olivier Bardet; Director, Frédéric Mitterrand; Photography, Philippe Welt; Costumes, Christian Gasc; Editor, Luc Barnier; Set Designer, Michelle Abbe-Vannier; from Erato Films/Ideale Audience/In Corporation with Imalyre-Vtcom/France Telecom/France 3 Cinema/Sony Classical, with the participation of Canal+/BBC/ZDF/S4C/Centre National de la Cinématographie; presented by Martin Scorsese; French-British; Dolby Digital Stereo; Panavision; Color; Not rated; 129 minutes; May release. CAST: Ying Huang (Cio-Cio-San), Ning Liang (Suzuki), Richard Troxell (Pinkerton), Richard Cowan (Sharpless), Jing-Ma Fan (Goro), Constance Hauman (Kate Pinkerton), Christopheren Nomura (Prince Yamadori)

RichardTtroxell, Ying Huang in *Madame Butterfly*
© Sony Classical

UNDER THE DOMIM TREE (Strand) Producers, Gila Almagor, Eitan Evan; Director, Eli Cohen; Screenplay, Gila Almagor, Eyal Sher, Eli Cohen; Photography, David Gurfinkel; Editor, Danny Shik; Music, Benny Nagari; Israeli; Dolby Stereo; Color; Not rated; 102 minutes; May release. CAST: Kaipo Cohen (Aviya), Gila Almagor (Aviya's Mother), Riki Blich (Mira), Orli Perl (Yola), Ohad Knoller (Yurek), Jeniya Catzan (Ze'evik)

Gila Almagor, Kaipo Cohen in *Under the Domim Tree*
© Strand Releasing

KILLING GRANDPA (Tara) Executive Producer, Pablo Rovito; Director/Editor, Luis César D'Angiolillo; Screenplay, Eduardo Mignona, Ariel Sienra, César D'Angiolillo; Based on an original idea by Ariel Sienra, César D'Angiolillo; Photography, Miguel Abal; Costumes, Cristina Tavano; an Aura Productions S.R.L.-Kankun S.A.-TVE production; Argentine; Fujicolor; Not rated; 114 minutes; May release. CAST: Federico Luppi (Don Mariano Aguero), Inés Estevez (Rosita), Alberto Segado (Fernando), Mirta Busnelli (Amelita), Atilio Vernoelli (Marcelo), Laura Novoa (Fabiana), Lidia Catalano (Deolinda), Horacio Peña (Jeff), Emilio Bardi (Ramón), Tina Serrano (Sister Matilde), Cecilia Etchegaray (Sabina), Maria Lorenzuti (Coca), Gustavo del Solar (Deolinda's Son), Roberto Berkunski (Dr. Kramer), Carlos Catalano (Father Estrada), Alicia Seguí (Alicia)

ASHES OF TIME (HKFM) Director/Screenplay, Wong Kare Wai; Cantonese; Color; Not rated; 100 minutes; May release. CAST: Leslie Cheung (Ouyang Feng), Tony Leung, Kar-fai, Brigitte Lin, Maggie Cheung

Frederico Luppi, Inés Estevez in *Killing Grandpa*
© Tara Releasing

THE MAN BY THE SHORE (KJM3) Producer, Pascal Verroust; Director/Screenplay, Raoul Peck; Photography, Armand Marco; Designer, Gilles Aird; Editor, Jacques Comets; Music, Amos Coulanges, Dominique Dejean; Haitian/Creole; Color; Not rated; 106 minutes; May release. CAST: Jennifer Zubar (Sarah), Toto Bissainthe (Grand-mére), Jean-Michel Martial (Janvier), Patrick Rameau (Sorel)

Falaba Issa Traore in *Guimba the Tyrant*
© Kino Intl.

GUIMBA THE TYRANT (Kino) Executive Producers, Idrissa Ouedraogo, Sophie Salbot; Director/Screenplay, Cheick Oumar Sissoko; Photography, Lionel Cousin; Editors, Kahena Attia, Joelle Dufour; Music, Pierre Sauvageot, Michel Risse; a Kora Films/Les Films de la Plaine/Mali National Center for Film Production/Direction of Film Production of Burkina Faso and W.D.R. production; Mali-Burkina Faso-France/Bambara-Peul; Color; Not rated; 93 minutes; May release. CAST: Falaba Issa Traore (Guimba), Lamine Diallo (Janguiné), Mouneissa Maiga (Kani), Héléne Diarra (Meya), Bala Moussa Keita (Mambi), Habib Dembele (Sambou, the Griot), Fatoumata Coulibaly (Sadio), Cheick Oumar Meiga (Siriman)

CARPATI: 50 MILES, 50 YEARS (Artistic License) Producers, David Notowitz, Yale Strom; Director/Screenplay/Music, Yale Strom; Photography/Editor, David Notowitz; Narrator, Leonard Nimoy; Color; Not rated; 80 minutes; May release. Documentary on Zev Godinger, a Carpathian Jew, and Auschwitz survivor

BILLY'S HOLIDAY (Miramax) Producers, Tristram Miall, Denis Whitburn; Director, Richard Wherrett; Screenplay, Denis Whitburn; Photography, Roger Lanser; Designer, Michael Scott-Mitchell; Editor, Sue Blainey; Music, Peter Cobbin; Costumes, Terry Ryan; Choreographer, Kim Walker; Australian; Color; Rated R; 93 minutes; May release. CAST: Max Cullen (Billy Apples), Kris McQuade (Kate Hammond), Tina Bursill (Louise), Drew Forythe (Sid Banks), Genevieve Lemon (Julie), Richard Roxburgh (Rob McSpedden), Rachel Coopes (Casey Appleby), Julie Haseler (Ricki Patterson), Maggie Kirkpatrick (Mauren O'Hara), Gary Scale (Reg Conroy), Arianthe Galani (Anna), Peter Colligwood (Anna's Gentleman), Stuart Nicholls (Gibson), Dylan Walters (Mack), Laurence Clifford (Jack), Sacher Horler (Kristin), Jade Gatt (Alex), Maryanne Puntoriero (Melody), Bridget Glover (Lady Day), Jeanette Cronin (Roz "Shutterbug"), Stuart Campbell (Kevin Freckle), Guntis Sics (Record Engineer), Paul Goddard (Gary "Stylist"), Lori Vallins, Sally Patience (Backing Singers), Phillip Scott ("Liberace")

Max Cullen (c) in Billy's Holiday
© Miramax Films

He Saifei, Wang Zhiwen in *Blush*
© First Run Features

THE PATRIOTS (Gaumont BVI) Producer, Xavier Amblard; Executive Producers, Katriel Schory, Gene Rosow; Director/Screenplay, Eric Rochant; Photography, Pierre Novion; Editor, Pascale Fenouillet; Music, Gerard Torikian; a Les Prods. Lazennec production with Gaumont/SFP Cinema/Glem Films, with the participation of Canal+; French; Dolby Stereo; Color; Not rated; 144 minutes; May release. CAST: Yvan Attal (Ariel), Yossi Banai (Yossi), Sandrine Kiberlain (Marie Claude), Richard Masur (Jeremy Pelman), Nancy Allen (Catherine Pelman), Allen Garfield (Eagleman)

BLUSH (First Run Features) Producers, Chen Kunming, Jimmy Tan; Executive Producer, Cheng Zhigu; Director, Li Shaohong; Screenplay, Ni Zhen, Li Shaohong; Based on the novel by Su Tong; Photography, Zeng Nianping; Editor, Zhou Xinxia; Music, Guo Wenjing; an Ocean Film Co., Ltd. presentation in association with Beijing Film Studio; Chinese-Hong Kong/Cantonese; Color; Not rated; 119 minutes; June release. CAST: Wang Ji (Qiuyi), Wang Zhiwen (Lao Pu), He Saifei (Xiao'e), Zhang Liwei (Liu Qing), Wang Rouli (Mrs. Pu), Song Xiuling (Ruifeng), Xing Yangchun (Mr. Zhang), Zhou Jianying (Mrs. Zhang), Yin Jimei (Wu Ma), Gu Zhifen (Aunt), Zhu Jiyong (Feng Lao Wu)

Andre Eisermann (hands raised) in *Kaspar Hauser*
© Leisure Time Features

KASPAR HAUSER (Leisure Time) Producer, Andreas Meyer; Director/Screenplay, Peter Sehr; Photography, Gernot Roll; Editor, Susanne Hartmann; Art Directors, O. Jochen Schmidt, Karel Vacek; Costumes, Dietmut Remy; German; Color; Not rated; 137 minutes; June release. CAST: Andre Eisermann (Kaspar Hauser), Katharina Thalbach (Countess Hochberg), Uwe Ochsenknecht (Ludwig of Baden), Udo Samel (Professor Daumer), Jeremy Clyde (Lord Stanhope), Hansa Czypionka (Hennehofer), Hermann Beyer (Anselm Ritter von Feurbach), Cecile Paoli (Stephanie of Baden)

MAGIC HUNTER (Low Distribution) Producers, Andras Hamori, Wieland Schulz-Keil; Director, Ildikó Enyedi; Screenplay, Ildikó Enyedi, László Lászlo Révész; Executive Producers, Susan Cavan, David Bowie, Robert D. Goodale; Photography, Tibor Máthé; Editor, Mária Rigó; Designer, Attila Ferenczfy-Kovács; an Alliance International release of an Accent/Gargantua Motion Pictures presentation; Presented by David Bowie; Hungarian; Color; Not rated; 106 minutes; June release. CAST: Gary Kemp (Max), Sadie Frost (Eva), Alexander Kaidanovsky (Maxim), Péter Vallai (Kaspar), Mathias Gnädinger (Police Chief), Alexandra Wasscher (Lili), Ildikó Tóth (Lina), Natalie Condé (The Virgin Mary), Zoltán Gera (Shoemaker), Philippe Duclos (Monk), Andor Lukáts (One-Eyed Monk), György Bárdy (Theologian), Eszter Csákányi (Nanny), Tibor Bitskey (Surgeon)

Gary Kemp, Sadie Frost in *Magic Hunter*
© Alliance

VIVE L'AMOUR (Strand) Producer, Hsu Li-kong; Executive Producer, Kiang Feng-chyi; Director, Tsai Ming-liang; Photography, Liao Pen-jung; Editor, Sung Shin-cheng; a Central Motion Pictures Corporation production; Taiwanese; Color; Not rated; 118 minutes; June release. CAST: Yang Kuei-mei (May), Chen Chao-jung (An-jung), Lee Kang-sheng (Hsiao-kang)

WHO KILLED PASOLINI? (Roxie Releasing) Producers, Vittorio & Rita Cecchi Gori, Claudio Bonivento; Director, Marco Tullio Giordana; Screenplay/Story, Marco Tullio Giordana, Stefano Rulli, Sandro Petraglia; Based on the book *Vita di Pasolini* by Enzo Siciliano; Photography, Franco Lecca; Music, Ennio Morricone; Italian-French; Color; Not rated; 100 minutes; July release. CAST: Carlo De Filippi (Pino Pelosi), Nicoletta Braschi (Graziella Chiarcossi), Toni Bertorelli (Inspector Pigna), Giulio Scarpati (Nino Marazzita), Andrea Occhipinti (Furio Columbo), Victor Cavallo (Antonio Pelosi)

WAR STORIES OUR MOTHERS NEVER TOLD US (First Run Features) Producer/Director, Gaylene Preston; Executive Producer, Robin Laing; Photography, Alun Bollinger; Editor, Paul Sutorius; Music, Jonathan Besser; a Gaylene Preston Productions presentation, produced in association with The New Zealand Film Commission and New Zealand on

Alfred Molina, Marianne Faithful, Rachael Bella in *When Pigs Fly*
© Panorama Entertainment

Air; New Zealand; Dolby Stereo; Color; Not rated; 95 minutes; June release. Documentary in which seven New Zealand women reminisce about how World War II effected their lives; with Pamela Quill, Flo Small, Tui Preston, Jean Andrews, Rita Graham, Neva Clarke McKenna and Mabel Waititi, interviewed by Judith Fyfe.

BYE BYE (Turbulent Arts) Producer, Alain Rozanes; Director/Screenplay, Karim Dridi; Photography, John Mathieson; Editor, Lise Beaulieu; Music, Steve Shean, Jimmy Oihid; Art Director, Gilles Bontemps; an ADR Prods. presentation of a Diaphana release of a Thelam Films/CMC/La Sept Cinema/La SNC production, with participation of Canal+ and Procirep; French; Dolby Stereo; Color; Not rated; 107 minutes; July release. CAST: Sami Bouajila (Ismaël), Nozha Khouadra (Yasmine), Ouassini Embarek (Mouloud), Philippe Ambrosini (Ludo), Frédéric Andrau (Jacky), Sofiane Mammeri (Rhida), Moussa Maaskri (Renard), Jamila Darwich-Farah (The Aunt)

WHEN PIGS FLY (Panorama) Producer, Kees Kasander; Executive Producers, Jim Jarmusch, Denis Wigman; Director, Sara Driver; Screenplay, Ray Dobbins; Photography, Robby Müller; Editor, Jay Rabinowitz; Music, Joe Strummer; a Nippon Film and Development Finance Inc. and Sumitomo Corp. presentation; Japanese-German-British; Color; Not rated; 94 minutes; July release. CAST: Alfred Molina (Marty), Marianne Faithfull (Lilly), Seymour Cassel (Frank), Rachael Bella (Ruthie), Maggie O'Neill (Sheila), Freddie Brooks (Stretch), Matyelok Gibbs (Mrs. Cleary), Carl Dennie (Tony), Tarzan (Dolphy the Dog)

JOHNNY SHORTWAVE (Independent/Film Forum) Producers/Screenplay, Michael Bockner, Peter Boboras; Director/Editor, Michael Bockner; Photography, Rick Fester, Andreas Trauttmansdorff; Music, Joel Rosenbaum; Canadian; Color; Not rated; 92 minutes; July release. CAST: Emmanuel Mark (Johnny Shortwave/John Howard Clayton), John Tench (The Photographer), Mona Matteo (Wilma Clayton), Dougie Richardson (Cosmo Unitas)

Lee Kang-Sheng in *Vive L'Amour*
© Strand Releasing

Emmanuel Mark in
Johnny Shortwave

THE GREEN HOUSE (Castle Hill) Producers, Harold Reichebner, Alain Clert, Yves Pasquier; Director, Philippe De Broca; Screenplay, Philippe De Broca, Alexandre Jardin; Photography, Janos Kende; Designer, Francois De Lamothe; Music, Charles Court; French; Dolby Stereo; Color; Not rated; 93 minutes; August release. CAST: Claude Rich (Fernand Bornard), Salomee Stevenin (Philippine Bornard), Catherine Jacob (Micheline), Rose Thiery (Jeanne), Samuel Labarthe (Armand), Gert Burkhard (Wenders)

MABOROSI (Milestone) Producer, Naoe Gozu; Executive Producer, Yutaka Shigenobu; Director, Hirokazu Kore-eda; Screenplay, Yoshihisa Ogita; Based on the story *Maborosi no Hikari* by Teru Miyamoto; Photography, Masao Nakabori; Music, Chen Ming-Chang; Japanese; Color; Not rated; 110 minutes; September release. CAST: Makiko Esumi (Yumiko), Takasi Naitoh (Tamio), Tadanobu Asano (Ikuo), Gohki Kashiyama (Yuichi), Naomi Watanabe (Tomoko), Midori Kiuchi (Michiko), Akira Emoto (Yoshihiro), Mutsuko Sakura (Tomeno), Hidekazu Akai (Master), Hiromi Ichida (Hatsuko), Minori Terada (Detective), Ren Ohsugi (Hiroshi), Kikuko Hasimoto (Kiyo)

Claude Rich, Salomee Stevenin in *The Green House*
© Castle Hill Productions

HIGHWAY OF HEARTACHE (Scorn-a-Rama Pictures) Producer/Director/Screenplay, Gregory Wild; Photography, Brian Pearson; Editor, Reginald Dean Harkema; Music, Barbara Chamberlin; Designers, Gregory Wild, Darcy Wild; Costumes/Wigs, Druh Ireland, Dean Ryane; Canadian; Color; Not rated; 86 minutes; September release. CAST: Barbara Chamberlin (Wynona-Sue Turnpike), Pat Patterson (Crawfish Crenshaw), Serge Houde, Klaus Kohlmeyer, Sean Pritchard, Willie Taylor, Dusty Ryane, Christy Russell, Manfred Janssen, Sidney Morozoff, Jana White, the Big Wigs

ERNESTO "CHE" GUEVARA: THE BOLIVIAN DIARY (Film Forum/Independent) Director/Screenplay, Richard Dindo; Photography, Pio Corradi; Editors, Richard Dindo, Georg Janett, Catherine Poitevin; Narrator, Judith Burnett; Produced by Cine-Manufacture/Les Films d'Ici; French-Swiss; Color; Not rated; 94 minutes; September release.

Makiko Esumi, Tadanobu Asano in *Maborosi*
© Milestone Film & Video

Predictions of Fire
© Kinetikon Pictures

Documentary on Che Guevara's attempts to forment revolution in Bolivia, featuring Robert Kramer as the voice of Che

PREDICTIONS OF FIRE (Artistic License) Producer/Director/Screenplay, Michael Benson; Photography, Teodoro Maniaci; Editor, Nika Lah; Music, Laibach; Narrator, Matej Russ; a TV Slovenia Arts Programs Production with Kinetikon Pictures; Slovenian; Black & white/color; Not rated; 90 minutes; October release. Documentary on the political and artistic history of Slovenia

NIKI DE SAINT PHALLE: WHO IS THE MONSTER—YOU OR ME? (Independent Film Forum) Producer/Director/Screenplay, Peter Schamoni; Narration/Scenery, Niki de Saint Phalle; Photography, Michael Bartlett, Rodger Hinrichs, Ernst Hirsch, Bernard Zitzermann, Francois de Menil, Peter Whitehead; German-Swiss; Color; Not rated; 93 minutes; October release. Documentary on French-American artist Niki de Saint Phalle, with excerpts from her own experimental films including *Daddy* and *A Dream: Longer Than the Night*

BIRD OF PREY (Northern Arts) Producers, Boyan Milushev, Jonathan Debin; Co-Producer, Lynette Prucha; Executive Producer, Steven J. Wolfe; Director, Temistocles Lopez; Screenplay, Boyan Milushev, James J. Mellon, Tracy Hall Adams, Lynette Prucha; a BM 5 Film Production and Sneak Preview Productions presentation in association with First Private Bank (Sofia, Bulgaria); Bulgarian-U.S.; Color; Rated R ; 105 minutes; October release. CAST: Jennifer Tilly (Kily Griffith), Boyan Milushev (Nick Milev), Lenny Von Dohlen (Johnny), Richard Chamberlain (John Griffith), Lesley Ann Warren (Carla Carr), Robert Carradine

Richard Chamberlain in *Bird of Prey*
© Northern Arts

Miguel Gutiérrez, René Lavan, Larry Villanueva in Bitter Sugar
© Overseas Filmgroup

BITTER SUGAR (First Look Pictures) Producers, Leon Ichaso, Jaime Pina, Lisa Rhoden; Director, Leon Ichaso; Screenplay, Leon Ichaso, Orestes Matacena; Story, Leon Ichaso, Pelayo Garcia; Executive Producer, Pelayo Garcia; Photography, Claudio Chea; Edtior, Yvette Pineyro; Music, Manuel Tejada; Designer, Lilian Soto; an Azucar Films S.A. production; Cuban; Dolby Stereo; Color; Not rated; 102 minutes; October release. CAST: Rene Lavan (Gustavo), Mayte Vilan (Yolanda), Miguel Guitierrez (Dr. Tomas Valdez), Larry Villanueva (Bobby), Luis Celeiro (Mr. Garcia), Teresa Maria Rojas (Belkis), Orestes Matacena (Claudio), Caridad Ravelo (Soraya), Jorge Pupo (Yiyo), Augusto Feria (Security—Hotel), Felix German (Security Guard—Beach)

CURTIS'S CHARM (Strand) Producer, Sandra Cunningham; Executive Producers, Atom Egoyan, Patricia Rozema; Director/Screenplay, John L'Ecuyer; Based on a story by Jim Carroll; Photography, Harald Bachmann; Designer, John Dondertman; Editor, Craig Webster; Music, Mark Korven; Costumes, Beth Pasternak; Canadian; Color; Not rated; 74 minutes; October release. CAST: Maurice Dean Wint (Curtis), Callum Keith Rennie (Jim), Rachael Crawford (Cookie), Barbara Barnes-Hopkins (Voodoo Ma), Aron Tager (Park Worker), Hugh Dillon (Spitting White Trash Thug), Trent Carr, Dale Harrison (Thugs), Brian Clancy (The Killer), John Dondertman (Furry Pimp), Bruce McDonald (Man in Restaurant), Bruno Bryniarski (Dealer), Mary Sylwester (Hooker), KEi, Trevor Black (Junkies), Mina Mushtaghi (Teen), Guy Sanvido (Patron), Conrod Ciandre (Afro Junkie), Ross Redfern (Exiting Man)

THE CHAMPAGNE SAFARI (First Run Features) Producer/Director, George Ungar; Executive Producer, John Walker; Screenplay, Steve Lucas, John Kramer, Harold Crooks; Photography, Floyd Crosby, Kirk Tougas, Douglas Kiefer, Ray Dumas, Susan Gourley; Music, Normand Roger, Denis Chartrand; Editor, John Kramer; Canadian; Color; Not rated; 100 minutes; November release. Documentary chronicles the failed 1934 expedition into the Canadian Rockies by millionaire Charles E. Bedaux; featuring Colm Feore (narrator), David Hemblen (voice of Bedaux)

Gard B. Eidsvold, Camilla Martens in *Zero Kelvin*
© Kino Intl.

ANNA (New Yorker) Producers, Nikita Mikhalkov, Michel Seydoux; Director, Nikita Mikhalkov; Screenplay, Nikita Mikhalkov, Sergei Mirochnitchenko; Photography, Pavel Lebechev, Elisbar Karavanev, Vadim Ioussov, Vadim Alissov; Editor, Eleonora Praskina; Music, Edward Artemyev; Russian-French, 1994; Color; Not rated; 100 minutes; November release. Documentary in which filmmaker Nikita Mikhalkov draws parallels to his daughter Anna's development as the Soviet Union crumbled.

NORTH STAR (Regency Enterprises) Producer, Anne Francois; Executive Producer, Christopher Lambert; Director, Nils Gaup; Screenplay, Sergio Donati, Lorenzo Donati, Paul Ohl; Story, Gilles Behat, Philippe Schwartz, Marc Pecase; Based on the novel *The North Star* by Will Henry; Photography, Bruno De Keyzer; Editors, Kant Pan, Michael A. Hoey; Music, Bruce Rowland; an AFCL Prods., M6 and Federal Films co-production, distributed by WB; French-British-Norwegian-Italian; Dolby Stereo; Color; Rated R; 88 minutes; November release. CAST: James Caan (Sean McLennon), Christopher Lambert (Hudson Ipsehawk), Catherine McCormack (Sarah), Burt Young (Reno)

PARIS WAS A WOMAN (Zeitgeist) Producers, Frances Berrigan, Greta Schiller, Andrea Weiss; Executive Producer, Frances Berrigan; Director/Editor, Greta Schiller; Screenplay, Andrea Weiss; Photography, Nurith Aviv, Greta Schiller, Renato Tonelli, Fawn Yacker; Music, Janette Mason; Narrator, Juliet Stevenson; German; Color/black and white; Not rated; 75 minutes; November release. Documentary on such notable women as Gertrude Stein, Janet Flanner, Romaine Brooks, and Alice B. Toklas and their lives as spent in Paris; featuring Gisele Freund, Berthe Cleyrergue, Catharine R. Stimpson, Sam Steward, Shari Benstock

A LEAP OF FAITH (Parallel Lines) Producers, Jenifer McShane, Tricia Regan, Dr. J. Brian Sheehan; Directors, Jenifer McShane, Tricia Regan; Photography, Eugene McVeigh; Editor, Toby Shimin; Narrator, Liam Neeson; Irish ; Color; Not rated; 86 minutes; November release.

BLUE JUICE (Filmopolis) Producers, Peter Salmi, Simon Relph; Director, Carl Prechezer; Screenplay, Carl Prechezer, Peter Salmi; Based on an idea by Peter Salmi, Carl Prechezer, Tim Veglio; Photography, Richard Greatrex; Editor, Michael Ellis; Designer, Mark Tildesley; Music, Simon Davison; a Film Four Intl./Pandora Cinema presentation of a Skreba Film production; British; Color; Not rated; 90 minutes; November release. CAST: Sean Pertwee (JC), Catherine Zeta Jones (Chloe), Steven Mackintosh (Josh Tambini), Ewan McGregor (Dean Raymond), Peter Gunn (Terry Colcott), Heathcote Williams, Colette Brown, Michelle Chadwick, Keith Allen, Robin Soans, Jenny Agutter, Guy Leverton, Mark Frost, Paul Reynolds, Edwin Starr

ZERO KELVIN (Kino) Producer, Bent Rognlien; Executive Producer, Esben Høilund Carlsen; Director, Hans Petter Moland; Screenplay, Lars Bill Lundholm, Hans Petter Moland; Photography, Philip Øgaard; Designer, Janusz Sosnowski; Editor, Einar Egeland; Music, Terje Rypdal; from Norsk Film AS; Norwegian, 1995; Dolby Stereo; Color; Not rated; 113 minutes; November release. CAST: Gard B. Eidsvold (Larsen), Stellan Skarsgard (Randbaek), Bjørn Sundquist (Holm), Camilla Martens (Gertrude), Paul Ottar Haga (Officer), Johannes Joner (Company Man), Erik Øksnes (Captain), Lars Andreas Larssen (Judge), Juni Dahr, Johan Rabaeus (Couple in Park), Frank Iversen (Poetry Buyer), Tinkas Qorfiq (Jane)

ORSON WELLES: THE ONE-MAN BAND (Independent/Film Forum) Producers, Dominique Antoine, Fredy Messmer, Roland Zag; Director, Vassili Silovic; Screenplay, Vassili Silovic, Roland Zag, Oja Kodar; Photography, Thomas Mauch; Editor, Marie-Joséph Yoyotte; Music, Simon Cloquet; German-French-Swiss; Color; Not rated; 90 minutes; December release. Documentary on filmmaker Orson Welles, featuring Oja Kodar

EVA PERON (Aleph Producciones S.A./Argentine Inst. for Cinema) Producer, Hugo Eduardo Lauria; Executive Producer, Maria de la Paz Marino; Director, Juan Carlos Desanzo; Screenplay, Jose Pablo Feinmann; Photography, Juan Carlos Lenardi; Editor, Sergio Zottola; Music, Jose Luis Castineira de Dios; Costumes, Leonor Puga Sabate; Argentine; Dolby Stereo; Color; Not rated; 119 minutes; December release. CAST: Esther Goris (Eva Duarte Peron), Victor Laplace (Juan Peron), Christnia Banegas (Juana de Ibarbian), Pepe Nuvoa (Lucero), Irma Cordoba (Marguarita Achaval Junco), Lorenzo Quinteros (Lonardi), Leandro Regunaga (Espejo), Carlos Roffe (Solari)

Maria Conchita Alonso

Richard Attenborough

Kevin Bacon

Diane Baker

Biographical Data

(Name, real name, place and date of birth, school attended)

AAMES, WILLIE (William Upton): Los Angeles, CA, July 15, 1960.

AARON, CAROLINE: Richmond, VA, Aug. 7, 1954. Catholic U.

ABBOTT, DIAHNNE: NYC, 1945.

ABBOTT, JOHN: London, June 5, 1905.

ABRAHAM, F. MURRAY: Pittsburgh, PA, Oct. 24, 1939. UTx.

ACKLAND, JOSS: London, Feb. 29, 1928.

ADAMS, BROOKE: NYC, Feb. 8, 1949. Dalton.

ADAMS, CATLIN: Los Angeles, Oct. 11, 1950.

ADAMS, DON: NYC, Apr. 13, 1926.

ADAMS, EDIE (Elizabeth Edith Enke): Kingston, PA, Apr. 16, 1927. Juilliard, Columbia.

ADAMS, JULIE (Betty May): Waterloo, IA, Oct. 17, 1926. Little Rock, Jr. College.

ADAMS, MASON: NYC, Feb. 26, 1919. UWi.

ADAMS, MAUD (Maud Wikstrom): Lulea, Sweden, Feb. 12, 1945.

ADJANI, ISABELLE: Germany, June 27, 1955.

AGAR, JOHN: Chicago, IL, Jan. 31, 1921.

AGUTTER, JENNY: Taunton, England, Dec. 20, 1952.

AIELLO, DANNY: NYC, June 20, 1933.

AIMEE, ANOUK (Dreyfus): Paris, France, Apr. 27, 1934. Bauer-Therond.

AKERS, KAREN: NYC, Oct. 13, 1945, Hunter College.

ALBERGHETTI, ANNA MARIA: Pesaro, Italy, May 15, 1936.

ALBERT, EDDIE (Eddie Albert Heimberger): Rock Island, IL, Apr. 22, 1908. U of Minn.

ALBERT, EDWARD: Los Angeles, Feb. 20. 1951. UCLA.

ALBRIGHT, LOLA: Akron, OH, July 20, 1925.

ALDA, ALAN: NYC, Jan. 28, 1936. Fordham.

ALEANDRO, NORMA: Buenos Aires, Dec. 6, 1936.

ALEJANDRO, MIGUEL: NYC, Feb. 21, 1958.

ALEXANDER, ERIKA: Philadelphia, PA, 1970.

ALEXANDER, JANE (Quigley): Boston, MA, Oct. 28, 1939. Sarah Lawrence.

ALEXANDER, JASON (Jay Greenspan): Newark, NJ, Sept. 23, 1959. Boston U.

ALICE, MARY: Indianola, MS, Dec. 3, 1941.

ALLEN, DEBBIE (Deborah): Houston, TX, Jan. 16, 1950. Howard U.

ALLEN, JOAN: Rochelle, IL, Aug. 20, 1956. EastIllU.

ALLEN, KAREN: Carrollton, IL, Oct. 5, 1951. UMd.

ALLEN, NANCY: NYC, June 24, 1950.

ALLEN, REX: Wilcox, AZ, Dec. 31, 1922.

ALLEN, STEVE: NYC, Dec. 26, 1921.

ALLEN, TIM: Denver, CO, June 13, 1953. W. MI. Univ.

ALLEN, WOODY (Allen Stewart Konigsberg): Brooklyn, Dec. 1, 1935.

ALLEY, KIRSTIE: Wichita, KS, Jan. 12, 1955.

ALLYSON, JUNE (Ella Geisman): Westchester, NY, Oct. 7, 1917.

ALONSO, MARIA CONCHITA: Cuba, 1957.

ALT, CAROL: Queens, NY, Dec. 1, 1960. HofstraU.

ALVARADO, TRINI: NYC, Jan. 10, 1967.

AMIS, SUZY: Oklahoma City, OK, Jan. 5, 1958. Actors Studio.

AMOS, JOHN: Newark, NJ, Dec. 27, 1940. Colo. U.

ANDERSON, KEVIN: Waukeegan, IL, Jan. 13, 1960.

ANDERSON, LONI: St. Paul, MN, Aug. 5, 1946.

ANDERSON, MELODY: Edmonton, Canada, 1955. Carlton U.

ANDERSON, MICHAEL, JR.: London, England, Aug. 6, 1943.

ANDERSON, RICHARD DEAN: Minneapolis, MN, Jan. 23, 1950.

ANDERSSON, BIBI: Stockholm, Sweden, Nov. 11, 1935. Royal Dramatic Sch.

ANDES, KEITH: Ocean City, NJ, July 12, 1920. Temple U., Oxford.

ANDRESS, URSULA: Bern, Switzerland, Mar. 19, 1936.

ANDREWS, ANTHONY: London, Dec. 1, 1948.

ANDREWS, JULIE (Julia Elizabeth Wells): Surrey, England, Oct. 1, 1935.

ANGLIM, PHILIP: San Francisco, CA, Feb. 11, 1953.

ANN-MARGRET (Olsson): Valsjobyn, Sweden, Apr. 28, 1941. Northwestern U.

ANSARA, MICHAEL: Lowell, MA, Apr. 15, 1922. Pasadena Playhouse.

ANSPACH, SUSAN: NYC, Nov. 23, 1945.

ANTHONY, LYSETTE: London, 1963.

ANTHONY, TONY: Clarksburg, WV, Oct. 16, 1937. Carnegie Tech.

ANTON, SUSAN: Yucaipa, CA, Oct. 12, 1950. Bemardino College.

ANTONELLI, LAURA: Pola, Italy, Nov. 28, 1941.

ANWAR, GABRIELLE: Lalehaam, England, Feb. 4, 1970

APPLEGATE, CHRISTINA: Hollywood CA, Nov. 25, 1972.

ARCHER, ANNE: Los Angeles, Aug. 25, 1947.

ARCHER, JOHN (Ralph Bowman): Osceola, NB, May 8, 1915. USC.

ARDANT, FANNY: Monte Carlo, Mar 22, 1949

ARKIN, ADAM: Brooklyn, NY, Aug. 19, 1956.

ARKIN, ALAN: NYC, Mar. 26, 1934. LACC.

Alec Baldwin

ARNAZ, DESI, JR.: Los Angeles, Jan. 19, 1953.

ARNAZ, LUCIE: Hollywood, July 17, 1951.

ARNESS, JAMES (Aurness): Minneapolis, MN, May 26, 1923. Beloit College.

ARQUETTE, PATRICIA: NYC, Apr. 8, 1968.

ARQUETTE, ROSANNA: NYC, Aug. 10, 1959.

ARTHUR, BEATRICE (Frankel): NYC, May 13, 1924. New School.

ASHER, JANE: London, Apr. 5, 1946.

ASHLEY, ELIZABETH (Elizabeth Ann Cole): Ocala, FL, Aug. 30, 1939.

ASHTON, JOHN: Springfield, MA, Feb. 22, 1948. USC.

ASNER, EDWARD: Kansas City, KS, Nov. 15, 1929.

ASSANTE, ARMAND: NYC, Oct. 4, 1949. AADA.

ASTIN, JOHN: Baltimore, MD, Mar. 30, 1930. U Minn.

ASTIN, MacKENZIE: Los Angeles, May 12, 1973.

ASTIN, SEAN: Santa Monica, Feb. 25, 1971.

ATHERTON, WILLIAM: Orange, CT, July 30, 1947. Carnegie Tech.

ATKINS, CHRISTOPHER: Rye, NY, Feb. 21, 1961.

ATKINSON, ROWAN: England, Jan. 6, 1955. Oxford.

ATTENBOROUGH, RICHARD: Cambridge, England, Aug. 29, 1923. RADA.

AUBERJONOIS, RENE: NYC, June 1, 1940. Carnegie Tech.

AUDRAN, STEPHANE: Versailles, France, Nov. 8, 1932.

AUGER, CLAUDINE: Paris, France, Apr. 26, 1942. Dramatic Cons.

AULIN, EWA: Stockholm, Sweden, Feb. 14, 1950.

AUMONT, JEAN PIERRE: Paris, France, Jan. 5, 1909. French Nat'l School of Drama.

AUTRY, GENE: Tioga, TX, Sept. 29, 1907.

AVALON, FRANKIE (Francis Thomas Avallone): Philadelphia, PA, Sept. 18, 1939.

AYKROYD, DAN: Ottawa, Canada, July 1, 1952.

AZNAVOUR, CHARLES (Varenagh Aznourian): Paris, France, May 22, 1924.

AZZARA, CANDICE: Brooklyn, NY, May 18, 1947.

BACH, CATHERINE: Warren, OH, Mar. 1, 1954.

BACALL, LAUREN (Betty Perske): NYC, Sept. 16, 1924. AADA.

BACH, BARBARA: Queens, NY, Aug. 27, 1946.

BACKER, BRIAN: NYC, Dec. 5, 1956. Neighborhood Playhouse.

BACON, KEVIN: Philadelphia, PA, July 8, 1958.

BAIN, BARBARA: Chicago, IL, Sept. 13, 1934. U Ill.

BAIO, SCOTT: Brooklyn, NY, Sept. 22, 1961.

BAKER, BLANCHE: NYC, Dec. 20, 1956.

BAKER, CARROLL: Johnstown, PA, May 28, 1931. St. Petersburg, Jr. College.

BAKER, DIANE: Hollywood, CA, Feb. 25, 1938. USC.

BAKER, JOE DON: Groesbeck, TX, Feb.12, 1936.

BAKER, KATHY: Midland, TX, June 8, 1950. UC Berkley.

BAKULA, SCOTT: St. Louis, MO, Oct. 9, 1955. KansasU.

BALABAN, BOB: Chicago, IL, Aug. 16, 1945. Colgate.

BALDWIN, ADAM: Chicago, IL, Feb. 27, 1962.

BALDWIN, ALEC: Massapequa, NY, Apr. 3, 1958. NYU.

BALDWIN, STEPHEN: Long Island, NY, 1966.

BALDWIN, WILLIAM: Massapequa, NY, Feb. 21, 1963.

BALE, CHRISTIAN: Pembrokeshire, West Wales, Jan. 30, 1974.

BALLARD, KAYE: Cleveland, OH, Nov. 20, 1926.

BANCROFT, ANNE (Anna Maria Italiano): Bronx, NY, Sept. 17, 1931. AADA.

BANDERAS, ANTONIO: Malaga, Spain, Aug. 10, 1960.

BANERJEE, VICTOR: Calcutta, India, Oct. 15, 1946.

BANES, LISA: Chagrin Falls, OH, July 9, 1955. Juilliard.

BANNEN, IAN: Airdrie, Scotland, June 29, 1928.

BARANSKI, CHRISTINE: Buffalo, NY, May 2, 1952. Juilliard.

BARBEAU, ADRIENNE: Sacramento, CA, June 11, 1945. Foothill College.

BARDOT, BRIGITTE: Paris, France, Sept. 28, 1934.

Antonio Banderas

BARKIN, ELLEN: Bronx, NY, Apr. 16, 1954. Hunter College.

BARNES, BINNIE (Gitelle Enoyce Barnes): London, Mar. 25, 1906.

BARNES, C. B. (Christopher): Portland, ME, 1973.

BARR, JEAN-MARC: San Diego, CA, Sept. 1960.

BARRAULT, JEAN-LOUIS: Vesinet, France, Sept. 8, 1910.

BARRAULT, MARIE-CHRISTINE: Paris, France, Mar. 21, 1944.

BARREN, KEITH: Mexborough, England, Aug. 8, 1936. Sheffield Playhouse.

BARRETT, MAJEL (Hudec): Columbus, OH, Feb. 23. Western Reserve U.

BARRIE, BARBARA: Chicago, IL, May 23, 1931.

BARRY, GENE (Eugene Klass): NYC, June 14, 1919.

BARRY, NEILL: NYC, Nov. 29, 1965.

BARRYMORE, DREW: Los Angeles, Feb. 22, 1975.

BARRYMORE, JOHN DREW: Beverly Hills, CA, June 4, 1932. St. John's Military Academy.

BARTEL, PAUL: Brooklyn, NY, Aug. 6, 1938. UCLA.

BARTY, BILLY: (William John Bertanzetti) Millsboro, PA, Oct. 25, 1924.

Christian Bale

Drew Barrymore

BARYSHNIKOV, MIKHAIL: Riga, Latvia, Jan. 27, 1948.

BASINGER, KIM: Athens, GA, Dec. 8, 1953. Neighborhood Playhouse.

BASSETT, ANGELA: NYC, Aug. 16, 1958.

BATEMAN, JASON: Rye, NY, Jan. 14, 1969.

BATEMAN, JUSTINE: Rye, NY, Feb. 19, 1966.

BATES, ALAN: Allestree, Derbyshire, England, Feb. 17, 1934. RADA.

BATES, JEANNE: San Francisco, CA, May 21. RADA.

BATES, KATHY: Memphis, TN, June 28, 1948. S. Methodist U.

BAUER, STEVEN (Steven Rocky Echevarria): Havana, Cuba, Dec. 2, 1956. U Miami.

BAXTER, KEITH: South Wales, England, Apr. 29, 1933. RADA.

BAXTER, MEREDITH: Los Angeles, June 21, 1947. Intelochen Acad.

BAYE, NATHALIE: Mainevile, France, July 6, 1948

BEACHAM, STEPHANIE: Casablanca, Morocco, Feb. 28, 1947.

BEAL, JOHN (J. Alexander Bliedung): Joplin, MO, Aug. 13, 1909. PA U.

BEALS, JENNIFER: Chicago, IL, Dec. 19, 1963.

BEAN, ORSON (Dallas Burrows): Burlington, VT, July 22, 1928.

BEAN, SEAN: Sheffield, Yorkshire, England, Apr. 17, 1958.

BEART, EMMANUELLE: Gassin, France, Aug. 14, 1965.

BEATTY, NED: Louisville, KY, July 6, 1937.

BEATTY, ROBERT: Hamilton, Ont., Canada, Oct. 19, 1909. U of Toronto.

BEATTY, WARREN: Richmond, VA, Mar. 30, 1937.

BECK, JOHN: Chicago, IL, Jan. 28, 1943.

BECK, MICHAEL: Memphis, TN, Feb. 4, 1949. Millsap College.

BEDELIA, BONNIE: NYC, Mar. 25, 1946. Hunter College.

BEDI, KABIR: India, 1945.

BEGLEY, ED, JR.: NYC, Sept. 16, 1949.

BELAFONTE, HARRY: NYC, Mar. 1, 1927.

BEL GEDDES, BARBARA: NYC, Oct. 31, 1922.

BELL, TOM: Liverpool, England, 1932.

BELLER, KATHLEEN: NYC, Feb. 10, 1957.

BELLWOOD, PAMELA (King): Scarsdale, NY, June 26.

BELMONDO, JEAN PAUL: Paris, France, Apr. 9, 1933.

BELUSHI, JAMES: Chicago, IL, June 15, 1954.

BELZER, RICHARD: Bridgeport, CT, Aug. 4, 1944.

BENEDICT, DIRK (Niewoehner): White Sulphur Springs, MT, March 1, 1945. Whitman College.

BENEDICT, PAUL: Silver City, NM, Sept. 17, 1938.

BENIGNI, ROBERTO: Tuscany, Italy, Oct. 27, 1952.

BENING, ANNETTE: Topeka, KS, May 29, 1958. SFSt. U.

BENJAMIN, RICHARD: NYC, May 22, 1938. Northwestern U.

BENNENT, DAVID: Lausanne, Sept. 9, 1966.

Angela Bassett

Richard Belzer

Peter Boyle

BENNETT, ALAN: Leeds, England, May 9, 1934. Oxford.

BENNETT, BRUCE (Herman Brix): Tacoma, WA, May 19, 1909. U Wash.

BENNETT, HYWEL: Garnant, So. Wales, Apr. 8, 1944.

BENSON, ROBBY: Dallas, TX, Jan. 21, 1957.

BERENGER, TOM: Chicago, IL, May 31, 1950, U Mo.

BERENSON, MARISA: NYC, Feb. 15, 1947.

BERG, PETER: NYC, 1964. Malcalester College.

BERGEN, CANDICE: Los Angeles, May 9, 1946. U PA.

BERGEN, POLLY: Knoxville, TN, July 14, 1930. Compton, Jr. College.

BERGER, HELMUT: Salzburg, Austria, May 29, 1942.

BERGER, SENTA: Vienna, Austria, May 13, 1941. Vienna Sch. of Acting.

BERGER, WILLIAM: Austria, Jan. 20, 1928. Columbia.

BERGERAC, JACQUES: Biarritz, France, May 26, 1927. Paris U.

BERGIN, PATRICK: Dublin, Feb. 4, 1951.

BERKOFF, STEVEN: London, England, Aug. 3, 1937.

BERLE, MILTON (Berlinger): NYC, July 12, 1908.

BERLIN, JEANNIE: Los Angeles, Nov. 1, 1949.

BERLINGER, WARREN: Brooklyn, Aug. 31, 1937. Columbia.

BERNHARD, SANDRA: Flint, MI, June 6, 1955.

BERNSEN, CORBIN: Los Angeles, Sept. 7, 1954. UCLA.

BERRI, CLAUDE (Langmann): Paris, France, July 1, 1934.

BERRIDGE, ELIZABETH: Westchester, NY, May 2, 1962. Strasberg Inst.

BERRY, HALLE: Cleveland, OH, Aug. 14, 1968.

BERRY, KEN: Moline, IL, Nov. 3, 1933.

BERTINELLI, VALERIE: Wilmington, DE, Apr. 23, 1960.

BEST, JAMES: Corydon, IN, July 26, 1926.

BETTGER, LYLE: Philadelphia, PA, Feb. 13, 1915. AADA.

BEY, TURHAN: Vienna, Austria, Mar. 30, 1921.

BEYMER, RICHARD: Avoca, IA, Feb. 21, 1939.

BIALIK, MAYIM: Dec. 12, 1975.

BIEHN, MICHAEL: Anniston, AL, July 31, 1956.

BIKEL, THEODORE: Vienna, May 2, 1924. RADA.

BILLINGSLEY, PETER: NYC, 1972.

BINOCHE, JULIETTE: Paris, France, Mar. 9, 1964.

BIRKIN, JANE: London, Dec. 14, 1947

BIRNEY, DAVID: Washington, DC, Apr. 23, 1939. Dartmouth, UCLA.

BIRNEY, REED: Alexandria, VA, Sept. 11, 1954. Boston U.

BISHOP, JOEY (Joseph Abraham Gotllieb): Bronx, NY, Feb. 3, 1918.

BISHOP, JULIE (Jacqueline Wells): Denver, CO, Aug. 30, 1917. Westlake School.

BISSET, JACQUELINE: Waybridge, England, Sept. 13, 1944.

BLACK, KAREN (Ziegler): Park Ridge, IL, July 1, 1942. Northwestern.

Kenneth Branagh

Matthew Broderick

Sandra Bullock

Chevy Chase

BLACKMAN, HONOR: London, 1926.
BLADES, RUBEN: Panama City, July 16, 1948. Harvard.
BLAIR, BETSY (Betsy Boger): NYC, Dec. 11, 1923.
BLAIR, JANET (Martha Jane Lafferty): Blair, PA, Apr. 23, 1921.
BLAIR, LINDA: Westport, CT, Jan. 22, 1959.
BLAKE, ROBERT (Michael Gubitosi): Nutley, NJ, Sept. 18, 1933.
BLAKELY, SUSAN: Frankfurt, Germany, Sept. 7, 1950. U TX.
BLAKLEY, RONEE: Stanley, ID, 1946. Stanford U.
BLOOM, CLAIRE: London, Feb. 15, 1931. Badminton School.
BLOOM, VERNA: Lynn, MA, Aug. 7, 1939. Boston U.
BLOUNT, LISA: Fayettville, AK, July 1, 1957. UAk.
BLUM, MARK: Newark, NJ, May 14, 1950. UMinn.
BLYTH, ANN: Mt. Kisco, NY, Aug. 16, 1928. New Waybum Dramatic School.
BOCHNER, HART: Toronto, Canada, Oct. 3, 1956. U San Diego.
BOCHNER, LLOYD: Toronto, Canada, July 29, 1924.
BOGARDE, DIRK: London, Mar. 28, 1921. Glasgow & Univ. College.
BOGOSIAN, ERIC: Woburn, MA, Apr. 24, 1953. Oberlin College.
BOHRINGER, RICHARD: Paris, France, 1942.
BOLKAN, FLORINDA (Florinda Soares Bulcao): Ceara, Brazil, Feb. 15, 1941.
BOLOGNA, JOSEPH: Brooklyn, NY, Dec. 30, 1938. Brown U.
BOND, DEREK: Glasgow, Scotland, Jan. 26, 1920. Askes School.
BONET, LISA: San Francisco, CA, Nov. 16, 1967.
BONHAM-CARTER, HELENA: London, England, May 26, 1966.
BONO, SONNY (Salvatore): Detroit, MI, Feb. 16, 1935.
BOONE, PAT: Jacksonville, FL, June 1, 1934. Columbia U.

BOOTHE, JAMES: Croydon, England, Dec.19, 1930
BOOTHE, POWERS: Snyder, TX, June 1, 1949. So. Methodist U.
BORGNINE, ERNEST (Borgnino): Hamden, CT, Jan. 24, 1917. Randall School.
BOSCO, PHILIP: Jersey City, NJ, Sept. 26, 1930. CatholicU.
BOSLEY, TOM: Chicago, IL, Oct. 1, 1927. DePaul U.
BOSTWICK, BARRY: San Mateo, CA, Feb. 24, 1945. NYU.
BOTTOMS, JOSEPH: Santa Barbara, CA, Aug. 30, 1954.
BOTTOMS, SAM: Santa Barbara, CA, Oct. 17, 1955.
BOTTOMS, TIMOTHY: Santa Barbara, CA, Aug. 30, 1951.
BOULTING, INGRID: Transvaal, So. Africa, 1947.
BOUTSIKARIS, DENNIS: Newark, NJ, Dec. 21, 1952. CatholicU.
BOVEE, LESLIE: Bend, OR, 1952.
BOWIE, DAVID (David Robert Jones): Brixton, South London, England, Jan. 8, 1947.
BOWKER, JUDI: Shawford, England, Apr. 6, 1954.
BOXLEITNER, BRUCE: Elgin, IL, May 12, 1950.
BOYLE, LARA FLYNN: Davenport, IA, Mar. 24, 1970.
BOYLE, PETER: Philadelphia, PA, Oct. 18, 1933. LaSalle College.
BRACCO, LORRAINE: Brooklyn, NY, 1955.
BRACKEN, EDDIE: NYC, Feb. 7, 1920. Professional Children's School.
BRAEDEN, ERIC (Hans Gudegast): Kiel, Germany, Apr. 3, 1942.
BRAGA, SONIA: Maringa, Brazil, June 8, 1950.
BRANAGH, KENNETH: Belfast, No. Ireland, Dec. 10, 1960.
BRANDAUER, KLAUS MARIA: Altaussee, Austria, June 22, 1944.
BRANDIS, JONATHAN: CT, Apr. 13, 1976.
BRANDO, JOCELYN: San Francisco, Nov. 18, 1919. Lake Forest College, AADA.
BRANDO, MARLON: Omaha, NB, Apr. 3, 1924. New School.

BRANDON, CLARK: NYC, 1959.
BRANDON, MICHAEL (Feldman): Brooklyn, NY.
BRANTLEY, BETSY: Rutherfordton, NC, 1955. London Central Sch. of Drama.
BRENNAN, EILEEN: Los Angeles, CA, Sept. 3, 1935. AADA.
BRIALY, JEAN-CLAUDE: Aumale, Algeria, 1933. Strasbourg Cons.
BRIDGES, BEAU: Los Angeles, Dec. 9, 1941. UCLA.
BRIDGES, JEFF: Los Angeles, Dec. 4, 1949.
BRIDGES, LLOYD: San Leandro, CA, Jan. 15, 1913.
BRIMLEY, WILFORD: Salt Lake City, UT, Sept. 27, 1934.
BRINKLEY, CHRISTIE: Malibu, CA, Feb. 2, 1954.
BRISEBOIS, DANIELLE: Brooklyn, NY, June 28, 1969.
BRITT, MAY (Maybritt Wilkins): Sweden, Mar. 22, 1936.
BRITTANY, MORGAN (Suzanne Cupito): Los Angeles, Dec. 5, 1950.
BRITTON, TONY: Birmingham, England, June 9, 1924.
BRODERICK, MATTHEW: NYC, Mar. 21, 1962.
BROLIN, JAMES: Los Angeles, July 18, 1940. UCLA.
BROMFIELD, JOHN (Farron Bromfield): South Bend, IN, June 11, 1922. St. Mary's College.
BRON, ELEANOR: Stanmore, England, 1934.
BRONSON, CHARLES (Buchinsky): Ehrenfield, PA, Nov. 3, 1920.
BROOKES, JACQUELINE: Montclair, NJ, July 24, 1930. RADA.
BROOKS, ALBERT (Einstein): Los Angeles, July 22, 1947.
BROOKS, MEL (Melvyn Kaminski): Brooklyn, NY, June 28, 1926.
BROSNAN, PIERCE: County Meath, Ireland. May 16, 1952.
BROWN, BLAIR: Washington, DC, Apr. 23, 1947. Pine Manor.
BROWN, BRYAN: Panania, Australia, June 23, 1947.

Cher

Christopher Collet

Sean Connery

Bill Cosby

BROWN, GARY (Christian Brando): Hollywood, CA, 1958.
BROWN, GEORG STANFORD: Havana, Cuba, June 24, 1943. AMDA.
BROWN, JAMES: Desdemona, TX, Mar. 22, 1920. Baylor U.
BROWN, JIM: St. Simons Island, NY, Feb. 17, 1935. Syracuse U.
BROWNE, LESLIE: NYC, 1958.
BROWNE, ROSCOE LEE: Woodbury, NJ, May 2, 1925.
BUCHHOLZ, HORST: Berlin, Germany, Dec. 4, 1933. Ludwig Dramatic School.
BUCKLEY, BETTY: Big Spring, TX, July 3, 1947. TxCU.
BUJOLD, GENEVIEVE: Montreal, Canada, July 1, 1942.
BULLOCK, SANDRA: Arlington, VA, June 26, 1964.
BURGHOFF, GARY: Bristol, CT, May 24, 1943.
BURGI, RICHARD: Montclair, NJ, July 30, 1958.
BURKE, PAUL: New Orleans, July 21, 1926. Pasadena Playhouse.
BURNETT, CAROL: San Antonio, TX, Apr. 26, 1933. UCLA.
BURNS, CATHERINE: NYC, Sept. 25, 1945. AADA.
BURROWS, DARREN E.: Winfield, KS, Sept. 12, 1966
BURSTYN, ELLEN (Edna Rae Gillhooly): Detroit, MI, Dec. 7, 1932.
BURTON, LeVAR: Los Angeles, CA, Feb. 16, 1958. UCLA.
BUSCEMI, STEVE: Brooklyn, NY, Dec. 13, 1957.
BUSEY, GARY: Goose Creek, TX, June 29, 1944.
BUSFIELD, TIMOTHY: Lansing, MI, June 12, 1957. E. Tenn. St. U.
BUSKER, RICKY: Rockford, IL, 1974.
BUTTONS, RED (Aaron Chwatt): NYC, Feb. 5, 1919.
BUZZI, RUTH: Westerly, RI, July 24, 1936. Pasadena Playhouse.
BYGRAVES, MAX: London, Oct. 16, 1922. St. Joseph's School.

BYRNE, DAVID: Dumbarton, Scotland, May 14, 1952.
BYRNE, GABRIEL: Dublin, Ireland, May 12, 1950.
BYRNES, EDD: NYC, July 30, 1933.
CAAN, JAMES: Bronx, NY, Mar. 26,1939.
CAESAR, SID: Yonkers, NY, Sept. 8, 1922.
CAGE, NICOLAS (Coppola): Long Beach, CA, Jan.7, 1964.
CAINE, MICHAEL (Maurice Micklewhite): London, Mar. 14, 1933.
CAINE, SHAKIRA (Baksh): Guyana, Feb. 23, 1947. Indian Trust College.
CALHOUN, RORY (Francis Timothy Durgin): Los Angeles, Aug. 8, 1922.
CALLAN, MICHAEL (Martin Calinieff): Philadelphia, Nov. 22, 1935.
CALLOW, SIMON: London, June 15, 1949. Queens U.
CALVERT, PHYLLIS: London, Feb. 18, 1917. Margaret Morris School.
CALVET, CORRINE (Corinne Dibos): Paris, France, Apr. 30, 1925. U Paris.
CAMERON, KIRK: Panorama City, CA, Oct. 12, 1970.
CAMP, COLLEEN: San Francisco, CA, 1953.
CAMPBELL, BILL: Chicago, IL, 1960.
CAMPBELL, GLEN: Delight, AR, Apr. 22, 1935.
CAMPBELL, TISHA: Newark, NJ, 1969.
CANALE, GIANNA MARIA: Reggio Calabria, Italy, Sept. 12, 1927.
CANNON, DYAN (Samille Diane Friesen): Tacoma, WA, Jan. 4, 1937.
CANTU, DOLORES: San Antonio, TX, 1957.
CAPERS, VIRGINIA: Sumter, SC, 1925. Juilliard.
CAPSHAW, KATE: Ft. Worth, TX, Nov. 3, 1953. UMo.
CARA, IRENE: NYC, Mar. 18, 1958.
CARDINALE, CLAUDIA: Tunis, N. Africa. Apr. 15, 1939. College Paul Cambon.
CAREY, HARRY, JR.: Saugus, CA, May 16, 1921. Black Fox Military Academy.
CAREY, PHILIP: Hackensack, NJ, July 15, 1925. U Miami.

CARIOU, LEN: Winnipeg, Canada, Sept. 30, 1939.
CARLIN, GEORGE: NYC, May 12, 1938.
CARMEN, JULIE: Mt. Vernon, NY, Apr. 4, 1954.
CARMICHAEL, IAN: Hull, England, June 18, 1920. Scarborough College.
CARNE, JUDY (Joyce Botterill): Northampton, England, 1939. Bush-Davis Theatre School.
CARNEY, ART: Mt. Vernon, NY, Nov. 4, 1918.
CARON, LESLIE: Paris, France, July 1, 1931. Nat'l Conservatory, Paris.
CARPENTER, CARLETON: Bennington, VT, July 10, 1926. Northwestern.
CARRADINE, DAVID: Hollywood, Dec. 8, 1936. San Francisco State.
CARRADINE, KEITH: San Mateo, CA, Aug. 8, 1950. Colo. State U.
CARRADINE, ROBERT: San Mateo, CA, Mar. 24, 1954.
CARREL, DANY: Tourane, Indochina, Sept. 20, 1936. Marseilles Cons.
CARRERA, BARBARA: Managua, Nicaragua, Dec. 31, 1945.
CARREY, JIM: Jacksons Point, Ontario, Canada, Jan. 17, 1962.
CARRIERE, MATHIEU: West Germany, 1950.
CARROLL, DIAHANN (Johnson): NYC, July 17, 1935. NYU.
CARROLL, PAT: Shreveport, LA, May 5, 1927. Catholic U.
CARSON, JOHN DAVID: California, 1951. Valley College.
CARSON, JOHNNY: Corning, IA, Oct. 23, 1925. U of Neb.
CARSTEN, PETER (Ransenthaler): Weissenberg, Bavaria, Apr. 30, 1929. Munich Akademie.
CARTER, NELL: Birmingham, AL, Sept. 13, 1948.
CARTWRIGHT, VERONICA: Bristol, England, Apr 20, 1949.
CARUSO, DAVID: Forest Hills, NY, 1956.
CARVEY, DANA: Missoula, MT, Apr. 2, 1955. SFST.Col.
CASELLA, MAX: Washington D.C, June 6, 1967

Ben Cross

Billy Crystal

Tim Daly

CASEY, BERNIE: Wyco, WV, June 8, 1939.

CASS, PEGGY (Mary Margaret Cass): Boston, MA, May 21, 1924.

CASSAVETES, NICK: NYC, 1959, Syracuse U, AADA.

CASSEL, JEAN-PIERRE: Paris, France, Oct. 27, 1932.

CASSEL, SEYMOUR: Detroit, MI, Jan. 22, 1935.

CASSIDY, DAVID: NYC, Apr. 12, 1950.

CASSIDY, JOANNA: Camden, NJ, Aug. 2, 1944. Syracuse U.

CASSIDY, PATRICK: Los Angeles, CA, Jan. 4, 1961.

CATES, PHOEBE: NYC, July 16, 1962.

CATTRALL, KIM: Liverpool, England, Aug. 21, 1956. AADA.

CAULFIELD, MAXWELL: Glasgow, Scotland, Nov. 23, 1959.

CAVANI, LILIANA: Bologna, Italy, Jan. 12, 1937. U Bologna.

CAVETT, DICK: Gibbon, NE, Nov. 19, 1936.

CHAKIRIS, GEORGE: Norwood, OH, Sept. 16, 1933.

CHAMBERLAIN, RICHARD: Beverly Hills, CA, March 31, 1935. Pomona.

CHAMPION, MARGE (Marjorie Belcher): Los Angeles, Sept. 2, 1923.

CHAN, JACKIE: Hong Kong, Apr. 7, 1954

CHANNING, CAROL: Seattle, WA, Jan. 31, 1921. Bennington.

CHANNING, STOCKARD (Susan Stockard): NYC, Feb. 13, 1944. Radcliffe.

CHAPIN, MILES: NYC, Dec. 6, 1954. HB Studio.

CHAPLIN, GERALDINE: Santa Monica, CA, July 31, 1944. Royal Ballet.

CHAPLIN, SYDNEY: Los Angeles, Mar. 31, 1926. Lawrenceville.

CHARISSE, CYD (Tula Ellice Finklea): Amarillo, TX, Mar. 3, 1922. Hollywood Professional School.

CHARLES, WALTER: East Strousburg, PA, Apr. 4, 1945. Boston U.

CHASE, CHEVY (Cornelius Crane Chase): NYC, Oct. 8, 1943.

CHAVES, RICHARD: Jacksonville, FL, Oct. 9, 1951. Occidental College.

CHAYKIN, MAURY: July 27, 1954

CHEN, JOAN: Shanghai, 1961. CalState.

CHER (Cherilyn Sarkisian): El Centro, CA, May 20, 1946.

CHILES, LOIS: Alice, TX, 1950.

CHONG, RAE DAWN: Vancouver, Canada, 1961.

CHONG, THOMAS: Edmonton, Alberta, Canada, May 24, 1938.

CHRISTIAN, LINDA (Blanca Rosa Welter): Tampico, Mexico, Nov. 13, 1923.

CHRISTIE, JULIE: Chukua, Assam, India, Apr. 14, 1941.

CHRISTOPHER, DENNIS (Carrelli): Philadelphia, PA, Dec. 2, 1955. Temple U.

CHRISTOPHER, JORDAN: Youngstown, OH, Oct. 23, 1940. Kent State.

CILENTO, DIANE: Queensland, Australia, Oct. 5, 1933. AADA.

CLAPTON, ERIC: London, Mar. 30, 1945.

CLARK, CANDY: Norman, OK, June 20, 1947.

CLARK, DANE: NYC, Feb. 18, 1915. Cornell, Johns Hopkins U.

CLARK, DICK: Mt. Vernon, NY, Nov. 30, 1929. Syracuse U.

CLARK, MATT: Washington, DC, Nov. 25, 1936.

CLARK, PETULA: Epsom, England, Nov. 15, 1932.

CLARK, SUSAN: Sarnid, Ont., Canada, Mar. 8, 1943. RADA.

CLAY, ANDREW DICE: Brooklyn, NY, 1958, Kingsborough College.

CLAYBURGH, JILL: NYC, Apr. 30, 1944. Sarah Lawrence.

CLEESE, JOHN: Weston-Super-Mare, England, Oct. 27, 1939, Cambridge.

CLERY, CORRINNE: Italy, 1950.

CLOONEY, ROSEMARY: Maysville, KY, May 23, 1928.

CLOSE, GLENN: Greenwich, CT, Mar. 19, 1947. William & Mary College.

COBURN, JAMES: Laurel, NB, Aug. 31, 1928. LACC.

COCA, IMOGENE: Philadelphia, Nov. 18, 1908.

CODY, KATHLEEN: Bronx, NY, Oct. 30, 1953.

COFFEY, SCOTT: HI, 1967.

COLE, GEORGE: London, Apr. 22, 1925.

COLEMAN, GARY: Zion, IL, Feb. 8, 1968.

COLEMAN, DABNEY: Austin, TX, Jan. 3, 1932.

COLEMAN, JACK: Easton, PA, 1958. Duke U.

COLIN, MARGARET: NYC, 1957.

COLLET, CHRISTOPHER: NYC, Mar. 13, 1968. Strasberg Inst.

COLLINS, JOAN: London, May 21, 1933. Francis Holland School.

COLLINS, PAULINE: Devon, England, Sept. 3, 1940.

COLLINS, STEPHEN: Des Moines, IA, Oct. 1, 1947. Amherst.

COLON, MIRIAM: Ponce, PR., 1945. UPR.

COLTRANE, ROBBIE: Ruthergien, Scotland, Mar. 30, 1950.

COMER, ANJANETTE: Dawson, TX, Aug. 7, 1942. Baylor, Tex. U.

CONANT, OLIVER: NYC, Nov. 15, 1955. Dalton.

CONAWAY, JEFF: NYC, Oct. 5, 1950. NYU.

CONNELLY, JENNIFER: NYC, Dec. 12, 1970

CONNERY, SEAN: Edinburgh, Scotland, Aug. 25, 1930.

CONNERY, JASON: London, 1962.

CONNICK, HARRY, JR.: New Orleans, LA, Sept. 11, 1967.

CONNORS, MIKE (Krekor Ohanian): Fresno, CA, Aug. 15, 1925. UCLA.

CONRAD, ROBERT (Conrad Robert Falk): Chicago, IL, Mar. 1, 1935. Northwestern U.

CONROY, KEVIN: Westport, CT, 1956. Juilliard.

CONSTANTINE, MICHAEL: Reading, PA, May 22, 1927.

CONTI, TOM: Paisley, Scotland, Nov. 22, 1941.

CONVERSE, FRANK: St. Louis, MO, May 22, 1938. Carnegie Tech.

CONWAY, GARY: Boston, Feb. 4, 1936.

CONWAY, KEVIN: NYC, May 29, 1942.

CONWAY, TIM (Thomas Daniel): Willoughby, OH, Dec. 15, 1933. Bowling Green State.

COOGAN, KEITH (Keith Mitchell Franklin): Palm Springs, CA, Jan. 13, 1970.

Jeff Daniels

Blythe Danner

Geena Davis

Dana Delany

COOPER, BEN: Hartford, CT, Sept. 30, 1930. Columbia U.

COOPER, CHRIS: Kansas City, MO, July 9, 1951. UMo.

COOPER, JACKIE: Los Angeles, Sept. 15, 1921.

COPELAND, JOAN: NYC, June 1, 1922. Brooklyn College, RADA.

CORBETT, GRETCHEN: Portland, OR, Aug. 13, 1947. Carnegie Tech.

CORBIN, BARRY: Dawson County, TX, Oct. 16, 1940. Texas Tech. U.

CORBY, ELLEN (Hansen): Racine, WI, June 13, 1913.

CORCORAN, DONNA: Quincy, MA, Sept. 29, 1942.

CORD, ALEX (Viespi): Floral Park, NY, Aug. 3, 1931. NYU, Actors Studio.

CORDAY, MARA (Marilyn Watts): Santa Monica, CA, Jan. 3, 1932.

COREY, JEFF: NYC, Aug. 10, 1914. Fagin School.

CORLEY, AL: Missouri, 1956. Actors Studio.

CORNTHWAITE, ROBERT: St. Helens, OR, Apr. 28, 1917. USC.

CORRI, ADRIENNE: Glasgow, Scot., Nov. 13, 1933. RADA.

CORT, BUD (Walter Edward Cox): New Rochelle, NY, Mar. 29, 1950. NYU.

CORTESA, VALENTINA: Milan, Italy, Jan. 1, 1924.

COSBY, BILL: Philadelphia, PA, July 12, 1937. Temple U.

COSTER, NICOLAS: London, Dec. 3, 1934. Neighborhood Playhouse.

COSTNER, KEVIN: Lynwood, CA, Jan. 18, 1955. CalStaU.

COURTENAY, TOM: Hull, England, Feb. 25, 1937. RADA.

COURTLAND, JEROME: Knoxville, TN, Dec. 27, 1926.

COX, BRIAN: Dundee, Scotland, June 1, 1946. LAMDA.

COX, COURTENEY: Birmingham, AL, June 15, 1964.

COX, RONNY: Cloudcroft, NM, Aug. 23, 1938.

COYOTE, PETER (Cohon): NYC, 1942.

CRAIG, MICHAEL: Poona, India, Jan. 27, 1929.

CRAIN, JEANNE: Barstow, CA, May 25, 1925.

CRAVEN, GEMMA: Dublin, Ireland, June 1, 1950.

CRAWFORD, MICHAEL (Dumbel-Smith): Salisbury, England, Jan. 19, 1942.

CREMER, BRUNO: Paris, France, 1929.

CRENNA, RICHARD: Los Angeles, Nov. 30, 1926. USC.

CRISTAL, LINDA (Victoria Moya): Buenos Aires, Feb. 25, 1934.

CRONYN, HUME (Blake): Ontario, Canada, July 18, 1911.

CROSBY, DENISE: Hollywood, CA, 1958.

CROSBY, HARRY: Los Angeles, CA, Aug. 8, 1958.

CROSBY, MARY FRANCES: Los Angeles, CA, Sept. 14, 1959.

CROSS, BEN: London, Dec. 16, 1947. RADA.

CROSS, MURPHY (Mary Jane): Laurelton, MD, June 22, 1950.

CROUSE, LINDSAY: NYC, May 12, 1948. Radcliffe.

CROWE, RUSSELL: New Zealand, 1964.

CROWLEY, PAT: Olyphant, PA, Sept. 17, 1932.

CRUISE, TOM (T. C. Mapother, IV): July 3, 1962, Syracuse, NY.

CRYER, JON: NYC, Apr. 16, 1965. RADA.

CRYSTAL, BILLY: Long Beach, NY, Mar. 14, 1947. Marshall U.

CULKIN, MACAULAY: NYC, Aug. 26, 1980.

CULLUM, JOHN: Knoxville, TN, Mar. 2, 1930. U Tenn.

CULLUM, JOHN DAVID: NYC, Mar. 1, 1966.

CULP, ROBERT: Oakland, CA, Aug. 16, 1930. U Wash.

CUMMINGS, CONSTANCE: Seattle, WA, May 15, 1910.

CUMMINGS, QUINN: Hollywood, Aug. 13, 1967.

CUMMINS, PEGGY: Prestatyn, N. Wales, Dec. 18, 1926. Alexandra School.

CURRY, TIM: Cheshire, England, Apr. 19, 1946. Birmingham U.

CURTIN, JANE: Cambridge, MA, Sept. 6, 1947.

CURTIS, JAMIE LEE: Los Angeles, CA, Nov. 22, 1958.

CURTIS, KEENE: Salt Lake City, UT, Feb. 15, 1925. U Utah.

CURTIS, TONY (Bernard Schwartz): NYC, June 3, 1924.

CUSACK, JOAN: Evanston, IL, Oct. 11, 1962.

CUSACK, JOHN: Chicago, IL, June 28, 1966.

CUSACK, SINEAD: Ireland, Feb. 18, 1948

DAFOE, WILLEM: Appleton, WI, July 22, 1955.

DAHL, ARLENE: Minneapolis, Aug. 11, 1928. U Minn.

DALE, JIM: Rothwell, England, Aug. 15, 1935.

DALLESANDRO, JOE: Pensacola, FL, Dec. 31, 1948.

DALTON, TIMOTHY: Colwyn Bay, Wales, Mar. 21, 1946. RADA.

DALTREY, ROGER: London, Mar. 1, 1944.

DALY, TIM: NYC, Mar. 1, 1956. Bennington College.

DALY, TYNE: Madison, WI, Feb. 21, 1947. AMDA.

DAMONE, VIC (Vito Farinola): Brooklyn, NY, June 12, 1928.

DANCE, CHARLES: Plymouth, England, Oct. 10, 1946.

D'ANGELO, BEVERLY: Columbus, OH, Nov. 15, 1953.

DANGERFIELD, RODNEY (Jacob Cohen): Babylon, NY, Nov. 22, 1921.

DANIELS, JEFF: Athens, GA, Feb. 19, 1955. EMichSt.

DANIELS, WILLIAM: Brooklyn, NY, Mar. 31, 1927. Northwestern.

DANNER, BLYTHE: Philadelphia, PA, Feb. 3, 1944. Bard College.

DANNING, SYBIL: Vienna, Austria, 1950.

Catherine Deneuve   Johnny Depp   Leonardo DiCaprio   Fran Drescher

DANSON, TED: San Diego, CA, Dec. 29, 1947. Stanford, Carnegie Tech.

DANTE, MICHAEL (Ralph Vitti): Stamford, CT, 1935. U Miami.

DANZA, TONY: Brooklyn, NY, Apr. 21, 1951. UDubuque.

D'ARBANVILLE-QUINN, PATTY: NYC, 1951.

DARBY, KIM (Deborah Zerby): North Hollywood, CA, July 8, 1948.

DARCEL, DENISE (Denise Billecard): Paris, France, Sept. 8, 1925. U Dijon.

DARREN, JAMES: Philadelphia, PA, June 8, 1936. Stella Adler School.

DARRIEUX, DANIELLE: Bordeaux, France, May 1, 1917. Lycee LaTour.

DAVENPORT, NIGEL: Cambridge, England, May 23, 1928. Trinity College.

DAVID, KEITH: NYC, June 4, 1954. Juilliard.

DAVIDOVICH, LOLITA: Toronto, Ontario, Canada, July 15, 1961.

DAVIDSON, JOHN: Pittsburgh, Dec. 13, 1941. Denison U.

DAVIS, CLIFTON: Chicago, IL, Oct. 4, 1945. Oakwood College.

DAVIS, GEENA: Wareham, MA, Jan. 21, 1957.

DAVIS, JUDY: Perth, Australia, Apr. 23, 1955.

DAVIS, MAC: Lubbock, TX, Jan. 21,1942.

DAVIS, NANCY (Anne Frances Robbins): NYC, July 6, 1921. Smith College.

DAVIS, OSSIE: Cogdell, GA, Dec. 18, 1917. Howard U.

DAVIS, SAMMI: Kidderminster, Worcestershire, England, June 21, 1964.

DAVIS, SKEETER (Mary Frances Penick): Dry Ridge, KY, Dec. 30, 1931.

DAVISON, BRUCE: Philadelphia, PA, June 28, 1946.

DAWBER, PAM: Detroit, MI, Oct. 18, 1954.

DAY, DORIS (Doris Kappelhoff): Cincinnati, Apr. 3, 1924.

DAY, LARAINE (Johnson): Roosevelt, UT, Oct. 13, 1917.

DAY LEWIS, DANIEL: London, Apr. 29, 1957. Bristol Old Vic.

DAYAN, ASSEF: Israel, 1945. U Jerusalem.

DEAKINS, LUCY: NYC, 1971.

DEAN, JIMMY: Plainview, TX, Aug. 10, 1928.

DEAN, LOREN: Las Vegas, NV, July 31, 1969.

DECAMP, ROSEMARY: Prescott, AZ, Nov. 14, 1913.

DeCARLO, YVONNE (Peggy Yvonne Middleton): Vancouver, B.C., Canada, Sept. 1, 1922. Vancouver School of Drama.

DEE, FRANCES: Los Angeles, Nov. 26, 1907. Chicago U.

DEE, JOEY (Joseph Di Nicola): Passaic, NJ, June 11, 1940. Patterson State College.

DEE, RUBY: Cleveland, OH, Oct. 27, 1924. Hunter College.

DEE, SANDRA (Alexandra Zuck): Bayonne, NJ, Apr. 23, 1942.

DeHAVEN, GLORIA: Los Angeles, July 23, 1923.

DeHAVILLAND, OLIVIA: Tokyo, Japan, July 1, 1916. Notre Dame Convent School.

DELAIR, SUZY: Paris, France, Dec. 31, 1916.

DELANY, DANA: NYC, March 13, 1956. Wesleyan U.

DELPY, JULIE: Paris. 1969.

DELON, ALAIN: Sceaux, France, Nov. 8, 1935.

DELORME, DANIELE: Paris, France, Oct. 9, 1927. Sorbonne.

DeLUISE, DOM: Brooklyn, NY, Aug. 1, 1933. Tufts College.

DeLUISE, PETER: Hollywood, CA, 1967.

DEMONGEOT, MYLENE: Nice, France, Sept. 29, 1938.

DeMORNAY, REBECCA: Los Angeles, Aug. 29, 1962. Strasberg Inst.

DEMPSEY, PATRICK: Lewiston, ME, Jan. 13, 1966.

DeMUNN, JEFFREY: Buffalo, NY, Apr. 25, 1947. Union College.

DENCH, JUDI: York, England, Dec. 9, 1934.

DENEUVE, CATHERINE: Paris, France, Oct. 22, 1943.

DeNIRO, ROBERT: NYC, Aug. 17, 1943. Stella Adler.

DENISON, MICHAEL: Doncaster, York, England, Nov. 1, 1915. Oxford.

DENNEHY, BRIAN: Bridgeport, CT, Jul. 9, 1938. Columbia.

DENVER, BOB: New Rochelle, NY, Jan. 9, 1935.

DENVER, JOHN: Roswell, NM, Dec. 31, 1943.

DEPARDIEU, GERARD: Chateauroux, France, Dec. 27, 1948.

DEPP, JOHNNY: Owensboro, KY, June 9, 1963.

DEREK, BO (Mary Cathleen Collins): Long Beach, CA, Nov. 20, 1956.

DEREK, JOHN: Hollywood, Aug. 12, 1926.

DERN, BRUCE: Chicago, IL, June 4, 1936. UPA.

DERN, LAURA: Los Angeles, Feb. 10, 1967.

DeSALVO, ANNE: Philadelphia, Apr. 3.

DEVANE, WILLIAM: Albany, NY, Sept. 5, 1939.

DEVINE, COLLEEN: San Gabriel, CA, June 22, 1960.

DeVITO, DANNY: Asbury Park, NJ, Nov. 17, 1944.

DEXTER, ANTHONY (Walter Reinhold Alfred Fleischmann): Talmadge, NB, Jan. 19, 1919. U Iowa.

DEY, SUSAN: Pekin, IL, Dec. 10, 1953.

DeYOUNG, CLIFF: Los Angeles, CA, Feb. 12, 1945. Cal State.

DIAMOND, NEIL: NYC, Jan. 24, 1941. NYU.

DICAPRIO, LEONARDO: Hollywood, CA, Nov.11, 1974.

DICKINSON, ANGIE (Angeline Brown): Kulm, ND, Sept. 30, 1932. Glendale College.

DILLER, PHYLLIS (Driver): Lima, OH, July 17, 1917. Bluffton College.

DILLMAN, BRADFORD: San Francisco, Apr. 14, 1930. Yale.

DILLON, KEVIN: Mamaroneck, NY, Aug. 19, 1965.

DILLON, MATT: Larchmont, NY, Feb. 18, 1964. AADA.

DILLON, MELINDA: Hope, AR, Oct. 13, 1939. Goodman Theatre School.

DIXON, DONNA: Alexandria, VA, July 20, 1957.

DOBSON, KEVIN: NYC, Mar. 18, 1944.

DOBSON, TAMARA: Baltimore, MD, 1947. MD Inst. of Art.

DOHERTY, SHANNEN: Memphis, TN, Apr. 12, 1971.

DOLAN, MICHAEL: Oklahoma City, OK, June 21, 1965.

DOMERGUE, FAITH: New Orleans, June 16, 1925.

DONAHUE, TROY (Merle Johnson): NYC, Jan. 27, 1937. Columbia U.

DONAT, PETER: Nova Scotia, Jan. 20, 1928. Yale.

DONNELLY, DONAL: Bradford, England, July 6, 1931.

D'ONOFRIO, VINCENT: Brooklyn, NY, June 30, 1959.

DONOHOE, AMANDA: London, June 29 1962.

DONOVAN, TATE: NYC, 1964.

DOOHAN, JAMES: Vancouver, BC, Mar. 3, 1920. Neighborhood Playhouse.

DOOLEY, PAUL: Parkersburg WV, Feb. 22, 1928. U WV.

DORFF, STEPHEN: July 29, 1973.

DOUGLAS, DONNA (Dorothy Bourgeois): Baywood, LA, Sept. 26, 1935.

DOUGLAS, KIRK (Issur Danielovitch): Amsterdam, NY, Dec. 9, 1916. St. Lawrence U.

DOUGLAS, MICHAEL: New Brunswick, NJ, Sept. 25, 1944. U Cal.

DOUGLASS, ROBYN: Sendai, Japan, June 21, 1953. UCDavis.

DOURIF, BRAD: Huntington, WV, Mar. 18, 1950. Marshall U.

DOVE, BILLIE: NYC, May 14, 1904.

DOWN, LESLEY-ANN: London, Mar. 17, 1954.

DOWNEY, ROBERT, JR.: NYC, Apr. 4, 1965.

DRAKE, BETSY: Paris, France, Sept. 11, 1923.

DREW, ELLEN (formerly Terry Ray): Kansas City, MO, Nov. 23, 1915.

DREYFUSS, RICHARD: Brooklyn, NY, Oct. 19, 1947.

DRILLINGER, BRIAN: Brooklyn, NY, June 27, 1960. SUNY/Purchase.

DRYER, JOHN: Hawthorne, CA, July 6, 1946.

DUCHOVNY, DAVID: NYC, Aug. 7, 1960. Yale.

DUDIKOFF, MICHAEL: Torrance, CA, Oct. 8, 1954.

DUGAN, DENNIS: Wheaton, IL, Sept. 5, 1946.

DUKAKIS, OLYMPIA: Lowell, MA, June 20, 1931.

DUKE, BILL: Poughkeepsie, NY, Feb. 26, 1943. NYU.

DUKE, PATTY (Anna Marie): NYC, Dec. 14, 1946.

DUKES, DAVID: San Francisco, June 6, 1945.

DULLEA, KEIR: Cleveland, NJ, May 30, 1936. SF State College.

DUNAWAY, FAYE: Bascom, FL, Jan. 14, 1941, Fla. U.

DUNCAN, SANDY: Henderson, TX, Feb. 20, 1946. Len Morris College.

DUNNE, GRIFFIN: NYC, June 8, 1955. Neighborhood Playhouse.

DUPEREY, ANNY: Paris, France, 1947.

DURBIN, DEANNA (Edna): Winnipeg, Canada, Dec. 4, 1921.

DURNING, CHARLES S. : Highland Falls, NY, Feb. 28, 1923. NYU.

Charles S. Dutton

Robert Duvall

Farrah Fawcett

DUSSOLLIER, ANDRE: Annecy, France, Feb. 17, 1946.

DUTTON, CHARLES: Baltimore, MD, Jan. 30, 1951. Yale.

DUVALL, ROBERT: San Diego, CA, Jan. 5, 1931. Principia College.

DUVALL, SHELLEY: Houston, TX, July 7, 1949.

DYSART, RICHARD: Brighton, ME, Mar. 30, 1929.

DZUNDZA, GEORGE: Rosenheim, Germ., July 19, 1945.

EASTON, ROBERT: Milwaukee, WI, Nov. 23, 1930. U Texas.

EASTWOOD, CLINT: San Francisco, May 31, 1931. LACC.

EATON, SHIRLEY: London, 1937. Aida Foster School.

EBSEN, BUDDY (Christian, Jr.): Belleville, IL, Apr. 2, 1910. U Fla.

ECKEMYR, AGNETA: Karlsborg, Sweden, July 2. Actors Studio.

EDELMAN, GREGG: Chicago, IL, Sept. 12, 1958. Northwestern U.

EDEN, BARBARA (Huffman): Tucson, AZ, Aug. 23, 1934.

EDWARDS, ANTHONY: Santa Barbara, CA, July 19, 1962. RADA.

EGGAR, SAMANTHA: London, Mar. 5, 1939.

EICHHORN, LISA: Reading, PA, Feb. 4, 1952. Queens Ont. U RADA.

EIKENBERRY, JILL: New Haven, CT, Jan. 21, 1947.

EILBER, JANET: Detroit, MI, July 27, 1951. Juilliard.

EKBERG, ANITA: Malmo, Sweden, Sept. 29, 1931.

EKLAND, BRITT: Stockholm, Sweden, Oct. 6, 1942.

ELDARD, RON: NYC, 1964.

ELIZONDO, HECTOR: NYC, Dec. 22, 1936.

ELLIOTT, CHRIS: NYC, May 31, 1960.

ELLIOTT, PATRICIA: Gunnison, CO, July 21, 1942. UCol.

ELLIOTT, SAM: Sacramento, CA, Aug. 9, 1944. U Ore.

ELWES, CARY: London, Oct. 26, 1962.

ELY, RON (Ronald Pierce): Hereford, TX, June 21, 1938.

ENGLISH, ALEX: USCar, 1954.

ENGLUND, ROBERT: Glendale, CA, June 6, 1949.

ERDMAN, RICHARD: Enid, OK, June 1, 1925.

ERICSON, JOHN: Dusseldorf, Ger., Sept. 25, 1926. AADA.

ERMEY, R. LEE (Ronald): Emporia, KS, Mar. 24, 1944

ESMOND, CARL: Vienna, June 14, 1906. U Vienna.

ESPOSITO, GIANCARLO: Copenhagen, Denmark, Apr. 26, 1958.

ESTEVEZ, EMILIO: NYC, May 12, 1962.

ESTRADA, ERIK: NYC, Mar. 16, 1949.

EVANS, DALE (Francis Smith): Uvalde, TX, Oct. 31, 1912.

EVANS, GENE: Holbrook, AZ, July 11, 1922.

EVANS, JOSH: NYC, Jan. 16, 1971.

EVANS, LINDA (Evanstad): Hartford, CT, Nov. 18, 1942.

EVERETT, CHAD (Ray Cramton): South Bend, IN, June 11, 1936.

EVERETT, RUPERT: Norfolk, England, 1959.

EVIGAN, GREG: South Amboy, NJ, Oct. 14, 1953.

FABARES, SHELLEY: Los Angeles, Jan. 19, 1944.

FABIAN (Fabian Forte): Philadelphia, Feb. 6, 1943.

FABRAY, NANETTE (Ruby Nanette Fabares): San Diego, Oct. 27, 1920.

FAHEY, JEFF: Olean, NY, Nov. 29, 1956.

FAIRBANKS, DOUGLAS, JR.: NYC, Dec. 9, 1907. Collegiate School.

FAIRCHILD, MORGAN (Patsy McClenny): Dallas, TX, Feb. 3, 1950. UCLA.

FALK, PETER: NYC, Sept. 16, 1927. New School.

FARENTINO, JAMES: Brooklyn, NY, Feb. 24, 1938. AADA.

FARGAS, ANTONIO: Bronx, NY, Aug. 14, 1946.

FARINA, DENNIS: Chicago, IL, Feb. 29, 1944.

FARINA, SANDY (Sandra Feldman): Newark, NJ, 1955.

FARLEY, CHRIS: Madison, WI, 1960. MarquetteU.

FARNSWORTH, RICHARD: Los Angeles, Sept. 1, 1920.

FARR, FELICIA: Westchester, NY, Oct. 4. 1932. Penn State College.

FARROW, MIA (Maria): Los Angeles, Feb. 9, 1945.

FAULKNER, GRAHAM: London, Sept. 26, 1947. Webber-Douglas.

FAWCETT, FARRAH: Corpus Christie, TX, Feb. 2, 1947. TexU.

FAYE, ALICE (Ann Leppert): NYC, May 5, 1912.

FEINSTEIN, ALAN: NYC, Sept. 8, 1941.

FELDMAN, COREY: Encino, CA, July 16, 1971.

FELDON, BARBARA (Hall): Pittsburgh, Mar. 12, 1941. Carnegie Tech.

FELDSHUH, TOVAH: NYC, Dec. 27, 1953, Sarah Lawrence College.

FELL, NORMAN: Philadelphia, PA, Mar. 24, 1924.

FELLOWS, EDITH: Boston, May 20, 1923.

FENN, SHERILYN: Detroit, MI, Feb. 1, 1965.

FERRELL, CONCHATA: Charleston, WV, Mar. 28, 1943. Marshall U.

FERRER, MEL: Elbeton, NJ, Aug. 25, 1912. Princeton U.

FERRER, MIGUEL: Santa Monica, CA, Feb. 7, 1954.

FERRIS, BARBARA: London, 1940.

FERZETTI, GABRIELE: Italy, 1927. Rome Acad. of Drama.

FIEDLER, JOHN: Plateville, WI, Feb. 3, 1925.

FIELD, SALLY: Pasadena, CA, Nov. 6, 1946.

FIELD, SHIRLEY-ANNE: London, June 27, 1938.

FIENNES, RALPH: Suffolk, England, Dec. 22, 1962. RADA.

FIERSTEIN, HARVEY: Brooklyn, NY, June 6, 1954. Pratt Inst.

FIGUEROA, RUBEN: NYC, 1958.

FINCH, JON: Caterham, England, Mar. 2, 1941.

FINLAY, FRANK: Farnworth, England, Aug. 6, 1926.

FINNEY, ALBERT: Salford, Lancashire, England, May 9, 1936. RADA.

FIORENTINO, LINDA: Philadelphia, PA, Mar. 9, 1960.

FIRESTONE, ROCHELLE: Kansas City, MO, June 14, 1949. NYU.

FIRTH, COLIN: Grayshott, Hampshire, England, Sept. 10, 1960.

FIRTH, PETER: Bradford, England, Oct. 27, 1953.

FISHBURNE, LAURENCE: Augusta, GA, July 30, 1961.

FISHER, CARRIE: Los Angeles, CA, Oct. 21, 1956. London Central School of Drama.

FISHER, EDDIE: Philadelphia, PA, Aug. 10, 1928.

FITZGERALD, BRIAN: Philadelphia, PA, 1960. West Chester U.

FITZGERALD, TARA: England, 1960.

FITZGERALD, GERALDINE: Dublin, Ireland, Nov. 24, 1914. Dublin Art School.

FLAGG, FANNIE: Birmingham, AL, Sept. 21, 1944. UAl.

FLANNERY, SUSAN: Jersey City, NJ, July 31, 1943.

FLEMING, RHONDA (Marilyn Louis): Los Angeles, Aug. 10, 1922.

FLEMYNG, ROBERT: Liverpool, England, Jan. 3, 1912. Haileybury College.

FLETCHER, LOUISE: Birmingham, AL, July 22 1934.

FOCH, NINA: Leyden, Holland, Apr. 20, 1924.

FOLDI, ERZSEBET: Queens, NY, 1967.

FOLLOWS, MEGAN: Toronto, Canada, 1967.

FONDA, BRIDGET: Los Angeles, Jan. 27, 1964.

FONDA, JANE: NYC, Dec. 21, 1937. Vassar.

FONDA, PETER: NYC, Feb. 23, 1939. U Omaha.

FONTAINE, JOAN: Tokyo, Japan, Oct. 22, 1917.

FOOTE, HALLIE: NYC, 1953. UNH.

FORD, GLENN (Gwyllyn Samuel Newton Ford): Quebec, Canada, May 1, 1916.

FORD, HARRISON: Chicago, IL, July 13, 1942. Ripon College.

FOREST, MARK (Lou Degni): Brooklyn, NY, Jan. 1933.

FORREST, FREDERIC: Waxahachie, TX, Dec. 23, 1936.

FORREST, STEVE: Huntsville, TX, Sept. 29, 1924. UCLA.

FORSLUND, CONNIE: San Diego, CA, June 19, 1950. NYU.

FORSTER, ROBERT (Foster, Jr.): Rochester, NY, July 13, 1941. Rochester U.

FORSYTHE, JOHN (Freund): Penn's Grove, NJ, Jan. 29, 1918.

FORSYTHE, WILLIAM: Brooklyn, NY, June 7, 1955

FOSSEY, BRIGITTE: Tourcoing, France, Mar. 11, 1947.

FOSTER, JODIE (Ariane Munker): Bronx, NY, Nov. 19, 1962. Yale.

FOSTER, MEG: Reading, PA, May 14, 1948.

FOX, EDWARD: London, Apr. 13, 1937. RADA.

FOX, JAMES: London, May 19, 1939.

Sally Field

Laurence Fishburne

Michael J. Fox

Dennis Franz

Brendan Fraser

Morgan Freeman

Edward Furlong

Andy Garcia

FOX, MICHAEL J.: Vancouver, BC, June 9, 1961.

FOXWORTH, ROBERT: Houston, TX, Nov. 1, 1941. Carnegie Tech.

FRAKES, JONATHAN: Bethlehem, PA, 1952. Harvard.

FRANCIOSA, ANTHONY (Papaleo): NYC, Oct. 25, 1928.

FRANCIS, ANNE: Ossining, NY, Sept. 16, 1932.

FRANCIS, ARLENE (Arlene Kazanjian): Boston, Oct. 20, 1908. Finch School.

FRANCIS, CONNIE (Constance Franconero): Newark, NJ, Dec. 12, 1938.

FRANCKS, DON: Vancouver, Canada, Feb. 28, 1932.

FRANK, JEFFREY: Jackson Heights, NY, 1965.

FRANKLIN, PAMELA: Tokyo, Feb. 4, 1950.

FRANZ, ARTHUR: Perth Amboy, NJ, Feb. 29, 1920. Blue Ridge College.

FRANZ, DENNIS: Chicago, IL, Oct. 28, 1944.

FRASER, BRENDAN: Indianapolis, IN, 1968.

FRAZIER, SHEILA: NYC, Nov. 13, 1948.

FRECHETTE, PETER: Warwick, RI, Oct. 1956. URI.

FREEMAN, AL, JR.: San Antonio, TX, Mar. 21, 1934. CCLA.

FREEMAN, KATHLEEN: Chicago, IL, Feb. 17, 1919.

FREEMAN, MONA: Baltimore, MD, June 9, 1926.

FREEMAN, MORGAN: Memphis, TN, June 1, 1937. LACC.

FREWER, MATT: Washington, DC, Jan. 4, 1958, Old Vic.

FRICKER, BRENDA: Dublin, Ireland, Feb. 17, 1945.

FRIELS, COLIN: Glasgow, Sept. 25, 1952.

FULLER, PENNY: Durham, NK, 1940. Northwestern U.

FUNICELLO, ANNETTE: Utica, NY, Oct. 22, 1942.

FURLONG, EDWARD: Glendale, CA, Aug. 2, 1977.

FURNEAUX, YVONNE: Lille, France, 1928. Oxford U.

FYODOROVA, VICTORIA: Russia, 1946.

GABLE, JOHN CLARK: Los Angeles, Mar. 20, 1961. Santa Monica College.

GABOR, EVA: Budapest, Hungary, Feb. 11, 1920.

GABOR, ZSA ZSA (Sari Gabor): Budapest, Hungary, Feb. 6, 1918.

GAIL, MAX: Derfoil, MI, Apr. 5, 1943.

GAINES, BOYD: Atlanta, GA, May 11, 1953. Juilliard.

GALLAGHER, PETER: NYC, Aug. 19, 1955. Tufts U.

GALLIGAN, ZACH: NYC, Feb. 14, 1963. ColumbiaU.

GAM, RITA: Pittsburgh, PA, Apr. 2, 1928.

GAMBON, MICHAEL: Dublin, Ireland, Oct. 19, 1940.

GANZ, BRUNO: Zurich, Switzerland, Mar. 22, 1941.

GARBER, VICTOR: Montreal, Canada, Mar. 16, 1949.

GARCIA, ANDY: Havana, Cuba, Apr. 12, 1956. FlaInt.

GARFIELD, ALLEN (Allen Goorwitz): Newark, NJ, Nov. 22, 1939. Actors Studio.

GARFUNKEL, ART: NYC, Nov. 5, 1941.

GARLAND, BEVERLY: Santa Cruz, CA, Oct. 17, 1926. Glendale College.

GARNER, JAMES (James Baumgarner): Norman, OK, Apr. 7, 1928. Okla. U.

GAROFALO, JANEANE: NJ, Sept. 28, 1964.

GARR, TERI: Lakewood, OH, Dec. 11, 1949.

GARRETT, BETTY: St. Joseph, MO, May 23, 1919. Annie Wright Seminary.

GARRISON, SEAN: NYC, Oct. 19, 1937.

GARY, LORRAINE: NYC, Aug. 16, 1937.

GASSMAN, VITTORIO: Genoa, Italy, Sept. 1,1922. Rome Academy of Dramatic Art.

GAVIN, JOHN: Los Angeles, Apr. 8, 1935. Stanford U.

GAYLORD, MITCH: Van Nuys, CA, 1961. UCLA.

GAYNOR, MITZI (Francesca Marlene Von Gerber): Chicago, IL, Sept. 4, 1930.

GAZZARA, BEN: NYC, Aug. 28, 1930. Actors Studio.

GEARY, ANTHONY: Coalsville, UT, May 29, 1947. UUt.

GEDRICK, JASON: Chicago, IL, Feb. 7, 1965. Drake U.

GEESON, JUDY: Arundel, England, Sept. 10, 1948. Corona.

GEOFFREYS, STEPHEN: Cincinnati, OH, Nov. 22, 1964. NYU.

GEORGE, SUSAN: West London, England, July 26, 1950.

GERARD, GIL: Little Rock, AR, Jan. 23, 1940.

GERE, RICHARD: Philadelphia, PA, Aug. 29, 1949. U Mass.

GERROLL, DANIEL: London, Oct. 16, 1951. Central.

GERTZ, JAMI: Chicago, IL, Oct. 28, 1965.

GETTY, BALTHAZAR: CA, Jan. 22, 1975.

GETTY, ESTELLE: NYC, July 25, 1923. New School.

GHOLSON, JULIE: Birmingham, AL, June 4, 1958.

GHOSTLEY, ALICE: Eve, MO, Aug. 14, 1926. Okla U.

GIAN, JOE: North Miami Beach, FL, 1962.

GIANNINI, CHERYL: Monessen, PA, June 15.

GIANNINI, GIANCARLO: Spezia, Italy, Aug. 1, 1942. Rome Acad. of Drama.

GIBB, CYNTHIA: Bennington, VT, Dec. 14, 1963.

GIBSON, HENRY: Germantown, PA, Sept. 21, 1935.

GIBSON, MEL: Peekskill, NY, Jan. 3, 1956. NIDA.

GIELGUD, JOHN: London, Apr. 14, 1904. RADA.

GIFT, ROLAND: Birmingham, England, May 28 1962.

GILBERT, MELISSA: Los Angeles, CA, May 8, 1964.

GILES, NANCY: NYC, July 17, 1960, Oberlin College.

GILLETTE, ANITA: Baltimore, MD, Aug. 16, 1938.

GILLIAM, TERRY: Minneapolis, MN, Nov. 22, 1940.

GILLIS, ANNE (Alma O'Connor): Little Rock, AR, Feb. 12, 1927.

Richard Gere

GINTY, ROBERT: NYC, Nov. 14, 1948. Yale.
GIRARDOT, ANNIE: Paris, France, Oct. 25, 1931.
GIROLAMI, STEFANIA: Rome, 1963.
GISH, ANNABETH: Albuquerque, NM, Mar. 13, 1971. DukeU.
GIVENS, ROBIN: NYC, Nov. 27, 1964.
GLASER, PAUL MICHAEL: Boston, MA, Mar. 25, 1943. Boston U.
GLASS, RON: Evansville, IN, July 10, 1945.
GLEASON, JOANNA: Winnipeg, Canada, June 2, 1950. UCLA.
GLEASON, PAUL: Jersey City, NJ, May 4, 1944.
GLENN, SCOTT: Pittsburgh, PA, Jan. 26, 1942. William and Mary College.
GLOVER, CRISPIN: NYC, Sept 20, 1964.
GLOVER, DANNY: San Francisco, CA, July 22, 1947. SFStateCol.
GLOVER, JOHN: Kingston, NY, Aug. 7, 1944.
GLYNN,CARLIN: Cleveland, Oh, Feb. 19, 1940. Actors Studio.
GOLDBERG, WHOOPI (Caryn Johnson): NYC, Nov. 13, 1949.
GOLDBLUM, JEFF: Pittsburgh, PA, Oct. 22, 1952. Neighborhood Playhouse.
GOLDEN, ANNIE: Brooklyn, NY, Oct. 19, 1951.

GOLDSTEIN, JENETTE: Beverly Hills, CA, 1960.
GOLDTHWAIT, BOB: Syracuse, NY, May 1, 1962.
GOLDWYN, TONY: Los Angeles, May 20, 1960. LAMDA.
GOLINO, VALERIA: Naples, Italy, Oct. 22, 1966.
GONZALEZ, CORDELIA: Aug. 11, 1958, San Juan, PR. UPR.
GONZALES-GONZALEZ, PEDRO: Aguilares, TX, Dec. 21, 1926.
GOODALL, CAROLINE: London, Nov. 13, 1959. BristolU.
GOODING, CUBA, JR.: Bronx, N.Y., 1968.
GOODMAN, DODY: Columbus, OH, Oct. 28, 1915.
GOODMAN, JOHN: St. Louis, MO, June 20, 1952.
GORDON, KEITH: NYC, Feb. 3, 1961.
GORMAN, CLIFF: Jamaica, NY, Oct. 13, 1936. NYU.
GORSHIN, FRANK: Pittsburgh, PA, Apr. 5, 1933.
GORTNER, MARJOE: Long Beach, CA, Jan. 14, 1944.
GOSSETT, LOUIS, JR.: Brooklyn, NY, May 27, 1936. NYU.
GOULD, ELLIOTT (Goldstein): Brooklyn, NY, Aug. 29, 1938. Columbia U.
GOULD, HAROLD: Schenectady, NY, Dec. 10, 1923. Cornell.
GOULD, JASON: NYC, Dec. 29, 1966.
GOULET, ROBERT: Lawrence, MA, Nov. 26, 1933. Edmonton.
GRAF, DAVID: Lancaster, OH, Apr. 1950. OhStateU.
GRAFF, TODD: NYC, Oct. 22, 1959. SUNY/Purchase.
GRANGER, FARLEY: San Jose, CA, July 1, 1925.
GRANT, DAVID MARSHALL: Westport, CT, June 21, 1955. Yale.
GRANT, HUGH: London, Sept. 9, 1960. Oxford.
GRANT, KATHRYN (Olive Grandstaff): Houston, TX, Nov. 25, 1933. UCLA.
GRANT, LEE: NYC, Oct. 31, 1927. Juilliard.
GRANT, RICHARD E: Mbabane, Swaziland, May 5, 1957. Cape Town U.
GRAVES, PETER (Aurness): Minneapolis, Mar. 18, 1926. U Minn.
GRAVES, RUPERT: Weston-Super-Mare, England, June 30, 1963.
GRAY, CHARLES: Bournemouth, England, 1928.
GRAY, COLEEN (Doris Jensen): Staplehurst, NB, Oct. 23, 1922. Hamline.
GRAY, LINDA: Santa Monica, CA, Sept. 12, 1940.
GRAY, SPALDING: Barrington, RI, June 5, 1941.
GRAYSON, KATHRYN (Zelma Hedrick): Winston-Salem, NC, Feb. 9, 1922.
GREEN, KERRI: Fort Lee, NJ, 1967. Vassar.
GREENE, ELLEN: NYC, Feb. 22, 1950. Ryder College.
GREENE, GRAHAM: Six Nations Reserve, Ontario, June 22, 1952
GREER, JANE: Washington, DC, Sept. 9, 1924.
GREER, MICHAEL: Galesburg, IL, Apr. 20, 1943.
GREGORY, MARK: Rome, Italy, 1965.

Caroline Goodall

GREIST, KIM: Stamford, CT, May 12, 1958.
GREY, JENNIFER: NYC, Mar. 26, 1960.
GREY, JOEL (Katz): Cleveland, OH, Apr. 11, 1932.
GREY, VIRGINIA: Los Angeles, Mar. 22, 1917.
GRIECO, RICHARD: Watertown, NY, 1966.
GRIEM, HELMUT: Hamburg, Germany, 1940. HamburgU.
GRIER, DAVID ALAN: Detroit, MI, June 30, 1955. Yale.
GRIER, PAM: Winston-Salem, NC, May 26, 1949.
GRIFFITH, ANDY: Mt. Airy, NC, June 1, 1926. UNC.
GRIFFITH, MELANIE: NYC, Aug. 9, 1957. Pierce College.
GRIMES, GARY: San Francisco, June 2, 1955.
GRIMES, SCOTT: Lowell, MA, July 9, 1971.
GRIMES, TAMMY: Lynn, MA, Jan. 30, 1934. Stephens College.
GRIZZARD, GEORGE: Roanoke Rapids, NC, Apr. 1, 1928. UNC.
GRODIN, CHARLES: Pittsburgh, PA, Apr. 21, 1935.
GROH, DAVID: NYC, May 21, 1939. Brown U, LAMDA.
GROSS, MARY: Chicago, IL, Mar. 25, 1953.

Whoopi Goldberg

Hugh Grant

Richard E. Grant

GROSS, MICHAEL: Chicago, IL, June 21, 1947.

GUEST, CHRISTOPHER: NYC, Feb. 5, 1948.

GUEST, LANCE: Saratoga, CA, July 21, 1960. UCLA.

GUILLAUME, ROBERT (Williams): St. Louis, MO, Nov. 30, 1937.

GUINNESS, ALEC: London, Apr. 2, 1914. Pembroke Lodge School.

GULAGER, CLU: Holdenville, OK, Nov. 16 1928.

GUTTENBERG, STEVE: Massapequa, NY, Aug. 24, 1958. UCLA.

GWILLIM, DAVID: Plymouth, England, Dec. 15, 1948. RADA.

GUY, JASMINE: Boston, Mar. 10, 1964.

HAAS, LUKAS: West Hollywood, CA, Apr. 16, 1976.

HACK, SHELLEY: Greenwich, CT, July 6, 1952.

HACKETT, BUDDY (Leonard Hacker): Brooklyn, NY, Aug. 31, 1924.

HACKMAN, GENE: San Bernardino, CA, Jan. 30, 1930.

HADDON, DALE: Montreal, Canada, May 26, 1949. Neighborhood Playhouse.

HAGERTY, JULIE: Cincinnati, OH, June 15, 1955. Juilliard.

HAGMAN, LARRY (Hageman): Weatherford, TX, Sept. 21, 1931. Bard.

HAID, CHARLES: San Francisco, June 2, 1943. CarnegieTech.

HAIM, COREY: Toronto, Canada, Dec. 23, 1972.

HALE, BARBARA: DeKalb, IL, Apr. 18, 1922. Chicago Academy of Fine Arts.

HALEY, JACKIE EARLE: Northridge, CA, July 14, 1961.

HALL, ALBERT: Boothton, AL, Nov. 10, 1937. Columbia.

HALL, ANTHONY MICHAEL: Boston, MA, Apr. 14, 1968.

HALL, ARSENIO: Cleveland, OH, Feb. 12, 1959.

HALL, HUNTZ: Boston, MA, Aug. 15, 1920.

HAMEL, VERONICA: Philadelphia, PA, Nov. 20, 1943.

HAMILL, MARK: Oakland, CA, Sept. 25, 1952. LACC.

HAMILTON, CARRIE: NYC, Dec. 5, 1963.

HAMILTON, GEORGE: Memphis, TN, Aug. 12, 1939. Hackley.

HAMILTON, LINDA: Salisbury, MD, Sept. 26, 1956.

HAMLIN, HARRY: Pasadena, CA, Oct. 30, 1951.

HAMPSHIRE, SUSAN: London, May 12, 1941.

HAMPTON, JAMES: Oklahoma City, OK, July 9, 1936. NTexasStU.

HAN, MAGGIE: Providence, RI, 1959.

HANDLER, EVAN: NYC, Jan. 10, 1961. Juillard.

HANKS, TOM: Concord, CA, Jul. 9, 1956. CalStateU.

HANNAH, DARYL: Chicago, IL, Dec. 3, 1960. UCLA.

HANNAH, PAGE: Chicago, IL, Apr. 13, 1964.

HARDIN, TY (Orison Whipple Hungerford, II): NYC, June 1, 1930.

HAREWOOD, DORIAN: Dayton, OH, Aug. 6, 1950. U Cinn.

HARMON, MARK: Los Angeles, CA, Sept. 2, 1951. UCLA.

HARPER, JESSICA: Chicago, IL, Oct. 10, 1949.

HARPER, TESS: Mammoth Spring, AK, 1952. SWMoState.

HARPER, VALERIE: Suffern, NY, Aug. 22, 1940.

HARRELSON, WOODY: Midland, TX, July 23, 1961. Hanover College.

HARRINGTON, PAT: NYC, Aug. 13, 1929. Fordham U.

HARRIS, BARBARA (Sandra Markowitz): Evanston, IL, July 25, 1935.

HARRIS, ED: Tenafly, NJ, Nov. 28, 1950. Columbia.

HARRIS, JULIE: Grosse Point, MI, Dec. 2, 1925. Yale Drama School.

HARRIS, MEL (Mary Ellen): Bethlehem, PA, 1957. Columbia.

HARRIS, RICHARD: Limerick, Ireland, Oct. 1, 1930. London Acad.

HARRIS, ROSEMARY: Ashby, England, Sept. 19, 1930. RADA.

HARRISON, GEORGE: Liverpool, England, Feb. 25, 1943.

HARRISON, GREGORY: Catalina Island, CA, May 31, 1950. Actors Studio.

HARRISON, NOEL: London, Jan. 29, 1936.

HARROLD, KATHRYN: Tazewell, VA, Aug. 2, 1950. Mills College.

Gene Hackman

HARRY, DEBORAH: Miami, IL, July 1, 1945.

HART, ROXANNE: Trenton, NJ, 1952, Princeton.

HARTLEY, MARIETTE: NYC, June 21, 1941.

HARTMAN, DAVID: Pawtucket, RI, May 19, 1935. Duke U.

HARTMAN, PHIL: Ontario, Canada, Sept. 24, 1948.

HASSETT, MARILYN: Los Angeles, CA, Dec. 17, 1947.

HATCHER, TERI: Sunnyvale, CA, Dec. 8, 1964.

HAUER, RUTGER: Amsterdam, Holland, Jan. 23, 1944.

HAVER, JUNE: Rock Island, IL, June 10, 1926.

HAVOC, JUNE (Hovick): Seattle, WA, Nov. 8, 1916.

HAWKE, ETHAN: Austin, TX, Nov. 6, 1970.

HAWN, GOLDIE: Washington, DC, Nov. 21, 1945.

HAYES, ISAAC: Covington, TN, Aug. 20, 1942.

HAYS, ROBERT: Bethesda, MD, July 24, 1947, SD State College.

HEADLY, GLENNE: New London, CT, Mar. 13, 1955. AmCollege.

Steve Guttenburg

Ethan Hawke

Goldie Hawn

Dan Hedaya

Paul Hogan

Anthony Hopkins

HEALD, ANTHONY: New Rochelle, NY, Aug. 25, 1944. MIStateU.

HEARD, JOHN: Washington, DC, Mar. 7, 1946. Clark U.

HEATHERTON, JOEY: NYC, Sept. 14, 1944.

HECKART, EILEEN: Columbus, OH, Mar. 29, 1919. Ohio State U.

HEDAYA, DAN: Brooklyn, NY, July 24, 1940.

HEDISON, DAVID: Providence, RI, May 20, 1929. Brown U.

HEDREN, TIPPI (Natalie): Lafayette, MN, Jan. 19, 1931.

HEGYES, ROBERT: NJ, May 7, 1951.

HELMOND, KATHERINE: Galveston, TX, July 5, 1934.

HEMINGWAY, MARIEL: Ketchum, ID, Nov. 22, 1961.

HEMMINGS, DAVID: Guilford, England, Nov. 18, 1941.

HEMSLEY, SHERMAN: Philadelphia, PA, Feb. 1, 1938.

HENDERSON, FLORENCE: Dale, IN, Feb. 14, 1934.

HENDRY, GLORIA: Jacksonville, FL, 1949.

HENNER, MARILU: Chicago, IL, Apr. 6, 1952.

HENRIKSEN, LANCE: NYC, May 5, 1940.

HENRY, BUCK (Henry Zuckerman): NYC, Dec. 9, 1930. Dartmouth.

HENRY, JUSTIN: Rye, NY, May 25, 1971.

HEPBURN, KATHARINE: Hartford, CT, May 12, 1907. Bryn Mawr.

HERMAN, PEE-WEE (Paul Reubenfeld): Peekskill, NY, Aug. 27, 1952.

HERRMANN, EDWARD: Washington, DC, July 21, 1943. Bucknell, LAMDA.

HERSHEY, BARBARA (Herzstein): Hollywood, CA, Feb. 5, 1948.

HESSEMAN. HOWARD: Lebanon, OR, Feb. 27, 1940.

HESTON, CHARLTON: Evanston, IL, Oct. 4, 1922. Northwestern U.

HEWITT, MARTIN: Claremont, CA, 1960. AADA.

HEYWOOD, ANNE (Violet Pretty): Birmingham, England, Dec. 11, 1932.

HICKEY, WILLIAM: Brooklyn, NY, Sept 19, 1928.

HICKMAN, DARRYL: Hollywood, CA, July 28, 1933. Loyola U.

HICKMAN, DWAYNE: Los Angeles, May 18, 1934. Loyola U.

HICKS, CATHERINE: NYC, Aug. 6, 1951. Notre Dame.

HIGGINS, ANTHONY (Corlan): Cork City, Ireland, May 9, 1947. Birmingham Sch. of Dramatic Arts.

HIGGINS, MICHAEL: Brooklyn, NY, Jan. 20, 1926. AmThWing.

HILL, ARTHUR: Saskatchewan, Canada, Aug. 1, 1922. U Brit. College.

HILL, BERNARD: Manchester, England, Dec. 17, 1944.

HILL, STEVEN: Seattle, WA, Feb. 24, 1922. U Wash.

HILL, TERRENCE (Mario Girotti): Venice, Italy, Mar. 29, 1941. U Rome.

HILLER, WENDY: Bramhall, Cheshire, England, Aug. 15, 1912. Winceby House School.

HILLERMAN, JOHN: Denison, TX, Dec. 20, 1932.

HINES, GREGORY: NYC, Feb.14, 1946.

HINGLE, PAT: Denver, CO, July 19, 1923. Tex. U.

HIRSCH, JUDD: NYC, Mar. 15, 1935. AADA.

HOBEL, MARA: NYC, June 18, 1971.

HODGE, PATRICIA: Lincolnshire, England, 1946. LAMDA.

HOFFMAN, DUSTIN: Los Angeles, Aug. 8, 1937. Pasadena Playhouse.

HOGAN, JONATHAN: Chicago, IL, June 13, 1951.

HOGAN, PAUL: Lightning Ridge, Australia, Oct. 8, 1939.

HOLBROOK, HAL (Harold): Cleveland, OH, Feb. 17, 1925. Denison.

HOLLIMAN, EARL: Tennass Swamp, Delhi, LA, Sept. 11, 1928. UCLA.

HOLM, CELESTE: NYC, Apr. 29, 1919.

HOLM, IAN: Ilford, Essex, England, Sept. 12, 1931. RADA.

HOMEIER, SKIP (George Vincent Homeier): Chicago, IL, Oct. 5, 1930. UCLA.

HOOKS, ROBERT: Washington, DC, Apr. 18, 1937. Temple.

HOPE, BOB (Leslie Townes Hope): London, May 26, 1903.

HOPKINS, ANTHONY: Port Talbot, So. Wales, Dec. 31, 1937. RADA.

HOPPER, DENNIS: Dodge City, KS, May 17, 1936.

HORNE, LENA: Brooklyn, NY, June 30, 1917.

HORSLEY, LEE: Muleshoe, TX, May 15, 1955.

HORTON, ROBERT: Los Angeles, July 29, 1924. UCLA.

HOSKINS, BOB: Bury St. Edmunds, England, Oct. 26, 1942.

HOUGHTON, KATHARINE: Hartford, CT, Mar. 10, 1945. Sarah Lawrence.

HOUSER, JERRY: Los Angeles, July 14, 1952. Valley, Jr. College.

HOWARD, ARLISS: Independence, MO, 1955. Columbia College.

HOWARD, KEN: El Centro, CA, Mar. 28, 1944. Yale.

HOWARD, RON: Duncan, OK, Mar. 1, 1954. USC.

HOWARD, RONALD: Norwood, England, Apr. 7, 1918. Jesus College.

HOWELL, C. THOMAS: Los Angeles, Dec. 7, 1966.

HOWELLS, URSULA: London, Sept. 17, 1922.

HOWES, SALLY ANN: London, July 20, 1930.

HOWLAND, BETH: Boston, MA, May 28, 1941.

HUBLEY, SEASON: NYC, May 14, 1951.

HUDDLESTON, DAVID: Vinton, VA, Sept. 17, 1930.

HUDDLESTON, MICHAEL: Roanoke, VA. AADA.

HUDSON, ERNIE: Benton Harbor, MI, Dec. 17, 1945.

HUGHES, BARNARD: Bedford Hills, NY, July 16, 1915. Manhattan College.

HUGHES, KATHLEEN (Betty von Gerkan): Hollywood, CA, Nov. 14, 1928. UCLA.

HULCE, TOM: Plymouth, MI, Dec. 6, 1953. N.C. Sch. of Arts.

HUNNICUT, GAYLE: Ft. Worth, TX, Feb. 6, 1943. UCLA.

HUNT, HELEN: Los Angeles, June 15, 1963.

HUNT, LINDA: Morristown, NJ, Apr. 1945. Goodman Theatre.

HUNT, MARSHA: Chicago, IL, Oct. 17, 1917.

HUNTER, HOLLY: Atlanta, GA, Mar. 20, 1958. Carnegie-Mellon.

HUNTER, KIM (Janet Cole): Detroit, Nov. 12, 1922.

HUNTER, TAB (Arthur Gelien): NYC, July 11, 1931.

HUPPERT, ISABELLE: Paris, France, Mar. 16, 1955.

HURT, JOHN: Lincolnshire, England, Jan. 22, 1940.

HURT, MARY BETH (Supinger): Marshalltown, IA, Sept. 26, 1948. NYU.

HURT, WILLIAM: Washington, DC, Mar. 20, 1950. Tufts, Juilliard.

HUSSEY, RUTH: Providence, RI, Oct. 30, 1917. U Mich.

HUSTON, ANJELICA: Santa Monica, CA, July 9, 1951.

HUTTON, BETTY (Betty Thornberg): Battle Creek, MI, Feb. 26, 1921.

HUTTON, LAUREN (Mary): Charleston, SC, Nov. 17, 1943. Newcomb College.

HUTTON, TIMOTHY: Malibu, CA, Aug. 16, 1960.

HYER, MARTHA: Fort Worth, TX, Aug. 10, 1924. Northwestern U.

ICE CUBE (O'Shea Jackson): Los Angeles, 1969.

IDLE, ERIC: South Shields, Durham, England, Mar. 29, 1943. Cambridge.

INGELS, MARTY: Brooklyn, NY, Mar. 9, 1936.

IRELAND, KATHY: Santa Barbara, CA, Mar. 8, 1963.

IRONS, JEREMY: Cowes, England, Sept. 19, 1948. Old Vic.

IRVING, AMY: Palo Alto, CA, Sept. 10, 1953. LADA.

IRWIN, BILL: Santa Monica, CA, Apr. 11, 1950.

ISAAK, CHRIS: Stockton, CA, June 26, 1956. UofPacific.

IVANEK, ZELJKO: Lujubljana, Yugo., Aug. 15, 1957. Yale, LAMDA.

IVEY, JUDITH: El Paso, TX, Sept. 4, 1951.

JACKSON, ANNE: Alleghany, PA, Sept. 3, 1926. Neighborhood Playhouse.

JACKSON, GLENDA: Hoylake, Cheshire, England, May 9, 1936. RADA.

JACKSON, JANET: Gary, IN, May 16, 1966.

JACKSON, KATE: Birmingham, AL, Oct. 29, 1948. AADA.

JACKSON, MICHAEL: Gary, IN, Aug. 29, 1958.

JACKSON, SAMUEL L.: Atlanta, Dec. 21, 1948.

JACKSON, VICTORIA: Miami, FL, Aug. 2, 1958.

JACOBI, DEREK: Leytonstone, London, Oct. 22, 1938. Cambridge.

JACOBI, LOU: Toronto, Canada, Dec. 28, 1913.

JACOBS, LAWRENCE-HILTON: Virgin Islands, 1954.

JACOBY, SCOTT: Chicago, IL, Nov. 19, 1956.

JAECKEL, RICHARD: Long Beach, NY, Oct. 10, 1926.

JAGGER, MICK: Dartford, Kent, England, July 26, 1943.

JAMES, CLIFTON: NYC, May 29, 1921. Ore. U.

JAMES, JOHN (Anderson): Apr. 18, 1956, New Canaan, CT. AADA.

JARMAN, CLAUDE, JR.: Nashville, TN, Sept. 27, 1934.

JASON, RICK: NYC, May 21, 1926. AADA.

JEAN, GLORIA (Gloria Jean Schoonover): Buffalo, NY, Apr. 14, 1927.

JEFFREYS, ANNE (Carmichael): Goldsboro, NC, Jan. 26, 1923. Anderson College.

JEFFRIES, LIONEL: London, 1927. RADA.

JERGENS, ADELE: Brooklyn, NY, Nov. 26, 1922.

JETER, MICHAEL: Lawrenceburg, TN, Aug. 26, 1952. Memphis St.U.

JETT, ROGER (Baker): Cumberland, MD, Oct. 2, 1946. AADA.

JILLIAN, ANN (Nauseda): Cambridge, MA, Jan. 29, 1951.

JOHANSEN, DAVID: Staten Island, NY, Jan. 9, 1950.

JOHN, ELTON (Reginald Dwight): Middlesex, England, Mar. 25, 1947. RAM.

JOHNS, GLYNIS: Durban, S. Africa, Oct. 5, 1923.

JOHNSON, DON: Galena, MO, Dec. 15, 1950. UKan.

JOHNSON, PAGE: Welch, WV, Aug. 25, 1930. Ithaca.

JOHNSON, RAFER: Hillsboro, TX, Aug. 18, 1935. UCLA.

JOHNSON, RICHARD: Essex, England, July 30, 1927. RADA.

JOHNSON, ROBIN: Brooklyn, NY, May 29, 1964.

JOHNSON, VAN: Newport, RI, Aug. 28, 1916.

JONES, CHRISTOPHER: Jackson, TN, Aug. 18, 1941. Actors Studio.

JONES, DEAN: Decatur, AL, Jan. 25, 1931. Actors Studio.

JONES, GRACE: Spanishtown, Jamaica, May 19, 1952.

JONES, JACK: Bel-Air, CA, Jan. 14, 1938.

JONES, JAMES EARL: Arkabutla, MS, Jan. 17, 1931. U Mich.

JONES, JEFFREY: Buffalo, NY, Sept. 28, 1947. LAMDA.

JONES, JENNIFER (Phyllis Isley): Tulsa, OK, Mar. 2, 1919. AADA.

JONES, L.Q. (Justice Ellis McQueen): Aug 19, 1927.

JONES, SAM J.: Chicago, IL, Aug. 12, 1954.

JONES, SHIRLEY: Smithton, PA, March 31, 1934.

JONES, TERRY: Colwyn Bay, Wales, Feb. 1, 1942.

JONES, TOMMY LEE: San Saba, TX, Sept. 15, 1946. Harvard.

JOURDAN, LOUIS: Marseilles, France, June 19, 1920.

JOY, ROBERT: Montreal, Canada, Aug. 17, 1951. Oxford.

Dennis Hopper

Ron Howard

Timothy Hutton

Samuel L. Jackson

JURADO, KATY (Maria Christina Jurado Garcia): Guadalajara, Mex., Jan. 16, 1927.

KACZMAREK, JANE: Milwaukee, WI, Dec. 21.

KAHN, MADELINE: Boston, MA, Sept. 29, 1942. Hofstra U.

KANE, CAROL: Cleveland, OH, June 18, 1952.

KAPLAN, MARVIN: Brooklyn, NY, Jan. 24, 1924.

KAPOOR, SHASHI: Bombay, India, 1940.

KAPRISKY, VALERIE: Paris, France, 1963.

KARRAS, ALEX: Gary, IN, July 15, 1935.

KATT, WILLIAM: Los Angeles, CA, Feb. 16, 1955.

KAUFMANN, CHRISTINE: Lansdorf, Graz, Austria, Jan. 11, 1945.

KAVNER, JULIE: Burbank, CA, Sept. 7, 1951. UCLA.

KAYE, STUBBY: NYC, Nov. 11, 1918.

KAZAN, LAINIE (Levine): Brooklyn, NY, May 15, 1942.

KAZURINSKY, TIM: Johnstown, PA, March 3, 1950.

KEACH, STACY: Savannah, GA, June 2, 1941. U Cal., Yale.

KEATON, DIANE (Hall): Los Angeles, CA, Jan. 5, 1946. Neighborhood Playhouse.

KEATON, MICHAEL: Coraopolis, PA, Sept. 9, 1951. KentStateU.

KEDROVA, LILA: Leningrad, 1918.

KEEL, HOWARD (Harold Leek): Gillespie, IL, Apr. 13, 1919.

KEITEL, HARVEY: Brooklyn, NY, May 13, 1939.

KEITH, BRIAN: Bayonne, NJ, Nov. 15, 1921.

KEITH, DAVID: Knoxville, TN, May 8, 1954. UTN.

KELLER, MARTHE: Basel, Switzerland, 1945. Munich Stanislavsky Sch.

KELLERMAN, SALLY: Long Beach, CA, June 2, 1936. Actors Studio West.

KELLEY, DeFOREST: Atlanta, GA, Jan. 20, 1920.

KEMP, JEREMY (Wacker): Chesterfield, England, Feb. 3, 1935. Central Sch.

KENNEDY, GEORGE: NYC, Feb. 18, 1925.

KENNEDY, LEON ISAAC: Cleveland, OH, 1949.

KENSIT, PATSY: London, Mar. 4, 1968.

KERR, DEBORAH: Helensburg, Scotland, Sept. 30, 1921. Smale Ballet School.

KERR, JOHN: NYC, Nov. 15, 1931. Harvard, Columbia.

KERWIN, BRIAN: Chicago, IL, Oct. 25, 1949.

KEYES, EVELYN: Port Arthur, TX, Nov. 20, 1919.

KHAMBATTA, PERSIS: Bombay, Oct. 2, 1950.

KIDDER, MARGOT: Yellow Knife, Canada, Oct. 17, 1948. UBC.

KIDMAN, NICOLE: Hawaii, June 20, 1967.

KIEL, RICHARD: Detroit, MI, Sept. 13, 1939.

KIER, UDO: Germany, Oct. 14, 1944.

KILEY, RICHARD: Chicago, IL, Mar. 31, 1922. Loyola.

KILMER, VAL: Los Angeles, Dec. 31, 1959. Juilliard.

KINCAID, ARON (Norman Neale Williams, III): Los Angeles, June 15, 1943. UCLA.

Diane Keaton

Brian Kerwin

Swoosie Kurtz

KING, ALAN (Irwin Kniberg): Brooklyn, NY, Dec. 26, 1927.

KING, PERRY: Alliance, OH, Apr. 30, 1948. Yale.

KINGSLEY, BEN (Krishna Bhanji): Snaiton, Yorkshire, England, Dec. 31, 1943.

KINSKI, NASTASSJA: Berlin, Ger., Jan. 24, 1960.

KIRBY, BRUNO: NYC, Apr. 28, 1949.

KIRK, TOMMY: Louisville, KY, Dec.10 1941.

KIRKLAND, SALLY: NYC, Oct. 31, 1944. Actors Studio.

KITT, EARTHA: North, SC, Jan. 26, 1928.

KLEIN, ROBERT: NYC, Feb. 8, 1942. Alfred U.

KLEMPERER, WERNER: Cologne, Mar. 22, 1920.

KLINE, KEVIN: St. Louis, MO, Oct. 24, 1947. Juilliard.

KLUGMAN, JACK: Philadelphia, PA, Apr. 27, 1922. Carnegie Tech.

KNIGHT, MICHAEL: Princeton, NJ, 1959.

KNIGHT, SHIRLEY: Goessel, KS, July 5, 1937. Wichita U.

KNOX, ELYSE: Hartford, CT, Dec. 14, 1917. Traphagen School.

KOENIG, WALTER: Chicago, IL, Sept. 14, 1936. UCLA.

KOHNER, SUSAN: Los Angeles, Nov. 11, 1936. U Calif.

KORMAN, HARVEY: Chicago, IL, Feb. 15, 1927. Goodman.

KORSMO, CHARLIE: Minneapolis, MN, 1978.

KORVIN, CHARLES (Geza Korvin Karpathi): Czechoslovakia, Nov. 21, 1907. Sorbonne.

KOTEAS, ELIAS: Montreal, Quebec, Canada, 1961. AADA.

KOTTO, YAPHET: NYC, Nov. 15, 1937.

KOZAK, HARLEY JANE: Wilkes-Barre, PA, Jan. 28, 1957. NYU.

KRABBE, JEROEN: Amsterdam, The Netherlands, Dec. 5, 1944.

KREUGER, KURT: St. Moritz, Switzerland, July 23, 1917. U London.

KRIGE, ALICE: Upington, So. Africa, June 28, 1955.

KRISTEL, SYLVIA: Amsterdam, The Netherlands, Sept. 28, 1952.

KRISTOFFERSON, KRIS: Brownsville, TX, June 22, 1936, Pomona College.

KRUGER, HARDY: Berlin, Germany, April 12, 1928.

KUNTSMANN, DORIS: Hamburg, Germany, 1944.

KURTZ, SWOOSIE: Omaha, NE, Sept. 6, 1944.

KWAN, NANCY: Hong Kong, May 19, 1939. Royal Ballet.

LaBELLE, PATTI: Philadelphia, PA, May 24, 1944.

LACY, JERRY: Sioux City, IA, Mar. 27, 1936. LACC.

LADD, CHERYL (Stoppelmoor): Huron, SD. July 12, 1951.

LADD, DIANE (Ladner): Meridian, MS, Nov. 29, 1932. Tulane U.

LaGRECA, PAUL: Bronx, NY, June 23, 1962. AADA.

LAHTI, CHRISTINE: Detroit, MI, Apr. 4, 1950. U Mich.

LAKE, RICKI: NYC, Sept. 21, 1968.

Diane Lane

LAMARR, HEDY (Hedwig Kiesler): Vienna, Sept. 11, 1913.

LAMAS, LORENZO: Los Angeles, Jan. 28, 1958.

LAMBERT, CHRISTOPHER: NYC, Mar. 29, 1958.

LANDAU, MARTIN: Brooklyn, NY, June 20, 1931. Actors Studio.

LANDRUM, TERI: Enid, OK, 1960.

LANE, ABBE: Brooklyn, NY, Dec. 14, 1935.

LANE, DIANE: NYC, Jan. 22, 1963.

LANE, NATHAN: Jersey City, NJ, Feb. 3, 1956.

LANG, STEPHEN: NYC, July 11, 1952. Swarthmore College.

LANGE, HOPE: Redding Ridge, CT, Nov. 28, 1931. Reed College.

LANGE, JESSICA: Cloquet, MN, Apr. 20, 1949. U Minn.

LANGELLA, FRANK: Bayonne, NJ, Jan. 1, 1940. SyracuseU.

LANSBURY, ANGELA: London, Oct. 16, 1925. London Academy of Music.

LaPAGLIA, ANTHONY: Adelaide, Australia. Jan 31, 1959.

LaPLANTE, LAURA: St. Louis, MO, Nov. 1, 1904.

LARROQUETTE, JOHN: New Orleans, LA, Nov. 25, 1947.

LASSER, LOUISE: NYC, Apr. 11, 1939. Brandeis U.

LATIFAH, QUEEN (Dana Owens): East Orange, NJ, 1970.

LAUGHLIN, JOHN: Memphis, TN, Apr. 3.

LAUGHLIN, TOM: Minneapolis, MN, 1938.

LAUPER, CYNDI: Astoria, Queens, NYC, June 20, 1953.

LAURE, CAROLE: Montreal, Canada, 1951.

LAURIE, PIPER (Rosetta Jacobs): Detroit, MI, Jan. 22, 1932.

LAUTER, ED: Long Beach, NY, Oct. 30, 1940.

LAVIN, LINDA: Portland, ME, Oct. 15 1939.

LAW, JOHN PHILLIP: Hollywood, CA, Sept. 7, 1937. Neighborhood Playhouse, U Hawaii.

LAWRENCE, BARBARA: Carnegie, OK, Feb. 24, 1930. UCLA.

LAWRENCE, CAROL (Laraia): Melrose Park, IL, Sept. 5, 1935.

LAWRENCE, VICKI: Inglewood, CA, Mar. 26, 1949.

LAWRENCE, MARTIN: Frankfurt, Germany, 1965.

LAWSON, LEIGH: Atherston, England, July 21, 1945. RADA.

LEACHMAN, CLORIS: Des Moines, IA, Apr. 30, 1930. Northwestern U.

LEAUD, JEAN-PIERRE: Paris, France, 1944.

LEDERER, FRANCIS: Karlin, Prague, Czech., Nov. 6, 1906.

LEE, CHRISTOPHER: London, May 27, 1922. Wellington College.

LEE, MARK: Australia, 1958.

LEE, MICHELE (Dusiak): Los Angeles, June 24, 1942. LACC.

LEE, PEGGY (Norma Delores Egstrom): Jamestown, ND, May 26, 1920.

LEE, SPIKE (Shelton Lee): Atlanta, GA, Mar. 20, 1957.

LEGROS, JAMES: Minneapolis, MN, Apr. 27, 1962.

LEGUIZAMO, JOHN: Columbia, July 22, 1965. NYU.

LEIBMAN, RON: NYC, Oct. 1l, 1937. Ohio Wesleyan.

LEIGH, JANET (Jeanette Helen Morrison): Merced, CA, July 6, 1926. ColofPacific.

LEIGH, JENNIFER JASON: Los Angeles, Feb. 5, 1962.

LeMAT, PAUL: Rahway, NJ, Sept. 22, 1945.

LEMMON, CHRIS: Los Angeles, Jan. 22, 1954.

LEMMON, JACK: Boston, Feb. 8, 1925. Harvard.

LENO, JAY: New Rochelle, NY, Apr. 28, 1950. Emerson College.

LENZ, KAY: Los Angeles, Mar. 4, 1953.

LENZ, RICK: Springfield, IL, Nov. 21, 1939. U Mich.

LEONARD, ROBERT SEAN: Westwood, NJ, Feb. 28, 1969.

LEONARD, SHELDON (Bershad): NYC, Feb. 22, 1907, Syracuse U.

LERNER, MICHAEL: Brooklyn, NY, June 22, 1941.

LEROY, PHILIPPE: Paris, France, Oct. 15, 1930. U Paris.

LESLIE, BETHEL: NYC, Aug. 3, 1929. Brearley School.

LESLIE, JOAN (Joan Brodell): Detroit, Jan. 26, 1925. St. Benedict's.

LESTER, MARK: Oxford, England, July 11, 1958.

John Leguizamo

LEVELS, CALVIN: Cleveland. OH, Sept. 30, 1954. CCC.

LEVEN, RACHEL: NYC, 1954. Goddard College.

LEVINE, JERRY: New Brunswick, NJ, Mar. 12, 1957, Boston U.

LEVY, EUGENE: Hamilton, Canada, Dec. 17, 1946. McMasterU.

LEWIS, CHARLOTTE: London, 1968.

LEWIS, GEOFFREY: San Diego, CA, Jan. 1, 1935.

LEWIS, JERRY (Joseph Levitch): Newark, NJ, Mar. 16, 1926.

LEWIS, JULIETTE: Los Angeles CA, June 21, 1973.

LIGON, TOM: New Orleans, LA, Sept. 10, 1945.

LINCOLN, ABBEY (Anna Marie Woolridge): Chicago, IL, Aug. 6, 1930.

LINDEN, HAL: Bronx, NY, Mar. 20, 1931. City College of NY.

LINDSAY, ROBERT: Ilketson, Derby-shire, England, Dec. 13, 1951. RADA.

LINN-BAKER, MARK: St. Louis, MO, June 17, 1954, Yale.

LIOTTA, RAY: Newark, NJ, Dec. 18, 1955. UMiami.

LISI, VIRNA: Rome, Nov. 8, 1937.

Jessica Lange

Robert Sean Leonard

LITHGOW, JOHN: Rochester, NY, Oct. 19, 1945. Harvard.

LLOYD, CHRISTOPHER: Stamford, CT, Oct. 22, 1938.

LLOYD, EMILY: London, Sept. 29, 1970.

LOCKE, SONDRA: Shelbyville, TN, May, 28, 1947.

LOCKHART, JUNE: NYC, June 25, 1925. Westlake School.

LOCKWOOD, GARY: Van Nuys, CA, Feb. 21, 1937.

LOGGIA, ROBERT: Staten Island, NY, Jan. 3, 1930. UMo.

LOLLOBRIGIDA, GINA: Subiaco, Italy, July 4, 1927. Rome Academy of Fine Arts.

LOM, HERBERT: Prague, Czechoslovakia, Jan. 9, 1917. Prague U.

LOMEZ, CELINE: Montreal, Canada, 1953.

LONDON, JULIE (Julie Peck): Santa Rosa, CA, Sept. 26, 1926.

LONE, JOHN: Hong Kong, Oct 13, 1952. AADA.

LONG, SHELLEY: Ft. Wayne, IN, Aug. 23, 1949. Northwestern U.

LOPEZ, PERRY: NYC, July 22, 1931. NYU.

LORD, JACK (John Joseph Ryan): NYC, Dec. 30, 1928. NYU.

LOREN, SOPHIA (Sophia Scicolone): Rome, Italy, Sept. 20, 1934.

LOUIS-DREYFUS, JULIA: NYC, Jan. 13, 1961.

LOUISE, TINA (Blacker): NYC, Feb. 11, 1934, Miami U.

LOVETT, LYLE: Klein, TX, Nov. 1, 1957.

LOVITZ, JON: Tarzana, CA, July 21, 1957.

LOWE, CHAD: Dayton, OH, Jan. 15, 1968.

LOWE, ROB: Charlottesville, VA, Mar. 17, 1964.

LOWITSCH, KLAUS: Berlin, Apr. 8, 1936, Vienna Academy.

LUCAS, LISA: Arizona, 1961.

LUCKINBILL, LAURENCE: Fort Smith, AK, Nov. 21, 1934.

LUFT, LORNA: Los Angeles, Nov. 21, 1952.

LULU (Marie Lawrie): Glasgow, Scotland, Nov. 3, 1948.

LUNA, BARBARA: NYC, Mar. 2, 1939.

LUNDGREN, DOLPH: Stockolm, Sweden, Nov. 3, 1959. Royal Inst.

LuPONE, PATTI: Northport, NY, Apr. 21, 1949, Juilliard.

LYDON, JAMES: Harrington Park, NJ, May 30, 1923.

LYNCH, KELLY: Minneapolis, MN, 1959.

LYNLEY, CAROL (Jones): NYC, Feb. 13, 1942.

LYON, SUE: Davenport, IA, July 10, 1946.

MacARTHUR, JAMES: Los Angeles, Dec. 8, 1937. Harvard.

MACCHIO, RALPH: Huntington, NY, Nov. 4, 1961.

MacCORKINDALE, SIMON: Cambridge, England, Feb. 12, 1953.

MacDOWELL, ANDIE (Rose Anderson MacDowell): Gaffney, SC, Apr. 21, 1958.

MacGINNIS, NIALL: Dublin, Ireland, Mar. 29, 1913. Dublin U.

MacGRAW, ALI: NYC, Apr. 1, 1938. Wellesley.

MacLACHLAN, KYLE: Yakima, WA, Feb. 22, 1959. UWa.

MacLAINE, SHIRLEY (Beaty): Richmond, VA, Apr. 24, 1934.

MacLEOD, GAVIN: Mt. Kisco, NY, Feb. 28, 1931.

MacNAUGHTON, ROBERT: NYC, Dec. 19, 1966.

MACNEE, PATRICK: London, Feb. 1922.

MacNICOL, PETER: Dallas, TX, Apr. 10, 1954. UMN.

MacPHERSON, ELLE: Sydney, Australia, 1965.

MACY, W. H. (William): Miami, FL, Mar. 13, 1950. Goddard College.

MADIGAN, AMY: Chicago, IL, Sept. 11, 1950. Marquette U.

MADONNA (Madonna Louise Veronica Cicone): Bay City, MI, Aug. 16, 1958. UMi.

MADSEN, MICHAEL: Chicago, IL, 1958.

MADSEN, VIRGINIA: Winnetka, IL, Sept. 11, 1963.

MAGNUSON, ANN: Charleston, WV, Jan. 4, 1956.

MAHARIS, GEORGE: Astoria, NY, Sept. 1, 1928. Actors Studio.

MAHONEY, JOHN: Manchester, England, June 20, 1940, WUIll.

MAILER, KATE: NYC, 1962.

MAILER, STEPHEN: NYC, Mar. 10, 1966. NYU.

MAJORS, LEE: Wyandotte, MI, Apr. 23, 1940. E. Ky. State College.

MAKEPEACE, CHRIS: Toronto, Canada, Apr. 22, 1964.

MAKO (Mako Iwamatsu): Kobe, Japan, Dec. 10, 1933. Pratt.

MALDEN, KARL (Mladen Sekulovich): Gary, IN, Mar. 22, 1914.

MALET, PIERRE: St. Tropez, France, 1955.

MALKOVICH, JOHN: Christopher, IL, Dec. 9, 1953, IllStateU.

MALONE, DOROTHY: Chicago, IL, Jan. 30, 1925.

MANN, KURT: Roslyn, NY, July 18, 1947.

MANN, TERRENCE: KY, 1945. NCSchl Arts.

MANOFF, DINAH: NYC, Jan. 25, 1958. CalArts.

MANTEGNA, JOE: Chicago, IL, Nov. 13, 1947. Goodman Theatre.

MANZ, LINDA: NYC, 1961.

MARAIS, JEAN: Cherbourg, France, Dec. 11, 1913, St. Germain.

MARCHAND, NANCY: Buffalo, NY, June 19, 1928.

MARCOVICCI, ANDREA: NYC, Nov. 18, 1948.

MARIN, CHEECH (Richard): Los Angeles, July 13, 1946.

MARIN, JACQUES: Paris, France, Sept. 9, 1919. Conservatoire National.

MARINARO, ED: NYC, 1951. Cornell.

MARS, KENNETH: Chicago, IL, 1936.

MARSH, JEAN: London, England, July 1, 1934.

MARSHALL, E. G.: Owatonna, MN, June 18, 1910. U Minn.

MARSHALL, KEN: NYC, 1953. Juilliard.

MARSHALL, PENNY: Bronx, NY, Oct. 15, 1942. UN. Mex.

MARSHALL, WILLIAM: Gary, IN, Aug. 19, 1924. NYU.

MARTIN, ANDREA: Portland, ME, Jan. 15, 1947.

MARTIN, DICK: Battle Creek, MI Jan. 30, 1923.

MARTIN, GEORGE N.: NYC, Aug. 15, 1929.

MARTIN, MILLICENT: Romford, England, June 8, 1934.

MARTIN, PAMELASUE: Westport, CT, Jan. 15, 1953.

MARTIN, STEVE: Waco, TX, Aug. 14, 1945. UCLA.

MARTIN, TONY (Alfred Norris): Oakland, CA, Dec. 25, 1913. St. Mary's College.

MASON, MARSHA: St. Louis, MO, Apr. 3, 1942. Webster College.

MASON, PAMELA (Pamela Kellino): Westgate, England, Mar. 10, 1918.

MASSEN, OSA: Copenhagen, Denmark, Jan. 13, 1916.

MASSEY, DANIEL: London, Oct. 10, 1933. Eton and King's Coll.

MASTERS, BEN: Corvallis, OR, May 6, 1947. UOr.

MASTERSON, MARY STUART: Los Angeles, June 28, 1966, NYU.

MASTERSON, PETER: Angleton, TX, June 1, 1934. Rice U.

MASTRANTONIO, MARY ELIZABETH: Chicago, IL, Nov. 17, 1958. UIll.

MASUR, RICHARD: NYC, Nov. 20, 1948.

MATHESON, TIM: Glendale, CA, Dec. 31, 1947. CalState.

MATHIS, SAMANTHA: Brooklyn, NY May 12, 1970.

MATLIN, MARLEE: Morton Grove, IL, Aug. 24, 1965.

MATTHAU, WALTER (Matuschanskayasky): NYC, Oct. 1, 1920.

MATTHEWS, BRIAN: Philadelphia, Jan. 24. 1953. St. Olaf.

MATURE, VICTOR: Louisville, KY, Jan. 29, 1915.

MAY, ELAINE (Berlin): Philadelphia, Apr. 21, 1932.

MAYO, VIRGINIA (Virginia Clara Jones): St. Louis, MO, Nov. 30, 1920.

MAYRON, MELANIE: Philadelphia, PA, Oct. 20, 1952. AADA.

MAZURSKY, PAUL: Brooklyn, NY, Apr. 25, 1930. Bklyn College.

MAZZELLO, JOSEPH: Rhinebeck, NY, Sept. 21, 1983.

McCALLUM, DAVID: Scotland, Sept. 19, 1933. Chapman College.

McCAMBRIDGE, MERCEDES: Jolliet, IL, Mar. 17, 1918. Mundelein College.

McCARTHY, ANDREW: NYC, Nov. 29, 1962, NYU.

McCARTHY, KEVIN: Seattle, WA, Feb. 15, 1914. Minn. U.

McCARTNEY, PAUL: Liverpool, Eng- land, June 18, 1942.

McCLANAHAN, RUE: Healdton, OK, Feb. 21, 1934.

McCLORY, SEAN: Dublin, Ireland, Mar. 8, 1924. U Galway.

McCLURE, MARC: San Mateo, CA, Mar. 31, 1957.

McCLURG, EDIE: Kansas City, MO, July 23, 1950.

McCONAUGHEY, MATTHEW: Uvalde, TX, Nov.4, 1969

McCOWEN, ALEC: Tunbridge Wells, England, May 26, 1925. RADA.

McCRANE, PAUL: Philadelphia, PA, Jan. 19. 1961.

McCRARY, DARIUS: Walnut, CA, 1976.

McDERMOTT, DYLAN: Waterbury, CT, Oct. 26, 1962. Neighborhood Playhouse.

McDONNELL, MARY: Wilkes Barre, PA, 1952.

Shirley MacLaine

Madonna

Steve Martin

Mary Stuart Masterson

McDORMAND, FRANCES: Illinois, June 23, 1957.

McDOWALL, RODDY: London, Sept. 17, 1928. St. Joseph's.

McDOWELL, MALCOLM (Taylor): Leeds, England, June 19, 1943. LAMDA.

McENERY, PETER: Walsall, England, Feb. 21, 1940.

McENTIRE, REBA: McAlester, OK, Mar. 28, 1955. SoutheasternStU.

McGAVIN, DARREN: Spokane, WA, May 7, 1922. College of Pacific.

McGILL, EVERETT: Miami Beach, FL, Oct. 21, 1945.

McGILLIS, KELLY: Newport Beach, CA, July 9, 1957. Juilliard.

McGINLEY, JOHN C.: NYC, Aug. 3, 1959. NYU.

McGOOHAN, PATRICK: NYC, Mar. 19, 1928.

McGOVERN, ELIZABETH: Evanston, IL. July 18, 1961. Juilliard.

McGOVERN, MAUREEN: Youngstown, OH, July 27, 1949.

McGREGOR, EWAN: Perth, Scotland, March 31, 1971.

McGREGOR, JEFF: Chicago, IL, 1957. UMn.

McGUIRE, BIFF: New Haven, CT, Oct. 25. 1926. Mass. Stale College.

McGUIRE, DOROTHY: Omaha, NE, June 14, 1918.

McHATTIE, STEPHEN: Antigonish, NS, Feb. 3. Acadia U AADA.

McKAY, GARDNER: NYC, June 10, 1932. Comell.

McKEAN, MICHAEL: NYC, Oct. 17, 1947.

McKEE, LONETTE: Detroit, MI, July 22, 1955.

McKELLEN, IAN: Burnley, England, May 25, 1939.

McKENNA, VIRGINIA: London, June 7, 1931.

McKEON, DOUG: Pompton Plains, NJ, June 10, 1966.

McKERN, LEO: Sydney, Australia, Mar. 16, 1920.

McKUEN, ROD: Oakland, CA, Apr. 29, 1933.

McLERIE, ALLYN ANN: Grand Mere, Canada, Dec. 1, 1926.

McMAHON, ED: Detroit, MI, Mar. 6, 1923.

McNAIR, BARBARA: Chicago, IL, Mar. 4, 1939. UCLA.

McNAMARA, WILLIAM: Dallas, TX, 1965.

McNICHOL, KRISTY: Los Angeles. CA, Sept. 11, 1962.

McQUEEN, ARMELIA: North Carolina, Jan. 6, 1952. Bklyn Consv.

McQUEEN, CHAD: Los Angeles, CA, Dec. 28, 1960. Actors Studio.

McRANEY, GERALD: Collins, MS, Aug. 19, 1948.

McSHANE, IAN: Blackburn, England, Sept. 29, 1942. RADA.

MEADOWS, JAYNE (formerly Jayne Cotter): Wuchang, China, Sept. 27, 1924. St. Margaret's.

MEARA, ANNE: Brooklyn, NY, Sept. 20, 1929.

MEAT LOAF (Marvin Lee Aday): Dallas, TX, Sept. 27, 1947.

MEDWIN, MICHAEL: London, 1925. Instut Fischer.

MEISNER, GUNTER: Bremen, Germany, Apr. 18, 1926. Municipal Drama School.

MEKKA, EDDIE: Worcester, MA, 1932. Boston Cons.

MELATO, MARIANGELA: Milan, Italy, 1941. Milan Theatre Acad.

MELL, MARISA: Vienna, Austria, Feb. 25, 1939.

MERCADO, HECTOR JAIME: NYC, 1949. HB Studio.

MEREDITH, BURGESS: Cleveland, OH, Nov. 16, 1907. Amherst.

MEREDITH, LEE (Judi Lee Sauls): Oct. 22, 1947. AADA.

MERKERSON, S. EPATHA: Saganaw, MI, Nov. 28, 1952. Wayne St. Univ.

MERRILL, DINA (Nedinia Hutton): NYC, Dec. 29, 1925. AADA.

METCALF, LAURIE: Edwardsville, IL, June 16, 1955., IIIStU.

METZLER, JIM: Oneonda, NY, June 23. Dartmouth.

MICHELL, KEITH: Adelaide, Australia, Dec. 1, 1926.

MIDLER, BETTE: Honolulu, HI, Dec. 1, 1945.

MIFUNE, TOSHIRO: Tsingtao, China, Apr. 1, 1920.

MILANO, ALYSSA: Brooklyn, NY, 1975.

MILES, JOANNA: Nice, France, Mar. 6, 1940.

MILES, SARAH: Ingatestone, England, Dec. 31, 1941. RADA.

MILES, SYLVIA: NYC, Sept. 9, 1934. Actors Studio.

MILES, VERA (Ralston): Boise City, OK, Aug. 23, 1929. UCLA.

MILLER, ANN (Lucille Ann Collier): Chireno, TX, Apr. 12, 1919. Lawler Professional School.

MILLER, BARRY: Los Angeles, CA, Feb. 6, 1958.

MILLER, DICK: NYC, Dec. 25, 1928.

MILLER, JASON: Long Island City, NY, Apr. 22, 1939. Catholic U.

MILLER, LINDA: NYC, Sept. 16, 1942. Catholic U.

MILLER, PENELOPE ANN: Santa Monica, CA, Jan. 13, 1964.

MILLER, REBECCA: Roxbury, CT, 1962. Yale.

MILLS, DONNA: Chicago, IL, Dec. 11, 1945. UII.

MILLS, HAYLEY: London, Apr. 18, 1946. Elmhurst School.

MILLS, JOHN: Suffolk, England, Feb. 22, 1908.

MILLS, JULIET: London, Nov. 21, 1941.

MILNER, MARTIN: Detroit, MI, Dec. 28, 1931.

MIMIEUX, YVETTE: Los Angeles, Jan. 8, 1941. Hollywood High.

MINNELLI, LIZA: Los Angeles, Mar. 19, 1946.

MIOU-MIOU (Sylvette Henry): Paris, France, Feb. 22, 1950.

MIRREN, HELEN: London, 1946.

MITCHELL, JAMES: Sacramento, CA, Feb. 29, 1920. LACC.

MITCHELL, JOHN CAMERON: El Paso, TX, Apr. 21, 1963. NorthwesternU.

Samantha Mathis

Joseph Mazzello

William McNamara

Armin Mueller-Stahl

MITCHUM, JAMES: Los Angeles, CA, May 8, 1941.

MITCHUM, ROBERT: Bridgeport, CT, Aug. 6, 1917.

MODINE, MATTHEW: Loma Linda, CA, Mar. 22, 1959.

MOFFAT, DONALD: Plymouth, England, Dec. 26, 1930. RADA.

MOFFETT, D. W.: Highland Park, IL, Oct. 26, 1954. Stanford U.

MOKAE, ZAKES: Johannesburg, So. Africa, Aug. 5, 1935. RADA.

MOLINA, ALFRED: London, May 24, 1953. Guildhall.

MOLL, RICHARD: Pasadena, CA, Jan. 13, 1943.

MONTALBAN, RICARDO: Mexico City, Nov. 25, 1920.

MONTGOMERY, BELINDA: Winnipeg, Canada, July 23, 1950.

MONTGOMERY, GEORGE (George Letz): Brady, MT, Aug. 29, 1916. U Mont.

MOODY, RON: London, Jan. 8, 1924. London U.

MOOR, BILL: Toledo, OH, July 13, 1931. Northwestern.

MOORE, CONSTANCE: Sioux City, IA, Jan. 18, 1919.

MOORE, DEMI (Guines): Roswell, NM, Nov. 11, 1962.

MOORE, DICK: Los Angeles, Sept. 12, 1925.

MOORE, DUDLEY: Dagenham, Essex, England, Apr. 19, 1935.

MOORE, FRANK: Bay-de-Verde, Newfoundland, 1946.

MOORE, KIERON: County Cork, Ireland, 1925. St. Mary's College.

MOORE, MARY TYLER: Brooklyn, NY, Dec. 29, 1936.

MOORE, ROGER: London, Oct. 14, 1927. RADA.

MOORE, TERRY (Helen Koford): Los Angeles, Jan. 7, 1929.

MORALES, ESAI: Brooklyn, NY, 1963.

MORANIS, RICK: Toronto, Canada, Apr. 18, 1954.

MOREAU, JEANNE: Paris, France, Jan. 23, 1928.

MORENO, RITA (Rosita Alverio): Humacao, P.R., Dec. 11, 1931.

MORGAN, HARRY (HENRY) (Harry Bratsburg): Detroit, Apr. 10, 1915. U Chicago.

MORGAN, MICHELE (Simone Roussel): Paris, France, Feb. 29, 1920. Paris Dramatic School.

MORIARTY, CATHY: Bronx, NY, Nov. 29, 1960.

MORIARTY, MICHAEL: Detroit, MI, Apr. 5, 1941. Dartmouth.

MORISON, PATRICIA: NYC, 1915.

MORITA, NORIYUKI "PAT": Isleton, CA, June 28, 1932.

MORRIS, GARRETT: New Orleans, LA, Feb. 1, 1937.

MORRIS, GREG: Cleveland, OH, Sept. 27, 1934. Ohio State.

MORRIS, HOWARD: NYC, Sept. 4, 1919. NYU.

MORROW, ROB: New Rochelle, NY, Sept. 21, 1962.

MORSE, DAVID: Hamilton, MA, Oct. 11, 1953.

MORSE, ROBERT: Newton, MA, May 18, 1931.

MORTON, JOE: NYC, Oct. 18, 1947. Hofstra U.

MOSES, WILLIAM: Los Angeles, Nov. 17, 1959.

MOSTEL, JOSH: NYC, Dec. 21, 1946. Brandeis U.

MOUCHET, CATHERINE: Paris, France, 1959. Ntl. Consv.

MOYA, EDDY: El Paso, TX, Apr. 11, 1963. LACC.

MUELLER-STAHL, ARMIN: Tilsit, East Prussia, Dec. 17, 1930.

MULDAUR, DIANA: NYC, Aug. 19, 1938. Sweet Briar College.

MULGREW, KATE: Dubuque, IA, Apr. 29, 1955. NYU.

MULHERN, MATT: Philadelphia, PA, July 21, 1960. Rutgers Univ.

MULL, MARTIN: N. Ridgefield, OH, Aug. 18, 1941. RISch. of Design.

MULLIGAN, RICHARD: NYC, Nov. 13, 1932.

MULRONEY, DERMOT: Alexandria, VA, Oct. 31, 1963. Northwestern.

MUMY, BILL (Charles William Mumy, Jr.): San Gabriel, CA, Feb. 1, 1954.

MURPHY, EDDIE: Brooklyn, NY, Apr. 3, 1961.

MURPHY, MICHAEL: Los Angeles, CA, May 5, 1938. UAz.

MURRAY, BILL: Wilmette, IL, Sept. 21, 1950. Regis College.

MURRAY, DON: Hollywood, CA, July 31, 1929.

MUSANTE, TONY: Bridgeport, CT, June 30, 1936. Oberlin College.

MYERS, MIKE: Scarborough, Canada, 1964.

NABORS, JIM: Sylacauga, GA, June 12, 1932.

NADER, GEORGE: Pasadena, CA, Oct. 19, 1921. Occidental College.

NADER, MICHAEL: Los Angeles, CA, 1945.

NAMATH, JOE: Beaver Falls, PA, May 31, 1943. UAla.

NAUGHTON, DAVID: Hartford, CT, Feb. 13, 1951.

NAUGHTON, JAMES: Middletown, CT, Dec. 6, 1945.

NEAL, PATRICIA: Packard, KY, Jan. 20, 1926. Northwestern U.

NEESOM, LIAM: Ballymena, Northern Ireland, June 7, 1952.

NEFF, HILDEGARDE (Hildegard Knef): Ulm, Germany, Dec. 28, 1925. Berlin Art Acad.

NEILL, SAM: No. Ireland, Sept. 14, 1947. U Canterbury.

NELL, NATHALIE: Paris, France, Oct. 1950.

NELLIGAN, KATE: London, Ont., Canada, Mar. 16, 1951. U Toronto.

NELSON, BARRY (Robert Nielsen): Oakland, CA, Apr. 16, 1920.

NELSON, CRAIG T.: Spokane, WA, Apr. 4, 1946.

NELSON, DAVID: NYC, Oct. 24, 1936. USC.

NELSON, JUDD: Portland, ME, Nov. 28, 1959. Haverford College.

NELSON, LORI (Dixie Kay Nelson): Santa Fe, NM, Aug. 15, 1933.

NELSON, TRACY: Santa Monica, CA, Oct. 25, 1963.

NELSON, WILLIE: Abbott, TX, Apr. 30, 1933.

NEMEC, CORIN: Little Rock, AK, Nov. 5, 1971.

NERO, FRANCO: Parma, Italy, 1941.

NESMITH, MICHAEL: Houston, TX, Dec. 30, 1942.

NETTLETON, LOIS: Oak Park, IL, 1931. Actors Studio.

Bette Midler

Dermot Mulroney

Bill Murray

Sam Neill

NEWHART, BOB: Chicago, IL, Sept. 5, 1929. Loyola U.

NEWLEY, ANTHONY: Hackney, London, Sept. 24, 1931.

NEWMAN, BARRY: Boston, MA, Nov. 7, 1938. Brandeis U.

NEWMAN, LARAINE: Los Angeles, Mar. 2, 1952.

NEWMAN, NANETTE: Northampton, England, 1934.

NEWMAN, PAUL: Cleveland, OH, Jan. 26, 1925. Yale.

NEWMAR, JULIE (Newmeyer): Los Angeles, Aug. 16, 1933.

NEWTON-JOHN, OLIVIA: Cambridge, England, Sept. 26, 1948.

NGUYEN, DUSTIN: Saigon, 1962.

NICHOLAS, DENISE: Detroit, MI, July 12, 1945.

NICHOLAS, PAUL: London, 1945.

NICHOLS, NICHELLE: Robbins, IL, 1936.

NICHOLSON, JACK: Neptune, NJ, Apr. 22, 1937.

NICKERSON, DENISE: NYC, 1959.

NICOL, ALEX: Ossining, NY, Jan. 20, 1919. Actors Studio.

NIELSEN, BRIGITTE: Denmark, July 15, 1963.

NIELSEN, LESLIE: Regina, Saskatchewan. Canada, Feb. 11, 1926. Neighborhood Playhouse.

NIMOY, LEONARD: Boston, MA, Mar. 26, 1931. Boston College, Antioch College.

NIXON, CYNTHIA: NYC, Apr. 9, 1966. Columbia U.

NOBLE, JAMES: Dallas, TX, Mar. 5, 1922, SMU.

NOIRET, PHILIPPE: Lille, France, Oct. 1, 1930.

NOLAN, KATHLEEN: St. Louis, MO, Sept. 27, 1933. Neighborhood Playhouse.

NOLTE, NICK: Omaha, NE, Feb. 8, 1940. Pasadena City College.

NORRIS, CHRISTOPHER: NYC, Oct. 7, 1943. Lincoln Square Acad.

NORRIS, CHUCK (Carlos Ray): Ryan, OK,Mar. 10, 1940.

NORTH, HEATHER: Pasadena, CA, Dec. 13, 1950. Actors Workshop.

NORTH, SHEREE (Dawn Bethel): Los Angeles. Jan. 17, 1933. Hollywood High.

NORTON, KEN: Jacksonville, Il, Aug. 9, 1945.

NOURI, MICHAEL: Washington, DC, Dec. 9, 1945.

NOVAK, KIM (Marilyn Novak): Chicago, IL, Feb. 13, 1933. LACC.

NOVELLO, DON: Ashtabula, OH, Jan. 1, 1943. UDayton.

NUYEN, FRANCE (Vannga): Marseilles, France, July 31, 1939. Beaux Arts School.

O'BRIAN, HUGH (Hugh J. Krampe): Rochester, N,. Apr. 19, 1928. Cincinnati U.

O'BRIEN, CLAY: Ray, AZ, May 6, 1961.

O'BRIEN, MARGARET (Angela Maxine O'Brien): Los Angeles, Jan. 15, 1937.

O'BRIEN, VIRGINIA: Los Angeles, Apr. 18, 1919.

O'CONNOR, CARROLL: Bronx, NY, Aug. 2, 1924. Dublin National Univ.

O'CONNOR, DONALD: Chicago, IL, Aug. 28, 1925.

O'CONNOR, GLYNNIS: NYC, Nov. 19, 1955. NYSU.

O'DONNELL, CHRIS: Winetka, IL, June 27, 1970.

O'DONNELL, ROSIE: Commack, NY, 1961.

O'HARA, CATHERINE: Toronto, Canada, Mar. 4, 1954.

O'HARA, MAUREEN (Maureen Fitz-Simons): Dublin, Ireland, Aug. 17, 1920.

O'HERLIHY, DAN: Wexford, Ireland, May 1, 1919. National U.

O'KEEFE, MICHAEL: Larchmont, NY, Apr. 24, 1955. NYU, AADA.

OLDMAN, GARY: New Cross, South London, England, Mar. 21, 1958.

OLIN, KEN: Chicago, IL, July 30, 1954. UPa.

OLIN, LENA: Stockholm, Sweden, Mar. 22, 1955.

OLMOS, EDWARD JAMES: Los Angeles, Feb. 24, 1947. CSLA.

O'LOUGHLIN, GERALD S.: NYC, Dec. 23, 1921. U Rochester.

OLSON, JAMES: Evanston, IL, Oct. 8, 1930.

OLSON, NANCY: Milwaukee, WI, July 14, 1928. UCLA.

O'NEAL, GRIFFIN: Los Angeles, 1965.

O'NEAL, RON: Utica, NY, Sept. 1, 1937. Ohio State.

O'NEAL, RYAN: Los Angeles, Apr. 20, 1941.

O'NEAL, TATUM: Los Angeles, Nov. 5, 1963.

O'NEIL, TRICIA: Shreveport, LA, Mar. 11, 1945. Baylor U.

O'NEILL, ED: Youngstown, OH, 1946.

O'NEILL, JENNIFER: Rio de Janeiro, Feb. 20, 1949. Neighborhood Playhouse.

ONTKEAN, MICHAEL: Vancouver, B.C., Canada, Jan. 24, 1946.

O'QUINN, TERRY: Newbury, MI, July 15, 1952.

ORBACH, JERRY: Bronx, NY, Oct. 20, 1935.

O'SHEA, MILO: Dublin, Ireland, June 2, 1926.

O'SULLIVAN, MAUREEN: Byle, Ireland, May 17, 1911. Sacred Heart Convent.

O'TOOLE, ANNETTE (Toole): Houston, TX, Apr. 1, 1953. UCLA.

O'TOOLE, PETER: Connemara, Ireland, Aug. 2, 1932. RADA.

OVERALL, PARK: Nashville, TN, Mar. 15, 1957. Tusculum College.

OZ, FRANK (Oznowicz): Hereford, England, May 25, 1944.

PACINO, AL: NYC, Apr. 25, 1940.

PACULA, JOANNA: Tamaszow Lubelski, Poland, Jan. 2, 1957. Polish Natl. Theatre Sch.

PAGE, TONY (Anthony Vitiello): Bronx, NY, 1940.

PAGET, DEBRA (Debralee Griffin): Denver, Aug. 19, 1933.

PAIGE, JANIS (Donna Mae Jaden): Tacoma, WA, Sept. 16, 1922.

PALANCE, JACK (Walter Palanuik): Lattimer, PA, Feb. 18, 1920. UNC.

PALIN, MICHAEL: Sheffield, Yorkshire, England, May 5, 1943, Oxford.

PALMER, BETSY: East Chicago, IN, Nov. 1, 1926. DePaul U.

PALMER, GREGG (Palmer Lee): San Francisco, Jan. 25, 1927. U Utah.

PALTROW, GWYNETH: Los Angeles, Sept 28, 1973

PAMPANINI, SILVANA: Rome, Sept. 25, 1925.

PANEBIANCO, RICHARD: NYC, 1971.

PANKIN, STUART: Philadelphia, Apr. 8, 1946.

PANTOLIANO, JOE: Jersey City, NJ, Sept. 12, 1954.

PAPAS, IRENE: Chiliomodion, Greece, Mar. 9, 1929.

PAQUIN, ANNA: Wellington, NZ, 1982.

PARE, MICHAEL: Brooklyn, NY, Oct. 9, 1959.

PARKER, COREY: NYC, July 8, 1965. NYU.

PARKER, ELEANOR: Cedarville, OH, June 26, 1922. Pasadena Playhouse.

PARKER, FESS: Fort Worth, TX, Aug. 16, 1925. USC.

PARKER, JAMESON: Baltimore, MD, Nov. 18, 1947. Beloit College.

PARKER, JEAN (Mae Green): Deer Lodge, MT, Aug. 11, 1912.

PARKER, MARY-LOUISE: Ft. Jackson, SC, Aug. 2, 1964. Bard College.

PARKER, NATHANIEL: London, 1963.

PARKER, SARAH JESSICA: Nelsonville, OH, Mar. 25, 1965.

PARKER, SUZY (Cecelia Parker): San Antonio, TX, Oct. 28, 1933.

PARKER, TREY: Auburn, AL, May 30, 1972.

PARKER, WILLARD (Worster Van Eps): NYC, Feb. 5, 1912.

PARKINS, BARBARA: Vancouver, Canada, May 22, 1943.

PARKS, MICHAEL: Corona, CA, Apr. 4, 1938.

PARSONS, ESTELLE: Lynn, MA, Nov. 20, 1927. Boston U.

PARTON, DOLLY: Sevierville, TN, Jan. 19, 1946.

PATINKIN, MANDY: Chicago, IL, Nov. 30, 1952. Juilliard.

PATRIC, JASON: NYC, June 17, 1966.

PATRICK, DENNIS: Philadelphia, Mar. 14, 1918.

PATTERSON, LEE: Vancouver, Canada, Mar. 31, 1929. Ontario College.

PATTON, WILL: Charleston, SC, June 14, 1954.

PAULIK, JOHAN: Prague, Czech., 1975.

PAVAN, MARISA (Marisa Pierangeli): Cagliari, Sardinia, June 19, 1932. Torquado Tasso College.

PAXTON, BILL: Fort Worth, TX, May. 17, 1955.

PAYS, AMANDA: Berkshire, England, June 6, 1959.

PEACH, MARY: Durban, S. Africa, 1934.

PEARL, MINNIE (Sarah Cannon): Centerville, TN, Oct. 25, 1912.

PEARSON, BEATRICE: Dennison, TX, July 27, 1920.

PECK, GREGORY: La Jolla, CA, Apr. 5, 1916. U Calif.

PEÑA, ELIZABETH: Cuba, Sept. 23, 1961.

PENDLETON, AUSTIN: Warren, OH, Mar. 27, 1940. Yale U.

PENHALL, BRUCE: Balboa, CA, Aug. 17, 1960.

PENN, SEAN: Burbank, CA, Aug. 17, 1960.

PEREZ, JOSE: NYC, 1940.

PEREZ, ROSIE: Brooklyn, NY, Sept. 6, 1964.

PERKINS, ELIZABETH: Queens, NY, Nov. 18, 1960. Goodman School.

PERKINS, MILLIE: Passaic, NJ, May 12, 1938.

PERLMAN, RHEA: Brooklyn, NY, Mar. 31, 1948.

PERLMAN, RON: NYC, Apr. 13, 1950. UMn.

PERREAU, GIGI (Ghislaine): Los Angeles, Feb. 6, 1941.

PERRINE, VALERIE: Galveston, TX, Sept. 3, 1943. U Ariz.

Gary Oldman

Chris O'Donnell

Edward James Olmos

PERRY, LUKE (Coy Luther Perry, III): Fredricktown, OH, Oct. 11, 1966.

PESCI, JOE: Newark, NJ. Feb. 9, 1943.

PESCOW, DONNA: Brooklyn, NY, Mar. 24, 1954.

PETERS, BERNADETTE (Lazzara): Jamaica, NY, Feb. 28, 1948.

PETERS, BROCK: NYC, July 2, 1927. CCNY.

PETERS. JEAN (Elizabeth): Caton, OH, Oct. 15, 1926. Ohio State U.

PETERS, MICHAEL: Brooklyn, NY, 1948.

PETERSEN, PAUL: Glendale, CA, Sept. 23, 1945. Valley College.

PETERSEN, WILLIAM: Chicago, IL, Feb. 21, 1953.

PETERSON, CASSANDRA: Colorado Springs, CO, Sept. 17, 1951.

PETTET, JOANNA: London, Nov. 16, 1944. Neighborhood Playhouse.

PETTY, LORI: Chattanooga, TN, 1965.

PFEIFFER, MICHELLE: Santa Ana, CA, Apr. 29, 1958.

PHILLIPS, LOU DIAMOND: Phillipines, Feb. 17, 1962, UTx.

PHILLIPS, MacKENZIE: Alexandria, VA, Nov. 10, 1959.

PHILLIPS, MICHELLE (Holly Gilliam): Long Beach, CA, June 4, 1944.

PHILLIPS, SIAN: Bettws, Wales, May 14, 1934. UWales.

PICARDO, ROBERT: Philadelphia, PA, Oct. 27, 1953. Yale.

PICERNI, PAUL: NYC, Dec. 1, 1922. Loyola U.

PIGOTT-SMITH, TIM: Rugby, England, May 13, 1946.

PINCHOT, BRONSON: NYC, May 20, 1959. Yale.

PINE, PHILLIP: Hanford, CA, July 16, 1925. Actors' Lab.

PISCOPO, JOE: Passaic. NJ, June 17, 1951.

PISIER, MARIE-FRANCE: Vietnam, May 10, 1944. U Paris.

PITILLO, MARIA: Mahwah, NJ, 1965.

PITT, BRAD (William Bradley Pitt): Shawnee, OK, Dec. 18, 1963.

PLACE, MARY KAY: Tulsa OK, Sept. 23, 1947. U Tulsa.

PLAYTEN, ALICE: NYC, Aug. 28, 1947. NYU.

PLESHETTE, SUZANNE: NYC, Jan. 31, 1937. Syracuse U.

PLIMPTON, MARTHA: NYC, Nov. 16, 1970.

PLOWRIGHT, JOAN: Scunthorpe, Brigg, Lincolnshire, England, Oct. 28, 1929. Old Vic.

PLUMB, EVE: Burbank, CA, Apr. 29, 1958.

PLUMMER, AMANDA: NYC, Mar. 23, 1957. Middlebury College.

PLUMMER, CHRISTOPHER: Toronto, Canada, Dec. 13, 1927.

PODESTA, ROSSANA: Tripoli, June 20, 1934.

POITIER, SIDNEY: Miami, FL, Feb. 27, 1927.

POLANSKI, ROMAN: Paris, France, Aug. 18, 1933.

POLITO, JON: Philadelphia, PA, Dec. 29, 1950. Villanova U.

POLITO, LINA: Naples, Italy, Aug. 11, 1954.

POLLACK, SYDNEY: South Bend, IN, July 1, 1934.

POLLAK, KEVIN: San Francisco, Oct. 30, 1958.

POLLAN, TRACY: NYC, June 22, 1960.

POLLARD, MICHAEL J.: Passaic, NJ, May 30, 1939.

PORTER, ERIC: London, Apr. 8, 1928. Wimbledon College.

POTTS, ANNIE: Nashville, TN, Oct. 28, 1952. Stephens College.

POWELL, JANE (Suzanne Burce): Port-land, OR, Apr. 1, 1928.

POWELL, ROBERT: Salford, England, June 1, 1944. Manchester U.

POWER, TARYN: Los Angeles, CA, 1954.

POWER, TYRONE, IV: Los Angeles, CA, Jan. 1959.

POWERS, MALA (Mary Ellen): San Francisco, CA, Dec. 29, 1921. UCLA.

POWERS, STEFANIE (Federkiewicz): Hollywood, CA, Oct. 12, 1942.

PRENTISS, PAULA (Paula Ragusa): San Antonio, TX, Mar. 4, 1939. Northwestern U.

PRESLE, MICHELINE (Micheline Chassagne): Paris, France, Aug. 22, 1922. Rouleau Drama School.

PRESLEY, PRISCILLA: Brooklyn, NY, May 24, 1945.

PRESNELL, HARVE: Modesto, CA, Sept. 14, 1933. USC.

PRESTON, KELLY: Honolulu, HI, Oct. 13, 1962. USC.

PRESTON, WILLIAM: Columbia, PA, Aug. 26, 1921. PaStateU.

PRICE, LONNY: NYC, Mar. 9, 1959. Juilliard.

PRIESTLEY, JASON: Vancouver, Canada, Aug, 28, 1969.

PRIMUS, BARRY: NYC, Feb. 16, 1938. CCNY.

PRINCE (P. Rogers Nelson): Minneapolis, MN, June 7, 1958.

PRINCIPAL, VICTORIA: Fukuoka, Japan, Jan. 3, 1945. Dade, Jr. College.

PROCHNOW, JURGEN: Berlin, June 10, 1941.

PROSKY, ROBERT: Philadelphia, PA, Dec. 13, 1930.

PROVAL, DAVID: Brooklyn, NY, 1943.

PROVINE, DOROTHY: Deadwood, SD, Jan. 20, 1937. U Wash.

PRYCE, JONATHAN: Wales, UK, June 1, 1947. RADA.

PRYOR, RICHARD: Peoria, IL, Dec. 1, 1940.

PULLMAN, BILL: Delphi, NY, Dec. 17, 1954. SUNY/Oneonta, UMass.

PURCELL, LEE: Cherry Point, NC, June 15, 1947. Stephens.

PURDOM, EDMUND: Welwyn Garden City, England, Dec. 19, 1924. St. Ignatius College.

PYLE, DENVER: Bethune, CO, May 11, 1920.

QUAID, DENNIS: Houston, TX, Apr. 9, 1954.

QUAID, RANDY: Houston, TX, Oct. 1, 1950. UHouston.

QUINLAN, KATHLEEN: Mill Valley, CA, Nov. 19, 1954.

QUINN, AIDAN: Chicago, IL, Mar. 8, 1959.

QUINN, ANTHONY: Chihuahua, Mex., Apr. 21, 1915.

RAFFERTY, FRANCES: Sioux City, IA, June 16, 1922. UCLA.

Mary-Louise Parker

Sarah Jessica Parker

Michelle Pfeiffer

RAFFIN, DEBORAH: Los Angeles, Mar. 13, 1953. Valley College.

RAGSDALE, WILLIAM: El Dorado, AK, Jan. 19, 1961. Hendrix College.

RAILSBACK, STEVE: Dallas, TX, 1948.

RAINER, LUISE: Vienna, Austria, Jan. 12, 1910.

RALSTON, VERA (Vera Helena Hruba): Prague, Czech., July 12, 1919.

RAMIS, HAROLD: Chicago, IL, Nov. 21, 1944. WashingtonU.

RAMPLING, CHARLOTTE: Surmer, England, Feb. 5, 1946. U Madrid.

RAMSEY, LOGAN: Long Beach, CA, Mar. 21, 1921. St. Joseph.

RANDALL, TONY (Leonard Rosenberg): Tulsa, OK, Feb. 26, 1920. Northwestern U.

RANDELL, RON: Sydney, Australia, Oct. 8, 1920. St. Mary's College.

RASCHE, DAVID: St. Louis, MO, Aug. 7, 1944.

RAYMOND, GENE (Raymond Guion): NYC, Aug. 13, 1908.

REA, STEPHEN: Belfast, No. Ireland, Oct. 31, 1949.

REAGAN, RONALD: Tampico, IL, Feb. 6, 1911. Eureka College.

REASON, REX: Berlin, Ger., Nov. 30, 1928. Pasadena Playhouse.

REDDY, HELEN: Melbourne, Australia, Oct. 25, 1942.

REDFORD, ROBERT: Santa Monica, CA, Aug. 18, 1937. AADA.

REDGRAVE, CORIN: London, July 16, 1939.

REDGRAVE, LYNN: London, Mar. 8, 1943.

REDGRAVE, VANESSA: London, Jan. 30, 1937.

REDMAN, JOYCE: County Mayo, Ireland, 1919. RADA.

REED, OLIVER: Wimbledon, England, Feb. 13, 1938.

REED, PAMELA: Tacoma, WA, Apr. 2, 1949.

REEMS, HARRY (Herbert Streicher): Bronx, NY, 1947. U Pittsburgh.

REES, ROGER: Aberystwyth, Wales, May 5, 1944.

REESE, DELLA: Detroit, MI, July 6, 1932.

REEVE, CHRISTOPHER: NYC, Sept. 25, 1952. Cornell, Juilliard.

REEVES, KEANU: Beiruit, Lebanon, Sept. 2, 1964.

REEVES, STEVE: Glasgow, MT, Jan. 21, 1926.

REGEHR, DUNCAN: Lethbridge, Canada, 1954.

REID, ELLIOTT: NYC, Jan. 16, 1920.

REID, TIM: Norfolk, VA, Dec, 19, 1944.

REILLY, CHARLES NELSON: NYC, Jan. 13, 1931. UCt.

REINER, CARL: NYC, Mar. 20, 1922. Georgetown.

REINER, ROB: NYC, Mar. 6, 1947. UCLA.

REINHOLD, JUDGE (Edward Ernest, Jr.): Wilmington, DE, May 21, 1957. NCSchool of Arts.

REINKING, ANN: Seattle, WA, Nov. 10, 1949.

REISER, PAUL: NYC, Mar. 30, 1957.

REMAR, JAMES: Boston, MA, Dec. 31, 1953. Neighborhood Playhouse.

REMSEN, BERT: Glen Cove, NY, Feb. 25, 1925. Ithaca.

Brad Pitt

Amanda Plummer

Jason Priestley

Dennis Quaid

REVILL, CLIVE: Wellington, NZ, Apr. 18, 1930.

REY, ANTONIA: Havana, Cuba, Oct. 12, 1927.

REYNOLDS, BURT: Waycross, GA, Feb. 11, 1935. Fla. State U.

REYNOLDS, DEBBIE (Mary Frances Reynolds): El Paso, TX, Apr. 1, 1932.

REYNOLDS, MARJORIE: Buhl, ID, Aug. 12, 1921.

RHOADES, BARBARA: Poughkeepsie, NY, 1947.

RHODES, CYNTHIA: Nashville, TN, Nov. 21, 1956.

RHYS-DAVIES, JOHN: Salisbury, England, May 5, 1944.

RICCI, CHRISTINA: Santa Monica, CA, 1980.

RICHARD, CLIFF: India, Oct. 14, 1940.

RICHARDS, MICHAEL: Culver City, CA, July 14, 1950.

RICHARDSON, JOELY: London, Jan. 9, 1965.

RICHARDSON, LEE: Chicago, IL, Sept. 11, 1926.

RICHARDSON, MIRANDA: Southport, England, Mar. 3, 1958.

RICHARDSON, NATASHA: London, May 11, 1963.

RICKLES, DON: NYC, May 8, 1926. AADA.

RICKMAN, ALAN: Hammersmith, England, Feb. 21, 1946.

RIEGERT, PETER: NYC, Apr. 11, 1947. U Buffalo.

RIGG, DIANA: Doncaster, England, July 20, 1938. RADA.

RINGWALD, MOLLY: Rosewood, CA, Feb. 16, 1968.

RITTER, JOHN: Burbank, CA, Sept. 17, 1948. US. Cal.

RIVERS, JOAN (Molinsky): Brooklyn, NY, NY, June 8, 1933.

ROBARDS, JASON: Chicago, IL, July 26, 1922. AADA.

ROBARDS, SAM: NYC, Dec. 16, 1963.

ROBBINS, TIM: NYC, Oct. 16, 1958. UCLA.

ROBERTS, ERIC: Biloxi, MS, Apr. 18, 1956. RADA.

ROBERTS, JULIA: Atlanta, GA, Oct. 28, 1967.

ROBERTS, RALPH: Salisbury, NC, Aug. 17, 1922. UNC.

ROBERTS, TANYA (Leigh): NYC, 1955.

ROBERTS, TONY: NYC, Oct. 22, 1939. Northwestern U.

ROBERTSON, CLIFF: La Jolla, CA, Sept. 9, 1925. Antioch College.

ROBERTSON, DALE: Oklahoma City, July 14, 1923.

ROBINSON, CHRIS: West Palm Beach, FL, Nov. 5, 1938. LACC.

ROBINSON, JAY: NYC, Apr. 14, 1930.

ROBINSON, ROGER: Seattle, WA, May 2, 1941. USC.

ROCHEFORT, JEAN: Paris, France, 1930.

ROCK-SAVAGE, STEVEN: Melville, LA, Dec. 14, 1958. LSU.

ROGERS, CHARLES "BUDDY": Olathe, KS, Aug. 13, 1904. U Kan.

ROGERS, MIMI: Coral Gables, FL, Jan. 27, 1956.

ROGERS, ROY (Leonard Slye): Cincinnati, Nov. 5, 1912.

ROGERS, WAYNE: Birmingham, AL, Apr. 7, 1933. Princeton.

ROLLE, ESTHER: Pompano Beach, FL, Nov. 8, 1922.

ROMAN, RUTH: Boston, Dec. 23, 1922. Bishop Lee Dramatic School.

RONSTADT, LINDA: Tucson, AZ, July 15, 1946.

ROOKER, MICHAEL: Jasper, AL, Apr. 6, 1955.

ROONEY, MICKEY (Joe Yule, Jr.): Brooklyn, NY, Sept. 23, 1920.

ROSE, REVA: Chicago, IL, July 30, 1940. Goodman.

ROSEANNE (Barr): Salt Lake City, UT, Nov. 3, 1952.

ROSS, DIANA: Detroit, MI, Mar. 26, 1944.

ROSS, JUSTIN: Brooklyn, NY, Dec. 15, 1954.

ROSS, KATHARINE: Hollywood, Jan. 29, 1943. Santa Rosa College.

ROSSELLINI, ISABELLA: Rome, June 18, 1952.

ROSSOVICH, RICK: Palo Alto, CA, Aug. 28, 1957.

ROTH, TIM: London, May 14, 1961.

ROUNDTREE, RICHARD: New Rochelle, NY, Sept. 7, 1942. Southern Ill.

ROURKE, MICKEY: Schenectady, NY, Sept. 1956.

ROWE, NICHOLAS: London, Nov. 22, 1966. Eton.

ROWLANDS, GENA: Cambria, WI, June 19, 1934.

RUBIN, ANDREW: New Bedford, MA, June 22, 1946. AADA.

RUBINEK, SAUL: Fohrenwold, Germany, July 2, 1948.

RUBINSTEIN, JOHN: Los Angeles, CA, Dec. 8, 1946. UCLA.

RUCKER, BO: Tampa, FL, Aug. 17, 1948.

RUDD, PAUL: Boston, MA, May 15, 1940.

RUDNER, RITA: Miami, FL, 1956.

RUEHL, MERCEDES: Queens, NY, Feb. 28, 1948.

RULE, JANICE: Cincinnati, OH, Aug. 15, 1931.

RUPERT, MICHAEL: Denver, CO, Oct. 23, 1951. Pasadena Playhouse.

RUSH, BARBARA: Denver, CO, Jan. 4, 1927. U Calif.

RUSH, GEOFFREY: Toowoomba, Australia, July 6, 1951.

RUSSELL, JANE: Bemidji, MI, June 21, 1921. Max Reinhardt School.

RUSSELL, KURT: Springfield, MA, Mar. 17, 1951.

RUSSELL, THERESA (Paup): San Diego, CA, Mar. 20, 1957.

RUSSO, JAMES: NYC, Apr. 23, 1953.

RUSSO, RENE: Burbank, CA, Feb. 17, 1954

RUTHERFORD, ANN: Toronto, Canada, Nov. 2, 1920.

RUYMEN, AYN: Brooklyn, NY, July 18, 1947. HB Studio.

RYAN, JOHN P.: NYC, July 30, 1936. CCNY.

RYAN, MEG: Fairfield, CT, Nov. 19, 1961. NYU.

RYAN, TIM (Meineslschmidt): Staten Island, NY, 1958. Rutgers U.

RYDER, WINONA: Winona, MN, Oct. 29, 1971.

SACCHI, ROBERT: Bronx, NY, 1941. NYU.

SÄGEBRECHT, MARIANNE: Starnberg, Bavaria, Aug. 27, 1945.

SAINT, EVA MARIE: Newark, NJ, July 4, 1924. Bowling Green State U.

SAINT JAMES, SUSAN (Suzie Jane Miller): Los Angeles, Aug. 14, 1946. Conn. College.

ST. JOHN, BETTA: Hawthorne, CA, Nov. 26, 1929.

ST. JOHN, JILL (Jill Oppenheim): Los Angeles, Aug. 19, 1940.

SALA, JOHN: Los Angeles, CA, Oct. 5, 1962.

SALDANA, THERESA: Brooklyn, NY, Aug. 20, 1954.

SALINGER, MATT: Windsor, VT, Feb. 13, 1960. Princeton, Columbia.

SALT, JENNIFER: Los Angeles, Sept. 4, 1944. Sarah Lawrence College.

SAMMS, EMMA: London, Aug. 28, 1960.

SAN GIACOMO, LAURA: Orange, NJ, Nov. 14, 1961.

SANDERS, JAY O.: Austin, TX, Apr. 16, 1953.

SANDS, JULIAN: Yorkshire, England, Jan 15, 1958.

SANDS, TOMMY: Chicago, IL, Aug. 27, 1937.

SAN JUAN, OLGA: NYC, Mar. 16, 1927.

SARA, MIA: Brooklyn, NY, 1968.

SARANDON, CHRIS: Beckley, WV, July 24, 1942. U WVa., Catholic U.

SARANDON, SUSAN (Tomalin): NYC, Oct. 4, 1946. Catholic U.

SARRAZIN, MICHAEL: Quebec City, Canada, May 22, 1940.

SAVAGE, FRED: Highland Park, IL, July 9, 1976.

SAVAGE, JOHN (Youngs): Long Island, NY, Aug. 25, 1949. AADA.

SAVIOLA, CAMILLE: Bronx, NY, July 16, 1950.

SAVOY, TERESA ANN: London, July 18, 1955.

SAXON, JOHN (Carmen Orrico): Brooklyn, NY, Aug. 5, 1935.

SBARGE, RAPHAEL: NYC, Feb. 12, 1964.

SCACCHI, GRETA: Milan, Italy, Feb. 18, 1960.

SCALIA, JACK: Brooklyn, NY, 1951.

SCARPELLI, GLEN: Staten Island, NY, July 1966.

SCARWID, DIANA: Savannah, GA, Aug. 27, 1955, AADA. Pace U.

SCHEIDER, ROY: Orange, NJ, Nov. 10, 1932. Franklin-Marshall.

SCHEINE, RAYNOR: Emporia, VA, Nov. 10. VaCommonwealthU.

SCHELL, MARIA: Vienna, Jan. 15, 1926.

SCHELL, MAXIMILIAN: Vienna, Dec. 8, 1930.

SCHLATTER, CHARLIE: NYC, 1967. Ithaca College.

SCHNEIDER, JOHN: Mt. Kisco, NY, Apr. 8, 1960.

SCHNEIDER, MARIA: Paris, France, Mar. 27, 1952.

SCHRODER, RICK: Staten Island, NY, Apr. 13, 1970.

SCHUCK, JOHN: Boston, MA, Feb. 4, 1940.

SCHULTZ, DWIGHT: Milwaukee, WI, Nov. 10, 1938. MarquetteU.

SCHWARZENEGGER, ARNOLD: Austria, July 30, 1947.

SCHYGULLA, HANNA: Katlowitz, Germany, Dec. 25, 1943.

SCIORRA, ANNABELLA: NYC, Mar. 24, 1964.

SCOFIELD, PAUL: Hurstpierpoint, England, Jan. 21, 1922. London Mask Theatre School.

SCOGGINS, TRACY: Galveston, TX, Nov. 13, 1959.

SCOLARI, PETER: Scarsdale, NY, Sept. 12, 1956. NYCC.

SCOTT,CAMPBELL: South Salem, NY, July 19, 1962. Lawrence.

SCOTT, DEBRALEE: Elizabeth, NJ, Apr. 2.

SCOTT, GEORGE C.: Wise, VA, Oct. 18, 1927. U Mo.

SCOTT, GORDON (Gordon M. Werschkul): Portland, OR, Aug. 3, 1927. Oregon U.

SCOTT, LIZABETH (Emma Matso): Scranton, PA, Sept. 29, 1922.

SCOTT, MARTHA: Jamesport, MO, Sept. 22, 1914. U Mich.

SCOTT-TAYLOR, JONATHAN: Brazil, 1962.

SEAGAL, STEVEN: Detroit, MI, Apr. 10, 1951.

SEARS, HEATHER: London, Sept. 28, 1935.

SECOMBE, HARRY: Swansea, Wales, Sept. 8, 1921.

SEDGWICK, KYRA: NYC, Aug. 19, 1965. USC.

SEGAL, GEORGE: NYC, Feb. 13, 1934. Columbia.

SELBY, DAVID: Morganstown, WV, Feb. 5, 1941. UWV.

SELLARS, ELIZABETH: Glasgow, Scotland, May 6, 1923.

SELLECK, TOM: Detroit, MI, Jan. 29, 1945. USCal.

SERNAS, JACQUES: Lithuania, July 30, 1925.

SERRAULT, MICHEL: Brunoy, France. 1928. Paris Consv.

SETH, ROSHAN: New Delhi, India. 1942.

SEYMOUR, JANE (Joyce Frankenberg): Hillingdon, England, Feb. 15, 1952.

SHARIF, OMAR (Michel Shalhoub): Alexandria, Egypt, Apr. 10, 1932. Victoria College.

SHANDLING, GARRY: Chicago, IL, Nov. 29, 1949.

SHATNER, WILLIAM: Montreal, Canada, Mar. 22, 1931. McGill U.

SHAVER, HELEN: St. Thomas, Ontario, Canada, Feb. 24, 1951.

SHAW, SEBASTIAN: Holt, England, May, 1905. Gresham School.

SHAW, STAN: Chicago, IL, 1952.

SHAWN, WALLACE: NYC, Nov. 12, 1943. Harvard.

SHEA, JOHN: North Conway, NH, Apr. 14, 1949. Bates, Yale.

SHEARER, HARRY: Los Angeles, Dec. 23, 1943. UCLA.

SHEARER, MOIRA: Dunfermline, Scotland, Jan. 17, 1926. London Theatre School.

SHEEDY, ALLY: NYC, June 13, 1962. USC.

Keanu Reeves

Miranda Richardson

Eric Roberts

SHEEN, CHARLIE (Carlos Irwin Estevez): Santa Monica, CA, Sept. 3, 1965.

SHEEN, MARTIN (Ramon Estevez): Dayton, OH, Aug. 3, 1940.

SHEFFER, CRAIG: York, PA, 1960. E. StroudsbergU.

SHEFFIELD, JOHN: Pasadena, CA, Apr. 11, 1931. UCLA.

SHELLEY, CAROL: London, England, Aug. 16, 1939.

SHEPARD, SAM (Rogers): Ft. Sheridan, IL, Nov. 5, 1943.

SHEPHERD, CYBILL: Memphis, TN, Feb. 18, 1950. Hunter, NYU.

SHERIDAN, JAMEY: Pasadena, CA, July 12, 1951.

SHIELDS, BROOKE: NYC, May 31, 1965.

SHIRE, TALIA: Lake Success, NY, Apr. 25, 1946. Yale.

SHORT, MARTIN: Toronto, Canada, Mar. 26, 1950. McMasterU.

SHOWALTER, MAX (formerly Casey Adams): Caldwell, KS, June 2, 1917. Pasadena Playhouse.

SHUE, ELISABETH: S. Orange, NJ, Oct. 6, 1963. Harvard.

SHULL, RICHARD B.: Evanston, IL, Feb. 24, 1929.

SIDNEY, SYLVIA: NYC, Aug. 8, 1910. Theatre Guild School.

SIEMASZKO, CASEY: Chicago, IL, March 17, 1961.

SIKKING, JAMES B.: Los Angeles, Mar. 5, 1934.

SILVA, HENRY: Puetro Rico, 1928.

SILVER, RON: NYC, July 2, 1946. SUNY.

SILVERMAN, JONATHAN: Los Angeles, CA, Aug. 5, 1966. USC.

SIMMONS, JEAN: London, Jan. 31, 1929. Aida Foster School.

SIMON, PAUL: Newark. NJ, Nov. 5, 1942.

SIMON, SIMONE: Marseilles, France, Apr. 23, 1910.

SIMPSON, O. J. (Orenthal James): San Francisco, CA, July 9, 1947. UCLA.

SINATRA, FRANK: Hoboken, NJ, Dec. 12, 1915.

SINBAD (David Adkins): Benton Harbor, MI, Nov. 10, 1956.

SINCLAIR, JOHN (Gianluigi Loffredo): Rome, Italy, 1946.

SINDEN, DONALD: Plymouth, England, Oct. 9, 1923. Webber-Douglas.

SINGER, LORI: Corpus Christi, TX, May 6, 1962. Juilliard.

SINISE, GARY: Chicago, Mar. 17. 1955.

SKELTON, RED (Richard): Vincennes, IN, July 18, 1910.

SKERRITT, TOM: Detroit, MI, Aug. 25, 1933. Wayne State U.

SKYE, IONE (Leitch): London, England, Sept. 4, 1971.

SLATER, CHRISTIAN: NYC, Aug. 18, 1969.

SLATER, HELEN: NYC, Dec. 15, 1965.

SMIRNOFF, YAKOV (Yakov Pokhis): Odessa, Russia, Jan. 24. 1951.

SMITH, CHARLES MARTIN: Los Angeles, CA, Oct. 30, 1953. CalState U.

SMITH, JACLYN: Houston, TX, Oct. 26, 1947.

SMITH, KURTWOOD: New Lisbon, WI, Jul. 3, 1942.

SMITH, LANE: Memphis, TN, Apr. 29, 1936.

SMITH, LEWIS: Chattanooga, TN, 1958. Actors Studio.

SMITH, LOIS: Topeka, KS, Nov. 3, 1930. U Wash.

SMITH, MAGGIE: Ilford, England, Dec. 28, 1934.

SMITH, ROGER: South Gate, CA, Dec. 18, 1932. U Ariz.

SMITH, WILL: Philadelphia, PA, Sept. 25, 1968.

SMITHERS, WILLIAM: Richmond, VA, July 10, 1927. Catholic U.

SMITS, JIMMY: Brooklyn, NY, July 9, 1955. Cornell U.

SNIPES, WESLEY: NYC, July 31, 1963. SUNY/Purchase.

SNODGRESS, CARRIE: Chicago, IL, Oct. 27, 1946. UNI.

SOLOMON, BRUCE: NYC, 1944. U Miami, Wayne State U.

SOMERS, SUZANNE (Mahoney): San Bruno, CA, Oct. 16, 1946. Lone Mt. College.

SOMMER, ELKE (Schletz): Berlin, Germany, Nov. 5, 1940.

SOMMER, JOSEF: Greifswald, Germany, June 26, 1934.

SORDI, ALBERTO: Rome, Italy, June 15, 1919.

SORVINO, MIRA: NYC, 1970.

SORVINO, PAUL: NYC, Apr. 13, 1939. AMDA.

SOTHERN, ANN (Harriet Lake): Chicago, IL, Aug. 28, 1943.

SOTO, TALISA: Brooklyn, NY, 1968.

SOUL, DAVID: Chicago, IL, Aug. 28, 1943.

SPACEK, SISSY: Quitman, TX, Dec. 25, 1949. Actors Studio.

SPACEY, KEVIN: So. Orange, NJ, July 26, 1959. Juilliard.

SPADER, JAMES: Buzzards Bay, MA, Feb. 7, 1960.

SPANO, VINCENT: Brooklyn, NY, Oct. 18, 1962.

SPENSER, JEREMY: Ceylon, 1937.

SPRINGFIELD, RICK (Richard Spring Thorpe): Sydney, Australia, Aug. 23, 1949.

STACK, ROBERT: Los Angeles, Jan. 13, 1919. USC.

STADLEN, LEWIS J.: Brooklyn, NY, Mar. 7, 1947. Neighborhood Playhouse.

STALLONE, FRANK: NYC, July 30, 1950.

STALLONE, SYLVESTER: NYC, July 6, 1946. U Miami.

STAMP, TERENCE: London, July 23, 1939.

STANG, ARNOLD: Chelsea, MA, Sept. 28, 1925.

STANLEY, KIM (Patricia Reid): Tularosa, NM, Feb. 11, 1925. U Tex.

STANTON, HARRY DEAN: Lexington, KY, July 14, 1926.

STAPLETON, JEAN: NYC, Jan. 19, 1923.

STAPLETON, MAUREEN: Troy, NY, June 21, 1925.

STARR, RINGO (Richard Starkey): Liverpool, England, July 7, 1940.

STEEL, ANTHONY: London, May 21, 1920. Cambridge.

STEELE, BARBARA: England, Dec. 29, 1937.

STEELE, TOMMY: London, Dec. 17, 1936.

STEENBURGEN, MARY: Newport, AR, 1953. Neighborhood Playhouse.

STEIGER, ROD: Westhampton, NY, Apr. 14, 1925.

STERLING, JAN (Jane Sterling Adriance): NYC, Apr. 3, 1923. Fay Compton School.

STERLING, ROBERT (William Sterling Hart): Newcastle, PA, Nov. 13, 1917. UPittsburgh.

Julia Roberts

Mimi Rogers

Tim Roth

Gena Rowlands

Winona Ryder

John Savage

Greta Scacchi

Kyra Sedgwick

STERN, DANIEL: Bethesda, MD, Aug. 28, 1957.
STERNHAGEN, FRANCES: Washington, DC, Jan. 13, 1932.
STEVENS, ANDREW: Memphis, TN, June 10, 1955.
STEVENS, CONNIE (Concetta Ann Ingolia): Brooklyn, NY, Aug. 8, 1938. Hollywood Professional School.
STEVENS, FISHER: Chicago, IL, Nov. 27, 1963. NYU.
STEVENS, KAYE (Catherine): Pittsburgh, July 21, 1933.
STEVENS, MARK (Richard): Cleveland, OH, Dec. 13, 1920.
STEVENS, STELLA (Estelle Eggleston): Hot Coffee, MS, Oct. 1, 1936.
STEVENSON, PARKER: Philadelphia, PA, June 4, 1953. Princeton.
STEWART, ALEXANDRA: Montreal, Canada, June 10, 1939. Louvre.
STEWART, ELAINE: Montclair, NJ, May 31, 1929.
STEWART, JAMES: Indiana, PA, May 20, 1908. Princeton.
STEWART, MARTHA (Martha Haworth): Bardwell, KY, Oct. 7, 1922.
STEWART, PATRICK: Mirfield, England, July 13, 1940.
STIERS, DAVID OGDEN: Peoria, IL, Oct. 31, 1942.
STILLER, BEN: NYC, 1966.
STILLER, JERRY: NYC, June 8, 1931.
STIMSON, SARA: Helotes, TX, 1973.
STING (Gordon Matthew Sumner): Wallsend, England, Oct. 2, 1951.
STOCKWELL, DEAN: Hollywood, Mar. 5, 1935.
STOCKWELL, JOHN (John Samuels, IV): Galveston, TX, Mar. 25, 1961. Harvard.
STOLER, SHIRLEY: Brooklyn, NY, Mar. 30, 1929.
STOLTZ, ERIC: California, Sept. 30, 1961. USC.
STONE, DEE WALLACE (Deanna Bowers): Kansas City, MO, Dec. 14, 1948. UKS.
STORM, GALE (Josephine Cottle): Bloomington, TX, Apr. 5, 1922.
STOWE, MADELEINE: Eagle Rock, CA, Aug. 18, 1958.

STRAIGHT, BEATRICE: Old Westbury, NY, Aug. 2, 1916. Dartington Hall.
STRASBERG, SUSAN: NYC, May 22, 1938.
STRASSMAN, MARCIA: New Jersey, Apr. 28, 1948.
STRATHAIRN, DAVID: San Francisco, Jan. 26, 1949.
STRAUSS, PETER: NYC, Feb. 20, 1947.
STREEP, MERYL (Mary Louise): Summit, NJ, June 22, 1949. Vassar, Yale.
STREISAND, BARBRA: Brooklyn, NY, Apr. 24, 1942.
STRITCH, ELAINE: Detroit, MI, Feb. 2, 1925. Drama Workshop.
STROUD, DON: Honolulu, HI, Sept. 1, 1937.
STRUTHERS, SALLY: Portland, OR, July 28, 1948. Pasadena Playhouse.
SUMMER, DONNA (LaDonna Gaines): Boston, MA, Dec. 31, 1948.
SUTHERLAND, DONALD: St. John, New Brunswick, Canada, July 17, 1935. U Toronto.
SUTHERLAND, KIEFER: Los Angeles, CA, Dec. 18, 1966.
SVENSON, BO: Goreborg, Sweden, Feb. 13, 1941. UCLA.
SWAYZE, PATRICK: Houston, TX, Aug. 18, 1952.
SWEENEY, D. B. (Daniel Bernard Sweeney): Shoreham, NY, 1961.
SWINBURNE, NORA: Bath, England, July 24, 1902. RADA.
SWIT, LORETTA: Passaic, NJ, Nov. 4, 1937. AADA.
SYLVESTER, WILLIAM: Oakland, CA, Jan. 31, 1922. RADA.
SYMONDS, ROBERT: Bistow, AK, Dec. 1, 1926. TexU.
SYMS, SYLVIA: London, June 1, 1934. Convent School.
SZARABAJKA, KEITH: Oak Park, IL, Dec. 2, 1952. UChicago.
T, MR. (Lawrence Tero): Chicago, IL, May 21, 1952.
TABORI, KRISTOFFER (Siegel): Los Angeles, Aug. 4, 1952.
TAKEI, GEORGE: Los Angeles, CA, Apr. 20, 1939. UCLA.
TALBOT, LYLE (Lysle Hollywood): Pittsburgh, Feb. 8, 1904.

TALBOT, NITA: NYC, Aug. 8, 1930. Irvine Studio School.
TAMBLYN, RUSS: Los Angeles, Dec. 30, 1934.
TARANTINO, QUENTIN: Knoxville, TN, Mar. 27, 1963.
TAYLOR, DON: Freeport, PA, Dec. 13, 1920. Penn State U.
TAYLOR, ELIZABETH: London, Feb. 27, 1932. Byron House School.
TAYLOR, RENEE: NYC, Mar. 19, 1935.
TAYLOR, ROD (Robert): Sydney, Aust., Jan. 11, 1929.
TAYLOR-YOUNG, LEIGH: Washington, DC, Jan. 25, 1945. Northwestern.
TEAGUE, ANTHONY SCOOTER: Jacksboro, TX, Jan. 4, 1940.
TEAGUE, MARSHALL: Newport, TN.
TEEFY, MAUREEN: Minneapolis, MN, 1954, Juilliard.
TEMPLE, SHIRLEY: Santa Monica, CA, Apr. 23, 1927.
TENNANT, VICTORIA: London, England, Sept. 30, 1950.
TERZIEFF, LAURENT: Paris, France, June 25, 1935.
TEWES, LAUREN: Pennsylvania, 1954.
THACKER, RUSS: Washington, DC, June 23, 1946. Montgomery College.
THAXTER, PHYLLIS: Portland, ME, Nov. 20, 1921. St. Genevieve.
THELEN, JODI: St. Cloud, MN, 1963.
THOMAS, HENRY: San Antonio, TX, Sept. 8, 1971.
THOMAS, JAY: New Orleans, July 12, 1948.
THOMAS, MARLO (Margaret): Detroit, Nov. 21, 1938. USC.
THOMAS, PHILIP MICHAEL: Columbus, OH, May 26, 1949. Oakwood College.
THOMAS, RICHARD: NYC, June 13, 1951. Columbia.
THOMPSON, EMMA: London, England, Apr. 15, 1959. Cambridge.
THOMPSON, FRED DALTON: Laurenceberg, TN, Aug. 19, 1942
THOMPSON, JACK (John Payne): Sydney, Australia, Aug. 31, 1940.
THOMPSON, LEA: Rochester, MN, May 31, 1961.
THOMPSON, REX: NYC, Dec. 14, 1942.

George Segal

Helen Shaver

Christian Slater

Wesley Snipes

THOMPSON, SADA: Des Moines, IA, Sept. 27, 1929. Carnegie Tech.

THOMSON, GORDON: Ottawa, Canada, 1945.

THORSON, LINDA: Toronto, Canada, June 18, 1947. RADA.

THULIN, INGRID: Solleftea, Sweden, Jan. 27, 1929. Royal Drama Theatre.

THURMAN, UMA: Boston, MA, Apr. 29, 1970.

TICOTIN, RACHEL: Bronx, NY, Nov. 1, 1958.

TIERNEY, LAWRENCE: Brooklyn, NY, Mar. 15, 1919. Manhattan College.

TIFFIN, PAMELA (Wonso): Oklahoma City, OK, Oct. 13, 1942.

TIGHE, KEVIN: Los Angeles, Aug. 13, 1944.

TILLY, MEG: Texada, Canada, Feb. 14, 1960.

TOBOLOWSKY, STEPHEN: Dallas, Tx, May 30, 1951. So. Methodist U.

TODD, BEVERLY: Chicago, IL, July 1, 1946.

TODD, RICHARD: Dublin, Ireland, June 11, 1919. Shrewsbury School.

TOLKAN, JAMES: Calumet, MI, June 20, 1931.

TOLO, MARILU: Rome, Italy, 1944.

TOMEI, MARISA: Brooklyn, NY, Dec. 4, 1964. NYU.

TOMLIN, LILY: Detroit, MI, Sept. 1, 1939. Wayne State U.

TOPOL (Chaim Topol): Tel-Aviv, Israel, Sept. 9, 1935.

TORN, RIP: Temple, TX, Feb. 6, 1931. UTex.

TORRES, LIZ: NYC, 1947. NYU.

TOTTER, AUDREY: Joliet, IL, Dec. 20, 1918.

TOWSEND, ROBERT: Chicago, IL, Feb. 6, 1957.

TRAVANTI, DANIEL J.: Kenosha, WI, Mar. 7, 1940.

TRAVIS, NANCY: Astoria, NY, Sept. 21, 1961.

TRAVOLTA, JOEY: Englewood, NJ, 1952.

TRAVOLTA, JOHN: Englewood, NJ, Feb. 18, 1954.

TREMAYNE, LES: London, Apr. 16, 1913. Northwestern, Columbia, UCLA.

TREVOR, CLAIRE (Wemlinger): NYC, March 8, 1909.

TRINTIGNANT, JEAN-LOUIS: Pont-St. Esprit, France, Dec. 11, 1930. DullinBalachova Drama School.

TSOPEI, CORINNA: Athens, Greece, June 21, 1944.

TUBB, BARRY: Snyder, TX, 1963. AmConsv Th.

TUCKER, MICHAEL: Baltimore, MD, Feb. 6, 1944.

TUNE, TOMMY: Wichita Falls, TX, Feb. 28, 1939.

TURNER, JANINE (Gauntt): Lincoln, NE, Dec. 6, 1963.

TURNER, KATHLEEN: Springfield, MO, June 19, 1954. UMd.

TURNER, TINA (Anna Mae Bullock): Nutbush, TN, Nov. 26, 1938.

TURTURRO, JOHN: Brooklyn, NY, Feb. 28, 1957. Yale.

TUSHINGHAM, RITA: Liverpool, England, Mar. 14, 1940.

TUTIN, DOROTHY: London, Apr. 8, 1930.

TWIGGY (Lesley Hornby): London, Sept. 19, 1949.

TWOMEY, ANNE: Boston, MA, June 7, 1951. Temple U.

TYLER, BEVERLY (Beverly Jean Saul): Scranton, PA, July 5, 1928.

TYRRELL, SUSAN: San Francisco, 1946.

TYSON, CATHY: Liverpool, England, 1966. Royal Shake. Co.

TYSON, CICELY: NYC, Dec. 19, 1933. NYU.

UGGAMS, LESLIE: NYC, May 25, 1943. Juilliard.

ULLMAN, TRACEY: Slough, England, Dec. 30, 1959.

ULLMANN, LIV: Tokyo, Dec. 10, 1938. Webber-Douglas Acad.

UMEKI, MIYOSHI: Otaru, Hokaido, Japan, 1929.

UNDERWOOD, BLAIR: Tacoma, WA, Aug. 25, 1964. Carnegie-Mellon U.

URICH, ROBERT: Toronto, Canada, Dec. 19, 1946.

USTINOV, PETER: London, Apr. 16, 1921. Westminster School.

VACCARO, BRENDA: Brooklyn, NY, Nov. 18, 1939. Neighborhood Playhouse.

VALANDREY, CHARLOTTE (Anne Charlone Pascal): Paris, France, 1968.

VALLI, ALIDA: Pola, Italy, May 31, 1921. Academy of Drama.

VALLONE, RAF: Riogio, Italy, Feb. 17, 1916. Turin U.

VAN ARK, JOAN: NYC, June 16, 1943. Yale.

VAN DAMME, JEAN-CLAUDE (J-C Vorenberg): Brussels, Belgium, Apr. 1, 1960.

VAN DE VEN, MONIQUE: Holland, 1957.

VAN DEVERE, TRISH (Patricia Dressel): Englewood Cliffs, NJ, Mar. 9, 1945. Ohio Wesleyan.

VAN DOREN, MAMIE (Joan Lucile Olander): Rowena SD, Feb. 6, 1933.

VAN DYKE, DICK: West Plains, MO, Dec. 13, 1925.

VANITY (Denise Mathews): Niagara, Ont., Can, 1963.

VAN PALLANDT, NINA: Copenhagen, Denmark, July 15, 1932.

VAN PATTEN, DICK: NYC, Dec. 9, 1928.

VAN PATTEN, JOYCE: NYC, Mar. 9, 1934.

VAN PEEBLES, MARIO: NYC, Jan. 15, 1958. Columbia U.

VAN PEEBLES, MELVIN: Chicago, IL, Aug. 21, 1932.

VANCE, COURTNEY B.: Detroit, MI, Mar. 12, 1960.

VARNEY, JIM: Lexington, KY, June 15, 1949.

VAUGHN, ROBERT: NYC, Nov. 22, 1932. USC.

VEGA, ISELA: Mexico, 1940.

VELJOHNSON, REGINALD: NYC, Aug. 16, 1952.

VENNERA, CHICK: Herkimer, NY, Mar. 27, 1952. Pasadena Playhouse.

VENORA, DIANE: Hartford, CT, 1952. Juilliard.

VERDON, GWEN: Culver City, CA, Jan. 13, 1925.

VERNON, JOHN: Montreal, Canada, Feb. 24, 1932.

VEREEN, BEN: Miami, FL, Oct. 10, 1946.

VICTOR, JAMES (Lincoln Rafael Peralta Diaz): Santiago, D.R., July 27, 1939. Haaren HS/NYC.

VINCENT, JAN-MICHAEL: Denver, CO, July 15, 1944. Ventura.

VIOLET, ULTRA (Isabelle Collin-Dufresne): Grenoble, France.

VITALE, MILLY: Rome, Italy, July 16, 1928. Lycee Chateaubriand.

VOHS, JOAN: St. Albans, NY, July 30, 1931.

VOIGHT, JON: Yonkers, NY, Dec. 29, 1938. Catholic U.

Patrick Swayze

Quentin Tarantino

Courtney B. Vance

Emma Thompson

VON DOHLEN, LENNY: Augusta, GA, Dec. 22, 1958. UTex.

VON SYDOW, MAX: Lund, Sweden, July 10, 1929. Royal Drama Theatre.

WAGNER, LINDSAY: Los Angeles, June 22. 1949.

WAGNER, ROBERT: Detroit, Feb. 10, 1930.

WAHL, KEN: Chicago, IL, Feb. 14, 1953.

WAITE, GENEVIEVE: South Africa, 1949.

WAITE, RALPH: White Plains, NY, June 22, 1929. Yale.

WAITS, TOM: Pomona, CA, Dec. 7, 1949.

WALKEN, CHRISTOPHER: Astoria, NY, Mar. 31, 1943. Hofstra.

WALKER, CLINT: Hartfold, IL, May 30, 1927. USC.

WALLACH, ELI: Brooklyn, NY, Dec. 7, 1915. CCNY, U Tex.

WALLACH, ROBERTA: NYC, Aug. 2, 1955.

WALLIS, SHANI: London, Apr. 5, 1941.

WALSH, J.T.: San Francisco,. CA. Sept. 28, 1943.

WALSH, M. EMMET: Ogdensburg, NY, Mar. 22, 1935. Clarkson College, AADA.

WALSTON, RAY: New Orleans, Nov. 22, 1917. Cleveland Playhouse.

WALTER, JESSICA: Brooklyn, NY, Jan. 31, 1944 Neighborhood Playhouse.

WALTER, TRACEY: Jersey City, NJ, Nov. 25, 1942.

WALTERS, JULIE: London, Feb. 22, 1950.

WALTON, EMMA: London, Nov. 1962. Brown U.

WARD, BURT (Gervis): Los Angeles, July 6, 1945.

WARD, FRED: San Diego, CA, Dec. 30, 1942.

WARD, RACHEL: London, Sept. 12, 1957.

WARD, SELA: Meridian, MS, July 11, 1956.

WARD, SIMON: London, Oct. 19, 1941.

WARDEN, JACK (Lebzelter): Newark, NJ, Sept. 18, 1920.

WARNER, DAVID: Manchester, England, July 29, 1941. RADA.

WARNER, MALCOLM-JAMAL: Jersey City, NJ, Aug. 18, 1970.

WARREN, JENNIFER: NYC, Aug. 12, 1941. U Wisc.

WARREN, LESLEY ANN: NYC, Aug. 16, 1946.

WARREN, MICHAEL: South Bend, IN, Mar. 5, 1946. UCLA.

WARRICK, RUTH: St. Joseph, MO, June 29, 1915. U Mo.

WASHINGTON, DENZEL: Mt. Vernon, NY, Dec. 28, 1954. Fordham.

WASSON, CRAIG: Ontario, OR, Mar. 15, 1954. UOre.

WATERSTON, SAM: Cambridge, MA, Nov. 15, 1940. Yale.

WATLING, JACK: London, Jan. 13, 1923. Italia Conti School.

WAYANS, DAMON: NYC, 1960.

WAYANS, KEENEN, IVORY: NYC, June 8, 1958. Tuskegee Inst.

WAYNE, PATRICK: Los Angeles, July 15, 1939. Loyola.

WEATHERS, CARL: New Orleans, LA, Jan. 14, 1948. Long Beach CC.

WEAVER, DENNIS: Joplin, MO, June 4, 1924. U Okla.

WEAVER, FRITZ: Pittsburgh, PA, Jan. 19, 1926.

WEAVER, MARJORIE: Crossville, TN, Mar. 2, 1913. Indiana U.

WEAVER, SIGOURNEY (Susan): NYC, Oct. 8, 1949. Stanford, Yale.

WEDGEWORTH, ANN: Abilene, TX, Jan. 21, 1935. U Tex.

WELCH, RAQUEL (Tejada): Chicago, IL, Sept. 5, 1940.

WELD, TUESDAY (Susan): NYC, Aug. 27, 1943. Hollywood Professional School.

WELDON, JOAN: San Francisco, Aug. 5, 1933. San Francisco Conservatory.

WELLER, PETER: Stevens Point, WI, June 24, 1947. AmThWing.

WENDT, GEORGE: Chicago, IL, Oct. 17, 1948.

WEST, ADAM (William Anderson): Walla Walla, WA, Sept. 19, 1929.

WETTIG, PATRICIA: Cincinatti, OH, Dec. 4, 1951. TempleU.

WHALEY, FRANK: Syracuse, NY, July 20, 1963. SUNY/Albany.

WHALLEY-KILMER, JOANNE: Manchester, England, Aug. 25, 1964.

Denzel Washington

Frank Whaley

Dianne Wiest

Shelley Winters

WHEATON, WIL: Burbank, CA, July 29, 1972.

WHITAKER, FOREST: Longview, TX, July 15, 1961.

WHITAKER, JOHNNY: Van Nuys, CA, Dec. 13, 1959.

WHITE, BETTY: Oak Park, IL, Jan. 17, 1922.

WHITE, CHARLES: Perth Amboy, NJ, Aug. 29, 1920. Rutgers U.

WHITE, JESSE: Buffalo, NY, Jan. 3, 1919.

WHITELAW, BILLIE: Coventry, England, June 6, 1932.

WHITMAN, STUART: San Francisco, Feb. 1, 1929. CCLA.

WHITMORE, JAMES: White Plains, NY, Oct. 1, 1921. Yale.

WHITNEY, GRACE LEE: Detroit, MI, Apr. 1, 1930.

WHITTON, MARGARET: Philadelphia, PA, Nov, 30, 1950.

WIDDOES, KATHLEEN: Wilmington, DE, Mar. 21, 1939.

WIDMARK, RICHARD: Sunrise, MN, Dec. 26, 1914. Lake Forest.

WIEST, DIANNE: Kansas City, MO, Mar. 28, 1948. UMd.

WILBY. JAMES: Burma, Feb. 20, 1958.

WILCOX, COLIN: Highlands, NC, Feb. 4, 1937. U Tenn.

WILDER, GENE (Jerome Silberman): Milwaukee, WI, June 11, 1935. UIowa.

WILLIAMS, BILLY DEE: NYC, Apr. 6, 1937.

WILLIAMS, CARA (Bernice Kamiat): Brooklyn, NY, 1925.

WILLIAMS, CINDY: Van Nuys, CA, Aug. 22, 1947. KACC.

WILLIAMS, CLARENCE, III: NYC, Aug. 21, 1939.

WILLIAMS, DICK A.: Chicago, IL, Aug. 9, 1938.

WILLIAMS, ESTHER: Los Angeles, Aug. 8, 1921.

WILLIAMS, JOBETH: Houston, TX, Dec 6, 1948. Brown U.

WILLIAMS, PAUL: Omaha, NE, Sept. 19, 1940.

WILLIAMS, ROBIN: Chicago, IL, July 21, 1951. Juilliard.

WILLIAMS, TREAT (Richard): Rowayton, CT, Dec. 1, 1951.

WILLIAMSON, FRED: Gary, IN, Mar. 5, 1938. Northwestern.

WILLIAMSON, NICOL: Hamilton, Scotland, Sept. 14, 1938.

WILLIS, BRUCE: Penns Grove, NJ, Mar. 19, 1955.

WILLISON, WALTER: Monterey Park, CA, June 24, 1947.

WILSON, DEMOND: NYC, Oct. 13, 1946. Hunter College.

WILSON, ELIZABETH: Grand Rapids, MI, Apr. 4, 1925.

WILSON, FLIP (Clerow Wilson): Jersey City, NJ, Dec. 8, 1933.

WILSON, LAMBERT: Paris, France, 1959.

WILSON, NANCY: Chillicothe, OH, Feb. 20, 1937.

WILSON, SCOTT: Atlanta, GA, 1942.

WINCOTT, JEFF: Toronto, Canada, 1957.

WINDE, BEATRICE: Chicago, IL, Jan. 6.

WINDOM, WILLIAM: NYC, Sept. 28, 1923. Williams College.

WINDSOR, MARIE (Emily Marie Bertelson): Marysvale, UT, Dec. 11, 1924. Brigham Young U.

WINFIELD, PAUL: Los Angeles, May 22, 1940. UCLA.

WINFREY, OPRAH: Kosciusko, MS, Jan. 29, 1954. TnStateU.

WINGER, DEBRA: Cleveland, OH, May 17, 1955. Cal State.

WINKLER, HENRY: NYC, Oct. 30, 1945. Yale.

WINN, KITTY: Washingtohn, D.C., 1944. Boston U.

WINNINGHAM, MARE: Phoenix, AZ, May 6, 1959.

WINSLOW, MICHAEL: Spokane, WA, Sept. 6, 1960.

WINTER, ALEX: London, July 17, 1965. NYU.

WINTERS, JONATHAN: Dayton, OH, Nov. 11, 1925. Kenyon College.

WINTERS, SHELLEY (Shirley Schrift): St. Louis, Aug. 18, 1922. Wayne U.

WITHERS, GOOGIE: Karachi, India, Mar. 12, 1917. Italia Conti.

WITHERS, JANE: Atlanta, GA, Apr. 12, 1926.

WONG, B.D.: San Francisco, Oct. 24,1962.

WONG, RUSSELL: Troy, NY, 1963. SantaMonica College.

WOOD, ELIJAH: Cedar Rapids, IA, Jan 28, 1981.

WOODARD, ALFRE: Tulsa, OK, Nov. 2, 1953. Boston U.

WOODLAWN, HOLLY (Harold Ajzen-berg): Juana Diaz, PR, 1947.

WOODS, JAMES: Vernal, UT, Apr. 18, 1947. MIT.

WOODWARD, EDWARD: Croyden, Surrey, England, June 1, 1930.

WOODWARD, JOANNE: Thomasville, GA, Feb. 27, 1930. Neighborhood Playhouse.

WORONOV, MARY: Brooklyn, NY, Dec. 8, 1946. Cornell.

WORTH, IRENE (Hattie Abrams): Nebraska, June 23, 1916. UCLA.

WRAY, FAY: Alberta, Canada, Sept. 15, 1907.

WRIGHT, AMY: Chicago, IL, Apr. 15, 1950.

WRIGHT, MAX: Detroit, MI, Aug. 2, 1943. WayneStateU.

WRIGHT, ROBIN: Dallas, TX, Apr. 8, 1966.

WRIGHT, TERESA: NYC, Oct. 27, 1918.

WUHL, ROBERT: Union City, NJ, Oct. 9, 1951. UHouston.

WYATT, JANE: NYC, Aug. 10, 1910. Barnard College.

WYMAN, JANE (Sarah Jane Fulks): St. Joseph, MO, Jan. 4, 1914.

WYMORE, PATRICE: Miltonvale, KS, Dec. 17, 1926.

WYNN, MAY (Donna Lee Hickey): NYC, Jan. 8, 1930.

WYNTER, DANA (Dagmar): London, June 8. 1927. Rhodes U.

YORK, DICK: Fort Wayne, IN, Sept. 4, 1928. De Paul U.

YORK, MICHAEL: Fulmer, England, Mar. 27, 1942. Oxford.

YORK, SUSANNAH: London, Jan. 9, 1941. RADA.

YOUNG, ALAN (Angus): North Shield, England, Nov. 19, 1919.

YOUNG, BURT: Queens, NY, Apr. 30, 1940.

YOUNG, CHRIS: Chambersburg, PA, Apr. 28, 1971.

YOUNG, LORETTA (Gretchen): Salt Lake City, UT, Jan. 6, 1912. Immaculate Heart College.

YOUNG, ROBERT: Chicago, IL, Feb. 22, 1907.

YOUNG, SEAN: Louisville, KY, Nov. 20, 1959. Interlochen.

ZACHARIAS, ANN: Stockholm, Sweden, Sweden, 1956.

ZADORA, PIA: Hoboken, NJ, 1954.

ZERBE, ANTHONY: Long Beach, CA, May 20, 1939.

294

OBITUARIES

WESLEY ADDY, 83, Omaha-born actor died on Dec. 31, 1996 in Danbury, CT. His movies include *The First Legion, My Six Convicts, Kiss Me Deadly, The Big Knife, The Garment Jungle, Ten Seconds in Hell, What Ever Happened to Baby Jane?, Seconds, Mister Buddwing, Network, The Europeans, The Bostonians,* and *Before and After.* He is survived by his wife, actress Celeste Holm.

JOHN ALTON, 94, Hungarian-born cinematographer who received an Academy Award for his work on *An American in Paris* died on June 2, 1996 in Santa Monica, CA. Among his other credits are *The Black Book, Devil's Doorway, Father of the Bride* (1950), *The People Against O'Hara, The Big Combo, Tea and Sympathy, The Teahouse of the August Moon, The Brothers Karamazov,* and *Elmer Gantry.*

MOREY AMSTERDAM, 87, film and tv comedian, best known for his role as Buddy Sorrell on the sitcom "The Dick Van Dyke Show" died of a heart attack in Los Angeles on Oct. 28, 1996. His films include *It Came From Outer Space, Machine Gun Kelly, Murder Inc., Beach Party, Don't Worry We'll Think of a Title,* and *Won Ton Ton the Dog Who Saved Hollywood.* Survived by his wife and a daughter.

Wesley Addy   Annabella

ANNABELLA (Suzanne Georgette Charpentier), 86, French actress who came to Hollywood in the 1930s after achieving fame in her native country, died on Sept. 18, 1996 at her home in Neuilly-sur-Seine, France. Her credits include *Le Million, Le Quartorze Julliet, Under the Red Robe, Dinner at the Ritz, Wings of the Morning, Suez* (co-starring Tyrone Power to whom she was once married), *Bridal Suite, Tonight We Raid Calais,* and *13 Rue Madeleine.* Survived by a daughter by Power.

LEW AYRES, 88, Minneapolis-born actor who came to prominence playing the disillusioned German soldier in the Oscar-winning *All Quiet on the Western Front* died in Los Angeles on Dec. 30, 1996, two days after his birthday. He also gained fame playing James Kildare in a series of nine films for MGM starting with *Young Dr. Kildare* in 1938 and ending with *Dr. Kildare's Victory* in 1942. In addition to *Johnny Belinda,* for which he received an Oscar-nomination he appeared in such movies as *The Kiss* (his debut, in 1929), *Common Clay, The Spirit of Notre Dame, Heaven on Earth, Okay America, State Fair* (1933), *My Weakness, Servants' Entrance, Lottery Lover, The Leathernecks Have Landed, The*

Lew Ayres

Crime Nobody Saw, Last Train From Madrid, Hold 'em Navy, Scandal Street, King of the Newsboys, Holiday (1938), *Spring Madness, Ice Follies of 1939, Broadway Serenade, Remember?, Maisie Was a Lady, The Dark Mirror, New Mexico, Donovan's Brain, Advise and Consent, The Carpetbaggers,* and *The Biscuit Eater.* He was previously married to actresses Lola Lane and Ginger Rogers and is survived by his third wife and a son.

MARTIN BALSAM, 76, Bronx-born screen, stage and tv character actor who won an Academy Award for his performance as Jason Robard's sensible brother in *A Thousand Clowns,* died of a stroke while on vacation in Rome on Feb. 13, 1996. Following his 1954 film debut in *On the Waterfront* he was seen in such movies as *12 Angry Men, Time Limit, Marjorie Morningstar, Middle of the Night, Psycho, Ada, Breakfast at Tiffany's, Cape Fear* (1962, and 1991 remake), *The Carpetbaggers, Seven Days in May, The Bedford Incident, After the Fox, Hombre, Me Natalie, Tora! Tora! Tora!, Catch-22, Little Big Man, Confessions of a Police Commissioner, Summer Wishes Winter Dreams, The Taking of Pelham One Two Three, Murder on the Orient Express, All the President's Men, Two-Minute Warning, Silver Bears, Cuba, The Goodbye People, Delta Force,* and *Two Evil Eyes.* Survived by three children, including actress Talia Balsam from his marriage to actress to Joyce Van Patten, and a brother.

SAUL BASS, 75, noted Hollywood title designer died of non-Hodgkins lymphoma on Apr. 25, 1996 in Los Angeles. His designs were seen in such movies as *Carmen Jones, The Man With the Golden Arm, Around the World in 80 Days, Vertigo, The Big Country, North by Northwest, Anatomy of a Murder, Psycho, Exodus, Ocean's Eleven, Walk on the Wild Side, It's a Mad Mad Mad Mad World, Bunny Lake Is Missing, That's Entertainment Part 2, GoodFellas,* and *The Age of Innocence* (1993). Survived by his wife, two daughters, two sons, and one granddaughter.

PANDRO S. BERMAN, 91, Pittsburgh-born producer whose lengthy output included such notable films as *Top Hat, Stage Door, Gunga Din, The Hunchback of Notre Dame* (1939), *National Velvet, Father of the Bride* (1950), and *Ivanhoe,* died at his home in Beverly Hills on July 13, 1996. His many other credits include *What Price Hollywood?, Morning Glory, The Gay Divorcee, Of Human Bondage* (1934), *Roberta, Alice Adams, The Informer, Follow the Fleet, Winterset, Vivacious Lady, Carefree, Bachelor Mother, Ziegfeld Girl, Honky Tonk, The Seventh Cross, Dragon Seed, The Picture of Dorian Gray, The Three Musketeers* (1948), *Madame Bovary, The Long Long Trailer, Blackboard Jungle, Tea and Sympathy, Something of Value, The Brothers Karamazov, Butterfield 8, Sweet Bird of Youth, The Prize, A Patch of Blue,* and *Move.* Survived by three children and several grandchildren.

Martin Balsam

BIBI BESCH, 54, Vienna-born American actress died of cancer on Sept. 7, 1996 in Los Angeles. The daughter of actress Gusti Huber she was seen in such movies as *Hardcore, The Promise, Meteor, The Beast Within, Star Trek II: The Wrath of Khan, The Lonely Lady, Date With an Angel, Tremors, Betsy's Wedding,* and *My Family/Mi Familia.* Survived by her daughter, actress Samantha Mathis, a brother, two sisters, and her stepfather.

TED BESSELL, 57, New York City-born actor-director, best known for his role on the 1960s sitcom "That Girl" died of an aortic aneurysm in Los Angeles on Oct. 6, 1996. He was also seen in the films *Billie* and *Don't Drink the Water.* Survived by his wife, two daughters, his mother, and a brother.

WHIT BISSELL (Whitner Bissell), 86, New York City-born character actor of screen, stage and tv died of an unspecified illness on March 5, 1996 in Woodland Hills, CA. His movie credits include *Holy Matrimony, Another Part of the Forest, It Should Happen to You, The Caine Mutiny, The Creature From the Black Lagoon, Invasion of the Body Snatchers* (1956), *The Young Stranger, Gunfight at the O.K. Corral, I Was a Teenage*

Bibi Besch   Lucille Bremer

Werewolf, I Was a Teenage Frankenstein, The Time Machine, Birdman of Alcatraz, The Manchurian Candidate, Hud, Seven Days in May, Airport, Pete 'n' Tillie, Soylent Green, and *Casey's Shadow.* Survived by a son, three daughters, and six grandchildren.

LUCILLE BREMER, 79, New York-born actress-dancer, best known for playing Rose, the eldest daughter of the Smith Family, in the 1944 musical classic *Meet Me in St. Louis,* died of complications following a heart attack on Apr. 16, 1996 in La Jolla, CA. Her other film credits are *Yolanda and the Thief, Ziegfeld Follies, Till the Clouds Roll By, Dark Delusion, Adventures of Casanova, Ruthless,* and *Behind Locked Doors,* in 1948, after which she married and retired from show business. Survived by four children and several grandchildren.

George Burns

GEORGE BURNS (Nathan Birnbaum), 100, New York City-born comedian-actor, one of the most beloved entertainers in show business history, died at his home in Beverly Hills on March 9, 1996, less than two months after celebrating reaching the century mark. He had never fully recovered from injuries sustained after a fall in his bathtub in 1994 which resulted in brain surgery. The first part of his long career was as straight man to his wife Gracie Allen in a successful partnership that took them from vaudeville to radio, films and tv. Together they appeared in several short films and the features *The Big Broadcast, International House, College Humor, Six of a Kind, We're Not Dressing, Many Happy Returns, Here Comes Cookie, Love in Bloom, Big Broadcast of 1936, Big Broadcast of 1937, College Holiday, A Damsel in Distress, College Swing* and *Honolulu.* Following Gracie's retirement in 1958 and eventual death in 1964 Burns embarked on a solo career, returning triumphantly to the movies in 1975 winning an Academy Award for *The Sunshine Boys.* He then went on to appear in the movies *Oh God!, Sgt. Pepper's Lonely Hearts Club Band, Movie Movie, Just You and Me Kid, Going in Style, Oh God Book II, Oh God You Devil, 18 Again,* and *Radioland Murders.* Survived by his son and daughter, seven grandchildren and five great-children.

DONALD CAMMELL, 62, Scottish writer-director who co-directed the 1970 cult film *Performance* died on Apr. 24, 1996 at his Hollywood home after shooting himself. In addition to writing *Duffy* he was the director of *Demon Seed, White of the Eye,* and *The Wild Ride.* Survived by his wife and a son by his first marriage.

MARCEL CARNE, 90, French director, best known for the 1946 classic *Children of Paradise* died on Oct. 31, 1996 in Clamart, France. His other films include *Drole de Drame, Hotel du Nord, Les Visiteurs du Soir, Therese Racquin,* and *Three Rooms in Manhattan.* No reported survivors.

Claudette Colbert

VIRGINIA CHERRILL, 88, Illinois-born actress best known for playing the Blind Girl in the 1931 Charlie Chaplin classic *City Lights* died in Santa Barbara, CA, on Nov. 14, 1996. Her other credits include *Girls Demand Excitement, The Brat, The Nuisance, Charlie Chan's Greatest Case, What Price Crime?,* and her last, *Troubled Waters,* in 1935. That same year she divorced actor Cary Grant (to whom she had been married for two years) and retired in 1937 following her marriage to the ninth Earl of Jersey. Survived by her third husband.

VIRGINIA CHRISTINE (Virginia Kraft), 76, screen and tv character actress, died of heart complications on July 24, 1996 at her home in Brentwood, CA. Best known for playing Mrs. Olson on the Folger's coffee commercials she was seen in such movies as *Edge of Darkness, The Mummy's Curse, The Killers* (1946), *Cyrano de Bergerac* (1950), *Never Wave at a WAC, Not as a Stranger, Invasion of the Body Snatchers* (1956), *The Careless Years, Judgment at Nuremberg, The Prize,* and *Guess Who's Coming to Dinner.* She had been married to the late Fritz Feld (who died in 1993) for 53 years. Survived by their two sons and two grandchildren.

Herb Edelman   Vince Edwards

Virginia Christine   Joanne Dru

RENE CLEMENT, 82, French director whose 1952 film *Forbidden Games* received the Academy Award for Best Foreign-Language film died in Southern France on March 17, 1996, two days before his 83rd birthday. His other films include *Bataille du Rail, Les Jeux Interdits, Knave of Hearts, Gervaise, The Day and the Hour, Love Cage, Is Paris Burning?,* and *And Hope to Die.* No reported survivors.

CLAUDETTE COLBERT (Lily Claudette Chauchoin), 92, French-born American film star, one of the top actresses of the 1930s and 40s who won an Academy Award for the classic screwball comedy *It Happened One Night,* died at her home in Barbados on July 29, 1996. Following her 1928 film debut in *For the Love of Mike* she was seen in such movies as *The Big Pond, Young Man of Manhattan, The Smiling Lieutenant, Secrets of a Secretary, The Wiser Sex, Misleading Lady, The Man From Yesterday, The Phantom President, The Sign of the Cross, I Cover the Waterfront, Three-Cornered Moon, Four Frightened People, Cleopatra* (1934), *Imitation of Life* (1934), *The Gilded Lily, Private Worlds* (Oscar nomination), *She Married Her Boss, The Bride Comes Home, Under Two Flags, Maid of Salem, I Met Him in Paris, Tovarich, Bluebeard's Eighth Wife, Midnight, It's a Wonderful World, Drums Along the Mohawk, Boom Town, Arise My Love, Skylark, The Palm Beach Story, So Proudly We Hail!, No Time for Love, Since You Went Away* (Oscar nomination), *Practically Yours, Tomorrow Is Forever, Without Reservations, The Egg and I, Family Honeymoon, Three Came Home, Thunder on the Hill, Let's Make It Legal, Texas Lady,* and *Parrish.* No immediate survivors.

JORDAN CRONENWETH, 61, Los Angeles-Born cinematographer died of Parkinson's Disease on Nov. 29, 1996 in Los Angeles. His credits as director of photography include *Brewster McCloud, Play It As It Lays, Zandy's Bride, The Front Page* (1974), *Citizen's Band, Altered States, Cutter and Bone, Blade Runner, Peggy Sue Got Married, Gardens of Stone,* and *State of Grace.* Survived by his mother and three children.

JOANNE DRU (Joanne LaCock), 74, West Virginia-born actress who rose to stardom via roles in such films as *Red River* and *All the King's Men,* died of a respiratory illness at her home in Beverly Hills on Sept. 10, 1996. After her debut in 1946 in *Abie's Irish Rose* she appeared in such movies as *She Wore a Yellow Ribbon, Wagonmaster, 711 Ocean Drive, Vengeance Valley, Mr. Belvedere Rings the Bell, Pride of St. Louis, Thunder Bay, The Siege at Red River, Duffy of San Quentin, Three Ring Circus, Day of Triumph, Hell on Frisco Bay, Sincerely Yours, The Light in the Forest, September Storm, Sylvia,* and *Super Fuzz.* Survived by two children, six grandchildren, several great-grandchildren, and two brothers, one of whom is entertainer Peter Marshall.

HERB EDELMAN, 62, Brooklyn-born screen, stage and tv character actor died of emphyssema in Woodland Hills, CA, on July 21, 1996. He was seen in such movies as *In Like Flint, Barefoot in the Park, I Love You Alice B. Toklas, The Odd Couple* (as Murray the Cop), *The War Between Men and Women, The Way We Were, The Front Page* (1974), *The Yakuza, Goin' Coconuts, California Suite,* and *On the Right Track.* Survived by two daughters, his father, a sister, a brother, and his companion, Christina Pickles.

Greer Garson

VINCE EDWARDS (Vincento Eduardo Zoino), 67, Brooklyn-born screen, stage and tv actor, best known for playing the title role in the hit 1960s medical tv series "Ben Casey," died on March 11, 1996 in Los Angeles of pancreatic cancer. His films include *Sailor Beware, Rogue Cop, The Night Holds Terror, The Killing, Serenade, The Three Faces of Eve, The Hired Gun, Murder by Contract, Too Late Blues, The Victors, The Devil's Brigade, Hammerhead,* and *Deal of the Century.* Survived by his wife, his brother, and three daughters.

Larry Gates   Peter Glenville

ELLA FITZGERALD, 79, Viriginia-born singer, one of the century's great jazz vocalists, died on June 15, 1996 at her home in Beverly Hills. Her few movie credits include *Ride 'em Cowboy, Pete Kelly's Blues, St. Louis Blues,* and *Let No Man Write My Epitaph.*

GREER GARSON, 92, Ireland-born American film star who earned an Academy Award for playing the title role in the 1942 classic *Mrs. Miniver* and became one of the most popular stars of the 1940s, died on Apr. 6, 1996 in Dallas following a history of heart problems. She made her film debut in 1939 in *Goodbye Mr. Chips* earning the first of her seven Oscar nominations. In addition to her win for *Miniver* she was nominated for *Blossoms in the Dust, Madame Curie, Mrs. Parkington, The Valley of Decision,* and *Sunrise at Campobello.* Her other films include *When Ladies Meet* (1941), *Random Harvest, Adventure, Desire Me, Julia Misbehaves, That Forsyte Woman, The Miniver Story, Scandal at Scourie, Julius Caesar* (1953), *Her Twelve Men, Strange Lady in Town, Pepe, The Singing Nun,* and *The Happiest Millionaire.* She had been previously wed to actor Richard Ney who played her son in *Mrs. Miniver.* Survived by her stepson from her marriage to oil developer Buddy Fogelson.

Margaux Hemingway   Barton Heyman

LARRY GATES, 81, St. Paul-born character actor died on Dec. 12, 1996 in Sharon, CT. His film appearances include *Has Anybody Seen My Gal?, The Girl Rush, Invasion of the Body Snatchers* (1956), *Jeanne Eagles, Cat on a Hot Tin Roof, The Hoodlum Priest, Toys in the Attic, The Sand Pebbles, Airport,* and *Funny Lady.* Survived by his wife and a sister.

PETER GLENVILLE, 82, London-born screen and stage director, who received an Oscar-nomination for helming the 1964 film *Becket,* died on June 3, 1996 while visiting his friend's home in Manhattan. His other film credits are *The Prisoner/Father Brown, Me and the Colonel, Summer and Smoke, Term of Trial, Hotel Paradiso,* and *The Comedians.* No immediate survivors.

BRIGITTE HELM (Eva Gisela Schittenhelm), 88, German actress who starred in the dual roles of Maria and her evil robotic alter-image in the 1926 classic *Metropolis,* died in Ascona, Switzerland, where she had lived in seclusion for more than 30 years, on June 11, 1996. Other films included *The Loves of Jeanne Ney, Countess of Monte Cristo,* and *The Blue Danube.* Survived by three sons and a daughter.

MARGAUX HEMINGWAY, 41, Oregon-born model-turned-actress was found dead at her Santa Monica home on July 1, 1996, an apparent suicide. Her movies included *Lipstick, Killer Fish, They Call Me Bruce, Over the Brooklyn Bridge,* and *Inner Sanctum.* The granddaughter of writer Ernest Hemingway, survivors include her younger sister, actress Mariel Hemingway.

Ross Hunter   Ben Johnson

BARTON HEYMAN, 59, screen and stage character actor died of heart failure at his Manhattan home on May 15, 1996. Among his movies were *The Exorcist, Awakenings, The Bonfire of the Vanities, Raising Cain,* and *Dead Man Walking.* Survived by his son and two grandchildren.

ROSS HUNTER (Martin Fuss), 75, Cleveland-born actor-turned-producer whose most notable productions included *Magnificent Obsession* (1954), *Pillow Talk, Thoroughly Modern Millie,* and *Airport* (for which he received an Oscar nomination), died of undisclosed causes in Los Angeles on March 10, 1996. After appearing in such films as *The Bandit of Sherwood Forest* and *The Groom Wore Spurs,* he became a producer for Universal where his movies included *Take Me to Town, All I Desire, Captain Lightfoot, The Spoilers* (1955), *All That Heaven Allows, Battle Hymn, Tammy and the Bachelor, My Man Godfrey* (1957), *The Restless Years, Stranger in My Arms, Imitation of Life* (1959), *Portrait in Black, Midnight Lace, Back Street* (1961), *Flower Drum Song, Tammy Tell Me True, If a Man Answers, The Thrill of It All, The Chalk Garden, I'd Rather Be Rich, The Art of Love, Madame X* (1966), *The Pad...and How to Use It,* and *Rosie!* No reported survivors.

Gene Kelly

BEN JOHNSON, 75, Oklahoma-born stunt man-turned-character actor who won an Academy Award in 1971 for his portrayal of Sam the Lion in the classic *The Last Picture Show* , died of a heart attack in Mesa, AZ, on Apr. 8, 1996. He began his acting career in 1949 with *Three Godfathers* followed by roles in such movies as *She Wore a Yellow Ribbon, Mighty Joe Young, Rio Grande, Wagonmaster, Shane, Slim Carter, One-Eyed Jacks, Major Dundee, The Rare Breed, Will Penny, The Wild Bunch, The Undefeated, Junior Bonner, Dillinger, The Sugarland Express, Bite the Bullet, Hustle, The Greatest, The Town That Dreaded Sundown, Terror Train, The Hunter, My Heroes Have Always Been Cowboys, Radio Flyer,* and *Angels in the Outfield.* Survivors include his mother.

Guy Madison   Audrey Meadows

KRZYSZTOF KIESLOWSKI, 54, Polish film director who became famous for his "Three Colors" trilogy, *Blue, White,* and *Red,* died in Warsaw on March 13, 1996 following a heart bypass operation. His other films include *The Scar, Blind Chance, The Double Life of Veronique,* and *A Short Film About Killing.* Survived by his wife and a daughter.

DOROTHY LAMOUR (Mary Leta Dorothy Slaton), 81, New Orleans-born actress-singer who became famous via her various screen adventures which often found her clad in a sarong and through the "Road" pictures, a series of hit comedies with Bing Crosby and Bob Hope, died at her home in North Hollywood on Sept. 22, 1996. After her 1936 debut in the Paramount production *The Jungle Princess* she was seen in such movies as *Swing High Swing Low, High Wide and Handsome, The Hurricane, Big Broadcast of 1938, Her Jungle Love, Spawn of the North, Man About Town, Typhoon, Road to Singapore, Chad Hanna, Road to Zanzibar, Caught in the Draft, Aloma of the South Seas, The Fleet's In, Beyond the Blue Horizon, Road to Morocco, Star Spangled Rhythm, They Got Me Covered, Dixie, And the Angels Sing, A Medal for Benny, Duffy's Tavern, Road to Utopia, My Favorite Brunette, Road to Rio, Wild Harvest, Variety Girl, On Our Merry Way, The Lucky Stiff, The Greatest Show on Earth, Road to Bali, The Road to Hong Kong, Donovan's Reef, Pajama Party, The Phynx, Won Ton Ton the Dog Who Saved Hollywood,* and her last, *Creepshow 2.* She is survived by two sons.

Dorothy Lamour

GENE KELLY (Eugene Curran Kelly), 83, Pittsburgh-born actor, dancer, singer, choreographer, and director, one of the screen's legendary performers whose infinite charm and amazing footwork brightened such notable musicals as *Cover Girl, Anchors Aweigh* (for which he received an Academy Award nomination), *On the Town* (his first credit as co-director), *An American in Paris,* and, perhaps, his greatest achievement, *Singin' in the Rain* (which he also co-directed), died in his sleep on Feb. 2, 1996 at his home in Beverly Hills, CA. He had never fully recovered from the strokes he had suffered in 1994 and 1995. After obtaining stardom on Broadway with the original production of *Pal Joey* he came to Hollywood where he made his movie debut in 1942 in *For Me and My Gal.* Eventually he would become, along with Fred Astaire, one of movie history's two greatest dancers, his athletic style and imaginative dance routines expanding the screen musical. His other movies are *Pilot No. 5, DuBarry Was a Lady, Thousands Cheer, The Cross of Lorraine, Christmas Holiday, Ziegfeld Follies* (in which he first danced with Astaire), *Living in a Big Way, The Pirate, The Three Musketeers* (1948), *Words and Music, Take Me Out to the Ball Game, Black Hand, Summer Stock, It's a Big Country, The Devil Makes Three, Love Is Better Than Ever, Brigadoon, The Crest of the Wave (Seagulls Over Sorrento), Deep in My Heart, It's Always Fair Weather* (also co-director), *Invitation to the Dance* (also director), *The Happy Road* (also director, producer), *Les Girls, Marjorie Morningstar, Inherit the Wind, Let's Make Love, What a Way to Go!, The Young Girls of Rochefort, 40 Carats, That's Entertainment, That's Entertainment Part 2* (also director), *Viva Knievel, Xanadu, That's Dancing!,* and *That's Entertainment! III.* He was also the director of the films *The Tunnel of Love, Gigot, A Guide for the Married Man, Hello Dolly!,* and *The Cheyenne Social Club* (also producer). His honors include a special Academy Award (1951), American Film Institute Life Achievement Award (1985) and the Kennedy Center Honors (1982). Survived by his third wife, his daughter from his first wife, actress Betsy Blair, and two children from his second marriage.

Marcello Mastroianni

Gene Nelson   Haing S. Ngor

JENNINGS LANG, 81, New York City-born studio executive and producer died on May 29, 1996 in Palm Desert, CA, one day after his 81st birthday. His credits for Universal Pictures include *Coogan's Bluff, Winning, Tell Them Willie Boy Is Here, They Might Be Giants, Play Misty for Me, Slaughterhouse 5, Joe Kidd, Pete 'n' Tillie, High Plains Drifter, Earthquake, Airport 1975, The Front Page* (1974), *The Hindenburg, Airport '77, Rollercoaster, House Calls, The Concorde—Airport '79, Little Miss Marker,* and *The Nude Bomb.* Survived by his wife, actress-singer Monica Lewis, three sons, one of whom is director Rocky Lang, and three grandchildren.

LASH LaRUE (Albert LaRue), 79, Michigan-born cowboy star of the 1940s known for his black attire and his bullwhip, died on May 21, 1996 in Burbank, CA. He had undergone triple-bypass surgery and had suffered from emphysema. His films include *Song of Old Wyoming, Law of the Lash, The Caravan Trail, Border Feud, Mark of the Lash,* and *King of the Bullwhip.* Survived by his wife, three sons and three daughters.

MARK LENARD, 68, Chicago-born character actor, best known for his appearances on the series "Star Trek" (as Spock's father) and "Here Come the Brides," died of multiple myeloma on Nov. 22, 1996 in Manhattan. He was seen in such movies as *The Greatest Story Ever Told, Hang 'em High, Annie Hall, Star Trek: The Motion Picture,* and *Star Trek III: The Search for Spock.* Survived by his wife and two daughters.

David Opatoshu   Luana Patten

GUY MADISON (Robert Moseley), 74, California-born screen and tv actor, died of emphysema in Palm Springs, CA, on Feb. 6, 1996. After making his debut in 1944's *Since You Went Away* he went on to appear in such movies as *Till the End of Time, Texas Brooklyn and Heaven, The Charge at Feather River, The Command, Five Against the House, The Beast of Hollow Mountain, Last Frontier, On the Threshold of Space, Hilda Crane, Jet Over the Atlantic, Slaves of Rome,* and *Won Ton Ton the Dog Who Saved Hollywood.* Survived by a sister, two brothers, three daughters, and a son.

MARCELLO MASTROIANNI, 72, Italy's greatest male international star, known for his performances in such movies as *Big Deal on Madonna Street, La Dolce Vita, Divorce—Italian Style* (Oscar nomination), *8 1/2,* and *A Special Day* (Oscar nomination), died at his home in Paris on Dec. 19, 1996. He had been suffering from cancer of the pancreas. His more than 100 movie credits include *I Miserabili* (debut, 1947), *Too Bad She's Bad, White Nights, Where the Hot Wind Blows, La Notte, A Very Private Affair, The Organizer, Yesterday Today and Tomorrow, Marriage—Italian Style, Casanova '70, The 10th Victim, Shoot Loud Louder...I Don't Understand, The Stranger, Kiss the Other Shiek, A Place for Lovers, Leo the Last, Sunflower, The Pizza Triangle, The Priest's Wife, What?, The Grand Bouffe, The Sunday Woman, Lunatics and Lovers, Wifemistress, Stay As You Are, City of Women, Gabriella, La Nuit de Varennes, Henry IV, Macaroni, Ginger and Fred, Intervista, Dark Eyes* (Oscar nomination), *Everybody's Fine, A Fine Romance, Used People, I Don't Want to Talk About It,* and *Ready to Wear (Pret-a-Porter).* He is survived by two daughters, one from his relationship with actress Catherine Deneuve.

William Prince   Juliet Prowse

AUDREY MEADOWS, 71, China-born screen, stage and tv actress, who became part of tv history with her Emmy Award-winning portrayal of Ralph Kramden's patient but sassy wife Alice in the sitcom "The Honeymooners," died of lung cancer on Feb. 3, 1996 in Los Angeles. On screen she appeared in the movies *That Touch of Mink, Take Her She's Mine,* and *Rosie!* Survivors include her sister, actress Jayne Meadows.

JEAN MUIR, 85, New York-born screen, stage and television actress died on July 23, 1996 in Mesa, AZ. Among her movie credits are *As the Earth Turns, Desirable, Gentlemen Are Born, The White Cockatoo, A Midsummer Night's Dream* (as Helena), *The Lone Wolf Meets the Lady,* and *The Constant Nymph.* After being blacklisted from television in the 1950s she spent much of the remainder of her career teaching acting. Survived by a daughter and two sons.

JACK NANCE, 53, character actor best known for playing the title character in David Lynch's 1978 cult film *Eraserhead,* was found dead in his South Pasadena, CA home on Dec. 30, 1996. He had been hit in the head during an argument at a donut shop the day before and had suffered blunt-force trauma. He also appeared for Lynch in his films *Dune, Blue Velvet, Wild at Heart,* and *Lost Highway,* released posthumously.

Beryl Reid   Tommy Rettig

GENE NELSON (Eugene Berg), 76, Seattle-born actor-dancer-director perhaps best known for playing Will Parker in the 1955 film version of the classic musical *Oklahoma!,* died on Sept. 16, 1996 in Calabasas, CA, of cancer. As a performer he was seen in such movies as *This Is the Army* (debut, 1943), *I Wonder Who's Kissing Her Now, Gentleman's Agreement, Apartment for Peggy, Tea for Two, The West Point Story, Lullaby of Broadway, She's Working Her Way Through College, She's Back on Broadway, Three Sailors and a Girl, Crime Wave, So This Is Paris, The Atomic Man, The Purple Hills,Thunder Island,* and *S.O.B.* Turning to directing he helmed the films *The Hand of Death, Hootenany Hoot, Your Cheatin' Heart, Kissin' Cousins, Harum Scarum,* and *The Cool Ones* (which he also wrote). Survived by his daughter, two sons, and three grandchildren.

HAING S. NGOR, 45, Cambodian physician-turned-actor who won an Academy Award for his debut in *The Killing Fields* in 1984 was shot to death outside of his home near the Chinatown section of Los Angeles on February 25, 1996. Like his character in the film, Dith Pran, he had experienced torture by the Khmer Rouge and continued to work in bringing the perpetrators of the massacres in Cambodia to justice. His other movies include *Iron Triangle, My Life,* and *Heaven and Earth* (1993). No reported survivors.

DAVID OPATOSHU, 78, New York City-born screen, stage and tv character actor died at his Los Angeles home on Apr. 30, 1996 following a long illness. Following his 1939 film debut in the Yiddish film *The Light Ahead* he was seen in such movies as *The Naked City, Molly, The Brothers Karamazov, Exodus* (as Akiva, the resistance leader), *Cimarron* (1961), *The Best of Enemies, Torn Curtain, The Defector, Enter Laughing, The Fixer, Romance of a Horse Thief* (which he also wrote), *Who'll Stop the Rain,* and *Beyond Evil.* Survived by his wife, a son, and three stepchildren.

CHRISTINE PASCAL, 42, French actress-director died on either Aug. 30 or 31, 1996 in Paris, a probable suicide. She was seen in such movies as *The Clockmaker, Black Thursday, Spoiled Children,* and *Round Midnight,* while she directed *The Little Prince Said* and *Adultery: A User's Guide.* Survivors include her husband.

LUANA PATTEN, 57, former child star and actress died on May 1, 1996 in Long Beach, CA, of respiratory failure. She made her debut in *Song of the South* in 1947 after which she was seen in such movies as *Melody Time, So Dear to My Heart, The Little Shepherd of Kingdom Come, A Thunder of Drums, Rock Pretty Baby, The Restless Years, Home From the Hill,* and *Go Naked in the World.* No reported survivors.

WILLIAM PRINCE, 83, New York-born screen, stage and television character actor died on Oct. 8, 1996 in Tarrytown, NY. His many films include *Destination Tokyo, Objective Burma, Cinderella Jones, Roughly Speaking, Pillow to Post, Carnegie Hall, Dead Reckoning, Lust for Gold, Cyrano de Bergerac, Macabre, The Heartbreak Kid, The Stepford Wives,*

Network, Rollercoaster, The Gauntlet, Bronco Billy, Kiss Me Goodbye, Spies Like Us, Nuts, and *The Paper.* Survived by his wife Augusta Dabney, a sister, two daughters, two sons, and three grandchildren.

JULIET PROWSE, 59, Bombay-born American actress-dancer died of pancreatic cancer on Sept. 14, 1996 at her home in Holmby Hills, CA. She was seen in such films as *Can-Can, G.I. Blues, The Fiercest Heart, The Second Time Around,* and *Who Killed Teddy Bear?* Survived by her son, her mother, a brother, and her companion, B.J. Allen.

BERYL REID, 76, British character actress best known for her Tony Award-winning performance as the lesbian soap opera actress in *The Killing of Sister George,* a role she repeated in the 1968 film version, died on Oct. 13, 1996 in England. She had developed pneumonia after a knee operation. Her other films include *The Belles of St. Trinian's, The Dock Brief, Star!, Inspector Clouseau, The Assassination Bureau, Entertaining Mr. Sloane, Dr. Phibes Rises Again, No Sex Please—We're British, Joseph Andrews, Yellowbeard,* and *The Doctor and the Devils.* There were no immediate survivors.

NORMAN RENE, 45, film and stage director died of AIDS on May 24, 1996 in Manhattan. He directed three films, *Longtime Companion, Prelude to a Kiss,* and *Reckless.* The latter two were adaptations of works he had also directed on stage. Survived by his companion, Kevin McKenna, his mother, and a sister.

Howard Rollins   Joe Seneca

TOMMY RETTIG, 54, former child actor who played the lead in the 1953 fantasy *The 5000 Fingers of Dr. T,* was found dead in his home in Marina del Rey, CA, on Feb. 15, 1996 of natural causes. In addition to starring in the 1950s tv series "Lassie" he was seen in such other feature films as *Panic in the Streets, Two Weeks With Love, The Jackpot, Paula, The Lady Wants Mink, The Egyptian, River of No Return, The Cobweb,* and *The Last Wagon.* No reported survivors.

ADAM ROARKE (Adam Gerler), 58, Brooklyn-born actor and acting teacher died of a heart attack on Apr. 27, 1996 at his home in Euless, TX. Among his movie credits were *Hell's Angels on Wheels, Dirty Mary Crazy Larry* and *The Stunt Man.* Survived by his wife, daughter, son, two sisters, and a brother.

HOWARD ROLLINS, 46, Baltimore-born screen and television actor died of complications from cancer on Dec. 8, 1996 in Manhattan. He received an Oscar nomination for his 1981 film debut in *Ragtime,* later appeared in the movies *A Soldier's Story,* and *Drunks,* and was perhaps best known for his starring role on the tv series "In the Heat of the Night." No reported survivors.

VITO SCOTTI, 78, screen and tv character actor died on June 5, 1996 in Woodland Hills, CA. His movie appearances included *Where the Boys Are, Von Ryan's Express, How Sweet It Is, The Godfather,* and *Herbie Rides Again,* while on television he was best known for the series "Life With Luigi." Survived by his wife, a daughter and a son.

Jo Van Fleet

Jack Weston

JOE SENECA, early 80s, Cleveland-born character actor-singer-songwriter died on Aug. 15, 1996 at his home on Roosevelt Island, NY of coronary arrest following an asthma attack. Following his 1982 movie debut in *The Verdict* he was seen in such movies as *Crossroads, Silverado, The Blob* (1988), *Mississippi Masala, The Saint of Fort Washington,* and *A Time to Kill.* Survived by his wife.

TUPAC SHAKUR, 25, New York City-born rap performer and actor died on Sept. 13, 1996 in Las Vegas of wounds he received from a drive-by shooting. He was seen in the films *Juice, Poetic Justice, Above the Rim, Gridlock'd* and *Gang Related.* Survived by his mother.

STIRLING SILLIPHANT, 78, Detroit-born screenwriter who won an Academy Award for his work on *In the Heat of the Night* died of cancer on Apr. 26, 1996 in Bangkok. His other credits include *Five Against the House, The Lineup, Village of the Damned* (1960), *The Slender Thread, Charly, The Liberation of L.B. Jones, Murphy's War, The New Centurions, The Poseidon Adventure, Shaft in Africa, The Towering Inferno, The Enforcer, When Time Ran Out, Over the Top,* and *The Grass Harp.* Survived by his wife and two children.

DON SIMPSON, 52, Seattle-born movie producer of such hits as *Flashdance, Beverly Hills Cop* and *Top Gun,* was found dead at his Bel Air, CA, home on Jan. 19, 1996. His other credits include *American Gigolo, Urban Cowboy, An Officer and a Gentleman, Days of Thunder, Crimson Tide,* and *Dangerous Minds.* Survived by his parents and a brother.

STEVE TESICH, 53, Yugoslav-born writer who won an Academy Award for his script for the 1979 film *Breaking Away* died of a heart attack on July 1, 1996 in Sydney, Nova Scotia where he was vacationing with his family. His other film credits are *Eyewitness, Four Friends, The World According to Garp, American Flyers,* and *Eleni.* Survived by his wife, daughter, mother, and sister.

TINY TIM (Herbert Khaury), 64 (?), New York City-born singer died on Nov. 30, 1996 of cardiac arrest in Minneapolis. He had recently collapsed from a heart attack on stage while performing his signature song "Tip Toe Through the Tulips." The bizarre, falsetto-voiced entertainer was seen in such movies as *You Are What You Eat* and *One-Trick Pony.* Survived by his third wife and his daughter from his first marriage.

TAMARA TOUMANOVA, 77, Siberian-born ballet dancer and actress died on May 29, 1996 in Santa Monica, CA, following a brief illness. She was seen on screen in such movies as *Days of Glory, Tonight We Sing, Deep in My Heart, Torn Curtain,* and *The Private Life of Sherlock Holmes.* No immediate survivors.

JAMIE UYS, 74, South African director of the international hit *The Gods Must Be Crazy* died of a heart attack at his home in Pretoria, South Africa on Jan. 29, 1996. His other movies include *The Hellions, Dingaka,* and *Animals Are Beautiful People.* Survived by his wife, a son and two daughters.

JO VAN FLEET, 81, Oakland-born screen, stage, and tv character actress, who won an Academy Award for Best Supporting Actress for her film debut playing James Dean's mother in *East of Eden,* died on June 10, 1996 in Queens, NY. Her other movies include *I'll Cry Tomorrow, The Rose Tattoo, Gunfight at the O.K. Corral, This Angry Age, Wild River, Cool Hand Luke, I Love You Alice B. Toklas, The Gang That Couldn't Shoot Straight,* and *The Tenant.* Survived by a son, and a granddaughter.

JACK WESTON, 71, Cleveland-born screen, stage and tv character actor who specialized in comedies including *Cactus Flower, The Ritz,* and *The Four Seasons,* died on May 3, 1996 in New York. He had had lymphoma for several years. Among his other films were *Stage Struck* (debut, 1958), *Imitation of Life* (1959), *Please Don't Eat the Daisies, All in a Night's Work, The Honeymoon Machine, It's Only Money, Palm Springs Weekend, The Incredible Mr. Limpet, Mirage, The Cincinnati Kid, Wait Until Dark, The Thomas Crown Affair, The April Fools, A New Leaf, Fuzz, Gator, Cuba, Can't Stop the Music, Ishtar,* and *Dirty Dancing.* Survived by his wife, a stepdaughter, and a brother.

FARON YOUNG, 64, country music singer and actor died on Dec. 10, 1996 in Nashville, TN, from a self-inflicted gunshot wound. He was seen in such movies as *Hidden Guns, Raiders of Old California, Country Music Holiday,* and *Road to Nashville.* Survived by four children.

Blacklisted Writers

Because of the blacklisting outrage brought on by the so-called "McCarthy Era" several screenwriters were denied final credit on films they worked on, starting in 1947 and continuing into the 1970s. The Writers Guild of America recently voted to reinstate the correct writer credits on several motion pictures. The following are the corrected credits listed according to the corresponding volume of *Screen World* in which they originally appeared. The title is followed by the original, incorrect credit in parenthese, then by the real writer who should be credited. Thanks to the Writers Guild of America/West for supplying us with this list.

Volume 2: 1950.

Broken Arrow. (Original Credit reads: Screenplay by Michael Blankfort). The actual writer is Albert Maltz.

Chain Lightning (Original credit reads: Story by J. Redmond Prior). Prior was a pseudonymn for Lester Cole.

Volume 3: 1951.

Joe Palooka in Triple Cross (Original credit reads: Screenplay by Jan Jeffries; Screen Story by Harold Bancroft). Jeffries and Bancroft were both pseudonymns for Henry Blankfort.

Passage West (Original credit reads: Story by Nedrick Young). Young fronted for Alvah Bessie.

Volume 4: 1952.

Adventures of Robinson Crusoe (Original credit reads: Screenplay by Philip Ansell Roll and Luis Bunuel). Philip Ansell Roll was a pseudonym for Hugo Butler.

Boots Malone (Original credit reads: Written by Milton Holmes). Harold Buchman's name was ommitted.

Cry, the Beloved Country (Original credit reads: Screenplay by Alan Paton). John Howard Lawson's name was ommitted.

Ivanhoe (Original credit reads: Screenplay by Noel Langley). Marguerite Roberts' name was ommitted.

Volume 5: 1953.

The Robe (Original credit reads: Screenplay by Philip Dunne). Albert Maltz's name was ommitted.

Roman Holiday (Original credit reads: Story by Ian McLellan Hunter). Hunter, one of the screenwriters, received story credit instead of Dalton Trumbo.

Shark River (Original credit reads: Screenplay by Joseph Carpenter and Lewis Meltzer). Carpenter was a pseudonymn for Louis Lantz.

Volume 6: 1954.

Go, Man, Go! (Original credit reads: Written by Arnold Becker). Becker fronted for Alfred Palca.

The Law vs. Billy the Kid (Original credit reads: Screenplay and Screen Story by John T. Williams). Williams fronted for Bernard Gordon.

Volume 7: 1955.

Autumn Leaves (Original credit reads: Written by Jack Jevne and Lewis Metzler and Robert Blees). Hugo Butler's name was ommitted.

The Naked Dawn (Original credit reads: Written by Nina & Herman Schneider). The actual writer is Julian Zimet.

Volume 8: 1956.

The Brave One (Original credit reads: Screenplay, Harry Franklin; Story by Robert Rich). Screenplay credit should also include Merrill G. White; Rich is a pseudonymn for Dalton Trumbo.

Earth vs. the Flying Saucers (Original credit reads: Screenplay by George Worthing Yates and Raymond T. Marcus). Marcus is a pseudonymn for Bernard Gordon.

Friendly Persuasion (No screenplay credit given). Screenplay was written by Michael Wilson.

Volume 9: 1957.

An Affair to Remember (Original credit reads: Screenplay by Delmer Daves and Leo McCarey). The name of Donald Ogden Stewart (who is credited on the '39 original version *Love Affair,* of which this was a re-make) was ommitted.

The Bridge on the River Kwai (Original credit reads: Screenplay by Pierre Boulle). Boulle, the novelist on whose work this film is based, was given credit in place of Carl Foreman and Michael Wilson.

Chicago Confidential (Original credit reads: Screenplay and Screen Story by Raymond T. Marcus). Marcus is a pseudonymn for Bernard Gordon. Story source credit should go to Hugh King.

Escape from San Quentin (Original credit reads: Written by Raymond T. Marcus). Marcus is a pseudonymn for Bernard Gordon.

Hellcats of the Navy (Original credit reads: Screenplay by David Lang and Raymond T. Marcus). Marcus is a pseudonymn for Bernard Gordon.

The Man Who Turned to Stone (original credit reads: Screenplay by Raymond T. Marcus). Marcus is a pseudonymn for Bernard Gordon.

Short Cut to Hell (Original credit reads: Based on a screenplay by W.R. Burnett). Albert Maltz's name was ommitted.

Zombies of Mora-Tau (Original credit reads: Screenplay by Raymond T. Marcus). Marcus is a pseudonymn for Bernard Gordon.

Volume 10: 1958.

The Case Against Brooklyn (Original credit reads: Screenplay by Raymond T. Marcus). Marcus is a pseudonymn for Bernard Gordon; Julian Zimet's name was ommitted.

The Defiant Ones (Original credit reads: Screenplay by Nathan E. Douglas and Harold Jacob Smith). Douglas' name should by replaced that of Nedrick Young.

The Naked Earth (Original credit reads: Screenplay by Milton Holmes). Harold Buchman's name was ommitted.

Volume 11: 1959.

Odds Against Tomorrow (Original credit reads: Screenplay by John O. Killens and Nelson Gidding). Killens' name should be replaced by that of Abraham Polonsky.

The Sheriff of Fractured Jaw (Original credit reads: Screenplay by Arthur Dales). Dales is a pseudonymn for Howard Dimsdale.

Volume 12: 1960.

Conspiracy of Hearts (Original credit reads: Story by Dale Pitt). Pitt fronted for Adrian Scott.

Inherit the Wind (Original credit reads: Screenplay by Nathan E. Douglas and Harold Jacob Smith). Douglas' name should be replaced by that of Nedrick Young.

Volume 13: 1961.

    Gorgo (Original credit reads: Screenplay by John Loring and Daniel Hyatt). Loring is a pseudonymn for Robert L. Richards; Hyatt is a pseudonymn for Daniel James.

    Operation Eichmann (Original credit reads: Screenplay by Lewis Copley). Copley is a pseudonymn for Lester Cole.

    The Young One (Original credit reads: Screenplay by Luis Bunuel and H.B. Addis). Addis is a pseudonymn for Hugo Butler.

Volume 14: 1962.

    Lawrence of Arabia (Original credit reads: Screenplay by Robert Bolt). Michael Wilson's name was ommitted.

Volume 15: 1963.

    Cairo (Original credit reads: Screenplay by Joanne Court). Court is a pseudonymn for Joan Scott.

    Captain Sinbad (Original credit reads: Screenplay by Samuel B. West and Harry Relis). Actual writers were Ian McLellan Hunter and Guy Endore.

    The Day of the Triffids (Original credit reads: Screenplay by Philip Yordan). Yordan, the executive producer, took credit in place of the actual writer, Bernard Gordon.

Volume 16: 1964.

    Circus World (Original credit reads: Screenplay by Ben Hecht and Julian Halevy and James Edward Grant). Halevy is a pseudonymn for Julian Zimet.

    The Misadventures of Merlin Jones (Original credit reads: Screenplay by Tom and Helen August). These are pseudonymns for Alfred Lewis Levitt and Helen Levitt).

    Psyche 59 (Original credit reads: Screenplay by Julian Halevy). Halevy is a pseudonymn for Julian Zimet.

Volume 17: 1965.

    Crack in the World (Original credit reads: Screenplay by Jon Machip White and Julia Halevy). Halevy is a pseudonymn for Julian Zimet.

    The Monkey's Uncle (Original credit reads: Screenplay by Tom and Helen August). These are pseudonymns for Alfred Lewis Levitt and Helen Levitt).

Volume 18: 1966.

    Born Free (Original credit reads: Screenplay by Gerald L.C. Copley). Copley is pseudonymn for Lester Cole.

Volume 20: 1968.

    Custer of the West (Original credt reads: Screenplay by Bernard Gordon and Julian Halevy). Halevy is a pseudonymn for Julian Zimet.

Volume 21: 1969.

    A Place for Lovers (Original credit reads: Screenplay by Julian Halevy & Peter Baldwin and Ennio de Concini and Tonino Guerra & Cesare Zavattini). Halevy is a pseudonymn for Julian Zimet.

Volume 26: 1974.

    Horror Express (Original on screen credit reads: Screenplay by Arnaud d'Usseau and Julian Halevy). Halevy is a pseudonymn for Julian Zimet.

Volume 27: 1975.

    Pancho Villa (Original on screen credit reads: Screenplay by Julian Halevy). Halevy is a pseudonymn for Julian Zimet.

INDEX